150 Best Jobs® for Your Skills

Part of JIST's Best Jobs® Series

Second Edition

Laurence Shatkin, Ph.D.

Foreword by Linda Kobylarz, President,
Kobylarz & Associates, Career Consultants

150 Best Jobs for Your Skills, Second Edition

© 2012 by JIST Publishing

Published by JIST Works, an imprint of JIST Publishing
875 Montreal Way
St. Paul, MN 55102

E-mail: info@jist.com   Website: www.jist.com

Some Other Books by Laurence Shatkin, Ph.D.

The Sequel: How to Change Your Career Without Starting Over

Best Jobs for the 21st Century

150 Best Jobs for a Secure Future

50 Best Jobs for Your Personality

10 Best College Majors for Your Personality

200 Best Jobs for College Graduates

300 Best Jobs Without a Four-Year Degree

200 Best Jobs Through Apprenticeships

250 Best-Paying Jobs

Visit www.jist.com for information on JIST, free job search tips, tables of contents, sample pages, and ordering information on our many products.

Acquisitions Editor: Susan Pines
Development Editors: Susan Pines, Stephanie Koutek
Production Editor: Jeanne Clark
Cover and Interior Designer: Aleata Halbig
Interior Layout: Jack Ross
Proofreader: Laura Bowman
Indexer: Cheryl Ann Lenser

Printed in the United States of America

17 16 15 14 13 12   9 8 7 6 5 4 3 2 1

Library of Congress Cataloging-in-Publication data is on file with the Library of Congress.

ISBN 978-1-59357-898-5

This Is a Big Book, But It Is Very Easy to Use

How do you earn a paycheck? With your skills. An impressive degree, personal contacts, and the slickest resume in town can only suggest your skills. They may get you hired, but to keep a job you need to own the relevant skills. That's why, when you are making career plans, you should think in terms of the jobs that match your skills—the skills you already have or believe you can develop.

This book can help you identify your top skills and learn about jobs that use those skills. It guides you through an exercise that makes you think about your skills in greater depth than you may ever have before. Then you can browse lists of jobs in which your top skills are used at a high level. The jobs on the lists are selected and ordered to emphasize those with the highest earnings and the highest demand for workers. Specialized lists arrange these jobs by the level of education or training required, by personality types, and by career clusters. You can also see lists of jobs that have high percentages of workers who are self-employed, male, female, urban, or rural.

Every job is described in detail later in the book, so you can explore the jobs that interest you the most. You'll learn the major work tasks, all the important skills, the relevant educational programs, and many other informative facts.

Using this book, you'll be surprised how quickly you'll get new ideas for career goals that can use your top skills and can suit you in many other ways.

Some Things You Can Do with This Book

- ❀ Identify jobs for your skills that don't require you to get additional training or education.

- ❀ Develop long-term career plans that may require additional training, education, or experience.

- ❀ Explore and select a training or educational program that relates to a career objective suited to your skills.

- ❀ Find skill information to emphasize on your resume.

- ❀ Prepare for interviews by learning how to connect your skills to your career goal.

These are a few of the many ways you can use this book. I hope you find it as interesting to browse as I did to put together. I have tried to make it easy to use and as interesting as occupational information can be. When you are done with this book, pass it along or tell someone else about it. I wish you well in your career and in your life.

Table of Contents

Summary of Major Sections

Introduction. A short overview to help you better understand and use the book. *Starts on page 1.*

Part I. Overview of Skills and Careers. Part I defines "skill" and discusses ways you can develop your skills. It clarifies the relationship between skills and career choice as well as the role skills play in the hiring process. *Starts on page 18.*

Part II. What Are Your Top Skills? Take an Assessment. This part helps you identify your strongest skills through an assessment. *Starts on page 25.*

Part III. The Best Jobs Lists: Jobs for Each of the 9 Skills. Very useful for exploring career options! Lists are arranged into easy-to-use groups based on skills. The first group of lists presents the best jobs with a high level of each skill. These jobs are selected to be outstanding for earnings, job growth, and job openings. Another series of lists gives the 20 best-paying jobs with a high level of each skill, the 20 fastest-growing jobs with a high level of each skill, and the 20 jobs with the most openings with a high level of each skill. More-specialized lists of high-skill jobs follow, presenting the best jobs with high percentages of workers that fit certain demographic categories, the best jobs by level of education or training, the best jobs by personality types, and the best jobs by career cluster, as well as several bonus lists. The detailed table of contents starting at right presents all the list titles. *Starts on page 45.*

Part IV. Descriptions of the Best Jobs for Your Skills. Provides complete descriptions of the jobs that appear on the lists in Part III. Each description contains information on skills, education and training required, earnings, projected growth, job duties, knowledge and courses, and many other details. Many descriptions include facts about job specializations. *Starts on page 144.*

Detailed Table of Contents

Table of Contents

Foreword

Today's workplace is one of rapid change, challenge, and opportunity. To survive and prosper, you need to keep up with changing job requirements and be able to bounce back from layoffs and move on to new opportunities. In a word, you need to be resilient. This is true whether you are just starting out or have many years of work experience.

Skills are at the heart of resilience in the workplace. Everybody has skills, but most people have a hard time talking about their skills. A prospective employer asks you to identify your top skills for a job and give examples of how you've used those skills in the past. You're looking for a new job and wondering which of your skills are transferable. You're trying to figure out what your best skills are. When it comes to skills, you probably have more questions than answers. Where to begin?

This book can help you find the answers to your questions about skills. It organizes the wide array of transferable skills into nine major types, gives you an exercise to clarify your strongest transferable skills, and helps you identify examples of how you used your skills effectively. It also provides lists and descriptions of the best jobs that require your key skills.

When you understand your skills, you can target jobs that use them, and you can make a powerful case in your resume, cover letter, and interview for why you're the person who should get hired. It's also important to know what skills are your weak spots so you can work on improving them or develop team strategies for getting help when necessary.

Ready to begin? Use this book as the launchpad for exploring your transferable skills and your career options. You'll find it's a handy guide throughout your career as you continue to face changes, meet challenges, and explore new work opportunities.

Linda Kobylarz
President, Kobylarz & Associates
Career Consultants

Introduction

Not everybody will want to read this introduction. You may want to skip this background information and go directly to Part I, which discusses what skills are, how to develop your skills, and how to use this book to identify your skills. If you're really impatient, you may want to jump directly to Part II and start assessing your skills.

But if you want to understand how and why I put this book together, where the information comes from, and what makes a job "best," this introduction can answer a lot of questions.

Why Skills Deserve Their Own Book

Ask employers what they look for when they hire, and they'll say, "Somebody with the right skills." A few of the skills they seek are technical skills that are uniquely related to the job at hand. For example, an all-around automobile mechanic must be able to change an oil filter, balance a tire, and adjust a timing belt. But employers mostly look for skills that are important on almost every job—for example, communication, problem-solving, and getting along with others. Automobile mechanics, accountants, and architects all need these skills, and somebody who moves from being an automobile mechanic to being an accountant can transfer many of these skills to the new job. For that reason, they are usually called *transferable* skills.

Not all transferable skills can transfer to *all* work settings. Some are much more important in certain jobs than in other jobs, and some combinations of skills—for example, the combination of managerial skills, math skills, and programming skills—are needed at a high level in a limited selection of jobs. In fact, each occupation in the U.S. economy demands a particular mix of transferable skills. That's how this book can help you. It uses information from the U.S. Department of Labor on skill requirements to help you identify the jobs that are the best match for your transferable skills. It also uses information about the economic rewards of jobs so you can identify the *best* jobs that match your skills.

Part I explains what skills are and how to develop them. In Part II, you can take a quick assessment of your transferable skills. Use your scores from this assessment to identify your top three skills and then turn to Part III, where you can see up to the best 50 jobs for each of your top three skills. (That's why the book is called *150 Best Jobs for Your Skills.*) Learn the details about the jobs that interest you by turning to Part IV, which is crammed with facts about each one.

This book can motivate you to build your skills and guide you toward jobs that suit you, but its most important purpose is to *inform* you about jobs and their skill requirements. The rest of this introduction focuses on the information in the book: where it came from, what it means, and how it is organized.

Where the Information Came From

The information I used in creating this book came from databases created by the U.S. Department of Labor and the Census Bureau:

❋ I started with the jobs and skill information included in the Department of Labor's O*NET (Occupational Information Network) database, which is the primary source of detailed information on occupations. The Labor Department updates the O*NET on a regular basis, and I used the most recent one available—O*NET release 16. The O*NET also provided the information about work tasks, knowledge/courses, and personality type.

❋ I linked the information from the O*NET to several other kinds of data that the U.S. Bureau of Labor Statistics (BLS) collects: earnings, projected growth, number of openings, self-employed workers, rural workers, and urban workers. I also linked the information to data from the Census Bureau on the number of male and female workers and workers in various age brackets. All of the figures from the BLS and Census Bureau are reported under a classifying system called Standard Occupational Classification (SOC), which organizes the U.S. workforce into approximately 800 job titles. The lists in Part III and the headings of the job descriptions in Part IV are based on SOC titles.

❋ Information about the level of education or training required for each occupation is taken mostly from a table on the Website of the Office of Occupational Statistics and Employment Projections (www.bls.gov/emp/ep_table_111.htm). For recently emerged job specializations not included in that table, I relied on other sources of information, such as professional associations.

❋ I used the Classification of Instructional Programs, a system developed by the U.S. Department of Education, for the names of the education and training programs related to each job. I linked programs to jobs by following the crosswalk developed jointly by the BLS and the National Center for Education Statistics (NCES). I modified the names of some education and training programs so that they would be more easily understood. In 11 cases, I abbreviated the listing of related programs for the sake of space; such entries end with "others."

⁂ Information about the career clusters and pathways linked to each occupation is based on materials developed for the U.S. Department of Education's Office of Vocational and Adult Education (OVAE).

As you can see, this information came from numerous databases housed in various government agencies. In its original database formats, the information would have been disjointed and sometimes confusing, so I did many things to connect related data and present it to you in a form that is easy to understand.

How the Best Jobs for Your Skills Were Selected

Here is the procedure I followed to select the jobs I included in this book:

1. Of the 1,110 job titles in the O*NET database, 862 have skills data. These are linked to 750 SOC occupational titles. To begin, I analyzed the O*NET skills data and simplified it so I could describe jobs using fewer skills than the 35 that the O*NET uses. I ended up with 9 important skills and ratings for the 750 SOC occupations on these skills. (I explain my methods in detail later in this introduction.)

2. I had to eliminate 39 jobs that had no skill with a rating that exceeded the average. It's not a coincidence that these low-skill jobs are not very rewarding and therefore don't belong in a book about "best jobs." For each of the remaining 711 jobs, I ordered the 9 skills by their ratings from highest to lowest. Thus I was able to identify the top three skills for each job. Some jobs had only one or two skills rated higher than average. For a few highly diverse jobs, I identified four, five, or even six top skills.

3. For each of the 9 skills, I listed the jobs that had that skill as one of its top skills. I then linked the jobs to economic data I obtained from other sources at the Department of Labor. I had to eliminate any jobs for which earnings or outlook figures were not available. I also removed any jobs that were expected to employ fewer than 500 workers per year and to shrink rather than grow in workforce size. I then had a list of 206 jobs for Communication Skills, 269 for Equipment Use/Maintenance Skills, 37 for Installation Skills, 135 for Management Skills, 198 for Mathematics Skills, 182 for Science Skills, 258 for Social Skills, 46 for Technology/Programming Skills, and 250 for Thought-Processing Skills. Because most jobs had more than one top skill and therefore appeared on multiple lists, I had a total of 625 unique jobs.

4. On each list, I ranked the jobs three times, based on these major criteria: median annual earnings, projected growth through 2018, and number of job openings projected per year.

5. I then added the three numerical rankings for each job to calculate its overall score.

6. To emphasize jobs that tend to pay more, are likely to grow more rapidly, and have more job openings, I selected up to 50 job titles from each list with the best numerical scores. For example, on the list of jobs linked to Communication Skills, the job with the best combined score for earnings, growth, and number of job openings is Management Analysts, so this job is listed first among the "50 Best Jobs with a High Level of Communication Skills" even though it is not the best-paying job (which is Orthodontists), the fastest-growing job (which is Financial Examiners), or the job with the most openings (which is Retail Salespersons, a job that is not even included among the top 50 because it is very low in earnings and in job openings). Because my lists of jobs high in Installation Skills and Technology/Programming Skills started with fewer than 50 jobs each, I selected the best 30 jobs for each of these skills.

In Part II you'll determine your top three skills, and then in Part III you'll consult the three corresponding lists to learn the best jobs for each skill. As noted earlier, two of the lists contain fewer than 50 jobs, and most jobs appear on multiple lists, so you may not actually find a total of 150 unique jobs on the lists for your skills. Nevertheless, you're sure to find a very large selection of jobs, probably including many job titles that you haven't previously considered, some of which may be unfamiliar to you. In fact, the 9 best jobs lists contain 199 unique jobs. These jobs are the focus of this book and are described in full in Part IV. These descriptions also cover 146 O*NET job specializations linked to the occupations from the lists.

Understand the Limits of the Data in This Book

In this book, I used the most reliable and up-to-date information available on earnings, projected growth, number of openings, and other topics. The earnings data came from the U.S. Department of Labor's Bureau of Labor Statistics. As you look at the figures, keep in mind that they are estimates. They give you a general idea about the number of workers employed, annual earnings, rate of job growth, and annual job openings.

Understand that a problem with such data is that it describes an average. Just as there is no precisely average person, there is no such thing as a statistically average example of a particular job. I say this because data, while helpful, can also be misleading.

Take, for example, the yearly earnings information in this book. This is highly reliable data obtained from a very large U.S. working population sample. It reports the average annual pay received as of May 2010 by people in various job titles (actually, it is the median annual pay, which means that half earned more and half less).

This sounds great, except that half of all people in the occupation earned less than that amount. For example, people who are new to the occupation or with only a few years of work experience often earn much less than the median amount.

Also keep in mind that the figures for job growth and number of openings are projections by labor economists—their best estimates of what we can expect between now and 2018. These projections are not guarantees. A catastrophic economic downturn, war, or technological breakthrough could change the outcome. The projections are also averages over a 10-year period. During economic slowdowns, you can expect job growth and openings to be lower; during recoveries, both will be higher.

Finally, don't forget that the job market consists of both job openings and job *seekers*. The figures on job growth and openings don't tell you how many people will be competing with you to be hired. The Department of Labor does not publish figures on the supply of job candidates, so I can't provide a number that tells how much competition you can expect. Competition is an important issue that you should research for any tentative career goal. You may find a discussion about the job's competition in the *Occupational Outlook Handbook* at www.bls.gov/oco/home.htm. You also should speak to people who educate or train tomorrow's workers; they probably have a good idea of how many graduates find rewarding employment and how quickly. People in the workforce can provide insights into this issue. Use your critical-thinking skills to evaluate what people tell you. For example, educators or trainers may be trying to recruit you, whereas people in the workforce may be trying to discourage you from competing. Get a variety of opinions to balance possible biases.

So, in reviewing the information in this book, please understand the limitations of the data. You need to use common sense in career decision making as in most other things in life. I hope that, by using that approach, you find the information helpful and interesting.

The Data Complexities

If you are curious about details, this section explains some of the complexities inherent in the sources of information I used and what I did to make sense of them. You don't need to know this information to use the book, so jump to the "How This Book Is Organized" section if you are bored with details.

Skills Covered in This Book

One of the best places to obtain information about the skill requirements of jobs is the O*NET database created by the U.S. Department of Labor. Job analysts, occupational experts, and workers created detailed lists of the tasks of each occupation. The job analysts then decided which skills were needed to perform these tasks. To be more precise, they considered each skill and gave a numerical rating for the *level* of mastery necessary for doing the work tasks and another numerical rating for the *importance* of the skill for doing the work tasks.

The 46 skills that O*NET originally covered have been simplified somewhat, so the skill information in the database now covers 35 skills. But the O*NET skills information is still too detailed to be useful to most people. If you wanted to use O*NET to identify jobs for which you already have many of the skills, you'd have to consider your level of mastery of 35 skills—a tedious procedure.

So in this book I further simplified the O*NET taxonomy of skills. I collapsed the 35 skills down to 9 major skill types. I did this by using a statistical analysis called correlation, which shows how well one variable can predict another. I applied it to the skill ratings (for level of mastery) in the O*NET database, and my thinking was that if the ratings for one skill can predict the ratings for another skill almost all the time, there's no need to consider the two skills separately. Another way of saying this is that I don't need to know about two skills if the two *don't say anything different about the jobs*. The two can be collapsed into one skill instead.

Note that this did not happen with all of the O*NET skills. Some, such as Mathematics, do not have very high correlations with any other O*NET skill, so I decided to let them stand alone.

For an example of highly correlated O*NET skills, consider Reading Comprehension and Writing. A perfect correlation of 1.0 between the ratings for these skills would mean that every occupation is rated exactly the same on both skills. In actuality, the correlation is 0.93, which is so close to perfect that there is no point in treating these as two separate skills. I also discovered very high correlations between these two skills and two other O*NET skills: Active Listening and Speaking. No correlation between any pair of skills in this group of four is lower than 0.89. That means that I would be wasting your time if I asked you to look at more than one of these skills when deciding which jobs are and are not a good match for your abilities. The other three skills provide no additional information, so you can focus on one O*NET skill and ignore the other three.

The next question was *which* one of the highly correlated skills to use as a stand-in for the whole set. A good approach was to see which skills tend to be the highest-rated skills for a large number of occupations. As I explain later in this introduction, I found it useful to compare skills by looking at the *difference* between the occupation's rating and the average rating for all occupations on that skill.

For each skill-rated occupation in the O*NET database, I ordered the 35 O*NET skills by this differential measure of their required level. Then I counted how many times each O*NET skill was included among the top five skills for all occupations. To continue the earlier example of the four highly correlated verbal skills, Writing appeared 119 times among the top five skills; Reading Comprehension 115 times; Speaking 91 times; and Active Listening 80 times. Reading Comprehension comes in at second place, but I decided to use it as the stand-in skill anyway, because many people have a good idea of their level of Reading Comprehension, thanks to standardized tests used for measuring progress in high school and for screening college applicants.

There was a limit, however, to how much I wanted single skills, such as Reading Comprehension, to stand in for a group of skills. Most advertisements for job openings do not list a single, highly specific skill such as Reading Comprehension. More often, you'll see a broader term, such as communication skills, used to embrace Reading Comprehension, Writing, Speaking, and Active Listening. Furthermore, you are not likely to convince an employer to hire you by mentioning only your high level of Reading Comprehension and assuming that the employer readily understands that this means you are also highly skilled at Writing, Speaking, and Active Listening. Therefore, I decided to focus on specific skills *only in the assessment* in Part II, where I can save you time by not asking you about skills that don't give us additional information about your fitness for various jobs. Everywhere else in this book, beginning with the scoring procedure for the assessment, I use a broader term such as Communication Skills to identify highly correlated skills. (The "s" on the end of "Skills" that I use for this and other skill terms is a reminder that many of them have several components.)

Here is a listing of the 35 O*NET skills that shows how I used them in creating my set of 9 skills. The left column lists the names that O*NET uses; the right column lists the names of the skills I use in this book. Where several O*NET skills are collapsed into one skill name for the book, I use bold type to indicate the O*NET skill that I focus on in the assessment in Part II.

O*NET Skill	Skill Used in This Book
Reading Comprehension	Communication Skills
Active Listening	Communication Skills
Speaking	Communication Skills
Writing	Communication Skills
Management of Financial Resources	Management Skills
Management of Material Resources	Management Skills
Management of Personnel Resources	Management Skills
Time Management	Management Skills
Mathematics	Mathematics Skills
Science	Science Skills
Service Orientation	Social Skills
Coordination	Social Skills
Instructing	Social Skills
Negotiation	Social Skills
Persuasion	Social Skills
Social Perceptiveness	Social Skills

O*NET Skill	Skill Used in This Book
Equipment Maintenance	Equipment Use/Maintenance Skills
Equipment Selection	Equipment Use/Maintenance Skills
Operation and Control	Equipment Use/Maintenance Skills
Operation Monitoring	Equipment Use/Maintenance Skills
Quality Control Analysis Skills	Equipment Use/Maintenance Skills
Repairing	Equipment Use/Maintenance Skills
Troubleshooting	Equipment Use/Maintenance Skills
Installation	Installation Skills
Computer Programming	Technology/Programming Skills
Technology Design	Technology/Programming Skills
Active Learning	Thought-Processing Skills
Complex Problem Solving	Thought-Processing Skills
Critical Thinking	Thought-Processing Skills
Judgment and Decision Making	Thought-Processing Skills
Learning Strategies	Thought-Processing Skills
Monitoring	Thought-Processing Skills
Operations Analysis	Thought-Processing Skills
Systems Analysis	Thought-Processing Skills
Systems Evaluation	Thought-Processing Skills

Assigning Skills to Occupations

In assembling the lists of occupations in Part III, I used the SOC taxonomy of job titles because the Department of Labor uses this scheme to report information about salaries and job outlook. However, I also wanted to organize the lists around the 9 skills that I defined, and skill data is reported according to the O*NET taxonomy, which in some cases is more detailed than the SOC taxonomy. For example, the SOC occupation Accountants and Auditors appears on the lists, but in the O*NET database you can find skill information only for the two separate job specializations contained within that SOC title. (Let's call these companion specializations "sibling occupations.") This did not really create a problem because the skills of most sibling occupations are so similar. For example, O*NET rates both Accountants and Auditors on Mathematics Skills with the exact same skill level, 3.75, so the rating of the parent SOC occupation obviously should be 3.75. Where ratings of sibling occupations differed, I used the average of the two ratings to characterize the parent SOC occupation.

However, some SOC occupations are highly diverse. This is particularly true for those with a job title that ends with "All Other," because they tend to be catch-all categories. A good example is Computer Occupations, All Other, which is a grab-bag that includes

Software Quality Assurance Engineers and Testers (rated 1.88 on Mathematics Skills), Web Administrators (rated 2.12), Computer Systems Engineers/Architects (2.88), Geospatial Information Scientists and Technologists (3.38), and Geographic Information Systems Technicians (4.38). By comparing the skill ratings of sibling occupations, I identified six SOC titles that are so diverse that it made sense to list more than three top skills for them. Five of these six jobs are included among the best jobs: Compliance Officers; Computer Occupations, All Other; Engineers, All Other; Engineering Technicians, Except Drafters, All Other; and Producers and Directors. As a result, you'll find that some of these jobs appear on the lists of the best jobs for more than three skills.

The ratings I use for Mathematics Skills are based on the ratings for the single O*NET skill Mathematics. But most of the skills I use in this book, such as Communication Skills or Social Skills, represent combinations of several highly correlated O*NET skills. In these cases, I computed the average of the O*NET skills that I was combining. For example, the O*NET ratings for Lawyers are 4.5 on Reading Comprehension, 4.5 on Active Listening, 4.9 on Speaking, and 4.6 on Writing, so for Communication Skills, I computed the average rating of 4.6 for Lawyers.

So far, the O*NET skill ratings I have been discussing and using as examples are ratings for *level* of skill required. The O*NET also rates every job on the *importance* of each skill. Although I focused on the ratings for level, I also eliminated any occupation that had a very low importance rating for a skill.

I also made some adjustments to the raw ratings for level of skill that appear in the O*NET database, because the distribution of ratings varies greatly. That is to say, although all skills are rated on a scale of 0 to 7, no skill has an average rating of 4, the midpoint of that scale. In fact, the average ratings vary from a high of 3.4 for Communication Skills to a low of 0.4 for Installation Skills. Therefore, for each skill and each occupation, I calculated the *difference* between that occupation's rating and the average rating. This figure, which I call the skill's *score,* indicates how exceptional the skill requirement really is. So, for example, the score on Communication Skills for Lawyers is not 4.6 (the raw rating on level) but rather 1.2 (the difference between 4.6 and the average of 3.4).

After I had computed the nine skill scores for each occupation, I arranged the scores in descending order and thus identified each job's **top skills** (three in most cases, although some low-skill jobs had fewer and I assigned more to the six highly diverse jobs). I used these skills to create the lists in Part III and to describe the jobs in Part IV.

Earnings

The employment security agency of each state gathers information on earnings for various jobs and forwards it to the U.S. Bureau of Labor Statistics. This information is organized in standardized ways by a BLS program called Occupational Employment Statistics (OES). To keep the earnings for the various jobs and regions comparable, the OES screens out certain types of earnings and includes others, so the OES earnings I use in this book represent straight-time gross pay exclusive of premium pay. More specifically, the OES earnings include the job's base rate; cost-of-living allowances; guaranteed pay; hazardous-duty pay; incentive pay, including commissions and production bonuses; on-call pay; and tips. They do not include back pay, jury duty pay, overtime pay, severance pay, shift differentials, nonproduction bonuses, or tuition reimbursements.

For each job, you'll find two facts related to earnings, both based on the OES survey:

❋ The Annual Earnings figure shows the median earnings (half earn more, half earn less).

❋ The Earnings Growth Potential statement represents the gap between the 10th percentile and the median. (The 10th percentile is the highest earnings figure among the lowest-paid 10 percent of the workers.) This information answers the question, "If I compared the wages of the low earners to the median, how much of a pay difference (in percentage terms) would I find?" If the difference is large, the job has great potential for increasing your earnings as you gain experience and skills. If the difference is small, you probably will need to move on to another occupation to improve your earnings substantially. Because a percentage figure, by itself, might be hard to interpret, I precede the figure with an easy-to-understand verbal tag that expresses the Earnings Growth Potential: "very low" when the percentage is 25 percent or less, "low" for 26 percent to 35 percent, "medium" for 36 percent to 40 percent, "high" for 41 percent to 50 percent, and "very high" for any figure 51 percent or higher.

The median earnings for all workers in all occupations were $33,840 in May 2010. The 199 unique jobs listed in this book were chosen partly on the basis of good earnings, so their average is a respectable $58,107. (This is a weighted average, which means that jobs with larger workforces are given greater weight in the computation.)

Projected Growth and Number of Job Openings

This information comes from the Office of Occupational Statistics and Employment Projections, a program within the Bureau of Labor Statistics that develops information about projected trends in the nation's labor market for the next 10 years. The most recent projections available cover 2008 to 2018. The projections are based on information about people moving into and out of occupations. The BLS uses data from various sources in projecting the growth and number of openings for each job title; some data comes from the Census Bureau's Current Population Survey and some comes from an OES survey.

In making the projections, the BLS economists assume that there will be no major war, depression, or other economic upheaval. They do assume that recessions may occur, in keeping with the business cycles we have experienced for several decades, but because the projections cover 10 years, they are intended to provide an average of both the good times and the bad times.

While salary figures are fairly straightforward, you may not know what to make of job-growth figures. For example, is a projected growth of 15 percent good or bad? Keep in mind that the average (mean) growth in all occupations, as projected by the Bureau of Labor Statistics, is 10.1 percent. One-quarter of the SOC occupations have a growth projection of 3.2 percent or lower. Growth of 11.6 percent is the median, meaning that half of the occupations have more, half less. Only one-quarter of the occupations have growth projected at more than 17.4 percent.

Because the jobs in this book were selected as "best" partly on the basis of job growth, their mean growth is 16.4 percent, which compares favorably to the mean for all jobs. Among these 199 jobs, the job ranked 50th by projected growth has a figure of 23.3 percent, the job ranked 99th (the median) has a projected growth of 16.8 percent, and the job ranked 150th has a projected growth of 11.9 percent.

The BLS projects an average of about 35,000 job openings per year for the 750 occupations that it studies, but for the 199 occupations included in this book, the average is 10,307 openings. You should not be surprised by this figure; most jobs in our economy with a very large number of openings are low-skill jobs with rapid turnover, such as fast-food workers. The jobs in this book tend to require higher skills and experience slower turnover. The job ranked 50th for job openings has a figure of 12,380 annual openings, the job ranked 99th (the median) has 4,820 openings projected, and the job ranked 150th has 2,000 openings projected.

Perhaps you're wondering why this book offers figures on both job growth *and* number of openings. Aren't these two ways of saying the same thing? Actually, you need to know both. Consider Prosthodontists, which is projected to grow at the impressive rate of 26.4 percent. There should be lots of opportunities in such a fast-growing job, right? Not exactly. This is a tiny occupation, with only about 500 people currently employed. So, even though it is growing rapidly, it will not create many new jobs (about 30 per year). Now consider General and Operations Managers. Because of the decline of domestic manufacturing, this occupation is not growing at all; it's expected to shrink by 0.1 percent. Nevertheless, this is a huge occupation that employs 1.7 million workers. So, even though the workforce size will not increase, the occupation is expected to take on 50,000 new workers each year as existing workers move on to other jobs, retire, or die. That's why I base my selection of the best jobs on both of these economic indicators and why you should pay attention to both when you scan the lists of best jobs.

How This Book Is Organized

The information in this book about best jobs for your skills moves from the general to the highly specific.

Part I. Overview of Skills and Careers

Part I is an overview of what skills are, how to develop them, and how they relate to career choice.

Part II. What Are Your Top Skills? Take an Assessment

Part II is a self-assessment exercise that presents 9 skills. It goes further than a simple checklist by doing all of the following:

 ❋ It defines each skill, sometimes by focusing on a specific skill as a way of measuring a more general skill.

 ❋ It gives you several contexts for understanding how the skill is learned and used: related school subjects, leisure activities, and work tasks at several levels of ability.

 ❋ It asks for your self-estimate of your level of skill.

 ❋ It challenges your self-estimate by asking you to provide examples from your own experiences of how you have demonstrated this skill.

You can complete the assessment in about 45 minutes—more or less, depending on how fast you work—and it will help you understand which skills are your best. As an extra benefit, the skill-related experiences that you jot down here can come in handy in the future when you are writing a resume or a cover letter for a job application.

Part III. The Best Jobs Lists: Jobs for Each of the 9 Skills

For many people, the 97 lists in Part III are the most interesting feature of the book. Here you can see titles of jobs that require a high level of one of your top skills and that have the best combination of high salaries, fast growth, and plentiful job openings. You can see which jobs are best for these factors combined or considered separately. Jobs are broken out further according to education levels, career clusters, and personality types and to highlight jobs with a high percentage of various types of workers, such as those who are self-employed. Look in the Table of Contents for a complete list of lists. Although there are a lot of lists, they are not difficult to understand because they have clear titles and are organized into groupings of related lists.

Following are the names of each group of lists along with short comments on each group.

Best Jobs Overall for Each Skill: Jobs with the Highest Pay, Fastest Growth, and Most Openings

These four sets of nine lists (one for each skill) are the ones that you probably want to see first. The first set of lists presents, for each skill, up to 50 jobs that have that skill among their three most important skills. (For two skills, 30 jobs are listed.) The second set presents the 20 best-paying jobs from the top jobs for each skill. The third set presents the 20 fastest-growing jobs from the top jobs for each skill. The fourth set presents the 20 jobs with the most openings from the top jobs for each skill.

Best High-Skill Jobs by Demographic

Like other books in the *Best Jobs* series, this one includes lists that show what sorts of jobs different types of people are most likely to have. For example, you can see which jobs have the highest percentage of men or young workers. I'm not saying that men or young people should consider these jobs over others based solely on this information, but it is interesting information to know.

In some cases, the lists can give you ideas for jobs to consider that you might otherwise overlook. For example, perhaps women should consider some jobs that traditionally have high percentages of men in them. Or older workers might consider some jobs typically held by young people. Although these aren't obvious ways of using these lists, the lists may give you some good ideas of jobs to consider. The lists may also help you identify jobs that work well for others in your situation—for example, jobs that are well represented in rural areas, if that's where you live.

All lists in this section were created through a similar process. I began with the 199 unique best jobs and sorted these jobs by the primary criterion for each set of lists. For example, I sorted the jobs based on the percentage of workers age 16–24 from highest to lowest percentage and selected the jobs with a high percentage (19 jobs with a percentage greater than 15). Then I sorted these jobs by their combined scores for earnings, growth rate, and number of openings. The lists show these three economic factors for each job. Because this book is about jobs for your skills, the lists have a column immediately to the right of each occupation name that shows abbreviations (such as "COM" for Communication Skills) for the top skills for the job.

The same basic process was used to create all the lists in this section, and they are all formatted the same way. The lists are very interesting, and I hope you find them helpful.

Best High-Skill Jobs by Education or Training Required

I created a separate list for each level of education and training as defined by the U.S. Department of Labor, and I assigned job titles to the lists based on the education, training, and experience usually required for entry. Jobs in these lists are presented in order of their total combined scores for earnings, growth, and number of openings. In addition to the economic information that guided the ordering, I show the top skills for each job on each list.

Best High-Skill Jobs by Career Cluster

These lists organize the 199 unique best jobs into the 16 career clusters that are used by many educational institutions and career information resources to divide up the world of work. For each cluster, you can see the jobs ordered by the combination of their scores for earnings, growth, and number of openings. You'll also see the top skills for each job.

Best High-Skill Jobs by Personality Type

These lists organize the 199 high-skill jobs into six personality types, which are described in the introduction to the lists: Realistic, Investigative, Artistic, Social, Enterprising, and Conventional. The jobs within each list are presented in order of their total scores for earnings, growth, and number of openings. For each job, I identify the top skills.

Bonus Lists About Skills

Unlike the other lists, these don't contain jobs, but they do contain interesting information on the relationship between skills and work:

- ❁ One list orders the 9 skills by how closely they are associated with **income**. Specifically, it orders them by how much a difference in skill level is accompanied by a difference in income.

- ❁ A second list orders the 9 skills by how closely they are associated with job **growth**. Specifically, it orders them by how much a difference in skill level is accompanied by a difference in projected job growth.

- ❁ A third list orders the 9 skills by the average number of job **openings** projected for the occupations with the highest levels of skill.

- ❁ A set of lists shows, for each of the 9 skills, the 10 **industries** where the skill is most concentrated in the workforce. Using this information, you can plan your career for a segment of the economy where demand for the skill is really hot.

- ❁ A set of lists shows, for each of the 9 skills, the 20 **metropolitan areas** where the skill is most concentrated in the workforce. Using this information, you can see how well your skills match employer needs in your geographical area or identify another area where your skills would be a better fit.

Part IV: Descriptions of the Best Jobs for Your Skills

This part describes the best jobs for your skills, using a format that is informative yet compact and easy to read. Because the jobs in this section are arranged in alphabetical order, you can easily find a job that you've identified from Part III and that you want to learn more about.

As explained earlier in this introduction, the job titles used in the lists are based on the Standard Occupational Classification (SOC), but in Part IV many SOC titles are linked to one or more "job specializations," which are O*NET occupation titles.

Although I've tried to make the descriptions easy to understand, the sample that follows—with an explanation of each of its parts—may help you better understand and use the descriptions. Note that the O*NET database provides much more detailed information about some jobs than others, and these differences in detail are reflected in the job descriptions in Part IV.

❋ **Job Title:** This is the title for the job as defined by the SOC taxonomy.

❋ **Data Elements:** The information comes from various U.S. Department of Labor and Census Bureau databases, as explained elsewhere in this introduction.

❋ **Skills:** The O*NET database provides data on 35 skills; I decided to collapse those into 9 skills, as explained in detail earlier. First I identify as many as three skills that are most important for each job—the skills that were used in the Part III lists. Following these are any other skills that were significantly higher than the average rating for that skill for all jobs. Taken together, the two sets of skills are ordered by descending level of mastery required.

❋ **Summary Description and Tasks:** The boldfaced sentence provides a summary description of the occupation. It is followed by a listing of tasks generally performed by people who work in this job. This information comes from the O*NET database but, where necessary, has been edited to avoid exceeding 1,500 characters.

❋ **Education/Training Required:** Based mostly on information from the BLS, this phrase identifies the most common level of education or training that is required of workers entering the career. Understand that a higher level of preparation may sometimes be beneficial, either to make you more competitive against other job seekers or to allow you to enter the job at a more responsible and better-paying level. On the other hand, if the demand for workers is high, it sometimes may be possible for you to enter the career with a lower level of preparation.

❋ **Education and Training Program(s):** This part of the job description provides the name of the educational or training program(s) for the job. It will help you identify sources of formal or informal training for a job that interests you.

Job Title

Healthcare Social Workers

Data Elements

- ❋ Annual Earnings: $47,230
- ❋ Earnings Growth Potential: Medium (37.6%)
- ❋ Growth: 22.4%
- ❋ Annual Job Openings: 6,590
- ❋ Self-Employed: 2.2%

Skills

Skills—Most Important: Science Skills; Social Skills; Communication Skills. **Other High-Level Skills:** Thought-Processing Skills; Management Skills.

Summary Description and Tasks

Provide persons, families, or vulnerable populations with the psychosocial support needed to cope with chronic, acute, or terminal illnesses such as Alzheimer's, cancer, or AIDS. Services include advising family caregivers, providing patient education and counseling, and making necessary referrals for other social services. Collaborate with other professionals to evaluate patients' medical or physical condition and to assess client needs. Investigate child abuse or neglect cases and take authorized protective action when necessary. Refer patient, client, or family to community resources to assist in recovery from mental or physical illness and to provide access to services such as financial assistance, legal aid, housing, job placement, or education. Counsel clients and patients in individual and group sessions to help them overcome dependencies, recover from illness, and adjust to life. Organize support groups or counsel family members to assist them in understanding, dealing with, and supporting the client or patient. Advocate for clients or patients to resolve crises. Identify environmental impediments to client or patient progress through interviews and review of patient records. Utilize consultation data and social work experience to plan and coordinate client or patient care and rehabilitation, following through to ensure service efficacy. Modify treatment plans to comply with changes in clients' status. Monitor, evaluate, and record client progress according to measurable goals described in treatment and care plan. Supervise and direct other workers providing services to clients or patients. Develop or advise on social policy and assist in community development. Oversee Medicaid- and Medicare-related paperwork and recordkeeping in hospitals.

Education/Training Required, Education and Training Program(s), Knowledge/Courses

Education/Training Required: Bachelor's degree. **Education and Training Program:** Clinical/Medical Social Work. **Knowledge/ Courses:** Therapy and Counseling; Sociology and Anthropology; Psychology; Philosophy and Theology; Customer and Personal Service; Medicine and Dentistry.

Personality Type, Career Cluster(s), Career Pathway(s), Other Jobs in This Pathway

Personality Type: Social-Investigative. **Career Cluster:** 10 Human Services. **Career Pathway:** 10.2 Counseling and Mental Health Services. **Other Jobs in This Pathway:** Clergy; Clinical Psychologists; Counseling Psychologists; Counselors, All Other; Directors, Religious Activities and Education; Epidemiologists; Health Educators; Marriage and Family Therapists; Mental Health and Substance Abuse Social Workers; Mental Health Counselors; Music Directors; Psychologists, All Other; Recreation Workers; Religious Workers, All Other; School Psychologists; Substance Abuse and Behavioral Disorder Counselors.

❋ **Knowledge/Courses:** This entry can help you understand the most important knowledge areas that are required for a job and the types of courses or programs you will likely need to take to prepare for it. I used information in the O*NET database for this entry. For each job, I identified any knowledge area with a rating that was higher than the average rating for that knowledge area for all jobs; then I listed as many as six in descending order.

❋ **Personality Type:** The O*NET database assigns each job to a primary personality type and to as many as two secondary types. These job descriptions include the names of the related personality types. You can find more information on the personality types as well as a brief definition of each type in the introduction to the lists of jobs based on personality types in Part III.

❋ **Career Cluster(s), Career Pathway(s),** and **Other Jobs in This Pathway:** This information cross-references the scheme of career clusters and pathways that was created by the U.S. Department of Education's Office of Vocational and Adult Education in 1999 and is now used by many states to organize career-oriented programs and career information. In identifying a career cluster and pathway for the job (sometimes more than one), I followed the assignments of the online O*NET database. Your state might assign this job to a different career pathway or even a different cluster.

Getting all the information I used in the job descriptions was not a simple process, and it is not always perfect. Even so, I used the best and most recent sources of data I could find, and I think that my efforts will be helpful to many people.

Credits and Acknowledgments: While the author created this book, it is based on the work of many others. The occupational information is based on data obtained from the U.S. Department of Labor, the Census Bureau, and the Department of Education. These sources provide the most authoritative occupational information available.

Part I

Overview of Skills and Careers

This part provides a useful look at skills and their importance to your career.

What Exactly Is a Skill?

A skill is a learned capability to perform actions. Let's look at the parts of that definition.

A skill is a capability because it gives you the potential to do something competently. It's not a guarantee of success, but it means you are *able* to succeed. It's not a preference for doing something, although people tend to prefer doing what they're good at.

A skill is learned because it is not something you're born with, and it is not acquired through normal sensory development (as depth perception is) or through special physical conditioning (as the ability to bench-press 250 pounds would be). It is not a talent or aptitude, which means a capacity for learning something easily; it is the fruit of learning. Not all learning comes from books or formal instructional programs. In fact, you may learn a skill without conscious intent or even awareness of the learning process. For example, you may acquire certain social skills, such as being sensitive to other people's feelings, through day-to-day experiences without realizing you are doing so.

A skill allows you to perform actions rather than just know or feel something, which is what makes it valuable to employers. It gets the job done. For example, some social skills may be referred to as "a positive attitude," but they require more than just a sunny feeling. They require such actions as seeing things from someone else's point of view, speaking in a cheerful tone of voice, or offering to help. Some skills are largely intellectual, but even these skills contribute to work tasks. For example, critical-thinking skills would enable you to decide which supplier to buy from or where to drill for oil.

People sometimes don't realize all the skills they have. For example, they may think that a positive attitude on the job is just a feeling or that critical thinking is just a matter of raw intelligence. Part II of this book can help you take stock of your skills so you can aspire toward appropriate jobs and use effective wording on your resume, on job application letters, and in interviews.

How Can I Develop My Skills?

If you're in school (and paying attention), you're making progress on developing your skills. But skill-building is not just for young people. Because skills are learned, you can develop them throughout your lifetime. In fact, you'd better. If you're working now, your present job will undergo changes. What if part of your job is taken over by a computer? What if your employer wants to expand to a world market? Will you have the skills to adjust easily? And if you lose your job for whatever reason, if you decide to change your job, or if you're not yet in the workforce, will you have the skills that employers are looking for? Employers often complain that younger job applicants lack certain vital social skills (they're "slackers," they're "surly," or they "have an attitude problem") and that older job applicants lack emerging technology skills (they're "fuddy-duddies" or "dinosaurs"). Don't be one of those rejects! Develop the skills that employers want.

Developing skills is never easy. The process requires you to accept challenges and learn how to overcome them. As an old African proverb says, "A smooth sea never made a skillful mariner." On the other hand, if you take on a challenge that's too far above your current abilities, you may get discouraged. The trick is to find a way you can learn in small steps and get support when you need it.

Informal Learning

The best way to learn work-related skills is on the job. Even for jobs that require certain educational credentials, most job-specific skills are learned after you're hired. When you see co-workers using skills that you don't have, watch what they do and ask them to show you how. Most co-workers will be happy to teach you, if it doesn't take up too much of their time. When you feel you have mastered the skill, ask your supervisor for an assignment that uses the skill—perhaps not a high-stakes project, but something that will demonstrate your new skill. Then be sure to ask for feedback that specifically targets your use of the skill. What did you do right? How could you have done it better? Try not to be defensive in response to criticism; use this feedback as part of the learning process.

If you're not working now, you can get informal on-the-job training in specific skills by doing volunteer work in a relevant setting. For example, to improve your social skills, do volunteer work at a senior center, a charity fundraising event, or some other setting where there's a lot of interaction with people. Some hobbies also provide opportunities for you to learn skills—for example, designing Web pages, customizing cars, or gardening. With hobbies, it helps to join a club so you can learn from more highly skilled hobbyists and get feedback on your accomplishments. Keep in mind that your volunteer work can do more than help others, and your hobby can be more than self-indulgence. Use informal activities as skill academies. Challenge yourself with new tasks; ask for feedback.

Sometimes you can create your own training program by studying a book or technical manual (maybe one aimed at "dummies"). In fact, if the skill you want to learn is very rare (for example, speaking Estonian) or on the cutting edge of technology (for example, using the very latest software), you may have no choice but to design your own curriculum because you can't find anyone to teach you. If you're very lucky, you may be able to convince your employer to pay for the books or other learning aids and to give you time in the workday for upgrading your skills. But most workers find that they have to use lunch hours, evenings, and weekends for this self-training. Consider the time and expense of self-training as investments in your future employability. Try to find a study partner to learn with you; study partners help reinforce each other's learning and keep the learning program on track.

For more details about how to study informally, including a sample e-mail you can send to your boss asking for a skills-testing assignment, see my book *The Sequel: How to Change Your Career Without Starting Over*.

Formal Learning

Some skills can be learned only in formal settings. Doctors, for example, must go to medical school. Often a specific college degree or apprenticeship is the accepted way of preparing for a certain career. Accountants usually have a degree in accounting or at least in business. Most electricians learn through a formal apprenticeship program.

But many other skills are taught in single classes rather than in long-term programs— and not because formal learning is required but because so many people want to learn these skills. Night schools and corporate training centers offer classes in technical skills, such as using spreadsheets or driving trucks, and in soft skills, such as conducting meetings or reading people's body language. Another setting for training is the annual conference of the professional association relevant to your career, where you can attend training workshops.

Because the need for these popular skills is so obvious, employers often are willing to cover the expenses and perhaps the time these classes require. Be sure to find out what classes your employer makes available and consider taking them if they are at all relevant to your work. Your employer will appreciate your desire to upgrade your skills.

Sometimes employers are not willing to set aside funding or time for classes that would add to your skills, especially if your workday is very busy or if the skills you are seeking are not obviously relevant to your job. In fact, your employer may fear that you would use your new skills to find work elsewhere—and, in fact, that is another good reason for upgrading your skills. If your employer is unwilling to help or you are not currently employed, you may need to find (and pay for) useful night classes at your local high school, vocational school, or community college. Alternatively, it may be worthwhile for you to invest your time and money in a very relevant night class at a proprietary technical school (or "institute"). First, talk to employers and get evidence that they will value this credential. Some shady education providers claim to be teaching in-demand skills but leave you with a lot of debt and insufficient preparation for the job you thought you'd get.

If you are still in college, you should consider an internship as a way of acquiring skills that can't be learned in the classroom. Much of the learning that takes place during an internship is equivalent to informal on-the-job training, but internship programs often have formal requirements and procedures for recruitment and sometimes include formal classes.

Just as you need nutritious food, exercise, and a good night's sleep to keep your body healthy, you need a regular program of upgrading your skills to keep your career healthy. It doesn't matter whether you learn formally or informally, from a book or by rolling up your sleeves, in cooperation with your employer or on your own. Just be sure you keep on learning.

How Are Skills and Career Choice Related?

A good career goal is one in which you will be successful and find satisfaction.

To be *successful* on the job, you need the specific skills that are relevant to the work tasks. For example, most health-care jobs involve tasks that require contact with patients, so the workers need social and communication skills, among others. Most teaching jobs involve tasks that require breaking ideas into bite-sized pieces, so the workers need thought-processing skills, among others.

Your *satisfaction* on the job also will depend on how well your skills match the job. How happy can you be in a job if you constantly feel overwhelmed by the duties? How happy can you be if the work is so lacking in challenge that you are bored most of the time? In a recent poll, 54 percent of professionals stated that their current job does not utilize their skills and that they transfer jobs frequently. These workers need to find a better match between their skills and their work.

Therefore this book is designed to help you clarify your outstanding skills and identify good jobs that can use those skills.

You may not yet have *all* the skills needed for the job you choose as your goal. In fact, you may need to take classes, get on-the-job training, or get work experience to qualify for the job. But it makes sense for you to aim for a job where you already have *some* of the skills. Here's why:

❀ As you seek a career goal that at least partly matches your skills, the learning curve will not be so steep.

⊛ You will have a track record of relevant accomplishments.

⊛ You will have self-confidence from having tried and succeeded at some of the required tasks (or tasks similar to them).

That's why I designed the next section of this book, Part II, to help you identify the skills you already have.

How Important Are Skills in the Hiring Process?

Whenever employers are looking at your resume, interviewing you, or talking to your references, the question that is uppermost in their minds is, "Does this job applicant have the skills needed to get the job done?"

As evidence, consider what the National Association of Manufacturers found in 2001 when they asked members why they reject job applicants. Of the 14 reasons most frequently cited, 6 were about skills deficiencies:

⊛ Inadequate reading/writing skills

⊛ Inadequate oral communication skills

⊛ Inadequate math skills

⊛ Inadequate technical/computer skills

⊛ Inadequate problem-solving skills

⊛ Inadequate basic employability skills (attendance, timeliness, work ethic, and so on)

A seventh reason, "inability to work in a team environment," may also be considered a skills deficiency.

Note that this research applies to only one industry: manufacturing. It is true that these same skills are vital in all career fields and at almost all worksites. However, the particular *blend* of skills, the emphasis on some skills in the mix rather than on others, varies from field to field and from job to job. One goal of this book is to help you identify the jobs that emphasize your strongest skills.

The "basic employability skills (attendance, timeliness, work ethic, and so on)" that manufacturers were not finding in job applicants are so fundamental to workplace success that they are equally important in *all* jobs. I don't include them in this book, but that's not because they are not essential. On the contrary, they are so vital that it would not be meaningful to say they are more important for one job than for another.

What Do I Need at Work Besides Skills?

Employers sometimes mention other important personal qualities, such as self-esteem, honesty, and comfort working with people from different backgrounds, as important at work. These traits are essential at work but arguably don't fit under the definition of skills. Because O*NET does not classify these qualities under skills, I do not include them in this book. Nevertheless, they're just as fundamental for success as the basic employability skills.

You may have all the skills required for an occupation and still not get hired. That's because being hired often depends on many other factors. For example, the occupation may require a license or certification for workers. Having the necessary skills will probably help you qualify for the license or certification, but you may also have to overcome other hurdles, such as completing required classes, earning a degree at an accredited institution, passing a test, completing supervised work experience, and paying a fee.

In addition, there needs to be a job opening and you need to be aware of it. You may need to relocate. Alternatively, you may create a job opening for yourself by convincing an employer that your skills are just what the company needs or by starting your own business.

Finally, skills are not the same thing as motivation. To get and keep a job, you must want to do the work. As Muhammad Ali once remarked, "Champions...have to have the skill and the will. But the will must be stronger than the skill." This book is designed to help you find a job that appeals to you because it's a good match for your skills, pays well, and has lots of job openings. But be sure to read all the details about the job in Part IV—and then do additional career exploration—to make sure that the job is one you'll really want to pursue and will enjoy once you're in it.

How Does This Book Help Me Identify My Outstanding Skills?

The best way to identify your outstanding skills would be to gather outside appraisals of *all* your previous experiences on the job, in school, and in leisure-time activities. This would require a huge effort. You'd need to get in touch with all your previous employers, co-workers, and customers; your teachers and trainers; and the people you spend time with on evenings and weekends. You'd need to remind them of all the tasks you performed in these settings and ask them for honest appraisals of your performance. Then you'd need to connect their responses to a consistent set of skill names and reconcile situations where one person thought you did well and another thought you did poorly. What a chore! But the results would be extremely well-informed and therefore extremely accurate.

At the other extreme, you could look at a listing of skills and check off the skills you think you have. This checklist approach often works very well for determining *interests*. But for a *skills* self-assessment to be accurate, it needs to give you some *contexts* for making decisions about which skills you have and which you lack. Specifically, you need a full understanding of what each skill is—a definition with examples, not just a name—and you need a way to connect the skill to your experiences at work, in school, and elsewhere.

That's the kind of depth that you'll find in the assessment in Part II. For each of the 9 skills, I give you a definition, examples of high school courses that teach it, examples of leisure activities that use it, and examples of work tasks that use it—many of which are the same tasks considered as examples by the job analysts, experts, and workers who develop the O*NET skill ratings. The assessment then asks you to give a preliminary self-estimate of your skill level.

And it doesn't stop there. If you think you have more than a low level of skill, it asks you to jot down *examples* of how you have demonstrated the skill, drawn from your experience on the job, in school, or in leisure activities. This additional step gives you a way to provide a context for confirming your self-estimate. You may also find these examples useful in the future when you will need to provide evidence of your qualifications for a job in a resume, a cover letter, or an interview.

Finally, the assessment asks you to review your responses and select the skills that have the highest self-estimates and the most examples of experiences. That means that your decisions about your skills are grounded in a context that allows you to make an informed judgment. If you are honest and thoughtful about your responses, you will gain a useful understanding of your top skills. Then you can use that understanding to identify good jobs that use your top skills.

So why not get started? Find out your most important skills by turning the page and doing the exercise in Part II.

Part II

What Are Your Top Skills? Take an Assessment

Before you look at the lists of best jobs, I want you to determine which skills are your strongest. That's what you'll do in this part. The exercise in this part takes about 45 minutes. It's time well spent, because the exercise can give you thoughtful insights into your skills, and it's linked to the U.S. Department of Labor's authoritative O*NET database of information about occupations. What you'll learn from this exercise will help you focus on one or more occupations as promising career goals.

This exercise will not *guarantee* you a particular job or *prove* that you're qualified for the job. However, what you say here about your experiences can provide useful material to include in resumes, cover letters, and interviews. This material, along with whatever formal credentials you possess (such as a certificate or a college degree), your natural abilities, the positive testimonials of your references, and your personal charm can prove that you're the candidate the employer should hire.

Keep in mind that this exercise focuses on *skills* but not on *abilities*, such as being able to carry 50 pounds—or a tune. It also does not emphasize interests. It focuses first on what you *can* do well, and only afterward asks you to consider what you *like* to do. For most people these two are closely linked, but in some people there are differences.

Step 1: Rate Your Skills

Nobody is going to grade you on your answers to this exercise. The most important thing is to answer honestly. If someone else will be using this book, do the writing on a separate piece of paper.

For each skill, read the definition and examples and then estimate your level of mastery. If you believe you command the skill at a moderate or high level, you'll confirm that estimate by providing examples from your own experiences of using the skill. At the end of the exercise, you'll review your self-estimates and examples and decide which are your outstanding skills.

You'll note that some skills have names that indicate they are "measured by" a more specific skill. For example, the first skill is called "Communication Skills (Measured by Reading Comprehension)." This indicates that the assessment is asking you about your ability with just *one specific skill* as a fast way of predicting how good you are at a family of related skills. Later, you'll use that family of skills (such as Communication Skills) to identify jobs that may be a good fit for you. These more general skills are also used in the lists in Part III and in the job descriptions in Part IV.

Communication Skills (Measured by Reading Comprehension)

Definition of Reading Comprehension: Understanding written sentences and paragraphs in work-related documents.

Examples of High School Subjects That Teach Reading Comprehension

- ❋ English
- ❋ Literature

Examples of Leisure Activities That Use Reading Comprehension

- ❋ Reading magazines, newspapers, and books
- ❋ Reading directions for a test
- ❋ Being able to summarize for a friend something you've read

Examples of Work Tasks That Use Reading Comprehension

- ❋ Following a restaurant's recipe for a beef stew
- ❋ Reading step-by-step instructions for completing a form
- ❋ Reading a memo from management describing new personnel policies
- ❋ Reading a schedule for freight pickups and deliveries
- ❋ Reading a licensing agreement before purchasing software
- ❋ Reading a scientific journal article describing surgical procedures

Using the examples of high school courses, leisure activities, and work tasks and your knowledge of yourself for guidance, circle a number to estimate your level of command of this skill.

Communication Skills Self-Estimate
(Based on Reading Comprehension)

Low Level			Moderate Level			High Level		
1	2	3	4	5	6	7	8	9

If your self-estimate is 3 or lower, move on to the next skill, **Equipment Use/Maintenance Skills**. Otherwise, continue.

Examples of How I Demonstrated Communication Skills Through Reading Comprehension

Think of examples of how you have demonstrated your command of this skill and write the examples in the following worksheet.

❋ Write as many examples as you can, but you don't have to fill all the space.

❋ If possible, base your examples on work you've done, following the style of the work examples listed earlier.

❋ If you have little or no relevant work experience, write examples from school or leisure activities.

Examples of How I Demonstrated Communication Skills
Through Reading Comprehension

_____

_____

_____

_____

_____

Based on the examples, do you now want to change your self-estimate? Feel free to do so. Then go on to the next skill.

Equipment Use/Maintenance Skills (Measured by Equipment Maintenance)

Definition of Equipment Maintenance: Performing routine maintenance and determining when and what kind of maintenance is needed.

Examples of High School Subjects That Teach Equipment Maintenance

❋ Laboratory components of science courses

❋ Technology education

Examples of Leisure Activities That Use Equipment Maintenance

❋ Repairing plumbing in the home

❋ Working on bicycles, minibikes, lawnmowers, or cars

❋ Running utility programs to improve computer performance

Examples of Work Tasks That Use Equipment Maintenance

❋ Identifying the source of a leak by looking under a machine

❋ Adding oil to an engine as indicated by a gauge or warning light

❋ Adjusting or replacing worn or defective parts in an escalator

❋ Cleaning moving parts in production machinery

❋ Soldering loose electronic connections using a soldering iron

❋ Conducting maintenance checks on an experimental aircraft

Using the examples of high school courses, leisure activities, and work tasks and your knowledge of yourself for guidance, circle a number to estimate your level of command of this skill.

Equipment Use/Maintenance Skills Self-Estimate (Based on Equipment Maintenance)

Low Level	Moderate Level	High Level
1 2 3	4 5 6	7 8 9

If your self-estimate is 3 or lower, move on to the next skill, **Installation Skills**. Otherwise, continue.

Examples of How I Demonstrated Equipment Use/Maintenance Skills Through Equipment Maintenance

Think of examples of how you have demonstrated your command of this skill and write the examples in the following worksheet.

❋ Write as many examples as you can, but you don't have to fill all the space.

❋ If possible, base your examples on work you've done, following the style of the work examples listed earlier.

❋ If you have little or no relevant work experience, write examples from school or leisure activities.

Examples of How I Demonstrated Equipment Use/Maintenance Skills Through Equipment Maintenance

_____

_____

_____

_____

_____

Based on the examples, do you now want to change your self-estimate? Feel free to do so. Then go on to the next skill.

Installation Skills

Definition of Installation Skills: Installing equipment, machines, wiring, or programs to meet specifications.

Examples of High School Subjects That Teach Installation Skills

❋ Laboratory components of science courses

❋ Technology education

Examples of Leisure Activities That Use Installation Skills

❋ Installing a new air filter in an air conditioner

❋ Installing and configuring a new computer program

❋ Installing weather stripping around a door

Examples of Work Tasks That Use Installation Skills

Level of Skill

- ❋ Installing a water cooler in an office building
- ❋ Installing new switches for a telephone exchange
- ❋ Installing a motion-detector security alarm system
- ❋ Installing a solar panel array on a rooftop
- ❋ Installing a one-of-a-kind production molding machine

Using the examples of high school courses, leisure activities, and work tasks and your knowledge of yourself for guidance, circle a number to estimate your level of command of this skill.

Installation Skills Self-Estimate

Low Level	Moderate Level	High Level
1 2 3	4 5 6	7 8 9

If your self-estimate is 3 or lower, move on to the next skill, **Management Skills.** Otherwise, continue.

Examples of How I Demonstrated Installation Skills

Think of examples of how you have demonstrated your command of this skill and write the examples in the following worksheet.

- ❋ Write as many examples as you can, but you don't have to fill all the space.
- ❋ If possible, base your examples on work you've done, following the style of the work examples listed earlier.
- ❋ If you have little or no relevant work experience, write examples from school or leisure activities.

Examples of How I Demonstrated Installation Skills

_____

_____

_____

_____

_____

Based on the examples, do you now want to change your self-estimate? Feel free to do so. Then go on to the next skill.

Management Skills (Measured by Management of Financial Resources)

Definition of Management of Financial Resources: Determining how money will be spent to get the work done and accounting for these expenditures.

Examples of High School Subjects That Teach Management of Financial Resources

❊ Accounting

❊ Family and consumer science

❊ Business education

Examples of Leisure Activities That Use Management of Financial Resources

❊ Acting as treasurer for a club or organization

❊ Balancing a checkbook

❊ Organizing a budget for household expenses

Examples of Work Tasks That Use Management of Financial Resources

Lowest

Level of Skill

Highest

❊ Taking money from petty cash to buy office supplies and recording the amount

❊ Preparing and managing a budget for a short-term project

❊ Projecting next year's expenses for a business, based on this year's expenditures to date

❊ Estimating how to combine loans with expected sales to finance the operations of a business

Using the examples of high school courses, leisure activities, and work tasks and your knowledge of yourself for guidance, circle a number to estimate your level of command of this skill.

Management Skills Self-Estimate
(Based on Management of Financial Resources)

Low Level				Moderate Level				High Level	
1	2	3	4	5	6	7	8	9

If your self-estimate is 3 or lower, move on to the next skill, **Mathematics Skills**. Otherwise, continue.

Examples of How I Demonstrated Management Skills Through Management of Financial Resources

Think of examples of how you have demonstrated your command of this skill and write the examples in the following worksheet.

❋ Write as many examples as you can, but you don't have to fill all the space.

❋ If possible, base your examples on work you've done, following the style of the work examples listed earlier.

❋ If you have little or no relevant work experience, write examples from school or leisure activities.

Examples of How I Demonstrated Management Skills
Through Management of Financial Resources

_____

_____

_____

_____

_____

Based on the examples, do you now want to change your self-estimate? Feel free to do so. Then go on to the next skill.

Mathematics Skills

Definition of Mathematics Skills: Using mathematics to solve problems: calculating, estimating, and constructing mathematical models.

Examples of High School Subjects That Teach Mathematics Skills

❋ Algebra

❋ Geometry

❋ Trigonometry

❋ Calculus

❋ Business/Applied Mathematics

Examples of Leisure Activities That Use Mathematics Skills

❋ Computing sports statistics

❋ Multiplying measurements to scale up a recipe

❋ Preparing family income tax returns

Examples of Work Tasks That Use Mathematics Skills

Lowest

Level of Skill

Highest

❋ Computing totals of orders placed by clients

❋ Counting the amount of change to be given to a customer

❋ Estimating how many cans of paint are needed to cover a house with two coats

❋ Computing reduction of heat loss from a house after application of attic insulation

❋ Applying a mathematical theory to develop a new way to encrypt data

❋ Developing a mathematical model of how a mutated gene spreads through a population

Using the examples of high school courses, leisure activities, and work tasks and your knowledge of yourself for guidance, circle a number to estimate your level of command of this skill.

Mathematics Skills Self-Estimate

Low Level		Moderate Level			High Level	
1	2	3	4	5	6	7	8	9

If your self-estimate is 3 or lower, move on to the next skill, **Science Skills.** Otherwise, continue.

Examples of How I Demonstrated Mathematics Skills

Think of examples of how you have demonstrated your command of this skill and write the examples in the following worksheet.

❋ Write as many examples as you can, but you don't have to fill all the space.

❋ If possible, base your examples on work you've done, following the style of the work examples listed earlier.

❋ If you have little or no relevant work experience, write examples from school or leisure activities.

Examples of How I Demonstrated Mathematics Skills

_____

_____

_____

_____

_____

Based on the examples, do you now want to change your self-estimate? Feel free to do so. Then go on to the next skill.

Science Skills

Definition of Science Skills: Using scientific rules and methods to solve problems: observing phenomena, proposing a hypothesis, making a prediction, designing and conducting experiments to test the prediction, and constructing theories.

Examples of High School Subjects That Teach Science Skills

❋ Biology

❋ Chemistry

❋ Earth science

❋ Physics

Examples of Leisure Activities That Use Science Skills

❈ Collecting rocks or minerals

❈ Conducting experiments involving plants

❈ Experimenting with a chemistry set

❈ Observing and studying the moon and stars

❈ Performing experiments for a science fair

❈ Studying the habits of wildlife

Examples of Work Tasks That Use Science Skills

Level of Skill — Lowest / Highest

❈ Collecting air samples to determine levels of radioactive contamination

❈ Conducting standard tests in a dairy to determine nutrient contents of milk

❈ Designing an experiment to test a hypothesis about what causes a product to fail

❈ Creating a questionnaire to measure public opinion during a political campaign

❈ Analyzing the effect of forest conditions on tree growth rates and populations of tree species

❈ Conducting a research study concerning important factors in animal nutrition

Using the examples of high school courses, leisure activities, and work tasks and your knowledge of yourself for guidance, circle a number to estimate your level of command of this skill.

Science Skills Self-Estimate

Low Level			Moderate Level			High Level		
1	2	3	4	5	6	7	8	9

If your self-estimate is 3 or lower, move on to the next skill, **Social Skills**. Otherwise, continue.

Examples of How I Demonstrated Science Skills

Think of examples of how you have demonstrated your command of this skill and write the examples in the following worksheet.

❈ Write as many examples as you can, but you don't have to fill all the space.

❈ If possible, base your examples on work you've done, following the style of the work examples listed earlier.

✳ If you have little or no relevant work experience, write examples from school or leisure activities.

Examples of How I Demonstrated Science Skills

_____

_____

_____

_____

_____

Based on the examples, do you now want to change your self-estimate? Feel free to do so. Then go on to the next skill.

Social Skills (Measured by Service Orientation)

Definition of Service Orientation: Actively looking for ways to help people.

Examples of High School Subjects That Teach Service Orientation

✳ First aid

✳ Family living

Examples of Leisure Activities That Use Service Orientation

✳ Helping sick relatives, friends, and neighbors

✳ Serving as a volunteer counselor at a youth camp or center

✳ Tutoring pupils in school subjects or adults in literacy

Examples of Work Tasks That Use Service Orientation

Level of Skill — Lowest / Highest

✳ Asking customers if they would like cups of coffee

✳ Visiting people in hospitals to provide them with comfort and support

✳ Making flight reservations for customers, using an airline reservation system

✳ Showing understanding while counseling people about personal problems

✳ Directing relief agency operations in a disaster area

Using the examples of high school courses, leisure activities, and work tasks and your knowledge of yourself for guidance, circle a number to estimate your level of command of this skill.

Social Skills Self-Estimate
(Based on Service Orientation)

Low Level			Moderate Level			High Level		
1	2	3	4	5	6	7	8	9

If your self-estimate is 3 or lower, move on to the next skill, **Technology/Programming Skills**. Otherwise, continue.

Examples of How I Demonstrated Social Skills Through Service Orientation

Think of examples of how you have demonstrated your command of this skill and write the examples in the following worksheet.

❋ Write as many examples as you can, but you don't have to fill all the space.

❋ If possible, base your examples on work you've done, following the style of the work examples listed earlier.

❋ If you have little or no relevant work experience, write examples from school or leisure activities.

Examples of How I Demonstrated Social Skills
Through Service Orientation

_____

_____

_____

_____

_____

Based on the examples, do you now want to change your self-estimate? Feel free to do so. Then go on to the next skill.

Technology/Programming Skills (Measured by Computer Programming)

Definition of Computer Programming: Writing computer programs for various purposes: structuring the algorithm for the task at hand, organizing data storage, determining methods of input and output, choosing the right commands and syntax, and correcting errors.

Example of High School Subject That Teaches Computer Programming

❋ Computer science

Examples of Leisure Activities That Use Computer Programming

❋ Creating and modifying a macro in a word-processing program to accomplish a complex task

❋ Programming computer games

❋ Writing computer programs to solve puzzles

Examples of Work Tasks That Use Computer Programming

Lowest

Level of Skill

Highest

❋ Writing a program to convert metric measurements to inches, pounds, and so forth

❋ Coding a BASIC program to sort objects in a database

❋ Writing a computer program to extract text from a Web page and reformat it for a book

❋ Coding a function to accomplish a common text-processing task

❋ Coding a statistical analysis program to analyze demographic data

❋ Writing a program to analyze coded messages by finding patterns of letters that resemble normal text

❋ Designing a program to search the Web, compare prices for similar items, and present them as a buying guide

Using the examples of high school courses, leisure activities, and work tasks and your knowledge of yourself for guidance, circle a number to estimate your level of command of this skill.

Technology/Programming Skills Self-Estimate
(Based on Computer Programming)

Low Level			Moderate Level			High Level		
1	2	3	4	5	6	7	8	9

If your self-estimate is 3 or lower, move on to the next skill, **Thought-Processing Skills**. Otherwise, continue.

Examples of How I Demonstrated Technology/Programming Skills Through Computer Programming

Think of examples of how you have demonstrated your command of this skill and write the examples in the following worksheet.

❋ Write as many examples as you can, but you don't have to fill all the space.

❋ If possible, base your examples on work you've done, following the style of the work examples listed earlier.

❋ If you have little or no relevant work experience, write examples from school or leisure activities.

Examples of How I Demonstrated Technology/Programming Skills
Through Computer Programming

_____

_____

_____

_____

_____

Based on the examples, do you now want to change your self-estimate? Feel free to do so. Then go on to the next skill.

Thought-Processing Skills (Measured by Learning Strategies)

Definition of Learning Strategies: Using multiple approaches when learning or teaching new things.

Examples of High School Subjects That Teach Learning Strategies

❋ Any advanced literature or social studies course that requires research, perhaps for a term paper

❋ Science lab, especially in an advanced course

Examples of Leisure Activities That Use Learning Strategies

❋ Using various kinds of records to research a family tree

❋ Using Web searches and phone calls to identify local stores that sell a particular product

❋ Reading articles and talking to other pet owners to learn how to deal with a problem pet

Examples of Work Tasks That Use Learning Strategies

Lowest

Level
of Skill

Highest

❋ Learning a different method of completing a task from a co-worker

❋ Identifying an alternative approach that might help trainees who are having difficulties

❋ Using observation, an opinion survey, and sales receipts to understand buyer behavior in a store

❋ Applying principles of educational psychology to develop a new teaching strategy

Using the examples of high school courses, leisure activities, and work tasks and your knowledge of yourself for guidance, circle a number to estimate your level of command of this skill.

Thought-Processing Skills Self-Estimate
(Based on Learning Strategies)

Low Level			Moderate Level			High Level		
1	2	3	4	5	6	7	8	9

If your self-estimate is 3 or lower, move on to **Decide on Your Top Skills**. Otherwise, continue.

Examples of How I Demonstrated Thought-Processing Skills Through Learning Strategies

Think of examples of how you have demonstrated your command of this skill and write the examples in the following worksheet.

❋ Write as many examples as you can, but you don't have to fill all the space.

❋ If possible, base your examples on work you've done, following the style of the work examples listed earlier.

❋ If you have little or no relevant work experience, write examples from school or leisure activities.

Examples of How I Demonstrated Thought-Processing Skills
Through Learning Strategies

_____

_____

_____

_____

_____

Based on the examples, do you now want to change your self-estimate? Feel free to do so. Then go on to **Decide on Your Top Skills**.

Step 2: Decide on Your Top Skills

Now that you have completed the skills exercise, it's time to draw some conclusions. Look back over your self-estimates and the examples you wrote on the worksheets.

❋ Which skills received your highest self-estimates?

❋ For which skills did you provide the most examples?

Identify the three skills that have **a combination of high self-estimates and lots of examples**. Write them in the spaces below. Don't agonize over the ordering; what matters most is which three you choose, not how you order them. And don't feel you have to choose three. If one or two skills stand out greatly from the others, choose fewer than three.

My Three Top Skills

1. _____

2. _____

3. _____

If you did not have trouble deciding on your three top skills, go on to Part III. But maybe you're having trouble choosing your top skills for one of the following reasons.

One of the skills with lots of examples does not have a high self-estimate. You may have had a good reason for this response. Perhaps you have used a certain skill many times but never at a high level. For example, with Mathematical Skills, maybe you have done a lot of adding and subtracting but rarely have done any more complicated math than that. If your situation is like this, stick with your self-estimate for this skill—it is not one of your top skills. Concentrate on the skills for which your self-estimates and the number of examples are most consistently high. Write these in the box for My Three Top Skills. Then go to Part III.

The skills with the highest self-estimates do not have many examples. This could happen if you feel you have excellent command of a skill but have had few opportunities to demonstrate it. However, you need to give some thought to *why* you believe you have a high level of this skill. Surely you must have had some occasions to show your high level of mastery. The examples you provide do not have to be from paid work. Did you excel in this skill while you were in school? (If you're a young person, perhaps you're *still* in school and are excelling at this skill.) Do you use a high level of this skill in a hobby or in a volunteer activity? If so, write examples from school or from your leisure activities on the worksheet and reconsider including this skill among My Three Top Skills.

If you have had few or no opportunities to demonstrate one of your high-rated skills, even in school or in leisure activities, then maybe your self-estimate is too high. Keep in mind that even though you may be convinced you excel at this skill, you will have a hard time convincing employers because you have so little evidence. Therefore you should downgrade your self-estimate and maybe not include this skill among My Three Top Skills.

None of my self-estimates is particularly high. Perhaps you're too modest. Look at the skills with lots of examples and reconsider your level of ability.

If you're a young person, don't forget to consider the skills you are demonstrating in school and in your leisure activities. Even without much work experience, you may have evidence that you command one or more of these skills at a moderate or high level.

It's possible that you don't have any of these skills at a high level, especially if you don't have much work experience yet or if no part of your academic record is above average. In that case, focus on your three highest-rated skills, even if the ratings are at the moderate level, and write them as My Three Top Skills. Then go to Part III.

I have more than three skills with high self-estimates and lots of examples. Perhaps you're overconfident. You may want to reconsider your self-estimates by comparing yourself with professionals. For example, if you said you have a high level of Communication Skills, think about how your skills stack up to those of people who communicate for a living: professional writers, radio announcers, clergy, or counseling psychologists.

If you really do have a high level of command of four or more skills, good for you. But you need to narrow down your options. A helpful strategy is to go back and ask yourself which three high-rated skills give you the most *satisfaction*. Which skills would you rather spend every workday using? Those belong on the list of My Three Top Skills. After you write them down, go on to Part III.

I have an outstanding skill that's not included here. This assessment focuses on general skills that are transferable from one kind of job to another. As you may remember from Part I, a skill is a learned capability. Some highly specific capabilities that you may consider to be skills—for example, musical or athletic talent—are better classified as *abilities* because they are not learned (although they may be cultivated), and therefore they are not included here. Anyway, if you have these abilities at an outstanding level, you probably know what careers make use of them.

A lot of people with special talents use them in hobbies rather than at work. For example, they may pursue a career in sales because of their strong Social and Communication Skills but use their evenings and weekends to play music in a band, play soccer in an amateur league, or find some other outlet for their special talents. Others establish themselves in a career that is not directly related to their special ability but then carve out a niche where they can exploit their other talent. For example, they might go into sales and eventually focus on selling musical instruments, sports equipment, or some other product or service where their special ability gives them an instant bond with clients.

I command a skill at a high level, but I don't enjoy it. Even though you are good at this skill, you probably should not include it among My Three Top Skills. The purpose of My Three Top Skills is to help you identify jobs (in Parts III and IV) that might suit you. Therefore, you probably should not seek jobs where this skill is important. Even though you may be capable of entering one of these jobs and performing the tasks, you are unlikely to be happy with the work.

Of course, millions of people are unhappy with their jobs, but often what irks them is not the skills and tasks involved, but rather the work conditions (for example, outdoor work exposed to the weather), low economic rewards, or their boss or co-workers. These discontented workers may be able to move into a more satisfying position that requires similar skills.

However, if you are unhappy with the job's core skills and the related work tasks, it will be much more difficult for you to find a satisfying position in the same kind of job. Your lack of interest will also probably show in your work output. You are not likely to build a good reputation as a worker while doing work you dislike.

For My Three Top Skills, list only the skills that you *enjoy* using, even if it means listing only one skill that may not be your strongest.

There's a skill that I enjoy using, but I'm not good at it. If you enjoy using a skill, it's likely that you will try to use it constantly and therefore will improve your mastery of it over time. Particularly if you are a young person with much of your schooling and training ahead of you, you may not yet have developed a certain skill that attracts you.

Consider including this skill among My Three Top Skills even though you understand that you have a long way to go until you may be ready to use this skill for your livelihood. But also be cautious about pinning all your career hopes on this skill. Try to construct a plan B that uses other skills in case you fail to master this one.

Step 3: Find Jobs That Match Your Top Skills

Now that you have decided on your top skills, it's time to identify jobs that use them. Part III contains lists with the names of jobs. Each list focuses on one of the 9 skills and consists of jobs that use that skill at a high level. Here are some pointers about identifying likely jobs:

❋ A good place to start is the set of lists called "Best Jobs for Each Skill." For example, if you have strong Communication Skills, start by looking at "50 Best Jobs with a High Level of Communication Skills."

❋ You will find other lists that identify jobs that use the skill and that also have some other features that may be important to you: for example, jobs that pay the best; jobs with lots of opportunities for self-employment; or jobs that require education or training at a certain level.

❋ Give some thought to your work-related interests. First, consider which one of My Three Top Skills you most *enjoy* using and note which jobs are linked to it. Secondly, look at the lists that are organized by career clusters and personality types. In the lists for clusters that suit you and personality types that describe you, find jobs that use your favorite skill.

❋ Look at the lists for *each* of the skills on My Three Top Skills. Compare the lists and try to find jobs that appear twice or even three times. These jobs use a skill set close to your own and therefore deserve particular attention.

❋ If a job looks promising or if you aren't sure what it is, turn to Part IV and read its description.

❋ Consider this effort the first step in a long process of career exploration. Although skills are very important for choosing a career goal, they are not the only issue you need to explore. Before you can decide whether the job is a good choice for you, you need to read more about it, talk to people who do it, talk to students or trainees who are preparing for it, and perhaps get a taste of actual work experience by visiting a job site. Preparing for a career usually means a big investment—perhaps of money, perhaps of time, and certainly of hopes. Invest wisely.

Part III

The Best Jobs Lists: Jobs for Each of the 9 Skills

If you have completed the exercise in Part II, you now have an idea of which skills are your strongest. In this part you can find jobs that use your top skills and that also have good rewards in terms of income and job opportunities. Browse the lists of high-skill jobs to get ideas about careers that might be good choices for you. Then turn to Part IV to read the job descriptions and get an overview of what the jobs are like.

Best Jobs Overall for Each Skill: Jobs with the Highest Pay, Fastest Growth, and Most Openings

The four sets of lists that follow are the most important lists in this book. The first set of nine lists presents, for each skill, the jobs with the highest combined scores for pay, growth, and number of openings. Note that a job appears in a list for a skill if that skill is one of its top skills. Since most jobs have three top skills, most jobs appear on three of these lists. This also means that although there are seven lists of 50 jobs and two of 30 jobs, the total number of unique job titles is 199, rather than 410.

Look at the lists for *all three* of your top skills and try to find jobs that appear on two or three of these lists. These jobs are the best match for your top skills. But if your number-one skill greatly outweighs all other skills, focus on the list for that skill.

These lists are very appealing because they represent jobs with the very highest quantifiable measures from our labor market. The 199 jobs in these nine lists are described in detail in Part IV.

The three additional sets of lists present, for each skill, 20 jobs with the highest scores in each of three measures: annual earnings, projected percentage growth through 2018, and largest number of openings.

Best Jobs for Each Skill

Most people want to see these lists first. For each skill, you can see the jobs that have the highest overall combined ratings for earnings, projected growth, and number of openings. The section in the Introduction called "How the Best Jobs for Your Skills Were Selected" explains how I sorted jobs to assemble this list.

Although each list covers one skill, you'll notice a wide variety of jobs on the list. For example, among the top 10 jobs with a high level of Communication Skills are some in the fields of business and medicine. Among the top 10 jobs with a high level of Equipment Use/Maintenance Skills are some in high tech, health, and construction.

A look at one list will clarify how I ordered the high-skill jobs—take the Communication Skills list as an example. Management Analysts was the occupation with the best total score, and it is on the top of the list. The other occupations follow in descending order based on their total scores. Many jobs had tied scores and were simply listed one after another, so there are often very small or even no differences between the scores of jobs that are near each other on the list. All other jobs lists use these jobs as their source list.

50 Best Jobs with a High Level of Communication Skills

Job	Annual Earnings	Percent Growth	Annual Openings
1. Management Analysts	$78,160	23.9%	30,650
2. Dental Hygienists	$68,250	36.1%	9,840
3. Physical Therapists	$76,310	30.3%	7,860
4. Physician Assistants	$86,410	39.0%	4,280
5. Pharmacists	$111,570	17.0%	10,580
6. Financial Analysts	$74,350	19.8%	9,520
7. Accountants and Auditors	$61,690	21.6%	49,750
8. Personal Financial Advisors	$64,750	30.1%	8,530
9. Compliance Officers	$58,720	31.0%	10,850
10. Veterinarians	$82,040	32.9%	3,020
11. Occupational Therapists	$72,320	25.6%	4,580
12. Cost Estimators	$57,860	25.3%	10,360
13. Lawyers	$112,760	13.0%	24,040
14. Biochemists and Biophysicists	$79,390	37.4%	1,620
15. Environmental Scientists and Specialists, Including Health	$61,700	27.9%	4,840

50 Best Jobs with a High Level of Communication Skills

Job	Annual Earnings	Percent Growth	Annual Openings
16. Human Resources Specialists	$52,690	27.9%	11,230
17. Financial Examiners	$74,940	41.2%	1,600
18. Public Relations Specialists	$52,090	24.0%	13,130
19. Instructional Coordinators	$58,830	23.2%	6,060
20. Health Specialties Teachers, Postsecondary	$85,270	15.1%	4,000
21. Speech-Language Pathologists	$66,920	18.5%	4,380
22. Paralegals and Legal Assistants	$46,680	28.1%	10,400
23. Elementary School Teachers, Except Special Education	$51,660	15.8%	59,650
24. Detectives and Criminal Investigators	$68,820	16.6%	4,160
25. Middle School Teachers, Except Special and Career/Technical Education	$51,960	15.3%	25,110
26. Self-Enrichment Education Teachers	$36,340	32.0%	12,030
27. Computer Occupations, All Other	$79,240	13.1%	7,260
28. Administrative Services Managers	$77,890	12.5%	8,660
29. Geoscientists, Except Hydrologists and Geographers	$82,500	17.5%	1,540
30. Sales Representatives, Wholesale and Manufacturing, Technical and Scientific Products	$73,710	9.7%	14,230
31. Medical Assistants	$28,860	33.9%	21,780
32. Chiropractors	$67,200	19.5%	1,820
33. Healthcare Social Workers	$47,230	22.4%	6,590
34. Business Teachers, Postsecondary	$73,760	15.1%	2,000
35. Orthodontists	$166,400+	19.7%	360
36. Physical Therapist Assistants	$49,690	33.3%	3,050
37. Engineering Teachers, Postsecondary	$89,670	15.1%	1,000
38. Biological Scientists, All Other	$68,220	18.8%	1,610
39. Fitness Trainers and Aerobics Instructors	$31,090	29.4%	12,380
40. Medical Secretaries	$30,530	26.6%	18,900
41. Pharmacy Technicians	$28,400	30.6%	18,200
42. Securities, Commodities, and Financial Services Sales Agents	$70,190	9.3%	12,680
43. Special Education Teachers, Middle School	$53,440	18.1%	4,410
44. Biological Science Teachers, Postsecondary	$72,700	15.1%	1,700
45. Agents and Business Managers of Artists, Performers, and Athletes	$63,130	22.4%	1,010
46. Real Estate Sales Agents	$40,030	16.2%	12,830
47. Political Scientists	$107,420	19.4%	280
48. Audiologists	$66,660	25.0%	580
49. Technical Writers	$63,280	18.2%	1,680
50. Legal Secretaries	$41,500	18.4%	8,380

50 Best Jobs with a High Level of Equipment Use/Maintenance Skills

Job	Annual Earnings	Percent Growth	Annual Openings
1. Computer Network Architects	$75,660	53.4%	20,830
2. Network and Computer Systems Administrators	$69,160	23.2%	13,550
3. Compliance Officers	$58,720	31.0%	10,850
4. Computer and Information Systems Managers	$115,780	16.9%	9,710
5. Supervisors of Construction and Extraction Workers	$58,680	15.4%	24,220
6. Heating, Air Conditioning, and Refrigeration Mechanics and Installers	$42,530	28.1%	13,620
7. Radiologic Technologists	$54,340	17.2%	6,800
8. Firefighters	$45,250	18.5%	15,280
9. Respiratory Therapists	$54,280	20.9%	4,140
10. Plumbers, Pipefitters, and Steamfitters	$46,660	15.3%	17,550
11. Computer User Support Specialists	$46,260	13.8%	23,460
12. Electricians	$48,250	11.9%	25,090
13. Construction and Building Inspectors	$52,360	16.8%	3,970
14. Medical and Clinical Laboratory Technologists	$56,130	11.9%	5,330
15. Commercial Pilots	$67,500	18.6%	2,060
16. Surgical Technologists	$39,920	25.3%	4,630
17. Carpenters	$39,530	12.9%	32,540
18. Water and Wastewater Treatment Plant and System Operators	$40,770	19.8%	4,690
19. Captains, Mates, and Pilots of Water Vessels	$64,180	17.3%	1,950
20. Producers and Directors	$68,440	9.8%	4,040
21. Heavy and Tractor-Trailer Truck Drivers	$37,770	12.9%	55,460
22. First-Line Supervisors of Landscaping, Lawn Service, and Groundskeeping Workers	$41,860	14.9%	5,600
23. Cardiovascular Technologists and Technicians	$49,410	24.1%	1,910
24. Dental Assistants	$33,470	35.7%	16,100
25. Diagnostic Medical Sonographers	$64,380	18.3%	1,650
26. Engineers, All Other	$90,270	6.7%	5,020
27. Medical Equipment Repairers	$44,490	27.2%	2,320
28. Operating Engineers and Other Construction Equipment Operators	$40,400	12.0%	11,820
29. Brickmasons and Blockmasons	$46,930	11.5%	5,000
30. Environmental Science and Protection Technicians, Including Health	$41,380	28.9%	2,520
31. Airline Pilots, Copilots, and Flight Engineers	$103,210	8.4%	3,250
32. First-Line Supervisors of Mechanics, Installers, and Repairers	$59,150	4.2%	13,650
33. First-Line Supervisors of Fire Fighting and Prevention Workers	$68,240	8.2%	3,250
34. Radiation Therapists	$74,980	27.1%	690
35. Security and Fire Alarm Systems Installers	$38,500	24.8%	2,780

50 Best Jobs with a High Level of Equipment Use/Maintenance Skills

Job	Annual Earnings	Percent Growth	Annual Openings
36. Medical and Clinical Laboratory Technicians	$36,280	16.1%	5,460
37. Health Technologists and Technicians, All Other	$38,460	18.7%	3,200
38. Life, Physical, and Social Science Technicians, All Other	$43,350	13.3%	3,640
39. Transportation Inspectors	$57,640	18.4%	1,130
40. Construction Laborers	$29,280	20.5%	33,940
41. Surveying and Mapping Technicians	$37,900	20.4%	2,940
42. Industrial Machinery Mechanics	$45,420	7.3%	6,240
43. Maintenance and Repair Workers, General	$34,730	10.9%	35,750
44. Refuse and Recyclable Material Collectors	$32,640	18.6%	7,110
45. Cement Masons and Concrete Finishers	$35,450	12.9%	7,640
46. Ship Engineers	$65,880	18.6%	700
47. Boilermakers	$54,640	18.8%	810
48. Electrical Power-Line Installers and Repairers	$58,030	4.5%	4,550
49. Drywall and Ceiling Tile Installers	$37,320	13.5%	3,700
50. Environmental Engineering Technicians	$43,390	30.1%	1,040

30 Best Jobs with a High Level of Installation Skills

Job	Annual Earnings	Percent Growth	Annual Openings
1. Network and Computer Systems Administrators	$69,160	23.2%	13,550
2. Computer Occupations, All Other	$79,240	13.1%	7,260
3. Biomedical Engineers	$81,540	72.0%	1,490
4. Plumbers, Pipefitters, and Steamfitters	$46,660	15.3%	17,550
5. Electricians	$48,250	11.9%	25,090
6. Heating, Air Conditioning, and Refrigeration Mechanics and Installers	$42,530	28.1%	13,620
7. Engineers, All Other	$90,270	6.7%	5,020
8. Security and Fire Alarm Systems Installers	$38,500	24.8%	2,780
9. Maintenance and Repair Workers, General	$34,730	10.9%	35,750
10. Audio and Video Equipment Technicians	$40,540	12.6%	2,370
11. Industrial Machinery Mechanics	$45,420	7.3%	6,240
12. Elevator Installers and Repairers	$70,910	9.2%	920
13. Engineering Technicians, Except Drafters, All Other	$58,020	5.2%	1,850
14. Mobile Heavy Equipment Mechanics, Except Engines	$44,830	8.7%	3,770
15. Helpers—Electricians	$27,220	24.7%	4,800
16. Avionics Technicians	$52,320	10.6%	520

(continued)

30 Best Jobs with a High Level of Installation Skills

Job	Annual Earnings	Percent Growth	Annual Openings
17. Installation, Maintenance, and Repair Workers, All Other	$36,420	9.2%	4,180
18. Aircraft Structure, Surfaces, Rigging, and Systems Assemblers	$44,820	9.3%	1,340
19. Telecommunications Equipment Installers and Repairers, Except Line Installers	$54,710	–0.2%	3,560
20. Automotive Service Technicians and Mechanics	$35,790	4.7%	18,170
21. Electrical and Electronics Repairers, Commercial and Industrial Equipment	$51,820	3.8%	1,640
22. Medical Equipment Preparers	$29,490	12.8%	1,120
23. Helpers—Installation, Maintenance, and Repair Workers	$24,260	8.3%	8,500
24. Locksmiths and Safe Repairers	$35,550	12.0%	610
25. Electronic Home Entertainment Equipment Installers and Repairers	$32,940	10.8%	1,430
26. Rail Car Repairers	$47,410	6.5%	590
27. Audio-Visual and Multimedia Collections Specialists	$42,710	10.3%	220
28. Millwrights	$48,360	1.4%	980
29. Mechanical Door Repairers	$35,780	10.8%	450
30. Commercial Divers	$51,360	5.5%	50

50 Best Jobs with a High Level of Management Skills

Job	Annual Earnings	Percent Growth	Annual Openings
1. Pharmacists	$111,570	17.0%	10,580
2. Civil Engineers	$77,560	24.3%	11,460
3. Construction Managers	$83,860	17.2%	13,770
4. Computer and Information Systems Managers	$115,780	16.9%	9,710
5. Sales Managers	$98,530	14.9%	12,660
6. Medical and Health Services Managers	$84,270	16.0%	9,940
7. Dentists, General	$141,040	15.3%	5,180
8. Cost Estimators	$57,860	25.3%	10,360
9. Supervisors of Construction and Extraction Workers	$58,680	15.4%	24,220
10. Marketing Managers	$112,800	12.5%	5,970
11. Logisticians	$70,800	19.5%	4,190
12. Industrial Engineers	$76,100	14.2%	8,540
13. Managers, All Other	$96,450	7.3%	29,750
14. Business Operations Specialists, All Other	$62,450	11.5%	36,830
15. Financial Managers	$103,910	7.6%	13,820
16. Architects, Except Landscape and Naval	$72,550	16.2%	4,680

50 Best Jobs with a High Level of Management Skills

Job	Annual Earnings	Percent Growth	Annual Openings
17. Sales Representatives, Wholesale and Manufacturing, Technical and Scientific Products	$73,710	9.7%	14,230
18. Purchasing Agents, Except Wholesale, Retail, and Farm Products	$56,580	13.9%	11,860
19. Administrative Services Managers	$77,890	12.5%	8,660
20. Natural Sciences Managers	$116,020	15.5%	2,010
21. Social Scientists and Related Workers, All Other	$74,620	22.5%	2,380
22. Education Administrators, Elementary and Secondary School	$86,970	8.6%	8,880
23. Executive Secretaries and Executive Administrative Assistants	$43,520	12.8%	41,920
24. First-Line Supervisors of Office and Administrative Support Workers	$47,460	11.0%	48,900
25. Human Resources Managers	$99,180	9.6%	4,140
26. Clergy	$43,970	12.7%	21,770
27. Petroleum Engineers	$114,080	18.4%	860
28. Social and Community Service Managers	$57,950	13.8%	4,820
29. Public Relations and Fundraising Managers	$91,810	12.9%	2,060
30. General and Operations Managers	$94,400	–0.1%	50,220
31. Captains, Mates, and Pilots of Water Vessels	$64,180	17.3%	1,950
32. Carpenters	$39,530	12.9%	32,540
33. Architectural and Engineering Managers	$119,260	6.2%	4,870
34. Budget Analysts	$68,200	15.1%	2,230
35. Graphic Designers	$43,500	12.9%	12,480
36. Art Directors	$80,630	11.7%	2,870
37. Surgical Technologists	$39,920	25.3%	4,630
38. Chief Executives	$165,080	–1.4%	11,250
39. Interior Designers	$46,280	19.4%	3,590
40. Agents and Business Managers of Artists, Performers, and Athletes	$63,130	22.4%	1,010
41. First-Line Supervisors of Police and Detectives	$78,260	8.1%	5,050
42. Preschool Teachers, Except Special Education	$25,700	19.0%	17,830
43. Producers and Directors	$68,440	9.8%	4,040
44. First-Line Supervisors of Non-Retail Sales Workers	$68,880	4.8%	12,950
45. Coaches and Scouts	$28,340	24.8%	9,920
46. Landscape Architects	$62,090	19.6%	980
47. Cargo and Freight Agents	$37,150	23.9%	4,030
48. First-Line Supervisors of Landscaping, Lawn Service, and Groundskeeping Workers	$41,860	14.9%	5,600
49. First-Line Supervisors of Personal Service Workers	$35,290	15.4%	9,080
50. Ship Engineers	$65,880	18.6%	700

50 Best Jobs with a High Level of Mathematics Skills

Job	Annual Earnings	Percent Growth	Annual Openings
1. Software Developers, Applications	$87,790	34.0%	21,840
2. Software Developers, Systems Software	$94,180	30.4%	15,340
3. Management Analysts	$78,160	23.9%	30,650
4. Medical Scientists, Except Epidemiologists	$76,700	40.4%	6,620
5. Computer Systems Analysts	$77,740	20.3%	22,280
6. Civil Engineers	$77,560	24.3%	11,460
7. Construction Managers	$83,860	17.2%	13,770
8. Accountants and Auditors	$61,690	21.6%	49,750
9. Personal Financial Advisors	$64,750	30.1%	8,530
10. Market Research Analysts and Marketing Specialists	$60,570	28.1%	13,730
11. Compliance Officers	$58,720	31.0%	10,850
12. Financial Analysts	$74,350	19.8%	9,520
13. Environmental Engineers	$78,740	30.6%	2,790
14. Optometrists	$94,990	24.4%	2,010
15. Cost Estimators	$57,860	25.3%	10,360
16. Environmental Scientists and Specialists, Including Health	$61,700	27.9%	4,840
17. Biochemists and Biophysicists	$79,390	37.4%	1,620
18. Database Administrators	$73,490	20.3%	4,440
19. Computer and Information Research Scientists	$100,660	24.2%	1,320
20. Financial Managers	$103,910	7.6%	13,820
21. Logisticians	$70,800	19.5%	4,190
22. Financial Examiners	$74,940	41.2%	1,600
23. Industrial Engineers	$76,100	14.2%	8,540
24. Natural Sciences Managers	$116,020	15.5%	2,010
25. Compensation, Benefits, and Job Analysis Specialists	$57,000	23.6%	6,050
26. Computer Occupations, All Other	$79,240	13.1%	7,260
27. Operations Research Analysts	$70,960	22.0%	3,220
28. Architects, Except Landscape and Naval	$72,550	16.2%	4,680
29. Social Scientists and Related Workers, All Other	$74,620	22.5%	2,380
30. Heating, Air Conditioning, and Refrigeration Mechanics and Installers	$42,530	28.1%	13,620
31. Actuaries	$87,650	21.3%	1,000
32. Business Operations Specialists, All Other	$62,450	11.5%	36,830
33. Petroleum Engineers	$114,080	18.4%	860
34. Architectural and Engineering Managers	$119,260	6.2%	4,870
35. Geoscientists, Except Hydrologists and Geographers	$82,500	17.5%	1,540
36. Engineers, All Other	$90,270	6.7%	5,020
37. Plumbers, Pipefitters, and Steamfitters	$46,660	15.3%	17,550

50 Best Jobs with a High Level of Mathematics Skills

Job	Annual Earnings	Percent Growth	Annual Openings
38. Purchasing Agents, Except Wholesale, Retail, and Farm Products	$56,580	13.9%	11,860
39. Pharmacy Technicians	$28,400	30.6%	18,200
40. Securities, Commodities, and Financial Services Sales Agents	$70,190	9.3%	12,680
41. Airline Pilots, Copilots, and Flight Engineers	$103,210	8.4%	3,250
42. Engineering Teachers, Postsecondary	$89,670	15.1%	1,000
43. Aerospace Engineers	$97,480	10.4%	2,230
44. Physicists	$106,370	15.9%	690
45. Air Traffic Controllers	$108,040	13.1%	1,230
46. Business Teachers, Postsecondary	$73,760	15.1%	2,000
47. Radiation Therapists	$74,980	27.1%	690
48. Sales Engineers	$87,390	8.8%	3,500
49. Biological Scientists, All Other	$68,220	18.8%	1,610
50. Mechanical Engineers	$78,160	6.0%	7,570

50 Best Jobs with a High Level of Science Skills

Job	Annual Earnings	Percent Growth	Annual Openings
1. Software Developers, Applications	$87,790	34.0%	21,840
2. Software Developers, Systems Software	$94,180	30.4%	15,340
3. Computer Network Architects	$75,660	53.4%	20,830
4. Physician Assistants	$86,410	39.0%	4,280
5. Medical Scientists, Except Epidemiologists	$76,700	40.4%	6,620
6. Physical Therapists	$76,310	30.3%	7,860
7. Civil Engineers	$77,560	24.3%	11,460
8. Pharmacists	$111,570	17.0%	10,580
9. Computer Systems Analysts	$77,740	20.3%	22,280
10. Dental Hygienists	$68,250	36.1%	9,840
11. Veterinarians	$82,040	32.9%	3,020
12. Environmental Engineers	$78,740	30.6%	2,790
13. Dentists, General	$141,040	15.3%	5,180
14. Optometrists	$94,990	24.4%	2,010
15. Medical and Health Services Managers	$84,270	16.0%	9,940
16. Biomedical Engineers	$81,540	72.0%	1,490
17. Biochemists and Biophysicists	$79,390	37.4%	1,620
18. Compliance Officers	$58,720	31.0%	10,850

(continued)

50 Best Jobs with a High Level of Science Skills

Job	Annual Earnings	Percent Growth	Annual Openings
19. Market Research Analysts and Marketing Specialists	$60,570	28.1%	13,730
20. Occupational Therapists	$72,320	25.6%	4,580
21. Registered Nurses	$64,690	22.2%	103,900
22. Computer and Information Research Scientists	$100,660	24.2%	1,320
23. Environmental Scientists and Specialists, Including Health	$61,700	27.9%	4,840
24. Human Resources Specialists	$52,690	27.9%	11,230
25. Natural Sciences Managers	$116,020	15.5%	2,010
26. Health Specialties Teachers, Postsecondary	$85,270	15.1%	4,000
27. Operations Research Analysts	$70,960	22.0%	3,220
28. Training and Development Specialists	$54,160	23.3%	10,710
29. Architects, Except Landscape and Naval	$72,550	16.2%	4,680
30. Compensation, Benefits, and Job Analysis Specialists	$57,000	23.6%	6,050
31. Computer Occupations, All Other	$79,240	13.1%	7,260
32. Petroleum Engineers	$114,080	18.4%	860
33. Speech-Language Pathologists	$66,920	18.5%	4,380
34. Medical Assistants	$28,860	33.9%	21,780
35. Detectives and Criminal Investigators	$68,820	16.6%	4,160
36. Geoscientists, Except Hydrologists and Geographers	$82,500	17.5%	1,540
37. Orthodontists	$166,400+	19.7%	360
38. Architectural and Engineering Managers	$119,260	6.2%	4,870
39. Radiation Therapists	$74,980	27.1%	690
40. Healthcare Social Workers	$47,230	22.4%	6,590
41. Licensed Practical and Licensed Vocational Nurses	$40,380	20.6%	39,130
42. Physical Therapist Assistants	$49,690	33.3%	3,050
43. Prosthodontists	$118,400	26.4%	30
44. Engineers, All Other	$90,270	6.7%	5,020
45. Physicists	$106,370	15.9%	690
46. Chiropractors	$67,200	19.5%	1,820
47. Commercial Pilots	$67,500	18.6%	2,060
48. Respiratory Therapists	$54,280	20.9%	4,140
49. Engineering Teachers, Postsecondary	$89,670	15.1%	1,000
50. Radiologic Technologists	$54,340	17.2%	6,800

50 Best Jobs with a High Level of Social Skills

Job	Annual Earnings	Percent Growth	Annual Openings
1. Registered Nurses	$64,690	22.2%	103,900
2. Dental Hygienists	$68,250	36.1%	9,840
3. Physical Therapists	$76,310	30.3%	7,860
4. Construction Managers	$83,860	17.2%	13,770
5. Compliance Officers	$58,720	31.0%	10,850
6. Physician Assistants	$86,410	39.0%	4,280
7. Lawyers	$112,760	13.0%	24,040
8. Sales Managers	$98,530	14.9%	12,660
9. Supervisors of Construction and Extraction Workers	$58,680	15.4%	24,220
10. Elementary School Teachers, Except Special Education	$51,660	15.8%	59,650
11. Human Resources Specialists	$52,690	27.9%	11,230
12. Public Relations Specialists	$52,090	24.0%	13,130
13. Occupational Therapists	$72,320	25.6%	4,580
14. Training and Development Specialists	$54,160	23.3%	10,710
15. Instructional Coordinators	$58,830	23.2%	6,060
16. Middle School Teachers, Except Special and Career/Technical Education	$51,960	15.3%	25,110
17. Licensed Practical and Licensed Vocational Nurses	$40,380	20.6%	39,130
18. Firefighters	$45,250	18.5%	15,280
19. Detectives and Criminal Investigators	$68,820	16.6%	4,160
20. Radiologic Technologists	$54,340	17.2%	6,800
21. Managers, All Other	$96,450	7.3%	29,750
22. Marketing Managers	$112,800	12.5%	5,970
23. Administrative Services Managers	$77,890	12.5%	8,660
24. Healthcare Social Workers	$47,230	22.4%	6,590
25. Sales Representatives, Wholesale and Manufacturing, Technical and Scientific Products	$73,710	9.7%	14,230
26. Dental Assistants	$33,470	35.7%	16,100
27. Self-Enrichment Education Teachers	$36,340	32.0%	12,030
28. Respiratory Therapists	$54,280	20.9%	4,140
29. Securities, Commodities, and Financial Services Sales Agents	$70,190	9.3%	12,680
30. Educational, Guidance, School, and Vocational Counselors	$53,380	14.0%	9,440
31. Special Education Teachers, Middle School	$53,440	18.1%	4,410
32. Real Estate Sales Agents	$40,030	16.2%	12,830
33. Medical Secretaries	$30,530	26.6%	18,900
34. Medical Assistants	$28,860	33.9%	21,780
35. Executive Secretaries and Executive Administrative Assistants	$43,520	12.8%	41,920
36. Physical Therapist Assistants	$49,690	33.3%	3,050

(continued)

50 Best Jobs with a High Level of Social Skills

Job	Annual Earnings	Percent Growth	Annual Openings
37. First-Line Supervisors of Office and Administrative Support Workers	$47,460	11.0%	48,900
38. Customer Service Representatives	$30,460	17.7%	110,840
39. Education Administrators, Elementary and Secondary School	$86,970	8.6%	8,880
40. Writers and Authors	$55,420	14.8%	5,420
41. General and Operations Managers	$94,400	–0.1%	50,220
42. Secondary School Teachers, Except Special and Career/Technical Education	$53,230	8.9%	41,240
43. Fitness Trainers and Aerobics Instructors	$31,090	29.4%	12,380
44. Home Health Aides	$20,560	50.0%	55,270
45. Pharmacy Technicians	$28,400	30.6%	18,200
46. Clergy	$43,970	12.7%	21,770
47. Probation Officers and Correctional Treatment Specialists	$47,200	19.3%	4,180
48. Social and Community Service Managers	$57,950	13.8%	4,820
49. Police and Sheriff's Patrol Officers	$53,540	8.7%	22,790
50. Special Education Teachers, Secondary School	$54,810	13.3%	5,750

30 Best Jobs with a High Level of Technology/Programming Skills

Job	Annual Earnings	Percent Growth	Annual Openings
1. Software Developers, Applications	$87,790	34.0%	21,840
2. Software Developers, Systems Software	$94,180	30.4%	15,340
3. Computer and Information Systems Managers	$115,780	16.9%	9,710
4. Computer Network Architects	$75,660	53.4%	20,830
5. Computer Systems Analysts	$77,740	20.3%	22,280
6. Computer and Information Research Scientists	$100,660	24.2%	1,320
7. Network and Computer Systems Administrators	$69,160	23.2%	13,550
8. Biomedical Engineers	$81,540	72.0%	1,490
9. Computer Occupations, All Other	$79,240	13.1%	7,260
10. Database Administrators	$73,490	20.3%	4,440
11. Engineers, All Other	$90,270	6.7%	5,020
12. Actuaries	$87,650	21.3%	1,000
13. Aerospace Engineers	$97,480	10.4%	2,230
14. Physicists	$106,370	15.9%	690
15. Sales Engineers	$87,390	8.8%	3,500
16. Mechanical Engineers	$78,160	6.0%	7,570
17. Industrial-Organizational Psychologists	$87,330	26.1%	130

30 Best Jobs with a High Level of Technology/Programming Skills

Job	Annual Earnings	Percent Growth	Annual Openings
18. Computer Hardware Engineers	$98,810	3.8%	2,350
19. Electronics Engineers, Except Computer	$90,170	0.3%	3,340
20. Surveying and Mapping Technicians	$37,900	20.4%	2,940
21. Hydrologists	$75,690	18.2%	380
22. Mining and Geological Engineers, Including Mining Safety Engineers	$82,870	15.2%	260
23. Computer Programmers	$71,380	–2.9%	8,030
24. Survey Researchers	$36,050	30.3%	1,340
25. Architectural and Civil Drafters	$46,430	9.1%	3,620
26. Computer Science Teachers, Postsecondary	$70,300	15.1%	1,000
27. Industrial Machinery Mechanics	$45,420	7.3%	6,240
28. Statisticians	$72,830	13.1%	960
29. Commercial and Industrial Designers	$58,230	9.0%	1,760
30. Social Science Research Assistants	$37,230	17.8%	1,270

50 Best Jobs with a High Level of Thought-Processing Skills

Job	Annual Earnings	Percent Growth	Annual Openings
1. Management Analysts	$78,160	23.9%	30,650
2. Medical Scientists, Except Epidemiologists	$76,700	40.4%	6,620
3. Registered Nurses	$64,690	22.2%	103,900
4. Financial Analysts	$74,350	19.8%	9,520
5. Accountants and Auditors	$61,690	21.6%	49,750
6. Dentists, General	$141,040	15.3%	5,180
7. Market Research Analysts and Marketing Specialists	$60,570	28.1%	13,730
8. Personal Financial Advisors	$64,750	30.1%	8,530
9. Veterinarians	$82,040	32.9%	3,020
10. Medical and Health Services Managers	$84,270	16.0%	9,940
11. Environmental Engineers	$78,740	30.6%	2,790
12. Sales Managers	$98,530	14.9%	12,660
13. Compliance Officers	$58,720	31.0%	10,850
14. Lawyers	$112,760	13.0%	24,040
15. Optometrists	$94,990	24.4%	2,010
16. Database Administrators	$73,490	20.3%	4,440
17. Logisticians	$70,800	19.5%	4,190
18. Operations Research Analysts	$70,960	22.0%	3,220

(continued)

50 Best Jobs with a High Level of Thought-Processing Skills

Job	Annual Earnings	Percent Growth	Annual Openings
19. Health Specialties Teachers, Postsecondary	$85,270	15.1%	4,000
20. Instructional Coordinators	$58,830	23.2%	6,060
21. Social Scientists and Related Workers, All Other	$74,620	22.5%	2,380
22. Public Relations Specialists	$52,090	24.0%	13,130
23. Training and Development Specialists	$54,160	23.3%	10,710
24. Financial Examiners	$74,940	41.2%	1,600
25. Compensation, Benefits, and Job Analysis Specialists	$57,000	23.6%	6,050
26. Speech-Language Pathologists	$66,920	18.5%	4,380
27. Marketing Managers	$112,800	12.5%	5,970
28. Industrial Engineers	$76,100	14.2%	8,540
29. Elementary School Teachers, Except Special Education	$51,660	15.8%	59,650
30. Computer Occupations, All Other	$79,240	13.1%	7,260
31. Managers, All Other	$96,450	7.3%	29,750
32. Actuaries	$87,650	21.3%	1,000
33. Financial Managers	$103,910	7.6%	13,820
34. Middle School Teachers, Except Special and Career/Technical Education	$51,960	15.3%	25,110
35. Licensed Practical and Licensed Vocational Nurses	$40,380	20.6%	39,130
36. Self-Enrichment Education Teachers	$36,340	32.0%	12,030
37. Commercial Pilots	$67,500	18.6%	2,060
38. Chiropractors	$67,200	19.5%	1,820
39. Business Teachers, Postsecondary	$73,760	15.1%	2,000
40. Business Operations Specialists, All Other	$62,450	11.5%	36,830
41. General and Operations Managers	$94,400	–0.1%	50,220
42. Education Administrators, Elementary and Secondary School	$86,970	8.6%	8,880
43. Human Resources Managers	$99,180	9.6%	4,140
44. Special Education Teachers, Middle School	$53,440	18.1%	4,410
45. Fitness Trainers and Aerobics Instructors	$31,090	29.4%	12,380
46. Biological Science Teachers, Postsecondary	$72,700	15.1%	1,700
47. Orthodontists	$166,400+	19.7%	360
48. Chief Executives	$165,080	–1.4%	11,250
49. Art, Drama, and Music Teachers, Postsecondary	$62,040	15.1%	2,500
50. Purchasing Agents, Except Wholesale, Retail, and Farm Products	$56,580	13.9%	11,860

20 Best-Paying Jobs for Each Skill

In the following nine lists you'll find the 20 best-paying jobs using each skill that met my criteria for this book. This is a popular set of lists, for obvious reasons.

If you compare these nine lists, you may notice that some skills have better income possibilities than others. For example, the best-paying jobs with a high level of Social Skills and Thought-Processing Skills command much higher incomes than the best-paying jobs with a high level of Installation Skills. To see which skills pay the best and worst on average, look at the bonus section called "Skills with the Best Payoff for Improvement."

Keep in mind that the earnings figures are averages. Earnings can vary by region of the country, by amount of experience, and because of many other factors.

20 Best-Paying Jobs with a High Level of Communication Skills

Job	Annual Earnings
1. Orthodontists	$166,400+
2. Lawyers	$112,760
3. Pharmacists	$111,570
4. Political Scientists	$107,420
5. Engineering Teachers, Postsecondary	$89,670
6. Physician Assistants	$86,410
7. Health Specialties Teachers, Postsecondary	$85,270
8. Geoscientists, Except Hydrologists and Geographers	$82,500
9. Veterinarians	$82,040
10. Biochemists and Biophysicists	$79,390
11. Computer Occupations, All Other	$79,240
12. Management Analysts	$78,160
13. Administrative Services Managers	$77,890
14. Physical Therapists	$76,310
15. Financial Examiners	$74,940
16. Financial Analysts	$74,350
17. Business Teachers, Postsecondary	$73,760
18. Sales Representatives, Wholesale and Manufacturing, Technical and Scientific Products	$73,710
19. Biological Science Teachers, Postsecondary	$72,700
20. Occupational Therapists	$72,320

20 Best-Paying Jobs with a High Level of Equipment Use/Maintenance Skills

Job	Annual Earnings
1. Computer and Information Systems Managers	$115,780
2. Airline Pilots, Copilots, and Flight Engineers	$103,210
3. Engineers, All Other	$90,270
4. Computer Network Architects	$75,660
5. Radiation Therapists	$74,980
6. Network and Computer Systems Administrators	$69,160
7. Producers and Directors	$68,440
8. First-Line Supervisors of Fire Fighting and Prevention Workers	$68,240
9. Commercial Pilots	$67,500
10. Ship Engineers	$65,880
11. Diagnostic Medical Sonographers	$64,380
12. Captains, Mates, and Pilots of Water Vessels	$64,180
13. First-Line Supervisors of Mechanics, Installers, and Repairers	$59,150
14. Compliance Officers	$58,720
15. Supervisors of Construction and Extraction Workers	$58,680
16. Electrical Power-Line Installers and Repairers	$58,030
17. Transportation Inspectors	$57,640
18. Medical and Clinical Laboratory Technologists	$56,130
19. Boilermakers	$54,640
20. Radiologic Technologists	$54,340

20 Best-Paying Jobs with a High Level of Installation Skills

Job	Annual Earnings
1. Engineers, All Other	$90,270
2. Biomedical Engineers	$81,540
3. Computer Occupations, All Other	$79,240
4. Elevator Installers and Repairers	$70,910
5. Network and Computer Systems Administrators	$69,160
6. Engineering Technicians, Except Drafters, All Other	$58,020
7. Telecommunications Equipment Installers and Repairers, Except Line Installers	$54,710
8. Avionics Technicians	$52,320
9. Electrical and Electronics Repairers, Commercial and Industrial Equipment	$51,820
10. Commercial Divers	$51,360
11. Millwrights	$48,360
12. Electricians	$48,250

20 Best-Paying Jobs with a High Level of Installation Skills

Job	Annual Earnings
13. Rail Car Repairers	$47,410
14. Plumbers, Pipefitters, and Steamfitters	$46,660
15. Industrial Machinery Mechanics	$45,420
16. Mobile Heavy Equipment Mechanics, Except Engines	$44,830
17. Aircraft Structure, Surfaces, Rigging, and Systems Assemblers	$44,820
18. Audio-Visual and Multimedia Collections Specialists	$42,710
19. Heating, Air Conditioning, and Refrigeration Mechanics and Installers	$42,530
20. Audio and Video Equipment Technicians	$40,540

20 Best-Paying Jobs with a High Level of Management Skills

Job	Annual Earnings
1. Chief Executives	$165,080
2. Dentists, General	$141,040
3. Architectural and Engineering Managers	$119,260
4. Natural Sciences Managers	$116,020
5. Computer and Information Systems Managers	$115,780
6. Petroleum Engineers	$114,080
7. Marketing Managers	$112,800
8. Pharmacists	$111,570
9. Financial Managers	$103,910
10. Human Resources Managers	$99,180
11. Sales Managers	$98,530
12. Managers, All Other	$96,450
13. General and Operations Managers	$94,400
14. Public Relations and Fundraising Managers	$91,810
15. Education Administrators, Elementary and Secondary School	$86,970
16. Medical and Health Services Managers	$84,270
17. Construction Managers	$83,860
18. Art Directors	$80,630
19. First-Line Supervisors of Police and Detectives	$78,260
20. Administrative Services Managers	$77,890

20 Best-Paying Jobs with a High Level of Mathematics Skills

Job	Annual Earnings
1. Architectural and Engineering Managers	$119,260
2. Natural Sciences Managers	$116,020
3. Petroleum Engineers	$114,080
4. Air Traffic Controllers	$108,040
5. Physicists	$106,370
6. Financial Managers	$103,910
7. Airline Pilots, Copilots, and Flight Engineers	$103,210
8. Computer and Information Research Scientists	$100,660
9. Aerospace Engineers	$97,480
10. Optometrists	$94,990
11. Software Developers, Systems Software	$94,180
12. Engineers, All Other	$90,270
13. Engineering Teachers, Postsecondary	$89,670
14. Software Developers, Applications	$87,790
15. Actuaries	$87,650
16. Sales Engineers	$87,390
17. Construction Managers	$83,860
18. Geoscientists, Except Hydrologists and Geographers	$82,500
19. Biochemists and Biophysicists	$79,390
20. Computer Occupations, All Other	$79,240

20 Best-Paying Jobs with a High Level of Science Skills

Job	Annual Earnings
1. Orthodontists	$166,400+
2. Dentists, General	$141,040
3. Architectural and Engineering Managers	$119,260
4. Prosthodontists	$118,400
5. Natural Sciences Managers	$116,020
6. Petroleum Engineers	$114,080
7. Pharmacists	$111,570
8. Physicists	$106,370
9. Computer and Information Research Scientists	$100,660
10. Optometrists	$94,990
11. Software Developers, Systems Software	$94,180
12. Engineers, All Other	$90,270
13. Engineering Teachers, Postsecondary	$89,670
14. Software Developers, Applications	$87,790
15. Physician Assistants	$86,410

20 Best-Paying Jobs with a High Level of Science Skills

Job	Annual Earnings
16. Health Specialties Teachers, Postsecondary	$85,270
17. Medical and Health Services Managers	$84,270
18. Geoscientists, Except Hydrologists and Geographers	$82,500
19. Veterinarians	$82,040
20. Biomedical Engineers	$81,540

20 Best-Paying Jobs with a High Level of Social Skills

Job	Annual Earnings
1. Marketing Managers	$112,800
2. Lawyers	$112,760
3. Sales Managers	$98,530
4. Managers, All Other	$96,450
5. General and Operations Managers	$94,400
6. Education Administrators, Elementary and Secondary School	$86,970
7. Physician Assistants	$86,410
8. Construction Managers	$83,860
9. Administrative Services Managers	$77,890
10. Physical Therapists	$76,310
11. Sales Representatives, Wholesale and Manufacturing, Technical and Scientific Products	$73,710
12. Occupational Therapists	$72,320
13. Securities, Commodities, and Financial Services Sales Agents	$70,190
14. Detectives and Criminal Investigators	$68,820
15. Dental Hygienists	$68,250
16. Registered Nurses	$64,690
17. Instructional Coordinators	$58,830
18. Compliance Officers	$58,720
19. Supervisors of Construction and Extraction Workers	$58,680
20. Social and Community Service Managers	$57,950

20 Best-Paying Jobs with a High Level of Technology/Programming Skills

Job	Annual Earnings
1. Computer and Information Systems Managers	$115,780
2. Physicists	$106,370
3. Computer and Information Research Scientists	$100,660
4. Computer Hardware Engineers	$98,810
5. Aerospace Engineers	$97,480
6. Software Developers, Systems Software	$94,180
7. Engineers, All Other	$90,270
8. Electronics Engineers, Except Computer	$90,170
9. Software Developers, Applications	$87,790
10. Actuaries	$87,650
11. Sales Engineers	$87,390
12. Industrial-Organizational Psychologists	$87,330
13. Mining and Geological Engineers, Including Mining Safety Engineers	$82,870
14. Biomedical Engineers	$81,540
15. Computer Occupations, All Other	$79,240
16. Mechanical Engineers	$78,160
17. Computer Systems Analysts	$77,740
18. Hydrologists	$75,690
19. Computer Network Architects	$75,660
20. Database Administrators	$73,490

20 Best-Paying Jobs with a High Level of Thought-Processing Skills

Job	Annual Earnings
1. Orthodontists	$166,400+
2. Chief Executives	$165,080
3. Dentists, General	$141,040
4. Marketing Managers	$112,800
5. Lawyers	$112,760
6. Financial Managers	$103,910
7. Human Resources Managers	$99,180
8. Sales Managers	$98,530
9. Managers, All Other	$96,450
10. Optometrists	$94,990
11. General and Operations Managers	$94,400
12. Actuaries	$87,650
13. Education Administrators, Elementary and Secondary School	$86,970
14. Health Specialties Teachers, Postsecondary	$85,270
15. Medical and Health Services Managers	$84,270

20 Best-Paying Jobs with a High Level of Thought-Processing Skills

Job	Annual Earnings
16. Veterinarians	$82,040
17. Computer Occupations, All Other	$79,240
18. Environmental Engineers	$78,740
19. Management Analysts	$78,160
20. Medical Scientists, Except Epidemiologists	$76,700

20 Fastest-Growing Jobs for Each Skill

From the nine lists of best jobs using each skill, these nine lists show the 20 jobs using each skill that are projected to have the highest percentage increase in the numbers of people employed through 2018. Notice that just as income levels vary among the lists, rates of job growth vary, although not as greatly. The top 50 jobs with a high level of Science Skills have somewhat better opportunities (an average of 21.4 percent growth) than do the top jobs in the other groups (ranging from 18.3 percent to 11.4 percent). This is partly because the jobs that require Science Skills tend to be in the booming health-care and technology fields. The jobs requiring Communication Skills are also growing rapidly, at the average rate of 18.3 percent. Many of them are in the health-care field, too, and because communication works best in face-to-face exchanges between people, these jobs cannot easily be automated or outsourced to overseas workers. Although the exporting of technology jobs has received much press coverage, jobs requiring Technology/ Programming Skills made third place, with average projected growth of 18.0 percent.

For more ways of looking at the relationship between skills and job growth, see the bonus lists at the end of this part.

20 Fastest-Growing Jobs with a High Level of Communication Skills

Job	Percent Growth
1. Financial Examiners	41.2%
2. Physician Assistants	39.0%
3. Biochemists and Biophysicists	37.4%
4. Dental Hygienists	36.1%
5. Medical Assistants	33.9%
6. Physical Therapist Assistants	33.3%
7. Veterinarians	32.9%
8. Self-Enrichment Education Teachers	32.0%
9. Compliance Officers	31.0%

(continued)

20 Fastest-Growing Jobs with a High Level of Communication Skills

Job	Percent Growth
10. Pharmacy Technicians	30.6%
11. Physical Therapists	30.3%
12. Personal Financial Advisors	30.1%
13. Fitness Trainers and Aerobics Instructors	29.4%
14. Paralegals and Legal Assistants	28.1%
15. Environmental Scientists and Specialists, Including Health	27.9%
16. Human Resources Specialists	27.9%
17. Medical Secretaries	26.6%
18. Occupational Therapists	25.6%
19. Cost Estimators	25.3%
20. Audiologists	25.0%

20 Fastest-Growing Jobs with a High Level of Equipment Use/Maintenance Skills

Job	Percent Growth
1. Computer Network Architects	53.4%
2. Dental Assistants	35.7%
3. Compliance Officers	31.0%
4. Environmental Engineering Technicians	30.1%
5. Environmental Science and Protection Technicians, Including Health	28.9%
6. Heating, Air Conditioning, and Refrigeration Mechanics and Installers	28.1%
7. Medical Equipment Repairers	27.2%
8. Radiation Therapists	27.1%
9. Surgical Technologists	25.3%
10. Security and Fire Alarm Systems Installers	24.8%
11. Cardiovascular Technologists and Technicians	24.1%
12. Network and Computer Systems Administrators	23.2%
13. Respiratory Therapists	20.9%
14. Construction Laborers	20.5%
15. Surveying and Mapping Technicians	20.4%
16. Water and Wastewater Treatment Plant and System Operators	19.8%
17. Boilermakers	18.8%
18. Health Technologists and Technicians, All Other	18.7%
19. Refuse and Recyclable Material Collectors	18.6%
20. Ship Engineers	18.6%

20 Fastest-Growing Jobs with a High Level of Installation Skills

Job	Percent Growth
1. Biomedical Engineers	72.0%
2. Heating, Air Conditioning, and Refrigeration Mechanics and Installers	28.1%
3. Security and Fire Alarm Systems Installers	24.8%
4. Helpers—Electricians	24.7%
5. Network and Computer Systems Administrators	23.2%
6. Plumbers, Pipefitters, and Steamfitters	15.3%
7. Computer Occupations, All Other	13.1%
8. Medical Equipment Preparers	12.8%
9. Audio and Video Equipment Technicians	12.6%
10. Locksmiths and Safe Repairers	12.0%
11. Electricians	11.9%
12. Maintenance and Repair Workers, General	10.9%
13. Electronic Home Entertainment Equipment Installers and Repairers	10.8%
14. Mechanical Door Repairers	10.8%
15. Avionics Technicians	10.6%
16. Audio-Visual and Multimedia Collections Specialists	10.3%
17. Aircraft Structure, Surfaces, Rigging, and Systems Assemblers	9.3%
18. Elevator Installers and Repairers	9.2%
19. Installation, Maintenance, and Repair Workers, All Other	9.2%
20. Mobile Heavy Equipment Mechanics, Except Engines	8.7%

20 Fastest-Growing Jobs with a High Level of Management Skills

Job	Percent Growth
1. Cost Estimators	25.3%
2. Surgical Technologists	25.3%
3. Coaches and Scouts	24.8%
4. Civil Engineers	24.3%
5. Cargo and Freight Agents	23.9%
6. Social Scientists and Related Workers, All Other	22.5%
7. Agents and Business Managers of Artists, Performers, and Athletes	22.4%
8. Landscape Architects	19.6%
9. Logisticians	19.5%
10. Interior Designers	19.4%
11. Preschool Teachers, Except Special Education	19.0%
12. Ship Engineers	18.6%
13. Petroleum Engineers	18.4%
14. Captains, Mates, and Pilots of Water Vessels	17.3%

(continued)

20 Fastest-Growing Jobs with a High Level of Management Skills

Job	Percent Growth
15. Construction Managers	17.2%
16. Pharmacists	17.0%
17. Computer and Information Systems Managers	16.9%
18. Architects, Except Landscape and Naval	16.2%
19. Medical and Health Services Managers	16.0%
20. Natural Sciences Managers	15.5%

20 Fastest-Growing Jobs with a High Level of Mathematics Skills

Job	Percent Growth
1. Financial Examiners	41.2%
2. Medical Scientists, Except Epidemiologists	40.4%
3. Biochemists and Biophysicists	37.4%
4. Software Developers, Applications	34.0%
5. Compliance Officers	31.0%
6. Environmental Engineers	30.6%
7. Pharmacy Technicians	30.6%
8. Software Developers, Systems Software	30.4%
9. Personal Financial Advisors	30.1%
10. Heating, Air Conditioning, and Refrigeration Mechanics and Installers	28.1%
11. Market Research Analysts and Marketing Specialists	28.1%
12. Environmental Scientists and Specialists, Including Health	27.9%
13. Radiation Therapists	27.1%
14. Cost Estimators	25.3%
15. Optometrists	24.4%
16. Civil Engineers	24.3%
17. Computer and Information Research Scientists	24.2%
18. Management Analysts	23.9%
19. Compensation, Benefits, and Job Analysis Specialists	23.6%
20. Social Scientists and Related Workers, All Other	22.5%

20 Fastest-Growing Jobs with a High Level of Science Skills

Job	Percent Growth
1. Biomedical Engineers	72.0%
2. Computer Network Architects	53.4%
3. Medical Scientists, Except Epidemiologists	40.4%
4. Physician Assistants	39.0%
5. Biochemists and Biophysicists	37.4%
6. Dental Hygienists	36.1%
7. Software Developers, Applications	34.0%
8. Medical Assistants	33.9%
9. Physical Therapist Assistants	33.3%
10. Veterinarians	32.9%
11. Compliance Officers	31.0%
12. Environmental Engineers	30.6%
13. Software Developers, Systems Software	30.4%
14. Physical Therapists	30.3%
15. Market Research Analysts and Marketing Specialists	28.1%
16. Human Resources Specialists	27.9%
17. Environmental Scientists and Specialists, Including Health	27.9%
18. Radiation Therapists	27.1%
19. Prosthodontists	26.4%
20. Occupational Therapists	25.6%

20 Fastest-Growing Jobs with a High Level of Social Skills

Job	Percent Growth
1. Home Health Aides	50.0%
2. Physician Assistants	39.0%
3. Dental Hygienists	36.1%
4. Dental Assistants	35.7%
5. Medical Assistants	33.9%
6. Physical Therapist Assistants	33.3%
7. Self-Enrichment Education Teachers	32.0%
8. Compliance Officers	31.0%
9. Pharmacy Technicians	30.6%
10. Physical Therapists	30.3%
11. Fitness Trainers and Aerobics Instructors	29.4%
12. Human Resources Specialists	27.9%
13. Medical Secretaries	26.6%
14. Occupational Therapists	25.6%

(continued)

20 Fastest-Growing Jobs with a High Level of Social Skills

Job	Percent Growth
15. Public Relations Specialists	24.0%
16. Training and Development Specialists	23.3%
17. Instructional Coordinators	23.2%
18. Healthcare Social Workers	22.4%
19. Registered Nurses	22.2%
20. Respiratory Therapists	20.9%

20 Fastest-Growing Jobs with a High Level of Technology/Programming Skills

Job	Percent Growth
1. Biomedical Engineers	72.0%
2. Computer Network Architects	53.4%
3. Software Developers, Applications	34.0%
4. Software Developers, Systems Software	30.4%
5. Survey Researchers	30.3%
6. Industrial-Organizational Psychologists	26.1%
7. Computer and Information Research Scientists	24.2%
8. Network and Computer Systems Administrators	23.2%
9. Actuaries	21.3%
10. Surveying and Mapping Technicians	20.4%
11. Computer Systems Analysts	20.3%
12. Database Administrators	20.3%
13. Hydrologists	18.2%
14. Social Science Research Assistants	17.8%
15. Computer and Information Systems Managers	16.9%
16. Physicists	15.9%
17. Mining and Geological Engineers, Including Mining Safety Engineers	15.2%
18. Computer Science Teachers, Postsecondary	15.1%
19. Computer Occupations, All Other	13.1%
20. Statisticians	13.1%

20 Fastest-Growing Jobs with a High Level of Thought-Processing Skills

Job	Percent Growth
1. Financial Examiners	41.2%
2. Medical Scientists, Except Epidemiologists	40.4%
3. Veterinarians	32.9%
4. Self-Enrichment Education Teachers	32.0%
5. Compliance Officers	31.0%
6. Environmental Engineers	30.6%
7. Personal Financial Advisors	30.1%
8. Fitness Trainers and Aerobics Instructors	29.4%
9. Market Research Analysts and Marketing Specialists	28.1%
10. Optometrists	24.4%
11. Public Relations Specialists	24.0%
12. Management Analysts	23.9%
13. Compensation, Benefits, and Job Analysis Specialists	23.6%
14. Training and Development Specialists	23.3%
15. Instructional Coordinators	23.2%
16. Social Scientists and Related Workers, All Other	22.5%
17. Registered Nurses	22.2%
18. Operations Research Analysts	22.0%
19. Accountants and Auditors	21.6%
20. Actuaries	21.3%

20 Jobs for Each Skill with the Most Openings

This set of lists shows the 20 jobs using each skill at a high level that are projected to have the largest number of job openings per year through 2018.

Jobs with many openings present advantages that may be attractive to you. Because they have many openings, these jobs can be easier to obtain, particularly for those just entering the job market. These jobs may offer more opportunities to move from one employer to another with relative ease. Though some of these jobs have average or below-average pay, some pay quite well and can provide good long-term opportunities or the ability to move up.

Jobs high in Social Skills and Thought-Processing Skills have the largest number of openings (an average of about 20,800 and 14,100 openings, respectively). Most of these jobs require face-to-face interactions and on-site decisions, so the tasks are not likely to be taken over by offshore workers or computers. Jobs high in Installation Skills, on the other hand, are more vulnerable to such competition and therefore promise far fewer openings (an average of about 6,200). It is interesting that the jobs high in Technology/ Programming Skills are the group with the lowest average number of openings (about 5,700), even though these occupations are among those growing fastest. That's because these high-tech occupations also have a relatively small number of workers, so though they are growing rapidly, they will not provide as many job openings as the other groups.

20 Jobs with a High Level of Communication Skills with the Most Openings

Job	Annual Openings
1. Elementary School Teachers, Except Special Education	59,650
2. Accountants and Auditors	49,750
3. Management Analysts	30,650
4. Middle School Teachers, Except Special and Career/Technical Education	25,110
5. Lawyers	24,040
6. Medical Assistants	21,780
7. Medical Secretaries	18,900
8. Pharmacy Technicians	18,200
9. Sales Representatives, Wholesale and Manufacturing, Technical and Scientific Products	14,230
10. Public Relations Specialists	13,130
11. Real Estate Sales Agents	12,830
12. Securities, Commodities, and Financial Services Sales Agents	12,680
13. Fitness Trainers and Aerobics Instructors	12,380
14. Self-Enrichment Education Teachers	12,030
15. Human Resources Specialists	11,230
16. Compliance Officers	10,850
17. Pharmacists	10,580
18. Paralegals and Legal Assistants	10,400
19. Cost Estimators	10,360
20. Dental Hygienists	9,840

20 Jobs with a High Level of Equipment Use/Maintenance Skills with the Most Openings

Job	Annual Openings
1. Heavy and Tractor-Trailer Truck Drivers	55,460
2. Maintenance and Repair Workers, General	35,750
3. Construction Laborers	33,940
4. Carpenters	32,540
5. Electricians	25,090
6. Supervisors of Construction and Extraction Workers	24,220
7. Computer User Support Specialists	23,460

20 Jobs with a High Level of Equipment Use/Maintenance Skills with the Most Openings

Job	Annual Openings
8. Computer Network Architects	20,830
9. Plumbers, Pipefitters, and Steamfitters	17,550
10. Dental Assistants	16,100
11. Firefighters	15,280
12. First-Line Supervisors of Mechanics, Installers, and Repairers	13,650
13. Heating, Air Conditioning, and Refrigeration Mechanics and Installers	13,620
14. Network and Computer Systems Administrators	13,550
15. Operating Engineers and Other Construction Equipment Operators	11,820
16. Compliance Officers	10,850
17. Computer and Information Systems Managers	9,710
18. Cement Masons and Concrete Finishers	7,640
19. Refuse and Recyclable Material Collectors	7,110
20. Radiologic Technologists	6,800

20 Jobs with a High Level of Installation Skills with the Most Openings

Job	Annual Openings
1. Maintenance and Repair Workers, General	35,750
2. Electricians	25,090
3. Automotive Service Technicians and Mechanics	18,170
4. Plumbers, Pipefitters, and Steamfitters	17,550
5. Heating, Air Conditioning, and Refrigeration Mechanics and Installers	13,620
6. Network and Computer Systems Administrators	13,550
7. Helpers—Installation, Maintenance, and Repair Workers	8,500
8. Computer Occupations, All Other	7,260
9. Industrial Machinery Mechanics	6,240
10. Engineers, All Other	5,020
11. Helpers—Electricians	4,800
12. Installation, Maintenance, and Repair Workers, All Other	4,180
13. Mobile Heavy Equipment Mechanics, Except Engines	3,770
14. Telecommunications Equipment Installers and Repairers, Except Line Installers	3,560
15. Security and Fire Alarm Systems Installers	2,780
16. Audio and Video Equipment Technicians	2,370
17. Engineering Technicians, Except Drafters, All Other	1,850
18. Electrical and Electronics Repairers, Commercial and Industrial Equipment	1,640
19. Biomedical Engineers	1,490
20. Electronic Home Entertainment Equipment Installers and Repairers	1,430

20 Jobs with a High Level of Management Skills with the Most Openings

Job	Annual Openings
1. General and Operations Managers	50,220
2. First-Line Supervisors of Office and Administrative Support Workers	48,900
3. Executive Secretaries and Executive Administrative Assistants	41,920
4. Business Operations Specialists, All Other	36,830
5. Carpenters	32,540
6. Managers, All Other	29,750
7. Supervisors of Construction and Extraction Workers	24,220
8. Clergy	21,770
9. Preschool Teachers, Except Special Education	17,830
10. Sales Representatives, Wholesale and Manufacturing, Technical and Scientific Products	14,230
11. Financial Managers	13,820
12. Construction Managers	13,770
13. First-Line Supervisors of Non-Retail Sales Workers	12,950
14. Sales Managers	12,660
15. Graphic Designers	12,480
16. Purchasing Agents, Except Wholesale, Retail, and Farm Products	11,860
17. Civil Engineers	11,460
18. Chief Executives	11,250
19. Pharmacists	10,580
20. Cost Estimators	10,360

20 Jobs with a High Level of Mathematics Skills with the Most Openings

Job	Annual Openings
1. Accountants and Auditors	49,750
2. Business Operations Specialists, All Other	36,830
3. Management Analysts	30,650
4. Computer Systems Analysts	22,280
5. Software Developers, Applications	21,840
6. Pharmacy Technicians	18,200
7. Plumbers, Pipefitters, and Steamfitters	17,550
8. Software Developers, Systems Software	15,340
9. Financial Managers	13,820
10. Construction Managers	13,770
11. Market Research Analysts and Marketing Specialists	13,730
12. Heating, Air Conditioning, and Refrigeration Mechanics and Installers	13,620
13. Securities, Commodities, and Financial Services Sales Agents	12,680

20 Jobs with a High Level of Mathematics Skills with the Most Openings

Job	Annual Openings
14. Purchasing Agents, Except Wholesale, Retail, and Farm Products	11,860
15. Civil Engineers	11,460
16. Compliance Officers	10,850
17. Cost Estimators	10,360
18. Financial Analysts	9,520
19. Industrial Engineers	8,540
20. Personal Financial Advisors	8,530

20 Jobs with a High Level of Science Skills with the Most Openings

Job	Annual Openings
1. Registered Nurses	103,900
2. Licensed Practical and Licensed Vocational Nurses	39,130
3. Computer Systems Analysts	22,280
4. Software Developers, Applications	21,840
5. Medical Assistants	21,780
6. Computer Network Architects	20,830
7. Software Developers, Systems Software	15,340
8. Market Research Analysts and Marketing Specialists	13,730
9. Civil Engineers	11,460
10. Human Resources Specialists	11,230
11. Compliance Officers	10,850
12. Training and Development Specialists	10,710
13. Pharmacists	10,580
14. Medical and Health Services Managers	9,940
15. Dental Hygienists	9,840
16. Physical Therapists	7,860
17. Computer Occupations, All Other	7,260
18. Radiologic Technologists	6,800
19. Medical Scientists, Except Epidemiologists	6,620
20. Healthcare Social Workers	6,590

20 Jobs with a High Level of Social Skills with the Most Openings

Job	Annual Openings
1. Customer Service Representatives	110,840
2. Registered Nurses	103,900
3. Elementary School Teachers, Except Special Education	59,650
4. Home Health Aides	55,270
5. General and Operations Managers	50,220
6. First-Line Supervisors of Office and Administrative Support Workers	48,900
7. Executive Secretaries and Executive Administrative Assistants	41,920
8. Secondary School Teachers, Except Special and Career/Technical Education	41,240
9. Licensed Practical and Licensed Vocational Nurses	39,130
10. Managers, All Other	29,750
11. Middle School Teachers, Except Special and Career/Technical Education	25,110
12. Supervisors of Construction and Extraction Workers	24,220
13. Lawyers	24,040
14. Police and Sheriff's Patrol Officers	22,790
15. Medical Assistants	21,780
16. Clergy	21,770
17. Medical Secretaries	18,900
18. Pharmacy Technicians	18,200
19. Dental Assistants	16,100
20. Firefighters	15,280

20 Jobs with a High Level of Technology/Programming Skills with the Most Openings

Job	Annual Openings
1. Computer Systems Analysts	22,280
2. Software Developers, Applications	21,840
3. Computer Network Architects	20,830
4. Software Developers, Systems Software	15,340
5. Network and Computer Systems Administrators	13,550
6. Computer and Information Systems Managers	9,710
7. Computer Programmers	8,030
8. Mechanical Engineers	7,570
9. Computer Occupations, All Other	7,260
10. Industrial Machinery Mechanics	6,240
11. Engineers, All Other	5,020
12. Database Administrators	4,440
13. Architectural and Civil Drafters	3,620

20 Jobs with a High Level of Technology/Programming Skills with the Most Openings

Job	Annual Openings
14. Sales Engineers	3,500
15. Electronics Engineers, Except Computer	3,340
16. Surveying and Mapping Technicians	2,940
17. Computer Hardware Engineers	2,350
18. Aerospace Engineers	2,230
19. Commercial and Industrial Designers	1,760
20. Biomedical Engineers	1,490

20 Jobs with a High Level of Thought-Processing Skills with the Most Openings

Job	Annual Openings
1. Registered Nurses	103,900
2. Elementary School Teachers, Except Special Education	59,650
3. General and Operations Managers	50,220
4. Accountants and Auditors	49,750
5. Licensed Practical and Licensed Vocational Nurses	39,130
6. Business Operations Specialists, All Other	36,830
7. Management Analysts	30,650
8. Managers, All Other	29,750
9. Middle School Teachers, Except Special and Career/Technical Education	25,110
10. Lawyers	24,040
11. Financial Managers	13,820
12. Market Research Analysts and Marketing Specialists	13,730
13. Public Relations Specialists	13,130
14. Sales Managers	12,660
15. Fitness Trainers and Aerobics Instructors	12,380
16. Self-Enrichment Education Teachers	12,030
17. Purchasing Agents, Except Wholesale, Retail, and Farm Products	11,860
18. Chief Executives	11,250
19. Compliance Officers	10,850
20. Training and Development Specialists	10,710

Best High-Skill Jobs by Demographic

Different types of jobs attract different types of workers. It's interesting to consider which high-skill jobs have the highest percentage of men or young workers. I'm not saying that men or young people should consider these jobs over others based solely on this information, but it is useful information to know.

In some cases, these lists can give you ideas for jobs to consider that you might otherwise overlook. For example, perhaps women should consider some jobs that traditionally have high percentages of men in them—especially women who have skills more typically held by men. Or older workers might consider some jobs typically held by young people. Although these aren't obvious ways of using these lists, the lists may give you some good ideas of jobs to consider. The lists may also help you identify high-skill jobs that work well for others like you—for example, jobs with plentiful opportunities for self-employment, if that's a work arrangement that appeals to you.

All lists in this section were created through a similar process. I began with the 199 unique best high-skill jobs and created a list that included only those jobs with a workforce that exceeded a certain minimum representation of a specific demographic, such as the percentage of self-employed workers. Then I sorted those jobs in order of their combined scores for earnings, growth rate, and number of openings.

Note that the economic criteria that were used to sort the jobs in these lists are based on the averages for *all* workers, not just workers who match the particular demographic group. For example, it was not possible to obtain earnings figures that applied specifically to young people, although it is known that they tend to earn less. Similarly, it was not possible to obtain separate figures for projected job growth of urban or rural workers.

For each job listed, I identify the top skills, arranged in descending order of the level of mastery they require. To save space, I use abbreviations—for example, COM for Communications Skills.

Best High-Skill Jobs with a High Percentage of Self-Employed Workers

About 8 percent of all working people are self-employed or own their own business. Among the high-skill jobs in this book, the average figure is about the same: 8.6 percent. This substantial part of our workforce gets little mention in most career books.

Many jobs in this list, such as the various types of designers, are held by people who operate one- or two-person businesses and who may also do this work part time. Those in other occupations, such as Carpenters, often work on a per-job basis under the supervision of others.

As you will see from these lists, self-employed people hold a wide range of jobs at all levels of pay. The skill most frequently represented here is Management Skills. This may say something about the kinds of people who are able to start their own business, but all skills except Installation Skills and Technology/Programming Skills appear here at least five times. While the lists do not include data on age and gender, you may be interested in the fact that older workers and women make up a rapidly growing part of the self-employed population. For example, some highly experienced older workers set up consulting and other small businesses following a layoff or as an alternative to full retirement. Large numbers of women are forming small businesses or creating self-employment opportunities as an alternative to traditional employment.

The jobs listed here all have 20 percent or more self-employed workers, and they are ranked by earnings, job growth, and job openings. It's important to remember that the earnings are based on a salary survey that does not include self-employed workers, whose earnings may be either higher or lower than the figures reported here.

Best High-Skill Jobs with a High Percentage of Self-Employed Workers

Job	Top Skills	Percent Self-Employed Workers	Annual Earnings	Percent Growth	Annual Openings
1. Management Analysts	COM MAT THO	25.8%	$78,160	23.9%	30,650
2. Construction Managers	MGT MAT SOC	60.9%	$83,860	17.2%	13,770
3. Lawyers	COM SOC THO	26.2%	$112,760	13.0%	24,040
4. Personal Financial Advisors	COM MAT THO	29.3%	$64,750	30.1%	8,530
5. Optometrists	MAT SCI THO	24.6%	$94,990	24.4%	2,010
6. Dentists, General	MGT SCI THO	28.0%	$141,040	15.3%	5,180
7. Prosthodontists	SCI	27.9%	$118,400	26.4%	30
8. Orthodontists	COM SCI THO	28.1%	$166,400+	19.7%	360
9. Construction Laborers	EQU	21.3%	$29,280	20.5%	33,940
10. Managers, All Other	MGT SOC THO	57.1%	$96,450	7.3%	29,750
11. Industrial-Organizational Psychologists	TEC	33.6%	$87,330	26.1%	130
12. Chief Executives	MGT THO	21.6%	$165,080	−1.4%	11,250
13. Architects, Except Landscape and Naval	MGT MAT SCI	21.2%	$72,550	16.2%	4,680
14. Chiropractors	COM SCI THO	44.5%	$67,200	19.5%	1,820
15. Real Estate Sales Agents	COM SOC	58.3%	$40,030	16.2%	12,830
16. Agents and Business Managers of Artists, Performers, and Athletes	COM MGT	45.8%	$63,130	22.4%	1,010

(continued)

COM=*Communication Skills*   EQU=*Equipment Use/Maintenance Skills*   INS=*Installation Skills*   MAT=*Mathematics Skills*
MGT=*Management Skills*   SCI=*Science Skills*   SOC=*Social Skills*   TEC=*Technology/Programming Skills*   THO=*Thought-Processing Skills*

Best High-Skill Jobs with a High Percentage of Self-Employed Workers

Job	Top Skills	Percent Self-Employed Workers	Annual Earnings	Percent Growth	Annual Openings
17. First-Line Supervisors of Non-Retail Sales Workers	MGT	45.6%	$68,880	4.8%	12,950
18. Carpenters	EQU MGT	32.0%	$39,530	12.9%	32,540
19. Art Directors	MGT	60.2%	$80,630	11.7%	2,870
20. Graphic Designers	MGT	26.3%	$43,500	12.9%	12,480
21. Interior Designers	MGT	26.7%	$46,280	19.4%	3,590
22. Writers and Authors	SOC	69.4%	$55,420	14.8%	5,420
23. First-Line Supervisors of Personal Service Workers	MGT	37.8%	$35,290	15.4%	9,080
24. Landscape Architects	MGT	21.3%	$62,090	19.6%	980
25. First-Line Supervisors of Landscaping, Lawn Service, and Groundskeeping Workers	EQU MGT	50.4%	$41,860	14.9%	5,600
26. Producers and Directors	MGT EQU	20.1%	$68,440	9.8%	4,040
27. Brickmasons and Blockmasons	EQU	27.3%	$46,930	11.5%	5,000
28. Commercial and Industrial Designers	TEC	26.7%	$58,230	9.0%	1,760
29. Electronic Home Entertainment Equipment Installers and Repairers	INS	25.8%	$32,940	10.8%	1,430

Best High-Skill Jobs with a High Percentage of Workers Age 16–24

From my list of 199 high-skill jobs used in this book, this list contains jobs with the highest percentage (more than 15 percent) of workers age 16–24, presented in order of their combined rankings on earnings, job growth, and job openings. Younger workers are found in all jobs, but jobs with higher percentages of younger workers may present more opportunities for initial entry or upward mobility.

This listing is dominated by jobs that require less than a bachelor's degree, and some can be learned through on-the-job training or a few years of experience in a related job. Given these entry routes, it's not surprising that Equipment Use/Maintenance Skills and Social Skills are well represented here, whereas Science Skills, Technology/Programming Skills, and Mathematics Skills are scarce.

Best High-Skill Jobs with a High Percentage of Workers Age 16–24

Job	Top Skills	Percent Workers 16–24	Annual Earnings	Percent Growth	Annual Openings
1. Dental Assistants	EQU SOC	17.6%	$33,470	35.7%	16,100
2. Self-Enrichment Education Teachers	COM SOC THO	16.7%	$36,340	32.0%	12,030
3. Medical Assistants	COM SCI SOC	18.6%	$28,860	33.9%	21,780
4. Physical Therapist Assistants	COM SCI SOC	21.6%	$49,690	33.3%	3,050
5. Home Health Aides	SOC	15.9%	$20,560	50.0%	55,270
6. Fitness Trainers and Aerobics Instructors	COM SOC THO	30.3%	$31,090	29.4%	12,380
7. Pharmacy Technicians	COM MAT SOC	21.5%	$28,400	30.6%	18,200
8. Surgical Technologists	EQU MGT	21.5%	$39,920	25.3%	4,630
9. Customer Service Representatives	SOC	21.6%	$30,460	17.7%	110,840
10. Construction Laborers	EQU	18.3%	$29,280	20.5%	33,940
11. Environmental Science and Protection Technicians, Including Health	EQU	23.8%	$41,380	28.9%	2,520
12. Refuse and Recyclable Material Collectors	EQU	15.5%	$32,640	18.6%	7,110
13. Life, Physical, and Social Science Technicians, All Other	EQU	23.8%	$43,350	13.3%	3,640
14. Coaches and Scouts	MGT	33.7%	$28,340	24.8%	9,920
15. Drywall and Ceiling Tile Installers	EQU	15.9%	$37,320	13.5%	3,700
16. Social Science Research Assistants	TEC	23.8%	$37,230	17.8%	1,270
17. Helpers—Electricians	INS	41.7%	$27,220	24.7%	4,800
18. Helpers—Installation, Maintenance, and Repair Workers	INS	40.1%	$24,260	8.3%	8,500
19. Medical Equipment Preparers	INS	18.6%	$29,490	12.8%	1,120

Best High-Skill Jobs with a High Percentage of Workers Age 55 or Higher

Many high-skill jobs with the highest percentages of workers age 55 and over require considerable preparation, either through experience or through education and training. Workers who have invested heavily in advanced education tend to delay retirement to recoup their investment. It helps that most of these jobs are not physically demanding.

This list includes jobs with more than 30 percent of older workers. All of the skills except Equipment Use/Maintenance Skills and Installation Skills are well represented here.

COM=Communication Skills   EQU=Equipment Use/Maintenance Skills   INS=Installation Skills   MAT=Mathematics Skills
MGT=Management Skills   SCI=Science Skills   SOC=Social Skills   TEC=Technology/Programming Skills   THO=Thought-Processing Skills

Best High-Skill Jobs with a High Percentage of Workers Age 55 or Higher

Job	Top Skills	Percent Workers 55 or Higher	Annual Earnings	Percent Growth	Annual Openings
1. Engineering Teachers, Postsecondary	COM MAT SCI	30.1%	$89,670	15.1%	1,000
2. Management Analysts	COM MAT THO	32.3%	$78,160	23.9%	30,650
3. Health Specialties Teachers, Postsecondary	COM SCI THO	30.1%	$85,270	15.1%	4,000
4. Dentists, General	MGT SCI THO	36.1%	$141,040	15.3%	5,180
5. Optometrists	MAT SCI THO	30.6%	$94,990	24.4%	2,010
6. Cost Estimators	COM MGT MAT	30.9%	$57,860	25.3%	10,360
7. Orthodontists	COM SCI THO	36.1%	$166,400+	19.7%	360
8. Prosthodontists	SCI	36.1%	$118,400	26.4%	30
9. Business Teachers, Postsecondary	COM MAT THO	30.1%	$73,760	15.1%	2,000
10. Chief Executives	MGT THO	35.5%	$165,080	−1.4%	11,250
11. Instructional Coordinators	COM SOC THO	31.9%	$58,830	23.2%	6,060
12. Biological Science Teachers, Postsecondary	COM THO	30.1%	$72,700	15.1%	1,700
13. Industrial-Organizational Psychologists	TEC	41.9%	$87,330	26.1%	130
14. Computer Science Teachers, Postsecondary	TEC	30.1%	$70,300	15.1%	1,000
15. Physicists	MAT SCI TEC	33.8%	$106,370	15.9%	690
16. Real Estate Sales Agents	COM SOC	35.7%	$40,030	16.2%	12,830
17. Education Administrators, Elementary and Secondary School	MGT SOC THO	32.2%	$86,970	8.6%	8,880
18. Administrative Services Managers	COM MGT SOC	31.9%	$77,890	12.5%	8,660
19. Construction and Building Inspectors	EQU	40.1%	$52,360	16.8%	3,970
20. Art, Drama, and Music Teachers, Postsecondary	THO	30.1%	$62,040	15.1%	2,500
21. Mining and Geological Engineers, Including Mining Safety Engineers	TEC	34.3%	$82,870	15.2%	260
22. Clergy	MGT SOC	41.5%	$43,970	12.7%	21,770
23. Transportation Inspectors	EQU	31.3%	$57,640	18.4%	1,130
24. Art Directors	MGT	35.0%	$80,630	11.7%	2,870
25. Social and Community Service Managers	MGT SOC	30.8%	$57,950	13.8%	4,820
26. Writers and Authors	SOC	31.9%	$55,420	14.8%	5,420
27. Audio-Visual and Multimedia Collections Specialists	INS	31.9%	$42,710	10.3%	220

Best High-Skill Jobs with a High Percentage of Women

To create the lists that follow, I sorted the 199 best high-skill jobs according to the percentages of women and men in the workforce. Similar lists of the best jobs with high percentages (more than 75 percent) of men and women are included in other books in the Best Jobs series. It's important to understand that these lists aren't meant to restrict women or men from considering job options. Actually, my reasoning for including them is the opposite: I hope the lists help people see possibilities that they might not otherwise have considered.

As you might expect, Social Skills dominate the list of jobs with a high percentage of women. Women are generally believed to be better at those skills than men and thus tend to be attracted to jobs where they interact with and help other people. The list of jobs with a high percentage of men shows a heavy representation of Equipment Use/Maintenance Skills, because men have traditionally been drawn to work that involves machines and tools. Nevertheless, I have known men who displayed excellent people skills and women who considered themselves "motor heads."

The fact is that jobs with high percentages of women or high percentages of men offer good opportunities for people of either gender who have the appropriate skills and want to do these jobs. So I suggest that women browse the list of jobs that employ high percentages of men and that men browse the list of jobs with high percentages of women. There are high-skill jobs in both lists that pay well, and women or men who are interested in them and who have or can obtain the necessary education and training should consider them.

An interesting and unfortunate tidbit to bring up at your next party is that the average earnings for the jobs with the highest percentage of women is $46,585, compared to average earnings of $53,918 for the jobs with the highest percentage of men. But the earnings gap (which has narrowed in recent years) doesn't tell the whole story. I computed the average growth and job openings of the jobs with the highest percentage of women and found averages of 23.0 percent growth and 19,511 openings, compared to 14.1 percent growth and 8,428 openings for the jobs with the highest percentage of men. This discrepancy reinforces the idea that men have had more problems than women in adapting to an economy dominated by service and information-based jobs. Many women may simply be better prepared, possessing more appropriate skills for the jobs that are now growing rapidly and have more job openings.

COM=Communication Skills   EQU=Equipment Use/Maintenance Skills   INS=Installation Skills   MAT=Mathematics Skills
MGT=Management Skills   SCI=Science Skills   SOC=Social Skills   TEC=Technology/Programming Skills   THO=Thought-Processing Skills

Best High-Skill Jobs with a High Percentage of Women

Job	Top Skills	Percent Women	Annual Earnings	Percent Growth	Annual Openings
1. Dental Hygienists	COM SCI SOC	96.1%	$68,250	36.1%	9,840
2. Registered Nurses	SCI SOC THO	90.7%	$64,690	22.2%	103,900
3. Home Health Aides	SOC	88.0%	$20,560	50.0%	55,270
4. Occupational Therapists	COM SCI SOC	81.7%	$72,320	25.6%	4,580
5. Elementary School Teachers, Except Special Education	COM SOC THO	81.3%	$51,660	15.8%	59,650
6. Paralegals and Legal Assistants	COM	86.7%	$46,680	28.1%	10,400
7. Dental Assistants	EQU SOC	96.7%	$33,470	35.7%	16,100
8. Medical Assistants	COM SCI SOC	90.4%	$28,860	33.9%	21,780
9. Instructional Coordinators	COM SOC THO	77.4%	$58,830	23.2%	6,060
10. Medical Secretaries	COM SOC	96.8%	$30,530	26.6%	18,900
11. Middle School Teachers, Except Special and Career/Technical Education	COM SOC THO	81.3%	$51,960	15.3%	25,110
12. Licensed Practical and Licensed Vocational Nurses	SCI SOC THO	91.4%	$40,380	20.6%	39,130
13. Pharmacy Technicians	COM MAT SOC	77.6%	$28,400	30.6%	18,200
14. Physical Therapist Assistants	COM SCI SOC	78.6%	$49,690	33.3%	3,050
15. Audiologists	COM	77.8%	$66,660	25.0%	580
16. Healthcare Social Workers	COM SCI SOC	81.5%	$47,230	22.4%	6,590
17. Executive Secretaries and Executive Administrative Assistants	MGT SOC	96.8%	$43,520	12.8%	41,920
18. Speech-Language Pathologists	COM SCI THO	97.7%	$66,920	18.5%	4,380
19. Medical Equipment Preparers	INS	90.4%	$29,490	12.8%	1,120
20. Special Education Teachers, Secondary School	SOC	85.0%	$54,810	13.3%	5,750
21. Surgical Technologists	EQU MGT	77.6%	$39,920	25.3%	4,630
22. Special Education Teachers, Middle School	COM SOC THO	85.0%	$53,440	18.1%	4,410
23. Legal Secretaries	COM	96.8%	$41,500	18.4%	8,380
24. Preschool Teachers, Except Special Education	MGT	98.4%	$25,700	19.0%	17,830
25. Audio-Visual and Multimedia Collections Specialists	INS	77.4%	$42,710	10.3%	220

Best High-Skill Jobs with a High Percentage of Men

If you haven't read the introduction to the previous list, "Best High-Skill Jobs with a High Percentage of Women," consider doing so. Much of the content there applies to this list as well.

I didn't include this list with the assumption that men should consider only jobs with high percentages of men or that women should consider only jobs with high percentages of women. Instead, these lists are here because I think they are interesting and helpful in considering nontraditional career options. For example, some men would do very well in and enjoy jobs with high percentages of women but may not have considered these jobs seriously. Similarly, some women would very much enjoy and do well in jobs that traditionally have been held by high percentages of men. I hope that these lists help you consider options that you didn't seriously consider because of gender stereotypes.

In the high-skill jobs on the following list, more than 75 percent of the workers are men, but increasing numbers of women are entering many of these jobs.

Best High-Skill Jobs with a High Percentage of Men

Job	Top Skills	Percent Men	Annual Earnings	Percent Growth	Annual Openings
1. Software Developers, Applications	MAT SCI TEC	78.7%	$87,790	34.0%	21,840
2. Software Developers, Systems Software	MAT SCI TEC	78.7%	$94,180	30.4%	15,340
3. Computer Network Architects	EQU SCI TEC	77.5%	$75,660	53.4%	20,830
4. Police and Sheriff's Patrol Officers	SOC	85.4%	$53,540	8.7%	22,790
5. Civil Engineers	MGT MAT SCI	91.7%	$77,560	24.3%	11,460
6. Construction Managers	MGT MAT SOC	93.6%	$83,860	17.2%	13,770
7. Network and Computer Systems Administrators	EQU INS TEC	78.4%	$69,160	23.2%	13,550
8. Cost Estimators	COM MGT MAT	85.6%	$57,860	25.3%	10,360
9. Heavy and Tractor-Trailer Truck Drivers	EQU	96.3%	$37,770	12.9%	55,460
10. Supervisors of Construction and Extraction Workers	EQU MGT SOC	97.4%	$58,680	15.4%	24,220
11. Biomedical Engineers	INS SCI TEC	88.2%	$81,540	72.0%	1,490
12. Industrial Engineers	MGT MAT THO	82.1%	$76,100	14.2%	8,540
13. Heating, Air Conditioning, and Refrigeration Mechanics and Installers	EQU INS MAT	99.4%	$42,530	28.1%	13,620

(continued)

COM=*Communication Skills*   EQU=*Equipment Use/Maintenance Skills*   INS=*Installation Skills*   MAT=*Mathematics Skills*
MGT=*Management Skills*   SCI=*Science Skills*   SOC=*Social Skills*   TEC=*Technology/Programming Skills*   THO=*Thought-Processing Skills*

Best High-Skill Jobs with a High Percentage of Men

Job	Top Skills	Percent Men	Annual Earnings	Percent Growth	Annual Openings
14. Operating Engineers and Other Construction Equipment Operators	EQU	99.1%	$40,400	12.0%	11,820
15. First-Line Supervisors of Fire Fighting and Prevention Workers	EQU	92.3%	$68,240	8.2%	3,250
16. Firefighters	EQU SOC	95.5%	$45,250	18.5%	15,280
17. Architects, Except Landscape and Naval	MGT MAT SCI	75.8%	$72,550	16.2%	4,680
18. Plumbers, Pipefitters, and Steamfitters	EQU INS MAT	99.0%	$46,660	15.3%	17,550
19. Construction Laborers	EQU	97.7%	$29,280	20.5%	33,940
20. Electricians	EQU INS	97.5%	$48,250	11.9%	25,090
21. Petroleum Engineers	MGT MAT SCI	78.9%	$114,080	18.4%	860
22. Cement Masons and Concrete Finishers	EQU	99.6%	$35,450	12.9%	7,640
23. Chief Executives	MGT THO	75.9%	$165,080	–1.4%	11,250
24. Ship Engineers	EQU MGT	100.0%	$65,880	18.6%	700
25. Transportation Inspectors	EQU	91.5%	$57,640	18.4%	1,130
26. Architectural and Engineering Managers	MGT MAT SCI	91.2%	$119,260	6.2%	4,870
27. Carpenters	EQU MGT	98.1%	$39,530	12.9%	32,540
28. Air Traffic Controllers	MAT	76.7%	$108,040	13.1%	1,230
29. Clergy	MGT SOC	86.2%	$43,970	12.7%	21,770
30. Commercial Pilots	EQU SCI THO	97.4%	$67,500	18.6%	2,060
31. Electrical and Electronics Repairers, Commercial and Industrial Equipment	INS	100.0%	$51,820	3.8%	1,640
32. Refuse and Recyclable Material Collectors	EQU	93.2%	$32,640	18.6%	7,110
33. Engineers, All Other	MAT SCI TEC EQU INS	86.4%	$90,270	6.7%	5,020
34. Coaches and Scouts	MGT	84.0%	$28,340	24.8%	9,920
35. Installation, Maintenance, and Repair Workers, All Other	INS	94.5%	$36,420	9.2%	4,180
36. Construction and Building Inspectors	EQU	94.4%	$52,360	16.8%	3,970
37. First-Line Supervisors of Police and Detectives	MGT	88.0%	$78,260	8.1%	5,050
38. Airline Pilots, Copilots, and Flight Engineers	EQU MAT	97.4%	$103,210	8.4%	3,250
39. Mechanical Engineers	MAT TEC	95.0%	$78,160	6.0%	7,570
40. Captains, Mates, and Pilots of Water Vessels	EQU MGT	100.0%	$64,180	17.3%	1,950
41. Water and Wastewater Treatment Plant and System Operators	EQU	93.0%	$40,770	19.8%	4,690

Best High-Skill Jobs with a High Percentage of Men

Job	Top Skills	Percent Men	Annual Earnings	Percent Growth	Annual Openings
42. Aerospace Engineers	MAT TEC	88.9%	$97,480	10.4%	2,230
43. Landscape Architects	MGT	75.8%	$62,090	19.6%	980
44. Sales Engineers	MAT TEC	90.3%	$87,390	8.8%	3,500
45. Medical Equipment Repairers	EQU	89.4%	$44,490	27.2%	2,320
46. Security and Fire Alarm Systems Installers	EQU INS	98.4%	$38,500	24.8%	2,780
47. First-Line Supervisors of Mechanics, Installers, and Repairers	EQU	90.6%	$59,150	4.2%	13,650
48. Millwrights	INS	99.1%	$48,360	1.4%	980
49. Maintenance and Repair Workers, General	EQU INS	97.3%	$34,730	10.9%	35,750
50. First-Line Supervisors of Landscaping, Lawn Service, and Groundskeeping Workers	EQU MGT	95.8%	$41,860	14.9%	5,600
51. Mining and Geological Engineers, Including Mining Safety Engineers	TEC	90.0%	$82,870	15.2%	260
52. Helpers—Electricians	INS	95.2%	$27,220	24.7%	4,800
53. Environmental Engineering Technicians	EQU	83.0%	$43,390	30.1%	1,040
54. Boilermakers	EQU	95.7%	$54,640	18.8%	810
55. Brickmasons and Blockmasons	EQU	100.0%	$46,930	11.5%	5,000
56. Computer Programmers	TEC	78.9%	$71,380	–2.9%	8,030
57. Surveying and Mapping Technicians	EQU TEC	93.5%	$37,900	20.4%	2,940
58. Computer Hardware Engineers	TEC	90.4%	$98,810	3.8%	2,350
59. Electronics Engineers, Except Computer	TEC	91.3%	$90,170	0.3%	3,340
60. Electrical Power-Line Installers and Repairers	EQU	98.4%	$58,030	4.5%	4,550
61. Industrial Machinery Mechanics	EQU INS TEC	97.0%	$45,420	7.3%	6,240
62. Elevator Installers and Repairers	INS	100.0%	$70,910	9.2%	920
63. Drywall and Ceiling Tile Installers	EQU	98.2%	$37,320	13.5%	3,700
64. Mechanical Door Repairers	INS	97.0%	$35,780	10.8%	450
65. Architectural and Civil Drafters	TEC	75.4%	$46,430	9.1%	3,620
66. Automotive Service Technicians and Mechanics	INS	98.4%	$35,790	4.7%	18,170
67. Mobile Heavy Equipment Mechanics, Except Engines	INS	98.6%	$44,830	8.7%	3,770

(continued)

COM=*Communication Skills* EQU=*Equipment Use/Maintenance Skills* INS=*Installation Skills* MAT=*Mathematics Skills*
MGT=*Management Skills* SCI=*Science Skills* SOC=*Social Skills* TEC=*Technology/Programming Skills* THO=*Thought-Processing Skills*

Best High-Skill Jobs with a High Percentage of Men

Job	Top Skills	Percent Men	Annual Earnings	Percent Growth	Annual Openings
68. Audio and Video Equipment Technicians	INS	91.8%	$40,540	12.6%	2,370
69. Telecommunications Equipment Installers and Repairers, Except Line Installers	INS	92.2%	$54,710	–0.2%	3,560
70. Engineering Technicians, Except Drafters, All Other	INS	83.0%	$58,020	5.2%	1,850
71. Helpers—Installation, Maintenance, and Repair Workers	INS	94.7%	$24,260	8.3%	8,500
72. Avionics Technicians	INS	92.3%	$52,320	10.6%	520
73. Electronic Home Entertainment Equipment Installers and Repairers	INS	94.8%	$32,940	10.8%	1,430
74. Rail Car Repairers	INS	97.0%	$47,410	6.5%	590
75. Locksmiths and Safe Repairers	INS	92.0%	$35,550	12.0%	610
76. Commercial Divers	INS	100.0%	$51,360	5.5%	50

Best High-Skill Jobs with a High Percentage of Urban or Rural Workers

Some people have a strong preference for an urban setting. They want to live and work where there's more energy and excitement, more access to the arts, more diversity, more really good restaurants, and better public transportation. On the other hand, some prefer the open spaces, closeness to nature, quiet, and inexpensive housing of rural locations. If you are strongly attracted to either setting, you'll be interested in the following lists.

I identified urban jobs as those for which 35 percent or more of the workforce is located in the 38 most populous metropolitan areas of the United States. These 38 metro areas—the most populous 10 percent of all U.S. metro areas, according to the Census Bureau—consist primarily of built-up communities, unlike smaller metro areas, which consist of a core city surrounded by a lot of countryside. In the following lists of high-skill urban jobs, you'll see a figure called the "urban ratio" for each job that represents the percentage of the total U.S. workforce for the job that is located in those 38 huge metro areas.

The Census Bureau also identifies 173 nonmetropolitan areas—areas that have no city of 50,000 people and a total population of less than 100,000. I identified rural jobs as those for which 15 percent or more of the total U.S. workforce is located in these nonmetropolitan areas. In the following lists of high-skill rural jobs, you'll see a figure called the "rural ratio" that represents the percentage of the total U.S. workforce for the job that is located in nonmetropolitan areas.

The Equipment Use/Maintenance Skills and Technology/Programming Skills are well represented among both the urban jobs and the rural jobs, but the urban jobs emphasize Thought-Processing Skills and Mathematics Skills much more than do the rural jobs. Cities are the location for much research and development, plus high-level business decision making.

The "best of" lists of both urban and rural jobs are ordered by the usual three economic measures: earnings, growth, and openings. The top skills for the jobs are identified by abbreviations.

Best High-Skill Jobs with a High Percentage of Urban Workers

Job	Top Skills	Percent Urban Workers	Annual Earnings	Percent Growth	Annual Openings
1. Medical Equipment Repairers	EQU	50.5%	$44,490	27.2%	2,320
2. Biomedical Engineers	INS SCI TEC	56.0%	$81,540	72.0%	1,490
3. Optometrists	MAT SCI THO	36.3%	$94,990	24.4%	2,010
4. Environmental Engineering Technicians	EQU	46.5%	$43,390	30.1%	1,040
5. Financial Examiners	COM MAT THO	38.1%	$74,940	41.2%	1,600
6. Actuaries	MAT TEC THO	54.6%	$87,650	21.3%	1,000
7. Art Directors	MGT	39.6%	$80,630	11.7%	2,870
8. Air Traffic Controllers	MAT	36.2%	$108,040	13.1%	1,230
9. Environmental Science and Protection Technicians, Including Health	EQU	40.1%	$41,380	28.9%	2,520
10. Chiropractors	COM SCI THO	42.3%	$67,200	19.5%	1,820
11. Biological Scientists, All Other	COM MAT	40.1%	$68,220	18.8%	1,610
12. Radiation Therapists	EQU MAT SCI	38.8%	$74,980	27.1%	690
13. Landscape Architects	MGT	58.6%	$62,090	19.6%	980
14. Audiologists	COM	42.6%	$66,660	25.0%	580
15. Statisticians	TEC	40.1%	$72,830	13.1%	960
16. Transportation Inspectors	EQU	37.9%	$57,640	18.4%	1,130
17. Hydrologists	TEC	47.8%	$75,690	18.2%	380
18. Ship Engineers	EQU MGT	39.5%	$65,880	18.6%	700
19. Elevator Installers and Repairers	INS	41.1%	$70,910	9.2%	920
20. Locksmiths and Safe Repairers	INS	45.2%	$35,550	12.0%	610
21. Audio-Visual and Multimedia Collections Specialists	INS	60.1%	$42,710	10.3%	220

COM=Communication Skills   EQU=Equipment Use/Maintenance Skills   INS=Installation Skills   MAT=Mathematics Skills
MGT=Management Skills   SCI=Science Skills   SOC=Social Skills   TEC=Technology/Programming Skills   THO=Thought-Processing Skills

Best High-Skill Jobs with a High Percentage of Rural Workers

Job	Top Skills	Percent Rural Workers	Annual Earnings	Percent Growth	Annual Openings
1. Operating Engineers and Other Construction Equipment Operators	EQU	17.4%	$40,400	12.0%	11,820
2. Education Administrators, Elementary and Secondary School	MGT SOC THO	18.2%	$86,970	8.6%	8,880
3. Water and Wastewater Treatment Plant and System Operators	EQU	28.1%	$40,770	19.8%	4,690
4. Mining and Geological Engineers, Including Mining Safety Engineers	TEC	20.4%	$82,870	15.2%	260
5. Refuse and Recyclable Material Collectors	EQU	18.2%	$32,640	18.6%	7,110
6. Industrial Machinery Mechanics	EQU INS TEC	16.0%	$45,420	7.3%	6,240
7. Surveying and Mapping Technicians	EQU TEC	15.3%	$37,900	20.4%	2,940
8. Electrical Power-Line Installers and Repairers	EQU	26.0%	$58,030	4.5%	4,550
9. Mobile Heavy Equipment Mechanics, Except Engines	INS	18.3%	$44,830	8.7%	3,770
10. Helpers—Installation, Maintenance, and Repair Workers	INS	15.5%	$24,260	8.3%	8,500
11. Millwrights	INS	16.1%	$48,360	1.4%	980

Best High-Skill Jobs by Education or Training Required

The section that follows separates the best high-skill jobs into lists based on the education or training typically required for entry. Next to each job title you'll find the job's top skills listed (as abbreviations) in descending order of the level of mastery required. You'll also find the job's annual earnings, percent growth, and annual job openings, and these economic measures are used to order the jobs within each grouping. Thus you can easily find the best overall jobs for a given level of education or training and see what skills they are linked to.

You can use these lists in a variety of ways. For example, they can help you identify a job with higher potential than a job you now hold that requires a similar level of education. You can also use these lists to figure out additional job possibilities that would open up if you were to get additional training, education, or work experience. For example, maybe you are a high school graduate working in a job associated with Thought-Processing Skills. There are many jobs in this field at all levels of education, but especially at higher levels. You can identify the job you're interested in and the training you need so you can move ahead yet still be doing work that involves the same skill.

The lists of jobs by education should also help you when you're planning your education. For example, you might be thinking about a job that uses Communication Skills, Science Skills, and Social Skills, but you aren't sure what kind of work you want to do. The lists show that Human Resources Specialists need a bachelor's degree and earn an average of $52,690, while Dental Hygienists need only an associate degree but earn an average of $68,250. If you want comparable or higher earnings without lengthy education or training, this information might make a difference in your choice.

Descriptions of the 11 Education and Training Levels

❋ **Short-term on-the-job training:** It is possible to work in these occupations and achieve an average level of performance within a few days or weeks through on-the-job training.

❋ **Moderate-term on-the-job training:** Occupations that require this type of training can be performed adequately after a 1- to 12-month period of combined on-the-job and informal training. Typically, untrained workers observe experienced workers performing tasks and are gradually moved into progressively more difficult assignments.

❋ **Long-term on-the-job training:** This preparation requires more than 12 months of on-the-job training or combined work experience and formal classroom instruction. This level includes occupations that train workers through formal apprenticeships that may take up to four years. It also includes intensive occupation-specific, employer-sponsored training such as police academies. Furthermore, it includes occupations that require natural talent that must be developed over many years.

❋ **Work experience in a related occupation:** This entry route is appropriate when experience in one job serves as preparation for another. For example, police detectives are selected based on their experience as police patrol officers.

❋ **Postsecondary vocational training:** This requirement can vary from training that involves a few months but is usually less than one year. In a few instances, there may be as many as four years of training.

❋ **Associate degree:** This degree usually requires two years of full-time academic work beyond high school.

❋ **Bachelor's degree:** This degree requires approximately four to five years of full-time academic work beyond high school.

❋ **Work experience plus degree:** Many jobs in this category are management-related and require some experience in a related nonmanagerial position. Others require completion of a specific formal training program.

- ❋ **Master's degree:** Completion of a master's degree usually requires one to two years of full-time study beyond the bachelor's degree.

- ❋ **Doctoral degree:** This degree normally requires two or more years of full-time academic work beyond the bachelor's degree.

- ❋ **First professional degree:** This type of degree normally requires a minimum of two years of education beyond the bachelor's degree and frequently requires three years.

Another Warning About the Data

I warned you in the Introduction to use caution in interpreting the data I use, and I want to do it again here. The occupational data I use is the most accurate available anywhere, but it has its limitations. For example, the lists throughout this part are based on job titles in the Standard Occupational Classification (SOC), but the Department of Labor identifies appropriate levels of education or training only for the O*NET job specializations that are linked to the SOC titles. Therefore, in the lists in this section, many of the best jobs are assigned to two or more of the 11 levels of education and training.

For example, most Computer Systems Analysts have a four-year bachelor's degree, but the specialization Informatics Nurse Specialists requires a master's degree. As a result, you will find Computer Systems Analysts on two lists here.

Although some occupations require a certain minimal amount of preparation, many careers are open to people with various levels of preparation. The general rule, however, is that the higher your level of preparation, the more skills you have, and the more earnings and responsibility you can expect when you're hired.

The jobs in the first list have only one high-level skill, but as you look at the lists of jobs requiring more education or training, you start seeing more and more jobs that require multiple high-level skills. Education and training impart skills, and that's what makes them so valuable. Therefore, I encourage you to get as much education and training as you can.

Best High-Skill Jobs Requiring Short-Term On-the-Job Training

Job	Top Skills	Annual Earnings	Percent Growth	Annual Openings
1. Home Health Aides	SOC	$20,560	50.0%	55,270
2. Refuse and Recyclable Material Collectors	EQU	$32,640	18.6%	7,110
3. Helpers—Electricians	INS	$27,220	24.7%	4,800
4. Helpers—Installation, Maintenance, and Repair Workers	INS	$24,260	8.3%	8,500
5. Medical Equipment Preparers	INS	$29,490	12.8%	1,120

Best High-Skill Jobs Requiring Moderate-Term On-the-Job Training

Job	Top Skills	Annual Earnings	Percent Growth	Annual Openings
1. Heavy and Tractor-Trailer Truck Drivers	EQU	$37,770	12.9%	55,460
2. Operating Engineers and Other Construction Equipment Operators	EQU	$40,400	12.0%	11,820
3. Dental Assistants	EQU SOC	$33,470	35.7%	16,100
4. Cargo and Freight Agents	MGT	$37,150	23.9%	4,030
5. Customer Service Representatives	SOC	$30,460	17.7%	110,840
6. Medical Assistants	COM SCI SOC	$28,860	33.9%	21,780
7. Medical Secretaries	COM SOC	$30,530	26.6%	18,900
8. Construction Laborers	EQU	$29,280	20.5%	33,940
9. Life, Physical, and Social Science Technicians, All Other	EQU	$43,350	13.3%	3,640
10. Surveying and Mapping Technicians	EQU TEC	$37,900	20.4%	2,940
11. Drywall and Ceiling Tile Installers	EQU	$37,320	13.5%	3,700
12. Pharmacy Technicians	COM MAT SOC	$28,400	30.6%	18,200
13. Maintenance and Repair Workers, General	EQU INS	$34,730	10.9%	35,750
14. Cement Masons and Concrete Finishers	EQU	$35,450	12.9%	7,640
15. Aircraft Structure, Surfaces, Rigging, and Systems Assemblers	INS	$44,820	9.3%	1,340
16. Installation, Maintenance, and Repair Workers, All Other	INS	$36,420	9.2%	4,180
17. Locksmiths and Safe Repairers	INS	$35,550	12.0%	610
18. Mechanical Door Repairers	INS	$35,780	10.8%	450

Best High-Skill Jobs Requiring Long-Term On-the-Job Training

Job	Top Skills	Annual Earnings	Percent Growth	Annual Openings
1. Police and Sheriff's Patrol Officers	SOC	$53,540	8.7%	22,790
2. Compliance Officers	COM SCI THO EQU MAT SOC	$58,720	31.0%	10,850
3. Purchasing Agents, Except Wholesale, Retail, and Farm Products	MGT MAT THO	$56,580	13.9%	11,860
4. Electricians	EQU INS	$48,250	11.9%	25,090
5. Plumbers, Pipefitters, and Steamfitters	EQU INS MAT	$46,660	15.3%	17,550
6. Heating, Air Conditioning, and Refrigeration Mechanics and Installers	EQU INS MAT	$42,530	28.1%	13,620

(continued)

COM=*Communication Skills*   EQU=*Equipment Use/Maintenance Skills*   INS=*Installation Skills*   MAT=*Mathematics Skills*
MGT=*Management Skills*   SCI=*Science Skills*   SOC=*Social Skills*   TEC=*Technology/Programming Skills*   THO=*Thought-Processing Skills*

Best High-Skill Jobs Requiring Long-Term On-the-Job Training

Job	Top Skills	Annual Earnings	Percent Growth	Annual Openings
7. Firefighters	EQU SOC	$45,250	18.5%	15,280
8. Air Traffic Controllers	MAT	$108,040	13.1%	1,230
9. Carpenters	EQU MGT	$39,530	12.9%	32,540
10. Producers and Directors	MGT EQU	$68,440	9.8%	4,040
11. Boilermakers	EQU	$54,640	18.8%	810
12. Coaches and Scouts	MGT	$28,340	24.8%	9,920
13. Water and Wastewater Treatment Plant and System Operators	EQU	$40,770	19.8%	4,690
14. Brickmasons and Blockmasons	EQU	$46,930	11.5%	5,000
15. Installation, Maintenance, and Repair Workers, All Other	INS	$36,420	9.2%	4,180
16. Elevator Installers and Repairers	INS	$70,910	9.2%	920
17. Electrical Power-Line Installers and Repairers	EQU	$58,030	4.5%	4,550
18. Industrial Machinery Mechanics	EQU INS TEC	$45,420	7.3%	6,240
19. Audio and Video Equipment Technicians	INS	$40,540	12.6%	2,370
20. Mobile Heavy Equipment Mechanics, Except Engines	INS	$44,830	8.7%	3,770
21. Millwrights	INS	$48,360	1.4%	980
22. Rail Car Repairers	INS	$47,410	6.5%	590

Best High-Skill Jobs Requiring Work Experience in a Related Occupation

Job	Top Skills	Annual Earnings	Percent Growth	Annual Openings
1. Supervisors of Construction and Extraction Workers	EQU MGT SOC	$58,680	15.4%	24,220
2. Compliance Officers	COM SCI THO EQU MAT SOC	$58,720	31.0%	10,850
3. Managers, All Other	MGT SOC THO	$96,450	7.3%	29,750
4. Natural Sciences Managers	MGT MAT SCI	$116,020	15.5%	2,010
5. Business Operations Specialists, All Other	MGT MAT THO	$62,450	11.5%	36,830
6. Computer Occupations, All Other	SCI TEC THO COM INS MAT	$79,240	13.1%	7,260
7. Sales Representatives, Wholesale and Manufacturing, Technical and Scientific Products	COM MGT SOC	$73,710	9.7%	14,230
8. Detectives and Criminal Investigators	COM SCI SOC	$68,820	16.6%	4,160
9. Self-Enrichment Education Teachers	COM SOC THO	$36,340	32.0%	12,030

Best High-Skill Jobs Requiring Work Experience in a Related Occupation

Job	Top Skills	Annual Earnings	Percent Growth	Annual Openings
10. First-Line Supervisors of Office and Administrative Support Workers	MGT SOC	$47,460	11.0%	48,900
11. Ship Engineers	EQU MGT	$65,880	18.6%	700
12. Captains, Mates, and Pilots of Water Vessels	EQU MGT	$64,180	17.3%	1,950
13. Executive Secretaries and Executive Administrative Assistants	MGT SOC	$43,520	12.8%	41,920
14. Computer User Support Specialists	EQU	$46,260	13.8%	23,460
15. First-Line Supervisors of Non-Retail Sales Workers	MGT	$68,880	4.8%	12,950
16. First-Line Supervisors of Police and Detectives	MGT	$78,260	8.1%	5,050
17. Construction and Building Inspectors	EQU	$52,360	16.8%	3,970
18. Transportation Inspectors	EQU	$57,640	18.4%	1,130
19. First-Line Supervisors of Mechanics, Installers, and Repairers	EQU	$59,150	4.2%	13,650
20. First-Line Supervisors of Personal Service Workers	MGT	$35,290	15.4%	9,080
21. First-Line Supervisors of Fire Fighting and Prevention Workers	EQU	$68,240	8.2%	3,250
22. First-Line Supervisors of Landscaping, Lawn Service, and Groundskeeping Workers	EQU MGT	$41,860	14.9%	5,600

Best High-Skill Jobs Requiring Postsecondary Vocational Training

Job	Top Skills	Annual Earnings	Percent Growth	Annual Openings
1. Business Operations Specialists, All Other	MGT MAT THO	$62,450	11.5%	36,830
2. Licensed Practical and Licensed Vocational Nurses	SCI SOC THO	$40,380	20.6%	39,130
3. Computer Occupations, All Other	SCI TEC THO COM INS MAT	$79,240	13.1%	7,260
4. Commercial Pilots	EQU SCI THO	$67,500	18.6%	2,060
5. Surgical Technologists	EQU MGT	$39,920	25.3%	4,630
6. Fitness Trainers and Aerobics Instructors	COM SOC THO	$31,090	29.4%	12,380
7. Real Estate Sales Agents	COM SOC	$40,030	16.2%	12,830

(continued)

COM=*Communication Skills*   EQU=*Equipment Use/Maintenance Skills*   INS=*Installation Skills*   MAT=*Mathematics Skills*
MGT=*Management Skills*   SCI=*Science Skills*   SOC=*Social Skills*   TEC=*Technology/Programming Skills*   THO=*Thought-Processing Skills*

Best High-Skill Jobs Requiring Postsecondary Vocational Training

Job	Top Skills	Annual Earnings	Percent Growth	Annual Openings
8. Life, Physical, and Social Science Technicians, All Other	EQU	$43,350	13.3%	3,640
9. Preschool Teachers, Except Special Education	MGT	$25,700	19.0%	17,830
10. Security and Fire Alarm Systems Installers	EQU INS	$38,500	24.8%	2,780
11. Architectural and Civil Drafters	TEC	$46,430	9.1%	3,620
12. Health Technologists and Technicians, All Other	EQU	$38,460	18.7%	3,200
13. Engineering Technicians, Except Drafters, All Other	INS	$58,020	5.2%	1,850
14. Telecommunications Equipment Installers and Repairers, Except Line Installers	INS	$54,710	–0.2%	3,560
15. Automotive Service Technicians and Mechanics	INS	$35,790	4.7%	18,170
16. Avionics Technicians	INS	$52,320	10.6%	520
17. Electrical and Electronics Repairers, Commercial and Industrial Equipment	INS	$51,820	3.8%	1,640
18. Commercial Divers	INS	$51,360	5.5%	50
19. Electronic Home Entertainment Equipment Installers and Repairers	INS	$32,940	10.8%	1,430

Best High-Skill Jobs Requiring an Associate Degree

Job	Top Skills	Annual Earnings	Percent Growth	Annual Openings
1. Dental Hygienists	COM SCI SOC	$68,250	36.1%	9,840
2. Registered Nurses	SCI SOC THO	$64,690	22.2%	103,900
3. Paralegals and Legal Assistants	COM	$46,680	28.1%	10,400
4. Computer Occupations, All Other	SCI TEC THO COM INS MAT	$79,240	13.1%	7,260
5. Physical Therapist Assistants	COM SCI SOC	$49,690	33.3%	3,050
6. Business Operations Specialists, All Other	MGT MAT THO	$62,450	11.5%	36,830
7. Respiratory Therapists	EQU SCI SOC	$54,280	20.9%	4,140
8. Radiation Therapists	EQU MAT SCI	$74,980	27.1%	690
9. Radiologic Technologists	EQU SCI SOC	$54,340	17.2%	6,800
10. Legal Secretaries	COM	$41,500	18.4%	8,380
11. Cardiovascular Technologists and Technicians	EQU	$49,410	24.1%	1,910
12. Interior Designers	MGT	$46,280	19.4%	3,590
13. Medical and Clinical Laboratory Technologists	EQU	$56,130	11.9%	5,330
14. Medical Equipment Repairers	EQU	$44,490	27.2%	2,320

Best High-Skill Jobs Requiring an Associate Degree

Job	Top Skills	Annual Earnings	Percent Growth	Annual Openings
15. Diagnostic Medical Sonographers	EQU	$64,380	18.3%	1,650
16. Environmental Science and Protection Technicians, Including Health	EQU	$41,380	28.9%	2,520
17. Environmental Engineering Technicians	EQU	$43,390	30.1%	1,040
18. Health Technologists and Technicians, All Other	EQU	$38,460	18.7%	3,200
19. Life, Physical, and Social Science Technicians, All Other	EQU	$43,350	13.3%	3,640
20. Engineering Technicians, Except Drafters, All Other	INS	$58,020	5.2%	1,850
21. Medical and Clinical Laboratory Technicians	EQU	$36,280	16.1%	5,460
22. Social Science Research Assistants	TEC	$37,230	17.8%	1,270

Best High-Skill Jobs Requiring a Bachelor's Degree

Job	Top Skills	Annual Earnings	Percent Growth	Annual Openings
1. Software Developers, Applications	MAT SCI TEC	$87,790	34.0%	21,840
2. Software Developers, Systems Software	MAT SCI TEC	$94,180	30.4%	15,340
3. Computer Network Architects	EQU SCI TEC	$75,660	53.4%	20,830
4. Network and Computer Systems Administrators	EQU INS TEC	$69,160	23.2%	13,550
5. Computer Systems Analysts	MAT SCI TEC	$77,740	20.3%	22,280
6. Civil Engineers	MGT MAT SCI	$77,560	24.3%	11,460
7. Registered Nurses	SCI SOC T-P	$64,690	22.2%	103,900
8. Construction Managers	MGT MAT SOC	$83,860	17.2%	13,770
9. Accountants and Auditors	COM MAT T-P	$61,690	21.6%	49,750
10. Market Research Analysts and Marketing Specialists	MAT SCI T-P	$60,570	28.1%	13,730
11. Database Administrators	MAT TEC T-P	$73,490	20.3%	4,440
12. Personal Financial Advisors	COM MAT T-P	$64,750	30.1%	8,530
13. Environmental Engineers	MAT SCI T-P	$78,740	30.6%	2,790
14. Managers, All Other	MGT SOC T-P	$96,450	7.3%	29,750
15. Biomedical Engineers	INS SCI TEC	$81,540	72.0%	1,490
16. Budget Analysts	MGT	$68,200	15.1%	2,230
17. Financial Analysts	COM MAT T-P	$74,350	19.8%	9,520

(continued)

COM=Communication Skills   EQU=Equipment Use/Maintenance Skills   INS=Installation Skills   MAT=Mathematics Skills
MGT=Management Skills   SCI=Science Skills   SOC=Social Skills   TEC=Technology/Programming Skills   THO=Thought-Processing Skills

Best High-Skill Jobs Requiring a Bachelor's Degree

Job	Top Skills	Annual Earnings	Percent Growth	Annual Openings
18. Cost Estimators	COM MGT MAT	$57,860	25.3%	10,360
19. Financial Examiners	COM MAT T-P	$74,940	41.2%	1,600
20. Human Resources Specialists	COM SCI SOC	$52,690	27.9%	11,230
21. Industrial Engineers	MGT MAT T-P	$76,100	14.2%	8,540
22. Public Relations Specialists	COM SOC T-P	$52,090	24.0%	13,130
23. Statisticians	TEC	$72,830	13.1%	960
24. Computer Occupations, All Other	SCI TEC T-P COM INS MAT	$79,240	13.1%	7,260
25. Instructional Coordinators	COM SOC T-P	$58,830	23.2%	6,060
26. Petroleum Engineers	MGT MAT SCI	$114,080	18.4%	860
27. Business Operations Specialists, All Other	MGT MAT T-P	$62,450	11.5%	36,830
28. Compensation, Benefits, and Job Analysis Specialists	MAT SCI T-P	$57,000	23.6%	6,050
29. Elementary School Teachers, Except Special Education	COM SOC T-P	$51,660	15.8%	59,650
30. Customer Service Representatives	SOC	$30,460	17.7%	110,840
31. Logisticians	MGT MAT T-P	$70,800	19.5%	4,190
32. Architects, Except Landscape and Naval	MGT MAT SCI	$72,550	16.2%	4,680
33. Middle School Teachers, Except Special and Career/Technical Education	COM SOC T-P	$51,960	15.3%	25,110
34. Securities, Commodities, and Financial Services Sales Agents	COM MAT SOC	$70,190	9.3%	12,680
35. Engineers, All Other	MAT SCI TEC EQU INS	$90,270	6.7%	5,020
36. Aerospace Engineers	MAT TEC	$97,480	10.4%	2,230
37. Airline Pilots, Copilots, and Flight Engineers	EQU MAT	$103,210	8.4%	3,250
38. Mechanical Engineers	MAT TEC	$78,160	6.0%	7,570
39. Healthcare Social Workers	COM SCI SOC	$47,230	22.4%	6,590
40. Sales Engineers	MAT TEC	$87,390	8.8%	3,500
41. Secondary School Teachers, Except Special and Career/Technical Education	SOC	$53,230	8.9%	41,240
42. Mining and Geological Engineers, Including Mining Safety Engineers	TEC	$82,870	15.2%	260
43. Computer Hardware Engineers	TEC	$98,810	3.8%	2,350
44. Electronics Engineers, Except Computer	TEC	$90,170	0.3%	3,340
45. Computer Programmers	TEC	$71,380	−2.9%	8,030
46. Technical Writers	COM	$63,280	18.2%	1,680
47. Landscape Architects	MGT	$62,090	19.6%	980
48. Special Education Teachers, Middle School	COM SOC T-P	$53,440	18.1%	4,410
49. Writers and Authors	SOC	$55,420	14.8%	5,420

Best High-Skill Jobs Requiring a Bachelor's Degree

Job	Top Skills	Annual Earnings	Percent Growth	Annual Openings
50. Social and Community Service Managers	MGT SOC	$57,950	13.8%	4,820
51. Graphic Designers	MGT	$43,500	12.9%	12,480
52. Special Education Teachers, Secondary School	SOC	$54,810	13.3%	5,750
53. Survey Researchers	TEC	$36,050	30.3%	1,340
54. Probation Officers and Correctional Treatment Specialists	SOC	$47,200	19.3%	4,180
55. Medical and Clinical Laboratory Technologists	EQU	$56,130	11.9%	5,330
56. Commercial and Industrial Designers	TEC	$58,230	9.0%	1,760
57. Engineering Technicians, Except Drafters, All Other	INS	$58,020	5.2%	1,850
58. Audio-Visual and Multimedia Collections Specialists	INS	$42,710	10.3%	220

Best High-Skill Jobs Requiring Work Experience Plus Degree

Job	Top Skills	Annual Earnings	Percent Growth	Annual Openings
1. Computer and Information Systems Managers	EQU MGT TEC	$115,780	16.9%	9,710
2. Marketing Managers	MGT SOC THO	$112,800	12.5%	5,970
3. Management Analysts	COM MAT THO	$78,160	23.9%	30,650
4. Sales Managers	MGT SOC THO	$98,530	14.9%	12,660
5. Financial Managers	MGT MAT THO	$103,910	7.6%	13,820
6. Medical and Health Services Managers	MGT SCI THO	$84,270	16.0%	9,940
7. Chief Executives	MGT THO	$165,080	−1.4%	11,250
8. Training and Development Specialists	SCI SOC THO	$54,160	23.3%	10,710
9. General and Operations Managers	MGT SOC THO	$94,400	−0.1%	50,220
10. Managers, All Other	MGT SOC THO	$96,450	7.3%	29,750
11. Natural Sciences Managers	MGT MAT SCI	$116,020	15.5%	2,010
12. Architectural and Engineering Managers	MGT MAT SCI	$119,260	6.2%	4,870
13. Actuaries	MAT TEC THO	$87,650	21.3%	1,000
14. Business Operations Specialists, All Other	MGT MAT THO	$62,450	11.5%	36,830
15. Computer Occupations, All Other	SCI TEC THO COM INS MAT	$79,240	13.1%	7,260
16. Detectives and Criminal Investigators	COM SCI SOC	$68,820	16.6%	4,160

(continued)

COM=*Communication Skills*   EQU=*Equipment Use/Maintenance Skills*   INS=*Installation Skills*   MAT=*Mathematics Skills*
MGT=*Management Skills*   SCI=*Science Skills*   SOC=*Social Skills*   TEC=*Technology/Programming Skills*   THO=*Thought-Processing Skills*

Best High-Skill Jobs Requiring Work Experience Plus Degree

Job	Top Skills	Annual Earnings	Percent Growth	Annual Openings
17. Human Resources Managers	MGT THO	$99,180	9.6%	4,140
18. Administrative Services Managers	COM MGT SOC	$77,890	12.5%	8,660
19. Education Administrators, Elementary and Secondary School	MGT SOC THO	$86,970	8.6%	8,880
20. Public Relations and Fundraising Managers	MGT	$91,810	12.9%	2,060
21. Agents and Business Managers of Artists, Performers, and Athletes	COM MGT	$63,130	22.4%	1,010
22. Health Technologists and Technicians, All Other	EQU	$38,460	18.7%	3,200
23. Art Directors	MGT	$80,630	11.7%	2,870
24. Producers and Directors	MGT EQU	$68,440	9.8%	4,040

Best High-Skill Jobs Requiring a Master's Degree

Job	Top Skills	Annual Earnings	Percent Growth	Annual Openings
1. Physical Therapists	COM SCI SOC	$76,310	30.3%	7,860
2. Physician Assistants	COM SCI SOC	$86,410	39.0%	4,280
3. Computer Systems Analysts	MAT SCI TEC	$77,740	20.3%	22,280
4. Registered Nurses	SCI SOC THO	$64,690	22.2%	103,900
5. Industrial-Organizational Psychologists	TEC	$87,330	26.1%	130
6. Occupational Therapists	COM SCI SOC	$72,320	25.6%	4,580
7. Environmental Scientists and Specialists, Including Health	COM MAT SCI	$61,700	27.9%	4,840
8. Instructional Coordinators	COM SOC THO	$58,830	23.2%	6,060
9. Social Scientists and Related Workers, All Other	MGT MAT THO	$74,620	22.5%	2,380
10. Political Scientists	COM	$107,420	19.4%	280
11. Geoscientists, Except Hydrologists and Geographers	COM MAT SCI	$82,500	17.5%	1,540
12. Operations Research Analysts	MAT SCI THO	$70,960	22.0%	3,220
13. Speech-Language Pathologists	COM SCI THO	$66,920	18.5%	4,380
14. Educational, Guidance, School, and Vocational Counselors	SOC	$53,380	14.0%	9,440
15. Hydrologists	TEC	$75,690	18.2%	380
16. Clergy	MGT SOC	$43,970	12.7%	21,770
17. Statisticians	TEC	$72,830	13.1%	960

Best High-Skill Jobs Requiring a Doctoral Degree

Job	Top Skills	Annual Earnings	Percent Growth	Annual Openings
1. Engineering Teachers, Postsecondary	COM MAT SCI	$89,670	15.1%	1,000
2. Health Specialties Teachers, Postsecondary	COM SCI THO	$85,270	15.1%	4,000
3. Medical Scientists, Except Epidemiologists	MAT SCI THO	$76,700	40.4%	6,620
4. Business Teachers, Postsecondary	COM MAT THO	$73,760	15.1%	2,000
5. Biochemists and Biophysicists	COM MAT SCI	$79,390	37.4%	1,620
6. Biological Science Teachers, Postsecondary	COM THO	$72,700	15.1%	1,700
7. Computer and Information Research Scientists	MAT SCI TEC	$100,660	24.2%	1,320
8. Physicists	MAT SCI TEC	$106,370	15.9%	690
9. Computer Science Teachers, Postsecondary	TEC	$70,300	15.1%	1,000
10. Art, Drama, and Music Teachers, Postsecondary	THO	$62,040	15.1%	2,500
11. Biological Scientists, All Other	COM MAT	$68,220	18.8%	1,610
12. Audiologists	COM	$66,660	25.0%	580

Best High-Skill Jobs Requiring a First Professional Degree

Job	Top Skills	Annual Earnings	Percent Growth	Annual Openings
1. Dentists, General	MGT SCI THO	$141,040	15.3%	5,180
2. Orthodontists	COM SCI THO	$166,400+	19.7%	360
3. Veterinarians	COM SCI THO	$82,040	32.9%	3,020
4. Lawyers	COM SOC THO	$112,760	13.0%	24,040
5. Pharmacists	COM MGT SCI	$111,570	17.0%	10,580
6. Prosthodontists	SCI	$118,400	26.4%	30
7. Optometrists	MAT SCI THO	$94,990	24.4%	2,010
8. Chiropractors	COM SCI THO	$67,200	19.5%	1,820

Best High-Skill Jobs by Career Cluster

This group of lists organizes the 199 best high-skill jobs into 16 career clusters. The U.S. Department of Education's Office of Vocational and Adult Education developed these career clusters in 1999, and many states now use them to organize their career-oriented programs and career information. You can use these lists to identify jobs quickly based on your interests. You can also review clusters that represent areas in which you've had past experience, education, or training to see whether other jobs in those areas would meet your current requirements.

COM=Communication Skills   EQU=Equipment Use/Maintenance Skills   INS=Installation Skills   MAT=Mathematics Skills
MGT=Management Skills   SCI=Science Skills   SOC=Social Skills   TEC=Technology/Programming Skills   THO=Thought-Processing Skills

In this set of lists, you may notice that some occupations appear on multiple lists. This happens when two or more industries commonly employ workers with the same occupation title. For example, Statisticians may analyze market research data (and thus work in the Business and Administration cluster) or data from scientific research (in the Scientific Research, Engineering, and Mathematics cluster). If you decide to pursue one of these multiple-cluster occupations, you may have to choose your intended industry early in your education or training pathway, or it may be possible to specialize later or (more rarely) even jump industries after you have worked for several years.

In each cluster, jobs are listed by combined score for earnings, job growth, and job openings, from highest to lowest.

Descriptions of the 16 Career Clusters

Brief descriptions follow for the career clusters. Some descriptions refer to jobs (as examples) that aren't in this book.

❋ **Agriculture, Food, and Natural Resources:** *Work with plants, animals, forests, or mineral resources for agriculture, horticulture, conservation, extraction, and other purposes.* In this cluster you can work in farming, landscaping, forestry, fishing, mining, and related fields. You may like doing physical work outdoors, such as on a farm or ranch, in a forest, or on a drilling rig. If you have scientific curiosity, you could study plants and animals or analyze biological or rock samples in a lab. If you have management ability, you could own, operate, or manage a fish hatchery, a landscaping business, or a greenhouse.

❋ **Architecture and Construction:** *Work designing, assembling, and maintaining components of buildings and other structures.* You may want to be part of the team of architects, drafters, and others who design buildings and render plans. If construction interests you, you might find fulfillment in the building projects that are being undertaken at all times. If you like to organize and plan, you can find careers in managing these projects. Or you can play a more direct role in putting up and finishing buildings by doing jobs such as plumbing, carpentry, masonry, painting, or roofing, either as a skilled craftsworker or as a helper. You can prepare the building site by operating heavy equipment or installing, maintaining, and repairing vital building equipment and systems such as electricity and heating.

❋ **Arts, Audio/Video Technology, and Communications:** *Work in creatively expressing feelings or ideas, in communicating news or information, or in performing.* This cluster involves creative, verbal, or performing activities. For example, if you enjoy literature, perhaps writing or editing would appeal to you. Journalism and public relations are other fields for people who like to use their writing or speaking skills. Do you prefer to work in the performing arts? If so, you could direct or perform in drama, music, or dance. If you especially enjoy the visual arts, you could create paintings, sculpture, or ceramics or design products or visual displays. A flair for technology might lead you to specialize in photography, broadcast production, or dispatching.

❀ **Business, Management, and Administration:** *Work that makes a business organization or function run smoothly.* In this cluster, you can work in a position of leadership or specialize in a function that contributes to the overall effort in a business, a nonprofit organization, or a government agency. If you especially enjoy working with people, you may find fulfillment from working in human resources. An interest in numbers may lead you to consider accounting, finance, budgeting, billing, or financial record-keeping. A job as an administrative assistant may interest you if you like a variety of tasks in a busy environment. If you are good with details and word processing, you may enjoy a job as an administrative assistant or data-entry clerk. Or perhaps you would do well as the manager of a business.

❀ **Education and Training:** *Work that helps people learn.* In this cluster, your students may be preschoolers, retirees, or any age in between. You may specialize in an academic field or work with learners of a particular age, with a particular interest, or with a particular learning problem. Working in a library or museum may give you an opportunity to expand people's understanding of the world.

❀ **Finance:** *Work that helps businesses and people be assured of a financially secure future.* This cluster involves work in a financial or insurance business in a leadership or support role. If you like gathering and analyzing information, you may find fulfillment as an insurance adjuster or financial analyst. Or you may deal with information at the clerical level as a banking or insurance clerk or in person-to-person situations providing customer service. Another way to interact with people is to sell financial or insurance services that will meet their needs.

❀ **Government and Public Administration:** *Work that helps a government agency serve the needs of the public.* In this cluster you can work in a position of leadership or specialize in a function that contributes to the role of government. You may help protect the public by working as an inspector or examiner to enforce standards. If you enjoy using clerical skills, you could work as a clerk in a law court or government office. Or perhaps you prefer the top-down perspective of a government executive or urban planner.

❀ **Health Science:** *Work that helps people and animals be healthy.* This cluster involves working on a health-care team as a professional, therapist, or nurse. You might specialize in one part of the body (such as the teeth or eyes) or in one type of care. Or you may want to be a generalist who deals with the whole patient. If you like technology, you might find satisfaction working with X-rays or new diagnostic methods. You might work with relatively healthy people, helping them to eat better. If you enjoy working with animals, you might care for them and keep them healthy.

❋ **Hospitality and Tourism:** *Work that caters to the personal wishes and needs of others so that they can enjoy a clean environment, good food and drink, comfortable lodging away from home, and recreation.* You can work in this cluster by providing services for the convenience, care, and pampering of others in hotels, restaurants, airplanes, beauty salons, and so on. You may want to use your love of cooking as a chef. If you like working with people, you may want to provide personal services by being a travel guide, a flight attendant, a concierge, a hairstylist, or a waiter. You may want to work in cleaning and building services if you like a clean environment. If you enjoy sports or games, you could work for an athletic team or casino.

❋ **Human Services:** *Work that improves people's social, mental, emotional, or spiritual well-being.* Workers in this cluster include counselors, social workers, or religious workers who help people sort out their complicated lives or solve personal problems. You may work as a caretaker for very young people or the elderly. Or you may interview people to help identify the social services they need.

❋ **Information Technology:** *Work that designs, develops, manages, and supports information systems.* This cluster involves working with hardware, software, multimedia, or integrated systems. If you like to use your organizational skills, you might work as a systems, database, or Web administrator. Or you can solve complex problems as a software engineer or systems analyst. If you enjoy getting your hands on hardware, you might find work servicing computers, peripherals, and information-intense machines such as cash registers and ATMs.

❋ **Law, Public Safety, Corrections, and Security:** *Work that upholds people's rights or protects people and property by using authority, inspecting, or investigating.* You can work in law, law enforcement, firefighting, the military, and related fields. For example, if you enjoy mental challenge and intrigue, you could investigate crimes or fires. If you enjoy working with verbal skills and research skills, you may want to defend citizens in court or research deeds, wills, and other legal documents. If you want to help people in critical situations, you may want to fight fires, work as a police officer, or become a paramedic. Or, if you want more routine work in public safety, perhaps a job in guarding, patrolling, or inspecting would appeal to you. If you have management ability, you could seek a leadership position in law enforcement and the protective services. Work in the military gives you a chance to use technical and leadership skills while serving your country.

❋ **Manufacturing:** *Work that processes materials into intermediate or final products or that maintains and repairs products by using machines or hand tools.* In this cluster, you can work in one of many industries that mass-produce goods or work for a utility that distributes electrical power or other resources. You might enjoy manual work, using your hands or hand tools in highly skilled jobs such as assembling engines or electronic equipment. If you enjoy making machines run efficiently or fixing them when they break down, you could seek a job installing or repairing such devices as copiers, aircraft engines, cars, or watches. Perhaps you prefer to set up or operate machines that are used to manufacture products made of food, glass, or paper. You could enjoy cutting and grinding metal and plastic parts to desired shapes and measurements. Or you may want to operate equipment in systems that provide water and process wastewater. You may like inspecting, sorting, counting, or weighing products. Another option is to work with your hands and machinery to move boxes and freight in a warehouse. If leadership appeals to you, you could manage people engaged in production and repair.

✸ **Marketing, Sales, and Service:** *Work that anticipates the needs of people and organizations and communicates the benefits of products and services.* The jobs in this cluster involve understanding customer demand and using persuasion and selling. If you like using knowledge of science, you may enjoy selling pharmaceutical, medical, or electronic products or services. Real estate offers several kinds of sales jobs as well. If you like speaking on the phone, you could work as a telemarketer. Or you may enjoy selling apparel and other merchandise in a retail setting. If you prefer to help people, you may want a job in customer service.

✸ **Science, Technology, Engineering, and Mathematics:** *Work that discovers, collects, and analyzes information about the natural world; applies scientific research findings to problems in medicine, the life sciences, human behavior, and the natural sciences; imagines and manipulates quantitative data; and applies technology to manufacturing, transportation, and other economic activities.* In this cluster, you can work with the knowledge and processes of the sciences. You may enjoy researching and developing knowledge in mathematics, or perhaps solving problems in the physical, life, or social sciences would appeal to you. You may want to study engineering and help create new machines, processes, and structures. If you want to work with scientific equipment and procedures, you could seek a job in a research or testing laboratory.

✸ **Transportation, Distribution, and Logistics:** *Work in operations that move people or materials.* In this cluster, you can manage a transportation service, help keep vehicles on their assigned schedules and routes, or drive or pilot a vehicle. If you enjoy taking responsibility, perhaps managing a rail line would appeal to you. If you work well with details and can take pressure on the job, you might consider being an air traffic controller. Or would you rather get out on the highway, on the water, or up in the air? If so, you could drive a truck from state to state, be employed on a ship, or fly a crop duster over a cornfield. If you prefer to stay closer to home, you could drive a delivery van, taxi, or school bus. You can use your physical strength to load freight and arrange it so that it gets to its destination in one piece.

Best Jobs for People Interested in Agriculture, Food, and Natural Resources

Job	Top Skills	Annual Earnings	Percent Growth	Annual Openings
1. Veterinarians	COM SCI THO	$82,040	32.9%	3,020
2. Environmental Scientists and Specialists, Including Health	COM MAT SCI	$61,700	27.9%	4,840
3. Biochemists and Biophysicists	COM MAT SCI	$79,390	37.4%	1,620
4. First-Line Supervisors of Office and Administrative Support Workers	MGT SOC	$47,460	11.0%	48,900
5. Graphic Designers	MGT	$43,500	12.9%	12,480
6. Biological Science Teachers, Postsecondary	COM THO	$72,700	15.1%	1,700
7. Biological Scientists, All Other	COM MAT	$68,220	18.8%	1,610
8. First-Line Supervisors of Landscaping, Lawn Service, and Groundskeeping Workers	EQU MGT	$41,860	14.9%	5,600
9. Refuse and Recyclable Material Collectors	EQU	$32,640	18.6%	7,110
10. Water and Wastewater Treatment Plant and System Operators	EQU	$40,770	19.8%	4,690
11. Environmental Science and Protection Technicians, Including Health	EQU	$41,380	28.9%	2,520
12. Environmental Engineering Technicians	EQU	$43,390	30.1%	1,040
13. Mobile Heavy Equipment Mechanics, Except Engines	INS	$44,830	8.7%	3,770
14. Life, Physical, and Social Science Technicians, All Other	EQU	$43,350	13.3%	3,640
15. Engineering Technicians, Except Drafters, All Other	INS	$58,020	5.2%	1,850

Best Jobs for People Interested in Architecture and Construction

Job	Top Skills	Annual Earnings	Percent Growth	Annual Openings
1. Construction Managers	MGT MAT SOC	$83,860	17.2%	13,770
2. Cost Estimators	COM MGT MAT	$57,860	25.3%	10,360
3. Supervisors of Construction and Extraction Workers	EQU MGT SOC	$58,680	15.4%	24,220
4. Heating, Air Conditioning, and Refrigeration Mechanics and Installers	EQU INS MAT	$42,530	28.1%	13,620
5. Construction Laborers	EQU	$29,280	20.5%	33,940
6. Architects, Except Landscape and Naval	MGT MAT SCI	$72,550	16.2%	4,680
7. Plumbers, Pipefitters, and Steamfitters	EQU INS MAT	$46,660	15.3%	17,550
8. Cement Masons and Concrete Finishers	EQU	$35,450	12.9%	7,640

Best Jobs for People Interested in Architecture and Construction

Job	Top Skills	Annual Earnings	Percent Growth	Annual Openings
9. Electricians	EQU INS	$48,250	11.9%	25,090
10. Engineers, All Other	MAT SCI TEC EQU INS	$90,270	6.7%	5,020
11. Architectural and Engineering Managers	MGT MAT SCI	$119,260	6.2%	4,870
12. Landscape Architects	MGT	$62,090	19.6%	980
13. Carpenters	EQU MGT	$39,530	12.9%	32,540
14. Construction and Building Inspectors	EQU	$52,360	16.8%	3,970
15. Engineering Teachers, Postsecondary	COM MAT SCI	$89,670	15.1%	1,000
16. Helpers—Electricians	INS	$27,220	24.7%	4,800
17. Interior Designers	MGT	$46,280	19.4%	3,590
18. Boilermakers	EQU	$54,640	18.8%	810
19. Operating Engineers and Other Construction Equipment Operators	EQU	$40,400	12.0%	11,820
20. Security and Fire Alarm Systems Installers	EQU INS	$38,500	24.8%	2,780
21. Brickmasons and Blockmasons	EQU	$46,930	11.5%	5,000
22. Surveying and Mapping Technicians	EQU TEC	$37,900	20.4%	2,940
23. Electrical Power-Line Installers and Repairers	EQU	$58,030	4.5%	4,550
24. Architectural and Civil Drafters	TEC	$46,430	9.1%	3,620
25. Drywall and Ceiling Tile Installers	EQU	$37,320	13.5%	3,700
26. Engineering Technicians, Except Drafters, All Other	INS	$58,020	5.2%	1,850

Best Jobs for People Interested in Arts, Audio/Video Technology, and Communications

Job	Top Skills	Annual Earnings	Percent Growth	Annual Openings
1. Computer Occupations, All Other	SCI TEC THO COM INS MAT	$79,240	13.1%	7,260
2. Public Relations Specialists	COM SOC THO	$52,090	24.0%	13,130
3. Managers, All Other	MGT SOC THO	$96,450	7.3%	29,750
4. Writers and Authors	SOC	$55,420	14.8%	5,420
5. Art Directors	MGT	$80,630	11.7%	2,870
6. Art, Drama, and Music Teachers, Postsecondary	THO	$62,040	15.1%	2,500

(continued)

COM=Communication Skills   EQU=Equipment Use/Maintenance Skills   INS=Installation Skills   MAT=Mathematics Skills
MGT=Management Skills   SCI=Science Skills   SOC=Social Skills   TEC=Technology/Programming Skills   THO=Thought-Processing Skills

Best Jobs for People Interested in Arts, Audio/Video Technology, and Communications

Job	Top Skills	Annual Earnings	Percent Growth	Annual Openings
7. Interior Designers	MGT	$46,280	19.4%	3,590
8. Producers and Directors	MGT EQU	$68,440	9.8%	4,040
9. Technical Writers	COM	$63,280	18.2%	1,680
10. Agents and Business Managers of Artists, Performers, and Athletes	COM MGT	$63,130	22.4%	1,010
11. Graphic Designers	MGT	$43,500	12.9%	12,480
12. Commercial and Industrial Designers	TEC	$58,230	9.0%	1,760
13. Telecommunications Equipment Installers and Repairers, Except Line Installers	INS	$54,710	−0.2%	3,560
14. Audio and Video Equipment Technicians	INS	$40,540	12.6%	2,370
15. Electronic Home Entertainment Equipment Installers and Repairers	INS	$32,940	10.8%	1,430

Best Jobs for People Interested in Business, Management, and Administration

Job	Top Skills	Annual Earnings	Percent Growth	Annual Openings
1. Management Analysts	COM MAT THO	$78,160	23.9%	30,650
2. Construction Managers	MGT MAT SOC	$83,860	17.2%	13,770
3. Market Research Analysts and Marketing Specialists	MAT SCI THO	$60,570	28.1%	13,730
4. Accountants and Auditors	COM MAT THO	$61,690	21.6%	49,750
5. Computer and Information Systems Managers	EQU MGT TEC	$115,780	16.9%	9,710
6. Sales Managers	MGT SOC THO	$98,530	14.9%	12,660
7. General and Operations Managers	MGT SOC THO	$94,400	−0.1%	50,220
8. Financial Managers	MGT MAT THO	$103,910	7.6%	13,820
9. Financial Analysts	COM MAT THO	$74,350	19.8%	9,520
10. Business Teachers, Postsecondary	COM MAT THO	$73,760	15.1%	2,000
11. Cost Estimators	COM MGT MAT	$57,860	25.3%	10,360
12. Financial Examiners	COM MAT THO	$74,940	41.2%	1,600
13. Human Resources Specialists	COM SCI SOC	$52,690	27.9%	11,230
14. Public Relations Specialists	COM SOC THO	$52,090	24.0%	13,130
15. Managers, All Other	MGT SOC THO	$96,450	7.3%	29,750
16. Chief Executives	MGT THO	$165,080	−1.4%	11,250
17. Natural Sciences Managers	MGT MAT SCI	$116,020	15.5%	2,010
18. Customer Service Representatives	SOC	$30,460	17.7%	110,840

Best Jobs for People Interested in Business, Management, and Administration

Job	Top Skills	Annual Earnings	Percent Growth	Annual Openings
19. Statisticians	TEC	$72,830	13.1%	960
20. Training and Development Specialists	SCI SOC THO	$54,160	23.3%	10,710
21. Operations Research Analysts	MAT SCI THO	$70,960	22.0%	3,220
22. Computer Occupations, All Other	SCI TEC THO COM INS MAT	$79,240	13.1%	7,260
23. Logisticians	MGT MAT THO	$70,800	19.5%	4,190
24. Business Operations Specialists, All Other	MGT MAT THO	$62,450	11.5%	36,830
25. Compensation, Benefits, and Job Analysis Specialists	MAT SCI THO	$57,000	23.6%	6,050
26. Administrative Services Managers	COM MGT SOC	$77,890	12.5%	8,660
27. Human Resources Managers	MGT THO	$99,180	9.6%	4,140
28. Executive Secretaries and Executive Administrative Assistants	MGT SOC	$43,520	12.8%	41,920
29. Public Relations and Fundraising Managers	MGT	$91,810	12.9%	2,060
30. Cargo and Freight Agents	MGT	$37,150	23.9%	4,030
31. First-Line Supervisors of Office and Administrative Support Workers	MGT SOC	$47,460	11.0%	48,900
32. Agents and Business Managers of Artists, Performers, and Athletes	COM MGT	$63,130	22.4%	1,010
33. Technical Writers	COM	$63,280	18.2%	1,680
34. Budget Analysts	MGT	$68,200	15.1%	2,230
35. Survey Researchers	TEC	$36,050	30.3%	1,340
36. Social and Community Service Managers	MGT SOC	$57,950	13.8%	4,820
37. First-Line Supervisors of Personal Service Workers	MGT	$35,290	15.4%	9,080

Best Jobs for People Interested in Education and Training

Job	Top Skills	Annual Earnings	Percent Growth	Annual Openings
1. Engineering Teachers, Postsecondary	COM MAT SCI	$89,670	15.1%	1,000
2. Health Specialties Teachers, Postsecondary	COM SCI THO	$85,270	15.1%	4,000
3. Business Teachers, Postsecondary	COM MAT THO	$73,760	15.1%	2,000
4. Training and Development Specialists	SCI SOC THO	$54,160	23.3%	10,710

(continued)

COM=*Communication Skills*   EQU=*Equipment Use/Maintenance Skills*   INS=*Installation Skills*   MAT=*Mathematics Skills*
MGT=*Management Skills*   SCI=*Science Skills*   SOC=*Social Skills*   TEC=*Technology/Programming Skills*   THO=*Thought-Processing Skills*

Best Jobs for People Interested in Education and Training

Job	Top Skills	Annual Earnings	Percent Growth	Annual Openings
5. Biological Science Teachers, Postsecondary	COM THO	$72,700	15.1%	1,700
6. Instructional Coordinators	COM SOC THO	$58,830	23.2%	6,060
7. Self-Enrichment Education Teachers	COM SOC THO	$36,340	32.0%	12,030
8. Computer Science Teachers, Postsecondary	TEC	$70,300	15.1%	1,000
9. Elementary School Teachers, Except Special Education	COM SOC THO	$51,660	15.8%	59,650
10. Fitness Trainers and Aerobics Instructors	COM SOC THO	$31,090	29.4%	12,380
11. Middle School Teachers, Except Special and Career/Technical Education	COM SOC THO	$51,960	15.3%	25,110
12. Physicists	MAT SCI TEC	$106,370	15.9%	690
13. Coaches and Scouts	MGT	$28,340	24.8%	9,920
14. Preschool Teachers, Except Special Education	MGT	$25,700	19.0%	17,830
15. Special Education Teachers, Middle School	COM SOC THO	$53,440	18.1%	4,410
16. Art, Drama, and Music Teachers, Postsecondary	THO	$62,040	15.1%	2,500
17. Education Administrators, Elementary and Secondary School	MGT SOC THO	$86,970	8.6%	8,880
18. Secondary School Teachers, Except Special and Career/Technical Education	SOC	$53,230	8.9%	41,240
19. Educational, Guidance, School, and Vocational Counselors	SOC	$53,380	14.0%	9,440
20. Special Education Teachers, Secondary School	SOC	$54,810	13.3%	5,750
21. Audio-Visual and Multimedia Collections Specialists	INS	$42,710	10.3%	220

Best Jobs for People Interested in Finance

Job	Top Skills	Annual Earnings	Percent Growth	Annual Openings
1. Financial Analysts	COM MAT THO	$74,350	19.8%	9,520
2. Financial Managers	MGT MAT THO	$103,910	7.6%	13,820
3. Actuaries	MAT TEC THO	$87,650	21.3%	1,000
4. Business Teachers, Postsecondary	COM MAT THO	$73,760	15.1%	2,000
5. Personal Financial Advisors	COM MAT THO	$64,750	30.1%	8,530
6. Securities, Commodities, and Financial Services Sales Agents	COM MAT SOC	$70,190	9.3%	12,680
7. Budget Analysts	MGT	$68,200	15.1%	2,230

Best Jobs for People Interested in Government and Public Administration

Job	Top Skills	Annual Earnings	Percent Growth	Annual Openings
1. Accountants and Auditors	COM MAT THO	$61,690	21.6%	49,750
2. General and Operations Managers	MGT SOC THO	$94,400	–0.1%	50,220
3. Managers, All Other	MGT SOC THO	$96,450	7.3%	29,750
4. Chief Executives	MGT THO	$165,080	–1.4%	11,250
5. Compliance Officers EQU MAT SOC	COM SCI THO	$58,720	31.0%	10,850
6. Financial Examiners	COM MAT THO	$74,940	41.2%	1,600
7. Political Scientists	COM	$107,420	19.4%	280
8. Administrative Services Managers	COM MGT SOC	$77,890	12.5%	8,660
9. Social and Community Service Managers	MGT SOC	$57,950	13.8%	4,820
10. Surveying and Mapping Technicians	EQU TEC	$37,900	20.4%	2,940

Best Jobs for People Interested in Health Science

Job	Top Skills	Annual Earnings	Percent Growth	Annual Openings
1. Medical Scientists, Except Epidemiologists	MAT SCI THO	$76,700	40.4%	6,620
2. Dental Hygienists	COM SCI SOC	$68,250	36.1%	9,840
3. Physician Assistants	COM SCI SOC	$86,410	39.0%	4,280
4. Physical Therapists	COM SCI SOC	$76,310	30.3%	7,860
5. Computer Systems Analysts	MAT SCI TEC	$77,740	20.3%	22,280
6. Registered Nurses	SCI SOC THO	$64,690	22.2%	103,900
7. Home Health Aides	SOC	$20,560	50.0%	55,270
8. Pharmacists	COM MGT SCI	$111,570	17.0%	10,580
9. Veterinarians	COM SCI THO	$82,040	32.9%	3,020
10. Dental Assistants	EQU SOC	$33,470	35.7%	16,100
11. Medical Assistants	COM SCI SOC	$28,860	33.9%	21,780
12. Occupational Therapists	COM SCI SOC	$72,320	25.6%	4,580
13. Optometrists	MAT SCI THO	$94,990	24.4%	2,010
14. Dentists, General	MGT SCI THO	$141,040	15.3%	5,180
15. Medical and Health Services Managers	MGT SCI THO	$84,270	16.0%	9,940
16. Medical Secretaries	COM SOC	$30,530	26.6%	18,900
17. Prosthodontists	SCI	$118,400	26.4%	30
18. Public Relations Specialists	COM SOC THO	$52,090	24.0%	13,130
19. Pharmacy Technicians	COM MAT SOC	$28,400	30.6%	18,200

(continued)

COM=*Communication Skills* EQU=*Equipment Use/Maintenance Skills* INS=*Installation Skills* MAT=*Mathematics Skills*
MGT=*Management Skills* SCI=*Science Skills* SOC=*Social Skills* TEC=*Technology/Programming Skills* THO=*Thought-Processing Skills*

Best Jobs for People Interested in Health Science

Job	Top Skills	Annual Earnings	Percent Growth	Annual Openings
20. Licensed Practical and Licensed Vocational Nurses	SCI SOC THO	$40,380	20.6%	39,130
21. Industrial-Organizational Psychologists	TEC	$87,330	26.1%	130
22. Radiation Therapists	EQU MAT SCI	$74,980	27.1%	690
23. Physical Therapist Assistants	COM SCI SOC	$49,690	33.3%	3,050
24. Orthodontists	COM SCI THO	$166,400+	19.7%	360
25. Engineers, All Other	MAT SCI TEC EQU INS	$90,270	6.7%	5,020
26. Health Specialties Teachers, Postsecondary	COM SCI THO	$85,270	15.1%	4,000
27. Radiologic Technologists	EQU SCI SOC	$54,340	17.2%	6,800
28. Surgical Technologists	EQU MGT	$39,920	25.3%	4,630
29. Executive Secretaries and Executive Administrative Assistants	MGT SOC	$43,520	12.8%	41,920
30. Speech-Language Pathologists	COM SCI THO	$66,920	18.5%	4,380
31. First-Line Supervisors of Office and Administrative Support Workers	MGT SOC	$47,460	11.0%	48,900
32. Respiratory Therapists	EQU SCI SOC	$54,280	20.9%	4,140
33. Audiologists	COM	$66,660	25.0%	580
34. Medical Equipment Preparers	INS	$29,490	12.8%	1,120
35. Chiropractors	COM SCI THO	$67,200	19.5%	1,820
36. Biological Scientists, All Other	COM MAT	$68,220	18.8%	1,610
37. Cardiovascular Technologists and Technicians	EQU	$49,410	24.1%	1,910
38. Medical and Clinical Laboratory Technologists	EQU	$56,130	11.9%	5,330
39. Medical and Clinical Laboratory Technicians	EQU	$36,280	16.1%	5,460
40. Diagnostic Medical Sonographers	EQU	$64,380	18.3%	1,650
41. Health Technologists and Technicians, All Other	EQU	$38,460	18.7%	3,200
42. Life, Physical, and Social Science Technicians, All Other	EQU	$43,350	13.3%	3,640

Best Job for People Interested in Hospitality and Tourism

Job	Top Skills	Annual Earnings	Percent Growth	Annual Openings
1. Managers, All Other	MGT SOC THO	$96,450	7.3%	29,750

Best Jobs for People Interested in Human Services

Job	Top Skills	Annual Earnings	Percent Growth	Annual Openings
1. Public Relations Specialists	COM SOC THO	$52,090	24.0%	13,130
2. Sales Managers	MGT SOC THO	$98,530	14.9%	12,660
3. Managers, All Other	MGT SOC THO	$96,450	7.3%	29,750
4. Social Scientists and Related Workers, All Other	MGT MAT THO	$74,620	22.5%	2,380
5. Healthcare Social Workers	COM SCI SOC	$47,230	22.4%	6,590
6. Chief Executives	MGT THO	$165,080	–1.4%	11,250
7. Preschool Teachers, Except Special Education	MGT	$25,700	19.0%	17,830
8. Clergy	MGT SOC	$43,970	12.7%	21,770
9. Writers and Authors	SOC	$55,420	14.8%	5,420
10. Probation Officers and Correctional Treatment Specialists	SOC	$47,200	19.3%	4,180
11. Social and Community Service Managers	MGT SOC	$57,950	13.8%	4,820
12. Social Science Research Assistants	TEC	$37,230	17.8%	1,270

Best Jobs for People Interested in Information Technology

Job	Top Skills	Annual Earnings	Percent Growth	Annual Openings
1. Engineering Teachers, Postsecondary	COM MAT SCI	$89,670	15.1%	1,000
2. Software Developers, Applications	MAT SCI TEC	$87,790	34.0%	21,840
3. Software Developers, Systems Software	MAT SCI TEC	$94,180	30.4%	15,340
4. Computer Network Architects	EQU SCI TEC	$75,660	53.4%	20,830
5. Computer Systems Analysts	MAT SCI TEC	$77,740	20.3%	22,280
6. Computer and Information Systems Managers	EQU MGT TEC	$115,780	16.9%	9,710
7. Computer and Information Research Scientists	MAT SCI TEC	$100,660	24.2%	1,320
8. Database Administrators	MAT TEC THO	$73,490	20.3%	4,440
9. Network and Computer Systems Administrators	EQU INS TEC	$69,160	23.2%	13,550
10. Architectural and Engineering Managers	MGT MAT SCI	$119,260	6.2%	4,870
11. Computer User Support Specialists	EQU	$46,260	13.8%	23,460
12. Computer Occupations, All Other	SCI TEC THO COM INS MAT	$79,240	13.1%	7,260
13. Computer Hardware Engineers	TEC	$98,810	3.8%	2,350
14. Biological Scientists, All Other	COM MAT	$68,220	18.8%	1,610

(continued)

COM=Communication Skills   EQU=Equipment Use/Maintenance Skills   INS=Installation Skills   MAT=Mathematics Skills
MGT=Management Skills   SCI=Science Skills   SOC=Social Skills   TEC=Technology/Programming Skills   THO=Thought-Processing Skills

Best Jobs for People Interested in Information Technology

Job	Top Skills	Annual Earnings	Percent Growth	Annual Openings
15. Computer Programmers	TEC	$71,380	−2.9%	8,030
16. Graphic Designers	MGT	$43,500	12.9%	12,480
17. Computer Science Teachers, Postsecondary	TEC	$70,300	15.1%	1,000
18. Life, Physical, and Social Science Technicians, All Other	EQU	$43,350	13.3%	3,640

Best Jobs for People Interested in Law, Public Safety, Corrections, and Security

Job	Top Skills	Annual Earnings	Percent Growth	Annual Openings
1. Lawyers	COM SOC THO	$112,760	13.0%	24,040
2. Compliance Officers	COM SCI THO EQU MAT SOC	$58,720	31.0%	10,850
3. Firefighters	EQU SOC	$45,250	18.5%	15,280
4. Paralegals and Legal Assistants	COM	$46,680	28.1%	10,400
5. Police and Sheriff's Patrol Officers	SOC	$53,540	8.7%	22,790
6. Detectives and Criminal Investigators	COM SCI SOC	$68,820	16.6%	4,160
7. First-Line Supervisors of Police and Detectives	MGT	$78,260	8.1%	5,050
8. Legal Secretaries	COM	$41,500	18.4%	8,380
9. First-Line Supervisors of Fire Fighting and Prevention Workers	EQU	$68,240	8.2%	3,250

Best Jobs for People Interested in Manufacturing

Job	Top Skills	Annual Earnings	Percent Growth	Annual Openings
1. Cost Estimators	COM MGT MAT	$57,860	25.3%	10,360
2. First-Line Supervisors of Mechanics, Installers, and Repairers	EQU	$59,150	4.2%	13,650
3. Installation, Maintenance, and Repair Workers, All Other	INS	$36,420	9.2%	4,180
4. Interior Designers	MGT	$46,280	19.4%	3,590
5. Medical Equipment Repairers	EQU	$44,490	27.2%	2,320
6. Environmental Science and Protection Technicians, Including Health	EQU	$41,380	28.9%	2,520
7. Environmental Engineering Technicians	EQU	$43,390	30.1%	1,040

Best Jobs for People Interested in Manufacturing

Job	Top Skills	Annual Earnings	Percent Growth	Annual Openings
8. Life, Physical, and Social Science Technicians, All Other	EQU	$43,350	13.3%	3,640
9. Elevator Installers and Repairers	INS	$70,910	9.2%	920
10. Maintenance and Repair Workers, General	EQU INS	$34,730	10.9%	35,750
11. Industrial Machinery Mechanics	EQU INS TEC	$45,420	7.3%	6,240
12. Surveying and Mapping Technicians	EQU TEC	$37,900	20.4%	2,940
13. Mobile Heavy Equipment Mechanics, Except Engines	INS	$44,830	8.7%	3,770
14. Engineering Technicians, Except Drafters, All Other	INS	$58,020	5.2%	1,850
15. Avionics Technicians	INS	$52,320	10.6%	520
16. Automotive Service Technicians and Mechanics	INS	$35,790	4.7%	18,170
17. Electrical and Electronics Repairers, Commercial and Industrial Equipment	INS	$51,820	3.8%	1,640
18. Helpers—Installation, Maintenance, and Repair Workers	INS	$24,260	8.3%	8,500
19. Rail Car Repairers	INS	$47,410	6.5%	590
20. Millwrights	INS	$48,360	1.4%	980
21. Locksmiths and Safe Repairers	INS	$35,550	12.0%	610
22. Mechanical Door Repairers	INS	$35,780	10.8%	450

Best Jobs for People Interested in Marketing, Sales, and Service

Job	Top Skills	Annual Earnings	Percent Growth	Annual Openings
1. Sales Managers	MGT SOC THO	$98,530	14.9%	12,660
2. Marketing Managers	MGT SOC THO	$112,800	12.5%	5,970
3. Business Operations Specialists, All Other	MGT MAT THO	$62,450	11.5%	36,830
4. Computer Occupations, All Other COM INS MAT	SCI TEC THO	$79,240	13.1%	7,260
5. Real Estate Sales Agents	COM SOC	$40,030	16.2%	12,830
6. Sales Representatives, Wholesale and Manufacturing, Technical and Scientific Products	COM MGT SOC	$73,710	9.7%	14,230
7. Business Teachers, Postsecondary	COM MAT THO	$73,760	15.1%	2,000

(continued)

COM=Communication Skills   EQU=Equipment Use/Maintenance Skills   INS=Installation Skills   MAT=Mathematics Skills
MGT=Management Skills   SCI=Science Skills   SOC=Social Skills   TEC=Technology/Programming Skills   THO=Thought-Processing Skills

Best Jobs for People Interested in Marketing, Sales, and Service

Job	Top Skills	Annual Earnings	Percent Growth	Annual Openings
8. Interior Designers	MGT	$46,280	19.4%	3,590
9. Purchasing Agents, Except Wholesale, Retail, and Farm Products	MGT MAT THO	$56,580	13.9%	11,860
10. First-Line Supervisors of Non-Retail Sales Workers	MGT	$68,880	4.8%	12,950
11. Sales Engineers	MAT TEC	$87,390	8.8%	3,500
12. Survey Researchers	TEC	$36,050	30.3%	1,340

Best Jobs for People Interested in Science, Technology, Engineering, and Mathematics

Job	Top Skills	Annual Earnings	Percent Growth	Annual Openings
1. Health Specialties Teachers, Postsecondary	COM SCI THO	$85,270	15.1%	4,000
2. Computer Network Architects	EQU SCI TEC	$75,660	53.4%	20,830
3. Civil Engineers	MGT MAT SCI	$77,560	24.3%	11,460
4. Medical Scientists, Except Epidemiologists	MAT SCI THO	$76,700	40.4%	6,620
5. Environmental Engineers	MAT SCI THO	$78,740	30.6%	2,790
6. Engineering Teachers, Postsecondary	COM MAT SCI	$89,670	15.1%	1,000
7. Architectural and Engineering Managers	MGT MAT SCI	$119,260	6.2%	4,870
8. Natural Sciences Managers	MGT MAT SCI	$116,020	15.5%	2,010
9. Biomedical Engineers	INS SCI TEC	$81,540	72.0%	1,490
10. Biochemists and Biophysicists	COM MAT SCI	$79,390	37.4%	1,620
11. Cost Estimators	COM MGT MAT	$57,860	25.3%	10,360
12. Engineers, All Other	MAT SCI TEC EQU INS	$90,270	6.7%	5,020
13. Petroleum Engineers	MGT MAT SCI	$114,080	18.4%	860
14. Political Scientists	COM	$107,420	19.4%	280
15. Social Scientists and Related Workers, All Other	MGT MAT THO	$74,620	22.5%	2,380
16. Aerospace Engineers	MAT TEC	$97,480	10.4%	2,230
17. Industrial Engineers	MGT MAT THO	$76,100	14.2%	8,540
18. Operations Research Analysts	MAT SCI THO	$70,960	22.0%	3,220
19. Physicists	MAT SCI TEC	$106,370	15.9%	690
20. Computer Hardware Engineers	TEC	$98,810	3.8%	2,350
21. Electronics Engineers, Except Computer	TEC	$90,170	0.3%	3,340
22. Geoscientists, Except Hydrologists and Geographers	COM MAT SCI	$82,500	17.5%	1,540

Best Jobs for People Interested in Science, Technology, Engineering, and Mathematics

Job	Top Skills	Annual Earnings	Percent Growth	Annual Openings
23. Mechanical Engineers	MAT TEC	$78,160	6.0%	7,570
24. Survey Researchers	TEC	$36,050	30.3%	1,340
25. Biological Scientists, All Other	COM MAT	$68,220	18.8%	1,610
26. Mining and Geological Engineers, Including Mining Safety Engineers	TEC	$82,870	15.2%	260
27. Biological Science Teachers, Postsecondary	COM THO	$72,700	15.1%	1,700
28. Hydrologists	TEC	$75,690	18.2%	380
29. Statisticians	TEC	$72,830	13.1%	960

Best Jobs for People Interested in Transportation, Distribution, and Logistics

Job	Top Skills	Annual Earnings	Percent Growth	Annual Openings
1. Compliance Officers	COM SCI THO EQU MAT SOC	$58,720	31.0%	10,850
2. Environmental Engineers	MAT SCI THO	$78,740	30.6%	2,790
3. Logisticians	MGT MAT THO	$70,800	19.5%	4,190
4. Environmental Scientists and Specialists, Including Health	COM MAT SCI	$61,700	27.9%	4,840
5. Managers, All Other	MGT SOC THO	$96,450	7.3%	29,750
6. Chief Executives	MGT THO	$165,080	−1.4%	11,250
7. Commercial Pilots	EQU SCI THO	$67,500	18.6%	2,060
8. Ship Engineers	EQU MGT	$65,880	18.6%	700
9. Air Traffic Controllers	MAT	$108,040	13.1%	1,230
10. Airline Pilots, Copilots, and Flight Engineers	EQU MAT	$103,210	8.4%	3,250
11. Heavy and Tractor-Trailer Truck Drivers	EQU	$37,770	12.9%	55,460
12. Environmental Science and Protection Technicians, Including Health	EQU	$41,380	28.9%	2,520
13. Captains, Mates, and Pilots of Water Vessels	EQU MGT	$64,180	17.3%	1,950
14. Operating Engineers and Other Construction Equipment Operators	EQU	$40,400	12.0%	11,820
15. Transportation Inspectors	EQU	$57,640	18.4%	1,130

(continued)

COM=Communication Skills   EQU=Equipment Use/Maintenance Skills   INS=Installation Skills   MAT=Mathematics Skills
MGT=Management Skills   SCI=Science Skills   SOC=Social Skills   TEC=Technology/Programming Skills   THO=Thought-Processing Skills

Best Jobs for People Interested in Transportation, Distribution, and Logistics

Job	Top Skills	Annual Earnings	Percent Growth	Annual Openings
16. Automotive Service Technicians and Mechanics	INS	$35,790	4.7%	18,170
17. Installation, Maintenance, and Repair Workers, All Other	INS	$36,420	9.2%	4,180
18. Aircraft Structure, Surfaces, Rigging, and Systems Assemblers	INS	$44,820	9.3%	1,340
19. Avionics Technicians	INS	$52,320	10.6%	520
20. Commercial Divers	INS	$51,360	5.5%	50

Best High-Skill Jobs by Personality Type

These lists organize the 199 best high-skill jobs into groups matching six personality types. Within each personality type, I ranked the jobs based on each job's total combined score for earnings, growth, and annual job openings. In the lists, I identify the top skills (abbreviated) for each job.

The personality types are Realistic, Investigative, Artistic, Social, Enterprising, and Conventional. This system was developed by occupational researcher John Holland and is used in the *Self-Directed Search (SDS)* and other career assessment inventories and information systems. If you have used one of these career inventories or systems, the lists will help you identify jobs that most closely match these personality types. Even if you have not used one of these systems, the concept of personality types and the jobs that are related to them can help you identify jobs that suit the type of person you are.

Like the initial set of lists based on skills, this set assigns a few highly diverse jobs to more than one list to match the differing characteristics of job specializations. For example, you will find the job Compliance Officers on three lists because it is linked to the specializations Environmental Compliance Inspectors (Conventional), Equal Opportunity Representatives and Officers (Social), and Coroners (Investigative). In addition, you should be aware that these lists are based on the primary personality type that describes the job, but most jobs also are linked to one or two secondary personality types. The job descriptions in Part IV indicate all significant personality types. Consider reviewing the jobs for more than one personality type so you don't overlook possible jobs that would interest you.

The O*NET database, which was my source for personality-type information about the best jobs, provided no information on this topic for one job: Installation, Maintenance, and Repair Workers, All Other.

Descriptions of the Six Personality Types

Following are brief descriptions for the six personality types used in the lists. Select the two or three types that most closely describe you and then use the lists to identify high-skill jobs that best fit these personality types.

* **Realistic:** These occupations frequently involve work activities that include practical, hands-on problems and solutions. They often deal with plants; animals; and real-world materials such as wood, tools, and machinery. Many of the occupations require working outside and don't involve a lot of paperwork or working closely with others.

* **Investigative:** These occupations frequently involve working with ideas and require an extensive amount of thinking. These occupations can involve searching for facts and figuring out problems mentally.

* **Artistic:** These occupations frequently involve working with forms, designs, and patterns. They often require self-expression, and the work can be done without following a clear set of rules.

* **Social:** These occupations frequently involve working with, communicating with, and teaching people. These occupations often involve helping or providing service to others.

* **Enterprising:** These occupations frequently involve starting up and carrying out projects. These occupations can involve leading people and making many decisions. They sometimes require risk taking and often deal with business.

* **Conventional:** These occupations frequently involve following set procedures and routines. These occupations can include working with data and details more than with ideas. Usually there is a clear line of authority to follow.

Best High-Skill Jobs for People with a Realistic Personality Type

Job	Top Skills	Annual Earnings	Percent Growth	Annual Openings
1. Business Operations Specialists, All Other	MGT MAT THO	$62,450	11.5%	36,830
2. Civil Engineers	MGT MAT SCI	$77,560	24.3%	11,460
3. Heavy and Tractor-Trailer Truck Drivers	EQU	$37,770	12.9%	55,460
4. Heating, Air Conditioning, and Refrigeration Mechanics and Installers	EQU INS MAT	$42,530	28.1%	13,620
5. Operating Engineers and Other Construction Equipment Operators	EQU	$40,400	12.0%	11,820

(continued)

COM=Communication Skills   EQU=Equipment Use/Maintenance Skills   INS=Installation Skills   MAT=Mathematics Skills
MGT=Management Skills   SCI=Science Skills   SOC=Social Skills   TEC=Technology/Programming Skills   THO=Thought-Processing Skills

Best High-Skill Jobs for People with a Realistic Personality Type

Job	Top Skills	Annual Earnings	Percent Growth	Annual Openings
6. Radiologic Technologists	EQU SCI SOC	$54,340	17.2%	6,800
7. Firefighters	EQU SOC	$45,250	18.5%	15,280
8. Commercial Pilots	EQU SCI THO	$67,500	18.6%	2,060
9. Plumbers, Pipefitters, and Steamfitters	EQU INS MAT	$46,660	15.3%	17,550
10. Computer User Support Specialists	EQU	$46,260	13.8%	23,460
11. Ship Engineers	EQU MGT	$65,880	18.6%	700
12. Electricians	EQU INS	$48,250	11.9%	25,090
13. Construction and Building Inspectors	EQU	$52,360	16.8%	3,970
14. Captains, Mates, and Pilots of Water Vessels	EQU MGT	$64,180	17.3%	1,950
15. Cement Masons and Concrete Finishers	EQU	$35,450	12.9%	7,640
16. Cardiovascular Technologists and Technicians	EQU	$49,410	24.1%	1,910
17. Construction Laborers	EQU	$29,280	20.5%	33,940
18. Surgical Technologists	EQU MGT	$39,920	25.3%	4,630
19. Refuse and Recyclable Material Collectors	EQU	$32,640	18.6%	7,110
20. Water and Wastewater Treatment Plant and System Operators	EQU	$40,770	19.8%	4,690
21. Engineers, All Other	MAT SCI TEC EQU INS	$90,270	6.7%	5,020
22. Carpenters	EQU MGT	$39,530	12.9%	32,540
23. Medical Equipment Repairers	EQU	$44,490	27.2%	2,320
24. Transportation Inspectors	EQU	$57,640	18.4%	1,130
25. Boilermakers	EQU	$54,640	18.8%	810
26. Airline Pilots, Copilots, and Flight Engineers	EQU MAT	$103,210	8.4%	3,250
27. Brickmasons and Blockmasons	EQU	$46,930	11.5%	5,000
28. Environmental Engineering Technicians	EQU	$43,390	30.1%	1,040
29. Security and Fire Alarm Systems Installers	EQU INS	$38,500	24.8%	2,780
30. Helpers—Electricians	INS	$27,220	24.7%	4,800
31. Medical and Clinical Laboratory Technicians	EQU	$36,280	16.1%	5,460
32. Electrical Power-Line Installers and Repairers	EQU	$58,030	4.5%	4,550
33. Health Technologists and Technicians, All Other	EQU	$38,460	18.7%	3,200
34. Life, Physical, and Social Science Technicians, All Other	EQU	$43,350	13.3%	3,640
35. Maintenance and Repair Workers, General	EQU INS	$34,730	10.9%	35,750
36. Industrial Machinery Mechanics	EQU INS TEC	$45,420	7.3%	6,240
37. Elevator Installers and Repairers	INS	$70,910	9.2%	920
38. Drywall and Ceiling Tile Installers	EQU	$37,320	13.5%	3,700
39. Architectural and Civil Drafters	TEC	$46,430	9.1%	3,620
40. Telecommunications Equipment Installers and Repairers, Except Line Installers	INS	$54,710	−0.2%	3,560

Best High-Skill Jobs for People with a Realistic Personality Type

Job	Top Skills	Annual Earnings	Percent Growth	Annual Openings
41. Mobile Heavy Equipment Mechanics, Except Engines	INS	$44,830	8.7%	3,770
42. Engineering Technicians, Except Drafters, All Other	INS	$58,020	5.2%	1,850
43. Audio and Video Equipment Technicians	INS	$40,540	12.6%	2,370
44. Mechanical Door Repairers	INS	$35,780	10.8%	450
45. Automotive Service Technicians and Mechanics	INS	$35,790	4.7%	18,170
46. Avionics Technicians	INS	$52,320	10.6%	520
47. Electrical and Electronics Repairers, Commercial and Industrial Equipment	INS	$51,820	3.8%	1,640
48. Aircraft Structure, Surfaces, Rigging, and Systems Assemblers	INS	$44,820	9.3%	1,340
49. Helpers—Installation, Maintenance, and Repair Workers	INS	$24,260	8.3%	8,500
50. Millwrights	INS	$48,360	1.4%	980
51. Commercial Divers	INS	$51,360	5.5%	50
52. Rail Car Repairers	INS	$47,410	6.5%	590
53. Medical Equipment Preparers	INS	$29,490	12.8%	1,120
54. Electronic Home Entertainment Equipment Installers and Repairers	INS	$32,940	10.8%	1,430
55. Locksmiths and Safe Repairers	INS	$35,550	12.0%	610

Best High-Skill Jobs for People with an Investigative Personality Type

Job	Top Skills	Annual Earnings	Percent Growth	Annual Openings
1. Software Developers, Applications	MAT SCI TEC	$87,790	34.0%	21,840
2. Software Developers, Systems Software	MAT SCI TEC	$94,180	30.4%	15,340
3. Computer Network Architects	EQU SCI TEC	$75,660	53.4%	20,830
4. Management Analysts	COM MAT THO	$78,160	23.9%	30,650
5. Medical Scientists, Except Epidemiologists	MAT SCI THO	$76,700	40.4%	6,620
6. Pharmacists	COM MGT SCI	$111,570	17.0%	10,580
7. Veterinarians	COM SCI THO	$82,040	32.9%	3,020
8. Computer Systems Analysts	MAT SCI TEC	$77,740	20.3%	22,280

(continued)

COM=Communication Skills   EQU=Equipment Use/Maintenance Skills   INS=Installation Skills   MAT=Mathematics Skills
MGT=Management Skills   SCI=Science Skills   SOC=Social Skills   TEC=Technology/Programming Skills   THO=Thought-Processing Skills

Best High-Skill Jobs for People with an Investigative Personality Type

Job	Top Skills	Annual Earnings	Percent Growth	Annual Openings
9. Dentists, General	MGT SCI THO	$141,040	15.3%	5,180
10. Environmental Engineers	MAT SCI THO	$78,740	30.6%	2,790
11. Mechanical Engineers	MAT TEC	$78,160	6.0%	7,570
12. Biomedical Engineers	INS SCI TEC	$81,540	72.0%	1,490
13. Biochemists and Biophysicists	COM MAT SCI	$79,390	37.4%	1,620
14. Compliance Officers	COM SCI THO EQU MAT SOC	$58,720	31.0%	10,850
15. Optometrists	MAT SCI THO	$94,990	24.4%	2,010
16. Market Research Analysts and Marketing Specialists	MAT SCI THO	$60,570	28.1%	13,730
17. Computer and Information Research Scientists	MAT SCI TEC	$100,660	24.2%	1,320
18. Network and Computer Systems Administrators	EQU INS TEC	$69,160	23.2%	13,550
19. Prosthodontists	SCI	$118,400	26.4%	30
20. Orthodontists	COM SCI THO	$166,400+	19.7%	360
21. Petroleum Engineers	MGT MAT SCI	$114,080	18.4%	860
22. Engineers, All Other	MAT SCI TEC EQU INS	$90,270	6.7%	5,020
23. Environmental Scientists and Specialists, Including Health	COM MAT SCI	$61,700	27.9%	4,840
24. Computer Occupations, All Other	SCI TEC THO COM INS MAT	$79,240	13.1%	7,260
25. Political Scientists	COM	$107,420	19.4%	280
26. Industrial Engineers	MGT MAT THO	$76,100	14.2%	8,540
27. Aerospace Engineers	MAT TEC	$97,480	10.4%	2,230
28. Industrial-Organizational Psychologists	TEC	$87,330	26.1%	130
29. Operations Research Analysts	MAT SCI THO	$70,960	22.0%	3,220
30. Computer Hardware Engineers	TEC	$98,810	3.8%	2,350
31. Electronics Engineers, Except Computer	TEC	$90,170	0.3%	3,340
32. Physicists	MAT SCI TEC	$106,370	15.9%	690
33. Social Scientists and Related Workers, All Other	MGT MAT THO	$74,620	22.5%	2,380
34. Environmental Science and Protection Technicians, Including Health	EQU	$41,380	28.9%	2,520
35. Geoscientists, Except Hydrologists and Geographers	COM MAT SCI	$82,500	17.5%	1,540
36. Computer Programmers	TEC	$71,380	–2.9%	8,030
37. Survey Researchers	TEC	$36,050	30.3%	1,340
38. Audiologists	COM	$66,660	25.0%	580

Best High-Skill Jobs for People with an Investigative Personality Type

Job	Top Skills	Annual Earnings	Percent Growth	Annual Openings
39. Biological Scientists, All Other	COM MAT	$68,220	18.8%	1,610
40. Mining and Geological Engineers, Including Mining Safety Engineers	TEC	$82,870	15.2%	260
41. Diagnostic Medical Sonographers	EQU	$64,380	18.3%	1,650
42. Medical and Clinical Laboratory Technologists	EQU	$56,130	11.9%	5,330
43. Hydrologists	TEC	$75,690	18.2%	380
44. Engineering Technicians, Except Drafters, All Other	INS	$58,020	5.2%	1,850

Best High-Skill Jobs for People with an Artistic Personality Type

Job	Top Skills	Annual Earnings	Percent Growth	Annual Openings
1. Architects, Except Landscape and Naval	MGT MAT SCI	$72,550	16.2%	4,680
2. Art Directors	MGT	$80,630	11.7%	2,870
3. Interior Designers	MGT	$46,280	19.4%	3,590
4. Landscape Architects	MGT	$62,090	19.6%	980
5. Technical Writers	COM	$63,280	18.2%	1,680
6. Writers and Authors	SOC	$55,420	14.8%	5,420
7. Graphic Designers	MGT	$43,500	12.9%	12,480
8. Commercial and Industrial Designers	TEC	$58,230	9.0%	1,760

Best High-Skill Jobs for People with a Social Personality Type

Job	Top Skills	Annual Earnings	Percent Growth	Annual Openings
1. Engineering Teachers, Postsecondary	COM MAT SCI	$89,670	15.1%	1,000
2. Dental Hygienists	COM SCI SOC	$68,250	36.1%	9,840
3. Physician Assistants	COM SCI SOC	$86,410	39.0%	4,280
4. Physical Therapists	COM SCI SOC	$76,310	30.3%	7,860
5. Registered Nurses	SCI SOC THO	$64,690	22.2%	103,900
6. Health Specialties Teachers, Postsecondary	COM SCI THO	$85,270	15.1%	4,000
7. Compliance Officers	COM SCI THO EQU MAT SOC	$58,720	31.0%	10,850

(continued)

COM=*Communication Skills*   EQU=*Equipment Use/Maintenance Skills*   INS=*Installation Skills*   MAT=*Mathematics Skills*
MGT=*Management Skills*   SCI=*Science Skills*   SOC=*Social Skills*   TEC=*Technology/Programming Skills*   THO=*Thought-Processing Skills*

Best High-Skill Jobs for People with a Social Personality Type

Job	Top Skills	Annual Earnings	Percent Growth	Annual Openings
8. Business Teachers, Postsecondary	COM MAT THO	$73,760	15.1%	2,000
9. Biological Science Teachers, Postsecondary	COM THO	$72,700	15.1%	1,700
10. Home Health Aides	SOC	$20,560	50.0%	55,270
11. Occupational Therapists	COM SCI SOC	$72,320	25.6%	4,580
12. Computer Science Teachers, Postsecondary	TEC	$70,300	15.1%	1,000
13. Medical Assistants	COM SCI SOC	$28,860	33.9%	21,780
14. Training and Development Specialists	SCI SOC THO	$54,160	23.3%	10,710
15. Self-Enrichment Education Teachers	COM SOC THO	$36,340	32.0%	12,030
16. Instructional Coordinators	COM SOC THO	$58,830	23.2%	6,060
17. Fitness Trainers and Aerobics Instructors	COM SOC THO	$31,090	29.4%	12,380
18. Radiation Therapists	EQU MAT SCI	$74,980	27.1%	690
19. Elementary School Teachers, Except Special Education	COM SOC THO	$51,660	15.8%	59,650
20. Licensed Practical and Licensed Vocational Nurses	SCI SOC THO	$40,380	20.6%	39,130
21. Middle School Teachers, Except Special and Career/Technical Education	COM SOC THO	$51,960	15.3%	25,110
22. Customer Service Representatives	SOC	$30,460	17.7%	110,840
23. Speech-Language Pathologists	COM SCI THO	$66,920	18.5%	4,380
24. Physical Therapist Assistants	COM SCI SOC	$49,690	33.3%	3,050
25. Healthcare Social Workers	COM SCI SOC	$47,230	22.4%	6,590
26. Coaches and Scouts	MGT	$28,340	24.8%	9,920
27. Chiropractors	COM SCI THO	$67,200	19.5%	1,820
28. Respiratory Therapists	EQU SCI SOC	$54,280	20.9%	4,140
29. Secondary School Teachers, Except Special and Career/Technical Education	SOC	$53,230	8.9%	41,240
30. Preschool Teachers, Except Special Education	MGT	$25,700	19.0%	17,830
31. Special Education Teachers, Middle School	COM SOC THO	$53,440	18.1%	4,410
32. Art, Drama, and Music Teachers, Postsecondary	THO	$62,040	15.1%	2,500
33. Educational, Guidance, School, and Vocational Counselors	SOC	$53,380	14.0%	9,440
34. Clergy	MGT SOC	$43,970	12.7%	21,770
35. Special Education Teachers, Secondary School	SOC	$54,810	13.3%	5,750
36. Probation Officers and Correctional Treatment Specialists	SOC	$47,200	19.3%	4,180

Best High-Skill Jobs for People with an Enterprising Personality Type

Job	Top Skills	Annual Earnings	Percent Growth	Annual Openings
1. Sales Managers	MGT SOC THO	$98,530	14.9%	12,660
2. Lawyers	COM SOC THO	$112,760	13.0%	24,040
3. Marketing Managers	MGT SOC THO	$112,800	12.5%	5,970
4. Computer and Information Systems Managers	EQU MGT TEC	$115,780	16.9%	9,710
5. Construction Managers	MGT MAT SOC	$83,860	17.2%	13,770
6. Registered Nurses	SCI SOC THO	$64,690	22.2%	103,900
7. Supervisors of Construction and Extraction Workers	EQU MGT SOC	$58,680	15.4%	24,220
8. Medical and Health Services Managers	MGT SCI THO	$84,270	16.0%	9,940
9. Managers, All Other	MGT SOC THO	$96,450	7.3%	29,750
10. Financial Managers	MGT MAT THO	$103,910	7.6%	13,820
11. General and Operations Managers	MGT SOC THO	$94,400	–0.1%	50,220
12. Natural Sciences Managers	MGT MAT SCI	$116,020	15.5%	2,010
13. Personal Financial Advisors	COM MAT THO	$64,750	30.1%	8,530
14. Public Relations Specialists	COM SOC THO	$52,090	24.0%	13,130
15. Sales Representatives, Wholesale and Manufacturing, Technical and Scientific Products	COM MGT SOC	$73,710	9.7%	14,230
16. Business Operations Specialists, All Other	MGT MAT THO	$62,450	11.5%	36,830
17. Cost Estimators	COM MGT MAT	$57,860	25.3%	10,360
18. Human Resources Specialists	COM SCI SOC	$52,690	27.9%	11,230
19. Chief Executives	MGT THO	$165,080	–1.4%	11,250
20. Financial Examiners	COM MAT THO	$74,940	41.2%	1,600
21. Administrative Services Managers	COM MGT SOC	$77,890	12.5%	8,660
22. Air Traffic Controllers	MAT	$108,040	13.1%	1,230
23. Detectives and Criminal Investigators	COM SCI SOC	$68,820	16.6%	4,160
24. First-Line Supervisors of Office and Administrative Support Workers	MGT SOC	$47,460	11.0%	48,900
25. Real Estate Sales Agents	COM SOC	$40,030	16.2%	12,830
26. Securities, Commodities, and Financial Services Sales Agents	COM MAT SOC	$70,190	9.3%	12,680
27. Architectural and Engineering Managers	MGT MAT SCI	$119,260	6.2%	4,870
28. Human Resources Managers	MGT THO	$99,180	9.6%	4,140
29. Education Administrators, Elementary and Secondary School	MGT SOC THO	$86,970	8.6%	8,880
30. Public Relations and Fundraising Managers	MGT	$91,810	12.9%	2,060
31. Police and Sheriff's Patrol Officers	SOC	$53,540	8.7%	22,790

(continued)

COM=*Communication Skills* EQU=*Equipment Use/Maintenance Skills* INS=*Installation Skills* MAT=*Mathematics Skills*
MGT=*Management Skills* SCI=*Science Skills* SOC=*Social Skills* TEC=*Technology/Programming Skills* THO=*Thought-Processing Skills*

Best High-Skill Jobs for People with an Enterprising Personality Type

Job	Top Skills	Annual Earnings	Percent Growth	Annual Openings
32. First-Line Supervisors of Non-Retail Sales Workers	MGT	$68,880	4.8%	12,950
33. Agents and Business Managers of Artists, Performers, and Athletes	COM MGT	$63,130	22.4%	1,010
34. First-Line Supervisors of Personal Service Workers	MGT	$35,290	15.4%	9,080
35. Sales Engineers	MAT TEC	$87,390	8.8%	3,500
36. First-Line Supervisors of Police and Detectives	MGT	$78,260	8.1%	5,050
37. First-Line Supervisors of Mechanics, Installers, and Repairers	EQU	$59,150	4.2%	13,650
38. Social and Community Service Managers	MGT SOC	$57,950	13.8%	4,820
39. First-Line Supervisors of Landscaping, Lawn Service, and Groundskeeping Workers	EQU MGT	$41,860	14.9%	5,600
40. Producers and Directors	MGT EQU	$68,440	9.8%	4,040
41. First-Line Supervisors of Fire Fighting and Prevention Workers	EQU	$68,240	8.2%	3,250

Best High-Skill Jobs for People with a Conventional Personality Type

Job	Top Skills	Annual Earnings	Percent Growth	Annual Openings
1. Accountants and Auditors	COM MAT THO	$61,690	21.6%	49,750
2. Compliance Officers	COM SCI THO EQU MAT SOC	$58,720	31.0%	10,850
3. Financial Analysts	COM MAT THO	$74,350	19.8%	9,520
4. Paralegals and Legal Assistants	COM	$46,680	28.1%	10,400
5. Dental Assistants	EQU SOC	$33,470	35.7%	16,100
6. Statisticians	TEC	$72,830	13.1%	960
7. Database Administrators	MAT TEC THO	$73,490	20.3%	4,440
8. Actuaries	MAT TEC THO	$87,650	21.3%	1,000
9. Medical Secretaries	COM SOC	$30,530	26.6%	18,900
10. Pharmacy Technicians	COM MAT SOC	$28,400	30.6%	18,200
11. Compensation, Benefits, and Job Analysis Specialists	MAT SCI THO	$57,000	23.6%	6,050
12. Business Operations Specialists, All Other	MGT MAT THO	$62,450	11.5%	36,830
13. Computer Occupations, All Other	SCI TEC THO COM INS MAT	$79,240	13.1%	7,260
14. Logisticians	MGT MAT THO	$70,800	19.5%	4,190

Best High-Skill Jobs for People with a Conventional Personality Type

Job	Top Skills	Annual Earnings	Percent Growth	Annual Openings
15. Executive Secretaries and Executive Administrative Assistants	MGT SOC	$43,520	12.8%	41,920
16. Purchasing Agents, Except Wholesale, Retail, and Farm Products	MGT MAT THO	$56,580	13.9%	11,860
17. Budget Analysts	MGT	$68,200	15.1%	2,230
18. Cargo and Freight Agents	MGT	$37,150	23.9%	4,030
19. Legal Secretaries	COM	$41,500	18.4%	8,380
20. Surveying and Mapping Technicians	EQU TEC	$37,900	20.4%	2,940
21. Social Science Research Assistants	TEC	$37,230	17.8%	1,270
22. Audio-Visual and Multimedia Collections Specialists	INS	$42,710	10.3%	220

Bonus Lists About Skills

The following lists do not contain jobs, but they are based on the relationships between skills and jobs. I think you'll find they add to your understanding of skills and career options.

These lists may also help with long-range career planning. During your working lifetime, some new occupations will emerge and some existing occupations will go into decline. In addition, if you are diligent about acquiring new skills, eventually you will be able to consider entering occupations that presently seem unreachable to you. That's why it's useful to step back from the 199 jobs in this book and look at the larger issues of what skills tend to be high-paid, what skills are growing in demand, what skills are associated with many job openings, which industries need your strongest skills, and which metropolitan areas are home to jobs needing skills like yours.

Skills with the Best Payoff for Improvement

To create this list, I started with the 750 SOC occupations for which skills data is available. For the 9 skills that I use in this book, I looked at the range of ratings that are given to these 750 jobs. For example, the scores for Thought-Processing Skills range from a low of -0.50 (for Tank Car, Truck, and Ship Loaders) to a high of 1.98 (for Chief Executives). I divided this range into five equal zones and divided the 750 jobs according to which zone they belong in. The number of occupations in each zone varies greatly. For example, only two occupations (Chief Executives and Purchasing Managers) have scores

COM=Communication Skills   EQU=Equipment Use/Maintenance Skills   INS=Installation Skills   MAT=Mathematics Skills
MGT=Management Skills   SCI=Science Skills   SOC=Social Skills   TEC=Technology/Programming Skills   THO=Thought-Processing Skills

that put them in the top zone for Management Skills, whereas 49 occupations (such as Electricians, Rail Car Repairers, and Avionics Technicians) have a top-zone level of Equipment Use/Maintenance Skills.

I computed the average annual income for the jobs in each zone and then computed the average difference between the earnings in each zone and in the next-highest zone. This procedure indicated, for each skill, the *average monetary difference* ("payoff") that is associated with a higher level ("improvement") of skill. Finally, I ordered the 9 skills from highest to lowest average payoff to produce the following list. In other words, the skills nearest the top of the list have the highest payoff for higher mastery. If high income is important to you, you should think about developing these skills.

Note that I'm not looking at literal "improvements" or "payoffs." I'm measuring differences between skill levels and between earnings. I'm not measuring the historical behavior of individuals or the rewards they've achieved by improving. For example, the average income difference between occupations at different levels of Management Skills is $32,002, but that doesn't mean you should assume that every manager who improves his or her managerial abilities will automatically achieve that boost in earnings.

On the other hand, smart employers recognize and reward workers who improve their skills, often with promotions or raises. The lesson to take away is that you should aim for a high level of skill when you first prepare for career entry and continue to improve your skills as you work.

Average Payoffs for Improvement of Skill, from Highest to Lowest	
Skill	Average Payoff for Skill Improvement
1. Management Skills	$32,002
2. Social Skills	$18,221
3. Thought-Processing Skills	$16,278
4. Communication Skills	$15,284
5. Mathematics Skills	$14,123
6. Science Skills	$13,061
7. Technology/Programming Skills	$10,747
8. Installation Skills	$1,059
9. Equipment Use/Maintenance Skills	$367

Skills with the Most Job Growth Linked to Improvement

This list shows the relationship between skills and job growth. I used the same methodology as I did for the previous list, except that this time I computed the average projected growth through 2018, rather than the average income, for the jobs at each level of skill. The figures in the list thus indicate, for each of the 9 skills, the average boost in projected job growth that is associated with a higher level of skill.

It's interesting to note that for three skills, workers with better abilities will see less job growth. Keep in mind, however, that job growth and job opportunity are not the same thing; some occupations that are not growing will still offer many job openings.

Average Change in Job Growth for Improving Level of Skill, from Highest to Lowest	
Skill	Average Change in Growth for Skill Improvement
1. Technology/Programming Skills	3.6%
2. Thought-Processing Skills	2.6%
3. Social Skills	1.6%
4. Science Skills	1.5%
5. Installation Skills	1.4%
6. Communication Skills	1.2%
7. Mathematics Skills	−0.4%
8. Equipment Use/Maintenance Skills	−0.7%
9. Management Skills	−1.7%

Skills with the Most Openings for Highest-Skill Jobs

This list looks at the relationship between a very high level of skill and job openings. For the previous two lists, I divided all occupations into five zones according to their level of ability with each of the 9 skills. To create this list, I computed the average number of annual job openings projected for the occupations in the two highest zones for each skill.

You may wonder why I didn't look at the differences associated with skill *improvement,* as I did in the previous two lists. But consider that opportunities for employment tend to be shaped like a pyramid, with fewer openings as you progress toward higher levels of skill. That's why, for this list, I pooled the jobs at the two highest levels of skill instead of comparing openings at different levels.

This list demonstrates a point I made in my comments on the previous list: Sometimes occupations that are not growing rapidly (or even shrinking) still offer plentiful openings. Note that the jobs with very high levels of Management Skills offer many job openings even though this skill appears at the bottom of the previous list.

Another idea to bear in mind is that figures for job openings don't tell you how much competition you may expect for those openings. Not many people qualify for jobs that demand very high levels of Mathematics Skills and Science Skills, so even though openings for these jobs are relatively scarce, the jobs may be easier for appropriately educated people to enter than jobs using other skills.

Average Job Openings for Occupations with the Highest Level of Skill, from Highest to Lowest

Skill	Average Change in Annual Job Openings for Skill Improvement
1. Social Skills	8,107
2. Management Skills	7,417
3. Technology/Programming Skills	6,418
4. Thought-Processing Skills	6,288
5. Communication Skills	5,707
6. Installation Skills	4,846
7. Mathematics Skills	3,498
8. Equipment Use/Maintenance Skills	3,289
9. Science Skills	2,103

Industries in Which the Skills Are Concentrated

Although most lists in this book are about jobs, another way of looking at the workforce is by industries. Industries are usually defined by their outputs. For example, the aerospace product and parts manufacturing industry produces airplanes and their parts, the broadcasting industry produces radio and television broadcasts, and the health-care industry produces healthy people.

Industries also require different *inputs*, and one of those inputs is skills. Each industry demands a different mix of skills from workers, so certain skills dominate one industry more than another. You may want to plan to pursue a career in an industry where your top skills are appreciated—that is, an industry with jobs that employ many workers with your skills. Of course, another important consideration is how fast an industry is growing.

So I created the next nine lists to show, for each skill, the 10 industries in which the skill is most highly concentrated in the workforce, plus the projected growth rate for each industry between 2008 and 2018. To create these lists, I began with the procedure I used for the previous set of lists, in which every occupation with skill data is assigned to one of five zones of ability for each of the 9 skills. Next, I calculated how many workers from the occupations in the two highest zones for each skill are employed in each of 89 industries surveyed by the BLS. I divided this figure by the total number of workers in each industry. This told me which 10 industries have the highest percentage of these very highly skilled workers. So, for example, in the professional, scientific, and technical services industry, 16.8 percent of the workers are in the occupations that I assigned to the top two zones for Mathematics Skills. In the clothing and clothing accessories stores industry, 66.9 percent of the workers have high levels of Social Skills.

In the following lists, one for each skill, I rank the top 10 industries by descending percentage of highly skilled workers. However, the percentage figures you'll find in the lists indicate the *job growth* projected for the industries from 2008 to 2018, which I expect is more useful information.

Note that several industries have a negative growth rate, which means they are shrinking. That does not mean you should not consider these industries. For certain jobs and in certain parts of the country, the workforce in these industries may be growing, and even in a shrinking workforce there will be openings caused by job turnover.

10 Industries with the Highest Concentration of Communication Skills in Their Workforce

Industry	Growth Rate
1. Securities, Commodity Contracts, and Other Financial Investments and Related Activities	11.8%
2. Hospitals, Public and Private	10.1%
3. Funds, Trusts, and Other Financial Vehicles	17.3%
4. Broadcasting (Except Internet)	7.4%
5. Professional, Scientific, and Technical Services	33.9%
6. Monetary Authorities, Credit Intermediation, and Related Activities	5.0%
7. Religious, Grantmaking, Civic, Professional, and Similar Organizations	12.8%
8. Monetary Authorities-Central Bank	3.6%
9. Management of Companies and Enterprises	5.4%
10. Credit Intermediation and Related Activities	5.0%

10 Industries with the Highest Concentration of Equipment Use/Maintenance Skills in Their Workforce

Industry	Growth Rate
1. Support Activities for Mining	–23.2%
2. Water Transportation	2.6%
3. Mining (Except Oil and Gas)	–0.9%
4. Petroleum and Coal Products Manufacturing	–22.5%
5. Pipeline Transportation	–9.0%
6. Repair and Maintenance	5.1%
7. Specialty Trade Contractors	19.4%
8. Paper Manufacturing	–24.3%
9. Chemical Manufacturing	–6.7%
10. Utilities	–10.5%

10 Industries with the Highest Concentration of Installation Skills in Their Workforce

Industry	Growth Rate
1. Specialty Trade Contractors	19.4%
2. Real Estate	13.2%
3. Machinery Manufacturing	–7.6%
4. Mining (Except Oil and Gas)	–0.9%
5. Transportation Equipment Manufacturing	–10.5%
6. Primary Metal Manufacturing	–9.9%
7. Fabricated Metal Product Manufacturing	–8.5%
8. Repair and Maintenance	5.1%
9. Pipeline Transportation	–9.0%
10. Petroleum and Coal Products Manufacturing	–22.5%

10 Industries with the Highest Concentration of Management Skills in Their Workforce

Industry	Growth Rate
1. Religious, Grantmaking, Civic, Professional, and Similar Organizations	12.8%
2. Management of Companies and Enterprises	5.4%
3. Construction of Buildings	19.8%
4. Lessors of Nonfinancial Intangible Assets (Except Copyrighted Works)	34.4%
5. Securities, Commodity Contracts, and Other Financial Investments and Related Activities	11.8%
6. Museums, Historical Sites, and Similar Institutions	21.9%
7. Professional, Scientific, and Technical Services	33.9%
8. Oil and Gas Extraction	−16.0%
9. Chemical Manufacturing	−6.7%
10. Computer and Electronic Product Manufacturing	−19.3%

10 Industries with the Highest Concentration of Mathematics Skills in Their Workforce

Industry	Growth Rate
1. Professional, Scientific, and Technical Services	33.9%
2. Oil and Gas Extraction	−16.0%
3. Chemical Manufacturing	−6.7%
4. Construction of Buildings	19.8%
5. Computer and Electronic Product Manufacturing	−19.3%
6. Utilities	−10.5%
7. Monetary Authorities-Central Bank	3.6%
8. Federal Government	3.4%
9. Management of Companies and Enterprises	5.4%
10. Petroleum and Coal Products Manufacturing	−22.5%

10 Industries with the Highest Concentration of Science Skills in Their Workforce

Industry	Growth Rate
1. Ambulatory Health Care Services	35.6%
2. Chemical Manufacturing	−6.7%
3. Hospitals, Public and Private	10.1%
4. Oil and Gas Extraction	−16.0%
5. Petroleum and Coal Products Manufacturing	−22.5%
6. Federal Government	3.4%
7. Professional, Scientific, and Technical Services	33.9%
8. Computer and Electronic Product Manufacturing	−19.3%
9. Machinery Manufacturing	−7.6%
10. Utilities	−10.5%

10 Industries with the Highest Concentration of Social Skills in Their Workforce

Industry	Growth Rate
1. Clothing and Clothing Accessories Stores	3.7%
2. Sporting Goods, Hobby, Book, and Music Stores	5.0%
3. Furniture and Home Furnishings Stores	5.1%
4. Electronics and Appliance Stores	3.5%
5. Hospitals, Public and Private	10.1%
6. Miscellaneous Store Retailers	−1.1%
7. Building Material and Garden Equipment and Supplies Dealers	5.6%
8. Insurance Carriers and Related Activities	2.9%
9. Religious, Grantmaking, Civic, Professional, and Similar Organizations	12.8%
10. Management of Companies and Enterprises	5.4%

10 Industries with the Highest Concentration of Technology/Programming Skills in Their Workforce

Industry	Growth Rate
1. Data Processing, Hosting, and Related Services	52.7%
2. Professional, Scientific, and Technical Services	33.9%
3. Computer and Electronic Product Manufacturing	−19.3%
4. Monetary Authorities-Central Bank	3.6%
5. Telecommunications	−8.8%
6. Other Information Services	30.8%
7. Publishing Industries (Except Internet)	−4.6%
8. Management of Companies and Enterprises	5.4%
9. Machinery Manufacturing	−7.6%
10. Chemical Manufacturing	−6.7%

10 Industries with the Highest Concentration of Thought-Processing Skills in Their Workforce

Industry	Growth Rate
1. Securities, Commodity Contracts, and Other Financial Investments and Related Activities	11.8%
2. Hospitals, Public and Private	10.1%
3. Professional, Scientific, and Technical Services	33.9%
4. Management of Companies and Enterprises	5.4%
5. Monetary Authorities-Central Bank	3.6%
6. Religious, Grantmaking, Civic, Professional, and Similar Organizations	12.8%
7. Funds, Trusts, and Other Financial Vehicles	17.3%
8. Computer and Electronic Product Manufacturing	−19.3%
9. Data Processing, Hosting, and Related Services	52.7%
10. Oil and Gas Extraction	−16.0%

Metropolitan Areas Where the Skills Are Concentrated

Different communities are home to different industries, which in turn have differing needs for work skills. I thought you would be interested in seeing which metropolitan areas of the United States most need your top skills.

To compile the following set of lists, I used essentially the same methodology as for the previous set, using metro areas instead of industries. That is, for each skill, I identified the occupations in the top two zones of ability and computed the total number of those highly skilled workers in 300 metropolitan areas. Then I divided that figure by the figure for the total workforce in each metro area, thus determining the percentage of highly skilled workers in each area. For each skill, I sorted the 300 metro areas by decreasing percentage of highly skilled workers and listed the top 20 metro areas. I was unable to obtain growth projections for each metro area, so the lists feature the percentage of highly skilled workers instead.

For example, Mathematics Skills are most highly concentrated in Huntsville, Alabama, a hub for aerospace, defense, technology research, and biosciences. In first place for Science Skills is Rochester, Minnesota, home of the Mayo Clinic and a campus of IBM. If some metro areas on these lists are unfamiliar to you or you don't understand their connection to the skill, it's likely that you need to learn more about the industries in those communities. If the skill is one of your strengths, maybe you should consider relocating to its skill hotspot.

On the other hand, by relocating you'll run up expenses, strain communication with your friends and relatives, and need to construct a local job-finding network. You should remember that the skills covered by this book are highly transferable and therefore are needed to some extent in every community, including those that lie outside metropolitan areas. If you like your present location, be sure you exhaust local employment possibilities for your skills before you put down a deposit on a U-Haul truck.

20 Metro Areas with the Highest Concentration of Communication Skills in Their Workforce

Metro Area	Percentage of Workers with Very High Skills
1. Durham, NC	39.1%
2. Washington-Arlington-Alexandria, DC-VA-MD-WV	32.8%
3. Trenton-Ewing, NJ	32.1%
4. San Jose–Sunnyvale–Santa Clara, CA	31.4%
5. Boston-Cambridge-Quincy, MA-NH	31.4%

20 Metro Areas with the Highest Concentration of Communication Skills in Their Workforce

Metro Area	Percentage of Workers with Very High Skills
6. Hartford–West Hartford–East Hartford, CT	29.7%
7. Gainesville, FL	29.4%
8. Bridgeport-Stamford-Norwalk, CT	29.2%
9. San Francisco–Oakland–Fremont, CA	29.1%
10. Rochester, MN	28.7%
11. New Haven, CT	28.7%
12. Huntsville, AL	28.3%
13. Albany-Schenectady-Troy, NY	28.2%
14. Madison, WI	28.0%
15. New York–Northern New Jersey–Long Island, NY-NJ-PA	28.0%
16. Baltimore-Towson, MD	28.0%
17. Worcester, MA-CT	27.9%
18. Raleigh-Cary, NC	27.6%
19. Tallahassee, FL	27.6%
20. Denver-Aurora, CO	27.4%

20 Metro Areas with the Highest Concentration of Equipment Use/Maintenance Skills in Their Workforce

Metro Area	Percentage of Workers with Very High Skills
1. Houma–Bayou Cane–Thibodaux, LA	24.8%
2. Dalton, GA	24.1%
3. Joplin, MO	21.3%
4. Odessa, TX	21.0%
5. Elkhart-Goshen, IN	20.8%
6. Mobile, AL	20.1%
7. Longview, TX	20.0%
8. Evansville, IN-KY	19.7%
9. Kingsport–Bristol–Bristol, TN-VA	19.5%
10. Farmington, NM	19.3%
11. Green Bay, WI	19.2%
12. Beaumont–Port Arthur, TX	19.2%
13. Chattanooga, TN-GA	19.0%
14. Decatur, AL	19.0%

(continued)

20 Metro Areas with the Highest Concentration of Equipment Use/Maintenance Skills in Their Workforce

Metro Area	Percentage of Workers with Very High Skills
15. Fort Smith, AR-OK	18.9%
16. Lafayette, LA	18.7%
17. Oshkosh-Neenah, WI	18.5%
18. Hickory-Lenoir-Morganton, NC	18.5%
19. Cedar Rapids, IA	18.5%
20. Lake Charles, LA	18.4%

20 Metro Areas with the Highest Concentration of Installation Skills in Their Workforce

Metro Area	Percentage of Workers with Very High Skills
1. Anniston-Oxford, AL	6.2%
2. Odessa, TX	5.6%
3. Saginaw–Saginaw Township North, MI	5.2%
4. Lafayette, LA	4.9%
5. Texarkana-Texarkana, TX-AR	4.9%
6. Decatur, AL	4.9%
7. Houma–Bayou Cane–Thibodaux, LA	4.8%
8. Sandusky, OH	4.8%
9. Evansville, IN-KY	4.7%
10. Appleton, WI	4.6%
11. Victoria, TX	4.5%
12. Bremerton-Silverdale, WA	4.5%
13. Greenville-Mauldin-Easley, SC	4.4%
14. Warner Robins, GA	4.3%
15. Spartanburg, SC	4.3%
16. Lake Charles, LA	4.3%
17. Kingsport–Bristol–Bristol, TN-VA	4.2%
18. Palm Bay–Melbourne–Titusville, FL	4.2%
19. Rockford, IL	4.1%
20. Dalton, GA	4.1%

20 Metro Areas with the Highest Concentration of Management Skills in Their Workforce

Metro Area	Percentage of Workers with Very High Skills
1. Bridgeport-Stamford-Norwalk, CT	11.0%
2. Santa Fe, NM	10.6%
3. San Jose–Sunnyvale–Santa Clara, CA	10.3%
4. Washington-Arlington-Alexandria, DC-VA-MD-WV	9.9%
5. Hartford–West Hartford–East Hartford, CT	9.9%
6. San Francisco–Oakland–Fremont, CA	9.3%
7. Atlanta–Sandy Springs–Marietta, GA	9.2%
8. Charlotte-Gastonia-Concord, NC-SC	9.1%
9. Raleigh-Cary, NC	9.0%
10. Boston-Cambridge-Quincy, MA-NH	9.0%
11. Boise City–Nampa, ID	8.9%
12. Danbury, CT	8.8%
13. New Haven, CT	8.8%
14. Tulsa, OK	8.7%
15. Portland–South Portland–Biddeford, ME	8.7%
16. Huntsville, AL	8.7%
17. Nashville-Davidson–Murfreesboro, TN	8.7%
18. Kennewick-Pasco-Richland, WA	8.7%
19. Baltimore-Towson, MD	8.6%
20. Minneapolis–St. Paul–Bloomington, MN-WI	8.5%

20 Metro Areas with the Highest Concentration of Mathematics Skills in Their Workforce

Metro Area	Percentage of Workers with Very High Skills
1. Huntsville, AL	8.8%
2. San Jose–Sunnyvale–Santa Clara, CA	8.7%
3. Kennewick-Pasco-Richland, WA	8.1%
4. Boulder, CO	7.3%
5. Washington-Arlington-Alexandria, DC-VA-MD-WV	6.6%
6. Palm Bay–Melbourne–Titusville, FL	6.5%
7. Durham, NC	6.3%
8. Seattle-Tacoma-Bellevue, WA	6.2%
9. Trenton-Ewing, NJ	5.9%

(continued)

20 Metro Areas with the Highest Concentration of Mathematics Skills in Their Workforce

Metro Area	Percentage of Workers with Very High Skills
10. Warner Robins, GA	5.6%
11. Denver-Aurora, CO	5.5%
12. San Francisco–Oakland–Fremont, CA	5.5%
13. Olympia, WA	5.5%
14. Boston-Cambridge-Quincy, MA-NH	5.3%
15. Raleigh-Cary, NC	5.3%
16. San Diego–Carlsbad–San Marcos, CA	5.3%
17. College Station–Bryan, TX	5.2%
18. Crestview–Fort Walton Beach–Destin, FL	5.2%
19. Portsmouth, NH-ME	5.1%
20. Madison, WI	5.1%

20 Metro Areas with the Highest Concentration of Science Skills in Their Workforce

Metro Area	Percentage of Workers with Very High Skills
1. Rochester, MN	18.3%
2. Durham, NC	15.5%
3. Gainesville, FL	12.3%
4. Morgantown, WV	11.5%
5. Huntington-Ashland, WV-KY-OH	11.4%
6. Saginaw–Saginaw Township North, MI	10.5%
7. Johnstown, PA	10.4%
8. Florence, SC	10.3%
9. Winston-Salem, NC	10.2%
10. Johnson City, TN	9.8%
11. Worcester, MA-CT	9.8%
12. Lima, OH	9.7%
13. Columbia, MO	9.7%
14. Rome, GA	9.6%
15. Boston-Cambridge-Quincy, MA-NH	9.6%
16. New Haven, CT	9.5%
17. Palm Bay–Melbourne–Titusville, FL	9.4%
18. Sioux Falls, SD	9.4%

20 Metro Areas with the Highest Concentration of Science Skills in Their Workforce

Metro Area	Percentage of Workers with Very High Skills
19. Asheville, NC	9.4%
20. Alexandria, LA	9.3%

20 Metro Areas with the Highest Concentration of Social Skills in Their Workforce

Metro Area	Percentage of Workers with Very High Skills
1. Durham, NC	57.6%
2. Rochester, MN	55.1%
3. Jackson, MS	48.9%
4. Washington-Arlington-Alexandria, DC-VA-MD-WV	48.8%
5. Trenton-Ewing, NJ	48.7%
6. Gainesville, FL	48.2%
7. Worcester, MA-CT	48.0%
8. Boston-Cambridge-Quincy, MA-NH	47.6%
9. Hartford–West Hartford–East Hartford, CT	47.4%
10. New Haven, CT	47.4%
11. Winston-Salem, NC	47.0%
12. Baltimore-Towson, MD	46.6%
13. Huntington-Ashland, WV-KY-OH	46.0%
14. Charlotte-Gastonia-Concord, NC-SC	46.0%
15. Columbia, SC	45.9%
16. Bridgeport-Stamford-Norwalk, CT	45.8%
17. Richmond, VA	45.7%
18. Little Rock–North Little Rock–Conway, AR	45.6%
19. Raleigh-Cary, NC	45.4%
20. Florence, SC	45.2%

20 Metro Areas with the Highest Concentration of Technology/Programming Skills in Their Workforce

Metro Area	Percentage of Workers with Very High Skills
1. San Jose–Sunnyvale–Santa Clara, CA	12.2%
2. Washington-Arlington-Alexandria, DC-VA-MD-WV	8.2%
3. Huntsville, AL	7.8%
4. Boulder, CO	7.5%
5. Seattle-Tacoma-Bellevue, WA	6.8%
6. Austin–Round Rock, TX	6.2%
7. Durham, NC	6.0%
8. Palm Bay–Melbourne–Titusville, FL	5.8%
9. Warner Robins, GA	5.8%
10. Trenton-Ewing, NJ	5.7%
11. Portsmouth, NH-ME	5.5%
12. Colorado Springs, CO	5.5%
13. Boston-Cambridge-Quincy, MA-NH	5.3%
14. San Francisco–Oakland–Fremont, CA	5.3%
15. Raleigh-Cary, NC	5.3%
16. Denver-Aurora, CO	5.1%
17. Crestview–Fort Walton Beach–Destin, FL	5.0%
18. Olympia, WA	4.9%
19. Kennewick-Pasco-Richland, WA	4.9%
20. Minneapolis–St. Paul–Bloomington, MN-WI	4.6%

20 Metro Areas with the Highest Concentration of Thought-Processing Skills in Their Workforce

Metro Area	Percentage of Workers with Very High Skills
1. Durham, NC	43.9%
2. San Jose–Sunnyvale–Santa Clara, CA	39.8%
3. Washington-Arlington-Alexandria, DC-VA-MD-WV	39.6%
4. Rochester, MN	36.1%
5. Trenton-Ewing, NJ	35.4%
6. Boston-Cambridge-Quincy, MA-NH	34.4%
7. Huntsville, AL	33.8%
8. Gainesville, FL	33.2%
9. San Francisco–Oakland–Fremont, CA	32.9%
10. Hartford–West Hartford–East Hartford, CT	31.8%
11. Baltimore-Towson, MD	31.6%
12. Bridgeport-Stamford-Norwalk, CT	31.4%
13. Boulder, CO	31.3%
14. Minneapolis–St. Paul–Bloomington, MN-WI	31.3%
15. Madison, WI	31.1%
16. Seattle-Tacoma-Bellevue, WA	30.8%
17. Worcester, MA-CT	30.8%
18. New Haven, CT	30.0%
19. Denver-Aurora, CO	29.9%
20. Raleigh-Cary, NC	29.9%

Part IV

Descriptions of the Best Jobs for Your Skills

This part provides descriptions for all the jobs included in the lists in Part III. The Introduction gives more details on how to use and interpret the job descriptions, but here is some basic information you need to know:

⊛ Job descriptions are arranged in alphabetical order by job title. This approach allows you to find a description quickly if you know its correct title from a list in Part III.

⊛ If you are using this section to browse for interesting job options, I suggest you begin with the Table of Contents. The job titles in Part IV are listed there.

⊛ Part III features many interesting lists that will help you identify job titles to explore in more detail. If you have not browsed the lists in Part III, consider spending some time there.

⊛ Many jobs in this part are linked to more-specialized job titles in the O*NET database. I include information about these O*NET jobs under the heading "Job Specialization."

Accountants and Auditors

- ❋ Annual Earnings: $61,690
- ❋ Earnings Growth Potential: Medium (36.9%)
- ❋ Growth: 21.6%
- ❋ Annual Job Openings: 49,750
- ❋ Self-Employed: 8.1%

Skills—Most Important: Mathematics Skills; Thought-Processing Skills; Communication Skills. **Other High-Level Skills:** Management Skills; Social Skills.

Job Specialization: Accountants

Analyze financial information and prepare financial reports to determine or maintain record of assets, liabilities, profit and loss, tax liability, or other financial activities within an organization. Prepare, examine, or analyze accounting records, financial statements, or other financial reports to assess accuracy, completeness, and conformance to reporting and procedural standards. Report to management on the finances of establishment. Establish tables of accounts and assign entries to proper accounts. Develop, implement, modify, and document recordkeeping and accounting systems, making use of current computer technology. Compute taxes owed and prepare tax returns, ensuring compliance with payment, reporting, or other tax requirements. Maintain or examine the records of government agencies. Advise clients in areas such as compensation, employee health-care benefits, the design of accounting or data processing systems, or long-range tax or estate plans. Develop, maintain, and analyze budgets, preparing periodic reports that compare budgeted costs to actual costs. Provide internal and external auditing services for businesses or individuals. Analyze business operations, trends, costs, revenues, financial commitments, and obligations to project future revenues and expenses or to provide advice. Advise management about issues such as resource utilization, tax strategies, and the assumptions underlying budget forecasts. Represent clients before taxing authorities and provide support during litigation involving financial issues. Prepare forms and manuals for accounting and bookkeeping personnel and direct their work activities.

Education/Training Required: Bachelor's degree. **Education and Training Programs:** Accounting; Accounting and Business/Management; Accounting and Computer Science; Accounting and Finance; Auditing; Taxation. **Knowledge/Courses:** Economics and Accounting; Clerical Practices; Mathematics; Computers and Electronics; Personnel and Human Resources; Administration and Management.

Personality Type: Conventional-Enterprising. **Career Cluster:** 04 Business, Management, and Administration. **Career Pathway:** 04.2 Business, Financial Management, and Accounting. **Other Jobs in This Pathway:** Auditors; Billing and Posting Clerks; Billing, Cost, and Rate Clerks; Bookkeeping, Accounting, and Auditing Clerks; Brokerage Clerks; Brownfield Redevelopment Specialists and Site Managers; Budget Analysts; Compliance Managers; Credit Analysts; Financial Analysts; Financial Managers, Branch or Department; Investment Fund Managers; Logistics Managers; Loss Prevention Managers; Managers, All Other; Natural Sciences Managers; Payroll and Timekeeping Clerks; Regulatory Affairs Managers; Security Managers; Statement Clerks; Supply Chain Managers; Tax Preparers; Treasurers and

Controllers; Wind Energy Operations Managers; Wind Energy Project Managers; others.

Job Specialization: Auditors

Examine and analyze accounting records to determine financial status of establishment and prepare financial reports concerning operating procedures. Collect and analyze data to detect deficient controls, duplicated effort, extravagance, fraud, or noncompliance with laws, regulations, and management policies. Report to management about asset utilization and audit results. Recommend changes in operations and financial activities. Prepare detailed reports on audit findings. Examine and evaluate financial and information systems, recommending controls to ensure system reliability and data integrity. Review data about material assets, net worth, liabilities, capital stock, surplus, income, and expenditures. Inspect account books and accounting systems for efficiency, effectiveness, and use of accepted accounting procedures to record transactions. Supervise auditing of establishments and determine scope of investigation required. Prepare, analyze, and verify annual reports, financial statements, and other records, using accepted accounting and statistical procedures to assess financial condition and facilitate financial planning. Confer with company officials about financial and regulatory matters. Inspect cash on hand, notes receivable and payable, negotiable securities, and canceled checks to confirm records are accurate. Examine inventory to verify journal and ledger entries. Examine whether the organization's objectives are reflected in its management activities and whether employees understand the objectives.

Education/Training Required: Bachelor's degree. **Education and Training Programs:** Accounting; Accounting and Business/Management; Accounting and Computer Science; Accounting and Finance; Auditing; Taxation. **Knowledge/Courses:** Economics and Accounting; Administration and Management; Personnel and Human Resources; Law and Government; Computers and Electronics; Mathematics.

Personality Type: Conventional-Enterprising-Investigative. **Career Cluster:** 04 Business, Management, and Administration. **Career Pathway:** 04.2 Business, Financial Management, and Accounting. **Other Jobs in This Pathway:** Accountants; Billing and Posting Clerks; Billing, Cost, and Rate Clerks; Bookkeeping, Accounting, and Auditing Clerks; Brokerage Clerks; Brownfield Redevelopment Specialists and Site Managers; Budget Analysts; Compliance Managers; Credit Analysts; Financial Analysts; Financial Managers, Branch or Department; Investment Fund Managers; Logistics Managers; Loss Prevention Managers; Managers, All Other; Natural Sciences Managers; Payroll and Timekeeping Clerks; Regulatory Affairs Managers; Security Managers; Statement Clerks; Supply Chain Managers; Tax Preparers; Treasurers and Controllers; Wind Energy Operations Managers; Wind Energy Project Managers; others.

Actuaries

* Annual Earnings: $87,650
* Earnings Growth Potential: Medium (39.4%)
* Growth: 21.3%
* Annual Job Openings: 1,000
* Self-Employed: 0.0%

Skills—Most Important: Mathematics Skills; Thought-Processing Skills; Technology/Programming Skills. **Other High-Level Skills:** Management Skills; Communication Skills; Social Skills.

Analyze statistical data, such as mortality, accident, sickness, disability, and retirement rates and construct probability tables to forecast risk and liability for payment of future benefits. May ascertain premium rates required and cash reserves necessary to ensure payment of future benefits. Determine or help determine company policy and explain complex technical matters to company executives, government officials, shareholders, policyholders, or the public. Design, review, and help administer insurance and annuity and pension plans, determining financial soundness and calculating premiums. Analyze statistical information to estimate mortality, accident, sickness, disability, and retirement rates. Provide advice to clients on a contract basis, working as a consultant. Collaborate with programmers, underwriters, accountants, claims experts, and senior management to help companies develop plans for new lines of business or improve existing business. Provide expertise to help financial institutions manage risks and maximize returns associated with investment products or credit offerings. Construct probability tables for events such as fires, natural disasters, and unemployment based on analysis of statistical data and other pertinent information. Determine equitable basis for distributing surplus earnings under participating insurance and annuity contracts in mutual companies. Testify before public agencies on proposed legislation affecting businesses. Determine policy contract provisions for each type of insurance.

Education/Training Required: Work experience plus degree. **Education and Training Program:** Actuarial Science. **Knowledge/Courses:** Economics and Accounting; Mathematics; Computers and Electronics; Administration and Management; Personnel and Human Resources; Sales and Marketing.

Personality Type: Conventional-Investigative-Enterprising. **Career Cluster:** 06 Finance. **Career Pathway:** 06.4 Insurance Services. **Other Jobs in This Pathway:** Claims Examiners, Property and Casualty Insurance; Insurance Adjusters, Examiners, and Investigators; Insurance Appraisers, Auto Damage; Insurance Sales Agents; Insurance Underwriters; Telemarketers.

Administrative Services Managers

* Annual Earnings: $77,890
* Earnings Growth Potential: High (46.8%)
* Growth: 12.5%
* Annual Job Openings: 8,660
* Self-Employed: 0.2%

Skills—Most Important: Management Skills; Social Skills; Communication Skills. **Other High-Level Skills:** Thought-Processing Skills.

Plan, direct, or coordinate an organization's supportive services, such as recordkeeping, mail distribution, telephone operator/receptionist, and other office support services. May oversee facilities planning and maintenance and custodial operations. Prepare and review operational reports and schedules to ensure accuracy and efficiency. Set goals and deadlines for the department. Acquire, distribute, and store supplies. Analyze internal processes and recommend and implement procedural or policy changes to improve operations, such as supply changes or the disposal of records. Plan, administer, and control budgets for contracts, equipment, and supplies. Monitor the facility to ensure that it remains safe, secure, and well-maintained. Hire and terminate clerical and administrative personnel. Oversee the maintenance and repair of machinery, equipment, and electrical and mechanical systems.

Education/Training Required: Work experience plus degree. **Education and Training Programs:** Business Administration and Management, General; Business/Commerce, General; Medical Staff Services Technology/Technician; Medical/Health Management and Clinical Assistant/Specialist Training; Public Administration; Purchasing, Procurement/Acquisitions, and Contracts Management; Transportation/Mobility Management. **Knowledge/Courses:** Clerical Practices; Economics and Accounting; Personnel and Human Resources; Customer and Personal Service; Sales and Marketing; Administration and Management.

Personality Type: Enterprising-Conventional. **Career Clusters:** 04 Business, Management, and Administration; 07 Government and Public Administration. **Career Pathways:** 04.1

Management; 07.1 Governance. **Other Jobs in These Pathways:** Brownfield Redevelopment Specialists and Site Managers; Business Continuity Planners; Business Operations Specialists, All Other; Chief Executives; Chief Sustainability Officers; Compliance Managers; Computer and Information Systems Managers; Construction Managers; Customs Brokers; Energy Auditors; First-Line Supervisors of Office and Administrative Support Workers; General and Operations Managers; Investment Fund Managers; Loss Prevention Managers; Management Analysts; Managers, All Other; Public Relations Specialists; Regulatory Affairs Managers; Sales Managers; Security Management Specialists; Security Managers; Supply Chain Managers; Sustainability Specialists; Wind Energy Operations Managers; Wind Energy Project Managers; others.

Aerospace Engineers

* Annual Earnings: $97,480
* Earnings Growth Potential: Medium (37.8%)
* Growth: 10.4%
* Annual Job Openings: 2,230
* Self-Employed: 3.3%

Skills—Most Important: Science Skills; Mathematics Skills; Technology/Programming Skills. **Other High-Level Skills:** Thought-Processing Skills; Communication Skills; Social Skills; Equipment Use/Maintenance Skills; Management Skills.

Perform a variety of engineering work in designing, constructing, and testing aircraft, missiles, and spacecraft. May conduct basic and applied research to evaluate adaptability of materials and equipment to aircraft

design and manufacture. May recommend improvements in testing equipment and techniques. Direct and coordinate activities of engineering or technical personnel designing, fabricating, modifying, or testing aircraft or aerospace products. Formulate conceptual design of aeronautical or aerospace products or systems to meet customer requirements. Plan and coordinate activities concerned with investigating and resolving customers' reports of technical problems with aircraft or aerospace vehicles. Plan and conduct experimental, environmental, operational, and stress tests on models and prototypes of aircraft and aerospace systems and equipment. Analyze project requests and proposals and engineering data to determine feasibility, productibility, cost, and production time of aerospace or aeronautical product. Evaluate product data and design from inspections and reports for conformance to engineering principles, customer requirements, and quality standards. Maintain records of performance reports for future reference. Write technical reports and other documentation for use by engineering staff, management, and customers. Develop design criteria for aeronautical or aerospace products or systems, including testing methods, production costs, quality standards, and completion dates. Review performance reports and documentation from customers and field engineers and inspect malfunctioning or damaged products to determine problem.

Education/Training Required: Bachelor's degree. **Education and Training Program:** Aerospace, Aeronautical, and Astronautical/Space Engineering. **Knowledge/Courses:** Engineering and Technology; Physics; Design; Mechanical Devices; Mathematics; Production and Processing.

Personality Type: Investigative-Realistic. **Career Cluster:** 15 Science, Technology, Engineering, and Mathematics. **Career Pathway:** 15.1 Engineering and Technology. **Other Jobs in This Pathway:** Architectural and Engineering Managers; Automotive Engineers; Biochemical Engineers; Biofuels/Biodiesel Technology and Product Development Managers; Civil Engineers; Cost Estimators; Electrical Engineers; Electronics Engineers, Except Computer; Energy Engineers; Engineers, All Other; Fuel Cell Engineers; Human Factors Engineers and Ergonomists; Industrial Engineers; Manufacturing Engineers; Mechanical Engineers; Mechatronics Engineers; Microsystems Engineers; Nanosystems Engineers; Photonics Engineers; Radio Frequency Identification Device Specialists; Robotics Engineers; Solar Energy Systems Engineers; Transportation Engineers; Validation Engineers; Wind Energy Engineers; others.

Agents and Business Managers of Artists, Performers, and Athletes

* Annual Earnings: $63,130
* Earnings Growth Potential: Very high (59.7%)
* Growth: 22.4%
* Annual Job Openings: 1,010
* Self-Employed: 45.8%

Skills—Most Important: Social Skills; Management Skills; Communication Skills. **Other High-Level Skills:** Thought-Processing Skills.

Represent and promote artists, performers, and athletes to prospective employers. May handle contract negotiation and

other business matters for clients. Manage business and financial affairs for clients, such as arranging travel and lodging, selling tickets, and directing marketing and advertising activities. Obtain information about and/or inspect performance facilities, equipment, and accommodations to ensure that they meet specifications. Negotiate with managers, promoters, union officials, and other persons on clients' contractual rights and obligations. Advise clients on financial and legal matters, such as investments and taxes. Hire trainers or coaches to advise clients on performance matters, such as training techniques or performance presentations. Prepare periodic accounting statements for clients. Keep informed of industry trends and deals. Develop contacts with individuals and organizations and apply effective strategies and techniques to ensure their clients' success. Confer with clients to develop strategies for their careers and to explain actions taken on their behalf. Conduct auditions or interviews to evaluate potential clients. Schedule promotional or performance engagements for clients. Arrange meetings concerning issues involving their clients. Collect fees, commissions, or other payments according to contract terms.

Education/Training Required: Work experience plus degree. **Education and Training Program:** Purchasing, Procurement/Acquisitions, and Contracts Management. **Knowledge/Courses:** Fine Arts; Sales and Marketing; Communications and Media; Clerical Practices; Customer and Personal Service; Economics and Accounting.

Personality Type: Enterprising-Social. **Career Clusters:** 03 Arts, Audio/Video Technology, and Communications; 04 Business, Management, and Administration. **Career Pathways:** 03.1 Audio and Video Technology

and Film; 04.1 Management. **Other Jobs in These Pathways:** Brownfield Redevelopment Specialists and Site Managers; Business Continuity Planners; Business Operations Specialists, All Other; Chief Executives; Chief Sustainability Officers; Compliance Managers; Computer and Information Systems Managers; Construction Managers; Customs Brokers; Energy Auditors; First-Line Supervisors of Office and Administrative Support Workers; General and Operations Managers; Graphic Designers; Investment Fund Managers; Loss Prevention Managers; Management Analysts; Managers, All Other; Regulatory Affairs Managers; Sales Managers; Security Management Specialists; Security Managers; Supply Chain Managers; Sustainability Specialists; Wind Energy Operations Managers; Wind Energy Project Managers; others.

Air Traffic Controllers

- ✳ Annual Earnings: $108,040
- ✳ Earnings Growth Potential: High (49.6%)
- ✳ Growth: 13.1%
- ✳ Annual Job Openings: 1,230
- ✳ Self-Employed: 0.0%

Skills—Most Important: Thought-Processing Skills; Mathematics Skills; Social Skills. **Other High-Level Skills:** Communication Skills; Equipment Use/Maintenance Skills; Management Skills.

Control air traffic at and within vicinity of airport and movement of air traffic between altitude sectors and control centers according to established procedures and policies. Authorize, regulate, and control commercial airline flights according to government or

company regulations to expedite flights and ensure flight safety. Issue landing and takeoff authorizations and instructions. Monitor and direct the movement of aircraft within an assigned air space and on the ground at airports to minimize delays and maximize safety. Monitor aircraft within a specific airspace using radar, computer equipment, and visual references. Inform pilots about nearby planes as well as potentially hazardous conditions such as weather, speed and direction of wind, and visibility problems. Provide flight path changes or directions to emergency landing fields for pilots traveling in bad weather or in emergency situations. Alert airport emergency services in cases of emergency and when aircrafts are experiencing difficulties. Direct pilots to runways when space is available or direct them to maintain a traffic pattern until there is space to land. Transfer control of departing flights to traffic control centers and accept control of arriving flights. Direct ground traffic, including taxiing aircraft, maintenance and baggage vehicles, and airport workers. Determine the timing and procedures for flight vector changes. Maintain radio and telephone contact with adjacent control towers, terminal control units, and other area control centers to coordinate aircraft movement. Contact pilots by radio to provide meteorological, navigational, and other information.

Education/Training Required: Long-term on-the-job training. **Education and Training Program:** Air Traffic Controller Training. **Knowledge/Courses:** Transportation; Geography; Telecommunications; Public Safety and Security; Physics; Education and Training.

Personality Type: Enterprising-Conventional. **Career Cluster:** 16 Transportation, Distribution, and Logistics. **Career Pathway:** 16.1

Transportation Operations. **Other Jobs in This Pathway:** Airline Pilots, Copilots, and Flight Engineers; Automotive and Watercraft Service Attendants; Automotive Master Mechanics; Bus Drivers, School or Special Client; Bus Drivers, Transit and Intercity; Commercial Pilots; Crane and Tower Operators; First-Line Supervisors of Helpers, Laborers, and Material Movers, Hand; First-Line Supervisors of Transportation and Material-Moving Machine and Vehicle Operators; Freight and Cargo Inspectors; Heavy and Tractor-Trailer Truck Drivers; Laborers and Freight, Stock, and Material Movers, Hand; Light Truck or Delivery Services Drivers; Mates—Ship, Boat, and Barge; Motor Vehicle Operators, All Other; Operating Engineers and Other Construction Equipment Operators; Parking Lot Attendants; Pilots, Ship; Railroad Conductors and Yardmasters; Sailors and Marine Oilers; Ship and Boat Captains; Storage and Distribution Managers; Taxi Drivers and Chauffeurs; Transportation Managers; Transportation Workers, All Other; others.

Aircraft Structure, Surfaces, Rigging, and Systems Assemblers

* Annual Earnings: $44,820
* Earnings Growth Potential: Medium (39.8%)
* Growth: 9.3%
* Annual Job Openings: 1,340
* Self-Employed: 0.0%

Skills—Most Important: Installation Skills; Equipment Use/Maintenance Skills; Mathematics Skills. **Other High-Level Skills:** Thought-Processing Skills; Social Skills.

Assemble, fit, fasten, and install parts of airplanes, space vehicles, or missiles, such as

tails, wings, fuselage, bulkheads, stabilizers, landing gear, rigging and control equipment, or heating and ventilating systems. Form loops or splices in cables using clamps and fittings or reweave cable strands. Align and fit structural assemblies manually or signal crane operators to position assemblies for joining. Align, fit, assemble, connect, and install system components using jigs, fixtures, measuring instruments, hand tools, and power tools. Assemble and fit prefabricated parts to form subassemblies. Assemble, install, and connect parts, fittings, and assemblies on aircraft using layout tools, hand tools, power tools, and fasteners such as bolts, screws, rivets, and clamps. Attach brackets, hinges, or clips to secure or support components and subassemblies using bolts, screws, rivets, chemical bonding, or welding. Select and install accessories in swaging machines using hand tools. Fit and fasten sheet metal coverings to surface areas and other sections of aircraft prior to welding or riveting. Lay out and mark reference points and locations for installation of parts and components using jigs, templates, and measuring and marking instruments. Inspect and test installed units, parts, systems, and assemblies for fit, alignment, performance, defects, and compliance with standards using measuring instruments and test equipment. Install mechanical linkages and actuators and verify tension of cables using tensiometers. Join structural assemblies such as wings, tails, and fuselage. Measure and cut cables and tubing using master templates, measuring instruments, and cable cutters or saws.

Education/Training Required: Moderate-term on-the-job training. **Education and Training Programs:** Aircraft Powerplant Technology/Technician; Airframe Mechanics and Aircraft Maintenance Technology/Technician; Avionics Maintenance Technology/Technician.

Knowledge/Courses: Mechanical Devices; Design; Chemistry; Public Safety and Security.

Personality Type: Realistic-Conventional. **Career Cluster:** 16 Transportation, Distribution, and Logistics. **Career Pathway:** 16.4 Facility and Mobile Equipment Maintenance. **Other Jobs in This Pathway:** Aircraft Mechanics and Service Technicians; Automotive Body and Related Repairers; Automotive Glass Installers and Repairers; Automotive Master Mechanics; Automotive Specialty Technicians; Bicycle Repairers; Bus and Truck Mechanics and Diesel Engine Specialists; Cleaners of Vehicles and Equipment; Electrical and Electronics Installers and Repairers, Transportation Equipment; Electronic Equipment Installers and Repairers, Motor Vehicles; Engine and Other Machine Assemblers; Gem and Diamond Workers; Installation, Maintenance, and Repair Workers, All Other; Motorboat Mechanics and Service Technicians; Motorcycle Mechanics; Outdoor Power Equipment and Other Small Engine Mechanics; Painters, Transportation Equipment.

Airline Pilots, Copilots, and Flight Engineers

* Annual Earnings: $103,210
* Earnings Growth Potential: High (46.7%)
* Growth: 8.4%
* Annual Job Openings: 3,250
* Self-Employed: 0.0%

Skills—Most Important: Science Skills; Equipment Use/Maintenance Skills; Mathematics Skills. **Other High-Level Skills:** Thought-Processing Skills; Communication Skills; Management Skills; Social Skills.

Pilot and navigate the flight of multi-engine aircraft in regularly scheduled service for the transport of passengers and cargo. Requires Federal Air Transport rating and certification in specific aircraft type used. Use instrumentation to guide flights when visibility is poor. Respond to and report in-flight emergencies and malfunctions. Work as part of a flight team with other crew members, especially during takeoffs and landings. Contact control towers for takeoff clearances, arrival instructions, and other information using radio equipment. Steer aircraft along planned routes with the assistance of autopilot and flight management computers. Monitor gauges, warning devices, and control panels to verify aircraft performance and to regulate engine speed. Start engines, operate controls, and pilot airplanes to transport passengers, mail, or freight while adhering to flight plans, regulations, and procedures. Inspect aircraft for defects and malfunctions according to pre-flight checklists. Check passenger and cargo distributions and fuel amounts to ensure that weight and balance specifications are met. Monitor engine operation, fuel consumption, and functioning of aircraft systems during flights. Confer with flight dispatchers and weather forecasters to keep abreast of flight conditions. Coordinate flight activities with ground crews and air-traffic control and inform crew members of flight and test procedures. Order changes in fuel supplies, loads, routes, or schedules to ensure safety of flights. Choose routes, altitudes, and speeds that will provide the fastest, safest, and smoothest flights. Direct activities of aircraft crews during flights.

Education/Training Required: Bachelor's degree. **Education and Training Programs:** Airline/Commercial/Professional Pilot and Flight Crew Training; Flight Instructor Training. **Knowledge/Courses:** Transportation; Geography; Physics; Public Safety and Security; Psychology; Mechanical.

Personality Type: Realistic-Conventional-Investigative. **Career Cluster:** 16 Transportation, Distribution, and Logistics. **Career Pathway:** 16.1 Transportation Operations. **Other Jobs in This Pathway:** Automotive and Watercraft Service Attendants; Automotive Master Mechanics; Bus Drivers, School or Special Client; Bus Drivers, Transit and Intercity; Commercial Pilots; Crane and Tower Operators; First-Line Supervisors of Helpers, Laborers, and Material Movers, Hand; First-Line Supervisors of Transportation and Material-Moving Machine and Vehicle Operators; Freight and Cargo Inspectors; Heavy and Tractor-Trailer Truck Drivers; Laborers and Freight, Stock, and Material Movers, Hand; Light Truck or Delivery Services Drivers; Mates—Ship, Boat, and Barge; Motor Vehicle Operators, All Other; Operating Engineers and Other Construction Equipment Operators; Parking Lot Attendants; Pilots, Ship; Railroad Conductors and Yardmasters; Sailors and Marine Oilers; Ship and Boat Captains; Storage and Distribution Managers; Taxi Drivers and Chauffeurs; Transportation Inspectors; Transportation Managers; Transportation Workers, All Other; others.

Architects, Except Landscape and Naval

❋ Annual Earnings: $72,550

❋ Earnings Growth Potential: Medium (40.9%)

❋ Growth: 16.2%

❋ Annual Job Openings: 4,680

❋ Self-Employed: 21.2%

Skills—Most Important: Mathematics Skills; Science Skills; Management Skills. **Other High-Level Skills:** Thought-Processing Skills; Communication Skills; Social Skills.

Plan and design structures such as private residences, office buildings, theaters, factories, and other structural property. Consult with client to determine functional and spatial requirements of structure. Prepare scale drawings. Plan layout of project. Prepare information on design, structure specifications, materials, color, equipment, estimated costs, or construction time. Prepare contract documents for building contractors. Integrate engineering element into unified design. Direct activities of workers engaged in preparing drawings and specification documents. Conduct periodic on-site observation of work during construction to monitor compliance with plans. Seek new work opportunities through marketing, writing proposals, or giving presentations. Administer construction contracts. Represent client in obtaining bids and awarding construction contracts. Prepare operating and maintenance manuals, studies, and reports.

Education/Training Required: Bachelor's degree. **Education and Training Programs:** Architectural History and Criticism, General; Architecture (BArch, BA/BS, MArch, MA/MS, PhD); Architecture and Related Services, Other; Environmental Design/Architecture. **Knowledge/Courses:** Design; Building and Construction; Engineering and Technology; Fine Arts; Sales and Marketing; Law and Government.

Personality Type: Artistic-Investigative. **Career Cluster:** 02 Architecture and Construction. **Career Pathway:** 02.1 Design/Pre-Construction. **Other Jobs in This Pathway:** Architectural and Engineering Managers; Architectural Drafters; Cartographers and Photogrammetrists; Civil Drafters; Civil Engineering Technicians; Drafters, All Other; Electrical Drafters; Electronic Drafters; Engineering Technicians, Except Drafters, All Other; Engineers, All Other; Geodetic Surveyors; Interior Designers; Landscape Architects; Mechanical Drafters; Surveying Technicians.

Architectural and Civil Drafters

❋ Annual Earnings: $46,430

❋ Earnings Growth Potential: Low (35.4%)

❋ Growth: 9.1%

❋ Annual Job Openings: 3,620

❋ Self-Employed: 2.9%

Skills—Most Important: Mathematics Skills; Thought-Processing Skills; Technology/Programming Skills. **Other High-Level Skills:** Management Skills; Communication Skills; Social Skills; Equipment Use/Maintenance Skills.

Job Specialization: Architectural Drafters

Prepare detailed drawings of architectural designs and plans for buildings and

structures according to specifications provided by architect. Analyze building codes, bylaws, space and site requirements, and other technical documents and reports to determine their effect on architectural designs. Operate computer-aided drafting (CAD) equipment or conventional drafting station to produce designs, working drawings, charts, forms, and records. Coordinate structural, electrical, and mechanical designs and determine a method of presentation to graphically represent building plans. Obtain and assemble data to complete architectural designs, visiting job sites to compile measurements as necessary. Draw rough and detailed scale plans for foundations, buildings, and structures based on preliminary concepts, sketches, engineering calculations, specification sheets, and other data. Lay out and plan interior room arrangements for commercial buildings using CAD equipment and software. Supervise, coordinate, and inspect the work of draftspersons, technicians, and technologists on construction projects.

Education/Training Required: Postsecondary vocational training. **Education and Training Programs:** Architectural Drafting and Architectural CAD/CADD; Architectural Technology/Technician; CAD/CADD Drafting and/or Design Technology/Technician; Civil Drafting and Civil Engineering CAD/CADD; Drafting and Design Technology/Technician, General. **Knowledge/Courses:** Design; Building and Construction; Engineering and Technology; Fine Arts; Computers and Electronics; Law and Government.

Personality Type: Artistic-Realistic-Investigative. **Career Cluster:** 02 Architecture and Construction. **Career Pathway:** 02.1 Design/Pre-Construction. **Other Jobs in This Pathway:** Architects, Except Landscape and

Naval; Architectural and Engineering Managers; Cartographers and Photogrammetrists; Civil Drafters; Civil Engineering Technicians; Drafters, All Other; Electrical Drafters; Electronic Drafters; Engineering Technicians, Except Drafters, All Other; Engineers, All Other; Geodetic Surveyors; Interior Designers; Landscape Architects; Mechanical Drafters; Surveying Technicians.

Job Specialization: Civil Drafters

Prepare drawings and topographical and relief maps used in civil engineering projects such as highways, bridges, pipelines, flood control projects, and water and sewerage control systems. Produce drawings using computer-assisted drafting systems (CAD) or drafting machines or by hand using compasses, dividers, protractors, triangles, and other drafting devices. Draft plans and detailed drawings for structures, installations, and construction projects such as highways, sewage disposal systems, and dikes, working from sketches or notes. Draw maps, diagrams, and profiles, using cross-sections and surveys, to represent elevations, topographical contours, subsurface formations, and structures. Correlate, interpret, and modify data obtained from topographical surveys, well logs, and geophysical prospecting reports. Finish and duplicate drawings and documentation packages according to required mediums and specifications for reproduction using blueprinting, photography, or other duplicating methods. Review rough sketches, drawings, specifications, and other engineering data received from civil engineers to ensure that they conform to design concepts. Supervise and train other technologists, technicians, and drafters. Supervise or conduct field surveys, inspections, or technical investigations to obtain data required to revise construction drawings. Determine the order of work and method of presentation, such as orthographic or isometric drawing. Calculate excavation tonnage and prepare graphs and fill-hauling diagrams for use in earth-moving operations. Explain drawings to production or construction teams and provide adjustments as necessary.

Education/Training Required: Postsecondary vocational training. **Education and Training Programs:** Architectural Drafting and Architectural CAD/CADD; Architectural Technology/Technician; CAD/CADD Drafting and/or Design Technology/Technician; Civil Drafting and Civil Engineering CAD/CADD; Drafting and Design Technology/Technician, General. **Knowledge/Courses:** Design; Engineering and Technology; Building and Construction; Geography; Mathematics; Physics.

Personality Type: Realistic-Conventional-Investigative. **Career Cluster:** 02 Architecture and Construction. **Career Pathway:** 02.1 Design/Pre-Construction. **Other Jobs in This Pathway:** Architects, Except Landscape and Naval; Architectural and Engineering Managers; Architectural Drafters; Cartographers and Photogrammetrists; Civil Engineering Technicians; Drafters, All Other; Electrical Drafters; Electronic Drafters; Engineering Technicians, Except Drafters, All Other; Engineers, All Other; Geodetic Surveyors; Interior Designers; Landscape Architects; Mechanical Drafters; Surveying Technicians.

Architectural and Engineering Managers

* Annual Earnings: $119,260
* Earnings Growth Potential: Low (35.1%)
* Growth: 6.2%
* Annual Job Openings: 4,870
* Self-Employed: 0.6%

Skills—Most Important: Science Skills; Mathematics Skills; Management Skills. **Other High-Level Skills:** Thought-Processing Skills; Communication Skills; Social Skills.

Plan, direct, or coordinate activities or research and development in such fields as architecture and engineering. Confer with management, production, and marketing staff to discuss project specifications and procedures. Coordinate and direct projects, making detailed plans to accomplish goals and directing the integration of technical activities. Analyze technology, resource needs, and market demand to plan and assess the feasibility of projects. Plan and direct the installation, testing, operation, maintenance, and repair of facilities and equipment. Direct, review, and approve product design and changes. Recruit employees; assign, direct, and evaluate their work; and oversee the development and maintenance of staff competence. Prepare budgets, bids, and contracts and direct the negotiation of research contracts. Develop and implement policies, standards, and procedures for the engineering and technical work performed in the department, service, laboratory, or firm. Review and recommend or approve contracts and cost estimates. Perform administrative functions such as reviewing and writing reports, approving expenditures, enforcing rules, and making decisions about the purchase of materials or services. Present and explain proposals, reports, and findings to clients. Consult or negotiate with clients to prepare project specifications. Set scientific and technical goals within broad outlines provided by top management. Administer highway planning, construction, and maintenance. Direct the engineering of water control, treatment, and distribution projects.

Education/Training Required: Work experience plus degree. **Education and Training Programs:** Aerospace, Aeronautical, and Astronautical/Space Engineering; Agricultural Engineering; Architectural Engineering; Architecture; Bioengineering and Biomedical Engineering; Ceramic Sciences and Engineering; Chemical Engineering; City/Urban, Community, and Regional Planning; Civil Engineering, General; Computer Engineering, General; Computer Hardware Engineering; Computer Software Engineering; Construction Engineering; Electrical and Electronics Engineering; Engineering Mechanics; Engineering Physics/Applied Physics; Engineering Science; Engineering, General; Environmental Design; Environmental Health Engineering; Forest Engineering; Geological Engineering; Geotechnical and Geoenvironmental Engineering; Industrial Engineering; Interior Architecture; Landscape Architecture; Manufacturing Engineering; Materials Engineering; Mechanical Engineering; Metallurgical Engineering; Mining and Mineral Engineering; Naval Architecture and Marine Engineering; Nuclear Engineering; Ocean Engineering; Petroleum Engineering; Polymer/Plastics Engineering; Structural Engineering; Surveying Engineering; Systems Engineering; Textile Sciences and Engineering; Transportation and Highway Engineering; Water Resources Engineering;

others. **Knowledge/Courses:** Engineering and Technology; Design; Physics; Building and Construction; Computers and Electronics; Mathematics.

Personality Type: Enterprising-Realistic-Investigative. **Career Clusters:** 02 Architecture and Construction; 11 Information Technology; 15 Science, Technology, Engineering, and Mathematics. **Career Pathways:** 11.4 Programming and Software Development; 15.1 Engineering and Technology; 15.2 Science and Mathematics; 02.1 Design/Pre-Construction. **Other Jobs in These Pathways:** Architects, Except Landscape and Naval; Automotive Engineers; Biochemical Engineers; Biofuels/Biodiesel Technology and Product Development Managers; Civil Engineers; Cost Estimators; Electrical Engineers; Electronics Engineers, Except Computer; Energy Engineers; Engineers, All Other; Fuel Cell Engineers; Human Factors Engineers and Ergonomists; Industrial Engineers; Manufacturing Engineers; Mechanical Engineers; Mechatronics Engineers; Microsystems Engineers; Nanosystems Engineers; Photonics Engineers; Radio Frequency Identification Device Specialists; Robotics Engineers; Solar Energy Systems Engineers; Transportation Engineers; Validation Engineers; Wind Energy Engineers; others.

Job Specialization: Biofuels/Biodiesel Technology and Product Development Managers

Define, plan, or execute biofuel/biodiesel research programs that evaluate alternative feedstock and process technologies with near-term commercial potential. Develop lab-scale models of industrial scale processes, such as fermentation. Develop computational tools or approaches to improve biofuels research and development activities. Develop carbohydrates arrays and associated methods for screening enzymes involved in biomass conversion. Provide technical or scientific guidance to technical staff in the conduct of biofuels research or development. Prepare or oversee the preparation of experimental plans for biofuels research or development. Prepare biofuels research and development reports for senior management or technical professionals. Perform protein functional analysis and engineering for processing of feedstock and creation of biofuels. Develop separation processes to recover biofuels. Develop methods to recover ethanol or other fuels from complex bioreactor liquid and gas streams. Develop methods to estimate the efficiency of biomass pretreatments. Design or execute solvent or product recovery experiments in laboratory or field settings. Design or conduct applied biodiesel or biofuels research projects on topics such as transport, thermodynamics, mixing, filtration, distillation, fermentation, extraction, and separation. Design chemical conversion processes, such as etherification, esterification, interesterification, transesterification, distillation, hydrogenation, oxidation or reduction of fats and oils, and vegetable oil refining. Conduct experiments on biomass or pretreatment technologies.

Education/Training Required: Work experience plus degree. **Education and Training Programs:** Agricultural Engineering; Bioengineering and Biomedical Engineering; Chemical Engineering; Engineering, Other; Manufacturing Engineering. **Knowledge/Courses:** No data available.

Personality Type: No data available. **Career Cluster:** 15 Science, Technology, Engineering, and Mathematics. **Career Pathways:** 15.1 Engineering and Technology; 15.2 Science and Mathematics. **Other Jobs in These Pathways:** Architectural and Engineering Managers; Automotive Engineers; Biochemical Engineers; Civil Engineers; Community and Social Service Specialists, All Other; Cost Estimators; Electrical Engineers; Electronics Engineers, Except Computer; Energy Engineers; Engineers, All Other; Fuel Cell Engineers; Human Factors Engineers and Ergonomists; Industrial Engineers; Manufacturing Engineers; Mechanical Engineers; Mechatronics Engineers; Microsystems Engineers; Nanosystems Engineers; Photonics Engineers; Radio Frequency Identification Device Specialists; Robotics Engineers; Solar Energy Systems Engineers; Transportation Engineers; Validation Engineers; Wind Energy Engineers; others.

Art Directors

- ✱ Annual Earnings: $80,630
- ✱ Earnings Growth Potential: High (46.9%)
- ✱ Growth: 11.7%
- ✱ Annual Job Openings: 2,870
- ✱ Self-Employed: 60.2%

Skills—Most Important: Management Skills; Thought-Processing Skills; Social Skills. **Other High-Level Skills:** Communication Skills.

Formulate design concepts and presentation approaches and direct workers engaged in artwork, layout design, and copywriting for visual communications media such as magazines, books, newspapers, and packaging. Formulate basic layout design or presentation approach and specify material details, such as style and size of type, photographs, graphics, animation, video, and sound. Review and approve proofs of printed copy and art and copy materials developed by staff members. Manage own accounts and projects, working within budget and scheduling requirements. Confer with creative, art, copywriting, or production department heads to discuss client requirements and presentation concepts and to coordinate creative activities. Present final layouts to clients for approval. Confer with clients to determine objectives, budget, background information, and presentation approaches, styles, and techniques. Hire, train, and direct staff members who develop design concepts into art layouts or who prepare layouts for printing. Work with creative directors to develop design solutions. Review illustrative material to determine if it conforms to standards and specifications. Attend photo shoots and printing sessions to ensure that the products needed are obtained. Create custom illustrations or other graphic elements. Mark up, paste, and complete layouts and write typography instructions to prepare materials for typesetting or printing. Negotiate with printers and estimators to determine what services will be performed. Conceptualize and help design interfaces for multimedia games, products, and devices.

Education/Training Required: Work experience plus degree. **Education and Training Programs:** Graphic Design; Intermedia/Multimedia. **Knowledge/Courses:** Fine Arts; Design; Communications and Media; Production and Processing; Computers and Electronics; Administration and Management.

Personality Type: Artistic-Enterprising. **Career Cluster:** 03 Arts, Audio/Video Technology, and Communications. **Career Pathway:** 03.3 Visual Arts. **Other Jobs in This Pathway:** Artists and Related Workers, All Other; Audio and Video Equipment Technicians; Commercial and Industrial Designers; Craft Artists; Designers, All Other; Fashion Designers; Fine Artists, Including Painters, Sculptors, and Illustrators; Graphic Designers; Interior Designers; Multimedia Artists and Animators; Painting, Coating, and Decorating Workers; Photographers; Set and Exhibit Designers.

Art, Drama, and Music Teachers, Postsecondary

* Annual Earnings: $62,040
* Earnings Growth Potential: High (46.5%)
* Growth: 15.1%
* Annual Job Openings: 2,500
* Self-Employed: 0.2%

Skills—Most Important: Communication Skills; Thought-Processing Skills; Social Skills. **Other High-Level Skills:** Management Skills.

Teach courses in drama, music, and the arts, including fine and applied art, such as painting and sculpture or design and crafts. Evaluate and grade students' classwork, performances, projects, assignments, and papers. Explain and demonstrate artistic techniques. Prepare students for performances, exams, or assessments. Prepare and deliver lectures to undergraduate or graduate students on topics such as acting techniques, fundamentals of music, and art history. Prepare course materials such as syllabi, homework assignments, and handouts. Initiate, facilitate, and moderate classroom discussions. Keep abreast of developments in the field by reading current literature, talking with colleagues, and participating in professional conferences. Advise students on academic and vocational curricula and on career issues. Maintain student attendance records, grades, and other required records. Plan, evaluate, and revise curricula, course content, course materials, and methods of instruction. Maintain regularly scheduled office hours to advise and assist students. Compile, administer, and grade examinations or assign this work to others. Participate in student recruitment, registration, and placement activities. Select and obtain materials and supplies such as textbooks and performance pieces. Collaborate with colleagues to address teaching and research issues. Serve on academic or administrative committees that deal with institutional policies, departmental matters, and academic issues.

Education/Training Required: Doctoral degree. **Education and Training Programs:** Art History, Criticism and Conservation; Art, General; Ceramic Arts and Ceramics; Cinematography and Film/Video Production; Commercial Photography; Conducting; Crafts/Craft Design, Folk Art, and Artisanry; Dance, General; Design and Visual Communications, General; Directing and Theatrical Production; Drama and Dramatics/Theatre Arts, General; Fashion/Apparel Design; Fiber, Textile, and Weaving Arts; Film/Cinema/Video Studies; Fine/Studio Arts, General; Graphic Design; Humanities/Humanistic Studies; Industrial and Product Design; Interior Design; Intermedia/Multimedia; Jazz/Jazz Studies; Keyboard Instruments; Metal and Jewelry Arts; Music History, Literature, and Theory; Music Pedagogy; Music Performance, General; Music Theory and Composition; Musicology and Ethnomusicology; Painting; Photography; Playwriting and Screenwriting; Printmaking; Sculpture; Stringed Instruments; Technical Theatre/Theatre Design and Technology; Theatre Literature, History and Criticism; Visual and Performing Arts, General; Voice and Opera; others. **Knowledge/Courses:**
Fine Arts; Philosophy and Theology; History and Archeology; Education and Training; Communications and Media; Sociology and Anthropology.

Personality Type: Social-Artistic. **Career Clusters:** 03 Arts, Audio/Video Technology, and Communications; 05 Education and Training. **Career Pathways:** 03.2 Printing Technology; 05.3 Teaching/Training; 03.3 Visual Arts; 03.1 Audio and Video Technology and Film; 03.4 Performing Arts. **Other Jobs in These Pathways:** Career/Technical Education Teachers, Secondary School; Coaches and Scouts; Data Entry Keyers; Directors—Stage, Motion Pictures, Television, and Radio; Elementary School Teachers, Except Special Education; Fitness Trainers and Aerobics Instructors; Graphic Designers; Instructional Coordinators; Instructional Designers and Technologists; Kindergarten Teachers, Except Special Education; Librarians; Managers, All Other; Middle School Teachers, Except Special and Career/Technical Education; Musicians, Instrumental; Photographers; Poets, Lyricists and Creative Writers; Preschool Teachers, Except Special Education; Producers; Recreation Workers; Secondary School Teachers, Except Special and Career/Technical Education; Self-Enrichment Education Teachers; Singers; Teacher Assistants; Tutors; 37 other postsecondary teaching occupations; others.

Audio and Video Equipment Technicians

* Annual Earnings: $40,540
* Earnings Growth Potential: High (43.6%)
* Growth: 12.6%
* Annual Job Openings: 2,370
* Self-Employed: 12.4%

Skills—Most Important: Installation Skills; Equipment Use/Maintenance Skills; Thought-Processing Skills. **Other High-Level Skills:** Social Skills; Communication Skills.

Set up or set up and operate audio and video equipment, including microphones, sound speakers, video screens, projectors, video monitors, recording equipment, connecting wires and cables, sound and mixing boards, and related electronic equipment for concerts, sports events, meetings and conventions, presentations, and news conferences. May also set up and operate associated spotlights and other custom lighting systems. Notify supervisors when major equipment repairs are needed. Mix and regulate sound inputs and feeds or coordinate audio feeds with television pictures. Design layouts of audio and video equipment and perform upgrades and maintenance. Perform minor repairs and routine cleaning of audio and video equipment. Switch sources of video input from one camera or studio to another, from film to live programming, or from network to local programming. Compress, digitize, duplicate, and store audio and video data. Conduct training sessions on selection, use, and design of audiovisual materials and on operation of presentation equipment. Install, adjust, and operate electronic equipment to record, edit, and transmit radio and television programs, motion pictures, video conferencing, or multimedia presentations. Diagnose and resolve media system problems.

Education/Training Required: Long-term on-the-job training. **Education and Training Programs:** Agricultural Communication/Journalism; Photographic and Film/Video Technology/Technician and Assistant; Recording Arts Technology/Technician. **Knowledge/Courses:** Telecommunications; Communications and Media; Fine Arts; Computers and Electronics; Engineering and Technology; Production and Processing.

Personality Type: Realistic-Investigative-Conventional. **Career Cluster:** 03 Arts, Audio/Video Technology, and Communications. **Career Pathways:** 03.3 Visual Arts; 03.5 Journalism and Broadcasting. **Other Jobs in These Pathways:** Art Directors; Artists and Related Workers, All Other; Broadcast Technicians; Camera Operators, Television, Video, and Motion Picture; Commercial and Industrial Designers; Copy Writers; Directors—Stage, Motion Pictures, Television, and Radio; Editors; Fashion Designers; Film and Video Editors; Fine Artists, Including Painters, Sculptors, and Illustrators; Graphic Designers; Interior Designers; Media and Communication Workers, All Other; Multimedia Artists and Animators; Painting, Coating, and Decorating Workers; Photographers; Producers; Program Directors; Public Relations Specialists; Radio and Television Announcers; Reporters and Correspondents; Talent Directors; Technical Directors/Managers; Technical Writers; others.

Audiologists

❋ Annual Earnings: $66,660

❋ Earnings Growth Potential: Medium (36.1%)

❋ Growth: 25.0%

❋ Annual Job Openings: 580

❋ Self-Employed: 1.3%

Skills—Most Important: Science Skills; Communication Skills; Thought-Processing Skills. **Other High-Level Skills:** Social Skills; Mathematics Skills; Equipment Use/Maintenance Skills; Management Skills.

Assess and treat persons with hearing and related disorders. May fit hearing aids and provide auditory training. May perform research related to hearing problems. Examine and clean patients' ear canals. Educate and supervise audiology students and health-care personnel. Develop and supervise hearing screening programs. Counsel and instruct patients and their families in techniques to improve hearing and communication related to hearing loss. Evaluate hearing and balance disorders to determine diagnoses and courses of treatment. Program and monitor cochlear implants to fit the needs of patients. Participate in conferences or training to update or share knowledge of new hearing or balance disorder treatment methods or technologies. Conduct or direct research on hearing or balance topics and report findings to help in the development of procedures, technology, or treatments. Plan and conduct treatment programs for patients' hearing or balance problems, consulting with educators, physicians, nurses, psychologists, speech-language pathologists, and other health-care personnel as necessary. Administer hearing tests and examine patients to collect information on type and degree of impairment using specialized instruments and electronic equipment. Engage in marketing activities, such as developing marketing plans, to promote business for private practices. Recommend assistive devices according to patients' needs or nature of impairments. Fit, dispense, and repair assistive devices, such as hearing aids. Advise educators or other medical staff on hearing or balance topics.

Education/Training Required: Doctoral degree. **Education and Training Programs:** Audiology/Audiologist; Audiology/Audiologist and Speech-Language Pathology/Pathologist; Communication Disorders Sciences and Services, Other; Communication Disorders, General; Communication Sciences and Disorders, General. **Knowledge/Courses:** Therapy and Counseling; Medicine and Dentistry; Sales and Marketing; Psychology; Biology; Sociology and Anthropology.

Personality Type: Investigative-Social. **Career Cluster:** 08 Health Science. **Career Pathway:** 08.1 Therapeutic Services. **Other Jobs in This Pathway:** Clinical Psychologists; Community and Social Service Specialists, All Other; Counseling Psychologists; Dental Assistants; Dental Hygienists; Dentists, General; Health Technologists and Technicians, All Other; Healthcare Support Workers, All Other; Home Health Aides; Licensed Practical and Licensed Vocational Nurses; Low Vision Therapists, Orientation and Mobility Specialists, and Vision Rehabilitation Therapists; Massage Therapists; Medical and Clinical Laboratory Technicians; Medical and Health Services Managers; Medical Scientists, Except Epidemiologists; Medical Secretaries; Occupational Therapists; Pharmacists; Pharmacy Technicians; Radiologic Technologists; School Psychologists; Social and

Human Service Assistants; Speech-Language Pathologists; Speech-Language Pathology Assistants; Substance Abuse and Behavioral Disorder Counselors; others.

Audio-Visual and Multimedia Collections Specialists

* Annual Earnings: $42,710
* Earnings Growth Potential: High (44.8%)
* Growth: 10.3%
* Annual Job Openings: 220
* Self-Employed: 2.9%

Skills—Most Important: Installation Skills; Equipment Use/Maintenance Skills; Management Skills. **Other High-Level Skills:** Communication Skills; Thought-Processing Skills; Social Skills.

Prepare, plan, and operate audiovisual teaching aids for use in education. May record, catalogue, and file audiovisual materials. Set up, adjust, and operate audiovisual equipment such as cameras, film and slide projectors, and recording equipment, for meetings, events, classes, seminars, and video conferences. Attend conventions and conferences, read trade journals, and communicate with industry insiders to keep abreast of industry developments. Instruct users in the selection, use, and design of audiovisual materials and assist them in the preparation of instructional materials and the rehearsal of presentations. Maintain hardware and software, including computers, scanners, color copiers, and color laser printers. Perform simple maintenance tasks such as cleaning monitors and lenses and changing batteries and light bulbs. Develop manuals, texts, workbooks, or related materials for use in conjunction with production materials. Direct and coordinate activities of assistants and other personnel during production.

Education/Training Required: Bachelor's degree. **Education and Training Program:** School Librarian/School Library Media Specialist. **Knowledge/Courses:** Computers and Electronics; Telecommunications; Communications and Media; Fine Arts; Clerical Practices; Design.

Personality Type: Conventional-Realistic-Social. **Career Cluster:** 05 Education and Training. **Career Pathway:** 05.3 Teaching/Training. **Other Jobs in This Pathway:** Adult Basic and Secondary Education and Literacy Teachers and Instructors; Athletes and Sports Competitors; Career/Technical Education Teachers, Middle School; Career/Technical Education Teachers, Secondary School; Chemists; Coaches and Scouts; Dietitians and Nutritionists; Elementary School Teachers, Except Special Education; Fitness Trainers and Aerobics Instructors; Historians; Instructional Coordinators; Instructional Designers and Technologists; Interpreters and Translators; Kindergarten Teachers, Except Special Education; Librarians; Middle School Teachers, Except Special and Career/Technical Education; Physicists; Preschool Teachers, Except Special Education; Recreation Workers; Secondary School Teachers, Except Special and Career/Technical Education; Self-Enrichment Education Teachers; Teacher Assistants; Teachers and Instructors, All Other; Tutors.

Automotive Service Technicians and Mechanics

* Annual Earnings: $35,790
* Earnings Growth Potential: High (43.6%)
* Growth: 4.7%
* Annual Job Openings: 18,170
* Self-Employed: 15.9%

Skills—Most Important: Equipment Use/ Maintenance Skills; Installation Skills; Thought-Processing Skills. **Other High-Level Skills:** Management Skills; Social Skills.

Job Specialization: Automotive Master Mechanics

Repair automobiles, trucks, buses, and other vehicles. Master mechanics repair virtually any part on the vehicle or specialize in the transmission system. Test drive vehicles. Test components and systems using equipment such as infrared engine analyzers, compression gauges, and computerized diagnostic devices. Examine vehicles to determine extent of damage or malfunctions. Repair, reline, replace, and adjust brakes. Follow checklists to ensure all important parts are examined, including belts, hoses, steering systems, spark plugs, brake and fuel systems, wheel bearings, and other potentially troublesome areas. Confer with customers to obtain descriptions of vehicle problems and to discuss work to be performed and future repair requirements. Perform routine and scheduled maintenance services such as oil changes, lubrications, and tune-ups. Repair and service air conditioning, heating, engine-cooling, and electrical systems. Test and adjust repaired systems to meet manufacturers' performance specifications. Review work orders and discuss work with supervisors. Tear down, repair, and rebuild faulty assemblies such as power systems, steering systems, and linkages. Plan work procedures using charts, technical manuals, and experience. Disassemble units and inspect parts for wear using micrometers, calipers, and gauges. Repair or replace parts such as pistons, rods, gears, valves, and bearings. Rewire ignition systems, lights, and instrument panels. Repair manual and automatic transmissions. Install and repair accessories such as radios, heaters, mirrors, and windshield wipers. Maintain cleanliness of work area.

Education/Training Required: Postsecondary vocational training. **Education and Training Programs:** Alternative Fuel Vehicle Technology/ Technician; Autobody/Collision and Repair Technology/Technician; Automobile/ Automotive Mechanics Technology/Technician; Automotive Engineering Technology/ Technician; Medium/Heavy Vehicle and Truck Technology/Technician; Vehicle Emissions Inspection and Maintenance Technology/ Technician. **Knowledge/Courses:** Mechanical Devices; Engineering and Technology; Physics; Design; Chemistry; Computers and Electronics.

Personality Type: Realistic-Investigative. **Career Cluster:** 16 Transportation, Distribution, and Logistics. **Career Pathways:** 16.1 Transportation Operations; 16.4 Facility and Mobile Equipment Maintenance. **Other Jobs in These Pathways:** Aircraft Mechanics and Service Technicians; Aircraft Structure, Surfaces, Rigging, and Systems Assemblers; Airline Pilots, Copilots, and Flight Engineers; Automotive and Watercraft Service Attendants; Automotive Body and Related Repairers; Automotive Specialty Technicians; Bus and Truck Mechanics and Diesel Engine Specialists; Bus Drivers, School or Special

Client; Bus Drivers, Transit and Intercity; Cleaners of Vehicles and Equipment; Crane and Tower Operators; First-Line Supervisors of Helpers, Laborers, and Material Movers, Hand; First-Line Supervisors of Transportation and Material-Moving Machine and Vehicle Operators; Gem and Diamond Workers; Heavy and Tractor-Trailer Truck Drivers; Installation, Maintenance, and Repair Workers, All Other; Laborers and Freight, Stock, and Material Movers, Hand; Light Truck or Delivery Services Drivers; Motor Vehicle Operators, All Other; Operating Engineers and Other Construction Equipment Operators; Painters, Transportation Equipment; Parking Lot Attendants; Storage and Distribution Managers; Taxi Drivers and Chauffeurs; Transportation Managers; others.

Job Specialization: Automotive Specialty Technicians

Repair only one system or component on a vehicle, such as brakes, suspension, or radiator. Examine vehicles, compile estimates of repair costs, and secure customers' approval to perform repairs. Repair, overhaul, and adjust automobile brake systems. Use electronic test equipment to locate and correct malfunctions in fuel, ignition, and emissions control systems. Repair and replace defective balljoint suspensions, brakeshoes, and wheelbearings. Inspect and test new vehicles for damage, and then record findings so that necessary repairs can be made. Test electronic computer components in automobiles to ensure that they are working properly. Tune automobile engines to ensure proper and efficient functioning. Install and repair air conditioners and service components such as compressors, condensers, and controls. Repair, replace, and adjust defective carburetor parts and gasoline filters. Remove and replace defective mufflers and

tailpipes. Repair and replace automobile leaf springs. Rebuild, repair, and test automotive fuel injection units. Align and repair wheels, axles, frames, torsion bars, and steering mechanisms of automobiles using special alignment equipment and wheel-balancing machines. Repair, install, and adjust hydraulic and electromagnetic automatic lift mechanisms used to raise and lower automobile windows, seats, and tops. Repair and rebuild clutch systems. Convert vehicle fuel systems from gasoline to butane gas operations. Repair and service operating butane fuel units.

Education/Training Required: Postsecondary vocational training. **Education and Training Programs:** Alternative Fuel Vehicle Technology/ Technician; Autobody/Collision and Repair Technology/Technician; Automobile/ Automotive Mechanics Technology/Technician; Automotive Engineering Technology/ Technician; Medium/Heavy Vehicle and Truck Technology/Technician; Vehicle Emissions Inspection and Maintenance Technology/ Technician. **Knowledge/Courses:** Mechanical Devices; Physics; Engineering and Technology; Customer and Personal Service; Sales and Marketing; Administration and Management.

Personality Type: Realistic-Investigative-Conventional. **Career Clusters:** 13 Manufacturing; 16 Transportation, Distribution, and Logistics. **Career Pathways:** 16.4 Facility and Mobile Equipment Maintenance; 13.3 Maintenance, Installation, and Repair. **Other Jobs in These Pathways:** Aircraft Mechanics and Service Technicians; Automotive Body and Related Repairers; Automotive Master Mechanics; Biological Technicians; Bus and Truck Mechanics and Diesel Engine Specialists; Civil Engineering Technicians; Cleaners of Vehicles and Equipment; Computer, Automated

Teller, and Office Machine Repairers; Electrical and Electronic Equipment Assemblers; Electrical and Electronics Repairers, Commercial and Industrial Equipment; Electrical Engineering Technicians; Electrical Engineering Technologists; Electromechanical Engineering Technologists; Electronics Engineering Technicians; Electronics Engineering Technologists; Engineering Technicians, Except Drafters, All Other; Fuel Cell Technicians; Helpers—Installation, Maintenance, and Repair Workers; Industrial Engineering Technologists; Industrial Machinery Mechanics; Installation, Maintenance, and Repair Workers, All Other; Manufacturing Engineering Technologists; Mobile Heavy Equipment Mechanics, Except Engines; Telecommunications Line Installers and Repairers; Tire Repairers and Changers; others.

Avionics Technicians

❀ Annual Earnings: $52,320

❀ Earnings Growth Potential: Low (29.6%)

❀ Growth: 10.6%

❀ Annual Job Openings: 520

❀ Self-Employed: 0.1%

Skills—Most Important: Equipment Use/Maintenance Skills; Installation Skills; Science Skills. **Other High-Level Skills:** Thought-Processing Skills; Management Skills; Social Skills.

Install, inspect, test, adjust, or repair avionics equipment, such as radar, radio, navigation, and missile control systems in aircraft or space vehicles. Set up and operate ground support and test equipment to perform functional flight tests of electrical and electronic systems. Test and troubleshoot instruments, components, and assemblies using circuit testers, oscilloscopes, and voltmeters. Keep records of maintenance and repair work. Coordinate work with that of engineers, technicians, and other aircraft maintenance personnel. Interpret flight test data to diagnose malfunctions and systemic performance problems. Install electrical and electronic components, assemblies, and systems in aircraft using hand tools, power tools, and/or soldering irons. Adjust, repair, or replace malfunctioning components or assemblies using hand tools and/or soldering irons. Connect components to assemblies such as radio systems, instruments, magnetos, inverters, and in-flight refueling systems, using hand tools and soldering irons. Assemble components such as switches, electrical controls, and junction boxes using hand tools and soldering irons. Fabricate parts and test aids as required. Lay out installation of aircraft assemblies and systems following documentation such as blueprints, manuals, and wiring diagrams. Assemble prototypes or models of circuits, instruments, and systems so that they can be used for testing. Operate computer-aided drafting and design applications to design avionics system modifications.

Education/Training Required: Postsecondary vocational training. **Education and Training Programs:** Airframe Mechanics and Aircraft Maintenance Technology/Technician; Avionics Maintenance Technology/Technician. **Knowledge/Courses:** Engineering and Technology; Mechanical Devices; Computers and Electronics; Telecommunications; Production and Processing; Design.

Personality Type: Realistic-Investigative-Conventional. **Career Clusters:** 13 Manufacturing; 16 Transportation, Distribution, and Logistics. **Career Pathways:** 13.1 Production; 16.7 Sales and Service; 13.3 Maintenance, Installation, and Repair. **Other Jobs in These**

Pathways: Assemblers and Fabricators, All Other; Automotive Specialty Technicians; Cost Estimators; Cutting, Punching, and Press Machine Setters, Operators, and Tenders, Metal and Plastic; Electrical and Electronic Equipment Assemblers; Electrical Engineering Technicians; Electronics Engineering Technicians; First-Line Supervisors of Mechanics, Installers, and Repairers; First-Line Supervisors of Production and Operating Workers; Geothermal Technicians; Helpers—Production Workers; Industrial Machinery Mechanics; Installation, Maintenance, and Repair Workers, All Other; Machinists; Packaging and Filling Machine Operators and Tenders; Packers and Packagers, Hand; Parts Salespersons; Production Workers, All Other; Recycling and Reclamation Workers; Recycling Coordinators; Sheet Metal Workers; Solderers and Brazers; Team Assemblers; Telecommunications Line Installers and Repairers; Welders, Cutters, and Welder Fitters; others.

Biochemists and Biophysicists

- ❋ Annual Earnings: $79,390
- ❋ Earnings Growth Potential: High (45.8%)
- ❋ Growth: 37.4%
- ❋ Annual Job Openings: 1,620
- ❋ Self-Employed: 2.7%

Skills—Most Important: Science Skills; Mathematics Skills; Communication Skills. **Other High-Level Skills:** Thought-Processing Skills; Technology/Programming Skills; Management Skills; Social Skills; Equipment Use/Maintenance Skills.

Study the chemical composition and physical principles of living cells and organisms and their electrical and mechanical energy and related phenomena. May conduct research to further understanding of the complex chemical combinations and reactions involved in metabolism, reproduction, growth, and heredity. May determine the effects of foods, drugs, serums, hormones, and other substances on tissues and vital processes of living organisms. Design and perform experiments with equipment such as lasers, accelerators, and mass spectrometers. Analyze brain functions such as learning, thinking, and memory, and the dynamics of seeing and hearing. Share research findings by writing scientific articles and by making presentations at scientific conferences. Develop and test new drugs and medications intended for commercial distribution. Develop methods to process, store, and use foods, drugs, and chemical compounds. Develop new methods to study the mechanisms of biological processes. Examine the molecular and chemical aspects of immune system functioning. Investigate the nature, composition, and expression of genes, and research how genetic engineering can impact these processes. Determine the three-dimensional structure of biological macromolecules. Prepare reports and recommendations based upon research outcomes. Design and build laboratory equipment needed for special research projects. Isolate, analyze, and synthesize vitamins, hormones, allergens, minerals, and enzymes, and determine their effects on body functions. Research cancer treatment, using radiation and nuclear particles. Research transformations of substances in cells, using atomic isotopes. Study how light is absorbed in processes such as photosynthesis or vision. Analyze foods to determine their nutritional values and the effects of cooking, canning, and processing on these values.

Education/Training Required: Doctoral degree. **Education and Training Programs:** Biochemistry; Biochemistry and Molecular Biology; Biophysics; Cell/Cellular Biology and Anatomical Sciences, Other; Molecular Biochemistry; Molecular Biophysics; Soil Chemistry and Physics; Soil Microbiology. **Knowledge/Courses:** Biology; Chemistry; Physics; Engineering and Technology; Medicine and Dentistry; Mechanical.

Personality Type: Investigative-Artistic-Realistic. **Career Clusters:** 01 Agriculture, Food, and Natural Resources; 15 Science, Technology, Engineering, and Mathematics. **Career Pathways:** 01.2 Plant Systems; 15.2 Science and Mathematics. **Other Jobs in These Pathways:** Architectural and Engineering Managers; Biofuels/Biodiesel Technology and Product Development Managers; Bioinformatics Scientists; Biological Scientists, All Other; Biologists; Chemists; Clinical Research Coordinators; Community and Social Service Specialists, All Other; Dietitians and Nutritionists; Education, Training, and Library Workers, All Other; First-Line Supervisors of Landscaping, Lawn Service, and Groundskeeping Workers; First-Line Supervisors of Retail Sales Workers; Floral Designers; Geneticists; Geoscientists, Except Hydrologists and Geographers; Landscaping and Groundskeeping Workers; Medical Scientists, Except Epidemiologists; Natural Sciences Managers; Operations Research Analysts; Precision Agriculture Technicians; Retail Salespersons; Social Scientists and Related Workers, All Other; Transportation Planners; Tree Trimmers and Pruners; Water Resource Specialists; others.

Biological Science Teachers, Postsecondary

* Annual Earnings: $72,700
* Earnings Growth Potential: High (44.5%)
* Growth: 15.1%
* Annual Job Openings: 1,700
* Self-Employed: 0.2%

Skills—Most Important: Science Skills; Communication Skills; Thought-Processing Skills. **Other High-Level Skills:** Mathematics Skills; Social Skills; Management Skills.

Teach courses in biological sciences. Prepare and deliver lectures to undergraduate or graduate students on topics such as molecular biology, marine biology, and botany. Evaluate and grade students' classwork, laboratory work, assignments, and papers. Compile, administer, and grade examinations or assign this work to others. Supervise students' laboratory work. Keep abreast of developments in the field by reading current literature, talking with colleagues, and participating in professional conferences. Maintain student attendance records, grades, and other required records. Initiate, facilitate, and moderate classroom discussions. Plan, evaluate, and revise curricula, course content, and course materials and methods of instruction. Advise students on academic and vocational curricula and on career issues. Maintain regularly scheduled office hours to advise and assist students. Supervise undergraduate or graduate teaching, internship, and research work. Select and obtain materials and supplies such as textbooks and laboratory equipment. Collaborate with colleagues to address teaching and research issues. Conduct research in a particular field of knowledge and publish findings in professional journals, books, or electronic media. Serve on academic or administrative committees that deal with institutional policies, departmental matters, and academic issues. Write grant proposals to procure research funding.

Education/Training Required: Doctoral degree. **Education and Training Programs:** Anatomy; Animal Physiology; Biochemistry; Biological and Biomedical Sciences, Other; Biology/Biological Sciences, General; Biometry/Biometrics; Biophysics; Biotechnology; Botany/Plant Biology; Cell/Cellular Biology and Histology; Ecology; Ecology, Evolution, Systematics, and Population Biology, Other; Entomology; Evolutionary Biology; Immunology; Marine Biology and Biological Oceanography; Microbiology, General; Molecular Biology; Nutrition Sciences; Parasitology; Pathology/Experimental Pathology; Pharmacology; Plant Genetics; Plant Pathology/Phytopathology; Plant Physiology; Radiation Biology/Radiobiology; Toxicology; Virology; Zoology/Animal Biology. **Knowledge/Courses:** Biology; Chemistry; Education and Training; Geography; Physics; English Language.

Personality Type: Social-Investigative. **Career Clusters:** 01 Agriculture, Food, and Natural Resources; 05 Education and Training; 15 Science, Technology, Engineering, and Mathematics. **Career Pathways:** 01.5 Natural Resources Systems; 05.3 Teaching/Training; 15.2 Science and Mathematics. **Other Jobs in These Pathways:** Adult Basic and Secondary Education and Literacy Teachers and Instructors; Architectural and Engineering Managers; Biofuels/Biodiesel Technology and Product Development Managers; Biologists; Career/Technical Education Teachers, Secondary School; Coaches and Scouts;

Community and Social Service Specialists, All Other; Education, Training, and Library Workers, All Other; Elementary School Teachers, Except Special Education; Fitness Trainers and Aerobics Instructors; Industrial Truck and Tractor Operators; Instructional Coordinators; Instructional Designers and Technologists; Kindergarten Teachers, Except Special Education; Librarians; Medical Scientists, Except Epidemiologists; Middle School Teachers, Except Special and Career/Technical Education; Preschool Teachers, Except Special Education; Recreation Workers; Refuse and Recyclable Material Collectors; Secondary School Teachers, Except Special and Career/Technical Education; Self-Enrichment Education Teachers; Teacher Assistants; Tutors; 37 other postsecondary teaching occupations; others.

Biological Scientists, All Other

* Annual Earnings: $68,220
* Earnings Growth Potential: High (43.2%)
* Growth: 18.8%
* Annual Job Openings: 1,610
* Self-Employed: 2.5%

Skills—Most Important: Science Skills; Mathematics Skills; Communication Skills. **Other High-Level Skills:** Thought-Processing Skills; Management Skills; Technology/Programming Skills; Social Skills; Equipment Use/Maintenance Skills.

This occupation includes all biological scientists not listed separately. Because this is a highly diverse occupation, no data is available for some information topics.

Education/Training Required: Doctoral degree. **Education and Training Program:**

Biological and Biomedical Sciences, Other. **Career Clusters:** 08 Health Science; 15 Science, Technology, Engineering, and Mathematics. **Career Pathways:** 15.2 Science and Mathematics; 08.5 Biotechnology Research and Development. **Other Jobs in These Pathways:** Architectural and Engineering Managers; Biochemists and Biophysicists; Biofuels/Biodiesel Technology and Product Development Managers; Bioinformatics Scientists; Biologists; Biostatisticians; Chemists; Clinical Data Managers; Clinical Research Coordinators; Community and Social Service Specialists, All Other; Dietitians and Nutritionists; Education, Training, and Library Workers, All Other; Geneticists; Geoscientists, Except Hydrologists and Geographers; Medical Scientists, Except Epidemiologists; Molecular and Cellular Biologists; Natural Sciences Managers; Operations Research Analysts; Pharmacists; Physical Scientists, All Other; Social Scientists and Related Workers, All Other; Statisticians; Survey Researchers; Transportation Planners; Water Resource Specialists; others.

Job Specialization: Bioinformatics Scientists

Conduct research using bioinformatics theory and methods in areas such as pharmaceuticals, medical technology, biotechnology, computational biology, proteomics, computer information science, biology, and medical informatics. May design databases and develop algorithms for processing and analyzing genomic information or other biological information. Recommend new systems and processes to improve operations. Keep abreast of new biochemistries, instrumentation, or software by reading scientific literature and attending professional conferences. Confer with

departments such as marketing, business development, and operations to coordinate product development or improvement. Collaborate with software developers in the development and modification of commercial bioinformatics software. Test new and updated bioinformatics tools and software. Provide statistical and computational tools for biologically based activities such as genetic analysis, measurement of gene expression, and gene function determination. Prepare summary statistics of information on human genomes. Instruct others in the selection and use of bioinformatics tools. Improve user interfaces to bioinformatics software and databases. Direct the work of technicians and information technology staff applying bioinformatics tools or applications in areas such as proteomics, transcriptomics, metabolomics, and clinical bioinformatics. Develop new software applications or customize existing applications to meet specific scientific project needs. Develop data models and databases. Create or modify Web-based bioinformatics tools. Design and apply bioinformatics algorithms including unsupervised and supervised machine learning, dynamic programming, or graphic algorithms. Create novel computational approaches and analytical tools as required by research goals.

Education/Training Required: Doctoral degree. **Education and Training Program:** Bioinformatics.

Personality Type: Investigative-Conventional-Realistic. **Career Clusters:** 11 Information Technology; 15 Science, Technology, Engineering, and Mathematics. **Career Pathways:** 15.2 Science and Mathematics; 11.4 Programming and Software Development. **Other Jobs in These Pathways:** Architectural and Engineering Managers; Biochemists and

Biophysicists; Biofuels/Biodiesel Technology and Product Development Managers; Biological Scientists, All Other; Biologists; Biostatisticians; Chemists; Clinical Data Managers; Clinical Research Coordinators; Community and Social Service Specialists, All Other; Computer Hardware Engineers; Dietitians and Nutritionists; Education, Training, and Library Workers, All Other; Geneticists; Geoscientists, Except Hydrologists and Geographers; Medical Scientists, Except Epidemiologists; Molecular and Cellular Biologists; Natural Sciences Managers; Operations Research Analysts; Physical Scientists, All Other; Social Scientists and Related Workers, All Other; Statisticians; Survey Researchers; Transportation Planners; Water Resource Specialists; others.

Job Specialization: Geneticists

Research and study the inheritance of traits at the molecular, organism, or population level. May evaluate or treat patients with genetic disorders. Write grants and papers or attend fundraising events to seek research funds. Verify that cytogenetic, molecular genetic, and related equipment and instrumentation are maintained in working condition to ensure accuracy and quality of experimental results. Maintain laboratory safety programs and train personnel in laboratory safety techniques. Design and maintain genetics computer databases. Confer with information technology specialists to develop computer applications for genetic data analysis. Collaborate with biologists and other professionals to conduct appropriate genetic and biochemical analyses. Attend clinical and research conferences and read scientific literature to keep abreast of technological advances and current genetic research findings. Supervise or direct the work of other geneticists, biologists, technicians, or

biometricians working on genetics research projects. Review, approve, or interpret genetic laboratory results.

Education/Training Required: Doctoral degree. **Education and Training Programs:** Animal Genetics; Genetics, General; Genetics, Other; Genome Sciences/Genomics; Human/Medical Genetics; Microbial and Eukaryotic Genetics; Molecular Genetics; Plant Genetics. **Knowledge/Courses:** Biology; Chemistry; Medicine and Dentistry; Education and Training; English Language; Mathematics.

Personality Type: Investigative-Artistic-Realistic. **Career Clusters:** 01 Agriculture, Food, and Natural Resources; 15 Science, Technology, Engineering, and Mathematics. **Career Pathways:** 15.2 Science and Mathematics; 01.2 Plant Systems; 01.3 Animal Systems. **Other Jobs in These Pathways:** Animal Trainers; Architectural and Engineering Managers; Biofuels/Biodiesel Technology and Product Development Managers; Biologists; Chemists; Clinical Research Coordinators; Community and Social Service Specialists, All Other; Dietitians and Nutritionists; Education, Training, and Library Workers, All Other; First-Line Supervisors of Landscaping, Lawn Service, and Groundskeeping Workers; First-Line Supervisors of Retail Sales Workers; Floral Designers; Geoscientists, Except Hydrologists and Geographers; Landscaping and Groundskeeping Workers; Medical Scientists, Except Epidemiologists; Natural Sciences Managers; Nonfarm Animal Caretakers; Operations Research Analysts; Precision Agriculture Technicians; Retail Salespersons; Social Scientists and Related Workers, All Other; Transportation Planners; Tree Trimmers and Pruners; Veterinarians; Water Resource Specialists; others.

Job Specialization: Molecular and Cellular Biologists

Research and study cellular molecules and organelles to understand cell function and organization. Verify all financial, physical, and human resources assigned to research or development projects are used as planned. Develop guidelines for procedures such as the management of viruses. Coordinate molecular or cellular research activities with scientists specializing in other fields. Supervise technical personnel and postdoctoral research fellows. Prepare reports, manuscripts, and meeting presentations. Provide scientific direction for project teams on the evaluation or handling of devices, drugs, or cells for in vitro and in vivo disease models. Perform laboratory procedures following protocols including deoxyribonucleic acid (DNA) sequencing, cloning and extraction, ribonucleic acid (RNA) purification, or gel electrophoresis. Monitor or operate specialized equipment such as gas chromatographs and high-pressure liquid chromatographs, electrophoresis units, thermocyclers, fluorescence activated cell sorters, and phosphoimagers. Maintain accurate laboratory records and data.

Education/Training Required: Doctoral degree. **Education and Training Program:** Cell/Cellular Biology and Histology. **Knowledge/Courses:** Biology; Chemistry; English Language; Medicine and Dentistry; Computers and Electronics; Mathematics.

Personality Type: Investigative-Realistic-Artistic. **Career Cluster:** 15 Science, Technology, Engineering, and Mathematics. **Career Pathway:** 15.2 Science and Mathematics. **Other Jobs in This Pathway:** Architectural and Engineering Managers; Biochemists and Biophysicists; Biofuels/Biodiesel Technology and Product Development Managers; Bioinformatics Scientists; Biological Scientists, All Other; Biologists; Biostatisticians; Chemists; Clinical Data Managers; Clinical Research Coordinators; Community and Social Service Specialists, All Other; Dietitians and Nutritionists; Education, Training, and Library Workers, All Other; Geneticists; Geoscientists, Except Hydrologists and Geographers; Medical Scientists, Except Epidemiologists; Natural Sciences Managers; Operations Research Analysts; Physical Scientists, All Other; Social Scientists and Related Workers, All Other; Statisticians; Survey Researchers; Transportation Planners; Water Resource Specialists; Zoologists and Wildlife Biologists; others.

Biomedical Engineers

* Annual Earnings: $81,540
* Earnings Growth Potential: Medium (39.1%)
* Growth: 72.0%
* Annual Job Openings: 1,490
* Self-Employed: 3.3%

Skills—Most Important: Science Skills; Technology/Programming Skills; Installation Skills. **Other High-Level Skills:** Mathematics Skills; Equipment Use/Maintenance Skills; Thought-Processing Skills; Communication Skills; Social Skills; Management Skills.

Apply knowledge of engineering, biology, and biomechanical principles to the design, development, and evaluation of biological and health systems and products, such as artificial organs, prostheses, instrumentation, medical information systems, and health management and care delivery systems. Evaluate the safety, efficiency, and effectiveness of biomedical equipment. Advise and assist in the application of instrumentation in clinical environments. Research new materials to be used for products, such as implanted artificial organs. Design and develop medical diagnostic and clinical instrumentation, equipment, and procedures using the principles of engineering and biobehavioral sciences. Conduct research, along with life scientists, chemists, and medical scientists, on the engineering aspects of the biological systems of humans and animals. Teach biomedical engineering or disseminate knowledge about field through writing or consulting. Design and deliver technology to assist people with disabilities. Analyze new medical procedures to forecast likely outcomes. Develop new applications for energy sources, such as using nuclear power for biomedical implants. Install, adjust, maintain, repair, or provide technical support for biomedical equipment.

Education/Training Required: Bachelor's degree. **Education and Training Program:** Bioengineering and Biomedical Engineering. **Knowledge/Courses:** Biology; Engineering and Technology; Physics; Design; Medicine and Dentistry; Chemistry.

Personality Type: Investigative-Realistic. **Career Cluster:** 15 Science, Technology, Engineering, and Mathematics. **Career Pathway:** 15.1 Engineering and Technology. **Other Jobs in This Pathway:** Architectural and Engineering Managers; Automotive Engineers; Biochemical Engineers; Biofuels/Biodiesel Technology and Product Development Managers; Civil Engineers; Cost Estimators; Electrical Engineers; Electronics Engineers, Except Computer; Energy Engineers; Engineers, All Other; Fuel Cell Engineers; Human Factors Engineers and Ergonomists;

Industrial Engineers; Manufacturing Engineers; Mechanical Engineers; Mechatronics Engineers; Microsystems Engineers; Nanosystems Engineers; Photonics Engineers; Radio Frequency Identification Device Specialists; Robotics Engineers; Solar Energy Systems Engineers; Transportation Engineers; Validation Engineers; Wind Energy Engineers; others.

Boilermakers

* Annual Earnings: $54,640
* Earnings Growth Potential: High (44.3%)
* Growth: 18.8%
* Annual Job Openings: 810
* Self-Employed: 0.0%

Skills—Most Important: Equipment Use/Maintenance Skills; Thought-Processing Skills.

Construct, assemble, maintain, and repair stationary steam boilers and boiler house auxiliaries. Align structures or plate sections to assemble boiler frame tanks or vats following blueprints. Work involves use of hand and power tools, plumb bobs, levels, wedges, dogs, or turnbuckles. Assist in testing assembled vessels. Direct cleaning of boilers and boiler furnaces. Inspect and repair boiler fittings, such as safety valves, regulators, automatic-control mechanisms, water columns, and auxiliary machines. Bolt or arc-weld pressure vessel structures and parts together using wrenches and welding equipment. Examine boilers, pressure vessels, tanks, and vats to locate defects such as leaks, weak spots, and defective sections so they can be repaired. Inspect assembled vessels and individual components, such as tubes, fittings, valves, controls, and auxiliary mechanisms, to locate defects. Repair or replace defective pressure vessel parts, such as safety valves and regulators, using torches, jacks, caulking hammers, power saws, threading dies, welding equipment, and metalworking machinery. Attach rigging and then signal crane or hoist operators to lift heavy frame and plate sections and other parts into place. Bell, bead with power hammers, or weld pressure vessel tube ends to ensure leakproof joints. Lay out plate, sheet steel, or other heavy metal and locate and mark bending and cutting lines using protractors, compasses, and drawing instruments or templates. Install manholes, handholes, taps, tubes, valves, gauges, and feedwater connections in drums of water tube boilers using hand tools. Study blueprints to determine locations, relationships, and dimensions of parts. Straighten or reshape bent pressure vessel plates and structure parts using hammers, jacks, and torches.

Education/Training Required: Long-term on-the-job training. **Education and Training Program:** Boilermaking/Boilermaker. **Knowledge/Courses:** Building and Construction; Mechanical Devices; Engineering and Technology; Design; Physics; Transportation.

Personality Type: Realistic-Conventional. **Career Cluster:** 02 Architecture and Construction. **Career Pathway:** 02.2 Construction. **Other Jobs in This Pathway:** Brickmasons and Blockmasons; Cement Masons and Concrete Finishers; Construction and Building Inspectors; Construction Carpenters; Construction Laborers; Construction Managers; Cost Estimators; Drywall and Ceiling Tile Installers; Electrical Power-Line Installers and Repairers; Electricians; Engineering Technicians, Except Drafters, All Other; First-Line Supervisors of Construction Trades

and Extraction Workers; Heating and Air Conditioning Mechanics and Installers; Helpers—Carpenters; Helpers—Electricians; Helpers—Pipelayers, Plumbers, Pipefitters, and Steamfitters; Highway Maintenance Workers; Operating Engineers and Other Construction Equipment Operators; Painters, Construction and Maintenance; Pipe Fitters and Steamfitters; Plumbers; Refrigeration Mechanics and Installers; Roofers; Rough Carpenters; Solar Energy Installation Managers; others.

Brickmasons and Blockmasons

- ❀ Annual Earnings: $46,930
- ❀ Earnings Growth Potential: Medium (38.7%)
- ❀ Growth: 11.5%
- ❀ Annual Job Openings: 5,000
- ❀ Self-Employed: 27.3%

Skills—Most Important: Mathematics Skills; Equipment Use/Maintenance Skills.

Lay and bind building materials, such as brick, structural tile, concrete block, cinderblock, glass block, and terra-cotta block with mortar and other substances to construct or repair walls, partitions, arches, sewers, and other structures. Construct corners by fastening in plumb position a corner pole or building a corner pyramid of bricks and filling in between the corners using a line from corner to corner to guide each course, or layer, of brick. Measure distance from reference points and mark guidelines to lay out work using plumb bobs and levels. Calculate angles and courses and determine vertical and horizontal alignment of courses. Fasten or fuse brick or other building material to structure with wire clamps, anchor holes, torch, or cement. Break or cut bricks, tiles, or blocks to size using trowel edge, hammer, or power saw. Remove excess mortar with trowels and hand tools and finish mortar joints with jointing tools for a sealed, uniform appearance. Interpret blueprints and drawings to determine specifications and to calculate the materials required. Apply and smooth mortar or other mixture over work surface. Mix specified amounts of sand, clay, dirt, or mortar powder with water to form refractory mixtures.

Education/Training Required: Long-term on-the-job training. **Education and Training Program:** Masonry/Mason Training. **Knowledge/Courses:** Building and Construction; Design; Engineering and Technology; Production and Processing; Physics; Public Safety and Security.

Personality Type: Realistic-Conventional-Investigative. **Career Cluster:** 02 Architecture and Construction. **Career Pathway:** 02.2 Construction. **Other Jobs in This Pathway:** Cement Masons and Concrete Finishers; Construction and Building Inspectors; Construction Carpenters; Construction Laborers; Construction Managers; Cost Estimators; Drywall and Ceiling Tile Installers; Electrical Power-Line Installers and Repairers; Electricians; Engineering Technicians, Except Drafters, All Other; Excavating and Loading Machine and Dragline Operators; First-Line Supervisors of Construction Trades and Extraction Workers; Heating and Air Conditioning Mechanics and Installers; Helpers—Carpenters; Helpers—Electricians; Helpers—Pipelayers, Plumbers, Pipefitters, and Steamfitters; Highway Maintenance Workers; Operating Engineers and Other Construction Equipment Operators; Painters, Construction and Maintenance; Pipe Fitters and Steamfitters;

Plumbers; Refrigeration Mechanics and Installers; Roofers; Rough Carpenters; Solar Energy Installation Managers; others.

Budget Analysts

* Annual Earnings: $68,200
* Earnings Growth Potential: Low (34.2%)
* Growth: 15.1%
* Annual Job Openings: 2,230
* Self-Employed: 0.0%

Skills—Most Important: Mathematics Skills; Management Skills; Thought-Processing Skills. **Other High-Level Skills:** Communication Skills.

Examine budget estimates for completeness, accuracy, and conformance with procedures and regulations. Analyze budgeting and accounting reports for maintaining expenditure controls. Direct the preparation of regular and special budget reports. Consult with managers to ensure that budget adjustments are made in accordance with program changes. Match appropriations for specific programs with appropriations for broader programs, including items for emergency funds. Provide advice and technical assistance with cost analysis, fiscal allocation, and budget preparation. Summarize budgets and submit recommendations for the approval or disapproval of funds requests. Seek new ways to improve efficiency and increase profits. Review operating budgets to analyze trends affecting budget needs. Examine budget estimates for completeness, accuracy, and conformance with procedures and regulations. Perform cost-benefit analyses to compare operating programs, review financial requests, or explore alternative financing methods. Interpret budget directives and establish policies for carrying out directives. Compile and analyze accounting records and other data to determine the financial resources required to implement a program. Testify before examining and fund-granting authorities, clarifying and promoting the proposed budgets.

Education/Training Required: Bachelor's degree. **Education and Training Programs:** Accounting; Finance, General. **Knowledge/ Courses:** Economics and Accounting; Clerical Practices; Administration and Management; Mathematics; Personnel and Human Resources; Law and Government.

Personality Type: Conventional-Enterprising-Investigative. **Career Clusters:** 04 Business, Management, and Administration; 06 Finance. **Career Pathways:** 04.2 Business, Financial Management, and Accounting; 06.1 Financial and Investment Planning. **Other Jobs in These Pathways:** Accountants; Auditors; Billing and Posting Clerks; Billing, Cost, and Rate Clerks; Bookkeeping, Accounting, and Auditing Clerks; Brownfield Redevelopment Specialists and Site Managers; Compliance Managers; Financial Analysts; Financial Managers, Branch or Department; Investment Fund Managers; Loss Prevention Managers; Managers, All Other; Payroll and Timekeeping Clerks; Personal Financial Advisors; Regulatory Affairs Managers; Sales Agents, Financial Services; Sales Agents, Securities and Commodities; Securities and Commodities Traders; Securities, Commodities, and Financial Services Sales Agents; Security Managers; Statement Clerks; Supply Chain Managers; Treasurers and Controllers; Wind Energy Operations Managers; Wind Energy Project Managers; others.

Business Operations Specialists, All Other

* Annual Earnings: $62,450
* Earnings Growth Potential: High (45.8%)
* Growth: 11.5%
* Annual Job Openings: 36,830
* Self-Employed: 0.6%

Skills—Most Important: Mathematics Skills; Thought-Processing Skills; Management Skills. **Other High-Level Skills:** Science Skills; Social Skills; Communication Skills; Equipment Use/ Maintenance Skills.

This occupation includes all business operations specialists not listed separately. Because this is a highly diverse occupation, no data is available for some information topics.

Education/Training Required: Bachelor's degree. **Education and Training Program:** Business Administration and Management, General. **Career Cluster:** 04 Business, Management, and Administration. **Career Pathway:** 04.1 Management. **Other Jobs in This Pathway:** Administrative Services Managers; Brownfield Redevelopment Specialists and Site Managers; Business Continuity Planners; Chief Executives; Chief Sustainability Officers; Compliance Managers; Computer and Information Systems Managers; Construction Managers; Customs Brokers; Energy Auditors; First-Line Supervisors of Office and Administrative Support Workers; General and Operations Managers; Investment Fund Managers; Loss Prevention Managers; Management Analysts; Managers, All Other; Public Relations Specialists; Regulatory Affairs Managers; Sales Managers; Security Management Specialists; Security Managers;

Supply Chain Managers; Sustainability Specialists; Wind Energy Operations Managers; Wind Energy Project Managers; others.

Job Specialization: Business Continuity Planners

Develop, maintain and implement business continuity and disaster recovery strategies and solutions. Perform risk analyses. Act as a coordinator for recovery efforts in emergency situations. Write reports to summarize testing activities, including descriptions of goals, planning, scheduling, execution, results, analysis, conclusions, and recommendations. Maintain and update organization information technology applications and network systems blueprints. Interpret government regulations and applicable codes to ensure compliance. Identify individual or transaction targets to direct intelligence collection. Establish, maintain, or test call trees to ensure appropriate communication during disaster. Design or implement products and services to mitigate risk or facilitate use of technology-based tools and methods. Create business continuity and disaster recovery budgets. Create or administer training and awareness presentations or materials. Attend professional meetings, read literature, and participate in training or other educational offerings to keep abreast of developments and technologies related to disaster recovery and business continuity. Test documented disaster recovery strategies and plans. Review existing disaster recovery, crisis management, or business continuity plans. Recommend or implement methods to monitor, evaluate, or enable resolution of safety, operations, or compliance interruptions. Prepare reports summarizing operational results, financial performance, or accomplishments.

Education/Training Required: Work experience plus degree. **Education and Training Program:** Business Administration and Management, General. **Knowledge/ Courses:** Public Safety and Security; Telecommunications; Administration and Management; Communications and Media; Geography; Economics and Accounting.

Career Cluster: 04 Business, Management, and Administration. **Career Pathway:** 04.1 Management. **Other Jobs in This Pathway:** Administrative Services Managers; Brownfield Redevelopment Specialists and Site Managers; Business Operations Specialists, All Other; Chief Executives; Chief Sustainability Officers; Compliance Managers; Computer and Information Systems Managers; Construction Managers; Customs Brokers; Energy Auditors; First-Line Supervisors of Office and Administrative Support Workers; General and Operations Managers; Investment Fund Managers; Loss Prevention Managers; Management Analysts; Managers, All Other; Public Relations Specialists; Regulatory Affairs Managers; Sales Managers; Security Management Specialists; Security Managers; Supply Chain Managers; Sustainability Specialists; Wind Energy Operations Managers; Wind Energy Project Managers; others.

Job Specialization: Customs Brokers

Prepare customs documentation and ensure that shipments meet all applicable laws to facilitate the import and export of goods. Determine and track duties and taxes payable and process payments on behalf of client. Sign documents under a power of attorney. Represent clients in meetings with customs officials and apply for duty refunds and tariff

reclassifications. Coordinate transportation and storage of imported goods. Provide advice on transportation options, types of carriers, or shipping routes. Post bonds for the products being imported or assist clients in obtaining bonds. Insure cargo against loss, damage, or pilferage. Obtain line releases for frequent shippers of low-risk commodities, high-volume entries, or multiple-container loads. Contract with freight forwarders for destination services. Arrange for transportation, warehousing, or product distribution of imported or exported products. Suggest best methods of packaging or labeling products. Request or compile necessary import documentation, such as customs invoices, certificates of origin, and cargo-control documents. Stay abreast of changes in import or export laws or regulations by reading current literature, attending meetings or conferences, or conferring with colleagues. Quote duty and tax rates on goods to be imported, based on federal tariffs and excise taxes. Prepare papers for shippers to appeal duty charges. Pay or arrange for payment of taxes and duties on shipments. Monitor or trace the location of goods. Maintain relationships with customs brokers in other ports to expedite clearing of cargo. Inform importers and exporters of steps to reduce duties and taxes. Confer with officials in various agencies to facilitate clearance of goods through customs and quarantine. Classify goods according to tariff coding system.

Education/Training Required: Postsecondary vocational training. **Education and Training Program:** Traffic, Customs, and Transportation Clerk/Technician Training. **Knowledge/Courses:** Clerical Practices; Geography; Transportation; Sales and Marketing; Law and Government; Economics and Accounting.

Personality Type: Enterprising-Conventional.

Career Cluster: 04 Business, Management, and Administration. **Career Pathway:** 04.1 Management. **Other Jobs in This Pathway:** Administrative Services Managers; Brownfield Redevelopment Specialists and Site Managers; Business Continuity Planners; Business Operations Specialists, All Other; Chief Executives; Chief Sustainability Officers; Compliance Managers; Computer and Information Systems Managers; Construction Managers; Energy Auditors; First-Line Supervisors of Office and Administrative Support Workers; General and Operations Managers; Investment Fund Managers; Loss Prevention Managers; Management Analysts; Managers, All Other; Public Relations Specialists; Regulatory Affairs Managers; Sales Managers; Security Management Specialists; Security Managers; Supply Chain Managers; Sustainability Specialists; Wind Energy Operations Managers; Wind Energy Project Managers; others.

Job Specialization: Energy Auditors

Conduct energy audits of buildings, building systems and process systems. May also conduct investment grade audits of buildings or systems. Identify and prioritize energy-saving measures. Prepare audit reports containing energy analysis results and recommendations for energy cost savings. Inspect or evaluate building envelopes, mechanical systems, electrical systems, or process systems to determine the energy consumption of each system. Collect and analyze field data related to energy usage. Perform tests such as blower-door tests to locate air leaks. Calculate potential for energy savings. Educate customers on energy efficiency or answer questions on topics such as the costs of running household appliances and the selection of energy-efficient appliances. Recommend energy-efficient technologies or alternate energy sources. Prepare job specification sheets for home energy improvements such as attic insulation, window retrofits, and heating system upgrades. Quantify energy consumption to establish baselines for energy use and need. Identify opportunities to improve the operation, maintenance, or energy efficiency of building or process systems. Analyze technical feasibility of energy-saving measures using knowledge of engineering, energy production, energy use, construction, maintenance, system operation, or process systems. Analyze energy bills including utility rates or tariffs to gather historical energy usage data.

Education/Training Required: Associate degree. **Education and Training Program:** Energy Management and Systems Technology/Technician. **Knowledge/Courses:** Building and Construction; Physics; Sales and Marketing; Design; Clerical Practices; Mechanical.

Personality Type: Conventional-Enterprising. **Career Cluster:** 04 Business, Management, and Administration. **Career Pathway:** 04.1 Management. **Other Jobs in This Pathway:** Administrative Services Managers; Brownfield Redevelopment Specialists and Site Managers; Business Continuity Planners; Business Operations Specialists, All Other; Chief Executives; Chief Sustainability Officers; Compliance Managers; Computer and Information Systems Managers; Construction Managers; Customs Brokers; First-Line Supervisors of Office and Administrative Support Workers; General and Operations Managers; Investment Fund Managers; Loss Prevention Managers; Management Analysts; Managers, All Other; Public Relations Specialists; Regulatory Affairs Managers; Sales Managers; Security Management Specialists; Security Managers; Supply Chain Managers; Sustainability Specialists; Wind Energy Operations Managers; Wind Energy Project Managers; others.

Job Specialization: Online Merchants

Plan, direct, or coordinate retail activities of businesses operating online. May perform duties such as preparing business strategies, buying merchandise, managing inventory, implementing marketing activities, fulfilling and shipping online orders, and balancing financial records. Participate in online forums and conferences to stay abreast of online retailing trends, techniques, and security threats. Upload digital media, such as photos, video, or scanned images, to online storefront, auction sites, or other shopping Websites. Order or purchase merchandise to maintain optimal inventory levels. Maintain inventory of shipping supplies, such as boxes, labels, tape, bubble wrap, loose packing materials, and tape guns. Integrate online retailing strategy with physical and catalog retailing operations. Determine and set product prices. Disclose merchant information and terms and policies of transactions in online and offline materials. Deliver e-mail confirmation of completed transactions and shipment. Create, manage, and automate orders and invoices using order management and invoicing software. Create and maintain database of customer accounts. Create and distribute offline promotional material, such as brochures, pamphlets, business cards, stationary, and signage. Collaborate with search engine shopping specialists to place marketing content in desired online locations. Cancel orders based on customer requests or inventory or delivery problems. Select and purchase technical Web services, such as Web hosting services, online merchant accounts, shopping cart software, payment gateway software, and spyware.

Education/Training Required: Work experience in a related occupation. **Education and Training Program:** E-Commerce/Electronic Commerce.

Personality Type: Enterprising-Conventional-Realistic. **Career Cluster:** 14 Marketing, Sales, and Service. **Career Pathway:** 14.2 Professional Sales and Marketing. **Other Jobs in This Pathway:** Cashiers; Counter and Rental Clerks; Door-To-Door Sales Workers, News and Street Vendors, and Related Workers; Driver/Sales Workers; Energy Brokers; First-Line Supervisors of Non-Retail Sales Workers; First-Line Supervisors of Retail Sales Workers; Hotel, Motel, and Resort Desk Clerks; Marketing Managers; Marking Clerks; Order Fillers, Wholesale and Retail Sales; Parts Salespersons; Property, Real Estate, and Community Association Managers; Real Estate Sales Agents; Reservation and Transportation Ticket Agents and Travel Clerks; Retail Salespersons; Sales and Related Workers, All Other; Sales Representatives, Services, All Other; Sales Representatives, Wholesale and Manufacturing, Except Technical and Scientific Products; Sales Representatives, Wholesale and Manufacturing, Technical and Scientific Products; Solar Sales Representatives and Assessors; Stock Clerks—Stockroom, Warehouse, or Storage Yard; Stock Clerks, Sales Floor; Telemarketers; Wholesale and Retail Buyers, Except Farm Products; others.

Job Specialization: Security Management Specialists

Conduct security assessments for organizations, and design security systems and processes. May specialize in areas such as physical security, personnel security, and information security. May work in fields such as health care, banking, gaming, security engineering, or manufacturing. Prepare documentation for case reports or court proceedings. Review design drawings or technical documents for completeness, correctness, or appropriateness. Monitor tapes or digital recordings to identify the source of losses. Interview witnesses or suspects to identify persons responsible for security breaches, establish losses, pursue prosecutions, or obtain restitution. Budget and schedule security design work. Develop conceptual designs of security systems. Respond to emergency situations on an on-call basis. Train personnel in security procedures or use of security equipment. Prepare, maintain, or update security procedures, security system drawings, or related documentation. Monitor the work of contractors in the design, construction, and startup phases of security systems. Inspect security design features, installations, or programs to ensure compliance with applicable standards or regulations. Inspect fire, intruder detection, or other security systems. Engineer, install, maintain, or repair security systems, programmable logic controls, or other security-related electronic systems. Recommend improvements in security systems or procedures. Develop or review specifications for design or construction of security systems. Design security policies, programs, or practices to ensure adequate security relating to protection of assets, alarm response, and access card use.

Education/Training Required: Bachelor's degree. **Education and Training Program:** Security and Loss Prevention Services.

Personality Type: Realistic-Investigative-Conventional. **Career Cluster:** 04 Business, Management, and Administration. **Career**

Pathway: 04.1 Management. **Other Jobs in This Pathway:** Administrative Services Managers; Brownfield Redevelopment Specialists and Site Managers; Business Continuity Planners; Business Operations Specialists, All Other; Chief Executives; Chief Sustainability Officers; Compliance Managers; Computer and Information Systems Managers; Construction Managers; Customs Brokers; Energy Auditors; First-Line Supervisors of Office and Administrative Support Workers; General and Operations Managers; Investment Fund Managers; Loss Prevention Managers; Management Analysts; Managers, All Other; Public Relations Specialists; Regulatory Affairs Managers; Sales Managers; Security Managers; Supply Chain Managers; Sustainability Specialists; Wind Energy Operations Managers; Wind Energy Project Managers; others.

Job Specialization: Sustainability Specialists

Address organizational sustainability issues, such as waste stream management, green building practices, and green procurement plans. Review and revise sustainability proposals or policies. Research or review regulatory, technical, or market issues related to sustainability. Identify or investigate violations of natural resources, waste management, recycling, or other environmental policies. Identify or create new sustainability indicators. Write grant applications, rebate applications, or project proposals to secure funding for sustainability projects. Provide technical or administrative support for sustainability programs or issues. Identify or procure needed resources to implement sustainability programs or projects. Create or maintain plans or other documents related to sustainability projects. Develop reports or presentations to communicate the effectiveness of sustainability initiatives. Create marketing or outreach media, such as brochures or Websites, to communicate sustainability issues, procedures, or objectives. Collect information about waste stream management or green building practices to inform decision makers. Assess or propose sustainability initiatives, considering factors such as cost-effectiveness, technical feasibility, and acceptance. Monitor or track sustainability indicators, such as energy usage, natural resource usage, waste generation, and recycling. Develop sustainability project goals, objectives, initiatives, or strategies in collaboration with other sustainability professionals.

Education/Training Required: Bachelor's degree. **Education and Training Program:** Business Administration and Management, General.

Career Cluster: 04 Business, Management, and Administration. **Career Pathway:** 04.1 Management. **Other Jobs in This Pathway:** Administrative Services Managers; Brownfield Redevelopment Specialists and Site Managers; Business Continuity Planners; Business Operations Specialists, All Other; Chief Executives; Chief Sustainability Officers; Compliance Managers; Computer and Information Systems Managers; Construction Managers; Customs Brokers; Energy Auditors; First-Line Supervisors of Office and Administrative Support Workers; General and Operations Managers; Investment Fund Managers; Loss Prevention Managers; Management Analysts; Managers, All Other; Public Relations Specialists; Regulatory Affairs Managers; Sales Managers; Security Management Specialists; Security Managers; Supply Chain Managers; Wind Energy Operations Managers; Wind Energy Project Managers; others.

Business Teachers, Postsecondary

❋ Annual Earnings: $73,760

❋ Earnings Growth Potential: Very high (53.0%)

❋ Growth: 15.1%

❋ Annual Job Openings: 2,000

❋ Self-Employed: 0.2%

Skills—Most Important: Communication Skills; Mathematics Skills; Thought-Processing Skills. **Other High-Level Skills:** Social Skills; Management Skills.

Teach courses in business administration and management, such as accounting, finance, human resources, labor relations, marketing, and operations research. Prepare and deliver lectures to undergraduate or graduate students on topics such as financial accounting, principles of marketing, and operations management. Evaluate and grade students' classwork, assignments, and papers. Compile, administer, and grade examinations or assign this work to others. Prepare course materials such as syllabi, homework assignments, and handouts. Maintain student attendance records, grades, and other required records. Initiate, facilitate, and moderate classroom discussions. Plan, evaluate, and revise curricula, course content, and course materials and methods of instruction. Maintain regularly scheduled office hours to advise and assist students. Keep abreast of developments in the field by reading current literature, talking with colleagues, and participating in professional organizations and conferences. Advise students on academic and vocational curricula and career issues. Select and obtain materials and supplies such as textbooks. Collaborate with colleagues to address teaching and research issues. Collaborate with members of the business community to improve programs, to develop new programs, and to provide student access to learning opportunities such as internships. Participate in student recruitment, registration, and placement activities. Serve on academic or administrative committees that deal with institutional policies, departmental matters, and academic issues.

Education/Training Required: Doctoral degree. **Education and Training Programs:** Accounting; Actuarial Science; Business Administration and Management, General; Business Statistics; Business Teacher Education; Business/Commerce, General; Business/Corporate Communications; Entrepreneurship/Entrepreneurial Studies; Finance, General; Financial Planning and Services; Franchising and Franchise Operations; Human Resources Management/Personnel Administration, General; Insurance; International Business/Trade/Commerce; International Finance; International Marketing; Investments and Securities; Labor and Industrial Relations; Logistics, Materials, and Supply Chain Management; Management Science; Marketing Research; Marketing/Marketing Management, General; Operations Management and Supervision; Organizational Behavior Studies; Public Finance; Purchasing, Procurement/Acquisitions, and Contracts Management. **Knowledge/Courses:** Sociology and Anthropology; Education and Training; Communications and Media; Sales and Marketing; Economics and Accounting; English Language.

Personality Type: Social-Enterprising-Investigative. **Career Clusters:** 04 Business, Management, and Administration; 05 Education and Training; 06 Finance; 14 Marketing, Sales, and Service. **Career Pathways:** 04.5 Marketing; 06.1 Financial and Investment Planning; 06.4 Insurance Services; 04.3 Human Resources;

05.3 Teaching/Training; 14.1 Management and Entrepreneurship; 14.5 Marketing Information Management and Research; 04.2 Business, Financial Management, and Accounting; 04.1 Management. **Other Jobs in These Pathways:** Accountants; Auditors; Bookkeeping, Accounting, and Auditing Clerks; Brownfield Redevelopment Specialists and Site Managers; Business Continuity Planners; Business Operations Specialists, All Other; Compliance Managers; Customs Brokers; Elementary School Teachers, Except Special Education; Energy Auditors; First-Line Supervisors of Office and Administrative Support Workers; First-Line Supervisors of Retail Sales Workers; General and Operations Managers; Investment Fund Managers; Loss Prevention Managers; Managers, All Other; Regulatory Affairs Managers; Secondary School Teachers, Except Special and Career/Technical Education; Security Management Specialists; Security Managers; Supply Chain Managers; Sustainability Specialists; Teacher Assistants; Wind Energy Operations Managers; Wind Energy Project Managers; 37 other postsecondary teaching occupations; others.

Captains, Mates, and Pilots of Water Vessels

- ❊ Annual Earnings: $64,180
- ❊ Earnings Growth Potential: Very high (52.2%)
- ❊ Growth: 17.3%
- ❊ Annual Job Openings: 1,950
- ❊ Self-Employed: 7.2%

Skills—Most Important: Equipment Use/Maintenance Skills; Management Skills;

Mathematics Skills. **Other High-Level Skills:** Social Skills; Thought-Processing Skills; Communication Skills.

Job Specialization: Mates—Ship, Boat, and Barge

Supervise and coordinate activities of crew aboard ships, boats, barges, or dredges. Determine geographical positions of ships using lorans, azimuths of celestial bodies, or computers. Use this information to determine the course and speed of a ship. Supervise crews in cleaning and maintaining decks, superstructures, and bridges. Supervise crew members in the repair or replacement of defective gear and equipment. Steer vessels utilizing navigational devices such as compasses and sextons and navigational aids such as lighthouses and buoys. Observe water from ships' mastheads to advise on navigational direction. Inspect equipment such as cargo-handling gear, lifesaving equipment, visual-signaling equipment, and fishing, towing, or dredging gear to detect problems. Arrange for ships to be stocked, fueled, and repaired. Assume command of vessels in the event that ships' masters become incapacitated. Participate in activities related to maintenance of vessel security. Stand watches on vessels during specified periods. Observe loading and unloading of cargo and equipment to ensure that handling and storage are performed according to specifications.

Education/Training Required: Work experience in a related occupation. **Education and Training Programs:** Commercial Fishing; Marine Science/Merchant Marine Officer; Marine Transportation Services, Other. **Knowledge/Courses:** Transportation; Geography; Public Safety and Security;

Telecommunications; Personnel and Human Resources; Mechanical.

Personality Type: Enterprising-Realistic-Conventional. **Career Cluster:** 16 Transportation, Distribution, and Logistics. **Career Pathway:** 16.1 Transportation Operations. **Other Jobs in This Pathway:** Airline Pilots, Copilots, and Flight Engineers; Automotive and Watercraft Service Attendants; Automotive Master Mechanics; Bus Drivers, School or Special Client; Bus Drivers, Transit and Intercity; Commercial Pilots; Crane and Tower Operators; First-Line Supervisors of Helpers, Laborers, and Material Movers, Hand; First-Line Supervisors of Transportation and Material-Moving Machine and Vehicle Operators; Freight and Cargo Inspectors; Heavy and Tractor-Trailer Truck Drivers; Laborers and Freight, Stock, and Material Movers, Hand; Light Truck or Delivery Services Drivers; Motor Vehicle Operators, All Other; Operating Engineers and Other Construction Equipment Operators; Parking Lot Attendants; Pilots, Ship; Railroad Conductors and Yardmasters; Sailors and Marine Oilers; Ship and Boat Captains; Storage and Distribution Managers; Taxi Drivers and Chauffeurs; Transportation Inspectors; Transportation Managers; Transportation Workers, All Other; others.

Job Specialization: Pilots, Ship

Command ships to steer them into and out of harbors, estuaries, straits, and sounds and on rivers, lakes, and bays. Must be licensed by U.S. Coast Guard with limitations indicating class and tonnage of vessels for which licenses are valid and routes and waters that may be piloted. Maintain and repair boats and equipment. Give directions to crew members who are steering ships. Make nautical maps. Set ships' courses that avoid reefs, outlying shoals, and other hazards utilizing navigational aids such as lighthouses and buoys. Report to appropriate authorities any violations of federal or state pilotage laws. Relieve crew members on tugs and launches. Provide assistance to vessels approaching or leaving seacoasts, navigating harbors, and docking and undocking. Provide assistance in maritime rescue operations. Prevent ships under their navigational control from engaging in unsafe operations. Operate amphibious craft during troop landings. Maintain ship logs. Learn to operate new technology systems and procedures through instruction, simulators, and models. Advise ships' masters on harbor rules and customs procedures. Steer ships into and out of berths or signal tugboat captains to berth and unberth ships. Serve as a vessel's docking master on arrival at a port and when at a berth. Operate ship-to-shore radios to exchange information for ship operations. Consult maps, charts, weather reports, and navigation equipment to determine and direct ship movements. Direct courses and speeds of ships based on specialized knowledge of local winds, weather, water depths, tides, currents, and hazards. Oversee cargo storage on or below decks.

Education/Training Required: Work experience in a related occupation. **Education and Training Programs:** Commercial Fishing; Marine Science/Merchant Marine Officer; Marine Transportation Services, Other. **Knowledge/Courses:** Transportation; Geography; Public Safety and Security; Telecommunications; Mechanical Devices; Law and Government.

Personality Type: Realistic-Conventional-Investigative. **Career Cluster:** 16 Transportation, Distribution, and Logistics. **Career Pathway:**

16.1 Transportation Operations. **Other Jobs in This Pathway:** Airline Pilots, Copilots, and Flight Engineers; Automotive and Watercraft Service Attendants; Automotive Master Mechanics; Bus Drivers, School or Special Client; Bus Drivers, Transit and Intercity; Commercial Pilots; Crane and Tower Operators; First-Line Supervisors of Helpers, Laborers, and Material Movers, Hand; First-Line Supervisors of Transportation and Material-Moving Machine and Vehicle Operators; Freight and Cargo Inspectors; Heavy and Tractor-Trailer Truck Drivers; Laborers and Freight, Stock, and Material Movers, Hand; Light Truck or Delivery Services Drivers; Mates—Ship, Boat, and Barge; Motor Vehicle Operators, All Other; Operating Engineers and Other Construction Equipment Operators; Parking Lot Attendants; Railroad Conductors and Yardmasters; Sailors and Marine Oilers; Ship and Boat Captains; Storage and Distribution Managers; Taxi Drivers and Chauffeurs; Transportation Inspectors; Transportation Managers; Transportation Workers, All Other; others.

Job Specialization: Ship and Boat Captains

Command vessels in oceans, bays, lakes, rivers, and coastal waters. Assign watches and living quarters to crew members. Sort logs, form log booms, and salvage lost logs. Perform various marine duties such as checking for oil spills or other pollutants around ports and harbors and patrolling beaches. Contact buyers to sell cargo such as fish. Tow and maneuver barges or signal tugboats to tow barges to destinations. Signal passing vessels using whistles, flashing lights, flags, and radios. Resolve questions or problems with customs officials. Read gauges to verify sufficient levels of hydraulic fluid, air pressure, and oxygen.

Purchase supplies and equipment. Measure depths of water using depth-measuring equipment. Maintain boats and equipment on board, including engines, winches, navigational systems, fire extinguishers, and life preservers. Collect fares from customers or signal ferryboat helpers to collect fares. Arrange for ships to be fueled, restocked with supplies, and repaired. Signal crew members or deckhands to rig tow lines, open or close gates and ramps, and pull guard chains across entries. Maintain records of daily activities, personnel reports, ship positions and movements, ports of call, weather and sea conditions, pollution control efforts, and/or cargo and passenger status. Inspect vessels to ensure efficient and safe operation and conformance to regulations.

Education/Training Required: Work experience in a related occupation. **Education and Training Programs:** Commercial Fishing; Marine Science/Merchant Marine Officer; Marine Transportation Services, Other. **Knowledge/Courses:** Transportation; Public Safety and Security; Geography; Telecommunications; Mechanical Devices; Psychology.

Personality Type: Enterprising-Realistic. **Career Cluster:** 16 Transportation, Distribution, and Logistics. **Career Pathway:** 16.1 Transportation Operations. **Other Jobs in This Pathway:** Airline Pilots, Copilots, and Flight Engineers; Automotive and Watercraft Service Attendants; Automotive Master Mechanics; Bus Drivers, School or Special Client; Bus Drivers, Transit and Intercity; Commercial Pilots; Crane and Tower Operators; First-Line Supervisors of Helpers, Laborers, and Material Movers, Hand; First-Line Supervisors of Transportation and Material-Moving Machine and Vehicle Operators; Freight and Cargo Inspectors; Heavy and Tractor-Trailer Truck Drivers; Laborers and Freight, Stock, and Material Movers, Hand; Light Truck or Delivery Services Drivers; Mates—Ship, Boat, and Barge; Motor Vehicle Operators, All Other; Operating Engineers and Other Construction Equipment Operators; Parking Lot Attendants; Pilots, Ship; Railroad Conductors and Yardmasters; Sailors and Marine Oilers; Storage and Distribution Managers; Taxi Drivers and Chauffeurs; Transportation Inspectors; Transportation Managers; Transportation Workers, All Other; others.

Cardiovascular Technologists and Technicians

- ❋ Annual Earnings: $49,410
- ❋ Earnings Growth Potential: High (46.1%)
- ❋ Growth: 24.1%
- ❋ Annual Job Openings: 1,910
- ❋ Self-Employed: 0.8%

Skills—Most Important: Science Skills; Equipment Use/Maintenance Skills; Communication Skills. **Other High-Level Skills:** Social Skills; Thought-Processing Skills.

Conduct tests on pulmonary or cardiovascular systems of patients for diagnostic purposes. May conduct or assist in electrocardiograms, cardiac catheterizations, pulmonary-functions, lung capacity, and similar tests. Monitor patients' blood pressure and heart rate using electrocardiogram (EKG) equipment during diagnostic and therapeutic procedures to notify the physician if something appears wrong. Monitor patients' comfort and safety during tests, alerting physicians to abnormalities or changes in patient responses. Explain testing procedures to patient to obtain cooperation and reduce anxiety. Prepare reports of diagnostic procedures for interpretation by physician. Observe gauges, recorder, and video screens of data analysis system during imaging of cardiovascular system. Conduct EKG, phonocardiogram, echocardiogram, stress testing, or other cardiovascular tests to record patients' cardiac activity using specialized electronic test equipment, recording devices, and laboratory instruments. Prepare and position patients for testing. Obtain and record patient identification, medical history, or test results. Attach electrodes to the patients' chests, arms, and legs; connect electrodes to leads from the EKG machine; and operate the EKG machine to obtain a reading. Adjust equipment and controls according to physicians' orders or established protocol. Check, test, and maintain cardiology equipment, making minor repairs when necessary. Supervise and train other cardiology technologists and students.

Education/Training Required: Associate degree. **Education and Training Programs:** Cardiopulmonary Technology/Technologist; Cardiovascular Technology/Technologist; Electrocardiograph Technology/Technician; Perfusion Technology/Perfusionist. **Knowledge/Courses:** Medicine and Dentistry; Biology; Psychology; Customer and Personal Service; Sociology and Anthropology; Chemistry.

Personality Type: Realistic-Investigative-Social. **Career Cluster:** 08 Health Science. **Career Pathway:** 08.2 Diagnostics Services. **Other Jobs in This Pathway:** Ambulance Drivers and Attendants, Except Emergency Medical Technicians; Anesthesiologist Assistants; Cytogenetic Technologists; Cytotechnologists; Diagnostic Medical Sonographers; Emergency Medical Technicians and Paramedics; Endoscopy Technicians; Health Diagnosing and Treating

Practitioners, All Other; Health Technologists and Technicians, All Other; Healthcare Practitioners and Technical Workers, All Other; Histotechnologists and Histologic Technicians; Medical and Clinical Laboratory Technicians; Medical and Clinical Laboratory Technologists; Medical and Health Services Managers; Medical Assistants; Medical Equipment Preparers; Neurodiagnostic Technologists; Nuclear Medicine Technologists; Ophthalmic Laboratory Technicians; Physical Scientists, All Other; Physician Assistants; Radiologic Technicians; Radiologic Technologists; Surgical Technologists; Veterinary Assistants and Laboratory Animal Caretakers; others.

Cargo and Freight Agents

❋ Annual Earnings: $37,150

❋ Earnings Growth Potential: Medium (40.5%)

❋ Growth: 23.9%

❋ Annual Job Openings: 4,030

❋ Self-Employed: 0.3%

Skills—Most Important: Social Skills; Management Skills; Communication Skills. **Other High-Level Skills:** Thought-Processing Skills.

Expedite and route movement of incoming and outgoing cargo and freight shipments in airline, train, and trucking terminals and shipping docks. Take orders from customers and arrange pickup of freight and cargo for delivery to loading platform. Prepare and examine bills of lading to determine shipping charges and tariffs. Negotiate and arrange transport of goods with shipping or freight companies. Notify consignees, passengers, or customers of the arrival of freight or baggage and arrange for delivery. Advise clients on transportation and payment methods. Prepare manifests showing baggage, mail, and freight weights and number of passengers on airplanes and transmit data to destinations. Determine method of shipment and prepare bills of lading, invoices, and other shipping documents. Check import/export documentation to determine cargo contents and classify goods into different fee or tariff groups using a tariff coding system. Estimate freight or postal rates and record shipment costs and weights. Enter shipping information into a computer by hand or by using a handheld scanner that reads barcodes on goods. Retrieve stored items and trace lost shipments as necessary. Pack goods for shipping using tools such as staplers, strapping machines, and hammers. Direct delivery trucks to shipping doors or designated marshalling areas and help load and unload goods safely. Inspect and count items received and check them against invoices or other documents, recording shortages and rejecting damaged goods. Install straps, braces, and padding to loads to prevent shifting or damage during shipment. Keep records of all goods shipped, received, and stored. Coordinate and supervise activities of workers engaged in packing and shipping merchandise. Arrange insurance coverage for goods.

Education/Training Required: Moderate-term on-the-job training. **Education and Training Program:** General Office Occupations and Clerical Services. **Knowledge/Courses:** Transportation; Geography; Customer and Personal Service; Clerical Practices; Administration and Management.

Personality Type: Conventional-Enterprising-Realistic. **Career Cluster:** 04 Business, Management, and Administration. **Career Pathway:** 04.6 Administrative and

Information Support. **Other Jobs in This Pathway:** Couriers and Messengers; Court Clerks; Court, Municipal, and License Clerks; Customer Service Representatives; Data Entry Keyers; Dispatchers, Except Police, Fire, and Ambulance; Executive Secretaries and Executive Administrative Assistants; File Clerks; Human Resources Assistants, Except Payroll and Timekeeping; Information and Record Clerks, All Other; Insurance Claims Clerks; Insurance Policy Processing Clerks; Interviewers, Except Eligibility and Loan; Mail Clerks and Mail Machine Operators, Except Postal Service; Office and Administrative Support Workers, All Other; Office Clerks, General; Order Clerks; Patient Representatives; Postal Service Mail Carriers; Postal Service Mail Sorters, Processors, and Processing Machine Operators; Receptionists and Information Clerks; Secretaries and Administrative Assistants, Except Legal, Medical, and Executive; Shipping, Receiving, and Traffic Clerks; Switchboard Operators, Including Answering Service; Word Processors and Typists; others.

Job Specialization: Freight Forwarders

Research rates, routings, or modes of transport for shipment of products. Maintain awareness of regulations affecting the international movement of cargo. Make arrangements for additional services such as storage and inland transportation. Select shipment routes based on nature of goods shipped, transit times, or security needs. Determine efficient and cost-effective methods of moving goods from one location to another. Reserve necessary space on ships, aircraft, trains, or trucks. Arrange delivery or storage of goods at destinations. Arrange for special transport of sensitive cargoes, such as

livestock, food, and medical supplies. Assist clients in obtaining insurance reimbursements. Calculate weight, volume, or cost of goods to be moved. Complete shipping documentation, including bills of lading, packing lists, dock receipts, and certificates of origin. Consolidate loads with a common destination to reduce costs to individual shippers. Inform clients of factors such as shipping options, timelines, transfers, and regulations affecting shipments. Keep records of goods dispatched and received. Maintain current knowledge of relevant legislation, political situations, or other factors that could affect freight shipping. Monitor and record locations of goods in transit. Negotiate shipping rates with freight carriers. Obtain or arrange cargo insurance. Pay or arrange for payment of freight and insurance fees. Prepare invoices and cost quotations for freight transportation. Recommend or arrange appropriate merchandise packing methods, according to climate, terrain, weight, nature of goods, or costs. Verify proper packaging and labeling of exported goods.

Education/Training Required: Moderate-term on-the-job training. **Education and Training Program:** General Office Occupations and Clerical Services. **Knowledge/Courses:** No data available.

Personality Type: Conventional-Enterprising. **Career Cluster:** 04 Business, Management, and Administration. **Career Pathway:** 04.6 Administrative and Information Support. **Other Jobs in This Pathway:** Couriers and Messengers; Court Clerks; Court, Municipal, and License Clerks; Customer Service Representatives; Data Entry Keyers; Dispatchers, Except Police, Fire, and Ambulance; Executive Secretaries and Executive Administrative Assistants; File Clerks; Human Resources

Assistants, Except Payroll and Timekeeping; Information and Record Clerks, All Other; Insurance Claims Clerks; Insurance Policy Processing Clerks; Interviewers, Except Eligibility and Loan; Mail Clerks and Mail Machine Operators, Except Postal Service; Office and Administrative Support Workers, All Other; Office Clerks, General; Order Clerks; Patient Representatives; Postal Service Mail Carriers; Postal Service Mail Sorters, Processors, and Processing Machine Operators; Receptionists and Information Clerks; Secretaries and Administrative Assistants, Except Legal, Medical, and Executive; Shipping, Receiving, and Traffic Clerks; Switchboard Operators, Including Answering Service; Word Processors and Typists; others.

Carpenters

- ❋ Annual Earnings: $39,530
- ❋ Earnings Growth Potential: Medium (37.6%)
- ❋ Growth: 12.9%
- ❋ Annual Job Openings: 32,540
- ❋ Self-Employed: 32.0%

Skills—Most Important: Mathematics Skills; Equipment Use/Maintenance Skills; Management Skills. **Other High-Level Skills:** Social Skills; Thought-Processing Skills.

Job Specialization: Construction Carpenters

Construct, erect, install, and repair structures and fixtures of wood, plywood, and wallboard using carpenter's hand tools and power tools. Study specifications in blueprints, sketches, or building plans to prepare project layout and determine dimensions and

materials. Shape or cut materials to specified measurements using hand tools, machines, or power saw. Follow safety rules and regulations and maintain a safe and clean environment. Measure and mark cutting lines on materials using ruler, pencil, chalk, and marking gauge. Install structures and fixtures, such as windows, frames, floorings, and trim, or hardware, using carpenter's hand and power tools. Verify trueness of structure using plumb bob and level. Build or repair cabinets, doors, frameworks, floors, and other wooden fixtures used in buildings. Assemble and fasten materials to make framework or props using hand tools and wood screws, nails, dowel pins, or glue. Remove damaged or defective parts or sections of structures and repair or replace. Inspect ceiling or floor tile, wall coverings, siding, glass, or woodwork to detect broken or damaged structures. Erect scaffolding and ladders for assembling structures above ground level. Finish surfaces of woodwork or wallboard in houses and buildings using paint, hand tools, and paneling. Fill cracks and other defects in plaster or plasterboard and sand patch using patching plaster, trowel, and sanding tool. Select and order lumber and other materials.

Education/Training Required: Long-term on-the-job training. **Education and Training Program:** Carpentry/Carpenter. **Knowledge/ Courses:** Building and Construction; Design; Mechanical Devices; Engineering and Technology; Production and Processing; Mathematics.

Personality Type: Realistic-Conventional-Investigative. **Career Cluster:** 02 Architecture and Construction. **Career Pathway:** 02.2 Construction. **Other Jobs in This Pathway:** Brickmasons and Blockmasons; Cement Masons and Concrete Finishers; Construction and

Building Inspectors; Construction Laborers; Construction Managers; Cost Estimators; Drywall and Ceiling Tile Installers; Electrical Power-Line Installers and Repairers; Electricians; Engineering Technicians, Except Drafters, All Other; Excavating and Loading Machine and Dragline Operators; First-Line Supervisors of Construction Trades and Extraction Workers; Heating and Air Conditioning Mechanics and Installers; Helpers—Carpenters; Helpers—Electricians; Helpers—Pipelayers, Plumbers, Pipefitters, and Steamfitters; Highway Maintenance Workers; Operating Engineers and Other Construction Equipment Operators; Painters, Construction and Maintenance; Pipe Fitters and Steamfitters; Plumbers; Refrigeration Mechanics and Installers; Roofers; Rough Carpenters; Solar Energy Installation Managers; others.

Job Specialization: Rough Carpenters

Build rough wooden structures, such as concrete forms, scaffolds, tunnel, bridge, or sewer supports, billboard signs, and temporary frame shelters according to sketches, blueprints, or oral instructions. Study blueprints and diagrams to determine dimensions of structure or form to be constructed. Measure materials or distances using square, measuring tape, or rule to lay out work. Cut or saw boards, timbers, or plywood to required size using handsaw, power saw, or woodworking machine. Assemble and fasten material together to construct wood or metal framework of structure using bolts, nails, or screws. Anchor and brace forms and other structures in place using nails, bolts, anchor rods, steel cables, planks, wedges, and timbers. Mark cutting lines on materials using pencil and scriber. Erect forms, framework, scaffolds, hoists,

roof supports, or chutes using hand tools, plumb rule, and level. Install rough door and window frames, subflooring, fixtures, or temporary supports in structures undergoing construction or repair. Examine structural timbers and supports to detect decay and replace timbers as required using hand tools, nuts, and bolts.

Education/Training Required: Long-term on-the-job training. **Education and Training Program:** Carpentry/Carpenter. **Knowledge/ Courses:** Building and Construction; Design; Mechanical Devices; Production and Processing; Public Safety and Security; Mathematics.

Personality Type: Realistic-Conventional-Investigative. **Career Cluster:** 02 Architecture and Construction. **Career Pathway:** 02.2 Construction. **Other Jobs in This Pathway:** Brickmasons and Blockmasons; Cement Masons and Concrete Finishers; Construction and Building Inspectors; Construction Carpenters; Construction Laborers; Construction Managers; Cost Estimators; Drywall and Ceiling Tile Installers; Electrical Power-Line Installers and Repairers; Electricians; Engineering Technicians, Except Drafters, All Other; Excavating and Loading Machine and Dragline Operators; First-Line Supervisors of Construction Trades and Extraction Workers; Heating and Air Conditioning Mechanics and Installers; Helpers—Carpenters; Helpers—Electricians; Helpers—Pipelayers, Plumbers, Pipefitters, and Steamfitters; Highway Maintenance Workers; Operating Engineers and Other Construction Equipment Operators; Painters, Construction and Maintenance; Pipe Fitters and Steamfitters; Plumbers; Refrigeration Mechanics and Installers; Roofers; Solar Energy Installation Managers; others.

Cement Masons and Concrete Finishers

❋ Annual Earnings: $35,450

❋ Earnings Growth Potential: Low (34.8%)

❋ Growth: 12.9%

❋ Annual Job Openings: 7,640

❋ Self-Employed: 4.7%

Skills—Most Important: Mathematics Skills; Equipment Use/Maintenance Skills; Social Skills.

Smooth and finish surfaces of poured concrete, such as floors, walks, sidewalks, roads, or curbs using hand and power tools. Align forms for sidewalks, curbs, or gutters; patch voids; and use saws to cut expansion joints. Check the forms that hold the concrete to see that they are properly constructed. Set the forms that hold concrete to the desired pitch and depth and align them. Spread, level, and smooth concrete using rake, shovel, hand or power trowel, hand or power screed, and float. Mold expansion joints and edges using edging tools, jointers, and straightedge. Monitor how the wind, heat, or cold affect the curing of the concrete throughout the entire process. Signal truck driver to position truck to facilitate pouring concrete and move chute to direct concrete on forms. Produce rough concrete surface using broom. Operate power vibrator to compact concrete. Direct the casting of the concrete and supervise laborers who use shovels or special tools to spread it. Cut out damaged areas, drill holes for reinforcing rods, and position reinforcing rods to repair concrete using power saw and drill. Wet concrete surface and rub with stone to smooth surface and obtain specified finish.

Education/Training Required: Moderate-term on-the-job training. **Education and Training Program:** Concrete Finishing/Concrete Finisher. **Knowledge/Courses:** Building and Construction; Mechanical Devices; Engineering and Technology; Design; Chemistry; Physics.

Personality Type: Realistic-Enterprising. **Career Cluster:** 02 Architecture and Construction. **Career Pathway:** 02.2 Construction. **Other Jobs in This Pathway:** Brickmasons and Blockmasons; Construction and Building Inspectors; Construction Carpenters; Construction Laborers; Construction Managers; Cost Estimators; Drywall and Ceiling Tile Installers; Electrical Power-Line Installers and Repairers; Electricians; Engineering Technicians, Except Drafters, All Other; Excavating and Loading Machine and Dragline Operators; First-Line Supervisors of Construction Trades and Extraction Workers; Heating and Air Conditioning Mechanics and Installers; Helpers—Carpenters; Helpers—Electricians; Helpers—Pipelayers, Plumbers, Pipefitters, and Steamfitters; Highway Maintenance Workers; Operating Engineers and Other Construction Equipment Operators; Painters, Construction and Maintenance; Pipe Fitters and Steamfitters; Plumbers; Refrigeration Mechanics and Installers; Roofers; Rough Carpenters; Solar Energy Installation Managers; others.

Chief Executives

- ❋ Annual Earnings: $165,080
- ❋ Earnings Growth Potential: Very high (54.5%)
- ❋ Growth: −1.4%
- ❋ Annual Job Openings: 11,250
- ❋ Self-Employed: 21.6%

Skills—Most Important: Management Skills; Thought-Processing Skills; Social Skills. **Other High-Level Skills:** Communication Skills; Mathematics Skills.

Determine and formulate policies and provide the overall direction of companies or private and public sector organizations within the guidelines set up by a board of directors or similar governing body. Plan, direct, or coordinate operational activities at the highest level of management with the help of subordinate executives and staff managers. Direct and coordinate an organization's financial and budget activities to fund operations, maximize investments, and increase efficiency. Confer with board members, organization officials, and staff members to discuss issues, coordinate activities, and resolve problems. Analyze operations to evaluate performance of a company and its staff in meeting objectives and to determine potential cost reduction, program improvement, or policy change. Direct, plan, and implement policies, objectives, and activities of organizations or businesses to ensure continuing operations, to maximize returns on investments, and to increase productivity. Prepare budgets for approval, including those for funding and implementation of programs. Direct and coordinate activities of businesses or departments concerned with production, pricing, sales, and/or distribution of products. Negotiate or approve contracts and agreements with suppliers, distributors, federal and state agencies, and other entities. Review reports submitted by staff members to recommend approval or to suggest changes. Appoint department heads or managers and assign or delegate responsibilities to them. Direct human resources activities, including the approval of human resource plans and activities, the selection of directors and other high-level staff, and establishment and organization of major departments.

Education/Training Required: Work experience plus degree. **Education and Training Programs:** Business Administration and Management, General; Business/Commerce, General; Entrepreneurship/Entrepreneurial Studies; International Business/Trade/Commerce; International Relations and Affairs; Public Administration; Public Administration and Social Service Professions, Other; Public Policy Analysis, General; Transportation/Mobility Management. **Knowledge/Courses:** Economics and Accounting; Administration and Management; Sales and Marketing; Personnel and Human Resources; Law and Government; Medicine and Dentistry.

Personality Type: Enterprising-Conventional. **Career Clusters:** 04 Business, Management, and Administration; 07 Government and Public Administration; 10 Human Services; 16 Transportation, Distribution, and Logistics. **Career Pathways:** 07.6 Regulation; 07.3 Foreign Service; 07.1 Governance; 04.1 Management; 16.2 Logistics, Planning, and Management Services; 10.3 Family and Community Services. **Other Jobs in These Pathways:** Brownfield Redevelopment Specialists and Site Managers; Business Continuity Planners;

Business Operations Specialists, All Other; Chief Sustainability Officers; Compliance Managers; Construction Managers; Customs Brokers; Energy Auditors; First-Line Supervisors of Office and Administrative Support Workers; General and Operations Managers; Investment Fund Managers; Loss Prevention Managers; Management Analysts; Managers, All Other; Nannies; Personal Care Aides; Regulatory Affairs Managers; Sales Managers; Security Management Specialists; Security Managers; Supply Chain Managers; Sustainability Specialists; Wind Energy Operations Managers; Wind Energy Project Managers; others.

Job Specialization: Chief Sustainability Officers

Communicate and coordinate with management, shareholders, customers, and employees to address sustainability issues. Enact or oversee a corporate sustainability strategy. Identify educational, training, or other development opportunities for sustainability employees or volunteers. Identify and evaluate pilot projects or programs to enhance the sustainability research agenda. Conduct sustainability- or environment-related risk assessments. Create and maintain sustainability program documents, such as schedules and budgets. Write project proposals, grant applications, or other documents to pursue funding for environmental initiatives. Supervise employees or volunteers working on sustainability projects. Write and distribute financial or environmental impact reports. Review sustainability program objectives, progress, or status to ensure compliance with policies, standards, regulations, or laws. Formulate or implement sustainability campaign or marketing strategies. Research environmental sustainability issues, concerns,

or stakeholder interests. Evaluate and approve proposals for sustainability projects, considering cost-effectiveness, technical feasibility, and integration with other initiatives. Develop sustainability reports, presentations, or proposals for supplier, employee, academia, media, government, public interest, or other groups. Develop or oversee the development of sustainability evaluation or monitoring systems. Develop or oversee the development of marketing or outreach media for sustainability projects or events. Develop methodologies to assess the viability or success of sustainability initiatives.

Education/Training Required: Work experience plus degree. **Education and Training Programs:** Business Administration and Management, General; Business/Commerce, General; Entrepreneurship/Entrepreneurial Studies; International Business/Trade/Commerce; International Relations and Affairs; Public Administration; Public Administration and Social Service Professions, Other; Public Policy Analysis, General; Transportation/Mobility Management. **Knowledge/Courses:** No data available.

Personality Type: No data available. **Career Clusters:** 04 Business, Management, and Administration; 07 Government and Public Administration; 16 Transportation, Distribution, and Logistics. **Career Pathways:** 04.1 Management; 07.1 Governance; 16.2 Logistics, Planning, and Management Services. **Other Jobs in These Pathways:** Administrative Services Managers; Brownfield Redevelopment Specialists and Site Managers; Business Continuity Planners; Business Operations Specialists, All Other; Chief Executives; Compliance Managers; Computer and Information Systems Managers;

Construction Managers; Customs Brokers; Energy Auditors; First-Line Supervisors of Office and Administrative Support Workers; General and Operations Managers; Investment Fund Managers; Loss Prevention Managers; Management Analysts; Managers, All Other; Public Relations Specialists; Regulatory Affairs Managers; Sales Managers; Security Management Specialists; Security Managers; Supply Chain Managers; Sustainability Specialists; Wind Energy Operations Managers; Wind Energy Project Managers; others.

Chiropractors

* Annual Earnings: $67,200
* Earnings Growth Potential: Very high (52.0%)
* Growth: 19.5%
* Annual Job Openings: 1,820
* Self-Employed: 44.5%

Skills—Most Important: Science Skills; Communication Skills; Thought-Processing Skills. **Other High-Level Skills:** Social Skills; Management Skills.

Adjust spinal column and other articulations of the body to correct abnormalities believed to be caused by interference with the nervous system. Examine patients to determine nature and extent of disorders. Manipulate spines or other involved areas. May utilize supplementary measures such as exercise, rest, water, light, heat, and nutritional therapy. Perform manual adjustments to the spine or other articulations of the body to correct the musculoskeletal system. Evaluate the functioning of the neuromuscularskeletal system and the spine using systems of chiropractic diagnosis. Diagnose health problems by reviewing patients' health and medical histories; questioning, observing, and examining patients; and interpreting X-rays. Maintain accurate case histories of patients. Advise patients about recommended courses of treatment. Obtain and record patients' medical histories. Analyze X-rays to locate the sources of patients' difficulties and to rule out fractures or diseases as sources of problems. Counsel patients about nutrition, exercise, sleeping habits, stress management, and other matters. Arrange for diagnostic X-rays to be taken. Consult with and refer patients to appropriate health practitioners when necessary. Suggest and apply the use of supports such as straps, tapes, bandages, and braces.

Education/Training Required: First professional degree. **Education and Training Program:** Chiropractic (DC). **Knowledge/ Courses:** Medicine and Dentistry; Therapy and Counseling; Biology; Psychology; Personnel and Human Resources; Sales and Marketing.

Personality Type: Social-Investigative-Realistic. **Career Cluster:** 08 Health Science. **Career Pathway:** 08.1 Therapeutic Services. **Other Jobs in This Pathway:** Clinical Psychologists; Community and Social Service Specialists, All Other; Counseling Psychologists; Dental Assistants; Dental Hygienists; Dentists, General; Health Technologists and Technicians, All Other; Healthcare Support Workers, All Other; Home Health Aides; Licensed Practical and Licensed Vocational Nurses; Low Vision Therapists, Orientation and Mobility Specialists, and Vision Rehabilitation Therapists; Massage Therapists; Medical and Clinical Laboratory Technicians; Medical and Health Services Managers; Medical Scientists, Except Epidemiologists; Medical Secretaries; Occupational Therapists;

Pharmacists; Pharmacy Technicians; Radiologic Technologists; School Psychologists; Social and Human Service Assistants; Speech-Language Pathologists; Speech-Language Pathology Assistants; Substance Abuse and Behavioral Disorder Counselors; others.

Civil Engineers

- ❈ Annual Earnings: $77,560
- ❈ Earnings Growth Potential: Low (34.8%)
- ❈ Growth: 24.3%
- ❈ Annual Job Openings: 11,460
- ❈ Self-Employed: 4.3%

Skills—Most Important: Mathematics Skills; Science Skills; Management Skills. **Other High-Level Skills:** Thought-Processing Skills; Communication Skills; Technology/Programming Skills; Social Skills.

Perform engineering duties in planning, designing, and overseeing construction and maintenance of building structures and facilities such as roads, railroads, airports, bridges, harbors, channels, dams, irrigation projects, pipelines, power plants, water and sewage systems, and waste disposal units. Includes architectural, structural, traffic, ocean, and geo-technical engineers. Analyze survey reports, maps, drawings, blueprints, aerial photography, and other topographical or geologic data to plan projects. Plan and design transportation or hydraulic systems and structures, following construction and government standards, using design software and drawing tools. Inspect project sites to monitor progress and ensure conformance to design specifications and safety or sanitation standards. Compute load and grade requirements, water flow rates, and material stress factors to determine design specifications. Direct construction, operations, and maintenance activities at project site. Direct or participate in surveying to lay out installations and establish reference points, grades, and elevations to guide construction. Estimate quantities and cost of materials, equipment, or labor to determine project feasibility. Prepare or present public reports on bid proposals, deeds, environmental impact statements, or property and right-of-way descriptions. Test soils and materials to determine the adequacy and strength of foundations, concrete, asphalt, or steel. Provide technical advice on design, construction, or program modifications and structural repairs to industrial and managerial personnel. Conduct studies of traffic patterns or environmental conditions to identify engineering problems and assess the potential impact of projects.

Education/Training Required: Bachelor's degree. **Education and Training Programs:** Civil Engineering, General; Civil Engineering, Other; Transportation and Highway Engineering; Water Resources Engineering. **Knowledge/Courses:** Engineering and Technology; Building and Construction; Design; Physics; Transportation; Mathematics.

Personality Type: Realistic-Investigative-Conventional. **Career Cluster:** 15 Science, Technology, Engineering, and Mathematics. **Career Pathway:** 15.1 Engineering and Technology. **Other Jobs in This Pathway:** Architectural and Engineering Managers; Automotive Engineers; Biochemical Engineers; Biofuels/Biodiesel Technology and Product Development Managers; Cost Estimators; Education, Training, and Library Workers, All Other; Electrical Engineers; Electronics

Engineers, Except Computer; Energy Engineers; Engineers, All Other; Fuel Cell Engineers; Human Factors Engineers and Ergonomists; Industrial Engineers; Manufacturing Engineers; Mechanical Engineers; Mechatronics Engineers; Microsystems Engineers; Nanosystems Engineers; Photonics Engineers; Radio Frequency Identification Device Specialists; Robotics Engineers; Solar Energy Systems Engineers; Transportation Engineers; Validation Engineers; Wind Energy Engineers; others.

Job Specialization: Transportation Engineers

Develop plans for surface transportation projects according to engineering standards and state or federal construction policy. Prepare plans, estimates, or specifications to design transportation facilities. Plan alterations and modifications of existing streets, highways, or freeways to improve traffic flow. Present data, maps, or other information at construction-related public hearings or meetings. Review development plans to determine potential traffic impact. Prepare administrative, technical, or statistical reports on traffic-operation matters such as accidents, safety measures, or pedestrian volume or practices. Evaluate transportation systems or traffic control devices or lighting systems to determine need for modification or expansion. Prepare project budgets, schedules, or specifications for labor or materials. Plan alteration or modification of existing transportation structures to improve safety or function. Participate in contract bidding, negotiation, or administration. Model transportation scenarios to evaluate the impacts of activities such as new development or to identify possible solutions to transportation problems. Investigate traffic problems and recommend methods to improve traffic flow or safety. Inspect completed transportation projects to ensure safety or compliance with applicable standards or regulations. Estimate transportation project costs. Confer with contractors, utility companies, or government agencies to discuss plans, specifications, or work schedules. Check construction plans, design calculations, or cost estimations to ensure completeness, accuracy, or conformity to engineering standards or practices.

Education/Training Required: Bachelor's degree. **Education and Training Programs:** Civil Engineering, General; Civil Engineering, Other; Transportation and Highway Engineering; Water Resources Engineering. **Knowledge/Courses:** Engineering and Technology; Design; Transportation; Building and Construction; Physics; Geography.

Personality Type: Realistic-Investigative. **Career Cluster:** 15 Science, Technology, Engineering, and Mathematics. **Career Pathway:** 15.1 Engineering and Technology. **Other Jobs in This Pathway:** Architectural and Engineering Managers; Automotive Engineers; Biochemical Engineers; Biofuels/Biodiesel Technology and Product Development Managers; Civil Engineers; Cost Estimators; Education, Training, and Library Workers, All Other; Electrical Engineers; Electronics Engineers, Except Computer; Energy Engineers; Engineers, All Other; Fuel Cell Engineers; Human Factors Engineers and Ergonomists; Industrial Engineers; Manufacturing Engineers; Mechanical Engineers; Mechatronics Engineers; Microsystems Engineers; Nanosystems Engineers; Photonics Engineers; Radio Frequency Identification Device Specialists; Robotics Engineers; Solar Energy Systems Engineers; Validation Engineers; Wind Energy Engineers; others.

Clergy

* Annual Earnings: $43,970
* Earnings Growth Potential: High (44.9%)
* Growth: 12.7%
* Annual Job Openings: 21,770
* Self-Employed: 0.1%

Skills—Most Important: Social Skills; Management Skills; Communication Skills. **Other High-Level Skills:** Thought-Processing Skills; Mathematics Skills.

Conduct religious worship and perform other spiritual functions associated with beliefs and practices of religious faith or denomination. Provide spiritual and moral guidance and assistance to members. Pray and promote spirituality. Read from sacred texts such as the Bible, Torah, or Koran. Prepare and deliver sermons and other talks. Organize and lead regular religious services. Share information about religious issues by writing articles, giving speeches, or teaching. Instruct people who seek conversion. Visit people in homes, hospitals, and prisons to provide comfort and support. Counsel individuals and groups concerning their spiritual, emotional, and personal needs. Train leaders of church, community, and youth groups. Administer religious rites or ordinances. Study and interpret religious laws, doctrines, and/or traditions. Conduct special ceremonies such as weddings, funerals, and confirmations. Plan and lead religious education programs for congregations. Respond to requests for assistance during emergencies or crises. Devise ways in which congregation membership can be expanded. Collaborate with committees and individuals to address financial and administrative issues. Prepare people for participation in religious ceremonies. Perform administrative duties such as overseeing building management, ordering supplies, contracting for services and repairs, and supervising the work of staff members and volunteers. Refer people to community support services, psychologists, and/or doctors. Participate in fundraising activities to support congregation activities and facilities.

Education/Training Required: Master's degree. **Education and Training Programs:** Clinical Pastoral Counseling/Patient Counseling; Divinity/Ministry (BD, MDiv.); Pastoral Counseling and Specialized Ministries, Other; Pastoral Studies/Counseling; Philosophy; Pre-Theology/Pre-Ministerial Studies; Rabbinical Studies (M.H.L./Rav); Religion/Religious Studies; Theological and Ministerial Studies, Other; Theology and Religious Vocations, Other; Theology/Theological Studies; Youth Ministry. **Knowledge/Courses:** Philosophy and Theology; Therapy and Counseling; Sociology and Anthropology; Psychology; Public Safety and Security; Customer and Personal Service.

Personality Type: Social-Enterprising-Artistic. **Career Cluster:** 10 Human Services. **Career Pathway:** 10.2 Counseling and Mental Health Services. **Other Jobs in This Pathway:** Clinical Psychologists; Counseling Psychologists; Counselors, All Other; Directors, Religious Activities and Education; Epidemiologists; Health Educators; Healthcare Social Workers; Marriage and Family Therapists; Mental Health and Substance Abuse Social Workers; Mental Health Counselors; Music Directors; Psychologists, All Other; Recreation Workers; Religious Workers, All Other; School Psychologists; Substance Abuse and Behavioral Disorder Counselors.

C

Coaches and Scouts

- ❋ Annual Earnings: $28,340
- ❋ Earnings Growth Potential: High (42.2%)
- ❋ Growth: 24.8%
- ❋ Annual Job Openings: 9,920
- ❋ Self-Employed: 16.2%

Skills—Most Important: Social Skills; Management Skills; Thought-Processing Skills. **Other High-Level Skills:** Communication Skills.

Instruct or coach groups or individuals in the fundamentals of sports. Demonstrate techniques and methods of participation. May evaluate athletes' strengths and weaknesses as possible recruits or to improve the athletes' technique to prepare them for competition. Plan, organize, and conduct practice sessions. Plan and direct physical conditioning programs that will enable athletes to achieve maximum performance. Adjust coaching techniques based on the strengths and weaknesses of athletes. Instruct individuals or groups in sports rules, game strategies, and performance principles, such as specific ways of moving the body, hands, or feet to achieve desired results. Analyze the strengths and weaknesses of opposing teams to develop game strategies. Evaluate athletes' skills and review performance records to determine their fitness and potential. Keep abreast of changing rules, techniques, technologies, and philosophies relevant to their sport. Monitor athletes' use of equipment to ensure safe and proper use. Develop and arrange competition schedules and programs. Explain and enforce safety rules and regulations. Explain and demonstrate the use of sports and training equipment, such as

trampolines or weights. Arrange and conduct sports-related activities, such as training camps, skill-improvement courses, clinics, and pre-season tryouts. Select, acquire, store, and issue equipment and other materials. Provide training direction, encouragement, motivation, and nutritional advice to prepare athletes for games, competitive events, or tours. Teach instructional courses and advise students. Contact the parents of players to provide information and answer questions.

Education/Training Required: Long-term on-the-job training. **Education and Training Programs:** Health and Physical Education, General; Physical Education Teaching and Coaching; Sport and Fitness Administration/Management. **Knowledge/Courses:** Education and Training; Therapy and Counseling; Sales and Marketing; Personnel and Human Resources; Psychology; English Language.

Personality Type: Social-Realistic-Enterprising. **Career Cluster:** 05 Education and Training. **Career Pathways:** 05.3 Teaching/Training; 05.1 Administration and Administrative Support. **Other Jobs in These Pathways:** Adult Basic and Secondary Education and Literacy Teachers and Instructors; Career/Technical Education Teachers, Secondary School; Chemists; Dietitians and Nutritionists; Distance Learning Coordinators; Education Administrators, All Other; Education Administrators, Elementary and Secondary School; Education Administrators, Postsecondary; Education Administrators, Preschool and Childcare Center/Program; Elementary School Teachers, Except Special Education; Fitness and Wellness Coordinators; Fitness Trainers and Aerobics Instructors; Instructional Coordinators; Instructional Designers and Technologists; Interpreters and Translators; Kindergarten

Teachers, Except Special Education; Librarians; Middle School Teachers, Except Special and Career/Technical Education; Preschool Teachers, Except Special Education; Recreation Workers; Secondary School Teachers, Except Special and Career/Technical Education; Self-Enrichment Education Teachers; Teacher Assistants; Teachers and Instructors, All Other; Tutors; others.

Commercial and Industrial Designers

❋ Annual Earnings: $58,230

❋ Earnings Growth Potential: High (43.0%)

❋ Growth: 9.0%

❋ Annual Job Openings: 1,760

❋ Self-Employed: 26.7%

Skills—Most Important: Technology/Programming Skills; Science Skills; Mathematics Skills. **Other High-Level Skills:** Thought-Processing Skills; Communication Skills; Social Skills; Management Skills.

Develop and design manufactured products, such as cars, home appliances, and children's toys. Combine artistic talent with research on product use, marketing, and materials to create the most functional and appealing product design. Prepare sketches of ideas, detailed drawings, illustrations, artwork, or blueprints using drafting instruments, paints and brushes, or computer-aided design equipment. Direct and coordinate the fabrication of models or samples and the drafting of working drawings and specification sheets from sketches. Modify and refine designs using working models to conform with customer specifications, production

limitations, or changes in design trends. Coordinate the look and function of product lines. Confer with engineering, marketing, production, sales departments, or customers to establish and evaluate design concepts for manufactured products. Present designs and reports to customers or design committees for approval and discuss need for modification. Evaluate feasibility of design ideas based on appearance, safety, function, serviceability, budget, production costs/methods, and market characteristics.

Education/Training Required: Bachelor's degree. **Education and Training Programs:** Commercial and Advertising Art; Design and Applied Arts, Other; Design and Visual Communications, General; Industrial and Product Design. **Knowledge/Courses:** Design; Engineering and Technology; Mechanical Devices; Production and Processing; Physics; Fine Arts.

Personality Type: Artistic-Enterprising-Realistic. **Career Cluster:** 03 Arts, Audio/Video Technology, and Communications. **Career Pathways:** 03.3 Visual Arts; 03.1 Audio and Video Technology and Film. **Other Jobs in These Pathways:** Agents and Business Managers of Artists, Performers, and Athletes; Art Directors; Artists and Related Workers, All Other; Audio and Video Equipment Technicians; Broadcast Technicians; Camera Operators, Television, Video, and Motion Picture; Choreographers; Craft Artists; Curators; Dancers; Designers, All Other; Fashion Designers; Film and Video Editors; Fine Artists, Including Painters, Sculptors, and Illustrators; Graphic Designers; Interior Designers; Managers, All Other; Media and Communication Equipment Workers, All Other; Media and Communication Workers,

C

All Other; Multimedia Artists and Animators; Museum Technicians and Conservators; Painting, Coating, and Decorating Workers; Photographers; Set and Exhibit Designers; Technical Directors/Managers; others.

Commercial Divers

⊛ Annual Earnings: $51,360

⊛ Earnings Growth Potential: Medium (37.9%)

⊛ Growth: 5.5%

⊛ Annual Job Openings: 50

⊛ Self-Employed: 0.0%

Skills—Most Important: Equipment Use/Maintenance Skills; Installation Skills; Science Skills. **Other High-Level Skills:** Social Skills; Thought-Processing Skills; Communication Skills; Management Skills.

Work below surface of water using scuba gear to inspect, repair, remove, or install equipment and structures. May use power and hand tools such as drills, sledgehammers, torches, and welding equipment. May conduct tests or experiments, rig explosives, or photograph structures or marine life. Perform activities related to underwater search and rescue, salvage, recovery, and cleanup operations. Take safety precautions, such as monitoring dive lengths and depths and registering with authorities before diving expeditions begin. Set or guide placement of pilings and sandbags to provide support for structures such as docks, bridges, cofferdams, and platforms. Salvage wrecked ships and/or their cargo using pneumatic power velocity and hydraulic tools, and explosive charges when necessary. Repair ships, bridge foundations, and other structures below the water line using caulk, bolts, and hand tools. Remove obstructions from strainers and marine railway or launching ways using pneumatic and power hand tools. Inspect and test docks, ships, bouyage systems, plant intakes and outflows, and underwater pipelines, cables, and sewers using closed-circuit television, still photography, and testing equipment. Perform offshore oil and gas exploration and extraction duties such as conducting underwater surveys and repairing and maintaining drilling rigs and platforms. Install, inspect, clean, and repair piping and valves. Carry out nondestructive testing such as tests for cracks on the legs of oil rigs at sea. Check and maintain diving equipment such as helmets, masks, air tanks, harnesses, and gauges. Communicate with workers on the surface while underwater using signal lines or telephones.

Education/Training Required: Postsecondary vocational training. **Education and Training Program:** Diver Training, Professional and Instructor. **Knowledge/Courses:** Building and Construction; Mechanical Devices; Physics; Engineering and Technology; Design; Biology.

Personality Type: Realistic. **Career Cluster:** 16 Transportation, Distribution, and Logistics. **Career Pathway:** 16.1 Transportation Operations. **Other Jobs in This Pathway:** Airline Pilots, Copilots, and Flight Engineers; Automotive and Watercraft Service Attendants; Automotive Master Mechanics; Bus Drivers, School or Special Client; Bus Drivers, Transit and Intercity; Commercial Pilots; Crane and Tower Operators; First-Line Supervisors of Helpers, Laborers, and Material Movers, Hand; First-Line Supervisors of Transportation and Material-Moving Machine and Vehicle Operators; Freight and Cargo Inspectors; Heavy and Tractor-Trailer Truck Drivers; Laborers and Freight, Stock, and Material Movers, Hand;

Light Truck or Delivery Services Drivers; Mates—Ship, Boat, and Barge; Motor Vehicle Operators, All Other; Operating Engineers and Other Construction Equipment Operators; Pilots, Ship; Railroad Conductors and Yardmasters; Sailors and Marine Oilers; Ship and Boat Captains; Storage and Distribution Managers; Taxi Drivers and Chauffeurs; Transportation Managers; Transportation Workers, All Other; others.

Commercial Pilots

❈ Annual Earnings: $67,500

❈ Earnings Growth Potential: High (48.4%)

❈ Growth: 18.6%

❈ Annual Job Openings: 2,060

❈ Self-Employed: 12.0%

Skills—Most Important: Science Skills; Equipment Use/Maintenance Skills; Thought-Processing Skills. **Other High-Level Skills:** Social Skills; Management Skills.

Pilot and navigate the flight of small fixed- or rotary-winged aircraft primarily for the transport of cargo and passengers. Requires Commercial Rating. Check aircraft prior to flights to ensure that the engines, controls, instruments, and other systems are functioning properly. Contact control towers for takeoff clearances, arrival instructions, and other information using radio equipment. Start engines, operate controls, and pilot airplanes to transport passengers, mail, or freight while adhering to flight plans, regulations, and procedures. Monitor engine operation, fuel consumption, and functioning of aircraft systems during flights. Consider airport altitudes, outside temperatures, plane weights,

and wind speeds and directions to calculate the speed needed to become airborne. Order changes in fuel supplies, loads, routes, or schedules to ensure safety of flights. Obtain and review data such as load weights, fuel supplies, weather conditions, and flight schedules to determine flight plans and to see if changes might be necessary. Plan flights following government and company regulations using aeronautical charts and navigation instruments. Use instrumentation to pilot aircraft when visibility is poor. Check baggage or cargo to ensure that it has been loaded correctly. Request changes in altitudes or routes as circumstances dictate. Choose routes, altitudes, and speeds that will provide the fastest, safest, and smoothest flights. Coordinate flight activities with ground crews and air-traffic control and inform crew members of flight and test procedures.

Education/Training Required: Postsecondary vocational training. **Education and Training Programs:** Airline/Commercial/Professional Pilot and Flight Crew Training; Flight Instructor Training. **Knowledge/Courses:** Transportation; Geography; Mechanical Devices; Physics; Telecommunications; Psychology.

Personality Type: Realistic-Investigative-Enterprising. **Career Cluster:** 16 Transportation, Distribution, and Logistics. **Career Pathway:** 16.1 Transportation Operations. **Other Jobs in This Pathway:** Airline Pilots, Copilots, and Flight Engineers; Automotive and Watercraft Service Attendants; Automotive Master Mechanics; Bus Drivers, School or Special Client; Bus Drivers, Transit and Intercity; Crane and Tower Operators; First-Line Supervisors of Helpers, Laborers, and Material Movers, Hand; First-Line Supervisors of Transportation and Material-Moving Machine and Vehicle

Operators; Freight and Cargo Inspectors; Heavy and Tractor-Trailer Truck Drivers; Laborers and Freight, Stock, and Material Movers, Hand; Light Truck or Delivery Services Drivers; Mates—Ship, Boat, and Barge; Motor Vehicle Operators, All Other; Operating Engineers and Other Construction Equipment Operators; Parking Lot Attendants; Pilots, Ship; Railroad Conductors and Yardmasters; Sailors and Marine Oilers; Ship and Boat Captains; Storage and Distribution Managers; Taxi Drivers and Chauffeurs; Transportation Inspectors; Transportation Managers; Transportation Workers, All Other; others.

Compensation, Benefits, and Job Analysis Specialists

❀ Annual Earnings: $57,000

❀ Earnings Growth Potential: Medium (37.4%)

❀ Growth: 23.6%

❀ Annual Job Openings: 6,050

❀ Self-Employed: 1.6%

Skills—Most Important: Science Skills; Mathematics Skills; Thought-Processing Skills. **Other High-Level Skills:** Communication Skills; Social Skills; Management Skills.

Conduct programs of compensation and benefits and job analysis for employer. May specialize in specific areas, such as position classification and pension programs. Evaluate job positions, determining classification, exempt or non-exempt status, and salary. Ensure company compliance with federal and state laws, including reporting requirements. Advise managers and employees on state and federal employment regulations, collective agreements, benefit and compensation policies, personnel procedures, and classification programs. Plan, develop, evaluate, improve, and communicate methods and techniques for selecting, promoting, compensating, evaluating, and training workers. Provide advice on the resolution of classification and salary complaints. Prepare occupational classifications, job descriptions, and salary scales. Assist in preparing and maintaining personnel records and handbooks. Prepare reports such as organization and flow charts and career path reports to summarize job analysis and evaluation and compensation analysis information. Administer employee insurance, pension, and savings plans, working with insurance brokers and plan carriers. Negotiate collective agreements on behalf of employers or workers and mediate labor disputes and grievances. Develop, implement, administer, and evaluate personnel and labor relations programs, including performance appraisal, affirmative action, and employment equity programs. Perform multifactor data and cost analyses that may be used in areas such as support of collective bargaining agreements.

Education/Training Required: Bachelor's degree. **Education and Training Program:** Human Resources Management/Personnel Administration, General. **Knowledge/Courses:** Personnel and Human Resources; Economics and Accounting; Law and Government; Administration and Management; Mathematics; English Language.

Personality Type: Conventional-Enterprising. **Career Cluster:** 04 Business, Management, and Administration. **Career Pathway:** 04.3 Human Resources. **Other Job in This Pathway:** Human Resources Specialists.

Compliance Officers

* Annual Earnings: $58,720
* Earnings Growth Potential: High (41.2%)
* Growth: 31.0%
* Annual Job Openings: 10,850
* Self-Employed: 1.4%

Skills—Most Important: Because this occupation is highly diverse, separate lists of skills are provided for each job specialization.

Job Specialization: Coroners

Direct activities such as autopsies, pathological and toxicological analyses, and inquests relating to the investigation of deaths occurring within a legal jurisdiction to determine cause of death or to fix responsibility for accidental, violent, or unexplained deaths. Perform medico-legal examinations and autopsies, conducting preliminary examinations of the body to identify victims, to locate signs of trauma, and to identify factors that would indicate time of death. Inquire into the cause, manner, and circumstances of human deaths and establish the identities of deceased persons. Direct activities of workers who conduct autopsies, perform pathological and toxicological analyses, and prepare documents for permanent records. Complete death certificates, including the assignment of a cause and manner of death. Collect and document any pertinent medical history. Observe and record the positions and conditions of bodies and of related evidence. Observe, record, and preserve objects or personal property related to deaths, including medication containers and suicide notes. Complete reports and forms required to finalize cases. Remove or supervise removal of bodies from death scenes using the proper equipment and supplies and arrange for transportation to morgues. Interview persons present at death scenes to obtain information useful in determining the manner of death. Testify at inquests, hearings, and court trials. Provide information concerning the circumstances of death to relatives of the deceased. Locate and document information on the next of kin, including relationship to the deceased and the status of notification attempts.

Skills—Most Important: Science Skills; Communication Skills; Social Skills. **Other High-Level Skills:** Thought-Processing Skills; Management Skills; Mathematics Skills.

Education/Training Required: Work experience in a related occupation. **Education and Training Program:** Public Administration. **Knowledge/Courses:** Medicine and Dentistry; Biology; Psychology; Therapy and Counseling; Chemistry; Law and Government.

Personality Type: Investigative-Realistic-Conventional. **Career Cluster:** 12 Law, Public Safety, Corrections, and Security. **Career Pathway:** 12.6 Inspection Services. **Other Jobs in This Pathway:** Compliance Officers; Environmental Compliance Inspectors; Equal Opportunity Representatives and Officers; Government Property Inspectors and Investigators; Licensing Examiners and Inspectors; Regulatory Affairs Specialists.

Job Specialization: Environmental Compliance Inspectors

Inspect and investigate sources of pollution to protect the public and environment and ensure conformance with federal, state, and local regulations and ordinances. Determine the nature of code violations and actions to be taken and issue written notices of violation; participate in enforcement hearings. Examine permits, licenses, applications, and records to ensure compliance with licensing requirements. Prepare, organize, and maintain inspection records. Interview individuals to determine the nature of suspected violations and to obtain evidence of violations. Prepare written, oral, tabular, and graphic reports summarizing requirements and regulations, including enforcement and chain of custody documentation. Monitor follow-up actions in cases where violations were found and review compliance monitoring reports. Investigate complaints and suspected violations regarding illegal dumping, pollution, pesticides, product quality, or labeling laws. Inspect waste pretreatment, treatment, and disposal facilities and systems for conformance to federal, state, or local regulations.

Skills—Most Important: Science Skills; Mathematics Skills; Communication Skills. **Other High-Level Skills:** Thought-Processing Skills; Equipment Use/Maintenance Skills; Social Skills; Management Skills.

Education/Training Required: Long-term on-the-job training. **Education and Training Program:** Natural Resources Management and Policy, Other. **Knowledge/Courses:** Biology; Chemistry; Law and Government; Geography; Physics; Engineering and Technology.

Personality Type: Conventional-Investigative-Realistic. **Career Clusters:** 07 Government and Public Administration; 12 Law, Public Safety, Corrections, and Security; 16 Transportation, Distribution, and Logistics. **Career Pathways:** 16.6 Health, Safety, and Environmental Management; 07.6 Regulation; 12.6 Inspection Services. **Other Jobs in These Pathways:** Chief Executives; Compliance Officers; Coroners; Environmental Engineers; Environmental

Science and Protection Technicians, Including Health; Environmental Scientists and Specialists, Including Health; Equal Opportunity Representatives and Officers; Government Property Inspectors and Investigators; Health and Safety Engineers, Except Mining Safety Engineers and Inspectors; Licensing Examiners and Inspectors; Regulatory Affairs Managers; Regulatory Affairs Specialists.

Job Specialization: Equal Opportunity Representatives and Officers

Monitor and evaluate compliance with equal opportunity laws, guidelines, and policies to ensure that employment practices and contracting arrangements give equal opportunity without regard to race, religion, color, national origin, sex, age, or disability. Investigate employment practices and alleged violations of laws to document and correct discriminatory factors. Interpret civil rights laws and equal opportunity regulations for individuals and employers. Study equal opportunity complaints to clarify issues. Meet with persons involved in equal opportunity complaints to verify case information and to arbitrate and settle disputes. Coordinate, monitor, and revise complaint procedures to ensure timely processing and review of complaints. Prepare reports of selection, survey, and other statistics and recommendations for corrective action. Conduct surveys and evaluate findings to determine if systematic discrimination exists. Develop guidelines for nondiscriminatory employment practices and monitor their implementation and impact. Review company contracts to determine actions required to meet governmental equal opportunity provisions.

Skills—Most Important: Communication Skills; Social Skills; Thought-Processing Skills. **Other High-Level Skills:** Mathematics Skills; Management Skills.

Education/Training Required: Long-term on-the-job training. **Education and Training Program:** Public Administration and Social Service Professions, Other. **Knowledge/ Courses:** Law and Government; Personnel and Human Resources; Clerical Practices; English Language; Customer and Personal Service; Administration and Management.

Personality Type: Social-Enterprising-Conventional. **Career Cluster:** 12 Law, Public Safety, Corrections, and Security. **Career Pathway:** 12.6 Inspection Services. **Other Jobs in This Pathway:** Compliance Officers; Coroners; Environmental Compliance Inspectors; Government Property Inspectors and Investigators; Licensing Examiners and Inspectors; Regulatory Affairs Specialists.

Job Specialization: Government Property Inspectors and Investigators

Investigate or inspect government property to ensure compliance with contract agreements and government regulations. Prepare correspondence, reports of inspections or investigations, and recommendations for action. Inspect government-owned equipment and materials in the possession of private contractors to ensure compliance with contracts and regulations and to prevent misuse. Examine records, reports, and documents to establish facts and detect discrepancies. Inspect manufactured or processed products to ensure compliance with contract specifications and legal requirements. Locate and interview plaintiffs, witnesses, or representatives of business or government to gather facts relevant to inspections or alleged violations. Recommend legal or administrative action to protect government property. Submit samples of products to government laboratories for testing. Coordinate with and assist law enforcement agencies in matters of mutual concern. Testify in court or at administrative proceedings concerning investigation findings. Collect, identify, evaluate, and preserve case evidence. Monitor investigations of suspected offenders to ensure that they are conducted in accordance with constitutional requirements. Investigate applications for special licenses or permits as well as alleged license or permit violations.

Skills—Most Important: Communication Skills; Mathematics Skills; Social Skills. **Other High-Level Skills:** Thought-Processing Skills; Equipment Use/Maintenance Skills; Management Skills.

Education/Training Required: Long-term on-the-job training. **Education and Training Program:** Building/Home/Construction Inspection/Inspector. **Knowledge/Courses:** Building and Construction; Engineering and Technology; Public Safety and Security; Mechanical Devices; Transportation; Computers and Electronics.

Personality Type: Conventional-Enterprising-Realistic. **Career Cluster:** 12 Law, Public Safety, Corrections, and Security. **Career Pathway:** 12.6 Inspection Services. **Other Jobs in This Pathway:** Compliance Officers; Coroners; Environmental Compliance Inspectors; Equal Opportunity Representatives and Officers; Licensing Examiners and Inspectors; Regulatory Affairs Specialists.

Job Specialization: Licensing Examiners and Inspectors

Examine, evaluate, and investigate eligibility for, conformity with, or liability under licenses or permits. Issue licenses to individuals meeting standards. Evaluate applications, records, and documents to gather information about eligibility or liability issues. Administer oral, written, road, or flight tests to license applicants. Score tests and observe equipment operation and control to rate ability of applicants. Advise licensees and other individuals or groups concerning licensing, permit, or passport regulations. Warn violators of infractions or penalties. Prepare reports of activities, evaluations, recommendations, and decisions. Prepare correspondence to inform concerned parties of licensing decisions and of appeals processes. Confer with and interview officials, technical or professional specialists, and applicants to obtain information or to clarify facts relevant to licensing decisions. Report law or regulation violations to appropriate boards and agencies.

Skills—Most Important: Communication Skills; Social Skills; Thought-Processing Skills. **Other High-Level Skills:** Equipment Use/Maintenance Skills.

Education/Training Required: Long-term on-the-job training. **Education and Training Program:** Public Administration and Social Service Professions, Other. **Knowledge/Courses:** Clerical Practices; Customer and Personal Service; Law and Government; Foreign Language; Psychology; Public Safety and Security.

Personality Type: Conventional-Enterprising. **Career Cluster:** 12 Law, Public Safety, Corrections, and Security. **Career Pathway:** 12.6 Inspection Services. **Other Jobs in This Pathway:** Compliance Officers; Coroners; Environmental Compliance Inspectors; Equal Opportunity Representatives and Officers; Government Property Inspectors and Investigators; Regulatory Affairs Specialists.

Job Specialization: Regulatory Affairs Specialists

Coordinate and document internal regulatory processes, such as internal audits, inspections, license renewals, or registrations. May compile and prepare materials for submission to regulatory agencies. Coordinate, prepare, or review regulatory submissions for domestic or international projects. Provide technical review of data or reports that will be incorporated into regulatory submissions to assure scientific rigor, accuracy, and clarity of presentation. Review product promotional materials, labeling, batch records, specification sheets, or test methods for compliance with regulations and policies. Maintain knowledge base of existing and emerging regulations, standards, or guidance documents. Interpret regulatory rules or rule changes and ensure that they are communicated through corporate policies and procedures. Advise project teams on premarket regulatory requirements, export and labeling requirements, and clinical study compliance issues. Determine the types of regulatory submissions or internal documentation required in situations such as proposed device changes and labeling changes. Prepare or maintain technical files to obtain and sustain product approval. Coordinate efforts associated with the preparation of regulatory documents or submissions. Prepare or direct the preparation of additional information or responses as requested by regulatory agencies. Analyze product complaints and make recommendations on their reportability. Escort government inspectors during inspections and provide post-inspection follow-up information as requested.

Skills—Most Important: Thought-Processing Skills; Communication Skills; Mathematics Skills. **Other High-Level Skills:** Social Skills; Management Skills.

Education/Training Required: Work experience in a related occupation. **Education and Training Program:** Business Administration and Management, General. **Knowledge/Courses:** Law and Government; Biology; Medicine and Dentistry; Clerical Practices; English Language; Chemistry.

Personality Type: Conventional-Enterprising. **Career Cluster:** 12 Law, Public Safety, Corrections, and Security. **Career Pathway:** 12.6 Inspection Services. **Other Jobs in This Pathway:** Compliance Officers; Coroners; Environmental Compliance Inspectors; Equal Opportunity Representatives and Officers; Government Property Inspectors and Investigators; Licensing Examiners and Inspectors.

Computer and Information Research Scientists

* Annual Earnings: $100,660
* Earnings Growth Potential: High (42.7%)
* Growth: 24.2%
* Annual Job Openings: 1,320
* Self-Employed: 4.6%

Skills—Most Important: Technology/ Programming Skills; Mathematics Skills; Science Skills. **Other High-Level Skills:** Management Skills; Thought-Processing Skills; Communication Skills; Social Skills; Equipment Use/Maintenance Skills.

Conduct research into fundamental computer and information science as theorists, designers, or inventors. Solve or develop solutions to problems in the field of computer hardware and software. Assign or schedule tasks to meet work priorities and goals. Evaluate project plans and proposals to assess feasibility issues. Apply theoretical expertise and innovation to create or apply new technology, such as adapting principles for applying computers to new uses. Consult with users, management, vendors, and technicians to determine computing needs and system requirements. Meet with managers, vendors, and others to solicit cooperation and resolve problems. Conduct logical analyses of business, scientific, engineering, and other technical problems, formulating mathematical models of problems for solution by computers. Develop and interpret organizational goals, policies, and procedures. Participate in staffing decisions and direct training of subordinates. Develop performance standards and evaluate work. Design computers and the software that runs them. Maintain network hardware and software, direct network security measures, and monitor networks to ensure availability to system users. Participate in multidisciplinary projects in areas such as virtual reality, human-computer interaction, or robotics. Approve, prepare, monitor, and adjust operational budgets. Direct daily operations of departments, coordinating project activities with other departments.

Education/Training Required: Doctoral degree. **Education and Training Programs:** Computer Graphics; Computer Science; Computer Software and Media Applications, Other; Computer Systems Networking and Telecommunications; Data Modeling/ Warehousing and Database Administration; Modeling, Virtual Environments and

Simulation; Web Page, Digital/Multimedia, and Information Resources Design. **Knowledge/ Courses:** Computers and Electronics; Telecommunications; Engineering and Technology; Mathematics; Design; Education and Training.

Personality Type: Investigative-Realistic-Conventional. **Career Cluster:** 11 Information Technology. **Career Pathways:** 11.4 Programming and Software Development; 11.3 Interactive Media; 11.2 Information Support Services; 08.3 Health Informatics; 11.1 Network Systems. **Other Jobs in These Pathways:** Architectural and Engineering Managers; Clinical Psychologists; Computer and Information Systems Managers; Computer Hardware Engineers; Computer Operators; Editors; Engineers, All Other; Executive Secretaries and Executive Administrative Assistants; First-Line Supervisors of Office and Administrative Support Workers; Graphic Designers; Health Educators; Medical and Health Services Managers; Medical Assistants; Medical Records and Health Information Technicians; Medical Secretaries; Medical Transcriptionists; Mental Health Counselors; Multimedia Artists and Animators; Physical Therapists; Psychiatric Aides; Public Relations Specialists; Receptionists and Information Clerks; Rehabilitation Counselors; Remote Sensing Technicians; Substance Abuse and Behavioral Disorder Counselors; others.

Computer and Information Systems Managers

- ❋ Annual Earnings: $115,780
- ❋ Earnings Growth Potential: Medium (38.3%)
- ❋ Growth: 16.9%
- ❋ Annual Job Openings: 9,710
- ❋ Self-Employed: 3.3%

Skills—Most Important: Technology/ Programming Skills; Management Skills; Equipment Use/Maintenance Skills. **Other High-Level Skills:** Thought-Processing Skills; Social Skills; Communication Skills; Mathematics Skills.

Plan, direct, or coordinate activities in electronic data processing, information systems, systems analysis, and computer programming. Manage backup, security, and user help systems. Consult with users, management, vendors, and technicians to assess computing needs and system requirements. Direct daily operations of department, analyzing workflow, establishing priorities, developing standards, and setting deadlines. Assign and review the work of systems analysts, programmers, and other computer-related workers. Stay abreast of advances in technology. Develop computer information resources, providing for data security and control, strategic computing, and disaster recovery. Review and approve all systems charts and programs prior to implementation. Evaluate the organization's technology use and needs and recommend improvements, such as hardware and software upgrades. Control operational budget and expenditures. Meet with department heads, managers, supervisors, vendors, and others to solicit cooperation and resolve problems.

Develop and interpret organizational goals, policies, and procedures.

Education/Training Required: Work experience plus degree. **Education and Training Programs:** Computer and Information Sciences, General; Computer Science; Information Resources Management/ CIO Training; Information Science/Studies; Knowledge Management; Management Information Systems, General; Network and System Administration/Administrator; Operations Management and Supervision. **Knowledge/Courses:** Telecommunications; Computers and Electronics; Economics and Accounting; Production and Processing; Personnel and Human Resources; Administration and Management.

Personality Type: Enterprising-Conventional-Investigative. **Career Clusters:** 04 Business, Management, and Administration; 11 Information Technology. **Career Pathways:** 04.1 Management; 04.4 Business Analysis; 11.1 Network Systems; 11.2 Information Support Services. **Other Jobs in These Pathways:** Brownfield Redevelopment Specialists and Site Managers; Business Continuity Planners; Business Operations Specialists, All Other; Chief Executives; Chief Sustainability Officers; Compliance Managers; Construction Managers; Customs Brokers; Energy Auditors; First-Line Supervisors of Office and Administrative Support Workers; General and Operations Managers; Graphic Designers; Investment Fund Managers; Loss Prevention Managers; Management Analysts; Managers, All Other; Public Relations Specialists; Regulatory Affairs Managers; Sales Managers; Security Management Specialists; Security Managers; Supply Chain Managers; Sustainability Specialists; Wind Energy Operations Managers; Wind Energy Project Managers; others.

Computer Hardware Engineers

- ❋ Annual Earnings: $98,810
- ❋ Earnings Growth Potential: Medium (37.9%)
- ❋ Growth: 3.8%
- ❋ Annual Job Openings: 2,350
- ❋ Self-Employed: 1.3%

Skills—Most Important: Science Skills; Thought-Processing Skills; Technology/ Programming Skills. **Other High-Level Skills:** Equipment Use/Maintenance Skills; Communication Skills; Social Skills; Management Skills.

Research, design, develop, and test computer or computer-related equipment for commercial, industrial, military, or scientific use. May supervise the manufacturing and installation of computer or computer-related equipment and components. Update knowledge and skills to keep up with rapid advancements in computer technology. Provide technical support to designers, marketing and sales departments, suppliers, engineers, and other team members throughout the product development and implementation process. Test and verify hardware and support peripherals to ensure that they meet specifications and requirements, analyzing and recording test data. Monitor functioning of equipment and make necessary modifications to ensure system operates in conformance with specifications. Analyze information to determine, recommend, and plan layout, including type of computers and peripheral equipment modifications. Build, test, and modify product prototypes, using working models or theoretical models constructed using computer simulation. Analyze user needs and recommend appropriate hardware. Direct technicians, engineering designers, or other technical support personnel. Confer with engineering staff and consult specifications to evaluate interface between hardware and software and operational and performance requirements of system. Select hardware and material, assuring compliance with specifications and product requirements. Store, retrieve, and manipulate data for analysis of system capabilities and requirements. Write detailed functional specifications that document the hardware development process and support hardware introduction.

Education/Training Required: Bachelor's degree. **Education and Training Programs:** Computer Engineering, General; Computer Hardware Engineering. **Knowledge/Courses:** Computers and Electronics; Engineering and Technology; Telecommunications; Design; Physics; Communications and Media.

Personality Type: Investigative-Realistic-Conventional. **Career Clusters:** 11 Information Technology; 15 Science, Technology, Engineering, and Mathematics. **Career Pathways:** 15.1 Engineering and Technology; 11.4 Programming and Software Development. **Other Jobs in These Pathways:** Architectural and Engineering Managers; Automotive Engineers; Biochemical Engineers; Biofuels/Biodiesel Technology and Product Development Managers; Civil Engineers; Cost Estimators; Electrical Engineers; Electronics Engineers, Except Computer; Energy Engineers; Engineers, All Other; Fuel Cell Engineers; Human Factors Engineers and Ergonomists; Industrial Engineers; Manufacturing Engineers; Mechanical Engineers; Mechatronics Engineers; Microsystems Engineers; Nanosystems Engineers; Photonics Engineers; Radio Frequency Identification Device Specialists;

Robotics Engineers; Solar Energy Systems Engineers; Transportation Engineers; Validation Engineers; Wind Energy Engineers; others.

Computer Network Architects

* Annual Earnings: $75,660
* Earnings Growth Potential: High (42.9%)
* Growth: 53.4%
* Annual Job Openings: 20,830
* Self-Employed: 19.4%

Skills—Most Important: Technology/Programming Skills; Equipment Use/Maintenance Skills; Science Skills. **Other High-Level Skills:** Thought-Processing Skills; Management Skills; Mathematics Skills; Social Skills; Communication Skills.

Design and implement computer and information networks, such as local area networks (LAN), wide area networks (WAN), intranets, extranets, and other data communications networks. Perform network modeling, analysis, and planning. May also design network and computer security measures. May research and recommend network and data communications hardware and software. Adjust network sizes to meet volume or capacity demands. Communicate with customers, sales staff, or marketing staff to determine customer needs. Communicate with system users to ensure accounts are set up properly or to diagnose and solve operational problems. Coordinate installation of new equipment. Coordinate network operations, maintenance, repairs, or upgrades. Coordinate network or design activities with designers of associated networks. Design, build, or operate equipment configuration prototypes, including network hardware, software, servers, or server operation systems. Design, organize, and deliver product awareness, skills transfer, or product education sessions for staff or suppliers. Determine specific network hardware or software requirements, such as platforms, interfaces, bandwidths, or routine schemas. Develop and implement solutions for network problems. Develop and write procedures for installation, use, or troubleshooting of communications hardware or software. Develop conceptual, logical, or physical network designs. Develop disaster recovery plans. Develop network-related documentation. Develop or maintain project reporting systems. Develop or recommend network security measures, such as firewalls, network security audits, or automated security probes. Develop plans or budgets for network equipment replacement. Develop procedures to track, project, or report network availability, reliability, capacity, or utilization.

Education/Training Required: Bachelor's degree. **Education and Training Program:** Computer Systems Networking and Telecommunications. **Knowledge/ Courses:** Telecommunications; Computers and Electronics; Design; Engineering and Technology; Communications and Media; Clerical.

Personality Type: Investigative-Conventional-Realistic. **Career Cluster:** 11 Information Technology. **Career Pathway:** 11.4 Programming and Software Development. **Other Jobs in This Pathway:** Architectural and Engineering Managers; Bioinformatics Scientists; Computer Hardware Engineers; Computer Numerically Controlled Machine Tool Programmers, Metal and Plastic.

Job Specialization: Telecommunications Engineering Specialists

Design or configure voice, video, and data communications systems. Supervise installation and post-installation service and maintenance. Keep abreast of changes in industry practices and emerging telecommunications technology by reviewing current literature, talking with colleagues, participating in educational programs, attending meetings or workshops, or participating in professional organizations or conferences. Estimate costs for system or component implementation and operation. Develop, maintain, or implement telecommunications disaster recovery plans to ensure business continuity. Test and evaluate hardware and software to determine efficiency, reliability, or compatibility with existing systems. Supervise maintenance of telecommunications equipment. Review and evaluate requests from engineers, managers, and technicians for system modifications. Provide user support by diagnosing network and device problems and implementing technical or procedural solutions. Prepare system activity and performance reports. Prepare purchase requisitions for computer hardware and software, networking and telecommunications equipment, test equipment, cabling, or tools. Use computer-aided design (CAD) software to prepare or evaluate network diagrams, floor plans, or site configurations for existing facilities, renovations, or new systems. Order or maintain inventory of telecommunications equipment, including telephone sets, headsets, cellular phones, switches, trunks, printed circuit boards, network routers, and cabling. Monitor and analyze system performance, such as network traffic, security, and capacity.

C

Education/Training Required: Bachelor's degree. **Education and Training Program:** Computer Systems Networking and Telecommunications. **Knowledge/Courses:** No data available.

Personality Type: No data available. **Career Clusters:** 11 Information Technology; 15 Science, Technology, Engineering, and Mathematics. **Career Pathway:** 11.4 Programming and Software Development. **Other Jobs in This Pathway:** Architectural and Engineering Managers; Bioinformatics Scientists; Computer Hardware Engineers; Computer Numerically Controlled Machine Tool Programmers, Metal and Plastic.

Computer Occupations, All Other

* Annual Earnings: $79,240
* Earnings Growth Potential: High (47.4%)
* Growth: 13.1%
* Annual Job Openings: 7,260
* Self-Employed: 3.9%

Skills—Most Important: Because this occupation is highly diverse, separate lists of skills are provided for each job specialization when available.

This occupation includes all computer occupations not listed separately. Because this is a highly diverse occupation, no data is available for some information topics.

Education and Training Program: Computer and Information Sciences and Support Services, Other. **Career Cluster:** 11 Information Technology. **Career Pathways:** 11.4 Programming and Software Development; 11.3 Interactive Media; 11.2 Information

Support Services. **Other Jobs in These Pathways:** Architectural and Engineering Managers; Bioinformatics Scientists; Computer and Information Systems Managers; Computer Hardware Engineers; Computer Numerically Controlled Machine Tool Programmers, Metal and Plastic; Computer Operators; Remote Sensing Scientists and Technologists; Remote Sensing Technicians.

Job Specialization: Business Intelligence Analysts

Produce financial and market intelligence by querying data repositories and generating periodic reports. Devise methods for identifying data patterns and trends in available information sources. Provide technical support for existing reports, dashboards, or other tools. Maintain library of model documents, templates, or other reusable knowledge assets. Identify or monitor current and potential customers, using business intelligence tools. Create or review technical design documentation to ensure the accurate development of reporting solutions. Communicate with customers, competitors, suppliers, professional organizations, or others to stay abreast of industry or business trends. Maintain or update business intelligence tools, databases, dashboards, systems, or methods. Manage timely flow of business intelligence information to users. Identify and analyze industry or geographic trends with business strategy implications. Document specifications for business intelligence or information technology reports, dashboards, or other outputs. Disseminate information on tools, reports, or metadata enhancements. Create business intelligence tools or systems, including design of related databases, spreadsheets, or outputs. Conduct or coordinate tests to ensure that intelligence is consistent with defined needs. Collect business intelligence data from industry reports, public information, field reports, or purchased sources. Analyze technology trends to identify markets for future product development or to improve sales of existing products. Analyze competitive market strategies through analysis of related product, market, or share trends.

Education/Training Required: Work experience plus degree. **Education and Training Program:** Computer and Information Sciences and Support Services, Other.

Career Cluster: 04 Business, Management, and Administration. **Career Pathway:** 11.2 Information Support Services. **Other Jobs in This Pathway:** Computer and Information Systems Managers; Computer Numerically Controlled Machine Tool Programmers, Metal and Plastic; Computer Operators; Remote Sensing Scientists and Technologists; Remote Sensing Technicians.

Job Specialization: Computer Systems Engineers/Architects

Design and develop solutions to complex applications problems, system administration issues, or network concerns. Perform systems management and integration functions. Communicate with staff or clients to understand specific system requirements. Provide advice on project costs, design concepts, or design changes. Document design specifications, installation instructions, and other system-related information. Verify stability, interoperability, portability, security, or scalability of system architecture. Collaborate with engineers or software developers to select appropriate design solutions or ensure the compatibility of system components. Evaluate current or emerging technologies to consider cost, portability, compatibility, or usability. Provide technical guidance or support for the development or troubleshooting of systems. Identify system data, hardware, or software components required to meet user needs. Provide guidelines for implementing secure systems to customers or installation teams. Monitor system operation to detect potential problems. Direct the analysis, development, and operation of complete computer systems. Investigate system component suitability for specified purposes and make recommendations on component use. Perform ongoing hardware and software maintenance operations, including installing or upgrading hardware or software. Configure servers to meet functional specifications. Develop or approve project plans, schedules, or budgets. Define and analyze objectives, scope, issues, or organizational impact of information systems.

Skills—Most Important: Science Skills; Technology/Programming Skills; Thought-Processing Skills. **Other High-Level Skills:** Management Skills; Communication Skills; Equipment Use/Maintenance Skills; Mathematics Skills; Social Skills.

Education/Training Required: Bachelor's degree. **Education and Training Programs:** Computer Engineering, General; Data Modeling/Warehousing and Database Administration. **Knowledge/Courses:** Computers and Electronics; Telecommunications; Engineering and Technology; Design; Mathematics; Sales and Marketing.

Personality Type: Investigative-Realistic-Conventional. **Career Cluster:** 11 Information Technology. **Career Pathway:** 11.4 Programming and Software Development. **Other Jobs in This Pathway:** Architectural and Engineering Managers; Bioinformatics Scientists; Computer Hardware Engineers; Computer Numerically Controlled Machine Tool Programmers, Metal and Plastic.

Job Specialization: Data Warehousing Specialists

Design, model, or implement corporate data warehousing activities. Program and configure warehouses of database information and provide support to warehouse users. Test software systems or applications for software enhancements or new products. Review designs, codes, test plans, or documentation to ensure quality. Provide or coordinate troubleshooting support for data warehouses. Prepare functional or technical documentation for data warehouses. Write new programs or modify existing programs to meet customer requirements using current programming languages and technologies. Verify the structure, accuracy, or quality of warehouse data. Select methods, techniques, or criteria for data warehousing evaluative procedures. Perform system analysis, data analysis, or programming using a variety of computer languages and procedures. Map data between source systems, data warehouses, and data marts. Implement business rules via stored procedures, middleware, or other technologies. Develop and implement data extraction procedures from other systems, such as administration, billing, or claims. Develop or maintain standards, such as organization, structure, or nomenclature, for the design of data warehouse elements, such as data architectures, models, tools, and databases. Design and implement warehouse database structures. Create supporting documentation, such as metadata and diagrams of entity relationships, business processes, and process flow. Create plans, test files, and scripts for data warehouse testing, ranging from unit to integration testing. Create or implement metadata processes and frameworks.

Education/Training Required: Bachelor's degree. **Education and Training Program:** Data Modeling/Warehousing and Database Administration.

Career Cluster: 11 Information Technology. **Career Pathway:** 11.2 Information Support Services. **Other Jobs in This Pathway:** Computer and Information Systems Managers; Computer Numerically Controlled Machine Tool Programmers, Metal and Plastic; Computer Operators; Remote Sensing Scientists and Technologists; Remote Sensing Technicians.

Job Specialization: Database Architects

Design strategies for enterprise database systems and set standards for operations, programming, and security. Design and construct large relational databases. Integrate new systems with existing warehouse structure and refine system performance and functionality. Test changes to database applications or systems. Provide technical support to junior staff or clients. Set up database clusters, backup, or recovery processes. Identify, evaluate, and recommend hardware or software technologies to achieve desired database performance. Plan and install upgrades of database management system software to enhance database performance. Monitor and report systems resource consumption trends to assure production systems meet availability requirements and hardware enhancements are scheduled appropriately. Identify and correct deviations from database development standards. Document and communicate database schemas using accepted notations. Develop or maintain archived procedures, procedural codes, or queries for applications. Develop load-balancing processes to eliminate down time for backup processes. Develop data models for applications, metadata tables, views, or related database structures. Design databases to support business applications, ensuring system scalability, security, performance, and reliability. Design database applications, such as interfaces, data transfer mechanisms, global temporary tables, data partitions, and function-based indexes to enable efficient access of the generic database structure. Demonstrate database technical functionality, such as performance, security, and reliability. Create and enforce database development standards.

Education/Training Required: Bachelor's degree. **Education and Training Program:** Data Modeling/Warehousing and Database Administration.

Career Cluster: 11 Information Technology. **Career Pathway:** 11.4 Programming and Software Development. **Other Jobs in This Pathway:** Architectural and Engineering Managers; Bioinformatics Scientists; Computer Hardware Engineers; Computer Numerically Controlled Machine Tool Programmers, Metal and Plastic.

Job Specialization: Document Management Specialists

Implement and administer enterprise-wide document management procedures for the capture, storage, retrieval, sharing, and destruction of electronic records and documents. Keep abreast of developments in document management by reviewing current literature, talking with colleagues, participating in educational programs, attending meetings or workshops, or participating in professional organizations or conferences. Monitor regulatory activity to maintain compliance with records and document management laws. Write, review, or execute plans for testing new or established document management systems. Search electronic sources or manual sources for information. Retrieve electronic assets from repository for distribution to users, collecting and returning to repository. Propose recommendations for improving content management system capabilities. Prepare support documentation and training materials for end users of document management systems. Prepare and record changes to official documents and confirm changes with legal and compliance management staff. Exercise security surveillance over document processing, reproduction, distribution, storage, or archiving. Implement scanning or other automated data entry procedures using imaging devices and document imaging software. Document technical functions and specifications for new or proposed content management systems. Develop, document, or maintain standards, best practices, or system usage procedures. Consult with end users on problems in accessing electronic content.

Education/Training Required: Associate degree. **Education and Training Program:** Computer and Information Sciences and Support Services, Other.

Career Cluster: 11 Information Technology. **Career Pathway:** 11.2 Information Support Services. **Other Jobs in This Pathway:** Computer and Information Systems Managers; Computer Numerically Controlled Machine Tool Programmers, Metal and Plastic; Computer Operators; Remote Sensing Scientists and Technologists; Remote Sensing Technicians.

Job Specialization: Geographic Information Systems Technicians

Assist scientists, technologists, and related professionals in building, maintaining, modifying, and using geographic information systems (GIS) databases. May also perform some custom application development and provide user support. Recommend procedures or equipment or software upgrades to increase data accessibility or ease of use. Provide technical support to users or clients on the maintenance, development, or operation of GIS databases, equipment, or applications. Read current literature, talk with colleagues, continue education, or participate in professional organizations or conferences to keep abreast of developments in GIS technology, equipment, or systems. Confer with users to analyze, configure, or troubleshoot applications. Select cartographic elements needed for effective presentation of information. Transfer or rescale information from original photographs to maps or other photographs. Review existing or incoming data for currency, accuracy, usefulness, quality, or completeness of documentation. Interpret aerial or ortho photographs. Analyze GIS data to identify spatial relationships or display results of analyses using maps, graphs, or tabular data. Perform geospatial data building, modeling, or analysis using advanced spatial analysis, data manipulation, or cartography software.

Skills—Most Important: Technology/ Programming Skills; Mathematics Skills; Science Skills. **Other High-Level Skills:** Thought-Processing Skills; Communication Skills; Social Skills.

Education/Training Required: Associate degree. **Education and Training Program:** Geographic Information Science and Cartography. **Knowledge/Courses:** Geography; Design; Computers and Electronics; Engineering and Technology; Mathematics; Biology.

Personality Type: Investigative-Realistic-Conventional. **Career Cluster:** 11 Information Technology. **Career Pathway:** 11.4 Programming and Software Development. **Other Jobs in This Pathway:** Architectural and Engineering Managers; Bioinformatics Scientists; Computer Hardware Engineers; Computer Numerically Controlled Machine Tool Programmers, Metal and Plastic.

Job Specialization: Geospatial Information Scientists and Technologists

Research and develop geospatial technologies. May produce databases, perform applications programming, or coordinate projects. May specialize in agriculture, mining, health care, retail trade, urban planning, or military intelligence. Perform integrated and computerized Geographic Information Systems (GIS) analyses to address scientific problems. Develop specialized computer software routines, Internet-based GIS databases, or business applications to customize geographic information. Provide technical support for GIS mapping software. Create visual representations of geospatial data using complex procedures such as analytical modeling, three-dimensional renderings, and plot creation. Perform computer programming, data analysis, or software development for GIS applications, including the maintenance of existing systems or research and development for future enhancements. Assist users in formulating GIS requirements or understanding the implications of alternatives. Collect, compile, or integrate GIS data such as remote sensing and cartographic data for inclusion in map manuscripts. Conduct or coordinate research, data analysis, systems design, or support for GIS or Global Positioning Systems (GPS) mapping software. Design, program, or model GIS applications or procedures. Document, design, code, or test GIS models, Internet mapping solutions, or other applications.

Skills—Most Important: Science Skills; Technology/Programming Skills; Mathematics Skills. **Other High-Level Skills:** Thought-Processing Skills; Communication Skills; Social Skills; Management Skills.

Education/Training Required: Bachelor's degree. **Education and Training Program:** Geographic Information Science and Cartography. **Knowledge/Courses:** Geography; Computers and Electronics; Design; Engineering and Technology; Mathematics; Education and Training.

Personality Type: Investigative-Realistic-Conventional. **Career Cluster:** 11 Information Technology. **Career Pathway:** 11.4 Programming and Software Development. **Other Jobs in This Pathway:** Architectural and Engineering Managers; Bioinformatics Scientists; Computer Hardware Engineers; Computer Numerically Controlled Machine Tool Programmers, Metal and Plastic.

Job Specialization: Information Technology Project Managers

Plan, initiate, and manage information technology projects. Lead and guide the work of technical staff. Serve as liaison between business and technical aspects of projects. Plan project stages and assess business implications for each stage. Monitor progress to assure deadlines, standards, and cost targets are met. Perform risk assessments to develop response strategies. Submit project deliverables, ensuring adherence to quality standards. Monitor the performance of project team members, providing and documenting performance feedback. Confer with project personnel to identify and resolve problems. Assess current or future customer needs and priorities through communication with customers, surveys, or other methods. Schedule and facilitate meetings related to information technology projects. Monitor or track project milestones and deliverables. Negotiate with project stakeholders or suppliers to obtain resources or materials. Initiate, review, or approve modifications to project plans. Identify, review, or select vendors or consultants to meet project needs. Establish and execute a project communication plan. Identify need for initial or supplemental project resources. Direct or coordinate activities of project personnel. Develop implementation plans that include analyses such as cost-benefit or return on investment. Coordinate recruitment or selection of project personnel. Develop and manage annual budgets for information technology projects. Assign duties, responsibilities, and spans of authority to project personnel. Prepare project status reports by collecting, analyzing, and summarizing information and trends.

Education/Training Required: Work experience in a related occupation. **Education and Training Program:** Information Technology Project Management.

Career Clusters: 04 Business, Management, and Administration; 11 Information Technology. **Career Pathway:** 11.4 Programming and Software Development. **Other Jobs in This Pathway:** Architectural and Engineering

Managers; Bioinformatics Scientists; Computer Hardware Engineers; Computer Numerically Controlled Machine Tool Programmers, Metal and Plastic.

Job Specialization: Search Marketing Strategists

Employ search marketing tactics to increase visibility and engagement with content, products, or services in Internet-enabled devices or interfaces. Examine search query behaviors on general or specialty search engines or other Internet-based content. Analyze research, data, or technology to understand user intent and measure outcomes for ongoing optimization. Keep abreast of government regulations and emerging Web technology to ensure regulatory compliance by reviewing current literature, talking with colleagues, participating in educational programs, attending meetings or workshops, or participating in professional organizations or conferences. Resolve product availability problems in collaboration with customer service staff. Implement online customer service processes to ensure positive and consistent user experiences. Identify, evaluate, or procure hardware or software for implementing online marketing campaigns. Identify methods for interfacing Web application technologies with enterprise resource planning or other system software. Define product requirements based on market research analysis in collaboration with design and engineering staff. Assist in the evaluation and negotiation of contracts with vendors and online partners. Propose online or multiple-sales-channel campaigns to marketing executives. Assist in the development of online transactional and security policies. Prepare electronic commerce designs and prototypes, such as storyboards, mock-ups, and other content, using graphic design software. Participate in the development of online marketing strategy. Identify and develop commercial or technical specifications to promote transactional Web site functionality, including usability, pricing, checkout, or data security.

Education/Training Required: Bachelor's degree. **Education and Training Program:** Web Page, Digital/Multimedia, and Information Resources Design.

Career Clusters: 11 Information Technology; 14 Marketing, Sales, and Service. **Career Pathway:** 14.2 Professional Sales and Marketing. **Other Jobs in This Pathway:** Cashiers; Counter and Rental Clerks; Door-To-Door Sales Workers, News and Street Vendors, and Related Workers; Driver/Sales Workers; Energy Brokers; First-Line Supervisors of Non-Retail Sales Workers; First-Line Supervisors of Retail Sales Workers; Hotel, Motel, and Resort Desk Clerks; Marketing Managers; Marking Clerks; Online Merchants; Order Fillers, Wholesale and Retail Sales; Parts Salespersons; Property, Real Estate, and Community Association Managers; Real Estate Sales Agents; Reservation and Transportation Ticket Agents and Travel Clerks; Retail Salespersons; Sales and Related Workers, All Other; Sales Representatives, Services, All Other; Sales Representatives, Wholesale and Manufacturing, Except Technical and Scientific Products; Sales Representatives, Wholesale and Manufacturing, Technical and Scientific Products; Solar Sales Representatives and Assessors; Stock Clerks—Stockroom, Warehouse, or Storage Yard; Stock Clerks, Sales Floor; Telemarketers; others.

Job Specialization: Software Quality Assurance Engineers and Testers

Develop and execute software test plans to identify software problems and their causes. Design test plans, scenarios, scripts, or procedures. Test system modifications to prepare for implementation. Develop testing programs that address areas such as database impacts, software scenarios, regression testing, negative testing, error or bug retests, or usability. Document software defects using a bug-tracking system and report defects to software developers. Identify, analyze, and document problems with program function, output, online screen, or content. Monitor bug resolution efforts and track successes. Create or maintain databases of known test defects. Plan test schedules or strategies in accordance with project scope or delivery dates. Participate in product design reviews to provide input on functional requirements, product designs, schedules, or potential problems. Review software documentation to ensure technical accuracy, compliance, or completeness or to mitigate risks. Document test procedures to ensure replicability and compliance with standards. Develop or specify standards, methods, or procedures to determine product quality or release readiness. Update automated test scripts to ensure currency. Investigate customer problems referred by technical support. Install, maintain, or use software testing programs. Provide feedback and recommendations to developers on software usability and functionality. Monitor program performance to ensure efficient and problem-free operations.

Skills—Most Important: Technology/ Programming Skills; Installation Skills; Science Skills. **Other High-Level Skills:** Thought-Processing Skills; Equipment Use/Maintenance Skills; Communication Skills; Management Skills.

Education/Training Required: Bachelor's degree. **Education and Training Program:** Computer Engineering, General. **Knowledge/ Courses:** Computers and Electronics; Engineering and Technology; Design; English Language; Mathematics; Clerical.

Personality Type: Investigative-Conventional-Realistic. **Career Cluster:** 11 Information Technology. **Career Pathway:** 11.4 Programming and Software Development. **Other Jobs in This Pathway:** Architectural and Engineering Managers; Bioinformatics Scientists; Computer Hardware Engineers; Computer Numerically Controlled Machine Tool Programmers, Metal and Plastic.

Job Specialization: Video Game Designers

Design core features of video games. Specify innovative game and role-play mechanics, storylines, and character biographies. Create and maintain design documentation. Guide and collaborate with production staff to produce games as designed. Review or evaluate competitive products, film, music, television, and other art forms to generate new game design ideas. Provide test specifications to quality assurance staff. Keep abreast of game design technology and techniques, industry trends, or audience interests, reactions, and needs by reviewing current literature, talking with colleagues, participating in educational programs, attending meetings or workshops, or participating in professional organizations or conferences. Create gameplay test plans for internal and external test groups. Provide feedback to designers and other colleagues on game design features. Balance and adjust gameplay experiences to ensure the critical and commercial success of the product. Write or supervise the writing of game text and dialogue. Solicit, obtain, and integrate feedback from design and technical staff into game design. Provide feedback to production staff on technical game qualities or adherence to original design. Prepare two-dimensional concept layouts or three-dimensional mock-ups. Present new game design concepts to management and technical colleagues, including artists, animators, and programmers. Prepare and revise initial game sketches using two- and three-dimensional graphical design software. Oversee gameplay testing to ensure intended gaming experience and game adherence to original vision.

Education/Training Required: Postsecondary vocational training. **Education and Training Program:** Game and Interactive Media Design.

Career Clusters: 03 Arts, Audio/Video Technology, and Communications; 11 Information Technology. **Career Pathway:** 11.4 Programming and Software Development. **Other Jobs in This Pathway:** Architectural and Engineering Managers; Bioinformatics Scientists; Computer Hardware Engineers; Computer Numerically Controlled Machine Tool Programmers, Metal and Plastic.

Job Specialization: Web Administrators

Manage Web environment design, deployment, development, and maintenance activities. Perform testing and quality assurance of Websites and Web applications. Back up or modify applications and related data to provide for disaster recovery. Determine sources of Web page or server problems and take action to correct problems. Review or update Web page content or links in a timely manner. Monitor systems for intrusions or denial of service attacks and report security breaches to appropriate personnel. Implement Website security measures, such as firewalls or message encryption. Administer Internet/intranet infrastructure, including components such as Web, file transfer protocol (FTP), and news and mail servers. Collaborate with development teams to discuss, analyze, or resolve usability issues. Test backup or recovery plans regularly and resolve any problems. Monitor Web developments through continuing education, reading, or professional conferences, workshops, or groups. Implement updates, upgrades, and patches in a timely manner to limit loss of service. Identify or document backup or recovery plans. Collaborate with Web developers to create and operate internal and external Websites or to manage projects such as e-marketing campaigns. Install or configure Web server software or hardware to ensure that directory structure is well-defined, logical, and secure and that files are named properly. Gather, analyze, or document user feedback to locate or resolve sources of problems. Develop Web site performance metrics. Identify or address interoperability requirements.

Skills—Most Important: Technology/Programming Skills; Science Skills; Thought-Processing Skills. **Other High-Level Skills:** Equipment Use/Maintenance Skills; Communication Skills; Social Skills.

Education/Training Required: Bachelor's degree. **Education and Training Programs:** Computer and Information Systems Security/Information Assurance; Network and System Administration/Administrator; System, Networking, and LAN/WAN Management/Manager; Web/Multimedia Management and Webmaster Training. **Knowledge/ Courses:** Computers and Electronics; Telecommunications; Design; Communications and Media; Sales and Marketing; Clerical.

Personality Type: Conventional-Enterprising-Investigative. **Career Cluster:** 11 Information Technology. **Career Pathway:** 11.4 Programming and Software Development. **Other Jobs in This Pathway:** Architectural and Engineering Managers; Bioinformatics Scientists; Computer Hardware Engineers; Computer Numerically Controlled Machine Tool Programmers, Metal and Plastic.

Computer Programmers

- ❋ Annual Earnings: $71,380
- ❋ Earnings Growth Potential: High (42.8%)
- ❋ Growth: –2.9%
- ❋ Annual Job Openings: 8,030
- ❋ Self-Employed: 5.5%

Skills—Most Important: Technology/ Programming Skills; Science Skills; Mathematics Skills. **Other High-Level Skills:** Thought-Processing Skills; Communication Skills; Management Skills.

Convert project specifications and statements of problems and procedures to detailed logical flow charts for coding into computer language. Develop and write computer programs to store, locate, and retrieve specific documents, data, and information. May program Websites. Correct errors by making appropriate changes and rechecking the program to ensure that the desired results are produced. Conduct trial runs of programs and software applications to be sure they will produce the desired information and that the instructions are correct. Compile and write documentation of program development and subsequent revisions, inserting comments in the coded instructions so others can understand the program. Write, update, and maintain computer programs or software packages to handle specific jobs such as tracking inventory, storing or retrieving data, or controlling other equipment. Consult with managerial, engineering, and technical personnel to clarify program intent, identify problems, and suggest changes. Perform or direct revision, repair, or expansion of existing programs to increase operating efficiency or adapt to new requirements. Write, analyze, review, and rewrite programs using workflow chart and diagram and applying knowledge of computer capabilities, subject matter, and symbolic logic. Write or contribute to instructions or manuals to guide end users. Investigate whether networks, workstations, the central processing unit of the system, or peripheral equipment are responding to a program's instructions. Prepare detailed workflow charts and diagrams that describe input, output, and logical operation and convert them into instructions coded in a computer language.

Education/Training Required: Bachelor's degree. **Education and Training Programs:** Computer Programming, Other; Computer Programming, Specific Applications; Computer Programming, Vendor/Product Certification; Computer Programming/Programmer Training, General; Computer Science. **Knowledge/ Courses:** Computers and Electronics; Mathematics; Design; Administration and Management; English Language; Communications and Media.

Personality Type: Investigative-Conventional. **Career Cluster:** 11 Information Technology. **Career Pathways:** 11.3 Interactive Media; 11.4 Programming and Software Development; 11.1 Network Systems; 08.3 Health Informatics;

15.2 Science and Mathematics. **Other Jobs in These Pathways:** Architectural and Engineering Managers; Biofuels/Biodiesel Technology and Product Development Managers; Biologists; Chemists; Clinical Psychologists; Community and Social Service Specialists, All Other; Computer and Information Systems Managers; Editors; Education, Training, and Library Workers, All Other; Engineers, All Other; Executive Secretaries and Executive Administrative Assistants; First-Line Supervisors of Office and Administrative Support Workers; Graphic Designers; Medical and Health Services Managers; Medical Assistants; Medical Records and Health Information Technicians; Medical Scientists, Except Epidemiologists; Medical Secretaries; Medical Transcriptionists; Mental Health Counselors; Physical Therapists; Public Relations Specialists; Receptionists and Information Clerks; Rehabilitation Counselors; Substance Abuse and Behavioral Disorder Counselors; others.

Computer Science Teachers, Postsecondary

- ✻ Annual Earnings: $70,300
- ✻ Earnings Growth Potential: High (48.5%)
- ✻ Growth: 15.1%
- ✻ Annual Job Openings: 1,000
- ✻ Self-Employed: 0.2%

Skills—Most Important: Communication Skills; Mathematics Skills; Technology/Programming Skills. **Other High-Level Skills:** Thought-Processing Skills; Science Skills; Social Skills; Management Skills.

Teach courses in computer science. May specialize in a field of computer science, such as the design and function of computers or operations and research analysis. Evaluate and grade students' classwork, laboratory work, assignments, and papers. Maintain student attendance records, grades, and other required records. Prepare and deliver lectures to undergraduate or graduate students on topics such as programming, data structures, and software design. Prepare course materials such as syllabi, homework assignments, and handouts. Compile, administer, and grade examinations or assign this work to others. Keep abreast of developments in the field by reading current literature, talking with colleagues, and participating in professional conferences. Initiate, facilitate, and moderate classroom discussions. Plan, evaluate, and revise curricula, course content, and course materials and methods of instruction. Supervise students' laboratory work. Maintain regularly scheduled office hours to advise and assist students. Select and obtain materials and supplies such as textbooks and laboratory equipment. Advise students on academic and vocational curricula and on career issues. Participate in student recruitment, registration, and placement activities. Collaborate with colleagues to address teaching and research issues. Serve on academic or administrative committees that deal with institutional policies, departmental matters, and academic issues. Conduct research and publish findings in professional journals, books, or electronic media.

Education/Training Required: Doctoral degree. **Education and Training Programs:** Computer and Information Sciences, General; Computer Programming/Programmer, General; Computer Science; Computer Systems Analysis/Analyst; Information Science/Studies. **Knowledge/Courses:** Computers and Electronics; Engineering and Technology; Education and Training; Telecommunications; Design; English Language.

Personality Type: Social-Investigative-Conventional. **Career Clusters:** 05 Education and Training; 11 Information Technology. **Career Pathways:** 05.3 Teaching/Training; 11.1 Network Systems; 11.2 Information Support Services; 11.4 Programming and Software Development. **Other Jobs in These Pathways:** Adult Basic and Secondary Education and Literacy Teachers and Instructors; Architectural and Engineering Managers; Career/Technical Education Teachers, Secondary School; Chemists; Coaches and Scouts; Computer and Information Systems Managers; Computer Hardware Engineers; Computer Operators; Elementary School Teachers, Except Special Education; Fitness Trainers and Aerobics Instructors; Graphic Designers; Instructional Coordinators; Instructional Designers and Technologists; Kindergarten Teachers, Except Special Education; Librarians; Middle School Teachers, Except Special and Career/Technical Education; Multimedia Artists and Animators; Preschool Teachers, Except Special Education; Recreation Workers; Remote Sensing Technicians; Secondary School Teachers, Except Special and Career/Technical Education; Self-Enrichment Education Teachers; Teacher Assistants; Tutors; 37 other postsecondary teaching occupations; others.

Computer Systems Analysts

- ❋ Annual Earnings: $77,740
- ❋ Earnings Growth Potential: Medium (37.8%)
- ❋ Growth: 20.3%
- ❋ Annual Job Openings: 22,280
- ❋ Self-Employed: 5.7%

Skills—Most Important: Technology/Programming Skills; Science Skills; Mathematics Skills. **Other High-Level Skills:** Thought-Processing Skills; Communication Skills; Social Skills; Equipment Use/Maintenance Skills; Management Skills.

Analyze science, engineering, business, and all other data-processing problems for application to electronic data-processing systems. Analyze user requirements, procedures, and problems to automate or improve existing systems and review computer system capabilities, workflow, and scheduling limitations. May analyze or recommend commercially available software. May supervise computer programmers. Provide staff and users with assistance solving computer-related problems, such as malfunctions and program problems. Test, maintain, and monitor computer programs and systems, including coordinating the installation of computer programs and systems. Use object-oriented programming languages as well as client and server applications development processes and multimedia and Internet technology. Confer with clients on the nature of the information-processing or computation needs a computer program is to address. Coordinate and link the computer systems in an organization to increase compatibility and so information can be shared. Consult with management to ensure agreement on system principles. Expand or modify system to serve new purposes or improve workflow. Interview or survey workers, observe job performance, or perform the job to determine what information is processed and how it is processed. Determine computer software or hardware needed to set up or alter system. Train staff and users to work with computer systems and programs. Analyze information-processing or computation needs and plan and design computer systems using structured analysis, data modeling, and information engineering. Assess the usefulness of pre-developed application packages and adapt them to a user environment. Define the goals of the system and devise flow charts and diagrams describing logical operational steps of programs.

Education/Training Required: Bachelor's degree. **Education and Training Programs:** Computer Systems Analysis/Analyst; Information Science/Studies. **Knowledge/ Courses:** Computers and Electronics; Engineering and Technology; Mathematics; Telecommunications; Clerical Practices; English Language.

Personality Type: Investigative-Conventional-Realistic. **Career Cluster:** 11 Information Technology. **Career Pathways:** 11.4 Programming and Software Development; 11.3 Interactive Media; 11.2 Information Support Services. **Other Jobs in These Pathways:** Architectural and Engineering Managers; Bioinformatics Scientists; Computer and Information Systems Managers; Computer Hardware Engineers; Computer Numerically Controlled Machine Tool Programmers, Metal and Plastic; Computer Operators; Remote Sensing Scientists and Technologists; Remote Sensing Technicians.

Job Specialization: Informatics Nurse Specialists

Apply knowledge of nursing and informatics to assist in the design, development, and ongoing modification of computerized health-care systems. May educate staff and assist in problem solving to promote the implementation of the health-care system. Design, develop, select, test, implement, and evaluate new or modified informatics solutions, data structures, and decision-support mechanisms to support patients, health-care professionals,

and their information management and human-computer and human-technology interactions within health-care contexts. Disseminate information about nursing informatics science and practice to the profession, other health-care professions, nursing students, and the public. Translate nursing practice information between nurses and systems engineers, analysts, or designers using object-oriented models or other techniques. Plan, install, repair, or troubleshoot telehealth technology applications or systems in homes. Use informatics science to design or implement health information technology applications to resolve clinical or health-care administrative problems. Develop, implement or evaluate health information technology applications, tools, processes, or structures to assist nurses with data management. Analyze and interpret patient, nursing, or information systems data to improve nursing services. Analyze computer and information technologies to determine applicability to nursing practice, education, administration, and research. Apply knowledge of computer science, information science, nursing, and informatics theory to nursing practice, education, administration, or research in collaboration with other health informatics specialists.

Education/Training Required: Master's degree. **Education and Training Programs:** Computer Systems Analysis/Analyst; Information Science/ Studies. **Knowledge/Courses:** Medicine and Dentistry; Sociology and Anthropology; Education and Training; Engineering and Technology; Computers and Electronics; Clerical.

Personality Type: Social-Investigative. **Career Clusters:** 08 Health Science; 11 Information Technology. **Career Pathway:** 08.1 Therapeutic Services. **Other Jobs in This Pathway:** Clinical Psychologists; Community and Social Service Specialists, All Other; Counseling Psychologists; Dental Assistants; Dental Hygienists; Dentists, General; Health Technologists and Technicians, All Other; Healthcare Support Workers, All Other; Home Health Aides; Licensed Practical and Licensed Vocational Nurses; Low Vision Therapists, Orientation and Mobility Specialists, and Vision Rehabilitation Therapists; Massage Therapists; Medical and Clinical Laboratory Technicians; Medical and Health Services Managers; Medical Scientists, Except Epidemiologists; Medical Secretaries; Occupational Therapists; Pharmacists; Pharmacy Technicians; Radiologic Technologists; School Psychologists; Social and Human Service Assistants; Speech-Language Pathologists; Speech-Language Pathology Assistants; Substance Abuse and Behavioral Disorder Counselors; others.

Computer User Support Specialists

❋ Annual Earnings: $46,260

❋ Earnings Growth Potential: Medium (38.8%)

❋ Growth: 13.8%

❋ Annual Job Openings: 23,460

❋ Self-Employed: 1.2%

Skills—Most Important: Equipment Use/Maintenance Skills; Communication Skills; Thought-Processing Skills. **Other High-Level Skills:** Social Skills; Management Skills.

Provide technical assistance to computer users. Answer questions or resolve computer problems for clients in person, via telephone, or electronically. May provide assistance on the use of computer hardware and software, including printing, installation, word-processing, electronic mail, and operating systems. Enter commands and observe system functioning to verify correct operations and detect errors. Install and perform minor repairs to hardware, software, or peripheral equipment following design or installation specifications. Oversee the daily performance of computer systems. Set up equipment for employee use, performing or ensuring proper installation of cables, operating systems, or appropriate software. Maintain records of daily data communication transactions, problems, remedial actions, or installation activities. Read technical manuals, confer with users, or conduct computer diagnostics to investigate and resolve problems or to provide technical assistance and support. Confer with staff, users, and management to establish requirements for new systems or modifications. Develop training materials and procedures or train users in the proper use of hardware or software. Refer major hardware or software problems or defective products to vendors or technicians for service. Prepare evaluations of software or hardware and recommend improvements or upgrades. Read trade magazines and technical manuals or attend conferences and seminars to maintain knowledge of hardware and software. Inspect equipment and read order sheets to prepare for delivery to users. Modify and customize commercial programs for internal needs.

Education/Training Required: Work experience in a related occupation. **Education and Training Program:** Computer Support Specialist Training. **Knowledge/Courses:** Computers and Electronics; Telecommunications; Engineering and Technology; Clerical Practices; Customer and Personal Service; Communications and Media.

Personality Type: Realistic-Investigative-Conventional. **Career Cluster:** 11 Information Technology. **Career Pathway:** 11.2 Information Support Services. **Other Jobs in This Pathway:** Computer and Information Systems Managers; Computer Numerically Controlled Machine Tool Programmers, Metal and Plastic; Computer Operators; Remote Sensing Scientists and Technologists; Remote Sensing Technicians.

Construction and Building Inspectors

* Annual Earnings: $52,360
* Earnings Growth Potential: Medium (38.9%)
* Growth: 16.8%
* Annual Job Openings: 3,970
* Self-Employed: 7.5%

Skills—Most Important: Science Skills; Mathematics Skills; Equipment Use/Maintenance Skills. **Other High-Level Skills:** Thought-Processing Skills; Social Skills; Management Skills; Communication Skills.

Inspect structures using engineering skills to determine structural soundness and compliance with specifications, building codes, and other regulations. Inspections may be general or may be limited to a specific area, such as electrical systems or plumbing. Use survey instruments, metering devices, tape measures, and test equipment such as concrete strength measurers to perform inspections. Inspect bridges, dams, highways, buildings, wiring, plumbing, electrical circuits, sewers, heating systems, and foundations during and after construction for structural quality, general safety, and conformance to specifications and codes. Maintain daily logs and supplement inspection records with photographs. Review and interpret plans, blueprints, site layouts, specifications, and construction methods to ensure compliance to legal requirements and safety regulations. Inspect and monitor construction sites to ensure adherence to safety standards, building codes, and specifications. Measure dimensions and verify level, alignment, and elevation of structures and fixtures to ensure compliance to building plans and codes. Issue violation notices and stop-work orders, conferring with owners, violators, and authorities to explain regulations and recommend rectifications. Issue permits for construction, relocation, demolition, and occupancy. Approve and sign plans that meet required specifications. Compute estimates of work completed or of needed renovations or upgrades and approve payment for contractors. Monitor installation of plumbing, wiring, equipment, and appliances to ensure that installation is performed properly and is in compliance with applicable regulations.

Education/Training Required: Work experience in a related occupation. **Education and Training Program:** Building/Home/Construction Inspection/Inspector. **Knowledge/Courses:** Building and Construction; Engineering and Technology; Design; Physics; Public Safety and Security; Mechanical.

Personality Type: Realistic-Conventional-Investigative. **Career Cluster:** 02 Architecture and Construction. **Career Pathway:** 02.2 Construction. **Other Jobs in This Pathway:** Brickmasons and Blockmasons; Cement Masons and Concrete Finishers; Construction Carpenters; Construction Laborers; Construction Managers; Cost Estimators; Drywall and Ceiling Tile Installers; Electrical Power-Line Installers and Repairers; Electricians; Engineering Technicians,

Except Drafters, All Other; Excavating and Loading Machine and Dragline Operators; First-Line Supervisors of Construction Trades and Extraction Workers; Heating and Air Conditioning Mechanics and Installers; Helpers—Carpenters; Helpers—Electricians; Helpers—Pipelayers, Plumbers, Pipefitters, and Steamfitters; Highway Maintenance Workers; Operating Engineers and Other Construction Equipment Operators; Painters, Construction and Maintenance; Pipe Fitters and Steamfitters; Plumbers; Refrigeration Mechanics and Installers; Roofers; Rough Carpenters; Solar Energy Installation Managers; others.

Construction Laborers

- ❋ Annual Earnings: $29,280
- ❋ Earnings Growth Potential: Medium (36.6%)
- ❋ Growth: 20.5%
- ❋ Annual Job Openings: 33,940
- ❋ Self-Employed: 21.3%

Skills—Most Important: Equipment Use/ Maintenance Skills.

Perform tasks involving physical labor at building, highway, and heavy construction projects; tunnel and shaft excavations; and demolition sites. May operate hand and power tools of all types: air hammers, earth tampers, cement mixers, small mechanical hoists, surveying and measuring equipment, and other equipment and instruments. May clean and prepare sites; dig trenches; set braces to support the sides of excavations; erect scaffolding; clean up rubble and debris; and remove asbestos, lead, and other hazardous waste materials. May assist other craft workers. Clean and prepare construction sites to eliminate possible hazards. Read and interpret plans, instructions, and specifications to determine work activities. Control traffic passing near, in, and around work zones. Signal equipment operators to facilitate alignment, movement, and adjustment of machinery, equipment, and materials. Dig ditches or trenches, backfill excavations, and compact and level earth to grade specifications using picks, shovels, pneumatic tampers, and rakes. Measure, mark, and record openings and distances to lay out areas where construction work will be performed. Position, join, align, and seal structural components such as concrete wall sections and pipes. Load, unload, and identify building materials, machinery, and tools and distribute them to the appropriate locations according to project plans and specifications. Erect and disassemble scaffolding, shoring, braces, traffic barricades, ramps, and other temporary structures. Build and position forms for pouring concrete and dismantle forms after use. Lubricate, clean, and repair machinery, equipment, and tools. Operate jackhammers and drills to break up concrete or pavement. Operate, read, and maintain air monitoring and other sampling devices in confined and/or hazardous environments. Smooth and finish freshly poured cement or concrete using floats, trowels, screeds, or powered cement finishing tools.

Education/Training Required: Moderate-term on-the-job training. **Education and Training Program:** Construction Trades, Other. **Knowledge/Courses:** Building and Construction; Design; Mechanical Devices; Transportation; Public Safety and Security; Engineering and Technology.

Personality Type: Realistic-Conventional. **Career Cluster:** 02 Architecture and Construction. **Career Pathway:** 02.2 Construction. **Other Jobs in This Pathway:**

Brickmasons and Blockmasons; Cement Masons and Concrete Finishers; Construction and Building Inspectors; Construction Carpenters; Construction Managers; Cost Estimators; Drywall and Ceiling Tile Installers; Electrical Power-Line Installers and Repairers; Electricians; Engineering Technicians, Except Drafters, All Other; Excavating and Loading Machine and Dragline Operators; First-Line Supervisors of Construction Trades and Extraction Workers; Heating and Air Conditioning Mechanics and Installers; Helpers—Carpenters; Helpers— Electricians; Helpers—Pipelayers, Plumbers, Pipefitters, and Steamfitters; Highway Maintenance Workers; Operating Engineers and Other Construction Equipment Operators; Painters, Construction and Maintenance; Pipe Fitters and Steamfitters; Plumbers; Refrigeration Mechanics and Installers; Roofers; Rough Carpenters; Solar Energy Installation Managers; others.

Construction Managers

- Annual Earnings: $83,860
- Earnings Growth Potential: Medium (40.1%)
- Growth: 17.2%
- Annual Job Openings: 13,770
- Self-Employed: 60.9%

Skills—Most Important: Management Skills; Mathematics Skills; Social Skills. **Other High-Level Skills:** Thought-Processing Skills; Science Skills; Communication Skills; Equipment Use/ Maintenance Skills.

Plan, direct, coordinate, or budget, usually through subordinate supervisory personnel, activities concerned with the construction and maintenance of structures, facilities, and systems. Participate in the conceptual development of a construction project and oversee its organization, scheduling, and implementation. Confer with supervisory personnel, owners, contractors, and design professionals to discuss and resolve matters such as work procedures, complaints, and construction problems. Plan, organize, and direct activities concerned with the construction and maintenance of structures, facilities, and systems. Schedule the project in logical steps and budget time required to meet deadlines. Determine labor requirements and dispatch workers to construction sites. Inspect and review projects to monitor compliance with building and safety codes and other regulations. Interpret and explain plans and contract terms to administrative staff, workers, and clients, representing the owner or developer. Prepare contracts and negotiate revisions, changes, and additions to contractual agreements with architects, consultants, clients, suppliers, and subcontractors. Obtain permits and licenses. Study job specifications to determine appropriate construction methods.

Education/Training Required: Bachelor's degree. **Education and Training Programs:** Business Administration and Management, General; Business/Commerce, General; Construction Engineering Technology/ Technician; Operations Management and Supervision. **Knowledge/Courses:** Building and Construction; Design; Engineering and Technology; Mechanical Devices; Administration and Management; Personnel and Human Resources.

Personality Type: Enterprising-Realistic-Conventional. **Career Clusters:** 02 Architecture and Construction; 04 Business, Management, and Administration. **Career Pathways:** 04.1

Management; 02.2 Construction. **Other Jobs in These Pathways:** Brownfield Redevelopment Specialists and Site Managers; Business Continuity Planners; Business Operations Specialists, All Other; Compliance Managers; Construction Carpenters; Construction Laborers; Customs Brokers; Electricians; Energy Auditors; First-Line Supervisors of Construction Trades and Extraction Workers; First-Line Supervisors of Office and Administrative Support Workers; General and Operations Managers; Investment Fund Managers; Loss Prevention Managers; Management Analysts; Managers, All Other; Regulatory Affairs Managers; Rough Carpenters; Security Management Specialists; Security Managers; Solar Energy Installation Managers; Supply Chain Managers; Sustainability Specialists; Wind Energy Operations Managers; Wind Energy Project Managers; others.

Cost Estimators

* Annual Earnings: $57,860
* Earnings Growth Potential: High (41.1%)
* Growth: 25.3%
* Annual Job Openings: 10,360
* Self-Employed: 2.0%

Skills—Most Important: Mathematics Skills; Management Skills; Communication Skills. **Other High-Level Skills:** Thought-Processing Skills; Social Skills.

Prepare cost estimates for product manufacturing, construction projects, or services to aid management in bidding on or determining prices of products or services. May specialize according to particular service performed or type of product manufactured.

Analyze blueprints and other documentation to prepare time, cost, materials, and labor estimates. Assess cost-effectiveness of products, projects, or services, tracking actual costs relative to bids as the project develops. Consult with clients, vendors, personnel in other departments, or construction foremen to discuss and formulate estimates and resolve issues. Confer with engineers, architects, owners, contractors, and subcontractors on changes and adjustments to cost estimates. Prepare estimates used by management for planning, organizing, and scheduling work. Prepare estimates for use in selecting vendors or subcontractors. Review material and labor requirements to decide whether it is more cost-effective to produce or purchase components. Prepare cost and expenditure statements and other documentation at regular intervals for the duration of the project. Prepare and maintain a directory of suppliers, contractors, and subcontractors. Set up cost monitoring and reporting systems and procedures. Establish and maintain tendering process and conduct negotiations. Conduct special studies to develop and establish standard hour and related cost data or to effect cost reduction. Visit site and record information about access, drainage, and topography and availability of services such as water and electricity.

Education/Training Required: Bachelor's degree. **Education and Training Programs:** Business Administration and Management, General; Business/Commerce, General; Construction Engineering; Construction Engineering Technology/Technician; Manufacturing Engineering; Materials Engineering; Mechanical Engineering. **Knowledge/Courses:** Engineering and Technology; Mathematics; Economics and Accounting; Building and Construction; Design; Computers and Electronics.

Personality Type: Conventional-Enterprising. **Career Clusters:** 02 Architecture and Construction; 04 Business, Management, and Administration; 13 Manufacturing; 15 Science, Technology, Engineering, and Mathematics. **Career Pathways:** 13.1 Production; 04.1 Management; 02.2 Construction; 15.1 Engineering and Technology. **Other Jobs in These Pathways:** Brownfield Redevelopment Specialists and Site Managers; Business Continuity Planners; Business Operations Specialists, All Other; Compliance Managers; Construction Carpenters; Construction Laborers; Customs Brokers; Energy Auditors; First-Line Supervisors of Construction Trades and Extraction Workers; First-Line Supervisors of Office and Administrative Support Workers; General and Operations Managers; Investment Fund Managers; Loss Prevention Managers; Management Analysts; Managers, All Other; Packers and Packagers, Hand; Regulatory Affairs Managers; Rough Carpenters; Security Management Specialists; Security Managers; Supply Chain Managers; Sustainability Specialists; Team Assemblers; Wind Energy Operations Managers; Wind Energy Project Managers; others.

Customer Service Representatives

❀ Annual Earnings: $30,460

❀ Earnings Growth Potential: Low (35.8%)

❀ Growth: 17.7%

❀ Annual Job Openings: 110,840

❀ Self-Employed: 0.4%

Skills—Most Important: Social Skills; Communication Skills; Thought-Processing Skills. **Other High-Level Skills:** Management Skills.

Interact with customers to provide information in response to inquiries about products and services and to handle and resolve complaints. Confer with customers by telephone or in person to provide information about products and services, to take or enter orders, cancel accounts, or to obtain details of complaints. Keep records of customer interactions and transactions, recording details of inquiries, complaints, and comments as well as actions taken. Check to ensure that appropriate changes were made to resolve customers' problems. Determine charges for services requested, collect deposits or payments, or arrange for billing. Refer unresolved customer grievances to designated departments for further investigation. Review insurance policy terms to determine whether a loss is covered by insurance. Contact customers to respond to inquiries or to notify them of claim investigation results and any planned adjustments. Resolve customers' service or billing complaints by exchanging merchandise, refunding money, and adjusting bills. Compare disputed merchandise with original requisitions and information from invoices and prepare invoices for returned goods. Obtain and examine all relevant information to assess validity of complaints and to determine possible causes, such as extreme weather conditions that could increase utility bills. Solicit sale of new or additional services or products. Complete contract forms, prepare change of address records, and issue service discontinuance orders.

Education/Training Required: Moderate-term on-the-job training. **Education and Training Programs:** Customer Service Support/Call Center/Teleservice Operation; Receptionist Training. **Knowledge/Courses:** Clerical Practices; Customer and Personal Service; English Language.

Personality Type: Enterprising-Social-Conventional. **Career Cluster:** 04 Business, Management, and Administration. **Career Pathway:** 04.6 Administrative and Information Support. **Other Jobs in This Pathway:** Couriers and Messengers; Court Clerks; Court, Municipal, and License Clerks; Data Entry Keyers; Dispatchers, Except Police, Fire, and Ambulance; Executive Secretaries and Executive Administrative Assistants; File Clerks; Human Resources Assistants, Except Payroll and Timekeeping; Information and Record Clerks, All Other; Insurance Claims Clerks; Insurance Policy Processing Clerks; Interviewers, Except Eligibility and Loan; License Clerks; Mail Clerks and Mail Machine Operators, Except Postal Service; Office and Administrative Support Workers, All Other; Office Clerks, General; Order Clerks; Patient Representatives; Postal Service Mail Carriers; Postal Service Mail Sorters, Processors, and Processing Machine Operators; Receptionists and Information Clerks; Secretaries and Administrative Assistants, Except Legal, Medical, and Executive; Shipping, Receiving, and Traffic Clerks; Switchboard Operators, Including Answering Service; Word Processors and Typists; others.

Job Specialization: Patient Representatives

Assist patients in obtaining services, understanding policies, and making health-care decisions. Explain policies, procedures, or services to patients using medical or administrative knowledge. Coordinate communication among patients, family members, medical staff, administrative staff, or regulatory agencies. Investigate and direct patient inquiries or complaints to appropriate medical staff members and follow up to ensure satisfactory resolution. Interview patients

or their representatives to identify problems relating to care. Refer patients to appropriate health-care services or resources. Collect and report data on topics such as patient encounters and inter-institutional problems, making recommendations for change when appropriate. Develop and distribute newsletters, brochures, or other printed materials to share information with patients or medical staff. Identify and share research, recommendations, or other information on legal liabilities, risk management, or quality of care. Read current literature, talk with colleagues, continue education, or participate in professional organizations or conferences to keep abreast of developments in the field. Maintain knowledge of community services and resources available to patients. Provide consultation or training to volunteers or staff on topics such as guest relations, patients' rights, and medical issues. Analyze patients' abilities to pay to determine charges on a sliding scale. Teach patients to use home health-care equipment.

Education/Training Required: Bachelor's degree. **Education and Training Programs:** Customer Service Support/Call Center/Teleservice Operation; Receptionist Training. **Knowledge/Courses:** Therapy and Counseling; Psychology; Customer and Personal Service; Sociology and Anthropology; Philosophy and Theology; Medicine and Dentistry.

Personality Type: Social-Enterprising. **Career Cluster:** 04 Business, Management, and Administration. **Career Pathway:** 04.6 Administrative and Information Support. **Other Jobs in This Pathway:** Couriers and Messengers; Court Clerks; Court, Municipal, and License Clerks; Customer Service Representatives; Data Entry Keyers; Dispatchers, Except Police, Fire, and Ambulance; Executive

Secretaries and Executive Administrative Assistants; File Clerks; Human Resources Assistants, Except Payroll and Timekeeping; Information and Record Clerks, All Other; Insurance Claims Clerks; Insurance Policy Processing Clerks; Interviewers, Except Eligibility and Loan; License Clerks; Mail Clerks and Mail Machine Operators, Except Postal Service; Office and Administrative Support Workers, All Other; Office Clerks, General; Order Clerks; Postal Service Mail Carriers; Postal Service Mail Sorters, Processors, and Processing Machine Operators; Receptionists and Information Clerks; Secretaries and Administrative Assistants, Except Legal, Medical, and Executive; Shipping, Receiving, and Traffic Clerks; Switchboard Operators, Including Answering Service; Word Processors and Typists; others.

Database Administrators

❋ Annual Earnings: $73,490

❋ Earnings Growth Potential: High (43.4%)

❋ Growth: 20.3%

❋ Annual Job Openings: 4,440

❋ Self-Employed: 0.6%

Skills—Most Important: Technology/ Programming Skills; Mathematics Skills; Thought-Processing Skills. **Other High-Level Skills:** Communication Skills; Equipment Use/ Maintenance Skills; Social Skills; Management Skills.

Coordinate changes to computer databases. Test and implement the databases, applying knowledge of database management systems. May plan, coordinate, and implement security measures to safeguard computer databases. Develop standards and guidelines to guide the use and acquisition of software and to protect vulnerable information. Modify existing databases and database management systems or direct programmers and analysts to make changes. Test programs or databases, correct errors, and make necessary modifications. Plan, coordinate, and implement security measures to safeguard information in computer files against accidental or unauthorized damage, modification, or disclosure. Approve, schedule, plan, and supervise the installation and testing of new products and improvements to computer systems such as the installation of new databases. Train users and answer questions. Establish and calculate optimum values for database parameters using manuals and calculator. Specify users and user access levels for each segment of database. Develop data model describing data elements and how they are used, following procedures and using pen, template, or computer software. Develop methods for integrating different products so they work properly together, such as customizing commercial databases to fit specific needs. Review project requests describing database user needs to estimate time and cost required to accomplish project. Review procedures in database management system manuals for making changes to database. Work as part of a project team to coordinate database development and determine project scope and limitations.

Education/Training Required: Bachelor's degree. **Education and Training Program:** Data Modeling/Warehousing and Database Administration. **Knowledge/ Courses:** Computers and Electronics; Telecommunications; Clerical Practices; Communications and Media; Engineering and Technology; Mathematics.

Personality Type: Conventional-Investigative.
Career Cluster: 11 Information Technology.
Career Pathways: 11.4 Programming and Software Development; 11.2 Information Support Services; 04.4 Business Analysis.
Other Jobs in These Pathways: Architectural and Engineering Managers; Bioinformatics Scientists; Computer and Information Systems Managers; Computer Hardware Engineers; Computer Numerically Controlled Machine Tool Programmers, Metal and Plastic; Computer Operators; Natural Sciences Managers; Operations Research Analysts; Remote Sensing Scientists and Technologists; Remote Sensing Technicians.

Dental Assistants

- ❈ Annual Earnings: $33,470
- ❈ Earnings Growth Potential: Low (32.2%)
- ❈ Growth: 35.7%
- ❈ Annual Job Openings: 16,100
- ❈ Self-Employed: 0.0%

Skills—Most Important: Equipment Use/Maintenance Skills; Social Skills.

Assist dentist, set up patient and equipment, and keep records. Prepare patient, sterilize and disinfect instruments, set up instrument trays, prepare materials, and assist dentist during dental procedures. Expose dental diagnostic X-rays. Record treatment information in patient records. Provide postoperative instructions prescribed by dentist. Assist dentist in management of medical and dental emergencies. Take and record medical and dental histories and vital signs of patients. Instruct patients in oral hygiene and plaque control programs. Order and monitor dental

supplies and equipment inventory. Clean and polish removable appliances. Make preliminary impressions for study casts and occlusal registrations for mounting study casts. Pour, trim, and polish study casts. Schedule appointments, prepare bills, receive payment for dental services, complete insurance forms, and maintain records manually or using computer. Fabricate temporary restorations and custom impressions from preliminary impressions. Clean teeth using dental instruments. Fabricate and fit orthodontic appliances and materials for patients, such as retainers, wires, and bands. Apply protective coating of fluoride to teeth.

Education/Training Required: Moderate-term on-the-job training. **Education and Training Program:** Dental Assisting/Assistant. **Knowledge/Courses:** Medicine and Dentistry; Customer and Personal Service; Psychology; Sales and Marketing.

Personality Type: Conventional-Realistic-Social. **Career Cluster:** 08 Health Science. **Career Pathway:** 08.1 Therapeutic Services. **Other Jobs in This Pathway:** Clinical Psychologists; Community and Social Service Specialists, All Other; Counseling Psychologists; Dental Hygienists; Dentists, General; Health Technologists and Technicians, All Other; Healthcare Support Workers, All Other; Home Health Aides; Licensed Practical and Licensed Vocational Nurses; Low Vision Therapists, Orientation and Mobility Specialists, and Vision Rehabilitation Therapists; Massage Therapists; Medical and Clinical Laboratory Technicians; Medical and Health Services Managers; Medical Scientists, Except Epidemiologists; Medical Secretaries; Occupational Therapists; Ophthalmic Medical Technologists; Pharmacists; Pharmacy Technicians; Radiologic Technologists; School Psychologists; Social and

D

Human Service Assistants; Speech-Language Pathologists; Speech-Language Pathology Assistants; Substance Abuse and Behavioral Disorder Counselors; others.

Dental Hygienists

- ❋ Annual Earnings: $68,250
- ❋ Earnings Growth Potential: Low (34.1%)
- ❋ Growth: 36.1%
- ❋ Annual Job Openings: 9,840
- ❋ Self-Employed: 0.1%

Skills—Most Important: Science Skills; Social Skills; Communication Skills. **Other High-Level Skills:** Equipment Use/Maintenance Skills; Thought-Processing Skills.

Clean teeth and examine oral areas, head, and neck for signs of oral disease. May educate patients on oral hygiene, take and develop X-rays, or apply fluoride or sealants. Clean calcareous deposits, accretions, and stains from teeth and beneath margins of gums using dental instruments. Record and review patient medical histories. Examine gums, using probes, to locate periodontal recessed gums and signs of gum disease. Provide clinical services and health education to improve and maintain the oral health of patients and the public. Feel and visually examine gums for sores and signs of disease. Expose and develop X-ray film. Chart conditions of decay and disease for diagnosis and treatment by dentist. Maintain dental equipment and sharpen and sterilize dental instruments. Apply fluorides and other cavity preventing agents to arrest dental decay. Feel lymph nodes under patient's chin to detect swelling or tenderness that could indicate presence of oral cancer. Maintain patient recall system. Remove excess cement from coronal surfaces of teeth. Administer local anesthetic agents. Conduct dental health clinics for community groups to augment services of dentist. Remove sutures and dressings. Make impressions for study casts. Place and remove rubber dams, matrices, and temporary restorations.

Education/Training Required: Associate degree. **Education and Training Program:** Dental Hygiene/Hygienist. **Knowledge/Courses:** Medicine and Dentistry; Psychology; Therapy and Counseling; Chemistry; Biology; Sales and Marketing.

Personality Type: Social-Realistic-Conventional. **Career Cluster:** 08 Health Science. **Career Pathway:** 08.1 Therapeutic Services. **Other Jobs in This Pathway:** Clinical Psychologists; Community and Social Service Specialists, All Other; Counseling Psychologists; Dental Assistants; Dentists, General; Health Technologists and Technicians, All Other; Healthcare Support Workers, All Other; Home Health Aides; Licensed Practical and Licensed Vocational Nurses; Low Vision Therapists, Orientation and Mobility Specialists, and Vision Rehabilitation Therapists; Massage Therapists; Medical and Clinical Laboratory Technicians; Medical and Health Services Managers; Medical Scientists, Except Epidemiologists; Medical Secretaries; Occupational Therapists; Ophthalmic Medical Technologists; Pharmacists; Pharmacy Technicians; Radiologic Technologists; School Psychologists; Social and Human Service Assistants; Speech-Language Pathologists; Speech-Language Pathology Assistants; Substance Abuse and Behavioral Disorder Counselors; others.

Dentists, General

- ❋ Annual Earnings: $141,040
- ❋ Earnings Growth Potential: High (49.4%)
- ❋ Growth: 15.3%
- ❋ Annual Job Openings: 5,180
- ❋ Self-Employed: 28.0%

Skills—Most Important: Science Skills; Management Skills; Thought-Processing Skills. **Other High-Level Skills:** Communication Skills; Social Skills; Mathematics Skills; Equipment Use/Maintenance Skills.

Diagnose and treat diseases, injuries, and malformations of teeth and gums and related oral structures. May treat diseases of nerve, pulp, and other dental tissues affecting vitality of teeth. Use masks, gloves, and safety glasses to protect themselves and their patients from infectious diseases. Administer anesthetics to limit the pain experienced by patients during procedures. Examine teeth, gums, and related tissues using dental instruments, X-rays, and other diagnostic equipment to evaluate dental health, diagnose diseases or abnormalities, and plan appropriate treatments. Formulate plan of treatment for patient's teeth and mouth tissue. Use air turbine and hand instruments, dental appliances, and surgical implements. Advise and instruct patients on preventive dental care, the causes and treatment of dental problems, and oral health-care services. Design, make, and fit prosthodontic appliances such as space maintainers, bridges, and dentures or write fabrication instructions or prescriptions for denturists and dental technicians. Fill pulp chamber and canal with endodontic materials. Write prescriptions for antibiotics and other medications.

Education/Training Required: First professional degree. **Education and Training Programs:** Advanced General Dentistry (Cert., MS, PhD); Dental Public Health and Education (Cert., MS/MPH, PhD/DPH); Dental Public Health Specialty; Dentistry (DDS, DMD); Pediatric Dentistry Residency Program; Pediatric Dentistry/Pedodontics (Cert., MS, PhD). **Knowledge/Courses:** Medicine and Dentistry; Biology; Psychology; Chemistry; Economics and Accounting; Customer and Personal Service.

Personality Type: Investigative-Realistic-Social. **Career Cluster:** 08 Health Science. **Career Pathway:** 08.1 Therapeutic Services. **Other Jobs in This Pathway:** Clinical Psychologists; Counseling Psychologists; Dental Assistants; Dental Hygienists; Dentists, All Other Specialists; Home Health Aides; Licensed Practical and Licensed Vocational Nurses; Low Vision Therapists, Orientation and Mobility Specialists, and Vision Rehabilitation Therapists; Massage Therapists; Medical and Clinical Laboratory Technicians; Medical and Health Services Managers; Medical Scientists, Except Epidemiologists; Medical Secretaries; Occupational Therapists; Ophthalmic Medical Technologists; Oral and Maxillofacial Surgeons; Orthodontists; Pharmacists; Pharmacy Technicians; Prosthodontists; Radiologic Technologists; School Psychologists; Social and Human Service Assistants; Speech-Language Pathologists; Substance Abuse and Behavioral Disorder Counselors; others.

Detectives and Criminal Investigators

* Annual Earnings: $68,820
* Earnings Growth Potential: High (43.5%)
* Growth: 16.6%
* Annual Job Openings: 4,160
* Self-Employed: 1.1%

Skills—Most Important: Science Skills; Social Skills; Communication Skills. **Other High-Level Skills:** Thought-Processing Skills; Equipment Use/Maintenance Skills; Management Skills.

Job Specialization: Criminal Investigators and Special Agents

Investigate alleged or suspected criminal violations of federal, state, or local laws to determine if evidence is sufficient to recommend prosecution. Obtain and verify evidence by interviewing and observing suspects and witnesses or by analyzing records. Record evidence and documents using equipment such as cameras and photocopy machines. Examine records to locate links in chains of evidence or information. Prepare reports that detail investigation findings. Collaborate with other offices and agencies to exchange information and coordinate activities. Determine scope, timing, and direction of investigations. Testify before grand juries concerning criminal activity investigations. Analyze evidence in laboratories or in the field. Investigate organized crime, public corruption, financial crime, copyright infringement, civil rights violations, bank robbery, extortion, kidnapping, and other violations of federal or state statutes. Identify case issues and evidence needed based on analysis of charges, complaints, or allegations of law violations. Obtain and use search and arrest warrants. Serve subpoenas or other official papers. Collaborate with other authorities on activities such as surveillance, transcription, and research. Develop relationships with informants to obtain information related to cases. Search for and collect evidence such as fingerprints using investigative equipment. Collect and record physical information about arrested suspects, including fingerprints, height and weight measurements, and photographs. Perform undercover assignments and maintain surveillance, including monitoring authorized wiretaps.

Education/Training Required: Work experience in a related occupation. **Education and Training Programs:** Criminal Justice/Police Science; Criminalistics and Criminal Science. **Knowledge/Courses:** Public Safety and Security; Psychology; Law and Government; Customer and Personal Service; Sociology and Anthropology; Therapy and Counseling.

Personality Type: Enterprising-Investigative. **Career Cluster:** 12 Law, Public Safety, Corrections, and Security. **Career Pathway:** 12.4 Law Enforcement Services. **Other Jobs in This Pathway:** Bailiffs; Correctional Officers and Jailers; First-Line Supervisors of Police and Detectives; Forensic Science Technicians; Immigration and Customs Inspectors; Intelligence Analysts; Police Detectives; Police Identification and Records Officers; Police Patrol Officers; Remote Sensing Scientists and Technologists; Sheriffs and Deputy Sheriffs.

Job Specialization: Immigration and Customs Inspectors

Investigate and inspect persons, common carriers, goods, and merchandise arriving in or departing from the United States or moving between states to detect violations of immigration and customs laws and regulations. Examine immigration applications, visas, and passports and interview persons to determine eligibility for admission, residence, and travel in U.S. Detain persons found to be in violation of customs or immigration laws and arrange for legal action such as deportation. Locate and seize contraband, undeclared merchandise, and vehicles, aircraft, or boats that contain such merchandise. Interpret and explain laws and regulations to travelers, prospective immigrants, shippers, and manufacturers. Inspect cargo, baggage, and personal articles entering or leaving U.S. for compliance with revenue laws and U.S. Customs Service regulations. Record and report job-related activities, findings, transactions, violations, discrepancies, and decisions. Institute civil and criminal prosecutions and cooperate with other law enforcement agencies in the investigation and prosecution of those in violation of immigration or customs laws. Testify on decisions at immigration appeals or in federal court. Determine duty and taxes to be paid on goods. Collect samples of merchandise for examination, appraisal, or testing. Investigate applications for duty refunds and petition for remission or mitigation of penalties when warranted.

Education/Training Required: Work experience in a related occupation. **Education and Training Programs:** Criminal Justice/Police Science; Criminalistics and Criminal Science. **Knowledge/Courses:** Public Safety and Security; Law and Government; Foreign Language; Geography; Customer and Personal Service; Philosophy and Theology.

Personality Type: Conventional-Enterprising-Realistic. **Career Cluster:** 12 Law, Public Safety, Corrections, and Security. **Career Pathway:** 12.4 Law Enforcement Services. **Other Jobs in This Pathway:** Bailiffs; Correctional Officers and Jailers; Criminal Investigators and Special Agents; First-Line Supervisors of Police and Detectives; Forensic Science Technicians; Intelligence Analysts; Police Detectives; Police Identification and Records Officers; Police Patrol Officers; Remote Sensing Scientists and Technologists; Sheriffs and Deputy Sheriffs.

Job Specialization: Intelligence Analysts

Gather, analyze, and evaluate information from a variety of sources, such as law enforcement databases, surveillance, intelligence networks, and geographic information systems (GIS). Use data to anticipate and prevent organized crime activities, such as terrorism. Predict future gang, organized crime, or terrorist activity using analyses of intelligence data. Study activities relating to narcotics, money laundering, gangs, auto theft rings, terrorism, or other national security threats. Design, use, or maintain databases and software applications, such as GIS mapping and artificial intelligence tools. Establish criminal profiles to aid in connecting criminal organizations with their members. Evaluate records of communications, such as telephone calls, to plot activity and determine the size and location of criminal groups and members. Gather and evaluate information using aerial photographs, radar equipment, or sensitive radio equipment. Gather intelligence information by field observation, confidential information sources, or public records. Gather, analyze, correlate, or evaluate information from a variety of resources, such as law enforcement databases. Link or chart suspects to criminal organizations or events to determine activities and interrelationships. Operate cameras, radios, or other surveillance equipment to intercept communications or document activities. Prepare comprehensive written reports, presentations, maps, or charts based on research, collection, and analysis of intelligence data. Prepare plans to intercept foreign communications transmissions. Study the assets of criminal suspects to determine the flow of money from or to targeted groups.

Education/Training Required: Work experience plus degree. **Education and Training Programs:** Criminal Justice/Police Science; Criminalistics and Criminal Science. **Knowledge/Courses:** No data available.

Personality Type: No data available. **Career Cluster:** 12 Law, Public Safety, Corrections, and Security. **Career Pathway:** 12.4 Law Enforcement Services. **Other Jobs in This Pathway:** Bailiffs; Correctional Officers and Jailers; Criminal Investigators and Special Agents; First-Line Supervisors of Police and Detectives; Forensic Science Technicians; Immigration and Customs Inspectors; Police Detectives; Police Identification and Records Officers; Police Patrol Officers; Remote Sensing Scientists and Technologists; Sheriffs and Deputy Sheriffs.

Job Specialization: Police Detectives

Conduct investigations to prevent crimes or solve criminal cases. Examine crime scenes to obtain clues and evidence, such as loose hairs, fibers, clothing, or weapons. Secure deceased body and obtain evidence from it, preventing bystanders from tampering with it prior to medical examiner's arrival. Obtain evidence from suspects. Provide testimony as a witness in court. Analyze completed police reports to determine what additional information and investigative work is needed. Prepare charges or responses to charges or information for court cases according to formalized procedures. Note, mark, and photograph location of objects found, such as footprints, tire tracks, bullets and bloodstains, and take measurements of the scene. Obtain facts or statements from complainants, witnesses, and accused persons and record interviews. Obtain summary of incident from officer in charge at crime scene, taking care to avoid disturbing evidence. Examine records and governmental agency files to find identifying data about suspects. Prepare and serve search and arrest warrants. Block or rope off scene and check perimeter to ensure that entire scene is secured. Summon medical help for injured individuals and alert medical personnel to take statements from them. Provide information to lab personnel concerning the source of an item of evidence and tests to be performed. Monitor conditions of victims who are unconscious so that arrangements can be made to take statements if consciousness is regained.

Education/Training Required: Work experience in a related occupation. **Education and Training Programs:** Criminal Justice/Police Science; Criminalistics and Criminal Science. **Knowledge/Courses:** Public Safety and Security; Law and Government; Psychology; Therapy and Counseling; Customer and Personal Service; Philosophy and Theology.

Personality Type: Enterprising-Investigative. **Career Cluster:** 12 Law, Public Safety, Corrections, and Security. **Career Pathway:** 12.4 Law Enforcement Services. **Other Jobs in This Pathway:** Bailiffs; Correctional Officers and Jailers; Criminal Investigators and Special

Agents; First-Line Supervisors of Police and Detectives; Forensic Science Technicians; Immigration and Customs Inspectors; Intelligence Analysts; Police Identification and Records Officers; Police Patrol Officers; Remote Sensing Scientists and Technologists; Sheriffs and Deputy Sheriffs.

Job Specialization: Police Identification and Records Officers

Collect evidence at crime scene, classify and identify fingerprints, and photograph evidence for use in criminal and civil cases. Photograph crime or accident scenes for evidence records. Testify in court and present evidence. Dust selected areas of crime scene and lift latent fingerprints, adhering to proper preservation procedures. Look for trace evidence, such as fingerprints, hairs, fibers, or shoe impressions, using alternative light sources when necessary. Analyze and process evidence at crime scenes and in the laboratory, wearing protective equipment and using powders and chemicals. Package, store, and retrieve evidence. Maintain records of evidence and write and review reports. Submit evidence to supervisors, crime labs, or court officials for legal proceedings. Identify, compare, classify, and file fingerprints using systems such as Automated Fingerprint Identification System (AFIS) or the Henry Classification System. Serve as technical advisor and coordinate with other law enforcement workers or legal personnel to exchange information on crime scene collection activities.

Education/Training Required: Work experience in a related occupation. **Education and Training Programs:** Criminal Justice/Police Science; Criminalistics and Criminal Science. **Knowledge/Courses:** Public Safety and Security; Law and Government; Chemistry; Customer and Personal Service; Clerical Practices; Telecommunications.

Personality Type: Conventional-Realistic-Investigative. **Career Cluster:** 12 Law, Public Safety, Corrections, and Security. **Career Pathway:** 12.4 Law Enforcement Services. **Other Jobs in This Pathway:** Bailiffs; Correctional Officers and Jailers; Criminal Investigators and Special Agents; First-Line Supervisors of Police and Detectives; Forensic Science Technicians; Immigration and Customs Inspectors; Intelligence Analysts; Police Detectives; Police Patrol Officers; Remote Sensing Scientists and Technologists; Sheriffs and Deputy Sheriffs.

Diagnostic Medical Sonographers

* Annual Earnings: $64,380
* Earnings Growth Potential: Low (30.3%)
* Growth: 18.3%
* Annual Job Openings: 1,650
* Self-Employed: 0.8%

Skills—Most Important: Science Skills; Equipment Use/Maintenance Skills; Social Skills. **Other High-Level Skills:** Communication Skills; Thought-Processing Skills.

Produce ultrasonic recordings of internal organs for use by physicians. Decide which images to include, looking for differences between healthy and pathological areas. Observe screen during scan to ensure that image produced is satisfactory for diagnostic purposes, making adjustments to equipment as required. Observe and care for patients throughout examinations to ensure their safety and comfort. Provide sonogram and oral or written summary of technical findings to physician for use in medical diagnosis. Operate ultrasound equipment to produce and record images of the motion, shape and composition of blood, organs, tissues, and bodily masses such as fluid accumulations. Select appropriate equipment settings and adjust patient positions to obtain the best sites and angles. Determine whether scope of exam should be extended based on findings. Process and code film from procedures and complete appropriate documentation. Obtain and record accurate patient history, including prior test results and information from physical examinations. Record and store suitable images using camera unit connected to the ultrasound equipment. Prepare patient for exam by explaining procedure, transferring them to ultrasound table, scrubbing skin, applying gel, and positioning them properly. Coordinate work with physicians and other health-care team members, including providing assistance during invasive procedures.

Education/Training Required: Associate degree. **Education and Training Programs:** Allied Health Diagnostic, Intervention, and Treatment Professions, Other; Diagnostic Medical Sonography/Sonographer and Ultrasound Technician Training. **Knowledge/ Courses:** Medicine and Dentistry; Physics; Biology; Customer and Personal Service; Psychology; Clerical.

Personality Type: Investigative-Social-Realistic. **Career Cluster:** 08 Health Science. **Career Pathways:** 08.1 Therapeutic Services; 08.2 Diagnostics Services. **Other Jobs in These Pathways:** Clinical Psychologists; Counseling Psychologists; Cytogenetic Technologists; Cytotechnologists; Dental Assistants; Dental Hygienists; Dentists, General; Emergency Medical Technicians and Paramedics; Endoscopy Technicians; Healthcare Support Workers, All

Other; Histotechnologists and Histologic Technicians; Home Health Aides; Licensed Practical and Licensed Vocational Nurses; Massage Therapists; Medical and Clinical Laboratory Technicians; Medical and Clinical Laboratory Technologists; Medical and Health Services Managers; Medical Assistants; Medical Secretaries; Pharmacists; Pharmacy Technicians; Radiologic Technologists; School Psychologists; Social and Human Service Assistants; Speech-Language Pathology Assistants; others.

Drywall and Ceiling Tile Installers

- ❋ Annual Earnings: $37,320
- ❋ Earnings Growth Potential: Low (34.4%)
- ❋ Growth: 13.5%
- ❋ Annual Job Openings: 3,700
- ❋ Self-Employed: 18.8%

Skills—Most Important: Equipment Use/ Maintenance Skills; Social Skills; Thought-Processing Skills.

Apply plasterboard or other wallboard to ceilings or interior walls of buildings. Apply or mount acoustical tiles or blocks, strips, or sheets of shock-absorbing materials to ceilings and walls of buildings to reduce or reflect sound. Materials may be of decorative quality. Includes lathers who fasten wooden, metal, or rockboard lath to walls, ceilings, or partitions of buildings to provide support base for plaster, fireproofing, or acoustical material. Inspect furrings, mechanical mountings, and masonry surface for plumbness and level, using spirit or water levels. Install metal lath where plaster applications will be exposed to weather or water or for curved or irregular surfaces. Install blanket insulation between studs and tack plastic moisture barriers over insulation. Coordinate work with drywall finishers who cover the seams between drywall panels. Trim rough edges from wallboard to maintain even joints. Seal joints between ceiling tiles and walls. Scribe and cut edges of tile to fit walls where wall molding is not specified. Read blueprints and other specifications to determine methods of installation, work procedures, and material and tool requirements. Nail channels or wood furring strips to surfaces to provide mounting for tile. Mount tile using adhesives or by nailing, screwing, stapling, or wire-tying lath directly to structural frameworks. Measure and mark surfaces to lay out work according to blueprints and drawings using tape measures, straightedges, squares, and marking devices. Hang drywall panels on metal frameworks of walls and ceilings in offices, schools, and other large buildings, using lifts or hoists to adjust panel heights when necessary. Install horizontal and vertical metal or wooden studs to frames so that wallboard can be attached to interior walls.

Education/Training Required: Moderate-term on-the-job training. **Education and Training Program:** Drywall Installation/Drywaller. **Knowledge/Courses:** Building and Construction; Design; Mechanical Devices; Mathematics; Production and Processing; Public Safety and Security.

Personality Type: Realistic-Conventional. **Career Cluster:** 02 Architecture and Construction. **Career Pathway:** 02.2 Construction. **Other Jobs in This Pathway:** Brickmasons and Blockmasons; Cement Masons and Concrete Finishers; Construction and Building Inspectors; Construction Carpenters; Construction Laborers; Construction Managers; Cost Estimators; Electrical Power-Line Installers and Repairers; Electricians; Engineering Technicians, Except Drafters, All Other; Excavating and Loading Machine and Dragline Operators; First-Line Supervisors of Construction Trades and Extraction Workers; Heating and Air Conditioning Mechanics and Installers; Helpers—Carpenters; Helpers—Electricians; Helpers—Pipelayers, Plumbers, Pipefitters, and Steamfitters; Highway Maintenance Workers; Operating Engineers and Other Construction Equipment Operators; Painters, Construction and Maintenance; Pipe Fitters and Steamfitters; Plumbers; Refrigeration Mechanics and Installers; Roofers; Rough Carpenters; Solar Energy Installation Managers; others.

Education Administrators, Elementary and Secondary School

- ❋ Annual Earnings: $86,970
- ❋ Earnings Growth Potential: Low (33.0%)
- ❋ Growth: 8.6%
- ❋ Annual Job Openings: 8,880
- ❋ Self-Employed: 4.7%

Skills—Most Important: Management Skills; Thought-Processing Skills; Social Skills. **Other High-Level Skills:** Communication Skills; Mathematics Skills.

Plan, direct, or coordinate the academic, clerical, or auxiliary activities of public or private elementary or secondary-level schools. Review and approve new programs or recommend modifications to existing programs, submitting program proposals for school board approval as necessary. Prepare, maintain, or oversee the preparation and maintenance of attendance, activity, planning, or personnel reports and records. Confer with parents and staff to discuss educational activities, policies, and student behavioral or learning problems. Prepare and submit budget requests and recommendations or grant proposals to solicit program funding. Direct and coordinate school maintenance services and the use of school facilities. Counsel and provide guidance to students on personal, academic, vocational, or behavioral issues. Organize and direct committees of specialists, volunteers, and staff to provide technical and advisory assistance for programs. Advocate for new schools to be built or for existing facilities to be repaired or remodeled.

Education/Training Required: Work experience plus degree. **Education and Training Programs:** Educational Administration and Supervision, Other; Educational Leadership and Administration, General; Educational, Instructional, and Curriculum Supervision; Elementary and Middle School Administration/ Principalship; Secondary School Administration/ Principalship. **Knowledge/Courses:** Therapy and Counseling; Education and Training; Philosophy and Theology; Sociology and Anthropology; Personnel and Human Resources; History and Archeology.

Personality Type: Enterprising-Social-Conventional. **Career Cluster:** 05 Education and Training. **Career Pathway:** 05.1 Administration and Administrative Support. **Other Jobs in This Pathway:** Coaches and Scouts; Distance Learning Coordinators; Education Administrators, All Other; Education Administrators, Postsecondary; Education Administrators, Preschool and Childcare Center/ Program; Fitness and Wellness Coordinators; Fitness Trainers and Aerobics Instructors; Instructional Coordinators; Instructional

Designers and Technologists; Umpires, Referees, and Other Sports Officials.

Educational, Guidance, School, and Vocational Counselors

* Annual Earnings: $53,380
* Earnings Growth Potential: Medium (40.7%)
* Growth: 14.0%
* Annual Job Openings: 9,440
* Self-Employed: 5.8%

Skills—Most Important: Social Skills; Communication Skills; Thought-Processing Skills. **Other High-Level Skills:** Management Skills.

Counsel individuals and provide group educational and vocational guidance services. Counsel individuals to help them understand and overcome personal, social, or behavioral problems affecting their educational or vocational situations. Maintain accurate and complete student records as required by laws, district policies, and administrative regulations. Provide crisis intervention to students when difficult situations occur at schools. Prepare students for later educational experiences by encouraging them to explore learning opportunities and to persevere with challenging tasks. Teach classes and present self-help or information sessions on subjects related to education and career planning. Conduct follow-up interviews with counselees to determine if their needs have been met. Prepare reports on students and activities as required by administration. Plan and conduct orientation programs and group conferences to promote the adjustment of individuals to new life experiences such as starting college.

Education/Training Required: Master's degree. **Education and Training Programs:** College Student Counseling and Personnel Services; Counselor Education/School Counseling and Guidance Services. **Knowledge/Courses:** Therapy and Counseling; Psychology; Sociology and Anthropology; Philosophy and Theology; Education and Training; Clerical.

Personality Type: Social. **Career Cluster:** 05 Education and Training. **Career Pathway:** 05.2 Professional Support Services. **Other Jobs in This Pathway:** Librarians; Library Assistants, Clerical Practices; Library Technicians.

Electrical and Electronics Repairers, Commercial and Industrial Equipment

❋ Annual Earnings: $51,820

❋ Earnings Growth Potential: Medium (37.2%)

❋ Growth: 3.8%

❋ Annual Job Openings: 1,640

❋ Self-Employed: 0.0%

Skills—Most Important: Installation Skills; Equipment Use/Maintenance Skills; Science Skills. **Other High-Level Skills:** Technology/Programming Skills; Mathematics Skills; Thought-Processing Skills; Social Skills.

Repair, test, adjust, or install electronic equipment, such as industrial controls, transmitters, and antennas. Test faulty equipment to diagnose malfunctions using test equipment and software and applying knowledge of the functional operation of electronic units and systems. Inspect components of industrial equipment for accurate assembly and installation and for defects such as loose connections and frayed wires. Install repaired equipment in various settings, such as industrial or military establishments. Examine work orders and converse with equipment operators to detect equipment problems and to ascertain whether mechanical or human errors contributed to the problems. Perform scheduled preventive maintenance tasks, such as checking, cleaning, and repairing equipment, to detect and prevent problems. Set up and test industrial equipment to ensure that it functions properly. Study blueprints, schematics, manuals, and other specifications to determine installation procedures. Repair and adjust equipment, machines, and defective components, replacing worn parts such as gaskets and seals in watertight electrical equipment. Calibrate testing instruments and installed or repaired equipment to prescribed specifications. Maintain equipment logs that record performance problems, repairs, calibrations, and tests. Develop or modify industrial electronic devices, circuits, and equipment according to available specifications. Coordinate efforts with other workers involved in installing and maintaining equipment or components.

Education/Training Required: Postsecondary vocational training. **Education and Training Programs:** Computer Installation and Repair Technology/Technician; Industrial Electronics Technology/Technician. **Knowledge/Courses:** Mechanical Devices; Computers and Electronics; Engineering and Technology; Design; Telecommunications; Physics.

Personality Type: Realistic-Investigative-Conventional. **Career Cluster:** 13 Manufacturing. **Career Pathway:** 13.3 Maintenance, Installation, and Repair. **Other Jobs in This Pathway:** Aircraft Mechanics and Service Technicians; Automotive Specialty

Technicians; Biological Technicians; Civil Engineering Technicians; Computer, Automated Teller, and Office Machine Repairers; Electrical and Electronic Equipment Assemblers; Electrical Engineering Technicians; Electrical Engineering Technologists; Electromechanical Engineering Technologists; Electronics Engineering Technicians; Electronics Engineering Technologists; Engineering Technicians, Except Drafters, All Other; Fuel Cell Technicians; Helpers—Installation, Maintenance, and Repair Workers; Industrial Engineering Technologists; Industrial Machinery Mechanics; Installation, Maintenance, and Repair Workers, All Other; Manufacturing Engineering Technologists; Manufacturing Production Technicians; Mapping Technicians; Mechanical Engineering Technologists; Mobile Heavy Equipment Mechanics, Except Engines; Nanotechnology Engineering Technicians; Telecommunications Line Installers and Repairers; Tire Repairers and Changers; others.

Electrical Power-Line Installers and Repairers

❀ Annual Earnings: $58,030

❀ Earnings Growth Potential: High (42.0%)

❀ Growth: 4.5%

❀ Annual Job Openings: 4,550

❀ Self-Employed: 1.4%

Skills—Most Important: Equipment Use/ Maintenance Skills; Thought-Processing Skills; Social Skills.

Install or repair cables or wires used in electrical power or distribution systems. May erect poles and light- or heavy-duty transmission towers. Adhere to safety practices and procedures, such as checking equipment regularly and erecting barriers around work areas. Open switches or attach grounding devices to remove electrical hazards from disturbed or fallen lines or to facilitate repairs. Climb poles or use truck-mounted buckets to access equipment. Place insulating or fireproofing materials over conductors and joints. Install, maintain, and repair electrical distribution and transmission systems, including conduits, cables, wires, and related equipment such as transformers, circuit breakers, and switches. Identify defective sectionalizing devices, circuit breakers, fuses, voltage regulators, transformers, switches, relays, or wiring using wiring diagrams and electrical-testing instruments. Drive vehicles equipped with tools and materials to job sites. Coordinate work assignment preparation and completion with other workers. Inspect and test power lines and auxiliary equipment to locate and identify problems using reading and testing instruments. String wire conductors and cables between poles, towers, trenches, pylons, and buildings, setting lines in place and using winches to adjust tension. Test conductors, according to electrical diagrams and specifications, to identify corresponding conductors and to prevent incorrect connections. Replace damaged poles with new poles and straighten the poles. Install watt-hour meters and connect service drops between power lines and consumers' facilities.

Education/Training Required: Long-term on-the-job training. **Education and Training Programs:** Electrical and Power Transmission Installation/Installer, General; Electrical and Power Transmission Installers, Other; Lineworker. **Knowledge/Courses:** Building and Construction; Mechanical Devices; Customer and Personal Service; Engineering and Technology; Transportation; Design.

Personality Type: Realistic-Investigative-Conventional. **Career Cluster:** 02 Architecture and Construction. **Career Pathway:** 02.2 Construction. **Other Jobs in This Pathway:** Brickmasons and Blockmasons; Cement Masons and Concrete Finishers; Construction and Building Inspectors; Construction Carpenters; Construction Laborers; Construction Managers; Cost Estimators; Drywall and Ceiling Tile Installers; Electricians; Engineering Technicians, Except Drafters, All Other; Excavating and Loading Machine and Dragline Operators; First-Line Supervisors of Construction Trades and Extraction Workers; Heating and Air Conditioning Mechanics and Installers; Helpers—Carpenters; Helpers—Electricians; Helpers—Pipelayers, Plumbers, Pipefitters, and Steamfitters; Highway Maintenance Workers; Operating Engineers and Other Construction Equipment Operators; Painters, Construction and Maintenance; Pipe Fitters and Steamfitters; Plumbers; Refrigeration Mechanics and Installers; Roofers; Rough Carpenters; Solar Energy Installation Managers; others.

Electricians

❋ Annual Earnings: $48,250

❋ Earnings Growth Potential: Medium (39.1%)

❋ Growth: 11.9%

❋ Annual Job Openings: 25,090

❋ Self-Employed: 9.3%

Skills—Most Important: Installation Skills; Equipment Use/Maintenance Skills; Mathematics Skills. **Other High-Level Skills:** Management Skills; Thought-Processing Skills; Social Skills.

Install, maintain, and repair electrical wiring, equipment, and fixtures. Ensure that work is in accordance with relevant codes. May install or service street lights, intercom systems, or electrical control systems. Assemble, install, test, and maintain electrical or electronic wiring, equipment, appliances, apparatus, and fixtures using hand tools and power tools. Diagnose malfunctioning systems, apparatus, and components, using test equipment and hand tools, to locate the cause of a breakdown and correct the problem. Connect wires to circuit breakers, transformers, or other components. Inspect electrical systems, equipment, and components to identify hazards, defects, and the need for adjustment or repair and to ensure compliance with codes. Advise management on whether continued operation of equipment could be hazardous. Test electrical systems and continuity of circuits in electrical wiring, equipment, and fixtures using testing devices such as ohmmeters, voltmeters, and oscilloscopes to ensure compatibility and safety of system. Maintain current electrician's license or identification card to meet governmental regulations. Plan layout and installation of electrical wiring, equipment, and fixtures based on job specifications and local codes. Direct and train workers to install, maintain, or repair electrical wiring, equipment, and fixtures. Prepare sketches or follow blueprints to determine the location of wiring and equipment and to ensure conformance to building and safety codes. Use a variety of tools and equipment such as power construction equipment, measuring devices, power tools, and testing equipment, including oscilloscopes, ammeters, and test lamps.

Education/Training Required: Long-term on-the-job training. **Education and Training Program:** Electrician. **Knowledge/Courses:** Building and Construction; Mechanical Devices; Design; Physics; Telecommunications; Engineering and Technology.

E

Personality Type: Realistic-Investigative-Conventional. **Career Cluster:** 02 Architecture and Construction. **Career Pathway:** 02.2 Construction. **Other Jobs in This Pathway:** Brickmasons and Blockmasons; Cement Masons and Concrete Finishers; Construction and Building Inspectors; Construction Carpenters; Construction Laborers; Construction Managers; Cost Estimators; Drywall and Ceiling Tile Installers; Electrical Power-Line Installers and Repairers; Engineering Technicians, Except Drafters, All Other; Excavating and Loading Machine and Dragline Operators; First-Line Supervisors of Construction Trades and Extraction Workers; Heating and Air Conditioning Mechanics and Installers; Helpers—Carpenters; Helpers—Electricians; Helpers—Pipelayers, Plumbers, Pipefitters, and Steamfitters; Highway Maintenance Workers; Operating Engineers and Other Construction Equipment Operators; Painters, Construction and Maintenance; Pipe Fitters and Steamfitters; Plumbers; Refrigeration Mechanics and Installers; Roofers; Rough Carpenters; Solar Energy Installation Managers; others.

Electronic Home Entertainment Equipment Installers and Repairers

* Annual Earnings: $32,940
* Earnings Growth Potential: Medium (37.3%)
* Growth: 10.8%
* Annual Job Openings: 1,430
* Self-Employed: 25.8%

Skills—Most Important: Installation Skills; Equipment Use/Maintenance Skills; Thought-Processing Skills. **Other High-Level Skills:** Social Skills; Management Skills.

Repair, adjust, or install audio or television receivers, stereo systems, camcorders, video systems, or other electronic home entertainment equipment. Tune or adjust equipment and instruments to obtain optimum visual or auditory reception according to specifications, manuals, and drawings. Compute cost estimates for labor and materials. Instruct customers on the safe and proper use of equipment. Keep records of work orders and test and maintenance reports. Make service calls to repair units in customers' homes, or return units to shops for major repairs. Position or mount speakers, and wire speakers to consoles. Install, service, and repair electronic equipment or instruments such as televisions and radios. Disassemble entertainment equipment and repair or replace loose, worn, or defective components and wiring using hand tools and soldering irons. Confer with customers to determine the nature of problems or to explain repairs. Calibrate and test equipment and locate circuit and component faults using hand and power tools and measuring and testing instruments such as resistance meters and oscilloscopes. Read and interpret electronic circuit diagrams, function block diagrams, specifications, engineering drawings, and service manuals.

Education/Training Required: Postsecondary vocational training. **Education and Training Program:** Communications Systems Installation and Repair Technology. **Knowledge/Courses:** Telecommunications; Engineering and Technology; Computers and Electronics; Mechanical Devices; Physics; Design.

Personality Type: Realistic-Conventional. **Career Cluster:** 03 Arts, Audio/Video Technology, and Communications. **Career Pathway:** 03.6 Telecommunications. **Other**

Jobs in This Pathway: Broadcast Technicians; Communications Equipment Operators, All Other; Film and Video Editors; Media and Communication Workers, All Other; Radio Mechanics; Radio Operators; Radio, Cellular, and Tower Equipment Installers and Repairers; Sound Engineering Technicians; Telecommunications Equipment Installers and Repairers, Except Line Installers.

Electronics Engineers, Except Computer

* Annual Earnings: $90,170
* Earnings Growth Potential: Low (35.8%)
* Growth: 0.3%
* Annual Job Openings: 3,340
* Self-Employed: 1.6%

Skills—Most Important: Technology/ Programming Skills; Equipment Use/ Maintenance Skills; Science Skills. **Other High-Level Skills:** Mathematics Skills; Management Skills; Thought-Processing Skills; Communication Skills; Social Skills.

Research, design, develop, and test electronic components and systems for commercial, industrial, military, or scientific use, utilizing knowledge of electronic theory and materials properties. Design electronic circuits and components for use in fields such as telecommunications, aerospace guidance and propulsion control, acoustics, or instruments and controls. Design electronic components, software, products, or systems for commercial, industrial, medical, military, or scientific applications. Provide technical support and instruction to staff or customers on equipment standards, assisting with specific, difficult in-service engineering. Operate computer-assisted engineering and design software and equipment to perform engineering tasks. Analyze system requirements, capacity, cost, and customer needs to determine feasibility of project and develop system plan. Confer with engineers, customers, vendors, or others to discuss existing and potential engineering projects or products. Review and evaluate work of others, inside and outside the organization, to ensure effectiveness, technical adequacy, and compatibility in the resolution of complex engineering problems. Determine material and equipment needs and order supplies.

Education/Training Required: Bachelor's degree. **Education and Training Program:** Electrical and Electronics Engineering. **Knowledge/Courses:** Design; Engineering and Technology; Physics; Computers and Electronics; Mathematics; Production and Processing.

Personality Type: Investigative-Realistic. **Career Cluster:** 15 Science, Technology, Engineering, and Mathematics. **Career Pathway:** 15.1 Engineering and Technology. **Other Jobs in This Pathway:** Architectural and Engineering Managers; Automotive Engineers; Biochemical Engineers; Biofuels/ Biodiesel Technology and Product Development Managers; Civil Engineers; Cost Estimators; Education, Training, and Library Workers, All Other; Electrical Engineers; Energy Engineers; Engineers, All Other; Fuel Cell Engineers; Human Factors Engineers and Ergonomists; Industrial Engineers; Manufacturing Engineers; Mechanical Engineers; Mechatronics Engineers; Microsystems Engineers; Nanosystems Engineers; Photonics Engineers; Radio Frequency Identification Device Specialists; Robotics Engineers; Solar Energy Systems Engineers; Transportation Engineers; Validation Engineers; Wind Energy Engineers; others.

Job Specialization: Radio Frequency Identification Device Specialists

Design and implement radio frequency identification device (RFID) systems used to track shipments or goods. Verify compliance of developed applications with architectural standards and established practices. Read current literature, attend meetings or conferences, or talk with colleagues to stay abreast of industry research about new technologies. Provide technical support for RFID technology. Perform systems analysis or programming of RFID technology. Document equipment or process details of RIFD technology. Train users in details of system operation. Analyze RFID-related supply chain data. Test tags or labels to ensure readability. Test RFID software to ensure proper functioning. Select appropriate RFID tags and determine placement locations. Perform site analyses to determine system configurations, processes to be impacted, or on-site obstacles to technology implementation. Perform acceptance testing on newly installed or updated systems. Identify operational requirements for new systems to inform selection of technological solutions. Determine usefulness of new RFID technologies. Develop process flows, work instructions, or standard operating procedures for RFID systems.

Education/Training Required: Bachelor's degree. **Education and Training Program:** Electrical and Electronics Engineering. **Knowledge/Courses:** No data available.

Personality Type: Realistic-Investigative-Conventional. **Career Cluster:** 15 Science, Technology, Engineering, and Mathematics. **Career Pathway:** 15.1 Engineering and Technology. **Other Jobs in This Pathway:** Architectural and Engineering Managers; Automotive Engineers; Biochemical Engineers; Biofuels/Biodiesel Technology and Product Development Managers; Civil Engineers; Cost Estimators; Education, Training, and Library Workers, All Other; Electrical Engineers; Electronics Engineers, Except Computer; Energy Engineers; Engineers, All Other; Fuel Cell Engineers; Human Factors Engineers and Ergonomists; Industrial Engineers; Manufacturing Engineers; Mechanical Engineers; Mechatronics Engineers; Microsystems Engineers; Nanosystems Engineers; Photonics Engineers; Robotics Engineers; Solar Energy Systems Engineers; Transportation Engineers; Validation Engineers; Wind Energy Engineers; others.

Elementary School Teachers, Except Special Education

- ❋ Annual Earnings: $51,660
- ❋ Earnings Growth Potential: Low (33.4%)
- ❋ Growth: 15.8%
- ❋ Annual Job Openings: 59,650
- ❋ Self-Employed: 0.0%

Skills—Most Important: Thought-Processing Skills; Social Skills; Communication Skills. **Other High-Level Skills:** Mathematics Skills; Management Skills.

Teach pupils in public or private schools at the elementary level basic academic, social, and other formative skills. Establish and enforce rules for behavior and procedures for maintaining order among students. Observe and evaluate students' performance, behavior, social development, and physical health. Prepare materials and classrooms for class activities.

Adapt teaching methods and instructional materials to meet students' varying needs and interests. Plan and conduct activities for a balanced program of instruction, demonstration, and work time that provides students with opportunities to observe, question, and investigate. Instruct students individually and in groups, using various teaching methods such as lectures, discussions, and demonstrations. Establish clear objectives for all lessons, units, and projects and communicate those objectives to students. Assign and grade classwork and homework. Read books to entire classes or small groups. Prepare, administer, and grade tests and assignments to evaluate students' progress.

Education/Training Required: Bachelor's degree. **Education and Training Programs:** Elementary Education and Teaching; Teacher Education, Multiple Levels. **Knowledge/ Courses:** History and Archeology; Geography; Philosophy and Theology; Sociology and Anthropology; Fine Arts; Therapy and Counseling.

Personality Type: Social-Artistic-Conventional. **Career Cluster:** 05 Education and Training. **Career Pathway:** 05.3 Teaching/Training. **Other Jobs in This Pathway:** Adult Basic and Secondary Education and Literacy Teachers and Instructors; Athletes and Sports Competitors; Audio-Visual and Multimedia Collections Specialists; Career/Technical Education Teachers, Middle School; Career/ Technical Education Teachers, Secondary School; Chemists; Coaches and Scouts; Dietitians and Nutritionists; Fitness Trainers and Aerobics Instructors; Historians; Instructional Coordinators; Instructional Designers and Technologists; Interpreters and Translators; Kindergarten Teachers, Except Special Education; Librarians; Middle School Teachers, Except Special and Career/Technical Education; Physicists; Preschool Teachers, Except Special Education; Recreation Workers; Secondary School Teachers, Except Special and Career/Technical Education; Self-Enrichment Education Teachers; Teacher Assistants; Teachers and Instructors, All Other; Tutors.

Elevator Installers and Repairers

- ✹ Annual Earnings: $70,910
- ✹ Earnings Growth Potential: High (44.9%)
- ✹ Growth: 9.2%
- ✹ Annual Job Openings: 920
- ✹ Self-Employed: 0.1%

Skills—Most Important: Installation Skills; Equipment Use/Maintenance Skills; Science Skills. **Other High-Level Skills:** Thought-Processing Skills.

Assemble, install, repair, or maintain electric or hydraulic freight or passenger elevators, escalators, or dumbwaiters. Assemble, install, repair, and maintain elevators, escalators, moving sidewalks, and dumbwaiters using hand and power tools and testing devices such as test lamps, ammeters, and voltmeters. Test newly installed equipment to ensure that it meets specifications, such as stopping at floors for set amounts of time. Locate malfunctions in brakes, motors, switches, and signal and control systems using test equipment. Check that safety regulations and building codes are met and complete service reports verifying conformance to standards. Connect electrical wiring to control panels and electric motors. Read and interpret blueprints to determine the layout of system components, frameworks, and foundations and to select installation equipment.

Adjust safety controls, counterweights, door mechanisms, and components such as valves, ratchets, seals, and brake linings. Inspect wiring connections, control panel hookups, door installations, and alignments and clearances of cars and hoistways to ensure that equipment will operate properly. Disassemble defective units and repair or replace parts such as locks, gears, cables, and electric wiring. Maintain log books that detail all repairs and checks performed. Attach guide shoes and rollers to minimize the lateral motion of cars as they travel through shafts. Connect car frames to counterweights, using steel cables.

Education/Training Required: Long-term on-the-job training. **Education and Training Program:** Industrial Mechanics and Maintenance Technology. **Knowledge/Courses:** Building and Construction; Mechanical Devices; Physics; Design; Engineering and Technology; Public Safety and Security.

Personality Type: Realistic-Investigative-Conventional. **Career Cluster:** 13 Manufacturing. **Career Pathway:** 13.3 Maintenance, Installation, and Repair. **Other Jobs in This Pathway:** Aircraft Mechanics and Service Technicians; Automotive Specialty Technicians; Biological Technicians; Civil Engineering Technicians; Computer, Automated Teller, and Office Machine Repairers; Electrical and Electronic Equipment Assemblers; Electrical and Electronics Repairers, Commercial and Industrial Equipment; Electrical Engineering Technicians; Electrical Engineering Technologists; Electromechanical Engineering Technologists; Electronics Engineering Technicians; Electronics Engineering Technologists; Engineering Technicians, Except Drafters, All Other; Fuel Cell Technicians; Helpers—Installation, Maintenance, and

Repair Workers; Industrial Engineering Technologists; Industrial Machinery Mechanics; Installation, Maintenance, and Repair Workers, All Other; Manufacturing Engineering Technologists; Manufacturing Production Technicians; Mapping Technicians; Mechanical Engineering Technologists; Mobile Heavy Equipment Mechanics, Except Engines; Telecommunications Line Installers and Repairers; Tire Repairers and Changers; others.

Engineering Teachers, Postsecondary

- ❋ Annual Earnings: $89,670
- ❋ Earnings Growth Potential: High (49.0%)
- ❋ Growth: 15.1%
- ❋ Annual Job Openings: 1,000
- ❋ Self-Employed: 0.2%

Skills—Most Important: Mathematics Skills; Science Skills; Communication Skills. **Other High-Level Skills:** Thought-Processing Skills; Social Skills; Management Skills.

Teach courses pertaining to the application of physical laws and principles of engineering for the development of machines, materials, instruments, processes, and services. Includes teachers of chemical, civil, electrical, industrial, mechanical, mineral, and petroleum engineering. Includes both teachers primarily engaged in teaching and those who do a combination of both teaching and research. Prepare and deliver lectures to undergraduate or graduate students on mechanics, hydraulics, and robotics. Keep abreast of developments in the field by reading current literature, talking with colleagues, and participating in professional conferences.

Supervise undergraduate or graduate teaching, internship, and research work. Evaluate and grade students' classwork, laboratory work, assignments, and papers. Conduct research and publish findings in professional journals, books, or electronic media. Prepare course materials such as syllabi, homework assignments, and handouts. Compile, administer, and grade examinations or assign this work to others. Write grant proposals to procure external research funding. Supervise students' laboratory work. Initiate, facilitate, and moderate class discussions. Maintain regularly scheduled office hours to advise and assist students. Plan, evaluate, and revise curricula, course content, and course materials and methods of instruction. Advise students on academic and vocational curricula and on career issues. Maintain student attendance records, grades, and other required records. Collaborate with colleagues to address teaching and research issues. Select and obtain materials and supplies such as textbooks and laboratory equipment.

Education/Training Required: Doctoral degree. **Education and Training Programs:** Aerospace, Aeronautical, and Astronautical/Space Engineering; Agricultural Engineering; Architectural Engineering; Bioengineering and Biomedical Engineering; Ceramic Sciences and Engineering; Chemical Engineering; Civil Engineering, General; Computer Engineering, General; Computer Hardware Engineering; Computer Software Engineering; Construction Engineering; Electrical and Electronics Engineering; Engineering Mechanics; Engineering Physics/Applied Physics; Engineering Science; Engineering, General; Environmental Health Engineering; Forest Engineering; Geological/Geophysical Engineering; Geotechnical and Geoenvironmental Engineering; Industrial Engineering; Manufacturing Engineering; Materials Engineering; Mechanical Engineering; Metallurgical Engineering; Mining and Mineral Engineering; Naval Architecture and Marine Engineering; Nuclear Engineering; Ocean Engineering; Petroleum Engineering; Polymer/Plastics Engineering; Structural Engineering; Surveying Engineering; Systems Engineering; Textile Sciences and Engineering; Transportation and Highway Engineering; Water Resources Engineering; others. **Knowledge/Courses:** Physics; Engineering and Technology; Design; Mathematics; Chemistry; Education and Training.

Personality Type: Investigative-Realistic-Social. **Career Clusters:** 02 Architecture and Construction; 05 Education and Training; 11 Information Technology; 15 Science, Technology, Engineering, and Mathematics. **Career Pathways:** 05.3 Teaching/Training; 15.2 Science and Mathematics; 11.4 Programming and Software Development; 02.1 Design/Pre-Construction; 15.1 Engineering and Technology. **Other Jobs in These Pathways:** Architectural and Engineering Managers; Automotive Engineers; Biochemical Engineers; Biofuels/Biodiesel Technology and Product Development Managers; Civil Engineers; Coaches and Scouts; Cost Estimators; Elementary School Teachers, Except Special Education; Energy Engineers; Engineers, All Other; Fitness Trainers and Aerobics Instructors; Fuel Cell Engineers; Human Factors Engineers and Ergonomists; Industrial Engineers; Manufacturing Engineers; Mechanical Engineers; Middle School Teachers, Except Special and Career/Technical Education; Preschool Teachers, Except Special Education; Recreation Workers; Secondary School Teachers, Except Special and Career/Technical Education; Self-Enrichment Education Teachers; Teacher Assistants; Transportation Engineers; Tutors; 37 other postsecondary teaching occupations; others.

Engineering Technicians, Except Drafters, All Other

⊛ Annual Earnings: $58,020

⊛ Earnings Growth Potential: High (46.1%)

⊛ Growth: 5.2%

⊛ Annual Job Openings: 1,850

⊛ Self-Employed: 0.7%

Skills—Most Important: Because this occupation is highly diverse, separate lists of skills are provided for each job specialization when available.

This occupation includes all engineering technicians, except drafters, not listed separately. Because this is a highly diverse occupation, no data is available for some information topics.

Education/Training Required: Associate degree. **Education and Training Program:** Drafting/Design Engineering Technologies/ Technicians, Other. **Career Clusters:** 01 Agriculture, Food, and Natural Resources; 02 Architecture and Construction; 13 Manufacturing. **Career Pathways:** 13.3 Maintenance, Installation, and Repair; 01.5 Natural Resources Systems; 02.2 Construction; 02.1 Design/Pre-Construction. **Other Jobs in These Pathways:** Architectural and Engineering Managers; Automotive Specialty Technicians; Cement Masons and Concrete Finishers; Construction Carpenters; Construction Laborers; Construction Managers; Cost Estimators; Electrical and Electronic Equipment Assemblers; Electrical Engineering Technicians; Electricians; Engineers, All Other; First-Line Supervisors of Construction Trades and Extraction Workers; Heating and Air Conditioning Mechanics and Installers; Industrial Machinery Mechanics; Industrial Truck and Tractor Operators; Installation, Maintenance, and Repair Workers, All Other; Operating Engineers and Other Construction Equipment Operators; Painters, Construction and Maintenance; Pipe Fitters and Steamfitters; Plumbers; Recreation Workers; Refrigeration Mechanics and Installers; Rough Carpenters; Solar Energy Installation Managers; Telecommunications Line Installers and Repairers; others.

Job Specialization: Electrical Engineering Technologists

Apply engineering theory and technical skills to support electrical engineering activities such as process control, electrical power distribution, and instrumentation design. Prepare layouts of machinery and equipment, plan the flow of work, conduct statistical studies, and analyze production costs. Participate in training and continuing education activities to stay abreast of engineering and industry advances. Assist engineers and scientists in conducting applied research in electrical engineering. Diagnose, test, or analyze the performance of electrical components, assemblies, and systems. Set up and operate standard and specialized testing equipment. Review installation and quality assurance documentation. Review, develop, and prepare maintenance standards. Compile and maintain records documenting engineering schematics, installed equipment, installation and operational problems, resources used, and repairs or corrective action performed. Supervise the construction and testing of electrical prototypes according to general instructions and established standards. Review electrical engineering plans to ensure adherence to design specifications and compliance with applicable electrical codes and standards. Install or maintain electrical control systems, industrial automation systems, and electrical equipment including control circuits, variable speed drives, or programmable logic controllers. Design or modify engineering schematics for electrical transmission and distribution systems or for electrical installation in residential, commercial, or industrial buildings using computer-aided design (CAD) software. Calculate design specifications or cost, material, and resource estimates and prepare project schedules and budgets.

Education/Training Required: Bachelor's degree. **Education and Training Program:** Electrical, Electronic, and Communications Engineering Technology/Technician.

Personality Type: Realistic-Investigative-Conventional. **Career Cluster:** 13 Manufacturing. **Career Pathway:** 13.3 Maintenance, Installation, and Repair. **Other Jobs in This Pathway:** Aircraft Mechanics and Service Technicians; Automotive Specialty Technicians; Biological Technicians; Civil Engineering Technicians; Computer, Automated Teller, and Office Machine Repairers; Electrical and Electronic Equipment Assemblers; Electrical and Electronics Repairers, Commercial and Industrial Equipment; Electrical Engineering Technicians; Electromechanical Engineering Technologists; Electronics Engineering Technicians; Electronics Engineering Technologists; Engineering Technicians, Except Drafters, All Other; Fuel Cell Technicians; Helpers—Installation, Maintenance, and Repair Workers; Industrial Engineering Technologists; Industrial Machinery Mechanics; Installation, Maintenance, and Repair Workers, All Other; Manufacturing Engineering Technologists; Manufacturing Production Technicians; Mapping Technicians; Mechanical Engineering

Technologists; Mobile Heavy Equipment Mechanics, Except Engines; Nanotechnology Engineering Technicians; Telecommunications Line Installers and Repairers; Tire Repairers and Changers; others.

Job Specialization: Electromechanical Engineering Technologists

Apply engineering theory and technical skills to support electromechanical engineering activities such as computer-based process control, instrumentation, and machine design. Prepare layouts of machinery and equipment, plan the flow of work, conduct statistical studies, and analyze production costs. Modify, maintain, or repair electrical, electronic, and mechanical components, equipment, and systems to ensure proper functioning. Specify, coordinate, and conduct quality-control and quality-assurance programs and procedures. Establish and maintain inventory, records, and documentation systems. Fabricate or assemble mechanical, electrical, and electronic components and assemblies. Select electromechanical equipment, materials, components, and systems to meet functional specifications. Select and use laboratory, operational, and diagnostic techniques and test equipment to assess electromechanical circuits, equipment, processes, systems, and subsystems. Produce electrical, electronic, and mechanical drawings and other related documents or graphics necessary for electromechanical design using computer-aided design (CAD) software. Install and program computer hardware and machine and instrumentation software in microprocessor-based systems. Consult with machinists and technicians to ensure that electromechanical equipment and systems meet design specifications. Translate electromechanical drawings into design specifications, applying principles of engineering, thermal and fluid sciences, mathematics, and statistics. Collaborate with engineers to implement electromechanical designs in industrial or other settings.

Education/Training Required: Bachelor's degree. **Education and Training Program:** Electrical, Electronic, and Communications Engineering Technology/Technician.

Personality Type: Realistic-Investigative-Conventional. **Career Cluster:** 13 Manufacturing. **Career Pathway:** 13.3 Maintenance, Installation, and Repair. **Other Jobs in This Pathway:** Aircraft Mechanics and Service Technicians; Automotive Specialty Technicians; Biological Technicians; Civil Engineering Technicians; Computer, Automated Teller, and Office Machine Repairers; Electrical and Electronic Equipment Assemblers; Electrical and Electronics Repairers, Commercial and Industrial Equipment; Electrical Engineering Technicians; Electrical Engineering Technologists; Electronics Engineering Technicians; Electronics Engineering Technologists; Engineering Technicians, Except Drafters, All Other; Fuel Cell Technicians; Helpers—Installation, Maintenance, and Repair Workers; Industrial Engineering Technologists; Industrial Machinery Mechanics; Installation, Maintenance, and Repair Workers, All Other; Manufacturing Engineering Technologists; Manufacturing Production Technicians; Mapping Technicians; Mechanical Engineering Technologists; Mobile Heavy Equipment Mechanics, Except Engines; Nanotechnology Engineering Technicians; Telecommunications Line Installers and Repairers; Tire Repairers and Changers; others.

Job Specialization: Electronics Engineering Technologists

Apply engineering theory and technical skills to support electronics engineering activities such as electronics systems and instrumentation design and digital signal processing. Provide support to technical sales staff on product characteristics. Educate equipment operators on the proper use of equipment. Modify, maintain, and repair electronics equipment and systems to ensure that they function properly. Assemble circuitry for electronic systems according to engineering instructions, production specifications, and technical manuals. Specify, coordinate, or conduct quality control and quality assurance programs and procedures. Prepare and maintain design, testing, or operational records and documentation. Troubleshoot microprocessors and electronic instruments, equipment, and systems using electronic test equipment such as logic analyzers. Set up and operate specialized and standard test equipment to diagnose, test, and analyze the performance of electronic components, assemblies, and systems.

Skills—Most Important: Installation Skills; Technology/Programming Skills; Equipment Use/Maintenance Skills. **Other High-Level Skills:** Science Skills; Mathematics Skills; Thought-Processing Skills; Communication Skills; Management Skills; Social Skills.

Education/Training Required: Associate degree. **Education and Training Program:** Electrical, Electronic, and Communications Engineering Technology/Technician. **Knowledge/Courses:** Engineering and Technology; Telecommunications; Physics; Computers and Electronics; Design; Mathematics.

Personality Type: Realistic-Investigative-Conventional. **Career Cluster:** 13 Manufacturing. **Career Pathway:** 13.3 Maintenance, Installation, and Repair. **Other Jobs in This Pathway:** Aircraft Mechanics and Service Technicians; Automotive Specialty Technicians; Biological Technicians; Civil Engineering Technicians; Computer, Automated Teller, and Office Machine Repairers; Electrical and Electronic Equipment Assemblers; Electrical and Electronics Repairers, Commercial and Industrial Equipment; Electrical Engineering Technicians; Electrical Engineering Technologists; Electromechanical Engineering Technologists; Electronics Engineering Technicians; Engineering Technicians, Except Drafters, All Other; Fuel Cell Technicians; Helpers—Installation, Maintenance, and Repair Workers; Industrial Engineering Technologists; Industrial Machinery Mechanics; Installation, Maintenance, and Repair Workers, All Other; Manufacturing Engineering Technologists; Manufacturing Production Technicians; Mapping Technicians; Mechanical Engineering Technologists; Mobile Heavy Equipment Mechanics, Except Engines; Nanotechnology Engineering Technicians; Telecommunications Line Installers and Repairers; Tire Repairers and Changers; others.

Job Specialization: Fuel Cell Technicians

Install, operate, and maintain integrated fuel cell systems in transportation, stationary, or portable applications. Troubleshoot test equipment. Recommend improvements to fuel cell design and performance. Perform routine vehicle maintenance procedures, such as part replacements and tune-ups. Build or test power plant systems, including pumps, blowers, heat exchangers, or sensors. Order testing materials. Build or test electrical systems, making electrical calculations as needed. Report results of fuel cell test results. Perform routine and preventive maintenance on test equipment. Document or analyze fuel cell test data using spreadsheets or other computer software. Collect and maintain fuel cell test data. Calibrate equipment used for fuel cell testing. Build prototypes following engineering specifications. Test fuel cells or fuel cell stacks using complex electronic equipment. Assemble fuel cells or fuel cell stacks according to mechanical or electrical assembly documents or schematics.

Education/Training Required: Associate degree. **Education and Training Program:** Manufacturing Engineering Technology/Technician.

Career Cluster: 13 Manufacturing. **Career Pathway:** 13.3 Maintenance, Installation, and Repair. **Other Jobs in This Pathway:** Aircraft Mechanics and Service Technicians; Automotive Specialty Technicians; Biological Technicians; Civil Engineering Technicians; Computer, Automated Teller, and Office Machine Repairers; Electrical and Electronic Equipment Assemblers; Electrical and Electronics Repairers, Commercial and Industrial Equipment; Electrical Engineering Technicians; Electrical Engineering Technologists; Electromechanical Engineering Technologists; Electronics Engineering Technicians; Electronics Engineering Technologists; Engineering Technicians, Except Drafters, All Other; Helpers—Installation, Maintenance, and Repair Workers; Industrial Engineering Technologists; Industrial Machinery Mechanics; Installation, Maintenance, and Repair Workers, All Other; Manufacturing Engineering Technologists; Manufacturing Production Technicians; Mapping Technicians; Mechanical Engineering Technologists; Mobile

E

Heavy Equipment Mechanics, Except Engines; Nanotechnology Engineering Technicians; Telecommunications Line Installers and Repairers; Tire Repairers and Changers; others.

Job Specialization: Industrial Engineering Technologists

Apply engineering theory and technical skills to support industrial engineering activities such as quality control, inventory control, and material flow methods. May conduct statistical studies and analyze production costs. Interpret engineering drawings, sketches, or diagrams. Prepare schedules for equipment use or routine maintenance. Request equipment upgrades or purchases. Supervise production workers. Create computer applications for manufacturing processes or operations using computer-aided design (CAD) or computer-assisted manufacturing (CAM) tools. Oversee and inspect production processes. Prepare reports on inventories of raw materials and finished products. Modify equipment or processes to improve resource or cost efficiency. Develop and conduct quality control tests to ensure consistent production quality. Compile operational data to develop cost or time estimates, schedules, or specifications. Collect and analyze data related to quality or industrial health and safety programs. Analyze operational, production, economic, or other data using statistical procedures. Prepare layouts of machinery and equipment using drafting equipment or CAD software. Plan the flow of work or materials to maximize efficiency. Monitor and control inventory. Conduct time and motion studies to identify opportunities to improve worker efficiency. Design plant or production facility layouts. Develop and implement programs to address problems related to production, materials, safety, or quality. Analyze, estimate, or report production costs.

Education/Training Required: Bachelor's degree. **Education and Training Program:** Quality Control Technology/Technician.

Personality Type: Investigative-Realistic-Conventional. **Career Cluster:** 13 Manufacturing. **Career Pathway:** 13.3 Maintenance, Installation, and Repair. **Other Jobs in This Pathway:** Aircraft Mechanics and Service Technicians; Automotive Specialty Technicians; Biological Technicians; Civil Engineering Technicians; Computer, Automated Teller, and Office Machine Repairers; Electrical and Electronic Equipment Assemblers; Electrical and Electronics Repairers, Commercial and Industrial Equipment; Electrical Engineering Technicians; Electrical Engineering Technologists; Electromechanical Engineering Technologists; Electronics Engineering Technicians; Electronics Engineering Technologists; Engineering Technicians, Except Drafters, All Other; Fuel Cell Technicians; Helpers—Installation, Maintenance, and Repair Workers; Industrial Machinery Mechanics; Installation, Maintenance, and Repair Workers, All Other; Manufacturing Engineering Technologists; Manufacturing Production Technicians; Mapping Technicians; Mechanical Engineering Technologists; Mobile Heavy Equipment Mechanics, Except Engines; Nanotechnology Engineering Technicians; Telecommunications Line Installers and Repairers; Tire Repairers and Changers; others.

Job Specialization: Manufacturing Engineering Technologists

Apply engineering theory and technical skills to support manufacturing engineering activities. Develop tools, implement designs, and integrate machinery, equipment, and computer technologies to ensure effective manufacturing processes. Recommend corrective or preventive actions to assure or improve product quality or reliability. Prepare layouts, drawings, or sketches of machinery and equipment such as shop tooling, scale layouts, and new equipment design using drafting equipment or computer-aided design software. Identify and implement new manufacturing technologies, processes, or equipment. Identify opportunities for improvements in quality, cost, or efficiency of automation equipment. Monitor or measure manufacturing processes to identify ways to reduce losses, decrease time requirements, or improve quality. Ensure adherence to safety rules and practices. Coordinate equipment purchases, installations, or transfers. Plan, estimate, or schedule production work. Select material quantities and processing methods needed to achieve efficient production. Develop or maintain programs associated with automated production equipment. Estimate manufacturing costs. Install and evaluate manufacturing equipment, materials, or components. Oversee equipment start-up, characterization, qualification, or release. Develop production, inventory, or quality assurance programs. Create computer applications for manufacturing processes or operations using computer-aided design (CAD) or computer-assisted manufacturing (CAM) tools. Develop manufacturing infrastructure to integrate or deploy new manufacturing processes. Verify weights, measurements, counts, or calculations and record results on batch records.

Skills—Most Important: Installation Skills; Technology/Programming Skills; Equipment Use/Maintenance Skills. **Other High-Level Skills:** Mathematics Skills; Management Skills; Thought-Processing Skills; Science Skills; Communication Skills; Social Skills.

Education/Training Required: Bachelor's degree. **Education and Training Program:** Manufacturing Engineering Technology/ Technician. **Knowledge/Courses:** Engineering and Technology; Design; Mechanical Devices; Physics; Production and Processing; Mathematics.

Personality Type: Realistic-Investigative-Conventional. **Career Cluster:** 13 Manufacturing. **Career Pathway:** 13.3 Maintenance, Installation, and Repair. **Other Jobs in This Pathway:** Aircraft Mechanics and Service Technicians; Automotive Specialty Technicians; Biological Technicians; Civil Engineering Technicians; Computer, Automated Teller, and Office Machine Repairers; Electrical and Electronic Equipment Assemblers; Electrical and Electronics Repairers, Commercial and Industrial Equipment; Electrical Engineering Technicians; Electrical Engineering Technologists; Electromechanical Engineering Technologists; Electronics Engineering Technicians; Electronics Engineering Technologists; Engineering Technicians, Except Drafters, All Other; Fuel Cell Technicians; Helpers—Installation, Maintenance, and Repair Workers; Industrial Engineering Technologists; Industrial Machinery Mechanics; Installation, Maintenance, and Repair Workers, All Other; Manufacturing Production Technicians; Mapping Technicians; Mechanical Engineering Technologists; Mobile Heavy Equipment Mechanics, Except Engines; Nanotechnology Engineering Technicians; Telecommunications Line Installers and Repairers; Tire Repairers and Changers; others.

E

Job Specialization: Manufacturing Production Technicians

Apply knowledge of manufacturing engineering systems and tools to set up, test, and adjust manufacturing machinery and equipment using any combination of electrical, electronic, mechanical, hydraulic, pneumatic, and computer technologies. Adhere to applicable regulations, policies, and procedures for health, safety, and environmental compliance. Inspect finished products for quality and adherence to customer specifications. Set up and operate production equipment in accordance with current good manufacturing practices and standard operating procedures. Calibrate or adjust equipment to ensure quality production using tools such as calipers, micrometers, height gauges, protractors, and ring gauges. Set up and verify the functionality of safety equipment. Troubleshoot problems with equipment, devices, or products. Monitor and adjust production processes or equipment for quality and productivity. Test products or subassemblies for functionality or quality. Plan and lay out work to meet production and schedule requirements. Start up and shut down processing equipment. Prepare and assemble materials. Provide advice or training to other technicians. Measure and record data associated with operating equipment. Assist engineers in developing, building, or testing prototypes, new products, processes, or procedures. Prepare production documents such as standard operating procedures, manufacturing batch records, inventory reports, and productivity reports. Install new equipment. Keep production logs. Clean production equipment and work areas. Provide production, progress, or changeover reports to shift supervisors.

Skills—Most Important: Equipment Use/Maintenance Skills; Science Skills; Thought-Processing Skills. **Other High-Level Skills:** Mathematics Skills; Social Skills; Installation Skills; Communication Skills; Technology/Programming Skills; Management Skills.

Education/Training Required: Postsecondary vocational training. **Education and Training Program:** Manufacturing Engineering Technology/Technician. **Knowledge/Courses:** Mechanical Devices; Design; Engineering and Technology; Production and Processing; Physics; Chemistry.

Personality Type: Realistic-Investigative. **Career Cluster:** 13 Manufacturing. **Career Pathway:** 13.3 Maintenance, Installation, and Repair. **Other Jobs in This Pathway:** Aircraft Mechanics and Service Technicians; Automotive Specialty Technicians; Biological Technicians; Civil Engineering Technicians; Computer, Automated Teller, and Office Machine Repairers; Electrical and Electronic Equipment Assemblers; Electrical and Electronics Repairers, Commercial and Industrial Equipment; Electrical Engineering Technicians; Electrical Engineering Technologists; Electromechanical Engineering Technologists; Electronics Engineering Technicians; Electronics Engineering Technologists; Engineering Technicians, Except Drafters, All Other; Fuel Cell Technicians; Helpers—Installation, Maintenance, and Repair Workers; Industrial Engineering Technologists; Industrial Machinery Mechanics; Installation, Maintenance, and Repair Workers, All Other; Manufacturing Engineering Technologists; Mapping Technicians; Mechanical Engineering Technologists; Mobile Heavy Equipment Mechanics, Except Engines; Nanotechnology Engineering Technicians; Telecommunications Line Installers and Repairers; Tire Repairers and Changers; others.

Job Specialization: Mechanical Engineering Technologists

Apply engineering theory and technical skills to support mechanical engineering activities such as generation, transmission, and use of mechanical and fluid energy. Prepare layouts of machinery and equipment and plan the flow of work. May conduct statistical studies and analyze production costs. Prepare equipment inspection schedules, reliability schedules, work plans, and other records. Prepare cost and materials estimates and project schedules. Provide technical support to other employees on mechanical design, fabrication, testing, or documentation. Interpret engineering sketches, specifications, and drawings. Perform routine maintenance on equipment such as leak detectors, glove boxes, and mechanical pumps. Design specialized or customized equipment, machines, or structures. Design molds, tools, dies, jigs, or fixtures for use in manufacturing processes. Conduct failure analyses, document results, and recommend corrective actions. Assist engineers to design, develop, test, or manufacture industrial machinery, consumer products, or other equipment. Analyze or estimate production costs such as labor, equipment, and plant space. Apply testing or monitoring apparatus to operating equipment. Test machines, components, materials, or products to determine characteristics such as performance, strength, and response to stress. Prepare specifications, designs, or sketches for machines, components, and systems related to the generation, transmission, or use of mechanical and fluid energy. Prepare layouts of machinery, tools, plants, and equipment. Inspect and test mechanical equipment. Oversee, monitor, or inspect mechanical installations or construction projects.

Education/Training Required: Bachelor's degree. **Education and Training Program:** Mechanical Engineering/Mechanical Technology/Technician.

Personality Type: Realistic-Investigative-Conventional. **Career Cluster:** 13 Manufacturing. **Career Pathway:** 13.3 Maintenance, Installation, and Repair. **Other Jobs in This Pathway:** Aircraft Mechanics and Service Technicians; Automotive Specialty Technicians; Biological Technicians; Civil Engineering Technicians; Computer, Automated Teller, and Office Machine Repairers; Electrical and Electronic Equipment Assemblers; Electrical and Electronics Repairers, Commercial and Industrial Equipment; Electrical Engineering Technicians; Electrical Engineering Technologists; Electromechanical Engineering Technologists; Electronics Engineering Technicians; Electronics Engineering Technologists; Engineering Technicians, Except Drafters, All Other; Fuel Cell Technicians; Helpers—Installation, Maintenance, and Repair Workers; Industrial Engineering Technologists; Industrial Machinery Mechanics; Installation, Maintenance, and Repair Workers, All Other; Manufacturing Engineering Technologists; Manufacturing Production Technicians; Mapping Technicians; Mobile Heavy Equipment Mechanics, Except Engines; Nanotechnology Engineering Technicians; Telecommunications Line Installers and Repairers; Tire Repairers and Changers; others.

Job Specialization: Nanotechnology Engineering Technicians

Operate commercial-scale production equipment to produce, test, and modify materials, devices, and systems of molecular

or macromolecular composition. Work under the supervision of engineering staff. Track inventory and order new supplies. Repair nanotechnology processing or testing equipment or submit work orders for equipment repair. Maintain work area according to processing standards. Set up and execute experiments according to detailed instructions. Compile information and prepare reports. Record test results in logs, laboratory notebooks, or spreadsheet software. Produce detailed images and measurement of objects using tools such as scanning tunneling microscopes and oscilloscopes. Perform functional tests of nano-enhanced assemblies, components, or systems using equipment such as torque gauges and conductivity meters. Operate computer-controlled machine tools. Monitor equipment during operation to ensure adherence to specifications for characteristics such as pressure, temperature, and flow. Measure or mix chemicals or compounds in accordance with detailed instructions or formulas. Calibrate nanotechnology equipment such as weighing, testing, and production equipment. Inspect work products to ensure quality and adherence to specifications. Maintain accurate production record or batch record documentation. Assist scientists, engineers, or technologists in writing process specifications or documentation. Assist scientists, engineers, or technologists in processing or characterizing materials according to physical and chemical properties.

Education/Training Required: Associate degree. **Education and Training Program:** Nanotechnology.

Career Cluster: 13 Manufacturing. **Career Pathway:** 13.3 Maintenance, Installation, and Repair. **Other Jobs in This Pathway:** Aircraft Mechanics and Service Technicians;

Automotive Specialty Technicians; Biological Technicians; Civil Engineering Technicians; Computer, Automated Teller, and Office Machine Repairers; Electrical and Electronic Equipment Assemblers; Electrical and Electronics Repairers, Commercial and Industrial Equipment; Electrical Engineering Technicians; Electrical Engineering Technologists; Electromechanical Engineering Technologists; Electronics Engineering Technicians; Electronics Engineering Technologists; Engineering Technicians, Except Drafters, All Other; Fuel Cell Technicians; Helpers—Installation, Maintenance, and Repair Workers; Industrial Engineering Technologists; Industrial Machinery Mechanics; Installation, Maintenance, and Repair Workers, All Other; Manufacturing Engineering Technologists; Manufacturing Production Technicians; Mapping Technicians; Mechanical Engineering Technologists; Mobile Heavy Equipment Mechanics, Except Engines; Telecommunications Line Installers and Repairers; Tire Repairers and Changers; others.

Job Specialization: Nanotechnology Engineering Technologists

Implement production processes for nanoscale designs to produce and modify materials, devices, and systems of unique molecular or macromolecular composition. Operate advanced microscopy equipment to manipulate nanoscale objects. Work under the supervision of engineering staff. Supervise or provide technical direction to technicians engaged in nanotechnology research or production. Install nanotechnology production equipment at customer or manufacturing sites. Contribute written material or data for grant or patent applications. Produce images and measurements using tools and techniques such as atomic force microscopy, scanning electron microscopy, optical microscopy, particle size analysis, and zeta potential analysis. Prepare detailed verbal or written presentations for scientists, engineers, project managers, or upper management. Prepare capability data, training materials, or other documentation for transfer of processes to production. Develop or modify wet chemical or industrial laboratory experimental techniques for nanoscale use. Collect and compile nanotechnology research and engineering data. Inspect or measure thin films of carbon nanotubes, polymers, or inorganic coatings using a variety of techniques and analytical tools. Implement new or enhanced methods and processes for the processing, testing, or manufacture of nanotechnology materials or products. Design or conduct experiments in collaboration with scientists or engineers supportive of the development of nanotechnology materials, components, devices, or systems.

Education/Training Required: Bachelor's degree. **Education and Training Program:** Nanotechnology.

Career Cluster: 13 Manufacturing. **Career Pathway:** 13.3 Maintenance, Installation, and Repair. **Other Jobs in This Pathway:** Aircraft Mechanics and Service Technicians; Automotive Specialty Technicians; Biological Technicians; Civil Engineering Technicians; Computer, Automated Teller, and Office Machine Repairers; Electrical and Electronic Equipment Assemblers; Electrical and Electronics Repairers, Commercial and Industrial Equipment; Electrical Engineering Technicians; Electrical Engineering Technologists; Electromechanical Engineering

Technologists; Electronics Engineering Technicians; Electronics Engineering Technologists; Engineering Technicians, Except Drafters, All Other; Fuel Cell Technicians; Helpers—Installation, Maintenance, and Repair Workers; Industrial Engineering Technologists; Industrial Machinery Mechanics; Installation, Maintenance, and Repair Workers, All Other; Manufacturing Engineering Technologists; Manufacturing Production Technicians; Mapping Technicians; Mechanical Engineering Technologists; Mobile Heavy Equipment Mechanics, Except Engines; Telecommunications Line Installers and Repairers; Tire Repairers and Changers; others.

Job Specialization: Non-Destructive Testing Specialists

Test the safety of structures, vehicles, or vessels using X-ray, ultrasound, fiber-optic, or related equipment. Supervise or direct the work of non-destructive testing (NDT) trainees or staff. Produce images of objects on film using radiographic techniques. Develop or use new NDT methods such as acoustic emission testing, leak testing, and thermal or infrared testing. Document NDT methods, processes, or results. Map the presence of imperfections within objects using sonic measurements. Make radiographic images to detect flaws in objects while leaving objects intact. Visually examine materials, structures, or components using tools and equipment such as endoscopes, closed circuit television systems, and fiber optics for signs of corrosion, metal fatigue, cracks, or other flaws. Interpret or evaluate test results in accordance with applicable codes, standards, specifications, or procedures. Identify defects in solid materials using ultrasonic testing techniques. Select, calibrate, or operate equipment used in NDT of products or materials. Conduct liquid penetrant tests to locate surface cracks by coating objects with fluorescent dyes, cleaning excess penetrant, and applying developer. Prepare reports on NDT results. Interpret the results of all methods of NDT such as acoustic emission, electromagnetic, leak, liquid penetrant, magnetic particle, neutron radiographic, radiographic, thermal or infrared, ultrasonic, vibration analysis, and visual testing.

Skills—Most Important: Equipment Use/Maintenance Skills; Science Skills; Mathematics Skills. **Other High-Level Skills:** Thought-Processing Skills; Management Skills; Social Skills.

Education/Training Required: Associate degree. **Education and Training Program:** Industrial Radiologic Technology/Technician. **Knowledge/Courses:** Engineering and Technology; Physics; Chemistry; Production and Processing; Mechanical Devices; Design.

Personality Type: Realistic-Investigative-Conventional. **Career Cluster:** 13 Manufacturing. **Career Pathway:** 13.3 Maintenance, Installation, and Repair. **Other Jobs in This Pathway:** Aircraft Mechanics and Service Technicians; Automotive Specialty Technicians; Biological Technicians; Civil Engineering Technicians; Computer, Automated Teller, and Office Machine Repairers; Electrical and Electronic Equipment Assemblers; Electrical and Electronics Repairers, Commercial and Industrial Equipment; Electrical Engineering Technicians; Electrical Engineering Technologists; Electromechanical Engineering Technologists; Electronics Engineering Technicians; Electronics Engineering Technologists; Engineering Technicians, Except Drafters, All Other; Fuel Cell Technicians; Helpers—Installation, Maintenance, and

Repair Workers; Industrial Engineering Technologists; Industrial Machinery Mechanics; Installation, Maintenance, and Repair Workers, All Other; Manufacturing Engineering Technologists; Manufacturing Production Technicians; Mapping Technicians; Mechanical Engineering Technologists; Mobile Heavy Equipment Mechanics, Except Engines; Telecommunications Line Installers and Repairers; Tire Repairers and Changers; others.

Job Specialization: Photonics Technicians

Build, install, test, and maintain optical and fiber-optic equipment such as lasers, lenses, and mirrors using spectrometers, interferometers, or related equipment. Recommend design or material changes to reduce costs or processing times. Monitor inventory levels and order supplies. Maintain clean working environments according to clean-room standards. Document procedures such as calibration. Maintain activity logs. Record test results and compute test data. Test and perform failure analysis for optomechanical or optoelectrical products according to test plans. Assist scientists or engineers in photonic experiments. Perform diagnostic analyses of processing steps using analytical or metrological tools such as microscopy, profilometry, and ellipsometry devices. Optimize process parameters by making prototype and production devices. Mix, pour, and use processing chemicals or gases according to safety standards and established operating procedures. Design, build, or modify fixtures used to assemble parts. Lay out cutting lines for machining using drafting tools. Assist engineers in the development of new products, fixtures, tools, or processes. Assemble and adjust parts or related electrical units of prototypes to prepare for testing. Splice fibers using fusion splicing or other techniques. Terminate, cure, polish, or test fiber cables with mechanical connectors. Set up or operate prototype or test apparatus such as control consoles, collimators, recording equipment, and cables.

Education/Training Required: Associate degree. **Education and Training Program:** Engineering-Related Technologies, Other.

Personality Type: Realistic-Investigative-Conventional. **Career Cluster:** 13 Manufacturing. **Career Pathway:** 13.3 Maintenance, Installation, and Repair. **Other Jobs in This Pathway:** Aircraft Mechanics and Service Technicians; Automotive Specialty Technicians; Biological Technicians; Civil Engineering Technicians; Computer, Automated Teller, and Office Machine Repairers; Electrical and Electronic Equipment Assemblers; Electrical and Electronics Repairers, Commercial and Industrial Equipment; Electrical Engineering Technicians; Electrical Engineering Technologists; Electromechanical Engineering Technologists; Electronics Engineering Technicians; Electronics Engineering Technologists; Engineering Technicians, Except Drafters, All Other; Fuel Cell Technicians; Helpers—Installation, Maintenance, and Repair Workers; Industrial Engineering Technologists; Industrial Machinery Mechanics; Installation, Maintenance, and Repair Workers, All Other; Manufacturing Engineering Technologists; Manufacturing Production Technicians; Mapping Technicians; Mechanical Engineering Technologists; Mobile Heavy Equipment Mechanics, Except Engines; Telecommunications Line Installers and Repairers; Tire Repairers and Changers; others.

Engineers, All Other

- ❋ Annual Earnings: $90,270
- ❋ Earnings Growth Potential: High (45.1%)
- ❋ Growth: 6.7%
- ❋ Annual Job Openings: 5,020
- ❋ Self-Employed: 6.4%

Skills—Most Important: Because this occupation is highly diverse, separate lists of skills are provided for each job specialization when available.

This occupation includes all engineers not listed separately. Because this is a highly diverse occupation, no data is available for some information topics.

Education/Training Required: Bachelor's degree. **Education and Training Program:** Engineering, Other. **Career Clusters:** 02 Architecture and Construction; 08 Health Science; 15 Science, Technology, Engineering, and Mathematics. **Career Pathways:** 02.1 Design/Pre-Construction; 15.1 Engineering and Technology; 08.3 Health Informatics. **Other Jobs in These Pathways:** Architectural and Engineering Managers; Automotive Engineers; Biochemical Engineers; Biofuels/Biodiesel Technology and Product Development Managers; Civil Engineers; Cost Estimators; Energy Engineers; Executive Secretaries and Executive Administrative Assistants; First-Line Supervisors of Office and Administrative Support Workers; Fuel Cell Engineers; Human Factors Engineers and Ergonomists; Industrial Engineers; Manufacturing Engineers; Mechanical Engineers; Mechatronics Engineers; Medical and Health Services Managers; Medical Assistants; Medical Secretaries; Microsystems Engineers; Nanosystems Engineers; Photonics

Engineers; Physical Therapists; Public Relations Specialists; Receptionists and Information Clerks; Transportation Engineers; others.

Job Specialization: Biochemical Engineers

Apply knowledge of biology, chemistry, and engineering to develop usable, tangible products. Solve problems related to materials, systems, and processes that interact with humans, plants, animals, microorganisms, and biological materials. Read current scientific or trade literature to stay abreast of scientific, industrial, or technological advances. Prepare technical reports, data summary documents, or research articles for scientific publication, regulatory submissions, or patent applications. Modify or control biological systems to replace, augment, or sustain chemical or mechanical processes. Maintain databases of experiment characteristics or results. Lead studies to examine or recommend changes in process sequences or operation protocols. Direct experimental or developmental activities at contracted laboratories. Consult with chemists or biologists to develop or evaluate novel technologies. Collaborate with manufacturing or quality assurance staff to prepare product specification or safety sheets, standard operating procedures, user manuals, or qualification and validation reports. Devise scalable recovery, purification, or fermentation processes for producing proteins or other biological substances for human or animal therapeutic use, food production or processing, biofuels, or effluent treatment. Develop methodologies for transferring procedures or biological processes from laboratories to commercial-scale manufacturing production. Design or direct bench or pilot production experiments to determine the scale of production methods that optimize product yield and minimize production costs.

Skills—Most Important: Science Skills; Mathematics Skills; Thought-Processing Skills. **Other High-Level Skills:** Communication Skills; Technology/Programming Skills; Management Skills; Equipment Use/ Maintenance Skills; Social Skills.

Education/Training Required: Bachelor's degree. **Education and Training Program:** Biochemical Engineering. **Knowledge/ Courses:** Biology; Chemistry; Engineering and Technology; Physics; Production and Processing; Design.

Personality Type: Investigative-Realistic. **Career Cluster:** 15 Science, Technology, Engineering, and Mathematics. **Career Pathway:** 15.1 Engineering and Technology. **Other Jobs in This Pathway:** Architectural and Engineering Managers; Automotive Engineers; Biofuels/Biodiesel Technology and Product Development Managers; Civil Engineers; Cost Estimators; Education, Training, and Library Workers, All Other; Electrical Engineers; Electronics Engineers, Except Computer; Energy Engineers; Engineers, All Other; Fuel Cell Engineers; Human Factors Engineers and Ergonomists; Industrial Engineers; Manufacturing Engineers; Mechanical Engineers; Mechatronics Engineers; Microsystems Engineers; Nanosystems Engineers; Photonics Engineers; Radio Frequency Identification Device Specialists; Robotics Engineers; Solar Energy Systems Engineers; Transportation Engineers; Validation Engineers; Wind Energy Engineers; others.

Job Specialization: Energy Engineers

Design, develop, and evaluate energy-related projects and programs to reduce energy costs or improve energy efficiency during the designing, building, or remodeling stages of construction. May specialize in electrical systems; heating, ventilation, and air-conditioning (HVAC) systems; green buildings; lighting; air quality; or energy procurement. Identify energy-savings opportunities and make recommendations to achieve more energy-efficient operation. Manage the development, design, or construction of energy conservation projects to ensure acceptability of budgets and timelines, conformance to federal and state laws, or adherence to approved specifications. Conduct energy audits to evaluate energy use, costs, or conservation measures. Monitor and analyze energy consumption. Perform energy modeling, measurement, verification, commissioning, or retro-commissioning. Oversee design or construction aspects related to energy such as energy engineering, energy management, and sustainable design. Conduct jobsite observations, field inspections, or sub-metering to collect data for energy conservation analyses. Review architectural, mechanical, or electrical plans and specifications to evaluate energy efficiency or determine economic, service, or engineering feasibility. Inspect or monitor energy systems including heating, HVAC, or daylighting systems to determine energy use or potential energy savings. Evaluate construction design information such as detail and assembly drawings, design calculations, system layouts and sketches, or specifications. Direct the work of contractors or staff in implementing energy-management projects. Prepare project reports and other program or technical documentation. Make recommendations on energy fuel selection.

Skills—Most Important: Science Skills; Mathematics Skills; Thought-Processing Skills. **Other High-Level Skills:** Communication Skills; Social Skills; Management Skills; Equipment Use/Maintenance Skills.

Education/Training Required: Bachelor's degree. **Education and Training Program:** Engineering, Other. **Knowledge/Courses:** Engineering and Technology; Building and Construction; Physics; Design; Economics and Accounting; Mechanical.

Personality Type: Investigative-Realistic. **Career Cluster:** 15 Science, Technology, Engineering, and Mathematics. **Career Pathway:** 15.1 Engineering and Technology. **Other Jobs in This Pathway:** Architectural and Engineering Managers; Automotive Engineers; Biochemical Engineers; Biofuels/Biodiesel Technology and Product Development Managers; Civil Engineers; Cost Estimators; Education, Training, and Library Workers, All Other; Electrical Engineers; Electronics Engineers, Except Computer; Engineers, All Other; Fuel Cell Engineers; Human Factors Engineers and Ergonomists; Industrial Engineers; Manufacturing Engineers; Mechanical Engineers; Mechatronics Engineers; Microsystems Engineers; Nanosystems Engineers; Photonics Engineers; Radio Frequency Identification Device Specialists; Robotics Engineers; Solar Energy Systems Engineers; Transportation Engineers; Validation Engineers; Wind Energy Engineers; others.

Job Specialization: Manufacturing Engineers

Apply knowledge of materials and engineering theory and methods to design, integrate, and improve manufacturing systems or related processes. May work with commercial or

industrial designers to refine product designs to increase producibility and decrease costs. Identify opportunities or implement changes to improve products or reduce costs using knowledge of fabrication processes, tooling and production equipment, assembly methods, quality control standards, or product design, materials, and parts. Provide technical expertise or support related to manufacturing. Determine root causes of failures using statistical methods and recommend changes in designs, tolerances, or processing methods. Incorporate new methods and processes to improve existing operations. Supervise technicians, technologists, analysts, administrative staff, or other engineers. Troubleshoot new and existing product problems involving designs, materials, or processes. Review product designs for manufacturability and completeness. Train production personnel in new or existing methods. Communicate manufacturing capabilities, production schedules, or other information to facilitate production processes. Design, install, or troubleshoot manufacturing equipment. Prepare documentation for new manufacturing processes or engineering procedures. Apply continuous improvement methods such as lean manufacturing to enhance manufacturing quality, reliability, or cost-effectiveness. Investigate or resolve operational problems such as material use variances and bottlenecks. Estimate costs, production times, or staffing requirements for new designs. Evaluate manufactured products according to specifications and quality standards. Purchase equipment, materials, or parts.

Skills—Most Important: Installation Skills; Equipment Use/Maintenance Skills; Mathematics Skills. **Other High-Level Skills:** Management Skills; Technology/Programming Skills; Science Skills; Thought-Processing Skills; Communication Skills; Social Skills.

Education/Training Required: Bachelor's degree. **Education and Training Program:** Manufacturing Engineering. **Knowledge/Courses:** Engineering and Technology; Design; Physics; Production and Processing; Mechanical Devices; Chemistry.

Personality Type: Realistic-Investigative. **Career Cluster:** 15 Science, Technology, Engineering, and Mathematics. **Career Pathway:** 15.1 Engineering and Technology. **Other Jobs in This Pathway:** Architectural and Engineering Managers; Automotive Engineers; Biochemical Engineers; Biofuels/Biodiesel Technology and Product Development Managers; Civil Engineers; Cost Estimators; Education, Training, and Library Workers, All Other; Electrical Engineers; Electronics Engineers, Except Computer; Energy Engineers; Engineers, All Other; Fuel Cell Engineers; Human Factors Engineers and Ergonomists; Industrial Engineers; Mechanical Engineers; Mechatronics Engineers; Microsystems Engineers; Nanosystems Engineers; Photonics Engineers; Radio Frequency Identification Device Specialists; Robotics Engineers; Solar Energy Systems Engineers; Transportation Engineers; Validation Engineers; Wind Energy Engineers; others.

Job Specialization: Mechatronics Engineers

Apply knowledge of mechanical, electrical, and computer engineering theory and methods to the design of automation, intelligent systems, smart devices, or industrial systems control. Publish engineering reports documenting design details and qualification test results. Provide consultation or training on topics such as mechatronics and automated control. Oversee the work of contractors in accordance with project requirements. Create mechanical design documents for parts, assemblies, or finished products. Maintain technical project files. Analyze existing development or manufacturing procedures and suggest improvements. Implement and test design solutions. Research, select, and apply sensors, communication technologies, or control devices for motion control, position sensing, pressure sensing, or electronic communication. Identify and select materials appropriate for mechatronic system designs. Design, develop, or implement control circuits and algorithms for electromechanical and pneumatic devices or systems. Design engineering systems for the automation of industrial tasks. Design advanced electronic control systems for mechanical systems. Create embedded software design programs. Create mechanical models and tolerance analyses to simulate mechatronic design concepts. Conduct studies to determine the feasibility, costs, or performance benefits of new mechatronic equipment. Upgrade the design of existing devices by adding mechatronic elements. Develop electronic, mechanical, or computerized processes to perform tasks in dangerous situations such as underwater exploration and extraterrestrial mining.

Education/Training Required: Bachelor's degree. **Education and Training Program:** Mechatronics, Robotics, and Automation Engineering.

Personality Type: Investigative-Realistic-Conventional. **Career Cluster:** 15 Science, Technology, Engineering, and Mathematics. **Career Pathway:** 15.1 Engineering and Technology. **Other Jobs in This Pathway:** Architectural and Engineering Managers; Automotive Engineers; Biochemical Engineers; Biofuels/Biodiesel Technology and Product Development Managers; Civil Engineers; Cost Estimators; Education, Training, and Library Workers, All Other; Electrical Engineers; Electronics Engineers, Except Computer; Energy Engineers; Engineers, All Other; Fuel Cell Engineers; Human Factors Engineers and Ergonomists; Industrial Engineers; Manufacturing Engineers; Mechanical Engineers; Microsystems Engineers; Nanosystems Engineers; Photonics Engineers; Radio Frequency Identification Device Specialists; Robotics Engineers; Solar Energy Systems Engineers; Transportation Engineers; Validation Engineers; Wind Energy Engineers; others.

Job Specialization: Microsystems Engineers

Apply knowledge of electronic and mechanical engineering theory and methods, as well as specialized manufacturing technologies, to design and develop microelectromechanical systems (MEMS) devices. Manage new product introduction projects to ensure effective deployment of MEMS devices and applications. Plan or schedule engineering research or development projects involving MEMS technology. Develop or implement MEMS processing tools, fixtures, gauges, dies, molds, and trays. Identify, procure, or develop test equipment, instrumentation, and facilities for characterization of MEMS applications. Develop and verify customer documentation, such as performance specifications, training manuals, and operating instructions. Develop and file intellectual property and patent disclosure or application documents related to MEMS devices, products, and systems. Develop and communicate operating characteristics or performance experience to other engineers and designers for training or new product development purposes. Demonstrate miniaturized systems that contain components such as microsensors, microactuators, or integrated electronic circuits fabricated on silicon or silicon carbide wafers. Create or maintain formal engineering documents, such as schematics, bill of materials, components and materials specifications, and packaging requirements.

Education/Training Required: Bachelor's degree. **Education and Training Program:** Nanotechnology.

Personality Type: Investigative-Realistic-Conventional. **Career Cluster:** 15 Science, Technology, Engineering, and Mathematics. **Career Pathway:** 15.1 Engineering and Technology. **Other Jobs in This Pathway:** Architectural and Engineering Managers; Automotive Engineers; Biochemical Engineers; Biofuels/Biodiesel Technology and Product Development Managers; Civil Engineers; Cost Estimators; Education, Training, and Library Workers, All Other; Electrical Engineers; Electronics Engineers, Except Computer; Energy Engineers; Engineers, All Other; Fuel Cell Engineers; Human Factors Engineers and Ergonomists; Industrial Engineers; Manufacturing Engineers; Mechanical Engineers; Mechatronics Engineers; Nanosystems Engineers; Photonics Engineers; Radio Frequency Identification Device Specialists; Robotics Engineers; Solar Energy Systems Engineers; Transportation Engineers; Validation Engineers; Wind Energy Engineers; others.

Job Specialization: Nanosystems Engineers

Design, develop, and supervise the production of materials, devices, and systems of unique molecular or macromolecular composition applying principles of nanoscale physics and electrical, chemical, and biological engineering. Write proposals to secure external funding or to partner with other companies. Supervise technologists or technicians engaged in nanotechnology research or production. Synthesize, process, or characterize nanomaterials using advanced tools and techniques. Identify new applications for existing nanotechnologies. Provide technical guidance and support to customers on topics such as nanosystem start-up, maintenance, or use. Generate high-resolution images or measure force-distance curves using techniques such as atomic force microscopy. Prepare reports, deliver presentations, or participate in program review activities to communicate engineering results and recommendations. Prepare nanotechnology-related invention disclosures or patent applications. Develop processes or identify equipment needed for pilot or commercial nanoscale scale production. Provide scientific or technical guidance and expertise to scientists, engineers, technologists, technicians, or others using knowledge of chemical, analytical, or biological processes as applied to micro and nanoscale systems. Engineer production processes for specific nanotechnology applications such as electroplating, nanofabrication, or epoxy. Design or conduct tests of new nanotechnology products, processes, or systems. Coordinate or supervise the work of suppliers or vendors in designing, building, or testing nanosystem devices such as lenses or probes.

Education/Training Required: Bachelor's degree. **Education and Training Program:** Nanotechnology.

Career Cluster: 15 Science, Technology, Engineering, and Mathematics. **Career Pathway:** 15.1 Engineering and Technology. **Other Jobs in This Pathway:** Architectural and Engineering

Managers; Automotive Engineers; Biochemical Engineers; Biofuels/Biodiesel Technology and Product Development Managers; Civil Engineers; Cost Estimators; Education, Training, and Library Workers, All Other; Electrical Engineers; Electronics Engineers, Except Computer; Energy Engineers; Engineers, All Other; Fuel Cell Engineers; Human Factors Engineers and Ergonomists; Industrial Engineers; Manufacturing Engineers; Mechanical Engineers; Mechatronics Engineers; Microsystems Engineers; Photonics Engineers; Radio Frequency Identification Device Specialists; Robotics Engineers; Solar Energy Systems Engineers; Transportation Engineers; Validation Engineers; Wind Energy Engineers; others.

Job Specialization: Photonics Engineers

Apply knowledge of engineering and mathematical theory and methods to design technologies specializing in light information and light energy. Design, integrate, or test photonics systems and components. Develop optical or imaging systems such as optical imaging products, optical components, image processes, signal process technologies, and optical systems. Analyze system performance or operational requirements. Write reports or research proposals. Assist in the transition of photonic prototypes to production. Develop and test photonic prototypes or models. Conduct testing to determine functionality and optimization or to establish limits of photonics systems or components. Design electro-optical sensing or imaging systems. Read current literature, talk with colleagues, continue education, or participate in professional organizations or conferences to keep abreast of developments in the field. Conduct research on new photonics technologies. Determine applications of photonics appropriate to meet product objectives and features. Document design processes including objectives, issues, and outcomes. Oversee or provide expertise on manufacturing, assembly, or fabrication processes. Train operators, engineers, or other personnel. Determine commercial, industrial, scientific, or other uses for electro-optical applications or devices. Design gas lasers, solid state lasers, infrared, or other light-emitting or light-sensitive devices. Analyze, fabricate, or test fiber-optic links. Create or maintain photonic design histories. Develop laser-processed designs such as laser-cut medical devices.

Skills—Most Important: Mathematics Skills; Technology/Programming Skills; Science Skills. **Other High-Level Skills:** Equipment Use/Maintenance Skills; Thought-Processing Skills; Communication Skills; Management Skills; Social Skills.

Education/Training Required: Bachelor's degree. **Education and Training Program:** Engineering, Other. **Knowledge/Courses:** Physics; Engineering and Technology; Design; Mathematics; Mechanical Devices; Computers and Electronics.

Personality Type: Investigative-Realistic-Conventional. **Career Cluster:** 15 Science, Technology, Engineering, and Mathematics. **Career Pathway:** 15.1 Engineering and Technology. **Other Jobs in This Pathway:** Architectural and Engineering Managers; Automotive Engineers; Biochemical Engineers; Biofuels/Biodiesel Technology and Product Development Managers; Civil Engineers; Cost Estimators; Education, Training, and Library Workers, All Other; Electrical Engineers; Electronics Engineers, Except Computer; Energy Engineers; Engineers, All Other; Fuel Cell Engineers; Human Factors Engineers and Ergonomists; Industrial Engineers; Manufacturing Engineers; Mechanical Engineers; Mechatronics Engineers; Microsystems Engineers; Nanosystems Engineers; Radio Frequency Identification Device Specialists; Robotics Engineers; Solar Energy Systems Engineers; Transportation Engineers; Validation Engineers; Wind Energy Engineers; others.

Job Specialization: Robotics Engineers

Research, design, develop, and test robotic applications. Supervise technicians, technologists, or other engineers. Integrate robotics with peripherals such as welders, controllers, or other equipment. Provide technical support for robotic systems. Review or approve designs, calculations, or cost estimates. Make system device lists and event-timing charts. Document robotic application development, maintenance, or changes. Write algorithms and programming code for ad-hoc robotic applications. Create backups of robot programs or parameters. Process and interpret signals or sensor data. Plan mobile robot paths and teach path plans to robots. Investigate mechanical failures or unexpected maintenance problems. Install, calibrate, operate, or maintain robots. Debug robotics programs. Design end-of-arm tooling. Conduct research on robotic technology to create new robotic systems or system capabilities.

Skills—Most Important: Installation Skills; Technology/Programming Skills; Mathematics Skills. **Other High-Level Skills:** Equipment Use/Maintenance Skills; Science Skills; Thought-Processing Skills; Management Skills; Communication Skills; Social Skills.

Education/Training Required: Bachelor's degree. **Education and Training Program:** Mechatronics, Robotics, and Automation

Engineering. **Knowledge/Courses:** Engineering and Technology; Design; Physics; Mechanical Devices; Computers and Electronics; Production and Processing.

Personality Type: Investigative-Realistic-Conventional. **Career Cluster:** 15 Science, Technology, Engineering, and Mathematics. **Career Pathway:** 15.1 Engineering and Technology. **Other Jobs in This Pathway:** Architectural and Engineering Managers; Automotive Engineers; Biochemical Engineers; Biofuels/Biodiesel Technology and Product Development Managers; Civil Engineers; Cost Estimators; Education, Training, and Library Workers, All Other; Electrical Engineers; Electronics Engineers, Except Computer; Energy Engineers; Engineers, All Other; Fuel Cell Engineers; Human Factors Engineers and Ergonomists; Industrial Engineers; Manufacturing Engineers; Mechanical Engineers; Mechatronics Engineers; Microsystems Engineers; Nanosystems Engineers; Photonics Engineers; Radio Frequency Identification Device Specialists; Solar Energy Systems Engineers; Transportation Engineers; Validation Engineers; Wind Energy Engineers; others.

Job Specialization: Solar Energy Systems Engineers

Perform site-specific engineering analysis or evaluation of energy efficiency and solar projects involving residential, commercial, or industrial customers. Design solar domestic hot water and space heating systems for new and existing structures applying knowledge of structural energy requirements, local climates, solar technology, and thermodynamics. Test or evaluate photovoltaic (PV) cells or modules. Review specifications and recommend engineering or manufacturing changes to achieve solar design objectives. Perform thermal, stress, or cost reduction analyses for solar systems. Develop standard operation procedures and quality or safety standards for solar installation work. Design or develop vacuum tube collector systems for solar applications. Provide technical direction or support to installation teams during installation, start-up, testing, system commissioning, or performance monitoring. Perform computer simulation of solar PV generation system performance or energy production to optimize efficiency. Develop design specifications and functional requirements for residential, commercial, or industrial solar energy systems or components. Create plans for solar energy system development, monitoring, and evaluation activities. Create electrical single-line diagrams, panel schedules, or connection diagrams for solar electric systems using computer-aided design (CAD) software. Create checklists for review or inspection of completed solar installation projects. Design or coordinate design of PV or solar thermal systems, including system components, for residential and commercial buildings. Conduct engineering site audits to collect structural, electrical, and related site information for use in the design of residential or commercial solar power systems.

Education/Training Required: Bachelor's degree. **Education and Training Program:** Engineering, Other.

Career Cluster: 15 Science, Technology, Engineering, and Mathematics. **Career Pathway:** 15.1 Engineering and Technology. **Other Jobs in This Pathway:** Architectural and Engineering Managers; Automotive Engineers; Biochemical Engineers; Biofuels/Biodiesel Technology and Product Development Managers; Civil

Engineers; Cost Estimators; Education, Training, and Library Workers, All Other; Electrical Engineers; Electronics Engineers, Except Computer; Energy Engineers; Engineers, All Other; Fuel Cell Engineers; Human Factors Engineers and Ergonomists; Industrial Engineers; Manufacturing Engineers; Mechanical Engineers; Mechatronics Engineers; Microsystems Engineers; Nanosystems Engineers; Photonics Engineers; Radio Frequency Identification Device Specialists; Robotics Engineers; Transportation Engineers; Validation Engineers; Wind Energy Engineers; others.

Job Specialization: Validation Engineers

Design and plan protocols for equipment and processes to produce products meeting internal and external purity, safety, and quality requirements. Analyze validation test data to determine whether systems or processes have met validation criteria and to identify root causes of production problems. Prepare validation and performance qualification protocols for new or modified manufacturing processes, systems, or equipment for pharmaceutical, electronics, and other types of production. Coordinate the implementation or scheduling of validation testing with affected departments and personnel. Study product characteristics or customer requirements and confer with management to determine validation objectives and standards. Prepare, maintain, or review validation and compliance documentation such as engineering change notices, schematics, and protocols. Resolve testing problems by modifying testing methods or revising test objectives and standards. Create, populate, or maintain databases for tracking validation activities, test results, or validated systems. Prepare detailed reports and design statements based on results of validation and qualification tests or reviews of procedures and protocols. Identify deviations from established product or process standards and provide recommendations for resolving deviations. Direct validation activities such as protocol creation or testing. Develop validation master plans, process flow diagrams, test cases, or standard operating procedures. Communicate with regulatory agencies on compliance documentation or validation results.

Skills—Most Important: Science Skills; Mathematics Skills; Thought-Processing Skills. **Other High-Level Skills:** Communication Skills; Management Skills; Equipment Use/ Maintenance Skills; Social Skills.

Education/Training Required: Bachelor's degree. **Education and Training Program:** Engineering, Other. **Knowledge/Courses:** Engineering and Technology; Design; Production and Processing; Chemistry; Physics; Mathematics.

Personality Type: Investigative-Realistic-Conventional. **Career Cluster:** 15 Science, Technology, Engineering, and Mathematics. **Career Pathway:** 15.1 Engineering and Technology. **Other Jobs in This Pathway:** Architectural and Engineering Managers; Automotive Engineers; Biochemical Engineers; Biofuels/Biodiesel Technology and Product Development Managers; Civil Engineers; Cost Estimators; Education, Training, and Library Workers, All Other; Electrical Engineers; Electronics Engineers, Except Computer; Energy Engineers; Engineers, All Other; Fuel Cell Engineers; Human Factors Engineers and Ergonomists; Industrial Engineers; Manufacturing Engineers; Mechanical Engineers; Mechatronics Engineers; Microsystems Engineers; Nanosystems

Engineers; Photonics Engineers; Radio Frequency Identification Device Specialists; Robotics Engineers; Solar Energy Systems Engineers; Transportation Engineers; Wind Energy Engineers; others.

Job Specialization: Wind Energy Engineers

Design underground or overhead wind farm collector systems and prepare and develop site specifications. Write reports to document wind farm collector system test results. Oversee the work activities of wind farm consultants or subcontractors. Recommend process or infrastructure changes to improve wind turbine performance, reduce operational costs, or comply with regulations. Investigate experimental wind turbines or wind turbine technologies for properties such as aerodynamics, production, noise, and load. Test wind turbine equipment to determine effects of stress or fatigue. Test wind turbine components using mechanical or electronic testing equipment. Provide engineering technical support to designers of prototype wind turbines. Perform root cause analysis on wind turbine tower component failures. Monitor wind farm construction to ensure compliance with regulatory standards or environmental requirements. Direct balance of plant (BOP) construction, generator installation, testing, commissioning, or supervisory control and data acquisition (SCADA) to ensure compliance with specifications. Develop specifications for wind technology components such as gearboxes, blades, generators, frequency converters, and pad transformers. Develop active control algorithms, electronics, software, electromechanical, or electrohydraulic systems for wind turbines. Create or maintain wind farm layouts, schematics, or other visual documentation for wind farms.

Education/Training Required: Bachelor's degree. **Education and Training Program:** Engineering, Other.

Career Cluster: 15 Science, Technology, Engineering, and Mathematics. **Career Pathway:** 15.1 Engineering and Technology. **Other Jobs in This Pathway:** Architectural and Engineering Managers; Automotive Engineers; Biochemical Engineers; Biofuels/Biodiesel Technology and Product Development Managers; Civil Engineers; Cost Estimators; Education, Training, and Library Workers, All Other; Electrical Engineers; Electronics Engineers, Except Computer; Energy Engineers; Engineers, All Other; Fuel Cell Engineers; Human Factors Engineers and Ergonomists; Industrial Engineers; Manufacturing Engineers; Mechanical Engineers; Mechatronics Engineers; Microsystems Engineers; Nanosystems Engineers; Photonics Engineers; Radio Frequency Identification Device Specialists; Robotics Engineers; Solar Energy Systems Engineers; Transportation Engineers; Validation Engineers; others.

Environmental Engineering Technicians

* Annual Earnings: $43,390
* Earnings Growth Potential: Low (35.5%)
* Growth: 30.1%
* Annual Job Openings: 1,040
* Self-Employed: 0.7%

Skills—Most Important: Science Skills; Mathematics Skills; Equipment Use/Maintenance Skills. **Other High-Level Skills:** Communication Skills; Thought-Processing Skills; Management Skills; Social Skills.

Apply theory and principles of environmental engineering to modify, test, and operate equipment and devices used in the prevention, control, and remediation of environmental pollution, including waste treatment and site remediation. May assist in the development of environmental pollution remediation devices under direction of engineer. Receive, set up, test, or decontaminate equipment. Maintain project logbook records or computer program files. Conduct pollution surveys, collecting and analyzing samples such as air and ground water. Perform environmental quality work in field or office settings. Review technical documents to ensure completeness and conformance to requirements. Perform laboratory work such as logging numerical and visual observations, preparing and packaging samples, recording test results, and performing photo documentation. Review work plans to schedule activities. Obtain product information, identify vendors or suppliers, or order materials or equipment to maintain inventory. Inspect facilities to monitor compliance with regulations governing substances such as asbestos, lead, or wastewater. Provide technical engineering support in planning projects, such as wastewater treatment plants, to ensure compliance with environmental regulations and policies. Oversee support staff. Assist in the clean up of hazardous material spills. Produce environmental assessment reports, tabulating data and preparing charts, graphs, or sketches. Maintain process parameters and evaluate process anomalies. Develop work plans, including writing specifications or establishing material, manpower, or facilities needs. Arrange for the disposal of lead, asbestos, or other hazardous materials. Improve chemical processes to reduce toxic emissions.

Education/Training Required: Associate degree. **Education and Training Programs:**

Environmental Engineering Technology/ Environmental Technology; Hazardous Materials Information Systems Technology/ Technician. **Knowledge/Courses:** Biology; Building and Construction; Physics; Chemistry; Engineering and Technology; Design.

Personality Type: Realistic-Investigative-Conventional. **Career Clusters:** 01 Agriculture, Food, and Natural Resources; 13 Manufacturing. **Career Pathways:** 01.6 Environmental Service Systems; 13.4 Quality Assurance. **Other Jobs in These Pathways:** Hazardous Materials Removal Workers; Inspectors, Testers, Sorters, Samplers, and Weighers; Occupational Health and Safety Specialists; Water and Wastewater Treatment Plant and System Operators.

Environmental Engineers

- ❋ Annual Earnings: $78,740
- ❋ Earnings Growth Potential: Medium (37.8%)
- ❋ Growth: 30.6%
- ❋ Annual Job Openings: 2,790
- ❋ Self-Employed: 0.6%

Skills—Most Important: Science Skills; Mathematics Skills; Thought-Processing Skills. **Other High-Level Skills:** Communication Skills; Management Skills; Social Skills; Equipment Use/Maintenance Skills.

Design, plan, or perform engineering duties in the prevention, control, and remediation of environmental health hazards using various engineering disciplines. Work may include waste treatment, site remediation, or pollution control technology. Prepare, review, and update environmental investigation and recommendation reports.

Collaborate with environmental scientists, planners, hazardous waste technicians, engineers, and experts in law and business to address environmental problems. Provide technical-level support for environmental remediation and litigation projects, including remediation system design and determination of regulatory applicability. Obtain, update, and maintain plans, permits, and standard operating procedures. Monitor progress of environmental improvement programs. Inspect industrial and municipal facilities and programs to evaluate operational effectiveness and ensure compliance with environmental regulations. Provide administrative support for projects by collecting data, providing project documentation, training staff, and performing other general administrative duties. Develop proposed project objectives and targets and report to management on progress in attaining them. Advise corporations and government agencies of procedures to follow in cleaning up contaminated sites to protect people and the environment. Advise industries and government agencies about environmental policies and standards. Inform company employees and other interested parties of environmental issues. Assess the existing or potential environmental impact of land use projects on air, water, and land. Assist in budget implementation, forecasts, and administration.

Education/Training Required: Bachelor's degree. **Education and Training Program:** Environmental Health Engineering. **Knowledge/Courses:** Engineering and Technology; Physics; Design; Chemistry; Building and Construction; Biology.

Personality Type: Investigative-Realistic-Conventional. **Career Clusters:** 15 Science, Technology, Engineering, and Mathematics;

16 Transportation, Distribution, and Logistics. **Career Pathways:** 15.1 Engineering and Technology; 16.6 Health, Safety, and Environmental Management. **Other Jobs in These Pathways:** Architectural and Engineering Managers; Automotive Engineers; Biochemical Engineers; Biofuels/Biodiesel Technology and Product Development Managers; Civil Engineers; Cost Estimators; Electrical Engineers; Electronics Engineers, Except Computer; Energy Engineers; Engineers, All Other; Environmental Compliance Inspectors; Fuel Cell Engineers; Human Factors Engineers and Ergonomists; Industrial Engineers; Manufacturing Engineers; Mechanical Engineers; Mechatronics Engineers; Microsystems Engineers; Nanosystems Engineers; Photonics Engineers; Robotics Engineers; Solar Energy Systems Engineers; Transportation Engineers; Validation Engineers; Wind Energy Engineers; others.

Job Specialization: Water/ Wastewater Engineers

Design or oversee projects involving provision of fresh water, disposal of wastewater and sewage, or prevention of flood-related damage. Prepare environmental documentation for water resources, regulatory program compliance, data management and analysis, and fieldwork. Perform hydraulic modeling and pipeline design. Write technical reports or publications related to water resources development or water use efficiency. Review and critique proposals, plans, or designs related to water and wastewater treatment systems. Provide technical support on water resource or treatment issues to government agencies. Provide technical direction or supervision to junior engineers, engineering or computer-aided design (CAD) technicians, or other technical personnel. Identify design

alternatives for the development of new water resources. Develop plans for new water resources or water-efficiency programs. Design or select equipment for use in wastewater processing to ensure compliance with government standards. Conduct water quality studies to identify and characterize water pollutant sources. Perform mathematical modeling of underground or surface water resources, such as floodplains, ocean coastlines, streams, rivers, and wetlands. Perform hydrological analyses using three-dimensional simulation software to model the movement of water or forecast the dispersion of chemical pollutants in the water supply. Perform hydraulic analyses of water supply systems or water distribution networks to model flow characteristics, test for pressure losses, or to identify opportunities to mitigate risks and improve operational efficiency. Oversee the construction of decentralized and on-site wastewater treatment systems, including reclaimed water facilities. Gather and analyze water use data to forecast water demand.

Education/Training Required: Bachelor's degree. **Education and Training Program:** Environmental Health Engineering. **Knowledge/Courses:** No data available.

Personality Type: No data available. **Career Cluster:** 15 Science, Technology, Engineering, and Mathematics. **Career Pathway:** 15.1 Engineering and Technology. **Other Jobs in This Pathway:** Architectural and Engineering Managers; Automotive Engineers; Biochemical Engineers; Biofuels/Biodiesel Technology and Product Development Managers; Civil Engineers; Cost Estimators; Electrical Engineers; Electronics Engineers, Except Computer; Energy Engineers; Engineers, All Other; Fuel Cell Engineers; Human Factors Engineers and Ergonomists; Industrial

Engineers; Manufacturing Engineers; Mechanical Engineers; Mechatronics Engineers; Microsystems Engineers; Nanosystems Engineers; Photonics Engineers; Radio Frequency Identification Device Specialists; Robotics Engineers; Solar Energy Systems Engineers; Transportation Engineers; Validation Engineers; Wind Energy Engineers; others.

Environmental Science and Protection Technicians, Including Health

* Annual Earnings: $41,380
* Earnings Growth Potential: Low (35.7%)
* Growth: 28.9%
* Annual Job Openings: 2,520
* Self-Employed: 1.7%

Skills—Most Important: Science Skills; Mathematics Skills; Equipment Use/Maintenance Skills. **Other High-Level Skills:** Thought-Processing Skills; Communication Skills; Social Skills; Management Skills.

Perform laboratory and field tests to monitor the environment and investigate sources of pollution, including those that affect health. Under direction of environmental scientists or specialists, may collect samples of gases, soil, water, and other materials for testing and take corrective actions as assigned. Record test data and prepare reports, summaries, and charts that interpret test results. Collect samples of gases, soils, water, industrial wastewater, and asbestos products to conduct tests on pollutant levels and identify sources of pollution. Respond to and investigate hazardous conditions or spills or outbreaks of disease or food poisoning, collecting samples for analysis. Provide information and technical and program assistance to government representatives, employers, and the general public on the issues of public health, environmental protection, or workplace safety. Calibrate microscopes and test instruments. Make recommendations to control or eliminate unsafe conditions at workplaces or public facilities. Inspect sanitary conditions at public facilities. Prepare samples or photomicrographs for testing and analysis. Calculate amount of pollutant in samples or compute air pollution or gas flow in industrial processes using chemical and mathematical formulas. Initiate procedures to close down or fine establishments violating environmental or health regulations. Determine amounts and kinds of chemicals to use in destroying harmful organisms and removing impurities from purification systems. Discuss test results and analyses with customers. Maintain files such as hazardous waste databases, chemical usage data, personnel exposure information, and diagrams showing equipment locations. Perform statistical analysis of environmental data.

Education/Training Required: Associate degree. **Education and Training Programs:** Environmental Science; Environmental Studies; Physical Science Technologies/Technicians, Other; Science Technologies/Technicians, Other. **Knowledge/Courses:** Biology; Chemistry; Geography; Physics; Computers and Electronics; Building and Construction.

Personality Type: Investigative-Realistic-Conventional. **Career Clusters:** 01 Agriculture, Food, and Natural Resources; 13 Manufacturing; 16 Transportation, Distribution, and Logistics. **Career Pathways:** 16.6 Health, Safety, and Environmental Management; 13.2 Manufacturing Production Process

Development; 01.5 Natural Resources Systems. **Other Jobs in These Pathways:** Chemical Plant and System Operators; Chemical Technicians; Climate Change Analysts; Conveyor Operators and Tenders; Electrical Engineering Technicians; Electromechanical Equipment Assemblers; Engineering Technicians, Except Drafters, All Other; Environmental Compliance Inspectors; Environmental Engineers; Environmental Restoration Planners; Environmental Scientists and Specialists, Including Health; Fishers and Related Fishing Workers; Forest and Conservation Technicians; Health and Safety Engineers, Except Mining Safety Engineers and Inspectors; Helpers— Extraction Workers; Industrial Ecologists; Industrial Truck and Tractor Operators; Life, Physical, and Social Science Technicians, All Other; Logging Equipment Operators; Mechanical Engineering Technicians; Quality Control Analysts; Recreation Workers; Refuse and Recyclable Material Collectors; Rotary Drill Operators, Oil and Gas; Service Unit Operators, Oil, Gas, and Mining; others.

Environmental Scientists and Specialists, Including Health

❁ Annual Earnings: $61,700

❁ Earnings Growth Potential: Medium (38.7%)

❁ Growth: 27.9%

❁ Annual Job Openings: 4,840

❁ Self-Employed: 2.4%

Skills—Most Important: Science Skills; Mathematics Skills; Communication Skills. **Other High-Level Skills:** Thought-Processing Skills; Technology/Programming Skills; Management Skills; Social Skills; Equipment Use/Maintenance Skills.

Conduct research or perform investigation for the purpose of identifying, abating, or eliminating sources of pollutants or hazards that affect either the environment or the health of the population. Using knowledge of various scientific disciplines, may collect, synthesize, study, report, and take action based on data derived from measurements or observations of air, food, soil, water, and other sources. Conduct environmental audits and inspections and investigations of violations. Evaluate violations or problems discovered during inspections to determine appropriate regulatory actions or to provide advice on the development and prosecution of regulatory cases. Communicate scientific and technical information through oral briefings, written documents, workshops, conferences, and public hearings. Review and implement environmental technical standards, guidelines, policies, and formal regulations that meet requirements. Provide technical guidance, support, and oversight to environmental programs, industry, and the public. Provide advice on proper standards and regulations or the development of policies, strategies, and codes of practice for environmental management. Analyze data to determine validity, quality, and scientific significance and to interpret correlations between human activities and environmental effects. Collect, synthesize, and analyze data derived from pollution emission measurements, atmospheric monitoring, meteorological and mineralogical information, and soil or water samples. Determine data collection methods to be employed in research projects and surveys. Prepare charts or graphs from data samples, providing summary information on the environmental relevance of the data. Develop the technical portions of legal documents, administrative orders, or consent decrees. Investigate and report on accidents affecting the environment.

Education/Training Required: Master's degree. **Education and Training Programs:** Environmental Science; Environmental Studies. **Knowledge/Courses:** Biology; Geography; Chemistry; Physics; Law and Government; Engineering and Technology.

Personality Type: Investigative-Realistic-Conventional. **Career Clusters:** 01 Agriculture, Food, and Natural Resources; 16 Transportation, Distribution, and Logistics. **Career Pathways:** 01.5 Natural Resources Systems; 16.6 Health, Safety, and Environmental Management. **Other Jobs in These Pathways:** Climate Change Analysts; Conveyor Operators and Tenders; Derrick Operators, Oil and Gas; Engineering Technicians, Except Drafters, All Other; Environmental Compliance Inspectors; Environmental Engineers; Environmental Restoration Planners; Environmental Science and Protection Technicians, Including Health; Fishers and Related Fishing Workers; Forest and Conservation Technicians; Health and Safety Engineers, Except Mining Safety Engineers and Inspectors; Helpers—Extraction Workers; Industrial Ecologists; Industrial Truck and Tractor Operators; Logging Equipment Operators; Mechanical Engineering Technicians; Park Naturalists; Range Managers; Recreation Workers; Refuse and Recyclable Material Collectors; Rotary Drill Operators, Oil and Gas; Service Unit Operators, Oil, Gas, and Mining; Soil and Water Conservationists; Wellhead Pumpers; Zoologists and Wildlife Biologists; others.

Job Specialization: Climate Change Analysts

Research and analyze policy developments related to climate change. Make climate-related recommendations for actions such as legislation, awareness campaigns, or fundraising approaches. Write reports or academic papers to communicate findings of climate-related studies. Promote initiatives to mitigate climate change with government or environmental groups. Present climate-related information at public interest, governmental, or other meetings. Present and defend proposals for climate change research projects. Prepare grant applications to obtain funding for programs related to climate change, environmental management, or sustainability. Gather and review climate-related studies from government agencies, research laboratories, and other organizations. Develop or contribute to the development of educational or outreach programs on the environment or climate change. Review existing policies or legislation to identify environmental impacts. Provide analytical support for policy briefs related to renewable energy, energy efficiency, or climate change. Prepare study reports, memoranda, briefs, testimonies, or other written materials to inform government or environmental groups on environmental issues such as climate change. Make legislative recommendations related to climate change or environmental management based on climate change policies, principles, programs, practices, and processes. Research policies, practices, or procedures for climate or environmental management. Propose new or modified policies involving use of traditional and alternative fuels, transportation of goods, and other factors relating to climate and climate change.

Education/Training Required: Master's degree. **Education and Training Programs:** Environmental Science; Environmental Studies. **Knowledge/Courses:** No data available.

Personality Type: No data available. **Career Cluster:** 01 Agriculture, Food, and Natural Resources. **Career Pathway:** 01.5 Natural Resources Systems. **Other Jobs in This Pathway:** Conveyor Operators and Tenders; Derrick Operators, Oil and Gas; Engineering Technicians, Except Drafters, All Other; Environmental Economists; Environmental Restoration Planners; Environmental Science and Protection Technicians, Including Health; Environmental Scientists and Specialists, Including Health; Fishers and Related Fishing Workers; Forest and Conservation Technicians; Geological Sample Test Technicians; Geophysical Data Technicians; Helpers— Extraction Workers; Industrial Ecologists; Industrial Truck and Tractor Operators; Logging Equipment Operators; Mechanical Engineering Technicians; Park Naturalists; Range Managers; Recreation Workers; Refuse and Recyclable Material Collectors; Rotary Drill Operators, Oil and Gas; Service Unit Operators, Oil, Gas, and Mining; Soil and Water Conservationists; Wellhead Pumpers; Zoologists and Wildlife Biologists; others.

Job Specialization: Environmental Restoration Planners

Collaborate with field and biology staff to oversee the implementation of restoration projects and to develop new products. Process and synthesize complex scientific data into practical strategies for restoration, monitoring, or management. Notify regulatory or permitting agencies of deviations from implemented remediation plans. Develop environmental restoration project schedules and budgets. Develop and communicate recommendations for landowners to maintain or restore environmental conditions. Create diagrams to communicate environmental remediation planning using geographic information systems (GIS), computer-aided design (CAD), or other mapping or diagramming software. Apply for permits required for the implementation of environmental remediation projects. Review existing environmental remediation designs. Supervise and provide technical guidance, training, or assistance to employees working in the field to restore habitats. Provide technical direction on environmental planning to energy engineers, biologists, geologists, or other professionals working to develop restoration plans or strategies. Plan or supervise environmental studies to achieve compliance with environmental regulations in construction, modification, operation, acquisition, or divestiture of facilities such as power plants. Inspect active remediation sites to ensure compliance with environmental or safety policies, standards, or regulations. Plan environmental restoration projects using biological databases, environmental strategies, and planning software. Identify short- and long-term impacts of environmental remediation activities.

Education/Training Required: Master's degree. **Education and Training Programs:** Environmental Science; Environmental Studies. **Knowledge/Courses:** No data available.

Personality Type: No data available. **Career Cluster:** 01 Agriculture, Food, and Natural Resources. **Career Pathway:** 01.5 Natural Resources Systems. **Other Jobs in This Pathway:** Climate Change Analysts; Conveyor

Operators and Tenders; Derrick Operators, Oil and Gas; Engineering Technicians, Except Drafters, All Other; Environmental Economists; Environmental Science and Protection Technicians, Including Health; Environmental Scientists and Specialists, Including Health; Fishers and Related Fishing Workers; Forest and Conservation Technicians; Geological Sample Test Technicians; Geophysical Data Technicians; Helpers—Extraction Workers; Industrial Ecologists; Industrial Truck and Tractor Operators; Logging Equipment Operators; Mechanical Engineering Technicians; Park Naturalists; Range Managers; Recreation Workers; Refuse and Recyclable Material Collectors; Rotary Drill Operators, Oil and Gas; Service Unit Operators, Oil, Gas, and Mining; Soil and Water Conservationists; Wellhead Pumpers; Zoologists and Wildlife Biologists; others.

Job Specialization: Industrial Ecologists

Study or investigate industrial production and natural ecosystems to achieve high production, sustainable resources, and environmental safety or protection. May apply principles and activities of natural ecosystems to develop models for industrial systems. Write ecological reports and other technical documents for publication in the research literature or in industrial or government reports. Recommend methods to protect the environment or minimize environmental damage. Investigate accidents affecting the environment to assess ecological impact. Investigate the adaptability of various animal and plant species to changed environmental conditions. Review industrial practices, such as the methods and materials used in construction or production, to identify potential liabilities and environmental hazards. Research sources of pollution to determine environmental impact or to develop methods of pollution abatement or control. Provide industrial managers with technical materials on environmental issues, regulatory guidelines, or compliance actions. Plan or conduct studies of the ecological implications of historic or projected changes in industrial processes or development. Plan or conduct field research on topics such as industrial production, industrial ecology, population ecology, and environmental production or sustainability. Monitor the environmental impact of development activities, pollution, or land degradation. Model alternative energy investment scenarios to compare economic and environmental costs and benefits. Identify or develop strategies or methods to minimize the environmental impact of industrial production processes. Investigate the impact of changed land management or land use practices on ecosystems.

Education/Training Required: Master's degree. **Education and Training Programs:** Environmental Science; Environmental Studies. **Knowledge/Courses:** No data available.

Personality Type: No data available. **Career Cluster:** 01 Agriculture, Food, and Natural Resources. **Career Pathway:** 01.5 Natural Resources Systems. **Other Jobs in This Pathway:** Climate Change Analysts; Conveyor Operators and Tenders; Derrick Operators, Oil and Gas; Engineering Technicians, Except Drafters, All Other; Environmental Economists; Environmental Restoration Planners; Environmental Science and Protection Technicians, Including Health; Environmental Scientists and Specialists, Including Health; Fishers and Related Fishing Workers; Forest and Conservation Technicians; Geological Sample Test Technicians; Geophysical Data Technicians;

Helpers—Extraction Workers; Industrial Truck and Tractor Operators; Logging Equipment Operators; Mechanical Engineering Technicians; Park Naturalists; Range Managers; Recreation Workers; Refuse and Recyclable Material Collectors; Rotary Drill Operators, Oil and Gas; Service Unit Operators, Oil, Gas, and Mining; Soil and Water Conservationists; Wellhead Pumpers; Zoologists and Wildlife Biologists; others.

Executive Secretaries and Executive Administrative Assistants

- ❋ Annual Earnings: $43,520
- ❋ Earnings Growth Potential: Low (34.0%)
- ❋ Growth: 12.8%
- ❋ Annual Job Openings: 41,920
- ❋ Self-Employed: 1.3%

Skills—Most Important: Communication Skills; Social Skills; Management Skills. **Other High-Level Skills:** Thought-Processing Skills.

Provide high-level administrative support by conducting research; preparing statistical reports; handling information requests; and performing clerical functions such as preparing correspondence, receiving visitors, arranging conference calls, and scheduling meetings. May also train and supervise lower-level clerical staff. Prepare invoices, reports, memos, letters, financial statements, and other documents using word processing, spreadsheet, database, or presentation software. Answer phone calls and direct calls to appropriate parties or take messages. Conduct research, compile data, and prepare papers for consideration and presentation by executives, committees, and boards of directors. Attend meetings to record minutes. Greet visitors and determine whether they should be given access to specific individuals. Read and analyze incoming memos, submissions, and reports to determine their significance and plan their distribution. Perform general office duties, such as ordering supplies, maintaining records management database systems, and performing basic bookkeeping work. File and retrieve corporate documents, records, and reports. Make travel arrangements for executives. Open, sort, and distribute incoming correspondence, including faxes and e-mail. Prepare responses to correspondence containing routine inquiries. Prepare agendas and make arrangements such as coordinating catering for luncheons for committee, board, and other meetings. Coordinate and direct office services, such as records, departmental finances, budget preparation, personnel issues, and housekeeping, to aid executives. Provide clerical support to other departments. Manage and maintain executives' schedules. Process payroll information. Compile, transcribe, and distribute minutes of meetings.

Education/Training Required: Work experience in a related occupation. **Education and Training Programs:** Administrative Assistant and Secretarial Science, General; Executive Assistant/Executive Secretary Training; Medical Administrative/Executive Assistant and Medical Secretary Training. **Knowledge/Courses:** Clerical Practices; Personnel and Human Resources.

Personality Type: Conventional-Enterprising. **Career Clusters:** 04 Business, Management, and Administration; 08 Health Science. **Career Pathways:** 04.6 Administrative and Information Support; 08.3 Health Informatics. **Other**

Jobs in These Pathways: Customer Service Representatives; Data Entry Keyers; Dispatchers, Except Police, Fire, and Ambulance; Engineers, All Other; File Clerks; First-Line Supervisors of Office and Administrative Support Workers; Information and Record Clerks, All Other; Insurance Claims Clerks; Insurance Policy Processing Clerks; Interviewers, Except Eligibility and Loan; Medical and Health Services Managers; Medical Assistants; Medical Records and Health Information Technicians; Medical Secretaries; Office and Administrative Support Workers, All Other; Office Clerks, General; Order Clerks; Patient Representatives; Physical Therapists; Postal Service Mail Carriers; Postal Service Mail Sorters, Processors, and Processing Machine Operators; Public Relations Specialists; Receptionists and Information Clerks; Secretaries and Administrative Assistants, Except Legal, Medical, and Executive; Shipping, Receiving, and Traffic Clerks; others.

Financial Analysts

❀ Annual Earnings: $74,350

❀ Earnings Growth Potential: Medium (40.2%)

❀ Growth: 19.8%

❀ Annual Job Openings: 9,520

❀ Self-Employed: 4.6%

Skills—Most Important: Mathematics Skills; Thought-Processing Skills; Communication Skills. **Other High-Level Skills:** Social Skills; Management Skills.

Conduct quantitative analyses of information affecting investment programs of public or private institutions. Assemble spreadsheets and draw charts and graphs used to illustrate technical reports. Analyze financial information to produce forecasts of business, industry, and economic conditions for making investment decisions. Maintain knowledge and stay abreast of developments in industrial technology, business, finance, and economic theory. Interpret data affecting investment programs, such as price, yield, stability, future trends in investment risks, and economic influences. Monitor fundamental economic, industrial, and corporate developments through the analysis of information obtained from financial publications and services, investment banking firms, government agencies, trade publications, company sources, and personal interviews. Recommend investments and investment timing to companies, investment firm staff, or the investing public. Determine the prices at which securities should be syndicated and offered to the public. Prepare plans of action for investment based on financial analyses. Evaluate and compare the relative quality of various securities in a given industry. Present oral and written reports on general economic trends, individual corporations, and entire industries. Contact brokers and purchase investments for companies according to company policy. Collaborate with investment bankers to attract new corporate clients to securities firms.

Education/Training Required: Bachelor's degree. **Education and Training Programs:** Accounting and Business/Management; Accounting and Finance; Finance, General. **Knowledge/Courses:** Economics and Accounting; Mathematics; Law and Government; Clerical Practices; Administration and Management; English Language.

Personality Type: Conventional-Investigative-Enterprising. **Career Clusters:** 04 Business, Management, and Administration; 06 Finance. **Career Pathways:** 06.2 Business Financial

Management; 06.1 Financial and Investment Planning; 04.2 Business, Financial Management, and Accounting. **Other Jobs in These Pathways:** Accountants; Auditors; Billing and Posting Clerks; Billing, Cost, and Rate Clerks; Bookkeeping, Accounting, and Auditing Clerks; Brownfield Redevelopment Specialists and Site Managers; Compliance Managers; Financial Managers, Branch or Department; Financial Quantitative Analysts; Investment Fund Managers; Loss Prevention Managers; Managers, All Other; Payroll and Timekeeping Clerks; Personal Financial Advisors; Regulatory Affairs Managers; Sales Agents, Financial Services; Sales Agents, Securities and Commodities; Securities and Commodities Traders; Securities, Commodities, and Financial Services Sales Agents; Security Managers; Statement Clerks; Supply Chain Managers; Treasurers and Controllers; Wind Energy Operations Managers; Wind Energy Project Managers; others.

Financial Examiners

❋ Annual Earnings: $74,940

❋ Earnings Growth Potential: High (42.4%)

❋ Growth: 41.2%

❋ Annual Job Openings: 1,600

❋ Self-Employed: 0.0%

Skills—Most Important: Mathematics Skills; Thought-Processing Skills; Communication Skills. **Other High-Level Skills:** Social Skills; Management Skills.

Enforce or ensure compliance with laws and regulations governing financial and securities institutions and financial and real estate transactions. May examine, verify correctness of, or establish authenticity of records. Investigate activities of institutions to enforce laws and regulations and to ensure legality of transactions and operations or financial solvency. Review and analyze new, proposed, or revised laws, regulations, policies, and procedures to interpret their meaning and determine their impact. Plan, supervise, and review work of assigned subordinates. Recommend actions to ensure compliance with laws and regulations or to protect solvency of institutions. Examine the minutes of meetings of directors, stockholders, and committees to investigate the specific authority extended at various levels of management. Prepare reports, exhibits, and other supporting schedules that detail an institution's safety and soundness, compliance with laws and regulations, and recommended solutions to questionable financial conditions. Review balance sheets, operating income and expense accounts, and loan documentation to confirm institution assets and liabilities. Review audit reports of internal and external auditors to monitor adequacy of scope of reports or to discover specific weaknesses in internal routines. Train other examiners in the financial examination process. Establish guidelines for procedures and policies that comply with new and revised regulations and direct their implementation.

Education/Training Required: Bachelor's degree. **Education and Training Programs:** Accounting; Taxation. **Knowledge/Courses:** Economics and Accounting; Law and Government; Clerical Practices; Mathematics; English Language; Administration and Management.

Personality Type: Enterprising-Conventional. **Career Clusters:** 04 Business, Management, and Administration; 07 Government and Public Administration. **Career Pathways:** 07.5 Revenue and Taxation; 04.2 Business, Financial

Management, and Accounting. **Other Jobs in These Pathways:** Accountants; Auditors; Billing and Posting Clerks; Billing, Cost, and Rate Clerks; Bookkeeping, Accounting, and Auditing Clerks; Brokerage Clerks; Brownfield Redevelopment Specialists and Site Managers; Compliance Managers; Credit Analysts; Financial Analysts; Financial Managers, Branch or Department; Investment Fund Managers; Logistics Managers; Loss Prevention Managers; Managers, All Other; Payroll and Timekeeping Clerks; Regulatory Affairs Managers; Security Managers; Statement Clerks; Supply Chain Managers; Tax Examiners and Collectors, and Revenue Agents; Tax Preparers; Treasurers and Controllers; Wind Energy Operations Managers; Wind Energy Project Managers; others.

Financial Managers

- ❀ Annual Earnings: $103,910
- ❀ Earnings Growth Potential: High (46.0%)
- ❀ Growth: 7.6%
- ❀ Annual Job Openings: 13,820
- ❀ Self-Employed: 5.3%

Skills—Most Important: Management Skills; Mathematics Skills; Thought-Processing Skills. **Other High-Level Skills:** Social Skills; Communication Skills.

Job Specialization: Financial Managers, Branch or Department

Direct and coordinate financial activities of workers in a branch, office, or department of an establishment, such as branch bank, brokerage firm, risk and insurance department, or credit department. Establish and maintain relationships with individual and business customers and provide assistance with problems these customers may encounter. Examine, evaluate, and process loan applications. Oversee the flow of cash and financial instruments. Recruit staff members and oversee training programs. Network in communities to find and attract new business. Approve or reject or coordinate the approval and rejection of lines of credit and commercial, real estate, and personal loans. Prepare financial and regulatory reports required by laws, regulations, and boards of directors. Establish procedures for custody and control of assets, records, loan collateral, and securities to ensure safekeeping. Review collection reports to determine the status of collections and the amounts of outstanding balances. Prepare operational and risk reports for management analysis. Evaluate financial reporting systems, accounting and collection procedures, and investment activities and make recommendations for changes to procedures, operating systems, budgets, and other financial control functions. Plan, direct, and coordinate risk and insurance programs of establishments to control risks and losses. Submit delinquent accounts to attorneys or outside agencies for collection.

Education/Training Required: Work experience plus degree. **Education and Training Programs:** Accounting and Business/Management; Accounting and Finance; Credit Management; Finance and Financial Management Services, Other; Finance, General; International Finance; Public Finance. **Knowledge/Courses:** Economics and Accounting; Sales and Marketing; Personnel and Human Resources; Clerical Practices; Customer and Personal Service; Mathematics.

Personality Type: Enterprising-Conventional. **Career Clusters:** 04 Business, Management, and Administration; 06 Finance. **Career**

Pathways: 06.1 Financial and Investment Planning; 04.2 Business, Financial Management, and Accounting. **Other Jobs in These Pathways:** Accountants; Auditors; Billing and Posting Clerks; Billing, Cost, and Rate Clerks; Bookkeeping, Accounting, and Auditing Clerks; Brownfield Redevelopment Specialists and Site Managers; Compliance Managers; Financial Analysts; Financial Quantitative Analysts; Investment Fund Managers; Loss Prevention Managers; Managers, All Other; Payroll and Timekeeping Clerks; Personal Financial Advisors; Regulatory Affairs Managers; Sales Agents, Financial Services; Sales Agents, Securities and Commodities; Securities and Commodities Traders; Securities, Commodities, and Financial Services Sales Agents; Security Managers; Statement Clerks; Supply Chain Managers; Treasurers and Controllers; Wind Energy Operations Managers; Wind Energy Project Managers; others.

Job Specialization: Treasurers and Controllers

Direct financial activities, such as planning, procurement, and investments, for all or part of an organization. Prepare and file annual tax returns or prepare financial information so that outside accountants can complete tax returns. Prepare or direct preparation of financial statements, business activity reports, financial position forecasts, annual budgets, and/or reports required by regulatory agencies. Supervise employees performing financial reporting, accounting, billing, collections, payroll, and budgeting duties. Delegate authority for the receipt, disbursement, banking, protection, and custody of funds, securities, and financial instruments. Maintain current knowledge of organizational policies and procedures, federal and state policies and directives, and current accounting standards. Receive and record requests for disbursements; authorize disbursements in accordance with policies and procedures. Conduct or coordinate audits of company accounts and financial transactions to ensure compliance with state and federal requirements and statutes. Monitor financial activities and details such as reserve levels to ensure that all legal and regulatory requirements are met. Monitor and evaluate the performance of accounting and other financial staff; recommend and implement personnel actions such as promotions and dismissals. Develop and maintain relationships with banking, insurance, and non-organizational accounting personnel to facilitate financial activities.

Education/Training Required: Work experience plus degree. **Education and Training Programs:** Accounting and Business/Management; Accounting and Finance; Credit Management; Finance and Financial Management Services, Other; Finance, General; International Finance; Public Finance. **Knowledge/Courses:** Economics and Accounting; Administration and Management; Personnel and Human Resources; Law and Government; Mathematics; English Language.

Personality Type: Conventional-Enterprising. **Career Clusters:** 04 Business, Management, and Administration; 06 Finance. **Career Pathways:** 04.2 Business, Financial Management, and Accounting; 06.1 Financial and Investment Planning. **Other Jobs in These Pathways:** Accountants; Auditors; Billing and Posting Clerks; Billing, Cost, and Rate Clerks; Bookkeeping, Accounting, and Auditing Clerks; Brownfield Redevelopment Specialists and Site Managers; Compliance Managers; Financial Analysts; Financial Managers, Branch or Department; Financial Quantitative Analysts;

Investment Fund Managers; Loss Prevention Managers; Managers, All Other; Payroll and Timekeeping Clerks; Personal Financial Advisors; Regulatory Affairs Managers; Sales Agents, Financial Services; Sales Agents, Securities and Commodities; Securities and Commodities Traders; Securities, Commodities, and Financial Services Sales Agents; Security Managers; Statement Clerks; Supply Chain Managers; Wind Energy Operations Managers; Wind Energy Project Managers; others.

Firefighters

* Annual Earnings: $45,250
* Earnings Growth Potential: High (49.1%)
* Growth: 18.5%
* Annual Job Openings: 15,280
* Self-Employed: 0.2%

Skills—Most Important: Equipment Use/Maintenance Skills; Science Skills; Social Skills. **Other High-Level Skills:** Thought-Processing Skills; Management Skills; Communication Skills.

Job Specialization: Forest Firefighters

Control and suppress fires in forests or vacant public land. Maintain contact with fire dispatchers at all times to notify them of the need for additional firefighters and supplies or to detail any difficulties encountered. Rescue fire victims and administer emergency medical aid. Collaborate with other firefighters as a member of a firefighting crew. Patrol burned areas after fires to locate and eliminate hot spots that may restart fires. Extinguish flames and embers to suppress fires using shovels or engine- or hand-driven water or chemical pumps. Fell trees, cut and clear brush, and dig trenches to create firelines using axes, chainsaws, or shovels. Maintain knowledge of current firefighting practices by participating in drills and by attending seminars, conventions, and conferences. Operate pumps connected to high-pressure hoses. Participate in physical training to maintain high levels of physical fitness. Establish water supplies, connect hoses, and direct water onto fires. Maintain fire equipment and firehouse living quarters.

Education/Training Required: Long-term on-the-job training. **Education and Training Programs:** Fire Protection, Other; Fire Science/Firefighting. **Knowledge/Courses:** Geography; Building and Construction; Telecommunications; Mechanical Devices; Public Safety and Security; Customer and Personal Service.

Personality Type: Realistic-Social. **Career Cluster:** 12 Law, Public Safety, Corrections, and Security. **Career Pathways:** 12.3 Security and Protective Services; 12.2 Emergency and Fire Management Services. **Other Jobs in These Pathways:** Animal Control Workers; Correctional Officers and Jailers; Crossing Guards; Fire Inspectors; Fire Investigators; First-Line Supervisors of Protective Service Workers, All Other; Forest Fire Fighting and Prevention Supervisors; Forest Fire Inspectors and Prevention Specialists; Gaming Surveillance Officers and Gaming Investigators; Lifeguards, Ski Patrol, and Other Recreational Protective Service Workers; Municipal Fire Fighting and Prevention Supervisors; Municipal Firefighters; Parking Enforcement Workers; Police, Fire, and Ambulance Dispatchers; Private Detectives and Investigators; Retail Loss Prevention Specialists; Security Guards; Sheriffs and Deputy Sheriffs; Transit and Railroad Police.

Job Specialization: Municipal Firefighters

Control and extinguish municipal fires, protect life and property, and conduct rescue efforts. Rescue victims from burning buildings and accident sites. Search burning buildings to locate fire victims. Administer first aid and cardiopulmonary resuscitation to injured persons. Dress with equipment such as fire-resistant clothing and breathing apparatus. Drive and operate firefighting vehicles and equipment. Move toward the source of a fire using knowledge of types of fires, construction design, building materials, and physical layout of properties. Respond to fire alarms and other calls for assistance, such as automobile and industrial accidents. Assess fires and situations and report conditions to superiors to receive instructions using two-way radios. Position and climb ladders to gain access to upper levels of buildings or to rescue individuals from burning structures. Create openings in buildings for ventilation or entrance using axes, chisels, crowbars, electric saws, or core cutters. Lay hose lines and connect them to water supplies. Operate pumps connected to high-pressure hoses. Collaborate with police to respond to accidents, disasters, and arson investigation calls. Take action to contain hazardous chemicals that might catch fire, leak, or spill. Select and attach hose nozzles, depending on fire type, and direct streams of water or chemicals onto fires. Participate in fire drills and demonstrations of firefighting techniques. Prepare written reports that detail specifics of fire incidents.

Education/Training Required: Long-term on-the-job training. **Education and Training Programs:** Fire Protection, Other; Fire Science/Firefighting. **Knowledge/Courses:** Building and Construction; Public Safety and Security; Mechanical Devices; Customer and Personal Service; Physics; Geography.

Personality Type: Realistic-Social-Enterprising. **Career Cluster:** 12 Law, Public Safety, Corrections, and Security. **Career Pathway:** 12.2 Emergency and Fire Management Services. **Other Jobs in This Pathway:** Correctional Officers and Jailers; Fire Inspectors; Fire Investigators; Forest Fire Fighting and Prevention Supervisors; Forest Fire Inspectors and Prevention Specialists; Forest Firefighters; Municipal Fire Fighting and Prevention Supervisors.

First-Line Supervisors of Fire Fighting and Prevention Workers

- ❋ Annual Earnings: $68,240
- ❋ Earnings Growth Potential: Medium (39.3%)
- ❋ Growth: 8.2%
- ❋ Annual Job Openings: 3,250
- ❋ Self-Employed: 0.0%

Skills—Most Important: Science Skills; Equipment Use/Maintenance Skills; Thought-Processing Skills. **Other High-Level Skills:** Social Skills; Management Skills; Mathematics Skills; Communication Skills.

Job Specialization: Forest Fire Fighting and Prevention Supervisors

Supervise firefighters who control and suppress fires in forests or vacant public land. Communicate fire details to superiors, subordinates, and interagency dispatch centers using two-way radios. Serve as working leader of an engine-, hand-, helicopter-, or prescribed fire crew of three or more firefighters. Maintain fire suppression equipment in good condition, checking equipment periodically to ensure that it is ready for use. Evaluate size, location, and condition of forest fires to request and dispatch crews and position equipment so fires can be contained safely and effectively. Operate wildland fire engines and hoselays. Monitor prescribed burns to ensure that they are conducted safely and effectively. Direct and supervise prescribed burn projects and prepare post-burn reports analyzing burn conditions and results. Identify staff training and development needs to ensure that appropriate training can be arranged. Maintain knowledge of forest fire laws and fire-prevention techniques and tactics. Recommend equipment modifications or new equipment purchases. Perform administrative duties such as compiling and maintaining records, completing forms, preparing reports, and composing correspondence. Recruit and hire forest firefighting personnel. Train workers in such skills as parachute jumping, fire suppression, aerial observation, and radio communication both in the classroom and on the job.

Education/Training Required: Work experience in a related occupation. **Education and Training Programs:** Fire Prevention and Safety Technology/Technician; Fire Services Administration. **Knowledge/Courses:** Public Safety and Security; Building and Construction; Mechanical Devices; Customer and Personal Service; Personnel and Human Resources; Transportation.

Personality Type: Enterprising-Realistic-Conventional. **Career Cluster:** 12 Law, Public Safety, Corrections, and Security. **Career Pathway:** 12.2 Emergency and Fire Management Services. **Other Jobs in This Pathway:** Correctional Officers and Jailers; Fire Inspectors; Fire Investigators; Forest Fire Inspectors and Prevention Specialists; Forest Firefighters; Municipal Fire Fighting and Prevention Supervisors; Municipal Firefighters.

Job Specialization: Municipal Fire Fighting and Prevention Supervisors

Supervise firefighters who control and extinguish municipal fires, protect life and property, and conduct rescue efforts. Assign firefighters to jobs at strategic locations to facilitate rescue of persons and maximize application of extinguishing agents. Provide emergency medical services and perform light-to-heavy rescue functions at emergencies. Assess nature and extent of fire, condition of building, danger to adjacent buildings, and water-supply status to determine crew or company requirements. Instruct and drill fire department personnel in assigned duties, including firefighting, medical care, hazardous materials response, fire prevention, and related subjects. Inspect and test new and existing fire-protection systems, fire-detection systems, and fire-safety equipment to ensure that they are operating properly. Compile and maintain records on personnel, accidents, equipment, and supplies. Perform maintenance and minor repairs on firefighting equipment, including vehicles, and write and submit proposals to modify, replace, and repair equipment. Prepare activity reports listing fire call locations, actions taken, fire types and probable causes, damage estimates, and situation dispositions. Evaluate the performance of assigned firefighting personnel. Direct the training of firefighters, assigning of instructors to training classes, and providing of supervisors with reports on training progress and status. Maintain required maps and records. Present and interpret fire-prevention and fire-code information to citizens' groups, organizations, contractors, engineers, and developers.

Education/Training Required: Work experience in a related occupation. **Education and Training Programs:** Fire Prevention and Safety Technology/Technician; Fire Services Administration. **Knowledge/Courses:** Building and Construction; Public Safety and Security; Medicine and Dentistry; Mechanical Devices; Chemistry; Personnel and Human Resources.

Personality Type: Enterprising-Realistic-Social. **Career Cluster:** 12 Law, Public Safety, Corrections, and Security. **Career Pathway:** 12.2 Emergency and Fire Management Services. **Other Jobs in This Pathway:** Correctional Officers and Jailers; Fire Inspectors; Fire Investigators; Forest Fire Fighting and Prevention Supervisors; Forest Fire Inspectors and Prevention Specialists; Forest Firefighters; Municipal Firefighters.

First-Line Supervisors of Landscaping, Lawn Service, and Groundskeeping Workers

- ❀ Annual Earnings: $41,860
- ❀ Earnings Growth Potential: Low (35.6%)
- ❀ Growth: 14.9%
- ❀ Annual Job Openings: 5,600
- ❀ Self-Employed: 50.4%

Skills—Most Important: Equipment Use/Maintenance Skills; Social Skills; Management Skills. **Other High-Level Skills:** Thought-Processing Skills; Communication Skills.

Plan, organize, direct, or coordinate activities of workers engaged in landscaping or groundskeeping activities such as planting and maintaining ornamental trees, shrubs, flowers, and lawns and applying fertilizers, pesticides, and other chemicals, according to contract specifications. May also coordinate activities of workers engaged in terracing hillsides, building retaining walls, constructing pathways, installing patios, and similar activities following a landscape design plan. Work may involve reviewing contracts to ascertain service, machine, and workforce requirements; answering inquiries from potential customers on methods, material, and price ranges; and preparing estimates according to labor, material, and machine costs. Establish and enforce operating procedures and work standards that will ensure adequate performance and personnel safety. Inspect completed work to ensure conformance to specifications, standards, and contract requirements. Direct activities of workers who perform duties such as landscaping, cultivating lawns, or pruning trees and shrubs. Schedule work for crews depending on work priorities, crew and equipment availability, and weather conditions. Plant and maintain vegetation through activities such as mulching, fertilizing, watering, mowing, and pruning. Monitor project activities to ensure that instructions are followed, deadlines are met, and schedules are maintained. Train workers in tasks such as transplanting and pruning trees and shrubs, finishing cement, using equipment, and caring for turf. Inventory tools, equipment, and materials to ensure that sufficient supplies are available and items are in usable condition. Provide workers with assistance in performing duties as necessary to meet deadlines. Confer with other supervisors to coordinate work activities with other departments or units. Perform personnel-related activities such as hiring workers, evaluating staff performance, and taking disciplinary actions when performance problems occur. Direct or perform mixing and application of fertilizers, insecticides, herbicides, and fungicides. Review contracts or work assignments to determine service, machine, and workforce requirements for jobs.

Education/Training Required: Work experience in a related occupation. **Education and Training Programs:** Landscaping and Groundskeeping; Ornamental Horticulture; Turf and Turfgrass Management. **Knowledge/ Courses:** Mechanical Devices; Building and Construction; Design; Biology; Chemistry; Education and Training.

Personality Type: Enterprising-Realistic-Conventional. **Career Cluster:** 01 Agriculture, Food, and Natural Resources. **Career Pathway:** 01.2 Plant Systems. **Other Jobs in This Pathway:** Agricultural Technicians; Animal Scientists; Biochemists and Biophysicists; Biologists; Economists; Environmental Economists; Farm and Home Management Advisors; First-Line Supervisors of Retail Sales Workers; Floral Designers; Food Science Technicians; Food Scientists and Technologists; Geneticists; Grounds Maintenance Workers, All Other; Landscaping and Groundskeeping Workers; Pesticide Handlers, Sprayers, and Applicators, Vegetation; Precision Agriculture Technicians; Retail Salespersons; Soil and Plant Scientists; Tree Trimmers and Pruners.

First-Line Supervisors of Mechanics, Installers, and Repairers

❀ Annual Earnings: $59,150

❀ Earnings Growth Potential: Medium (39.2%)

❀ Growth: 4.2%

❀ Annual Job Openings: 13,650

❀ Self-Employed: 0.4%

Skills—Most Important: Equipment Use/ Maintenance Skills; Management Skills; Social Skills. **Other High-Level Skills:** Mathematics Skills; Thought-Processing Skills; Communication Skills.

Supervise and coordinate the activities of mechanics, installers, and repairers. Determine schedules, sequences, and assignments for work activities based on work priority, quantity of equipment, and skill of personnel. Patrol and monitor work areas and examine tools and equipment to detect unsafe conditions or violations of procedures or safety rules. Monitor employees' work levels and review work performance. Examine objects, systems, or facilities and analyze information to determine needed installations, services, or repairs. Participate in budget preparation and administration, coordinating purchasing and documentation and monitoring departmental expenditures. Counsel employees about work-related issues and assist employees to correct job-skill deficiencies. Requisition materials and supplies such as tools, equipment, and replacement parts. Compute estimates and actual costs of factors such as materials, labor, and outside contractors. Conduct or arrange for worker training in safety, repair, and maintenance techniques, operational procedures, or equipment use. Interpret specifications, blueprints, and job orders to construct templates and lay out reference points for workers. Investigate accidents and injuries and prepare reports of findings. Confer with personnel such as management, engineering, quality control, customer, and union workers' representatives to coordinate work activities, resolve employee grievances, and identify and review resource needs.

Education/Training Required: Work experience in a related occupation. **Education and Training Program:** Operations Management and Supervision. **Knowledge/ Courses:** Mechanical Devices; Personnel and Human Resources; Production and Processing; Building and Construction; Engineering and Technology; Economics and Accounting.

Personality Type: Enterprising-Conventional-Realistic. **Career Cluster:** 13 Manufacturing. **Career Pathway:** 13.1 Production. **Other Jobs in This Pathway:** Assemblers and Fabricators, All Other; Cabinetmakers and Bench Carpenters; Coating, Painting, and Spraying Machine Setters, Operators, and Tenders; Computer-Controlled Machine Tool Operators, Metal and Plastic; Cost Estimators; Cutting, Punching, and Press Machine Setters, Operators, and Tenders, Metal and Plastic; First-Line Supervisors of Production and Operating Workers; Geothermal Technicians; Grinding, Lapping, Polishing, and Buffing Machine Tool Setters, Operators, and Tenders, Metal and Plastic; Helpers—Production Workers; Machine Feeders and Offbearers; Machinists; Mixing and Blending Machine Setters, Operators, and Tenders; Molding, Coremaking, and Casting Machine Setters, Operators, and Tenders, Metal and Plastic; Packaging and Filling Machine Operators and Tenders; Packers and Packagers, Hand; Paper Goods Machine Setters, Operators,

and Tenders; Production Workers, All Other; Recycling and Reclamation Workers; Recycling Coordinators; Sheet Metal Workers; Solderers and Brazers; Structural Metal Fabricators and Fitters; Team Assemblers; Welders, Cutters, and Welder Fitters; others.

First-Line Supervisors of Non-Retail Sales Workers

* Annual Earnings: $68,880
* Earnings Growth Potential: High (46.2%)
* Growth: 4.8%
* Annual Job Openings: 12,950
* Self-Employed: 45.6%

Skills—Most Important: Management Skills; Social Skills; Thought-Processing Skills. **Other High-Level Skills:** Mathematics Skills; Communication Skills.

Directly supervise and coordinate activities of sales workers other than retail sales workers. May perform duties such as budgeting, accounting, and personnel work in addition to supervisory duties. Listen to and resolve customer complaints on services, products, or personnel. Monitor sales staff performance to ensure that goals are met. Hire, train, and evaluate personnel. Confer with company officials to develop methods and procedures to increase sales, expand markets, and promote business. Direct and supervise employees engaged in sales, taking inventory, reconciling cash receipts, or performing specific services such as pumping gasoline for customers. Provide staff with assistance in performing difficult or complicated duties. Plan and prepare work schedules and assign employees to specific duties. Attend company meetings to exchange product information and coordinate work activities with other departments. Prepare sales and inventory reports for management and budget departments. Formulate pricing policies on merchandise according to profitability requirements. Examine merchandise to ensure correct pricing and display and that it functions as advertised. Analyze details of sales territories to assess their growth potential and to set quotas. Visit retailers and sales representatives to promote products and gather information. Keep records pertaining to purchases, sales, and requisitions. Coordinate sales promotion activities and prepare merchandise displays and advertising copy. Prepare rental or lease agreements, specifying charges and payment procedures for use of machinery, tools, or other items.

Education/Training Required: Work experience in a related occupation. **Education and Training Programs:** Business, Management, Marketing, and Related Support Services, Other; General Merchandising, Sales, and Related Marketing Operations, Other; Special Products Marketing Operations; Specialized Merchandising, Sales, and Marketing Operations, Other. **Knowledge/Courses:** Sales and Marketing; Economics and Accounting; Personnel and Human Resources; Administration and Management; Mathematics; Clerical.

Personality Type: Enterprising-Conventional-Social. **Career Cluster:** 14 Marketing, Sales, and Service. **Career Pathway:** 14.2 Professional Sales and Marketing. **Other Jobs in This Pathway:** Cashiers; Counter and Rental Clerks; Door-To-Door Sales Workers, News and Street Vendors, and Related Workers; Driver/Sales Workers; Energy Brokers; First-Line Supervisors of Retail Sales Workers; Hotel, Motel, and Resort Desk Clerks; Marketing Managers; Marking Clerks; Online Merchants;

Order Fillers, Wholesale and Retail Sales; Parts Salespersons; Property, Real Estate, and Community Association Managers; Real Estate Sales Agents; Reservation and Transportation Ticket Agents and Travel Clerks; Retail Salespersons; Sales and Related Workers, All Other; Sales Representatives, Services, All Other; Sales Representatives, Wholesale and Manufacturing, Except Technical and Scientific Products; Sales Representatives, Wholesale and Manufacturing, Technical and Scientific Products; Solar Sales Representatives and Assessors; Stock Clerks—Stockroom, Warehouse, or Storage Yard; Stock Clerks, Sales Floor; Telemarketers; Wholesale and Retail Buyers, Except Farm Products; others.

First-Line Supervisors of Office and Administrative Support Workers

* Annual Earnings: $47,460
* Earnings Growth Potential: Medium (39.2%)
* Growth: 11.0%
* Annual Job Openings: 48,900
* Self-Employed: 1.4%

Skills—Most Important: Management Skills; Social Skills; Thought-Processing Skills. **Other High-Level Skills:** Communication Skills; Mathematics Skills.

Supervise and coordinate the activities of clerical and administrative support workers. Resolve customer complaints and answer customers' questions on policies and procedures. Supervise the work of office, administrative, or customer service employees to ensure adherence to quality standards, deadlines, and proper procedures, correcting errors or problems. Provide employees with guidance in handling difficult or complex problems and in resolving escalated complaints or disputes. Implement corporate and departmental policies, procedures, and service standards in conjunction with management. Train and instruct employees in job duties and company policies or arrange for training to be provided. Discuss job performance problems with employees to identify causes and issues and to work on resolving problems. Evaluate employees' job performance and conformance to regulations and recommend appropriate personnel action. Recruit, interview, and select employees. Review records and reports pertaining to activities such as production, payroll, and shipping to verify details, monitor work activities, and evaluate performance. Interpret and communicate work procedures and company policies to staff. Prepare and issue work schedules, deadlines, and duty assignments of office or administrative staff. Maintain records pertaining to inventory, personnel, orders, supplies, and machine maintenance. Compute figures such as balances, totals, and commissions.

Education/Training Required: Work experience in a related occupation. **Education and Training Programs:** Agricultural Business Technology; Customer Service Management; Medical Staff Services Technology/Technician; Medical/Health Management and Clinical Assistant/Specialist Training; Office Management and Supervision. **Knowledge/ Courses:** Clerical Practices; Economics and Accounting; Administration and Management; Personnel and Human Resources; Customer and Personal Service; Education and Training.

Personality Type: Enterprising-Conventional-Social. **Career Clusters:** 01 Agriculture, Food, and Natural Resources; 04 Business, Management, and Administration; 08 Health Science. **Career Pathways:** 01.1 Food Products and Processing Systems; 08.3 Health Informatics; 04.1 Management. **Other Jobs in These Pathways:** Brownfield Redevelopment Specialists and Site Managers; Business Continuity Planners; Business Operations Specialists, All Other; Chief Executives; Chief Sustainability Officers; Compliance Managers; Construction Managers; Customs Brokers; Energy Auditors; Executive Secretaries and Executive Administrative Assistants; General and Operations Managers; Investment Fund Managers; Loss Prevention Managers; Management Analysts; Managers, All Other; Medical Assistants; Medical Secretaries; Receptionists and Information Clerks; Regulatory Affairs Managers; Security Management Specialists; Security Managers; Supply Chain Managers; Sustainability Specialists; Wind Energy Operations Managers; Wind Energy Project Managers; others.

First-Line Supervisors of Personal Service Workers

* Annual Earnings: $35,290
* Earnings Growth Potential: Medium (37.9%)
* Growth: 15.4%
* Annual Job Openings: 9,080
* Self-Employed: 37.8%

Skills—Most Important: Management Skills; Social Skills; Communication Skills. **Other High-Level Skills:** Equipment Use/Maintenance Skills; Thought-Processing Skills.

Supervise and coordinate activities of personal service workers such as flight

attendants, hairdressers, or caddies.
Requisition supplies, equipment, and services. Inform workers about interests and special needs of specific groups. Participate in continuing education to stay abreast of industry trends and developments. Meet with managers and other supervisors to stay informed of changes affecting operations. Collaborate with staff members to plan and develop programs of events, schedules of activities, or menus. Train workers in proper operational procedures and functions and explain company policies. Furnish customers with information on events and activities. Resolve customer complaints on worker performance and services rendered. Analyze and record personnel and operational data and write related activity reports. Observe and evaluate workers' appearance and performance to ensure quality service and compliance with specifications. Inspect work areas and operating equipment to ensure conformance to established standards in areas such as cleanliness and maintenance. Direct and coordinate the activities of workers such as flight attendants, hotel staff, or hairstylists. Assign work schedules, following work requirements, to ensure quality and timely delivery of service. Apply customer/guest feedback to service improvement efforts. Direct marketing, advertising, and other customer recruitment efforts. Take disciplinary action to address performance problems. Recruit and hire staff members.

Education/Training Required: Work experience in a related occupation. **Education and Training Program:** Business, Management, Marketing, and Related Support Services, Other. **Knowledge/Courses:** Psychology; Therapy and Counseling; Education and Training; Philosophy and Theology; Public Safety and Security; Medicine and Dentistry.

Personality Type: Enterprising-Conventional-Social. **Career Cluster:** 04 Business, Management, and Administration. **Career Pathway:** 04.1 Management. **Other Jobs in This Pathway:** Brownfield Redevelopment Specialists and Site Managers; Business Continuity Planners; Business Operations Specialists, All Other; Chief Executives; Chief Sustainability Officers; Compliance Managers; Computer and Information Systems Managers; Construction Managers; Customs Brokers; Energy Auditors; First-Line Supervisors of Office and Administrative Support Workers; General and Operations Managers; Investment Fund Managers; Loss Prevention Managers; Management Analysts; Managers, All Other; Public Relations Specialists; Regulatory Affairs Managers; Sales Managers; Security Management Specialists; Security Managers; Supply Chain Managers; Sustainability Specialists; Wind Energy Operations Managers; Wind Energy Project Managers; others.

Job Specialization: Spa Managers

Plan, direct, or coordinate activities of a spa facility. Coordinate programs, schedule and direct staff, and oversee financial activities.
Inform staff of job responsibilities, performance expectations, client service standards, or corporate policies and guidelines. Plan or direct spa services and programs. Train staff in the use or sale of products, programs, or activities. Assess employee performance and suggest ways to improve work. Check spa equipment to ensure proper functioning. Coordinate facility schedules to maximize usage and efficiency. Develop staff service or retail goals and guide staff in goal achievement. Establish spa budgets and financial goals. Inventory products and order supplies. Monitor operations to ensure compliance with applicable health, safety, or

hygiene standards. Perform accounting duties, such as recording daily cash flow, preparing bank deposits, or generating financial statements. Recruit, interview, or hire employees. Respond to customer inquiries or complaints. Schedule staff or supervise scheduling. Verify staff credentials, such as educational and certification requirements. Develop or implement marketing strategies. Direct facility maintenance or repair. Maintain client databases. Participate in continuing education classes to maintain current knowledge of industry. Schedule guest appointments. Sell products, services, or memberships.

Education/Training Required: Work experience in a related occupation. **Education and Training Program:** Resort Management. **Knowledge/Courses:** No data available.

Personality Type: Enterprising-Conventional-Social. **Career Cluster:** 04 Business, Management, and Administration. **Career Pathway:** 04.1 Management. **Other Jobs in This Pathway:** Brownfield Redevelopment Specialists and Site Managers; Business Continuity Planners; Business Operations Specialists, All Other; Chief Executives; Chief Sustainability Officers; Compliance Managers; Computer and Information Systems Managers; Construction Managers; Customs Brokers; Energy Auditors; First-Line Supervisors of Office and Administrative Support Workers; General and Operations Managers; Investment Fund Managers; Loss Prevention Managers; Management Analysts; Managers, All Other; Public Relations Specialists; Regulatory Affairs Managers; Sales Managers; Security Management Specialists; Security Managers; Supply Chain Managers; Sustainability Specialists; Wind Energy Operations Managers; Wind Energy Project Managers; others.

First-Line Supervisors of Police and Detectives

- ❋ Annual Earnings: $78,260
- ❋ Earnings Growth Potential: Medium (40.4%)
- ❋ Growth: 8.1%
- ❋ Annual Job Openings: 5,050
- ❋ Self-Employed: 0.0%

Skills—Most Important: Management Skills; Social Skills; Thought-Processing Skills. **Other High-Level Skills:** Communication Skills; Mathematics Skills; Equipment Use/Maintenance Skills.

Supervise and coordinate activities of members of police force. Explain police operations to subordinates to assist them in performing their job duties. Inform personnel of changes in regulations and policies, implications of new or amended laws, and new techniques of police work. Supervise and coordinate the investigation of criminal cases, offering guidance and expertise to investigators and ensuring that procedures are conducted in accordance with laws and regulations. Investigate and resolve personnel problems within organization and charges of misconduct against staff. Train staff in proper police work procedures. Maintain logs, prepare reports, and direct the preparation, handling, and maintenance of departmental records. Monitor and evaluate the job performance of subordinates and authorize promotions and transfers. Direct collection, preparation, and handling of evidence and personal property of prisoners. Develop, implement, and revise departmental policies and procedures. Conduct raids and order detention of witnesses and suspects for questioning. Prepare work schedules and assign duties to subordinates. Discipline staff for violation of department rules and regulations. Cooperate with court personnel and officials from other law enforcement agencies and testify in court as necessary. Review contents of written orders to ensure adherence to legal requirements. Inspect facilities, supplies, vehicles, and equipment to ensure conformance to standards. Prepare news releases and respond to police correspondence.

Education/Training Required: Work experience in a related occupation. **Education and Training Programs:** Corrections; Criminal Justice/Law Enforcement Administration; Criminal Justice/Safety Studies. **Knowledge/Courses:** Public Safety and Security; Law and Government; Psychology; Sociology and Anthropology; Therapy and Counseling; Personnel and Human Resources.

Personality Type: Enterprising-Social-Conventional. **Career Cluster:** 12 Law, Public Safety, Corrections, and Security. **Career Pathways:** 12.4 Law Enforcement Services; 12.1 Correction Services. **Other Jobs in These Pathways:** Bailiffs; Child, Family, and School Social Workers; Correctional Officers and Jailers; Criminal Investigators and Special Agents; First-Line Supervisors of Correctional Officers; Forensic Science Technicians; Immigration and Customs Inspectors; Intelligence Analysts; Police Detectives; Police Identification and Records Officers; Police Patrol Officers; Protective Service Workers, All Other; Remote Sensing Scientists and Technologists; Security Guards; Sheriffs and Deputy Sheriffs.

Fitness Trainers and Aerobics Instructors

- ✷ Annual Earnings: $31,090
- ✷ Earnings Growth Potential: High (45.1%)
- ✷ Growth: 29.4%
- ✷ Annual Job Openings: 12,380
- ✷ Self-Employed: 9.2%

Skills—Most Important: Social Skills; Thought-Processing Skills; Communication Skills.

Instruct or coach groups or individuals in exercise activities and the fundamentals of sports. Demonstrate techniques and methods of participation. Observe participants and inform them of corrective measures necessary to improve their skills. Instruct participants in maintaining exertion levels to maximize benefits from exercise routines. Offer alternatives during classes to accommodate different levels of fitness. Plan routines, choose appropriate music, and choose different movements for each set of muscles depending on participants' capabilities and limitations. Teach proper breathing techniques used during physical exertion. Evaluate individuals' abilities, needs, and physical conditions and develop suitable training programs to meet any special requirements. Explain and enforce safety rules and regulations governing sports, recreational activities, and the use of exercise equipment. Monitor participants' progress and adapt programs as needed. Provide students with information and resources on nutrition, weight control, and lifestyle issues. Administer emergency first aid, wrap injuries, treat minor chronic disabilities, or refer injured persons to physicians. Advise clients about proper clothing and shoes. Maintain fitness equipment. Teach and demonstrate use of gymnastic and training equipment such as trampolines and weights. Plan physical education programs to promote development of participants' physical attributes and social skills. Wrap ankles, fingers, wrists, or other body parts with synthetic skin, gauze, or adhesive tape to support muscles and ligaments.

Education/Training Required: Postsecondary vocational training. **Education and Training Programs:** Health and Physical Education, General; Physical Education Teaching and Coaching; Sport and Fitness Administration/Management. **Knowledge/Courses:** Education and Training; Therapy and Counseling; Psychology; Customer and Personal Service; Medicine and Dentistry; Biology.

Personality Type: Social-Realistic-Enterprising. **Career Cluster:** 05 Education and Training. **Career Pathways:** 05.3 Teaching/Training; 05.1 Administration and Administrative Support. **Other Jobs in These Pathways:** Adult Basic and Secondary Education and Literacy Teachers and Instructors; Career/Technical Education Teachers, Secondary School; Chemists; Coaches and Scouts; Dietitians and Nutritionists; Distance Learning Coordinators; Education Administrators, All Other; Education Administrators, Elementary and Secondary School; Education Administrators, Postsecondary; Education Administrators, Preschool and Childcare Center/Program; Elementary School Teachers, Except Special Education; Fitness and Wellness Coordinators; Instructional Coordinators; Instructional Designers and Technologists; Interpreters and Translators; Kindergarten Teachers, Except Special Education; Librarians; Middle School Teachers, Except Special and Career/Technical Education; Preschool Teachers, Except Special

Education; Recreation Workers; Secondary School Teachers, Except Special and Career/Technical Education; Self-Enrichment Education Teachers; Teacher Assistants; Teachers and Instructors, All Other; Tutors; others.

General and Operations Managers

- ❋ Annual Earnings: $94,400
- ❋ Earnings Growth Potential: High (49.9%)
- ❋ Growth: −0.1%
- ❋ Annual Job Openings: 50,220
- ❋ Self-Employed: 0.9%

Skills—Most Important: Management Skills; Thought-Processing Skills; Social Skills. **Other High-Level Skills:** Communication Skills; Equipment Use/Maintenance Skills.

Plan, direct, or coordinate the operations of companies or public- and private-sector organizations. Duties and responsibilities include formulating policies, managing daily operations, and planning the use of materials and human resources but are too diverse and general to be classified in any one functional area of management or administration, such as personnel, purchasing, or administrative services. Includes owners and managers who head small business establishments whose duties are primarily managerial. Direct and coordinate activities of businesses or departments concerned with the production, pricing, sales, or distribution of products. Manage staff, preparing work schedules and assigning specific duties. Review financial statements, sales and activity reports, and other performance data to measure productivity and goal achievement and to determine areas needing cost reduction and program improvement. Establish and implement departmental policies, goals, objectives, and procedures, conferring with board members, organization officials, and staff members as necessary. Determine staffing requirements and interview, hire, and train new employees or oversee those personnel processes. Monitor businesses and agencies to ensure that they efficiently and effectively provide needed services while staying within budgetary limits. Oversee activities directly related to making products or providing services.

Education/Training Required: Work experience plus degree. **Education and Training Programs:** Business Administration and Management, General; Entrepreneurship/Entrepreneurial Studies; International Business/Trade/Commerce; Public Administration. **Knowledge/Courses:** Economics and Accounting; Personnel and Human Resources; Administration and Management; Sales and Marketing; Building and Construction; Clerical.

Personality Type: Enterprising-Conventional-Social. **Career Clusters:** 04 Business, Management, and Administration; 07 Government and Public Administration. **Career Pathways:** 04.1 Management; 07.1 Governance. **Other Jobs in These Pathways:** Administrative Services Managers; Brownfield Redevelopment Specialists and Site Managers; Business Continuity Planners; Business Operations Specialists, All Other; Chief Executives; Chief Sustainability Officers; Compliance Managers; Computer and Information Systems Managers; Construction Managers; Customs Brokers; Energy Auditors; First-Line Supervisors of Office and Administrative Support Workers; Investment Fund Managers; Loss Prevention Managers; Management Analysts; Managers, All

Other; Public Relations Specialists; Regulatory Affairs Managers; Sales Managers; Security Management Specialists; Security Managers; Supply Chain Managers; Sustainability Specialists; Wind Energy Operations Managers; Wind Energy Project Managers; others.

Geoscientists, Except Hydrologists and Geographers

* Annual Earnings: $82,500
* Earnings Growth Potential: High (46.9%)
* Growth: 17.5%
* Annual Job Openings: 1,540
* Self-Employed: 2.4%

Skills—Most Important: Science Skills; Mathematics Skills; Communication Skills. **Other High-Level Skills:** Thought-Processing Skills; Management Skills; Social Skills.

Study the composition, structure, and other physical aspects of Earth. May use knowledge of geology, physics, and mathematics in exploration for oil, gas, minerals, or underground water or in waste disposal, land reclamation, or other environmental problems. May study Earth's internal composition, atmospheres, and oceans and its magnetic, electrical, and gravitational forces. Includes mineralogists, crystallographers, paleontologists, stratigraphers, geodesists, and seismologists. Analyze and interpret geological, geochemical, and geophysical information from sources such as survey data, well logs, bore holes, and aerial photos. Plan and conduct geological, geochemical, and geophysical field studies and surveys, sample collection, or drilling and testing programs used to collect data for research or application. Investigate the composition, structure, and history of the earth's crust through the collection, examination, measurement, and classification of soils, minerals, rocks, or fossil remains. Prepare geological maps, cross-sectional diagrams, charts, and reports on mineral extraction, land use, and resource management using results of field work and laboratory research. Locate and estimate probable natural gas, oil, and mineral ore deposits and underground water resources using aerial photographs, charts, or research and survey results. Assess ground and surface water movement to provide advice on issues such as waste management, route and site selection, and the restoration of contaminated sites. Identify risks for natural disasters such as mud slides, earthquakes, and volcanic eruptions, providing advice on mitigation of potential damage. Conduct geological and geophysical studies to provide information for use in regional development, site selection, and development of public works projects.

Education/Training Required: Master's degree. **Education and Training Programs:** Geochemistry; Geochemistry and Petrology; Geological and Earth Sciences/Geosciences, Other; Geology/Earth Science, General; Geophysics and Seismology; Oceanography, Chemical and Physical; Paleontology. **Knowledge/Courses:** Geography; Engineering and Technology; Physics; Chemistry; Mathematics; Design.

Personality Type: Investigative-Realistic. **Career Cluster:** 15 Science, Technology, Engineering, and Mathematics. **Career Pathway:** 15.2 Science and Mathematics. **Other Jobs in This Pathway:** Architectural and Engineering Managers; Biochemists and Biophysicists; Biofuels/Biodiesel Technology and Product Development Managers; Bioinformatics Scientists; Biological Scientists, All Other; Biologists; Biostatisticians; Chemists; Clinical Data Managers; Clinical Research Coordinators; Community and Social Service Specialists, All Other; Dietitians and Nutritionists; Education, Training, and Library Workers, All Other; Geneticists; Medical Scientists, Except Epidemiologists; Molecular and Cellular Biologists; Natural Sciences Managers; Operations Research Analysts; Physical Scientists, All Other; Social Scientists and Related Workers, All Other; Statisticians; Survey Researchers; Transportation Planners; Water Resource Specialists; Zoologists and Wildlife Biologists; others.

Graphic Designers

- ❋ Annual Earnings: $43,500
- ❋ Earnings Growth Potential: Medium (39.8%)
- ❋ Growth: 12.9%
- ❋ Annual Job Openings: 12,480
- ❋ Self-Employed: 26.3%

Skills—Most Important: Thought-Processing Skills; Management Skills; Social Skills.

Design or create graphics to meet specific commercial or promotional needs such as packaging, displays, or logos. May use a variety of media to achieve artistic or decorative effects. Create designs, concepts, and sample layouts based on knowledge of layout principles and aesthetic design concepts. Determine size and arrangement of illustrative material and copy and select style and size of type. Use computer software to generate new images. Draw and print charts, graphs, illustrations, and other artwork using computer.

Review final layouts and suggest improvements as needed. Confer with clients to discuss and determine layout design. Key information into computer equipment to create layouts for client or supervisor. Develop graphics and layouts for product illustrations, company logos, and Internet Websites. Prepare illustrations or rough sketches of material, discussing them with clients or supervisors and making necessary changes. Study illustrations and photographs to plan presentation of materials, products, or services. Prepare notes and instructions for workers who assemble and prepare final layouts for printing. Produce still and animated graphics for on-air and taped portions of television news broadcasts.

Education/Training Required: Bachelor's degree. **Education and Training Programs:** Agricultural Communication/Journalism; Commercial and Advertising Art; Computer Graphics; Design and Visual Communications, General; Graphic Design; Industrial and Product Design; Web Page, Digital/Multimedia and Information Resources Design. **Knowledge/Courses:** Fine Arts; Design; Communications and Media; Sales and Marketing; Sociology and Anthropology; Computers and Electronics.

Personality Type: Artistic-Realistic-Enterprising. **Career Clusters:** 03 Arts, Audio/Video Technology, and Communications; 11 Information Technology. **Career Pathways:** 11.1 Network Systems; 03.1 Audio and Video Technology and Film; 03.3 Visual Arts. **Other Jobs in These Pathways:** Agents and Business Managers of Artists, Performers, and Athletes; Art Directors; Artists and Related Workers, All Other; Audio and Video Equipment Technicians; Broadcast Technicians; Camera Operators, Television, Video, and Motion Picture; Choreographers; Commercial and Industrial Designers; Computer and Information Systems Managers; Craft Artists; Dancers; Designers, All Other; Farm and Home Management Advisors; Fashion Designers; Film and Video Editors; Fine Artists, Including Painters, Sculptors, and Illustrators; Interior Designers; Managers, All Other; Media and Communication Equipment Workers, All Other; Media and Communication Workers, All Other; Multimedia Artists and Animators; Painting, Coating, and Decorating Workers; Photographers; Reporters and Correspondents; Technical Directors/Managers; others.

Health Specialties Teachers, Postsecondary

- ❀ Annual Earnings: $85,270
- ❀ Earnings Growth Potential: Very high (52.7%)
- ❀ Growth: 15.1%
- ❀ Annual Job Openings: 4,000
- ❀ Self-Employed: 0.2%

Skills—Most Important: Science Skills; Communication Skills; Thought-Processing Skills. **Other High-Level Skills:** Social Skills; Mathematics Skills; Management Skills.

Teach courses in health specialties, such as veterinary medicine, dentistry, pharmacy, therapy, laboratory technology, and public health. Initiate, facilitate, and moderate classroom discussions. Keep abreast of developments in the field by reading current literature, talking with colleagues, and participating in professional conferences. Compile, administer, and grade examinations or assign this work to others. Evaluate and grade students' classwork, assignments, and papers. Prepare course materials such as syllabi, homework assignments, and handouts. Prepare and deliver lectures to undergraduate or graduate students on topics such as public health, stress management, and work-site health promotion. Plan, evaluate, and revise curricula, course content, course materials, and methods of instruction. Supervise undergraduate or graduate teaching, internship, and research work. Conduct research in a particular field of knowledge and publish findings in professional journals, books, or electronic media. Collaborate with colleagues to address teaching and research issues. Supervise laboratory sessions. Maintain student attendance records, grades, and other required records. Maintain regularly scheduled office hours to advise and assist students. Advise students on academic and vocational curricula and on career issues. Participate in student recruitment, registration, and placement activities. Serve on academic or administrative committees that deal with institutional policies, departmental matters, and academic issues. Select and obtain materials and supplies such as textbooks and laboratory equipment.

Education/Training Required: Doctoral degree. **Education and Training Programs:** Art Therapy; Asian Bodywork Therapy; Audiology and Speech-Language Pathology; Biostatistics; Blood Bank Technology Specialist Training; Cardiovascular Technology; Chiropractic; Clinical Laboratory Science/Medical Technology; Clinical Laboratory Assistant Training; Clinical Laboratory Technician; Cytotechnology; Dance Therapy; Dental Assisting; Dental Hygiene; Dental Laboratory Technology; Dentistry; Diagnostic Medical Sonography and Ultrasound Technician Training; Electrocardiograph Technology; Emergency Medical Technology; Environmental Health; Medical Radiologic

Technology; Music Therapy; Nuclear Medical Technology; Occupational Health and Industrial Hygiene; Occupational Therapist Assistant Training; Occupational Therapy; Orthotist/ Prosthetist; Pharmacy; Pharmacy Technician Training; Physical Therapy Assistant Training; Physical Therapy; Physician Assistant Training; Respiratory Care Therapy; Speech-Language Pathology; Surgical Technology; Therapeutic Recreation/Recreational Therapy; Veterinary Medicine; Veterinary Clinical Sciences, General; Veterinary Technology; Vocational Rehabilitation Counseling; others. **Knowledge/Courses:** Medicine and Dentistry; Biology; Education and Training; Therapy and Counseling; Sociology and Anthropology; Psychology.

Personality Type: Social-Investigative. **Career Clusters:** 05 Education and Training; 08 Health Science; 15 Science, Technology, Engineering, and Mathematics. **Career Pathways:** 08.5 Biotechnology Research and Development; 15.2 Science and Mathematics; 05.3 Teaching/Training; 08.1 Therapeutic Services; 08.2 Diagnostics Services; 08.3 Health Informatics. **Other Jobs in These Pathways:** Coaches and Scouts; Dental Assistants; Elementary School Teachers, Except Special Education; Executive Secretaries and Executive Administrative Assistants; First-Line Supervisors of Office and Administrative Support Workers; Fitness Trainers and Aerobics Instructors; Home Health Aides; Licensed Practical and Licensed Vocational Nurses; Medical and Health Services Managers; Medical Assistants; Medical Secretaries; Middle School Teachers, Except Special and Career/Technical Education; Pharmacists; Pharmacy Technicians; Preschool Teachers, Except Special Education; Public Relations Specialists; Radiologic Technologists; Receptionists and Information Clerks; Recreation Workers; Secondary School Teachers,

Except Special and Career/Technical Education; Self-Enrichment Education Teachers; Social and Human Service Assistants; Teacher Assistants; Tutors; 37 other postsecondary teaching occupations; others.

Health Technologists and Technicians, All Other

❋ Annual Earnings: $38,460

❋ Earnings Growth Potential: Low (33.5%)

❋ Growth: 18.7%

❋ Annual Job Openings: 3,200

❋ Self-Employed: 5.7%

Skills—Most Important: Science Skills; Equipment Use/Maintenance Skills; Communication Skills. **Other High-Level Skills:** Social Skills; Thought-Processing Skills; Management Skills.

This occupation includes all health technologists and technicians not listed separately. Because this is a highly diverse occupation, no data is available for some information topics.

Education/Training Required: Postsecondary vocational training. **Education and Training Program:** Allied Health Diagnostic, Intervention, and Treatment Professions, Other. **Career Cluster:** 08 Health Science. **Career Pathways:** 08.1 Therapeutic Services; 08.2 Diagnostics Services. **Other Jobs in These Pathways:** Clinical Psychologists; Counseling Psychologists; Cytogenetic Technologists; Cytotechnologists; Dental Assistants; Dental Hygienists; Dentists, General; Emergency Medical Technicians and Paramedics; Endoscopy Technicians; Healthcare Support Workers, All

Other; Histotechnologists and Histologic Technicians; Home Health Aides; Licensed Practical and Licensed Vocational Nurses; Massage Therapists; Medical and Clinical Laboratory Technicians; Medical and Clinical Laboratory Technologists; Medical and Health Services Managers; Medical Assistants; Medical Secretaries; Pharmacists; Pharmacy Technicians; Radiologic Technologists; School Psychologists; Social and Human Service Assistants; Speech-Language Pathology Assistants; others.

Job Specialization: Neurodiagnostic Technologists

Conduct electroneurodiagnostic (END) tests such as electroencephalograms, evoked potentials, polysomnograms, or electronystagmograms. May perform nerve conduction studies. Attach electrodes to patients using adhesives. Summarize technical data to assist physicians to diagnose brain, sleep, or nervous system disorders. Conduct tests or studies such as electroencephalography (EEG), polysomnography (PSG), nerve conduction studies (NCS), electromyography (EMG), and intraoperative monitoring (IOM). Calibrate, troubleshoot, or repair equipment and correct malfunctions as needed. Conduct tests to determine cerebral death, the absence of brain activity, or the probability of recovery from a coma. Measure visual, auditory, or somatosensory evoked potentials (EPs) to determine responses to stimuli. Indicate artifacts or interferences derived from sources outside of the brain such as poor electrode contact or patient movement on electroneurodiagnostic recordings. Measure patients' body parts and mark locations where electrodes are to be placed.

Education/Training Required: Associate degree. **Education and Training Program:**

Electroneurodiagnostic/Electroencephalographic Technology/Technologist. **Knowledge/Courses:** Medicine and Dentistry; Biology; Psychology; Computers and Electronics; Customer and Personal Service; Clerical.

Personality Type: Realistic-Investigative. **Career Cluster:** 08 Health Science. **Career Pathway:** 08.2 Diagnostics Services. **Other Jobs in This Pathway:** Ambulance Drivers and Attendants, Except Emergency Medical Technicians; Anesthesiologist Assistants; Cardiovascular Technologists and Technicians; Cytogenetic Technologists; Cytotechnologists; Diagnostic Medical Sonographers; Emergency Medical Technicians and Paramedics; Endoscopy Technicians; Health Diagnosing and Treating Practitioners, All Other; Health Technologists and Technicians, All Other; Healthcare Practitioners and Technical Workers, All Other; Histotechnologists and Histologic Technicians; Medical and Clinical Laboratory Technicians; Medical and Clinical Laboratory Technologists; Medical and Health Services Managers; Medical Assistants; Medical Equipment Preparers; Nuclear Medicine Technologists; Ophthalmic Laboratory Technicians; Physical Scientists, All Other; Physician Assistants; Radiologic Technicians; Radiologic Technologists; Surgical Technologists; Veterinary Assistants and Laboratory Animal Caretakers; others.

Job Specialization: Ophthalmic Medical Technologists

Assist ophthalmologists by performing ophthalmic clinical functions and ophthalmic photography. Provide instruction and supervision to other ophthalmic personnel. Assist with minor surgical procedures, applying aseptic techniques and preparing instruments. May perform eye exams, administer eye medications, and instruct patients in care and use of corrective lenses. Administer topical ophthalmic or oral medications. Assess abnormalities of color vision, such as amblyopia. Assess refractive condition of eyes using retinoscope. Assist physicians in performing ophthalmic procedures, including surgery. Calculate corrections for refractive errors. Collect ophthalmic measurements or other diagnostic information using ultrasound equipment such as A-scan ultrasound biometry or B-scan ultrasonography equipment. Conduct binocular disparity tests to assess depth perception. Conduct ocular motility tests to measure function of eye muscles. Conduct tests, such as the Amsler Grid test, to measure central visual field used in the early diagnosis of macular degeneration, glaucoma, or diseases of the eye. Conduct tonometry or tonography tests to measure intraocular pressure. Conduct visual field tests to measure field of vision. Create three-dimensional images of the eye, using computed tomography (CT). Measure and record lens power using lensometers. Measure corneal curvature with keratometers or ophthalmometers to aid in the diagnosis of conditions, such as astigmatism. Measure corneal thickness using pachymeter or contact ultrasound methods. Measure the thickness of the retinal nerve using scanning laser polarimetry techniques to aid in diagnosis of glaucoma. Measure visual acuity, including near, distance, pinhole, or dynamic visual acuity using appropriate tests.

Education/Training Required: Associate degree. **Education and Training Program:** Ophthalmic Technician/Technologist Training.

Career Cluster: 08 Health Science. **Career Pathway:** 08.1 Therapeutic Services. **Other Jobs in This Pathway:** Clinical Psychologists; Community and Social Service Specialists, All Other; Counseling Psychologists; Dental Assistants; Dental Hygienists; Dentists, General; Health Technologists and Technicians, All Other; Healthcare Support Workers, All Other; Home Health Aides; Licensed Practical and Licensed Vocational Nurses; Low Vision Therapists, Orientation and Mobility Specialists, and Vision Rehabilitation Therapists; Massage Therapists; Medical and Clinical Laboratory Technicians; Medical and Health Services Managers; Medical Scientists, Except Epidemiologists; Medical Secretaries; Occupational Therapists; Pharmacists; Pharmacy Technicians; Radiologic Technologists; School Psychologists; Social and Human Service Assistants; Speech-Language Pathologists; Speech-Language Pathology Assistants; Substance Abuse and Behavioral Disorder Counselors; others.

Job Specialization: Radiologic Technicians

Maintain and use equipment and supplies necessary to demonstrate portions of the human body on X-ray film or fluoroscopic screen for diagnostic purposes. Use beam-restrictive devices and patient-shielding techniques to minimize radiation exposure to patient and staff. Position X-ray equipment and adjust controls to set exposure factors, such as time and distance. Position patient on examining table and set up and adjust equipment to obtain optimum view of specific body area as requested by physician. Determine patients' X-ray needs by reading requests or instructions from physicians. Make exposures necessary for the requested procedures, rejecting and repeating work that does not meet established standards. Process exposed radiographs using film processors or computer-generated methods. Explain procedures to patients to reduce anxieties and obtain cooperation. Perform procedures such as linear tomography, mammography, sonograms, joint and cyst aspirations, routine contrast studies, routine fluoroscopy, and examinations of the head, trunk, and extremities under supervision of physician. Prepare and set up X-ray room for patient. Provide assistance to physicians or other technologists in the performance of more complex procedures. Provide students and other technologists with suggestions of additional views, alternate positioning, or improved techniques to ensure the images produced are of the highest quality. Coordinate work of other technicians or technologists when procedures require more than one person.

Education/Training Required: Associate degree. **Education and Training Program:** Medical Radiologic Technology/Science—Radiation Therapist. **Knowledge/Courses:** Physics; Medicine and Dentistry; Psychology; Biology; Chemistry; Customer and Personal Service.

Personality Type: Realistic-Conventional-Social. **Career Cluster:** 08 Health Science. **Career Pathways:** 08.2 Diagnostics Services; 08.1 Therapeutic Services. **Other Jobs in These Pathways:** Clinical Psychologists; Counseling Psychologists; Cytogenetic Technologists; Cytotechnologists; Dental Assistants; Dental Hygienists; Dentists, General; Emergency Medical Technicians and Paramedics; Endoscopy Technicians; Healthcare Support Workers, All Other; Histotechnologists and Histologic Technicians; Home Health Aides; Licensed Practical and Licensed Vocational

Nurses; Massage Therapists; Medical and Clinical Laboratory Technicians; Medical and Clinical Laboratory Technologists; Medical and Health Services Managers; Medical Assistants; Medical Secretaries; Pharmacists; Pharmacy Technicians; Radiologic Technologists; School Psychologists; Social and Human Service Assistants; Speech-Language Pathology Assistants; others.

Job Specialization: Surgical Assistants

Assist surgeons during surgery by performing duties such as tissue retraction, insertion of tubes and intravenous lines, or closure of surgical wounds. Perform preoperative and postoperative duties to facilitate patient care. Adjust and maintain operating room temperature, humidity, or lighting according to surgeon's specifications. Apply sutures, staples, clips, or other materials to close skin, facia, or subcutaneous wound layers. Assess skin integrity or other body conditions upon completion of the procedure to determine if damage has occurred from body positioning. Assist in the insertion, positioning, or suturing of closed-wound drainage systems. Assist members of surgical team with gowning or gloving. Clamp, ligate, or cauterize blood vessels to control bleeding during surgical entry using hemostatic clamps, suture ligatures, or electrocautery equipment. Coordinate or participate in the positioning of patients using body-stabilizing equipment or protective padding to provide appropriate exposure for the procedure or to protect against nerve damage or circulation impairment. Coordinate with anesthesia personnel to maintain patient temperature. Discuss with surgeon the nature of the surgical procedure, including operative consent, methods of operative exposure, diagnostic or laboratory data, patient-advanced directives, or other needs. Incise tissue layers in lower extremities to harvest veins. Maintain an unobstructed operative field using surgical retractors, sponges, or suctioning and irrigating equipment. Monitor and maintain aseptic technique throughout procedures. Monitor patient intra-operative status, including patient position, vital signs, or volume or color of blood.

Education/Training Required: Work experience plus degree. **Education and Training Program:** Surgical Technology/Technologist.

Career Cluster: 08 Health Science. **Career Pathway:** 08.1 Therapeutic Services. **Other Jobs in This Pathway:** Clinical Psychologists; Community and Social Service Specialists, All Other; Counseling Psychologists; Dental Assistants; Dental Hygienists; Dentists, General; Health Technologists and Technicians, All Other; Healthcare Support Workers, All Other; Home Health Aides; Licensed Practical and Licensed Vocational Nurses; Low Vision Therapists, Orientation and Mobility Specialists, and Vision Rehabilitation Therapists; Massage Therapists; Medical and Clinical Laboratory Technicians; Medical and Health Services Managers; Medical Scientists, Except Epidemiologists; Medical Secretaries; Occupational Therapists; Pharmacists; Pharmacy Technicians; Radiologic Technologists; School Psychologists; Social and Human Service Assistants; Speech-Language Pathologists; Speech-Language Pathology Assistants; Substance Abuse and Behavioral Disorder Counselors; others.

Healthcare Social Workers

✳ Annual Earnings: $47,230

✳ Earnings Growth Potential: Medium (37.6%)

✳ Growth: 22.4%

✳ Annual Job Openings: 6,590

✳ Self-Employed: 2.2%

Skills—Most Important: Science Skills; Social Skills; Communication Skills. **Other High-Level Skills:** Thought-Processing Skills; Management Skills.

Provide persons, families, or vulnerable populations with the psychosocial support needed to cope with chronic, acute, or terminal illnesses such as Alzheimer's, cancer, or AIDS. Services include advising family caregivers, providing patient education and counseling, and making necessary referrals for other social services. Collaborate with other professionals to evaluate patients' medical or physical condition and to assess client needs. Investigate child abuse or neglect cases and take authorized protective action when necessary. Refer patient, client, or family to community resources to assist in recovery from mental or physical illness and to provide access to services such as financial assistance, legal aid, housing, job placement, or education. Counsel clients and patients in individual and group sessions to help them overcome dependencies, recover from illness, and adjust to life. Organize support groups or counsel family members to assist them in understanding, dealing with, and supporting the client or patient. Advocate for clients or patients to resolve crises. Identify environmental impediments to client or patient progress through interviews and review of patient records. Utilize consultation data and social work experience to plan and coordinate client or patient care and rehabilitation, following through to ensure service efficacy. Modify treatment plans to comply with changes in clients' status. Monitor, evaluate, and record client progress according to measurable goals described in treatment and care plan. Supervise and direct other workers providing services to clients or patients. Develop or advise on social policy and assist in community development. Oversee Medicaid- and Medicare-related paperwork and recordkeeping in hospitals.

Education/Training Required: Bachelor's degree. **Education and Training Program:** Clinical/Medical Social Work. **Knowledge/Courses:** Therapy and Counseling; Sociology and Anthropology; Psychology; Philosophy and Theology; Customer and Personal Service; Medicine and Dentistry.

Personality Type: Social-Investigative. **Career Cluster:** 10 Human Services. **Career Pathway:** 10.2 Counseling and Mental Health Services. **Other Jobs in This Pathway:** Clergy; Clinical Psychologists; Counseling Psychologists; Counselors, All Other; Directors, Religious Activities and Education; Epidemiologists; Health Educators; Marriage and Family Therapists; Mental Health and Substance Abuse Social Workers; Mental Health Counselors; Music Directors; Psychologists, All Other; Recreation Workers; Religious Workers, All Other; School Psychologists; Substance Abuse and Behavioral Disorder Counselors.

Heating, Air Conditioning, and Refrigeration Mechanics and Installers

❋ Annual Earnings: $42,530

❋ Earnings Growth Potential: Medium (37.7%)

❋ Growth: 28.1%

❋ Annual Job Openings: 13,620

❋ Self-Employed: 15.5%

Skills—Most Important: Installation Skills; Equipment Use/Maintenance Skills; Mathematics Skills. **Other High-Level Skills:** Management Skills; Thought-Processing Skills; Social Skills.

Job Specialization: Heating and Air Conditioning Mechanics and Installers

Install, service, and repair heating and air conditioning systems in residences and commercial establishments. Obtain and maintain required certifications. Comply with all applicable standards, policies, and procedures, including safety procedures and the maintenance of a clean work area. Repair or replace defective equipment, components, or wiring. Test electrical circuits and components for continuity using electrical test equipment. Reassemble and test equipment following repairs. Inspect and test system to verify system compliance with plans and specifications and to detect and locate malfunctions. Discuss heating-cooling system malfunctions with users to isolate problems or to verify that malfunctions have been corrected. Record and report all faults, deficiencies, and other unusual occurrences as well as the time and materials expended on work orders. Test pipe or tubing joints and connections for leaks using pressure gauge or soap-and-water solution. Adjust system controls to setting recommended by manufacturer to balance system using hand tools.

Education/Training Required: Long-term on-the-job training. **Education and Training Programs:** Heating, Air Conditioning, Ventilation, and Refrigeration Maintenance Technology/Technician (HAC, HACR, HVAC, HVACR); Heating, Ventilation, Air Conditioning, and Refrigeration Engineering Technology/Technician; Solar Energy Technology/Technician. **Knowledge/ Courses:** Mechanical Devices; Building and Construction; Physics; Chemistry; Design; Engineering and Technology.

Personality Type: Realistic-Conventional-Investigative. **Career Cluster:** 02 Architecture and Construction. **Career Pathways:** 02.3 Maintenance/Operations; 02.2 Construction. **Other Jobs in These Pathways:** Brickmasons and Blockmasons; Cement Masons and Concrete Finishers; Construction and Building Inspectors; Construction Carpenters; Construction Laborers; Construction Managers; Cost Estimators; Drywall and Ceiling Tile Installers; Electrical Power-Line Installers and Repairers; Electricians; Engineering Technicians, Except Drafters, All Other; Excavating and Loading Machine and Dragline Operators; First-Line Supervisors of Construction Trades and Extraction Workers; Helpers—Carpenters; Helpers—Electricians; Helpers—Pipelayers, Plumbers, Pipefitters, and Steamfitters; Highway Maintenance Workers; Operating Engineers and Other Construction Equipment Operators; Painters, Construction and Maintenance; Pipe Fitters and Steamfitters; Plumbers; Refrigeration Mechanics and Installers; Roofers; Rough Carpenters; Solar Energy Installation Managers; others.

Job Specialization—Refrigeration Mechanics and Installers

Install and repair industrial and commercial refrigerating systems. Braze or solder parts to repair defective joints and leaks. Observe and test system operation using gauges and instruments. Test lines, components, and connections for leaks. Dismantle malfunctioning systems and test components using electrical, mechanical, and pneumatic testing equipment. Adjust or replace worn or defective mechanisms and parts and reassemble repaired systems. Read blueprints to determine location, size, capacity, and type of components needed to build refrigeration system. Supervise and instruct assistants. Install wiring to connect components to an electric power source. Perform mechanical overhauls and refrigerant reclaiming. Cut, bend, thread, and connect pipe to functional components and water, power, or refrigeration system. Adjust valves according to specifications and charge system with proper type of refrigerant by pumping the specified gas or fluid into the system.

Education/Training Required: Long-term on-the-job training. **Education and Training Programs:** Heating, Air Conditioning, Ventilation, and Refrigeration Maintenance Technology/Technician (HAC, HACR, HVAC, HVACR); Heating, Ventilation, Air Conditioning, and Refrigeration Engineering Technology/Technician. **Knowledge/Courses:** Mechanical Devices; Physics; Building and Construction; Engineering and Technology; Design; Chemistry.

Personality Type: Realistic-Conventional-Enterprising. **Career Cluster:** 02 Architecture and Construction. **Career Pathways:** 02.2 Construction; 02.3 Maintenance/Operations. **Other Jobs in These Pathways:** Brickmasons and Blockmasons; Cement Masons and Concrete Finishers; Construction and Building Inspectors; Construction Carpenters; Construction Laborers; Construction Managers; Cost Estimators; Drywall and Ceiling Tile Installers; Electrical Power-Line Installers and Repairers; Electricians; Engineering Technicians, Except Drafters, All Other; Excavating and Loading Machine and Dragline Operators; First-Line Supervisors of Construction Trades and Extraction Workers; Heating and Air Conditioning Mechanics and Installers; Helpers—Carpenters; Helpers—Electricians; Helpers—Pipelayers, Plumbers, Pipefitters, and Steamfitters; Highway Maintenance Workers; Operating Engineers and Other Construction Equipment Operators; Painters, Construction and Maintenance; Pipe Fitters and Steamfitters; Plumbers; Roofers; Rough Carpenters; Solar Energy Installation Managers; others.

Heavy and Tractor-Trailer Truck Drivers

* Annual Earnings: $37,770
* Earnings Growth Potential: Low (34.5%)
* Growth: 12.9%
* Annual Job Openings: 55,460
* Self-Employed: 8.3%

Skills—Most Important: Equipment Use/Maintenance Skills.

Drive a tractor-trailer combination or a truck with a capacity of at least 26,000 GVW to transport and deliver goods, livestock, or materials in liquid, loose, or packaged form. May be required to unload truck. May require use of automated routing equipment. Requires commercial driver's license. Check vehicles to ensure that mechanical, safety, and emergency equipment is in good working order. Maintain logs of working hours or of vehicle service or repair status following applicable state and federal regulations. Obtain receipts or signatures for delivered goods and collect payment for services when required. Check all load-related documentation to ensure that it is complete and accurate. Maneuver trucks into loading or unloading positions following signals from loading crew and checking that vehicle and loading equipment are properly positioned. Drive trucks with capacities greater than 3 tons, including tractor-trailer combinations, to transport and deliver products, livestock, or other materials. Secure cargo for transport using ropes, blocks, chain, binders, or covers. Read bills of lading to determine assignment details. Report vehicle defects, accidents, traffic violations, or damage to the vehicles. Read and interpret maps to determine vehicle routes. Couple or uncouple trailers by changing trailer jack positions, connecting or disconnecting air or electrical lines, or manipulating fifth-wheel locks. Collect delivery instructions from appropriate sources, verifying instructions and routes. Drive trucks to weigh stations before and after loading and along routes to document weights and to comply with state regulations.

Education/Training Required: Moderate-term on-the-job training. **Education and Training Program:** Truck and Bus Driver Training/Commercial Vehicle Operator and Instructor Training. **Knowledge/Courses:** Transportation; Food Production; Mechanical Devices; Building and Construction; Design; Personnel and Human Resources.

Personality Type: Realistic-Conventional. **Career Cluster:** 16 Transportation, Distribution, and Logistics. **Career Pathway:** 16.1 Transportation Operations. **Other Jobs in This Pathway:** Airline Pilots, Copilots, and Flight Engineers; Automotive and Watercraft Service Attendants; Automotive Master Mechanics; Bus Drivers, School or Special Client; Bus Drivers, Transit and Intercity; Commercial Pilots; Crane and Tower Operators; First-Line Supervisors of Helpers, Laborers, and Material Movers, Hand; First-Line Supervisors of Transportation and Material-Moving Machine and Vehicle Operators; Freight and Cargo Inspectors; Laborers and Freight, Stock, and Material Movers, Hand; Light Truck or Delivery Services Drivers; Mates—Ship, Boat, and Barge; Motor Vehicle Operators, All Other; Operating Engineers and Other Construction Equipment Operators; Parking Lot Attendants; Pilots, Ship; Railroad Conductors and Yardmasters; Sailors and Marine Oilers; Ship and Boat Captains; Storage and Distribution Managers; Taxi Drivers and Chauffeurs; Transportation Inspectors; Transportation Managers; Transportation Workers, All Other; others.

Helpers—Electricians

- ❋ Annual Earnings: $27,220
- ❋ Earnings Growth Potential: Low (28.1%)
- ❋ Growth: 24.7%
- ❋ Annual Job Openings: 4,800
- ❋ Self-Employed: 2.1%

Skills—Most Important: Installation Skills; Equipment Use/Maintenance Skills.

Help electricians by performing duties of lesser skill. Duties include using, supplying, or holding materials or tools and cleaning work area and equipment. Trace out short circuits in wiring using test meter. Measure, cut, and bend wire and conduit using measuring instruments and hand tools. Maintain tools, vehicles, and equipment and keep parts and supplies in order. Drill holes and pull or push wiring through openings using hand and power tools. Perform semi-skilled and unskilled laboring duties related to the installation, maintenance, and repair of a wide variety of electrical systems and equipment. Disassemble defective electrical equipment, replace defective or worn parts, and reassemble equipment using hand tools. Transport tools, materials, equipment, and supplies to work site by hand, handtruck, or heavy, motorized truck. Examine electrical units for loose connections and broken insulation and tighten connections using hand tools. Strip insulation from wire ends using wire-stripping pliers and attach wires to terminals for soldering. Thread conduit ends, connect couplings, and fabricate and secure conduit support brackets using hand tools. Construct controllers and panels using power drills, drill presses, taps, saws, and punches. Clean work area and wash parts. Erect electrical system components and barricades and rig scaffolds, hoists, and shoring. Install copper-clad ground rods using a manual post driver. Raise, lower, or position equipment, tools, and materials using hoist, hand line, or block and tackle. Dig trenches or holes for installation of conduit or supports.

Education/Training Required: Short-term on-the-job training. **Education and Training Program:** Electrician. **Knowledge/Courses:** Mechanical Devices; Building and Construction; Design; Transportation; Physics; English Language.

Personality Type: Realistic-Conventional. **Career Cluster:** 02 Architecture and Construction. **Career Pathway:** 02.2 Construction. **Other Jobs in This Pathway:** Brickmasons and Blockmasons; Cement Masons and Concrete Finishers; Construction and Building Inspectors; Construction Carpenters; Construction Laborers; Construction Managers; Cost Estimators; Drywall and Ceiling Tile Installers; Electrical Power-Line Installers and Repairers; Electricians; Engineering Technicians, Except Drafters, All Other; Excavating and Loading Machine and Dragline Operators; First-Line Supervisors of Construction Trades and Extraction Workers; Heating and Air Conditioning Mechanics and Installers; Helpers—Carpenters; Helpers—Pipelayers, Plumbers, Pipefitters, and Steamfitters; Highway Maintenance Workers; Operating Engineers and Other Construction Equipment Operators; Painters, Construction and Maintenance; Pipe Fitters and Steamfitters; Plumbers; Refrigeration Mechanics and Installers; Roofers; Rough Carpenters; Solar Energy Installation Managers; others.

Helpers—Installation, Maintenance, and Repair Workers

* Annual Earnings: $24,260
* Earnings Growth Potential: Low (30.3%)
* Growth: 8.3%
* Annual Job Openings: 8,500
* Self-Employed: 0.6%

Skills—Most Important: Installation Skills; Equipment Use/Maintenance Skills.

Help installation, maintenance, and repair workers in maintenance, parts replacement, and repair of vehicles, industrial machinery, and electrical and electronic equipment. Perform duties such as furnishing tools, materials, and supplies to other workers; cleaning work area, machines, and tools; and holding materials or tools for other workers.

Tend and observe equipment and machinery to verify efficient and safe operation. Examine and test machinery, equipment, components, and parts for defects to ensure proper functioning. Adjust, connect, or disconnect wiring, piping, tubing, and other parts using hand or power tools. Install or replace machinery, equipment, and new or replacement parts and instruments using hand or power tools. Clean or lubricate vehicles, machinery, equipment, instruments, tools, work areas, and other objects using hand tools, power tools, and cleaning equipment. Apply protective materials to equipment, components, and parts to prevent defects and corrosion. Transfer tools, parts, equipment, and supplies to and from work stations and other areas. Disassemble broken or defective equipment to facilitate repair and reassemble equipment when repairs are complete. Assemble and maintain physical structures using hand or power tools. Position vehicles, machinery, equipment, physical structures, and other objects for assembly or installation using hand tools, power tools, and moving equipment. Hold or supply tools, parts, equipment, and supplies for other workers. Adjust, maintain, and repair tools, equipment, and machines and assist more skilled workers with similar tasks. Prepare work stations for use by mechanics and repairers. Order new parts to maintain inventory. Diagnose electrical problems and install and rewire electrical components.

Education/Training Required: Short-term on-the-job training. **Education and Training Program:** Industrial Mechanics and Maintenance Technology. **Knowledge/Courses:** Mechanical Devices; Building and Construction; Physics.

Personality Type: Realistic-Conventional-Investigative. **Career Cluster:** 13 Manufacturing. **Career Pathway:** 13.3 Maintenance, Installation,

and Repair. **Other Jobs in This Pathway:** Aircraft Mechanics and Service Technicians; Automotive Specialty Technicians; Biological Technicians; Civil Engineering Technicians; Computer, Automated Teller, and Office Machine Repairers; Electrical and Electronic Equipment Assemblers; Electrical and Electronics Repairers, Commercial and Industrial Equipment; Electrical Engineering Technicians; Electrical Engineering Technologists; Electromechanical Engineering Technologists; Electronics Engineering Technicians; Electronics Engineering Technologists; Engineering Technicians, Except Drafters, All Other; Fuel Cell Technicians; Industrial Engineering Technologists; Industrial Machinery Mechanics; Installation, Maintenance, and Repair Workers, All Other; Manufacturing Engineering Technologists; Manufacturing Production Technicians; Mapping Technicians; Mechanical Engineering Technologists; Mobile Heavy Equipment Mechanics, Except Engines; Nanotechnology Engineering Technicians; Telecommunications Line Installers and Repairers; Tire Repairers and Changers; others.

Home Health Aides

* Annual Earnings: $20,560
* Earnings Growth Potential: Very low (20.7%)
* Growth: 50.0%
* Annual Job Openings: 55,270
* Self-Employed: 1.8%

Skills—Most Important: Social Skills.

Provide routine personal health care—such as bathing, dressing, or grooming—to elderly, convalescent, or disabled persons in the home of patients or in a residential care facility.

Maintain records of patient care, condition, progress, or problems to report and discuss observations with supervisor or case manager. Provide patients with help moving in and out of beds, baths, wheelchairs, or automobiles and with dressing and grooming. Entertain, converse with, or read aloud to patients to keep them mentally healthy and alert. Check patients' pulse, temperature, and respiration. Care for patients by changing bed linens, washing and ironing laundry, cleaning, or assisting with their personal care.

Education/Training Required: Short-term on-the-job training. **Education and Training Program:** Home Health Aide/Home Attendant Training. **Knowledge/Courses:** Psychology; Medicine and Dentistry; Therapy and Counseling; Philosophy and Theology; Customer and Personal Service; Personnel and Human Resources.

Personality Type: Social-Realistic. **Career Cluster:** 08 Health Science. **Career Pathway:** 08.1 Therapeutic Services. **Other Jobs in This Pathway:** Clinical Psychologists; Community and Social Service Specialists, All Other; Counseling Psychologists; Dental Assistants; Dental Hygienists; Dentists, General; Health Technologists and Technicians, All Other; Healthcare Support Workers, All Other; Licensed Practical and Licensed Vocational Nurses; Low Vision Therapists, Orientation and Mobility Specialists, and Vision Rehabilitation Therapists; Massage Therapists; Medical and Clinical Laboratory Technicians; Medical and Health Services Managers; Medical Scientists, Except Epidemiologists; Medical Secretaries; Occupational Therapists; Ophthalmic Medical Technologists; Pharmacists; Pharmacy Technicians; Radiologic Technologists; School Psychologists; Social and Human Service Assistants; Speech-Language Pathologists; Speech-Language Pathology Assistants; Substance Abuse and Behavioral Disorder Counselors; others.

Human Resources Managers

* Annual Earnings: $99,180
* Earnings Growth Potential: Medium (37.9%)
* Growth: 9.6%
* Annual Job Openings: 4,140
* Self-Employed: 0.6%

Skills—Most Important: Management Skills; Social Skills; Thought-Processing Skills. **Other High-Level Skills:** Mathematics Skills; Communication Skills.

Plan, direct, and coordinate human resource management activities of an organization to maximize the strategic use of human resources and maintain functions such as employee compensation, recruitment, personnel policies, and regulatory compliance. Administer compensation, benefits and performance management systems, and safety and recreation programs. Identify staff vacancies and recruit, interview, and select applicants. Allocate human resources, ensuring appropriate matches between personnel. Provide current and prospective employees with information about policies, job duties, working conditions, wages, opportunities for promotion, and employee benefits. Perform difficult staffing duties, including dealing with understaffing, refereeing disputes, firing employees, and administering disciplinary procedures. Advise managers on organizational policy matters such as equal employment opportunity and sexual harassment and recommend needed changes. Analyze and modify compensation and benefits policies to establish competitive programs and ensure compliance with legal requirements. Plan and conduct new employee orientation to foster positive attitude toward organizational objectives. Serve as a link between management and employees by handling questions, interpreting and administering contracts, and helping resolve work-related problems. Plan, direct, supervise, and coordinate work activities of subordinates and staff relating to employment, compensation, labor relations, and employee relations. Analyze training needs to design employee development, language training, and health and safety programs.

Education/Training Required: Work experience plus degree. **Education and Training Program:** Human Resources Management/Personnel Administration, General. **Knowledge/Courses:** Personnel and Human Resources; Therapy and Counseling; Sociology and Anthropology; Psychology; Clerical Practices; Administration and Management.

Personality Type: Enterprising-Social-Conventional. **Career Cluster:** 04 Business, Management, and Administration. **Career Pathway:** 04.3 Human Resources. **Other Jobs in This Pathway:** Human Resources Specialists.

Human Resources Specialists

- ❋ Annual Earnings: $52,690
- ❋ Earnings Growth Potential: High (44.9%)
- ❋ Growth: 27.9%
- ❋ Annual Job Openings: 11,230
- ❋ Self-Employed: 1.6%

Skills—Most Important: Science Skills; Communication Skills; Social Skills. **Other High-Level Skills:** Thought-Processing Skills; Management Skills.

Recruit and place workers. Address employee relations issues, such as harassment allegations, work complaints, or other employee concerns. Analyze employment-related data and prepare required reports. Conduct exit interviews and ensure that necessary employment termination paperwork is completed. Conduct reference or background checks on job applicants. Confer with management to develop or implement personnel policies or procedures. Contact job applicants to inform them of the status of their applications. Develop or implement recruiting strategies to meet current or anticipated staffing needs. Hire employees and process hiring-related paperwork. Inform job applicants of details such as duties and responsibilities, compensation, benefits, schedules, working conditions, or promotion opportunities. Interpret and explain human resources policies, procedures, laws, standards, or regulations. Interview job applicants to obtain information on work history, training, education, or job skills. Maintain and update human resources documents, such as organizational charts, employee handbooks or directories, or performance evaluation forms. Maintain current knowledge of Equal Employment Opportunity (EEO) and affirmative action guidelines and laws, such as the Americans with Disabilities Act (ADA). Perform searches for qualified job candidates, using sources such as computer databases, networking, Internet recruiting resources, media advertisements, job fairs, recruiting firms, or employee referrals.

Education/Training Required: Bachelor's degree. **Education and Training Programs:** Human Resources Management/Personnel Administration, General; Labor and Industrial Relations. **Knowledge/Courses:** Personnel and Human Resources; Sales and Marketing; Clerical Practices; Law and

Government; Customer and Personal Service; Communications and Media.

Personality Type: Enterprising-Social-Conventional. **Career Cluster:** 04 Business, Management, and Administration. **Career Pathway:** 04.3 Human Resources. **Other Jobs in This Pathway:** Business Teachers, Postsecondary; Compensation, Benefits, and Job Analysis Specialists; Employment, Recruitment, and Placement Specialists; Labor Relations Specialists; Training and Development Specialists.

Hydrologists

* Annual Earnings: $75,690
* Earnings Growth Potential: Medium (36.2%)
* Growth: 18.2%
* Annual Job Openings: 380
* Self-Employed: 2.4%

Skills—Most Important: Science Skills; Mathematics Skills; Technology/Programming Skills. **Other High-Level Skills:** Communication Skills; Thought-Processing Skills; Social Skills; Management Skills; Equipment Use/Maintenance Skills.

Research the distribution, circulation, and physical properties of underground and surface waters. Study the form and intensity of precipitation and its rate of infiltration into the soil, its movement through the earth, and its return to the ocean and atmosphere. Study and document quantities, distribution, disposition, and development of underground and surface waters. Prepare hydrogeologic evaluations of known or suspected hazardous waste sites and land treatment and feedlot facilities. Design and conduct scientific hydrogeological investigations to ensure that accurate and appropriate

information is available for use in water resource management decisions. Collect and analyze water samples as part of field investigations or to validate data from automatic monitors. Apply research findings to help minimize the environmental impacts of pollution, waterborne diseases, erosion, and sedimentation. Measure and graph phenomena such as lake levels, stream flows, and changes in water volumes. Investigate complaints or conflicts related to the alteration of public waters, gathering information, recommending alternatives, informing participants of progress, and preparing draft orders.

Education/Training Required: Master's degree. **Education and Training Programs:** Geology/Earth Science, General; Hydrology and Water Resources Science; Oceanography, Chemical and Physical. **Knowledge/Courses:** Geography; Biology; Engineering and Technology; Physics; Chemistry; Design.

Personality Type: Investigative-Realistic. **Career Cluster:** 15 Science, Technology, Engineering, and Mathematics. **Career Pathway:** 15.2 Science and Mathematics. **Other Jobs in This Pathway:** Architectural and Engineering Managers; Biochemists and Biophysicists; Biofuels/Biodiesel Technology and Product Development Managers; Bioinformatics Scientists; Biological Scientists, All Other; Biologists; Biostatisticians; Chemists; Clinical Data Managers; Clinical Research Coordinators; Community and Social Service Specialists, All Other; Dietitians and Nutritionists; Education, Training, and Library Workers, All Other; Geneticists; Geoscientists, Except Hydrologists and Geographers; Medical Scientists, Except Epidemiologists; Molecular and Cellular Biologists; Natural Sciences Managers; Operations Research Analysts; Physical Scientists, All Other; Social Scientists and Related Workers, All Other; Statisticians; Survey Researchers; Transportation Planners; Water Resource Specialists; others.

Industrial Engineers

- ✳ Annual Earnings: $76,100
- ✳ Earnings Growth Potential: Low (34.7%)
- ✳ Growth: 14.2%
- ✳ Annual Job Openings: 8,540
- ✳ Self-Employed: 0.7%

Skills—Most Important: Mathematics Skills; Management Skills; Thought-Processing Skills. **Other High-Level Skills:** Communication Skills; Social Skills; Equipment Use/Maintenance Skills.

Design, develop, test, and evaluate integrated systems for managing industrial production processes, including human work factors, quality control, inventory control, logistics and material flow, cost analysis, and production coordination. Develop manufacturing methods, labor utilization standards, and cost analysis systems to promote efficient staff and facility utilization. Recommend methods for improving utilization of personnel, material, and utilities. Plan and establish sequence of operations to fabricate and assemble parts or products and to promote efficient utilization. Apply statistical methods and perform mathematical calculations to determine manufacturing processes, staff requirements, and production standards. Draft and design layout of equipment, materials, and workspace to illustrate maximum efficiency using drafting tools and computer. Review production schedules, engineering specifications, orders, and related information to obtain knowledge of manufacturing methods, procedures, and activities. Communicate with management and user personnel to develop production and design standards.

Education/Training Required: Bachelor's degree. **Education and Training Program:** Industrial Engineering. **Knowledge/Courses:** Engineering and Technology; Design; Production and Processing; Mechanical Devices; Physics; Mathematics.

Personality Type: Investigative-Conventional-Enterprising. **Career Cluster:** 15 Science, Technology, Engineering, and Mathematics. **Career Pathway:** 15.1 Engineering and Technology. **Other Jobs in This Pathway:** Architectural and Engineering Managers; Automotive Engineers; Biochemical Engineers; Biofuels/Biodiesel Technology and Product Development Managers; Civil Engineers; Cost Estimators; Education, Training, and Library Workers, All Other; Electrical Engineers; Electronics Engineers, Except Computer; Energy Engineers; Engineers, All Other; Fuel Cell Engineers; Human Factors Engineers and Ergonomists; Manufacturing Engineers; Mechanical Engineers; Mechatronics Engineers; Microsystems Engineers; Nanosystems Engineers; Photonics Engineers; Radio Frequency Identification Device Specialists; Robotics Engineers; Solar Energy Systems Engineers; Transportation Engineers; Validation Engineers; Wind Energy Engineers; others.

Job Specialization: Human Factors Engineers and Ergonomists

Design objects, facilities, and environments to optimize human well-being and overall system performance, applying theory, principles, and data on the relationship between humans and respective technology. Investigate and

analyze characteristics of human behavior and performance as it relates to the use of technology. Write, review, or comment on documents such as proposals, test plans, and procedures. Train users in task techniques or ergonomic principles. Review health, safety, accident, or worker compensation records to evaluate safety program effectiveness or to identify jobs with high incidents of injury. Provide human factors technical expertise on topics such as advanced user-interface technology development and the role of human users in automated or autonomous sub-systems in advanced vehicle systems. Investigate theoretical or conceptual issues, such as the human design considerations of lunar landers or habitats. Estimate time and resource requirements for ergonomic or human factors research or development projects. Conduct interviews or surveys of users or customers to collect information on topics such as requirements, needs, fatigue, ergonomics, and interface. Recommend workplace changes to improve health and safety using knowledge of potentially harmful factors, such as heavy loads and repetitive motions. Provide technical support to clients through activities such as rearranging workplace fixtures to reduce physical hazards or discomfort and modifying task sequences to reduce cycle time. Prepare reports or presentations summarizing results or conclusions of human factors engineering or ergonomics activities, such as testing, investigation, and validation.

Education/Training Required: Bachelor's degree. **Education and Training Program:** Industrial Engineering. **Knowledge/Courses:** No data available.

Personality Type: No data available. **Career Cluster:** 15 Science, Technology, Engineering, and Mathematics. **Career Pathway:** 15.1 Engineering and Technology. **Other Jobs in**

This Pathway: Architectural and Engineering Managers; Automotive Engineers; Biochemical Engineers; Biofuels/Biodiesel Technology and Product Development Managers; Civil Engineers; Cost Estimators; Education, Training, and Library Workers, All Other; Electrical Engineers; Electronics Engineers, Except Computer; Energy Engineers; Engineers, All Other; Fuel Cell Engineers; Industrial Engineers; Manufacturing Engineers; Mechanical Engineers; Mechatronics Engineers; Microsystems Engineers; Nanosystems Engineers; Photonics Engineers; Radio Frequency Identification Device Specialists; Robotics Engineers; Solar Energy Systems Engineers; Transportation Engineers; Validation Engineers; Wind Energy Engineers; others.

Industrial Machinery Mechanics

- Annual Earnings: $45,420
- Earnings Growth Potential: Low (34.2%)
- Growth: 7.3%
- Annual Job Openings: 6,240
- Self-Employed: 2.2%

Skills—Most Important: Equipment Use/Maintenance Skills; Installation Skills; Technology/Programming Skills. **Other High-Level Skills:** Thought-Processing Skills; Social Skills.

Repair, install, adjust, or maintain industrial production and processing machinery or refinery and pipeline distribution systems. Disassemble machinery and equipment to remove parts and make repairs. Repair and replace broken or malfunctioning components of machinery and equipment. Repair and maintain the operating condition of industrial production and processing machinery and equipment. Examine parts for defects such as breakage and excessive wear. Reassemble equipment after completion of inspections, testing, or repairs. Observe and test the operation of machinery and equipment to diagnose malfunctions using voltmeters and other testing devices. Operate newly repaired machinery and equipment to verify the adequacy of repairs. Clean, lubricate, and adjust parts, equipment, and machinery. Analyze test results, machine error messages, and information obtained from operators to diagnose equipment problems. Record repairs and maintenance performed. Record parts and materials used and order or requisition new parts and materials as necessary. Study blueprints and manufacturers' manuals to determine correct installation and operation of machinery. Cut and weld metal to repair broken metal parts, fabricate new parts, and assemble new equipment. Demonstrate equipment functions and features to machine operators. Enter codes and instructions to program computer-controlled machinery.

Education/Training Required: Long-term on-the-job training. **Education and Training Programs:** Heavy/Industrial Equipment Maintenance Technologies, Other; Industrial Mechanics and Maintenance Technology. **Knowledge/Courses:** Mechanical Devices; Engineering and Technology; Building and Construction; Design; Chemistry; Physics.

Personality Type: Realistic-Investigative-Conventional. **Career Cluster:** 13 Manufacturing. **Career Pathway:** 13.3 Maintenance, Installation, and Repair. **Other Jobs in This Pathway:** Aircraft Mechanics and Service Technicians; Automotive Specialty Technicians; Biological Technicians; Civil Engineering Technicians; Computer, Automated Teller, and Office Machine Repairers; Electrical and Electronic Equipment Assemblers; Electrical and Electronics Repairers, Commercial and Industrial Equipment; Electrical Engineering Technicians; Electrical Engineering Technologists; Electromechanical Engineering Technologists; Electronics Engineering Technicians; Electronics Engineering Technologists; Engineering Technicians, Except Drafters, All Other; Fuel Cell Technicians; Helpers—Installation, Maintenance, and Repair Workers; Industrial Engineering Technologists; Installation, Maintenance, and Repair Workers, All Other; Manufacturing Engineering Technologists; Manufacturing Production Technicians; Mapping Technicians; Mechanical Engineering Technologists; Mobile Heavy Equipment Mechanics, Except Engines; Nanotechnology Engineering Technicians; Telecommunications Line Installers and Repairers; Tire Repairers and Changers; others.

Industrial-Organizational Psychologists

* Annual Earnings: $87,330
* Earnings Growth Potential: High (43.6%)
* Growth: 26.1%
* Annual Job Openings: 130
* Self-Employed: 33.6%

Skills—Most Important: Science Skills; Mathematics Skills; Technology/Programming Skills. **Other High-Level Skills:** Thought-Processing Skills; Communication Skills; Social Skills; Management Skills.

Apply principles of psychology to personnel, administration, management, sales, and marketing problems. Activities may include policy planning; employee screening, training, and development; and

organizational development and analysis. May work with management to reorganize the work setting to improve worker productivity. Develop and implement employee selection and placement programs. Analyze job requirements and content to establish criteria for classification, selection, training, and other related personnel functions. Observe and interview workers to obtain information about the physical, mental, and educational requirements of jobs as well as information about aspects such as job satisfaction. Write reports on research findings and implications to contribute to general knowledge and to suggest potential changes in organizational functioning. Advise management on personnel, managerial, and marketing policies and practices and their potential effects on organizational effectiveness and efficiency. Identify training and development needs. Conduct research studies of physical work environments, organizational structures, communication systems, group interactions, morale, and motivation to assess organizational functioning. Formulate and implement training programs, applying principles of learning and individual differences. Develop interview techniques, rating scales, and psychological tests used to assess skills, abilities, and interests for employee selection, placement, and promotion. Study organizational effectiveness, productivity, and efficiency, including the nature of workplace supervision and leadership. Assess employee performance.

Education/Training Required: Master's degree. **Education and Training Program:** Psychology, General. **Knowledge/Courses:** Personnel and Human Resources; Psychology; Sociology and Anthropology; Education and Training; Therapy and Counseling; Mathematics.

Personality Type: Investigative-Enterprising-Artistic. **Career Cluster:** 08 Health Science. **Career Pathway:** 08.1 Therapeutic Services. **Other Jobs in This Pathway:** Clinical Psychologists; Community and Social Service Specialists, All Other; Counseling Psychologists; Dental Assistants; Dental Hygienists; Dentists, General; Health Technologists and Technicians, All Other; Healthcare Support Workers, All Other; Home Health Aides; Licensed Practical and Licensed Vocational Nurses; Low Vision Therapists, Orientation and Mobility Specialists, and Vision Rehabilitation Therapists; Massage Therapists; Medical and Clinical Laboratory Technicians; Medical and Health Services Managers; Medical Scientists, Except Epidemiologists; Medical Secretaries; Occupational Therapists; Pharmacists; Pharmacy Technicians; Radiologic Technologists; School Psychologists; Social and Human Service Assistants; Speech-Language Pathologists; Speech-Language Pathology Assistants; Substance Abuse and Behavioral Disorder Counselors; others.

Installation, Maintenance, and Repair Workers, All Other

- ❋ Annual Earnings: $36,420
- ❋ Earnings Growth Potential: High (43.5%)
- ❋ Growth: 9.2%
- ❋ Annual Job Openings: 4,180
- ❋ Self-Employed: 17.4%

Skills—Most Important: Installation Skills; Equipment Use/Maintenance Skills; Mathematics Skills. **Other High-Level Skills:** Thought-Processing Skills.

This occupation includes all mechanical, installation, and repair workers and helpers

not listed separately. Because this is a highly diverse occupation, no data is available for some information topics.

Education/Training Required: Moderate-term on-the-job training. **Career Clusters:** 13 Manufacturing; 16 Transportation, Distribution, and Logistics. **Career Pathways:** 16.4 Facility and Mobile Equipment Maintenance; 13.3 Maintenance, Installation, and Repair. **Other Jobs in These Pathways:** Aircraft Mechanics and Service Technicians; Automotive Body and Related Repairers; Automotive Master Mechanics; Automotive Specialty Technicians; Biological Technicians; Bus and Truck Mechanics and Diesel Engine Specialists; Civil Engineering Technicians; Cleaners of Vehicles and Equipment; Computer, Automated Teller, and Office Machine Repairers; Electrical and Electronic Equipment Assemblers; Electrical and Electronics Repairers, Commercial and Industrial Equipment; Electrical Engineering Technicians; Electrical Engineering Technologists; Electromechanical Engineering Technologists; Electronics Engineering Technicians; Electronics Engineering Technologists; Engineering Technicians, Except Drafters, All Other; Fuel Cell Technicians; Helpers—Installation, Maintenance, and Repair Workers; Industrial Engineering Technologists; Industrial Machinery Mechanics; Manufacturing Engineering Technologists; Mobile Heavy Equipment Mechanics, Except Engines; Telecommunications Line Installers and Repairers; Tire Repairers and Changers; others.

Job Specialization: Geothermal Technicians

Perform technical activities at power plants or individual installations for the generation of power from geothermal energy sources.

Monitor and control operating activities at geothermal power generation facilities and perform maintenance and repairs. Install, test, and maintain residential and commercial geothermal heat pumps. Identify and correct malfunctions of geothermal plant equipment, electrical systems, instrumentation, or controls. Monitor and adjust operations of geothermal power plant equipment or systems. Adjust power production systems to meet load and distribution demands. Collect and record data associated with operating geothermal power plants or well fields. Prepare and maintain logs, reports, or other documentation of work performed. Install, maintain, or repair ground or water source-coupled heat pumps to heat and cool residential or commercial building air or water. Backfill piping trenches to protect pipes from damage. Calculate heat loss and heat gain factors for residential properties to determine heating and cooling required by installed geothermal systems. Design and lay out geothermal heat systems according to property characteristics, heating and cooling requirements, piping and equipment requirements, applicable regulations, or other factors. Determine the type of geothermal loop system most suitable to a specific property and its heating and cooling needs. Dig trenches for system piping to appropriate depths and lay piping in trenches. Prepare newly installed geothermal heat systems for operation by flushing, purging, or other actions. Identify equipment options, such as compressors, and make appropriate selections. Install and maintain geothermal system instrumentation or controls.

Education/Training Required: Long-term on-the-job training. **Education and Training Program:** Heating, Air Conditioning, Ventilation, and Refrigeration Maintenance Technology/Technician (HAC, HACR, HVAC,

HVACR). **Knowledge/Courses:** Mechanical Devices; Physics; Chemistry; Building and Construction; Design; Production and Processing.

Career Cluster: 13 Manufacturing. **Career Pathway:** 13.1 Production. **Other Jobs in This Pathway:** Assemblers and Fabricators, All Other; Cabinetmakers and Bench Carpenters; Coating, Painting, and Spraying Machine Setters, Operators, and Tenders; Computer-Controlled Machine Tool Operators, Metal and Plastic; Cost Estimators; Cutting, Punching, and Press Machine Setters, Operators, and Tenders, Metal and Plastic; First-Line Supervisors of Mechanics, Installers, and Repairers; First-Line Supervisors of Production and Operating Workers; Grinding, Lapping, Polishing, and Buffing Machine Tool Setters, Operators, and Tenders, Metal and Plastic; Helpers—Production Workers; Machine Feeders and Offbearers; Machinists; Mixing and Blending Machine Setters, Operators, and Tenders; Molding, Coremaking, and Casting Machine Setters, Operators, and Tenders, Metal and Plastic; Packaging and Filling Machine Operators and Tenders; Packers and Packagers, Hand; Paper Goods Machine Setters, Operators, and Tenders; Production Workers, All Other; Recycling and Reclamation Workers; Recycling Coordinators; Sheet Metal Workers; Solderers and Brazers; Structural Metal Fabricators and Fitters; Team Assemblers; Welders, Cutters, and Welder Fitters; others.

Instructional Coordinators

- ❋ Annual Earnings: $58,830
- ❋ Earnings Growth Potential: High (43.1%)
- ❋ Growth: 23.2%
- ❋ Annual Job Openings: 6,060
- ❋ Self-Employed: 2.9%

Skills—Most Important: Social Skills; Communication Skills; Thought-Processing Skills. **Other High-Level Skills:** Management Skills; Mathematics Skills.

Develop instructional material, coordinate educational content, and incorporate current technology in specialized fields that provide guidelines to educators and instructors for developing curricula and conducting courses. Conduct or participate in workshops, committees, and conferences designed to promote the intellectual, social, and physical welfare of students. Plan and conduct teacher training programs and conferences dealing with new classroom procedures, instructional materials and equipment, and teaching aids. Advise teaching and administrative staff in curriculum development, use of materials and equipment, and implementation of state and federal programs and procedures. Recommend, order, or authorize purchase of instructional materials, supplies, equipment, and visual aids designed to meet student educational needs and district standards. Interpret and enforce provisions of state education codes and rules and regulations of state education boards. Confer with members of educational committees and advisory groups to obtain knowledge of subject areas and to relate curriculum materials to specific subjects, individual student needs, and occupational areas.

Education/Training Required: Master's degree. **Education and Training Programs:** Curriculum and Instruction; Educational/Instructional Technology. **Knowledge/Courses:** Education and Training; Therapy and Counseling; Philosophy and Theology; Sociology and Anthropology; Personnel and Human Resources; Psychology.

Personality Type: Social-Investigative-Enterprising. **Career Cluster:** 05 Education and Training. **Career Pathways:** 05.1 Administration and Administrative Support; 05.3 Teaching/Training. **Other Jobs in These Pathways:** Adult Basic and Secondary Education and Literacy Teachers and Instructors; Career/Technical Education Teachers, Secondary School; Chemists; Coaches and Scouts; Dietitians and Nutritionists; Distance Learning Coordinators; Education Administrators, All Other; Education Administrators, Elementary and Secondary School; Education Administrators, Postsecondary; Education Administrators, Preschool and Childcare Center/Program; Elementary School Teachers, Except Special Education; Fitness and Wellness Coordinators; Fitness Trainers and Aerobics Instructors; Instructional Designers and Technologists; Interpreters and Translators; Kindergarten Teachers, Except Special Education; Librarians; Middle School Teachers, Except Special and Career/Technical Education; Preschool Teachers, Except Special Education; Recreation Workers; Secondary School Teachers, Except Special and Career/Technical Education; Self-Enrichment Education Teachers; Teacher Assistants; Teachers and Instructors, All Other; Tutors; others.

Job Specialization: Instructional Designers and Technologists

Develop instructional materials and products and assist in the technology-based redesign of courses. Assist faculty in learning about, becoming proficient in, and applying instructional technology. Observe and provide feedback on instructional techniques, presentation methods, or instructional aids. Edit instructional materials, such as books, simulation exercises, lesson plans, instructor guides, and tests. Develop measurement tools to evaluate the effectiveness of instruction or training interventions. Develop instructional materials, such as lesson plans, handouts, or examinations. Define instructional, learning, or performance objectives. Assess effectiveness and efficiency of instruction according to ease of instructional technology use and student learning, knowledge transfer, and satisfaction. Analyze performance data to determine effectiveness of instructional systems, courses, or instructional materials. Research and evaluate emerging instructional technologies or methods. Recommend instructional methods, such as individual or group instruction, self-study, lectures, demonstrations, simulation exercises, and role-playing, appropriate for content and learner characteristics. Recommend changes to curricula or delivery methods based on information such as instructional effectiveness data, current or future performance requirements, feasibility, and costs. Provide technical support to clients in the implementation of designed instruction or in task analyses and instructional systems design.

Education/Training Required: Bachelor's degree. **Education and Training Programs:** Curriculum and Instruction; Educational/

Instructional Technology. **Knowledge/ Courses**—No data available.

Personality Type: No data available.
Career Cluster: 05 Education and Training.
Career Pathways: 05.1 Administration and Administrative Support; 05.3 Teaching/ Training. **Other Jobs in These Pathways:** Adult Basic and Secondary Education and Literacy Teachers and Instructors; Career/Technical Education Teachers, Secondary School; Chemists; Coaches and Scouts; Dietitians and Nutritionists; Distance Learning Coordinators; Education Administrators, All Other; Education Administrators, Elementary and Secondary School; Education Administrators, Postsecondary; Education Administrators, Preschool and Childcare Center/Program; Elementary School Teachers, Except Special Education; Fitness and Wellness Coordinators; Fitness Trainers and Aerobics Instructors; Instructional Coordinators; Interpreters and Translators; Kindergarten Teachers, Except Special Education; Librarians; Middle School Teachers, Except Special and Career/Technical Education; Preschool Teachers, Except Special Education; Recreation Workers; Secondary School Teachers, Except Special and Career/ Technical Education; Self-Enrichment Education Teachers; Teacher Assistants; Teachers and Instructors, All Other; Tutors; others.

Interior Designers

❋ Annual Earnings: $46,280

❋ Earnings Growth Potential: High (43.0%)

❋ Growth: 19.4%

❋ Annual Job Openings: 3,590

❋ Self-Employed: 26.7%

Skills—Most Important: Management Skills; Mathematics Skills; Social Skills. **Other High-Level Skills:** Communication Skills; Thought-Processing Skills.

Plan, design, and furnish interiors of residential, commercial, or industrial buildings. Formulate design that is practical, aesthetic, and conducive to intended purposes, such as raising productivity, selling merchandise, or improving lifestyle. May specialize in a particular field, style, or phase of interior design. Confer with client to determine factors affecting planning interior environments, such as budget, architectural preferences, and purpose and function. Advise client on interior design factors such as space planning, layout and utilization of furnishings or equipment, and color coordination. Coordinate with other professionals, such as contractors, architects, engineers, and plumbers, to ensure job success. Review and detail shop drawings for construction plans. Estimate material requirements and costs and present design to client for approval. Subcontract fabrication, installation, and arrangement of carpeting, fixtures, accessories, draperies, paint and wall coverings, artwork, furniture, and related items. Formulate environmental plan to be practical, aesthetic, and conducive to intended purposes, such as raising productivity or selling merchandise. Select or design and purchase furnishings, artwork, and accessories. Use computer-aided drafting (CAD) and related software to produce construction documents. Plan and design interior environments for boats, planes, buses, trains, and other enclosed spaces.

Education/Training Required: Associate degree. **Education and Training Programs:** Facilities Planning and Management; Interior Architecture; Interior Design; Textile Science. **Knowledge/Courses:** Design; Fine Arts; Building and Construction; Sales and Marketing; History and Archeology; Psychology.

Personality Type: Artistic-Enterprising. **Career Clusters:** 02 Architecture and Construction; 03 Arts, Audio/Video Technology, and Communications; 13 Manufacturing; 14 Marketing, Sales, and Service. **Career Pathways:** 14.2 Professional Sales and Marketing; 13.3 Maintenance, Installation, and Repair; 03.3 Visual Arts; 02.1 Design/Pre-Construction.

Other Jobs in These Pathways: Automotive Specialty Technicians; Cashiers; Counter and Rental Clerks; Driver/Sales Workers; Electrical and Electronic Equipment Assemblers; Energy Brokers; First-Line Supervisors of Non-Retail Sales Workers; First-Line Supervisors of Retail Sales Workers; Graphic Designers; Hotel, Motel, and Resort Desk Clerks; Industrial Machinery Mechanics; Marking Clerks; Online Merchants; Order Fillers, Wholesale and Retail Sales; Parts Salespersons; Property, Real Estate, and Community Association Managers; Real Estate Sales Agents; Retail Salespersons; Sales Representatives, Services, All Other; Sales Representatives, Wholesale and Manufacturing, Except Technical and Scientific Products; Sales Representatives, Wholesale and Manufacturing, Technical and Scientific Products; Solar Sales Representatives and Assessors; Stock Clerks—Stockroom, Warehouse, or Storage Yard; Stock Clerks, Sales Floor; Telemarketers; others.

Landscape Architects

❋ Annual Earnings: $62,090

❋ Earnings Growth Potential: Medium (40.6%)

❋ Growth: 19.6%

❋ Annual Job Openings: 980

❋ Self-Employed: 21.3%

Skills—Most Important: Science Skills; Management Skills; Thought-Processing Skills. **Other High-Level Skills:** Social Skills; Mathematics Skills; Communication Skills; Equipment Use/Maintenance Skills.

Plan and design land areas for such projects as parks and other recreational facilities; airports; highways; hospitals; schools; land subdivisions; and commercial, industrial, and residential sites. Confer with clients, engineering personnel, and architects on overall program. Prepare site plans, specifications, and cost estimates for land development, coordinating arrangement of existing and proposed land features and structures. Seek new work opportunities through marketing, writing proposals or giving presentations. Inspect landscape work to ensure compliance with specifications, approve quality of materials and work, and advise client and construction personnel. Compile and analyze data on conditions such as location, drainage, and location of structures for environmental reports and landscaping plans. Prepare graphic representations and drawings of proposed plans and designs.

Education/Training Required: Bachelor's degree. **Education and Training Programs:** Environmental Design/Architecture; Landscape Architecture (BS, BSLA, BLA, MSLA, MLA, PhD). **Knowledge/Courses:** Design;

Geography; Building and Construction; Fine Arts; Biology; History and Archeology.

Personality Type: Artistic-Investigative-Realistic. **Career Cluster:** 02 Architecture and Construction. **Career Pathway:** 02.1 Design/Pre-Construction. **Other Jobs in This Pathway:** Architects, Except Landscape and Naval; Architectural and Engineering Managers; Architectural Drafters; Cartographers and Photogrammetrists; Civil Drafters; Civil Engineering Technicians; Drafters, All Other; Electrical Drafters; Electronic Drafters; Engineering Technicians, Except Drafters, All Other; Engineers, All Other; Geodetic Surveyors; Interior Designers; Mechanical Drafters; Surveying Technicians.

Lawyers

* Annual Earnings: $112,760
* Earnings Growth Potential: Very high (52.0%)
* Growth: 13.0%
* Annual Job Openings: 24,040
* Self-Employed: 26.2%

Skills—Most Important: Communication Skills; Social Skills; Thought-Processing Skills. **Other High-Level Skills:** Management Skills.

Represent clients in criminal and civil litigation and other legal proceedings, draw up legal documents, and manage or advise clients on legal transactions. May specialize in a single area or may practice broadly in many areas of law. Represent clients in court or before government agencies. Select jurors, argue motions, meet with judges, and question witnesses during a trial. Present evidence to defend clients or prosecute defendants in criminal or civil litigation. Interpret laws, rulings, and regulations for individuals and businesses. Study Constitution, statutes, decisions, regulations, and ordinances of quasi-judicial bodies to determine ramifications for cases. Present and summarize cases to judges and juries. Prepare legal briefs and opinions and file appeals in state and federal courts of appeal. Analyze the probable outcomes of cases, using knowledge of legal precedents. Examine legal data to determine advisability of defending or prosecuting lawsuits. Evaluate findings and develop strategies and arguments in preparation for presentation of cases. Advise clients concerning business transactions, claim liability, advisability of prosecuting or defending lawsuits, or legal rights and obligations.

Education/Training Required: First professional degree. **Education and Training Programs:** Advanced Legal Research/Studies, General (LL.M., M.C.L., M.L.I., M.S.L., J.S.D./S.J.D.); American/U.S. Law/Legal Studies/Jurisprudence (LL.M., M.C.J., J.S.D./ S.J.D.); Banking, Corporate, Finance, and Securities Law (LL.M., J.S.D./S.J.D.); Canadian Law/Legal Studies/Jurisprudence (LL.M., M.C.J., J.S.D./S.J.D.); Comparative Law (LL.M., M.C.L., J.S.D./S.J.D.); Energy, Environment, and Natural Resources Law (LL.M., M.S., J.S.D./S.J.D.); Health Law (LL.M., M.J., J.S.D./ S.J.D.); International Business, Trade, and Tax Law (LL.M., J.S.D./S.J.D.); International Law and Legal Studies (LL.M., J.S.D./S.J.D.); Law (LL.B, J.D.); Legal Professions and Studies, Other; Legal Research and Advanced Professional Studies, Other; Legal Studies, General; Pre-Law Studies; Programs for Foreign Lawyers (LL.M., M.C.L.); Tax Law/Taxation (LL.M., J.S.D./S.J.D.). **Knowledge/Courses:** Law and Government; English Language; Personnel and Human Resources; Customer and

Personal Service; Economics and Accounting; Administration and Management.

Personality Type: Enterprising-Investigative. **Career Cluster:** 12 Law, Public Safety, Corrections, and Security. **Career Pathway:** 12.5 Legal Services. **Other Jobs in This Pathway:** Administrative Law Judges, Adjudicators, and Hearing Officers; Arbitrators, Mediators, and Conciliators; Court Reporters; Farm and Home Management Advisors; Judges, Magistrate Judges, and Magistrates; Legal Secretaries; Legal Support Workers, All Other; Paralegals and Legal Assistants; Title Examiners, Abstractors, and Searchers.

Legal Secretaries

- ❋ Annual Earnings: $41,500
- ❋ Earnings Growth Potential: Medium (36.5%)
- ❋ Growth: 18.4%
- ❋ Annual Job Openings: 8,380
- ❋ Self-Employed: 1.4%

Skills—Most Important: Communication Skills.

Perform secretarial duties, utilizing legal terminology, procedures, and documents. Prepare legal papers and correspondence, such as summonses, complaints, motions, and subpoenas. May assist with legal research. Prepare and process legal documents and papers, such as summonses, subpoenas, complaints, appeals, motions, and pretrial agreements. Mail, fax, or arrange for delivery of legal correspondence to clients, witnesses, and court officials. Receive and place telephone calls. Schedule and make appointments. Make photocopies of correspondence, documents, and other printed matter. Organize and maintain

law libraries, documents, and case files. Assist attorneys in collecting information such as employment, medical, and other records. Draft and type office memos. Complete various forms, such as accident reports, trial and courtroom requests, and applications for clients.

Education/Training Required: Associate degree. **Education and Training Program:** Legal Administrative Assistant/Secretary Training. **Knowledge/Courses:** Clerical Practices; Law and Government; Computers and Electronics; English Language; Customer and Personal Service.

Personality Type: Conventional-Enterprising. **Career Cluster:** 12 Law, Public Safety, Corrections, and Security. **Career Pathway:** 12.5 Legal Services. **Other Jobs in This Pathway:** Administrative Law Judges, Adjudicators, and Hearing Officers; Arbitrators, Mediators, and Conciliators; Court Reporters; Farm and Home Management Advisors; Judges, Magistrate Judges, and Magistrates; Lawyers; Legal Support Workers, All Other; Paralegals and Legal Assistants; Title Examiners, Abstractors, and Searchers.

Licensed Practical and Licensed Vocational Nurses

- ❋ Annual Earnings: $40,380
- ❋ Earnings Growth Potential: Low (26.5%)
- ❋ Growth: 20.6%
- ❋ Annual Job Openings: 39,130
- ❋ Self-Employed: 1.2%

Skills—Most Important: Science Skills; Social Skills; Thought-Processing Skills. **Other High-Level Skills:** Equipment Use/Maintenance Skills; Communication Skills; Management Skills.

Care for ill, injured, convalescent, or disabled persons in hospitals, nursing homes, clinics, private homes, group homes, and similar institutions. May work under the supervision of a registered nurse. Licensing required. Observe patients, charting and reporting changes in patients' conditions, such as adverse reactions to medication or treatment, and taking necessary action. Administer prescribed medications or start intravenous fluids and note times and amounts on patients' charts. Answer patients' calls and determine how to assist them. Measure and record patients' vital signs, such as height, weight, temperature, blood pressure, pulse, and respiration. Provide basic patient care and treatments, such as taking temperatures or blood pressures, dressing wounds, treating bedsores, giving enemas or douches, rubbing with alcohol, massaging, or performing catheterizations. Help patients with bathing, dressing, maintaining personal hygiene, moving in bed, or standing and walking. Supervise nurses' aides and assistants. Record food and fluid intake and output. Work as part of a health-care team to assess patient needs, plan and modify care, and implement interventions. Evaluate nursing intervention outcomes, conferring with other health-care team members as necessary. Assemble and use equipment such as catheters, tracheotomy tubes, and oxygen suppliers. Collect samples such as blood, urine, and sputum from patients and perform routine laboratory tests on samples. Prepare patients for examinations, tests, or treatments and explain procedures. Prepare food trays and examine them for conformance to prescribed diet. Apply compresses, ice bags, and hot water bottles. Clean rooms and make beds.

Education/Training Required: Postsecondary vocational training. **Education and Training Program:** Licensed Practical/Vocational Nurse Training. **Knowledge/Courses:** Psychology; Medicine and Dentistry; Therapy and Counseling; Biology; Philosophy and Theology; Customer and Personal Service.

Personality Type: Social-Realistic. **Career Cluster:** 08 Health Science. **Career Pathway:** 08.1 Therapeutic Services. **Other Jobs in This Pathway:** Clinical Psychologists; Community and Social Service Specialists, All Other; Counseling Psychologists; Dental Assistants; Dental Hygienists; Dentists, General; Health Technologists and Technicians, All Other; Healthcare Support Workers, All Other; Home Health Aides; Low Vision Therapists, Orientation and Mobility Specialists, and Vision Rehabilitation Therapists; Massage Therapists; Medical and Clinical Laboratory Technicians; Medical and Health Services Managers; Medical Scientists, Except Epidemiologists; Medical Secretaries; Occupational Therapists; Ophthalmic Medical Technologists; Pharmacists; Pharmacy Technicians; Radiologic Technologists; School Psychologists; Social and Human Service Assistants; Speech-Language Pathologists; Speech-Language Pathology Assistants; Substance Abuse and Behavioral Disorder Counselors; others.

Life, Physical, and Social Science Technicians, All Other

* Annual Earnings: $43,350
* Earnings Growth Potential: Medium (40.9%)
* Growth: 13.3%
* Annual Job Openings: 3,640
* Self-Employed: 1.6%

Skills—Most Important: Science Skills; Equipment Use/Maintenance Skills; Mathematics Skills. **Other High-Level Skills:**

Thought-Processing Skills; Communication Skills; Social Skills; Management Skills.

This occupation includes all life, physical, and social science technicians not listed separately. Because this is a highly diverse occupation, no data is available for some information topics.

Education/Training Required: Associate degree. **Education and Training Program:** Science Technologies/Technicians, Other. **Career Clusters:** 08 Health Science; 13 Manufacturing. **Career Pathways:** 08.1 Therapeutic Services; 13.2 Manufacturing Production Process Development. **Other Jobs in These Pathways:** Clinical Psychologists; Community and Social Service Specialists, All Other; Counseling Psychologists; Dental Assistants; Dental Hygienists; Dentists, General; Electrical Engineering Technicians; Healthcare Support Workers, All Other; Home Health Aides; Licensed Practical and Licensed Vocational Nurses; Low Vision Therapists, Orientation and Mobility Specialists, and Vision Rehabilitation Therapists; Massage Therapists; Medical and Clinical Laboratory Technicians; Medical and Health Services Managers; Medical Scientists, Except Epidemiologists; Medical Secretaries; Occupational Therapists; Pharmacists; Pharmacy Technicians; Radiologic Technologists; School Psychologists; Social and Human Service Assistants; Speech-Language Pathologists; Speech-Language Pathology Assistants; Substance Abuse and Behavioral Disorder Counselors; others.

Job Specialization: Precision Agriculture Technicians

Apply geospatial technologies, including geographic information systems (GIS) and Global Positioning System (GPS), to agricultural production and management activities, such as pest scouting, site-specific pesticide application, yield mapping, and variable-rate irrigation. May use computers to develop and analyze maps and remote sensing images to compare physical topography with data on soils, fertilizer, pests, or weather. Collect information about soil and field attributes, yield data, or field boundaries using field data recorders and basic GIS. Create, layer, and analyze maps showing precision agricultural data such as crop yields, soil characteristics, input applications, terrain, drainage patterns, and field management history. Document and maintain records of precision agriculture information. Compile and analyze geospatial data to determine agricultural implications of factors such as soil quality, terrain, field productivity, fertilizers, and weather conditions. Divide agricultural fields into georeferenced zones based on soil characteristics and production potentials. Develop soil sampling grids or identify sampling sites using geospatial technology for soil testing on characteristics such as nitrogen, phosphorus, and potassium content; pH; and micronutrients. Compare crop yield maps with maps of soil test data, chemical application patterns, or other information to develop site-specific crop management plans. Apply knowledge of government regulations when making agricultural recommendations. Recommend best crop varieties and seeding rates for specific field areas based on analysis of geospatial data. Draw and read maps such as soil, contour, and plat maps. Process and analyze data from harvester monitors to develop yield maps.

Education/Training Required: Moderate-term on-the-job training. **Education and Training Program:** Agricultural Mechanics and Equipment/Machine Technology. **Knowledge/**

Courses: Food Production; Geography; Biology; Chemistry; Sales and Marketing; Mechanical.

Personality Type: Realistic-Investigative-Conventional. **Career Cluster:** 01 Agriculture, Food, and Natural Resources. **Career Pathways:** 01.3 Animal Systems; 01.2 Plant Systems. **Other Jobs in These Pathways:** Agricultural Technicians; Animal Breeders; Animal Scientists; Animal Trainers; Biochemists and Biophysicists; Biologists; Economists; Environmental Economists; Farm and Home Management Advisors; First-Line Supervisors of Landscaping, Lawn Service, and Groundskeeping Workers; First-Line Supervisors of Retail Sales Workers; Floral Designers; Food Science Technicians; Food Scientists and Technologists; Geneticists; Grounds Maintenance Workers, All Other; Landscaping and Groundskeeping Workers; Nonfarm Animal Caretakers; Pesticide Handlers, Sprayers, and Applicators, Vegetation; Retail Salespersons; Soil and Plant Scientists; Tree Trimmers and Pruners; Veterinarians.

Job Specialization: Quality Control Analysts

Conduct tests to determine quality of raw materials and bulk intermediate and finished products. May conduct stability sample tests. Train other analysts to perform laboratory procedures and assays. Perform visual inspections of finished products. Serve as a technical liaison between quality control and other departments, vendors, or contractors. Participate in internal assessments and audits as required. Identify and troubleshoot equipment problems. Evaluate new technologies and methods to make recommendations on their use. Ensure that lab cleanliness and safety standards are maintained. Develop and

qualify new testing methods. Coordinate testing with contract laboratories and vendors. Write technical reports or documentation such as deviation reports, testing protocols, and trend analyses. Write or revise standard quality control operating procedures. Supply quality control data necessary for regulatory submissions. Receive and inspect raw materials. Review data from contract laboratories to ensure accuracy and regulatory compliance.

Education/Training Required: Postsecondary vocational training. **Education and Training Program:** Quality Control Technology/ Technician.

Personality Type: Conventional-Investigative-Realistic. **Career Cluster:** 13 Manufacturing. **Career Pathway:** 13.2 Manufacturing Production Process Development. **Other Jobs in This Pathway:** Biofuels Processing Technicians; Biomass Plant Technicians; Chemical Plant and System Operators; Chemical Technicians; Electrical Engineering Technicians; Electromechanical Equipment Assemblers; Environmental Science and Protection Technicians, Including Health; Fabric and Apparel Patternmakers; Farm and Home Management Advisors; Fashion Designers; Hydroelectric Plant Technicians; Life, Physical, and Social Science Technicians, All Other; Methane/Landfill Gas Generation System Technicians; Nuclear Monitoring Technicians; Textile, Apparel, and Furnishings Workers, All Other.

Job Specialization: Remote Sensing Technicians

Apply remote sensing technologies to assist scientists in areas such as natural resources, urban planning, and homeland security. May prepare flight plans and sensor

configurations for flight trips. Participate in the planning and development of mapping projects. Maintain records of survey data. Document methods used and write technical reports containing information collected. Develop specialized computer software routines to customize and integrate image analysis. Collect verification data on the ground using equipment such as global positioning receivers, digital cameras, and notebook computers. Verify integrity and accuracy of data contained in remote sensing image analysis systems. Prepare documentation and presentations, including charts, photos, or graphs. Operate airborne remote sensing equipment such as survey cameras, sensors, and scanners. Monitor raw data quality during collection and make equipment corrections as necessary. Merge scanned images or build photo mosaics of large areas using image processing software. Integrate remotely sensed data with other geospatial data. Evaluate remote sensing project requirements to determine the types of equipment or computer software necessary to meet project requirements such as specific image types and output resolutions. Develop and maintain geospatial information databases. Correct raw data for errors due to factors such as skew and atmospheric variation. Calibrate data collection equipment. Consult with remote sensing scientists, surveyors, cartographers, or engineers to determine project needs.

Education/Training Required: Associate degree. **Education and Training Programs:** Geographic Information Science and Cartography; Signal/Geospatial Intelligence.

Personality Type: Realistic-Investigative-Conventional. **Career Cluster:** 11 Information Technology. **Career Pathway:** 11.2 Information Support Services. **Other Jobs in This Pathway:**

Computer and Information Systems Managers; Computer Numerically Controlled Machine Tool Programmers, Metal and Plastic; Computer Operators; Remote Sensing Scientists and Technologists.

Locksmiths and Safe Repairers

- ✸ Annual Earnings: $35,550
- ✸ Earnings Growth Potential: High (41.1%)
- ✸ Growth: 12.0%
- ✸ Annual Job Openings: 610
- ✸ Self-Employed: 15.8%

Skills—Most Important: Installation Skills; Equipment Use/Maintenance Skills.

Repair and open locks, make keys, change locks and safe combinations, and install and repair safes. Cut new or duplicate keys using keycutting machines. Keep records of company locks and keys. Insert new or repaired tumblers into locks to change combinations. Move picklocks in cylinders to open door locks without keys. Disassemble mechanical or electrical locking devices and repair or replace worn tumblers, springs, and other parts using hand tools. Repair and adjust safes, vault doors, and vault components using hand tools, lathes, drill presses, and welding and acetylene cutting apparatus. Open safe locks by drilling. Cut new or duplicate keys using impressions or code key machines. Set up and maintain master key systems. Install door hardware such as locks and closers. Install alarm and electronic access systems. Unlock cars and other vehicles.

Education/Training Required: Moderate-term on-the-job training. **Education and Training Program:** Locksmithing and Safe Repair. **Knowledge/Courses:** Mechanical Devices;

Public Safety and Security; Building and Construction; Sales and Marketing; Law and Government; Design.

Personality Type: Realistic-Conventional. **Career Cluster:** 13 Manufacturing. **Career Pathway:** 13.3 Maintenance, Installation, and Repair. **Other Jobs in This Pathway:** Aircraft Mechanics and Service Technicians; Automotive Specialty Technicians; Biological Technicians; Civil Engineering Technicians; Computer, Automated Teller, and Office Machine Repairers; Electrical and Electronic Equipment Assemblers; Electrical and Electronics Repairers, Commercial and Industrial Equipment; Electrical Engineering Technicians; Electrical Engineering Technologists; Electromechanical Engineering Technologists; Electronics Engineering Technicians; Electronics Engineering Technologists; Engineering Technicians, Except Drafters, All Other; Fuel Cell Technicians; Helpers—Installation, Maintenance, and Repair Workers; Industrial Engineering Technologists; Industrial Machinery Mechanics; Installation, Maintenance, and Repair Workers, All Other; Manufacturing Engineering Technologists; Manufacturing Production Technicians; Mapping Technicians; Mechanical Engineering Technologists; Mobile Heavy Equipment Mechanics, Except Engines; Telecommunications Line Installers and Repairers; Tire Repairers and Changers; others.

Logisticians

- ❋ Annual Earnings: $70,800
- ❋ Earnings Growth Potential: Medium (38.5%)
- ❋ Growth: 19.5%
- ❋ Annual Job Openings: 4,190
- ❋ Self-Employed: 0.0%

Skills—Most Important: Mathematics Skills; Thought-Processing Skills; Management Skills. **Other High-Level Skills:** Communication Skills; Technology/Programming Skills; Social Skills; Science Skills; Equipment Use/Maintenance Skills.

Analyze and coordinate the logistical functions of a firm or organization. Responsible for the entire life cycle of a product, including acquisition, distribution, internal allocation, delivery, and final disposal of resources. Maintain and develop positive business relationships with a customer's key personnel involved in or directly relevant to a logistics activity. Develop an understanding of customers' needs and take actions to ensure that such needs are met. Direct availability and allocation of materials, supplies, and finished products. Collaborate with other departments to meet customer requirements, to take advantage of sales opportunities, or in the case of shortages, to minimize negative impacts on a business. Protect and control proprietary materials. Review logistics performance with customers against targets, benchmarks, and service agreements. Develop and implement technical project management tools such as plans, schedules, and responsibility and compliance matrices. Direct team activities, establishing task priorities, scheduling and tracking work assignments, providing guidance, and ensuring the availability of resources. Report project plans, progress, and results. Direct and support the compilation and analysis of technical source data necessary for product development. Explain proposed solutions to customers, management, or other interested parties through written proposals and oral presentations. Plan, organize, and execute logistics support activities such as maintenance planning, repair analysis, and test equipment recommendations. Provide project management services, including the provision and analysis of technical data.

Education/Training Required: Bachelor's degree. **Education and Training Programs:** Logistics, Materials, and Supply Chain Management; Operations Management and Supervision; Transportation/Mobility Management. **Knowledge/Courses:** Telecommunications; Geography; Computers and Electronics; Economics and Accounting; Administration and Management; Public Safety and Security.

Personality Type: Enterprising-Conventional. **Career Clusters:** 04 Business, Management, and Administration; 16 Transportation, Distribution, and Logistics. **Career Pathways:** 16.2 Logistics, Planning, and Management Services; 04.1 Management. **Other Jobs in These Pathways:** Brownfield Redevelopment Specialists and Site Managers; Business Continuity Planners; Business Operations Specialists, All Other; Chief Executives; Chief Sustainability Officers; Compliance Managers; Computer and Information Systems Managers; Construction Managers; Customs Brokers; Energy Auditors; First-Line Supervisors of Office and Administrative Support Workers; General and Operations Managers; Investment Fund Managers; Loss Prevention Managers; Management Analysts; Managers, All Other;

Public Relations Specialists; Regulatory Affairs Managers; Sales Managers; Security Management Specialists; Security Managers; Supply Chain Managers; Sustainability Specialists; Wind Energy Operations Managers; Wind Energy Project Managers; others.

Job Specialization: Logistics Analysts

Analyze product delivery or supply chain processes to identify or recommend changes. May manage route activity including invoicing, electronic bills, and shipment tracing. Identify opportunities for inventory reductions. Monitor industry standards, trends, or practices to identify developments in logistics planning or execution. Enter logistics-related data into databases. Track product flow from origin to final delivery. Write or revise standard operating procedures for logistics processes. Review procedures such as distribution or inventory management to ensure maximum efficiency or minimum cost. Recommend improvements to existing or planned logistics processes. Provide ongoing analyses in areas such as transportation costs, parts procurement, back orders, or delivery processes. Prepare reports on logistics performance measures. Monitor inventory transactions at warehouse facilities to assess receiving, storage, shipping, or inventory integrity. Maintain databases of logistics information. Maintain logistics records in accordance with corporate policies. Develop or maintain models for logistics uses, such as cost estimating or demand forecasting. Confer with logistics management teams to determine ways to optimize service levels, maintain supply chain efficiency, or minimize cost. Compute reporting metrics, such as on-time delivery rates, order fulfillment rates, or inventory turns. Interpret data on logistics elements, such as availability, maintainability, reliability, supply chain management, strategic sourcing or distribution, supplier management, or transportation.

Education/Training Required: Bachelor's degree. **Education and Training Programs:** Logistics, Materials, and Supply Chain Management; Operations Management and Supervision; Transportation/Mobility Management. **Knowledge/Courses:** Transportation; Geography; Computers and Electronics; Production and Processing; Mathematics; Engineering and Technology.

Personality Type: Conventional-Enterprising-Investigative. **Career Clusters:** 04 Business, Management, and Administration; 16 Transportation, Distribution, and Logistics. **Career Pathways:** 04.1 Management; 16.3 Warehousing and Distribution Center Operations. **Other Jobs in These Pathways:** Brownfield Redevelopment Specialists and Site Managers; Business Continuity Planners; Business Operations Specialists, All Other; Chief Executives; Chief Sustainability Officers; Compliance Managers; Computer and Information Systems Managers; Construction Managers; Customs Brokers; Energy Auditors; First-Line Supervisors of Office and Administrative Support Workers; General and Operations Managers; Investment Fund Managers; Loss Prevention Managers; Management Analysts; Managers, All Other; Regulatory Affairs Managers; Sales Managers; Security Management Specialists; Security Managers; Shipping, Receiving, and Traffic Clerks; Supply Chain Managers; Sustainability Specialists; Wind Energy Operations Managers; Wind Energy Project Managers; others.

Job Specialization: Logistics Engineers

Design and analyze operational solutions for projects such as transportation optimization, network modeling, process and methods analysis, cost containment, capacity enhancement, routing and shipment optimization, and information management. Propose logistics solutions for customers. Interview key staff or tour facilities to identify efficiency-improvement, cost-reduction, or service-delivery opportunities. Direct the work of logistics analysts. Develop specifications for equipment, tools, facility layouts, or material-handling systems. Review contractual commitments, customer specifications, or related information to determine logistics or support requirements. Prepare or validate documentation on automated logistics or maintenance-data reporting or management information systems. Identify or develop business rules or standard operating procedures to streamline operating processes. Develop or maintain cost estimates, forecasts, or cost models. Determine logistics support requirements, such as facility details, staffing needs, or safety or maintenance plans. Conduct logistics studies or analyses, such as time studies, zero-base analyses, rate analyses, network analyses, flow-path analyses, or supply chain analyses. Analyze or interpret logistics data involving customer service, forecasting, procurement, manufacturing, inventory, transportation, or warehousing. Provide logistics technology or information for effective and efficient support of product, equipment, or system manufacturing or service. Evaluate effectiveness of current or future logistical processes. Apply logistics modeling techniques to address issues such as operational process improvement or facility design or layout.

Education/Training Required: Bachelor's degree. **Education and Training Programs:** Logistics, Materials, and Supply Chain Management; Operations Management and Supervision; Transportation/Mobility Management. **Knowledge/Courses:** Engineering and Technology; Design; Transportation; Telecommunications; Mechanical Devices; Production and Processing.

Personality Type: Investigative-Conventional-Realistic. **Career Clusters:** 04 Business, Management, and Administration; 16 Transportation, Distribution, and Logistics. **Career Pathways:** 04.1 Management; 16.2 Logistics, Planning, and Management Services. **Other Jobs in These Pathways:** Brownfield Redevelopment Specialists and Site Managers; Business Continuity Planners; Business Operations Specialists, All Other; Chief Executives; Chief Sustainability Officers; Compliance Managers; Computer and Information Systems Managers; Construction Managers; Customs Brokers; Energy Auditors; First-Line Supervisors of Office and Administrative Support Workers; General and Operations Managers; Investment Fund Managers; Loss Prevention Managers; Management Analysts; Managers, All Other; Public Relations Specialists; Regulatory Affairs Managers; Sales Managers; Security Management Specialists; Security Managers; Supply Chain Managers; Sustainability Specialists; Wind Energy Operations Managers; Wind Energy Project Managers; others.

Maintenance and Repair Workers, General

❀ Annual Earnings: $34,730

❀ Earnings Growth Potential: Medium (40.1%)

❀ Growth: 10.9%

❀ Annual Job Openings: 35,750

❀ Self-Employed: 1.1%

Skills—Most Important: Installation Skills; Equipment Use/Maintenance Skills.

Perform work involving the skills of two or more maintenance or craft occupations to keep machines, mechanical equipment, or the structure of an establishment in repair. Duties may involve pipe fitting; boiler making; insulating; welding; machining; carpentry; repairing electrical or mechanical equipment; installing, aligning, and balancing new equipment; and repairing buildings, floors, or stairs. Repair or replace defective equipment parts using hand tools and power tools and reassemble equipment. Perform routine preventive maintenance to ensure that machines continue to run smoothly, building systems operate efficiently, or the physical condition of buildings does not deteriorate. Inspect drives, motors, and belts; check fluid levels; replace filters; or perform other maintenance actions following checklists. Use tools ranging from common hand and power tools, such as hammers, hoists, saws, drills, and wrenches, to precision measuring instruments and electrical and electronic testing devices. Assemble, install, or repair the following: wiring, electrical or electronic components, pipe systems, plumbing, machinery, or equipment. Diagnose mechanical problems and determine how to correct them, checking blueprints, repair manuals, or parts catalogs. Inspect, operate, or test machinery or equipment to diagnose machine malfunctions. Record type and cost of maintenance or repair work. Clean or lubricate shafts, bearings, gears, or other parts of machinery. Dismantle devices to access and remove defective parts using hoists, cranes, hand tools, and power tools. Plan and lay out repair work using diagrams, drawings, blueprints, maintenance manuals, or schematic diagrams. Order parts, supplies, and equipment from catalogs and suppliers or obtain them from storerooms.

Education/Training Required: Moderate-term on-the-job training. **Education and Training Program:** Industrial Mechanics and Maintenance Technology. **Knowledge/Courses:** Building and Construction; Mechanical Devices; Design; Public Safety and Security; Physics; Engineering and Technology.

Personality Type: Realistic-Conventional-Investigative. **Career Cluster:** 13 Manufacturing. **Career Pathway:** 02.2 Construction. **Other Jobs in This Pathway:** Brickmasons and Blockmasons; Cement Masons and Concrete Finishers; Construction and Building Inspectors; Construction Carpenters; Construction Laborers; Construction Managers; Cost Estimators; Drywall and Ceiling Tile Installers; Electrical Power-Line Installers and Repairers; Electricians; Engineering Technicians, Except Drafters, All Other; First-Line Supervisors of Construction Trades and Extraction Workers; Heating and Air Conditioning Mechanics and Installers; Helpers—Carpenters; Helpers—Electricians; Helpers—Pipelayers, Plumbers, Pipefitters, and Steamfitters; Highway Maintenance Workers; Operating Engineers and Other Construction Equipment Operators; Painters, Construction and Maintenance; Pipe Fitters and Steamfitters; Plumbers; Refrigeration Mechanics and Installers; Roofers; Rough Carpenters; Solar Energy Installation Managers; others.

Management Analysts

❋ Annual Earnings: $78,160

❋ Earnings Growth Potential: High (43.8%)

❋ Growth: 23.9%

❋ Annual Job Openings: 30,650

❋ Self-Employed: 25.8%

Skills—Most Important: Thought-Processing Skills; Mathematics Skills; Communication Skills. **Other High-Level Skills:** Social Skills; Management Skills.

Conduct organizational studies and evaluations, design systems and procedures, conduct work simplifications and measurement studies, and prepare operations and procedures manuals to assist management in operating more efficiently and effectively. Includes program analysts and management consultants. Gather and organize information on problems or procedures. Analyze data and develop solutions or alternative methods of proceeding. Confer with personnel to ensure successful functioning of newly implemented systems or procedures. Develop and implement records management program for filing, protection, and retrieval of records and assure compliance with program. Review forms and reports and confer with management and users about format, distribution, and purpose and to identify problems and improvements. Document findings of study and prepare recommendations for implementation of new systems, procedures, or organizational changes. Interview personnel and conduct on-site observation to ascertain unit functions; work performed; and methods, equipment, and personnel used. Prepare manuals and train workers in use of new forms, reports, procedures, or equipment according to organizational policy. Plan study of work problems and procedures, such as organizational change, communications, information flow, integrated production methods, inventory control, or cost analysis. Design, evaluate, recommend, and approve changes of forms and reports. Recommend purchase of storage equipment and design area layout to locate equipment in space available.

Education/Training Required: Work experience plus degree. **Education and Training Programs:** Business Administration and Management, General; Business/Commerce, General. **Knowledge/Courses:** Personnel and Human Resources; Clerical Practices; Sales and Marketing; Economics and Accounting; Customer and Personal Service; Administration and Management.

Personality Type: Investigative-Enterprising-Conventional. **Career Cluster:** 04 Business, Management, and Administration. **Career Pathway:** 04.1 Management. **Other Jobs in This Pathway:** Administrative Services Managers; Brownfield Redevelopment Specialists and Site Managers; Business Continuity Planners; Business Operations Specialists, All Other; Chief Executives; Chief Sustainability Officers; Compliance Managers; Computer and Information Systems Managers; Construction Managers; Customs Brokers; Energy Auditors; First-Line Supervisors of Office and Administrative Support Workers; General and Operations Managers; Investment Fund Managers; Loss Prevention Managers; Managers, All Other; Public Relations

Specialists; Regulatory Affairs Managers; Sales Managers; Security Management Specialists; Security Managers; Supply Chain Managers; Sustainability Specialists; Wind Energy Operations Managers; Wind Energy Project Managers; others.

Managers, All Other

- ❀ Annual Earnings: $96,450
- ❀ Earnings Growth Potential: High (48.2%)
- ❀ Growth: 7.3%
- ❀ Annual Job Openings: 29,750
- ❀ Self-Employed: 57.1%

Skills—Most Important: Management Skills; Thought-Processing Skills; Social Skills. **Other High-Level Skills:** Communication Skills; Science Skills; Mathematics Skills.

This occupation includes all managers not listed separately. Because this is a highly diverse occupation, no data is available for some information topics.

Education/Training Required: Work experience in a related occupation. **Education and Training Program:** Business/Commerce, General. **Career Clusters:** 03 Arts, Audio/Video Technology, and Communications; 04 Business, Management, and Administration; 07 Government and Public Administration; 09 Hospitality and Tourism; 10 Human Services; 16 Transportation, Distribution, and Logistics. **Career Pathways:** 09.3 Travel and Tourism; 10.3 Family and Community Services; 07.7 Public Management and Administration; 07.1 Governance; 04.2 Business, Financial Management, and Accounting; 04.1 Management; 03.4 Performing Arts; 03.1 Audio and Video Technology and Film; 16.2 Logistics,

Planning, and Management Services. **Other Jobs in These Pathways:** Accountants; Auditors; Bookkeeping, Accounting, and Auditing Clerks; Brownfield Redevelopment Specialists and Site Managers; Business Continuity Planners; Business Operations Specialists, All Other; Childcare Workers; Compliance Managers; Construction Managers; Customs Brokers; Energy Auditors; First-Line Supervisors of Office and Administrative Support Workers; General and Operations Managers; Investment Fund Managers; Loss Prevention Managers; Management Analysts; Nannies; Personal Care Aides; Regulatory Affairs Managers; Security Management Specialists; Security Managers; Supply Chain Managers; Sustainability Specialists; Wind Energy Operations Managers; Wind Energy Project Managers; others.

Job Specialization: Brownfield Redevelopment Specialists and Site Managers

Participate in planning and directing clean up and redevelopment of contaminated properties for reuse. Does not include properties sufficiently contaminated to qualify as Superfund sites. Review or evaluate environmental remediation project proposals. Review or evaluate designs for contaminant treatment or disposal facilities. Provide training on hazardous material or waste cleanup procedures and technologies. Provide expert witness testimony on issues such as soil, air, or water contamination and associated cleanup measures. Prepare reports or presentations to communicate brownfield redevelopment needs, status, or progress. Negotiate contracts for services or materials needed for environmental remediation. Prepare and submit permit applications for demolition, clean up,

remediation, or construction projects. Maintain records of decisions, actions, and progress on environmental redevelopment projects. Inspect sites to assess environmental damage or monitor cleanup progress. Plan or implement brownfield redevelopment projects to ensure safety, quality, and compliance with applicable standards or requirements. Identify environmental contamination sources. Estimate costs for environmental clean up and remediation of land redevelopment projects. Develop or implement plans for revegetation of brownfield sites. Design or implement plans for surface or ground water remediation. Design or implement plans for structural demolition and debris removal. Design or implement measures to improve the water, air, and soil quality of military test sites, abandoned mine land, or other contaminated sites. Design or conduct environmental restoration studies.

Education/Training Required: Bachelor's degree. **Education and Training Program:** Hazardous Materials Management and Waste Technology/Technician.

Career Cluster: 04 Business, Management, and Administration. **Career Pathways:** 04.2 Business, Financial Management, and Accounting; 04.1 Management. **Other Jobs in These Pathways:** Accountants; Auditors; Billing and Posting Clerks; Bookkeeping, Accounting, and Auditing Clerks; Business Continuity Planners; Business Operations Specialists, All Other; Compliance Managers; Construction Managers; Customs Brokers; Energy Auditors; Financial Managers, Branch or Department; First-Line Supervisors of Office and Administrative Support Workers; General and Operations Managers; Investment Fund Managers; Loss Prevention Managers; Management Analysts; Managers, All Other;

Regulatory Affairs Managers; Security Management Specialists; Security Managers; Supply Chain Managers; Sustainability Specialists; Treasurers and Controllers; Wind Energy Operations Managers; Wind Energy Project Managers; others.

Job Specialization: Compliance Managers

Plan, direct, or coordinate activities of an organization to ensure compliance with ethical or regulatory standards. Verify that software technology is in place to adequately provide oversight and monitoring in all required areas. Serve as a confidential point of contact for employees to communicate with management, seek clarification on issues or dilemmas, or report irregularities. Maintain documentation of compliance activities such as complaints received and investigation outcomes. Consult with corporate attorneys to address difficult legal compliance issues. Discuss emerging compliance issues with management or employees. Collaborate with human resources departments to ensure the implementation of consistent disciplinary action strategies in cases of compliance standard violations. Advise internal management or business partners on the implementation and operation of compliance programs. Review communications such as securities sales advertising to ensure no violations of standards or regulations. Provide employee training on compliance-related topics, policies, or procedures. Report violations of compliance or regulatory standards to enforcement agencies as appropriate or required. Provide assistance to internal and external auditors in compliance reviews. Prepare management reports on compliance operations and progress. Oversee internal reporting systems such as corporate compliance hotlines and inform employees about these systems. Monitor compliance systems to ensure their effectiveness.

Education/Training Required: Work experience plus degree. **Education and Training Program:** Business Administration and Management, General.

Personality Type: Conventional-Enterprising-Realistic. **Career Clusters:** 04 Business, Management, and Administration; 07 Government and Public Administration. **Career Pathways:** 04.2 Business, Financial Management, and Accounting; 04.1 Management; 07.1 Governance. **Other Jobs in These Pathways:** Accountants; Auditors; Billing and Posting Clerks; Bookkeeping, Accounting, and Auditing Clerks; Brownfield Redevelopment Specialists and Site Managers; Business Continuity Planners; Business Operations Specialists, All Other; Construction Managers; Customs Brokers; Energy Auditors; Financial Managers, Branch or Department; First-Line Supervisors of Office and Administrative Support Workers; General and Operations Managers; Investment Fund Managers; Loss Prevention Managers; Management Analysts; Managers, All Other; Regulatory Affairs Managers; Security Management Specialists; Security Managers; Supply Chain Managers; Sustainability Specialists; Treasurers and Controllers; Wind Energy Operations Managers; Wind Energy Project Managers; others.

Job Specialization: Investment Fund Managers

Plan, direct, or coordinate investment strategy or operations for a large pool of liquid assets supplied by institutional investors or individual investors. Prepare for and respond to regulatory inquiries. Verify regulatory compliance of transaction reporting.

Hire and evaluate staff. Direct activities of accounting or operations departments. Develop, implement, or monitor security valuation policies. Attend investment briefings or consult financial media to stay abreast of relevant investment markets. Review offering documents or marketing materials to ensure regulatory compliance. Perform or evaluate research, such as detailed company and industry analyses, to inform financial forecasting, decision making, or valuation. Present investment information, such as product risks, fees, and fund performance statistics. Monitor financial or operational performance of individual investments to ensure portfolios meet risk goals. Monitor regulatory or tax law changes to ensure fund compliance or to capitalize on development opportunities. Meet with investors to determine investment goals or to discuss investment strategies. Identify group and individual target investors for a specific fund. Develop or direct development of offering documents or marketing materials. Evaluate the potential of new product developments or market opportunities according to factors such as business plans, technologies, and market potential. Develop and implement fund investment policies and strategies. Select and direct the execution of trades. Analyze acquisitions to ensure conformance with strategic goals or regulatory requirements.

Education/Training Required: Work experience plus degree. **Education and Training Program:** Investments and Securities.

Personality Type: Enterprising-Conventional. **Career Cluster:** 04 Business, Management, and Administration. **Career Pathways:** 04.1 Management; 04.2 Business, Financial Management, and Accounting. **Other Jobs in These Pathways:** Accountants; Auditors; Billing and Posting Clerks; Bookkeeping,

Accounting, and Auditing Clerks; Brownfield Redevelopment Specialists and Site Managers; Business Continuity Planners; Business Operations Specialists, All Other; Compliance Managers; Construction Managers; Customs Brokers; Energy Auditors; Financial Managers, Branch or Department; First-Line Supervisors of Office and Administrative Support Workers; General and Operations Managers; Loss Prevention Managers; Management Analysts; Managers, All Other; Regulatory Affairs Managers; Security Management Specialists; Security Managers; Supply Chain Managers; Sustainability Specialists; Treasurers and Controllers; Wind Energy Operations Managers; Wind Energy Project Managers; others.

Job Specialization: Loss Prevention Managers

Plan and direct policies, procedures, or systems to prevent the loss of assets. Determine risk exposure or potential liability and develop risk control measures. Review loss-prevention exception reports and cash discrepancies to ensure adherence to guidelines. Perform cash audits and deposit investigations to fully account for store cash. Provide recommendations and solutions in crisis situations such as workplace violence, protests, and demonstrations. Monitor and review paperwork procedures and systems to prevent error-related shortages. Maintain databases such as bad check logs, reports on multiple offenders, and alarm activation lists. Investigate or interview individuals suspected of shoplifting or internal theft. Direct installation of covert surveillance equipment, such as security cameras. Advise retail establishments on development of loss-investigation procedures. Visit stores to ensure compliance with company policies and procedures. Verify correct use and maintenance of physical security systems, such as closed-circuit television, merchandise tags, and burglar alarms. Train loss-prevention staff, retail managers, or store employees on loss control and prevention measures. Supervise surveillance, detection, or criminal processing related to theft and criminal cases. Recommend improvements in loss-prevention programs, staffing, scheduling, or training. Perform or direct inventory investigations in response to shrink results outside of acceptable ranges. Hire or supervise loss-prevention staff.

Education/Training Required: Bachelor's degree. **Education and Training Program:** Security and Loss Prevention Services.

Personality Type: Enterprising-Conventional. **Career Cluster:** 04 Business, Management, and Administration. **Career Pathways:** 04.2 Business, Financial Management, and Accounting; 04.1 Management. **Other Jobs in These Pathways:** Accountants; Auditors; Billing and Posting Clerks; Bookkeeping, Accounting, and Auditing Clerks; Brownfield Redevelopment Specialists and Site Managers; Business Continuity Planners; Business Operations Specialists, All Other; Compliance Managers; Construction Managers; Customs Brokers; Energy Auditors; Financial Managers, Branch or Department; First-Line Supervisors of Office and Administrative Support Workers; General and Operations Managers; Investment Fund Managers; Management Analysts; Managers, All Other; Regulatory Affairs Managers; Security Management Specialists; Security Managers; Supply Chain Managers; Sustainability Specialists; Treasurers and Controllers; Wind Energy Operations Managers; Wind Energy Project Managers; others.

Job Specialization: Regulatory Affairs Managers

Plan, direct, or coordinate production activities of an organization to ensure compliance with regulations and standard operating procedures. Direct the preparation and submission of regulatory agency applications, reports, or correspondence. Review all regulatory agency submission materials to ensure timeliness, accuracy, comprehensiveness, and compliance with regulatory standards. Provide regulatory guidance to departments or development project teams on design, development, evaluation, or marketing of products. Formulate or implement regulatory affairs policies and procedures to ensure that regulatory compliance is maintained or enhanced. Manage activities such as audits, regulatory agency inspections, and product recalls. Communicate regulatory information to multiple departments and ensure that information is interpreted correctly. Develop regulatory strategies and implementation plans for the preparation and submission of new products. Provide responses to regulatory agencies on product information or issues. Maintain current knowledge of relevant regulations including proposed and final rules. Investigate product complaints and prepare documentation and submissions to appropriate regulatory agencies as necessary. Review materials such as marketing literature and user manuals to ensure that regulatory agency requirements are met. Implement or monitor complaint-processing systems to ensure effective and timely resolution of all complaint investigations. Represent organizations before domestic or international regulatory agencies on major policy matters or decisions regarding company products.

Education/Training Required: Work experience plus degree. **Education and Training Program:** Business Administration and Management, General. **Knowledge/Courses:** Biology; Medicine and Dentistry; Law and Government; Chemistry; Clerical Practices; Personnel and Human Resources.

Personality Type: Enterprising-Conventional. **Career Clusters:** 04 Business, Management, and Administration; 07 Government and Public Administration. **Career Pathways:** 07.1 Governance; 07.6 Regulation; 04.2 Business, Financial Management, and Accounting; 04.1 Management. **Other Jobs in These Pathways:** Accountants; Auditors; Billing and Posting Clerks; Bookkeeping, Accounting, and Auditing Clerks; Brownfield Redevelopment Specialists and Site Managers; Business Continuity Planners; Business Operations Specialists, All Other; Compliance Managers; Construction Managers; Customs Brokers; Energy Auditors; Financial Managers, Branch or Department; First-Line Supervisors of Office and Administrative Support Workers; General and Operations Managers; Investment Fund Managers; Loss Prevention Managers; Management Analysts; Managers, All Other; Security Management Specialists; Security Managers; Supply Chain Managers; Sustainability Specialists; Treasurers and Controllers; Wind Energy Operations Managers; Wind Energy Project Managers; others.

Job Specialization: Security Managers

Direct an organization's security functions, including physical security and safety of employees, facilities, and assets. Write or review security-related documents, such as incident reports, proposals, and tactical or strategic initiatives. Train subordinate security professionals or other organization members in security rules and procedures. Plan security for special and high-risk events. Review financial reports to ensure efficiency and quality of security operations. Develop budgets for security operations. Order security-related supplies and equipment. Coordinate security operations or activities with public law enforcement, fire deparments, and other agencies. Attend meetings, professional seminars, or conferences to keep abreast of changes in executive legislative directives or new technologies impacting security operations. Assist in emergency management and contingency planning. Arrange for or perform executive protection activities. Respond to medical emergencies, bomb threats, fire alarms, or intrusion alarms following emergency response procedures. Recommend security procedures for security call centers, operations centers, domains, asset classification systems, system acquisition, system development, system maintenance, access control, program models, or reporting tools. Prepare reports or make presentations on internal investigations, losses, or violations of regulations, policies, and procedures. Identify, investigate, or resolve security breaches.

Education/Training Required: Work experience plus degree. **Education and Training Program:** Security and Loss Prevention Services.

Career Cluster: 04 Business, Management, and Administration. **Career Pathways:** 04.2 Business, Financial Management, and Accounting; 04.1 Management. **Other Jobs in These Pathways:** Accountants; Auditors; Billing and Posting Clerks; Bookkeeping, Accounting, and Auditing Clerks; Brownfield Redevelopment Specialists and Site Managers; Business Continuity Planners; Business Operations Specialists, All Other;

Compliance Managers; Construction Managers; Customs Brokers; Energy Auditors; Financial Managers, Branch or Department; First-Line Supervisors of Office and Administrative Support Workers; General and Operations Managers; Investment Fund Managers; Loss Prevention Managers; Management Analysts; Managers, All Other; Regulatory Affairs Managers; Security Management Specialists; Supply Chain Managers; Sustainability Specialists; Treasurers and Controllers; Wind Energy Operations Managers; Wind Energy Project Managers; others.

Job Specialization: Supply Chain Managers

Direct, or coordinate production, purchasing, warehousing, distribution, or financial forecasting services and activities to limit costs and improve accuracy, customer service and safety. Examine existing procedures and opportunities for streamlining activities to meet product distribution needs. Direct the movement, storage, and processing of inventory. Select transportation routes to maximize economy by combining shipments and consolidating warehousing and distribution. Develop material costs forecasts or standard cost lists. Assess appropriate material handling equipment needs and staffing levels to load, unload, move, or store materials. Appraise vendor manufacturing ability through on-site visits and measurements. Negotiate prices and terms with suppliers, vendors, or freight forwarders. Monitor supplier performance to assess ability to meet quality and delivery requirements. Monitor forecasts and quotas to identify changes or to determine their effect on supply chain activities. Meet with suppliers to discuss performance metrics, to provide performance feedback, or to discuss production

forecasts or changes. Implement new or improved supply chain processes. Collaborate with other departments, such as procurement, engineering, and quality assurance, to identify or qualify new suppliers.

Education/Training Required: Work experience plus degree. **Education and Training Program:** Logistics, Materials, and Supply Chain Management. **Knowledge/Courses:** Production and Processing; Transportation; Economics and Accounting; Administration and Management; Geography; Sales and Marketing.

Personality Type: Enterprising-Conventional. **Career Clusters:** 04 Business, Management, and Administration; 09 Hospitality and Tourism; 10 Human Services; 16 Transportation, Distribution, and Logistics. **Career Pathways:** 04.1 Management; 04.2 Business, Financial Management, and Accounting; 09.3 Travel and Tourism; 10.3 Family and Community Services; 16.2 Logistics, Planning, and Management Services. **Other Jobs in These Pathways:** Accountants; Auditors; Bookkeeping, Accounting, and Auditing Clerks; Brownfield Redevelopment Specialists and Site Managers; Business Continuity Planners; Business Operations Specialists, All Other; Childcare Workers; Compliance Managers; Construction Managers; Customs Brokers; Energy Auditors; First-Line Supervisors of Office and Administrative Support Workers; General and Operations Managers; Investment Fund Managers; Loss Prevention Managers; Management Analysts; Managers, All Other; Nannies; Personal Care Aides; Regulatory Affairs Managers; Security Management Specialists; Security Managers; Sustainability Specialists; Wind Energy Operations Managers; Wind Energy Project Managers; others.

Job Specialization: Wind Energy Operations Managers

Manage wind field operations, including personnel, maintenance activities, financial activities, and planning. Train or coordinate the training of employees in operations, safety, environmental issues, or technical issues. Track and maintain records for wind operations, such as site performance, downtime events, parts usage, and substation events. Provide technical support to wind field customers, employees, or subcontractors. Manage warranty repair or replacement services. Order parts, tools, or equipment needed to maintain, restore, or improve wind field operations. Maintain operations records, such as work orders, site inspection forms, or other documentation. Negotiate or review and approve wind farm contracts. Recruit or select wind operations employees, contractors, or subcontractors. Monitor and maintain records of daily facility operations. Estimate costs associated with operations, including repairs and preventive maintenance. Establish goals, objectives, or priorities for wind field operations. Develop relationships and communicate with customers, site managers, developers, land owners, authorities, utility representatives, or residents. Develop processes and procedures for wind operations, including transitioning from construction to commercial operations. Prepare wind field operational budgets. Supervise employees or subcontractors to ensure quality of work or adherence to safety regulations or policies. Oversee the maintenance of wind field equipment or structures, such as towers, transformers, electrical collector systems, roadways, and other site assets.

Education/Training Required: Work experience plus degree. **Education and Training Program:** Energy Management and Systems Technology/Technician.

Career Cluster: 04 Business, Management, and Administration. **Career Pathways:** 04.1 Management; 04.2 Business, Financial Management, and Accounting. **Other Jobs in These Pathways:** Accountants; Auditors; Billing and Posting Clerks; Bookkeeping, Accounting, and Auditing Clerks; Brownfield Redevelopment Specialists and Site Managers; Business Continuity Planners; Business Operations Specialists, All Other; Compliance Managers; Construction Managers; Customs Brokers; Energy Auditors; Financial Managers, Branch or Department; First-Line Supervisors of Office and Administrative Support Workers; General and Operations Managers; Investment Fund Managers; Loss Prevention Managers; Management Analysts; Managers, All Other; Regulatory Affairs Managers; Security Management Specialists; Security Managers; Supply Chain Managers; Sustainability Specialists; Treasurers and Controllers; Wind Energy Project Managers; others.

Job Specialization: Wind Energy Project Managers

Lead or manage the development and evaluation of potential wind energy business opportunities, including environmental studies, permitting, and proposals. May also manage construction of projects. Supervise the work of subcontractors or consultants to ensure quality and conformance to specifications or budgets. Prepare requests for proposals for wind project construction or equipment acquisition. Manage site assessments or environmental studies for wind fields. Lead or support negotiations involving tax agreements or abatements, power purchase agreements, land use, or interconnection agreements. Update schedules, estimates, forecasts, or budgets for wind projects. Review or evaluate proposals or bids to make recommendations on awarding of contracts. Provide verbal or written project status reports to project teams, management, subcontractors, customers, or owners. Review civil design, engineering, or construction technical documentation to ensure compliance with applicable government or industrial codes, standards, requirements, or regulations. Provide technical support for the design, construction, or commissioning of wind farm projects. Prepare wind project documentation, including diagrams or layouts. Manage wind project costs to stay within budget. Develop scope of work for wind project functions, such as design, site assessment, environmental studies, surveying, and field support services. Coordinate or direct development, energy assessment, engineering, or construction activities to ensure that wind project needs and objectives are met.

Education/Training Required: Work experience plus degree. **Education and Training Program:** Energy Management and Systems Technology/Technician.

Career Cluster: 04 Business, Management, and Administration. **Career Pathways:** 04.1 Management; 04.2 Business, Financial Management, and Accounting. **Other Jobs in These Pathways:** Accountants; Auditors; Billing and Posting Clerks; Bookkeeping, Accounting, and Auditing Clerks; Brownfield Redevelopment Specialists and Site Managers; Business Continuity Planners; Business Operations Specialists, All Other; Compliance Managers; Construction Managers; Customs Brokers; Energy Auditors; Financial Managers, Branch or Department; First-Line Supervisors of Office and Administrative Support Workers; General and Operations Managers; Investment Fund Managers; Loss Prevention Managers;

Management Analysts; Managers, All Other; Regulatory Affairs Managers; Security Management Specialists; Security Managers; Supply Chain Managers; Sustainability Specialists; Treasurers and Controllers; Wind Energy Operations Managers; others.

Market Research Analysts and Marketing Specialists

* Annual Earnings: $60,570
* Earnings Growth Potential: High (44.9%)
* Growth: 28.1%
* Annual Job Openings: 13,730
* Self-Employed: 6.8%

Skills—Most Important: Mathematics Skills; Science Skills; Thought-Processing Skills. **Other High-Level Skills:** Communication Skills; Social Skills; Management Skills.

Research market conditions in local, regional, or national areas to determine potential sales of a product or service. May gather information on competitors, prices, sales, and methods of marketing and distribution. May use survey results to create a marketing campaign based on regional preferences and buying habits. Collect and analyze data on customer demographics, preferences, needs, and buying habits to identify potential markets and factors affecting product demand. Prepare reports of findings, illustrating data graphically and translating complex findings into written text. Measure and assess customer and employee satisfaction. Forecast and track marketing and sales trends, analyzing collected data. Seek and provide information to help companies determine their position in the marketplace. Measure the effectiveness of marketing, advertising, and communications programs and strategies. Conduct research on consumer opinions and marketing strategies, collaborating with marketing professionals, statisticians, pollsters, and other professionals. Attend staff conferences to provide management with information and proposals concerning the promotion, distribution, design, and pricing of company products or services. Gather data on competitors and analyze their prices, sales, and method of marketing and distribution. Monitor industry statistics and follow trends in trade literature. Devise and evaluate methods and procedures for collecting data, such as surveys, opinion polls, or questionnaires, or arrange to obtain existing data. Develop and implement procedures for identifying advertising needs. Direct trained survey interviewers.

Education/Training Required: Bachelor's degree. **Education and Training Programs:** Apparel and Textile Marketing Management; Consumer Merchandising/Retailing Management; International Marketing; Marketing Research; Marketing, Other; Marketing/Marketing Management, General. **Knowledge/Courses:** Sales and Marketing; Clerical Practices; Sociology and Anthropology; Economics and Accounting; Personnel and Human Resources; Computers and Electronics.

Personality Type: Investigative-Enterprising-Conventional. **Career Cluster:** 04 Business, Management, and Administration. **Career Pathways:** 14.5 Marketing Information Management and Research; 04.1 Management; 15.2 Science and Mathematics. **Other Jobs in These Pathways:** Brownfield Redevelopment Specialists and Site Managers; Business Continuity Planners; Business Operations Specialists, All Other; Chief Executives; Chief

Sustainability Officers; Compliance Managers; Computer and Information Systems Managers; Construction Managers; Customs Brokers; Energy Auditors; First-Line Supervisors of Office and Administrative Support Workers; First-Line Supervisors of Retail Sales Workers; General and Operations Managers; Investment Fund Managers; Loss Prevention Managers; Management Analysts; Managers, All Other; Regulatory Affairs Managers; Sales Managers; Security Management Specialists; Security Managers; Supply Chain Managers; Sustainability Specialists; Wind Energy Operations Managers; Wind Energy Project Managers; others.

Marketing Managers

- ❋ Annual Earnings: $112,800
- ❋ Earnings Growth Potential: High (48.8%)
- ❋ Growth: 12.5%
- ❋ Annual Job Openings: 5,970
- ❋ Self-Employed: 4.1%

Skills—Most Important: Management Skills; Thought-Processing Skills; Social Skills. **Other High-Level Skills:** Mathematics Skills; Communication Skills.

Determine the demand for products and services offered by firms and their competitors and identify potential customers. Develop pricing strategies with the goal of maximizing firms' profits or shares of the market while ensuring that firms' customers are satisfied. Oversee product development or monitor trends that indicate the need for new products and services. Develop pricing strategies, balancing firm objectives and customer satisfaction. Identify, develop, and evaluate marketing strategy based on knowledge of

M

establishment objectives, market characteristics, and cost and markup factors. Evaluate the financial aspects of product development, such as budgets, expenditures, research and development appropriations, and return-on-investment and profit-loss projections. Formulate, direct, and coordinate marketing activities and policies to promote products and services, working with advertising and promotion managers. Direct the hiring, training, and performance evaluations of marketing and sales staff and oversee their daily activities. Negotiate contracts with vendors and distributors to manage product distribution, establishing distribution networks and developing distribution strategies. Compile lists describing product or service offerings.

Education/Training Required: Work experience plus degree. **Education and Training Programs:** Apparel and Textile Marketing Management; Consumer Merchandising/Retailing Management; International Marketing; Marketing Research; Marketing, Other; Marketing/Marketing Management, General. **Knowledge/Courses:** Sales and Marketing; Customer and Personal Service; Personnel and Human Resources; Communications and Media; Economics and Accounting; Sociology and Anthropology.

Personality Type: Enterprising-Conventional. **Career Cluster:** 14 Marketing, Sales, and Service. **Career Pathways:** 14.5 Marketing Information Management and Research; 14.2 Professional Sales and Marketing; 14.1 Management and Entrepreneurship. **Other Jobs in These Pathways:** Cashiers; Counter and Rental Clerks; Door-To-Door Sales Workers, News and Street Vendors, and Related Workers; Driver/Sales Workers; Energy Brokers; First-Line Supervisors of Non-Retail Sales Workers; First-Line Supervisors of Retail Sales Workers; Hotel,

Motel, and Resort Desk Clerks; Marking Clerks; Online Merchants; Order Fillers, Wholesale and Retail Sales; Parts Salespersons; Property, Real Estate, and Community Association Managers; Real Estate Sales Agents; Reservation and Transportation Ticket Agents and Travel Clerks; Retail Salespersons; Sales and Related Workers, All Other; Sales Managers; Sales Representatives, Services, All Other; Sales Representatives, Wholesale and Manufacturing, Except Technical and Scientific Products; Sales Representatives, Wholesale and Manufacturing, Technical and Scientific Products; Solar Sales Representatives and Assessors; Stock Clerks—Stockroom, Warehouse, or Storage Yard; Stock Clerks, Sales Floor; Telemarketers; others.

Mechanical Door Repairers

* Annual Earnings: $35,780
* Earnings Growth Potential: Medium (36.6%)
* Growth: 10.8%
* Annual Job Openings: 450
* Self-Employed: 0.4%

Skills—Most Important: Installation Skills; Equipment Use/Maintenance Skills.

Install, service, or repair opening and closing mechanisms of automatic doors and hydraulic door closers. Includes garage door mechanics. Adjust doors to open or close with the correct amount of effort and make simple adjustments to electric openers. Wind large springs with upward motion of arm. Inspect job sites, assessing headroom, side room, and other conditions to determine appropriateness of door for a given location. Collect payment on job completion. Complete required paperwork, such as work orders, according to services performed or required. Fasten angle iron back-hangers to ceilings and tracks using fasteners or welding equipment. Repair or replace worn or broken door parts using hand tools. Carry springs to tops of doors using ladders or scaffolding and attach springs to tracks to install spring systems. Set doors in place or stack hardware sections into openings after rail or track installation. Install door frames, rails, steel rolling curtains, electronic-eye mechanisms, and electric door openers and closers using power tools, hand tools, and electronic test equipment. Remove or disassemble defective automatic mechanical door closers using hand tools. Apply hardware to door sections. Assemble and fasten tracks to structures or bucks using impact wrenches or welding equipment. Run low-voltage wiring on ceiling surfaces using insulated staples. Cut door stops and angle irons to fit openings. Study blueprints and schematic diagrams to determine appropriate methods of installing and repairing automated door openers.

Education/Training Required: Moderate-term on-the-job training. **Education and Training Program:** Industrial Mechanics and Maintenance Technology. **Knowledge/Courses:** Building and Construction; Mechanical Devices; Engineering and Technology; Sales and Marketing; Design.

Personality Type: Realistic. **Career Cluster:** 13 Manufacturing. **Career Pathway:** 13.3 Maintenance, Installation, and Repair. **Other Jobs in This Pathway:** Aircraft Mechanics and Service Technicians; Automotive Specialty Technicians; Biological Technicians; Civil Engineering Technicians; Computer, Automated Teller, and Office Machine Repairers; Electrical and Electronic Equipment Assemblers; Electrical and Electronics Repairers, Commercial and Industrial Equipment; Electrical Engineering Technicians; Electrical Engineering Technologists; Electromechanical Engineering Technologists; Electronics Engineering Technicians; Electronics Engineering Technologists; Engineering Technicians, Except Drafters, All Other; Fuel Cell Technicians; Helpers—Installation, Maintenance, and Repair Workers; Industrial Engineering Technologists; Industrial Machinery Mechanics; Installation, Maintenance, and Repair Workers, All Other; Manufacturing Engineering Technologists; Manufacturing Production Technicians; Mapping Technicians; Mechanical Engineering Technologists; Mobile Heavy Equipment Mechanics, Except Engines; Telecommunications Line Installers and Repairers; Tire Repairers and Changers; others.

Mechanical Engineers

- ❋ Annual Earnings: $78,160
- ❋ Earnings Growth Potential: Low (35.3%)
- ❋ Growth: 6.0%
- ❋ Annual Job Openings: 7,570
- ❋ Self-Employed: 2.3%

Skills—Most Important: Science Skills; Technology/Programming Skills; Mathematics Skills. **Other High-Level Skills:** Thought-Processing Skills; Communication Skills; Management Skills; Equipment Use/Maintenance Skills; Social Skills.

Perform engineering duties in planning and designing tools, engines, machines, and other mechanically functioning equipment. Oversee installation, operation, maintenance, and repair of such equipment as centralized heat, gas, water, and steam systems. Read and interpret blueprints, technical drawings, schematics, and computer-generated reports. Assist drafters in developing the structural design of products using drafting tools or computer-assisted design (CAD) or drafting equipment and software. Research, design, evaluate, install, operate, and maintain mechanical products, equipment, systems and processes to meet requirements, applying knowledge of engineering principles. Confer with engineers and other personnel to implement operating procedures, resolve system malfunctions, and provide technical information. Recommend design modifications to eliminate machine or system malfunctions. Conduct research that tests and analyzes the feasibility, design, operation, and performance of equipment, components, and systems. Investigate equipment failures and difficulties to diagnose faulty operation and to make recommendations to maintenance crew. Develop and test models of alternate designs and processing methods to assess feasibility, operating condition effects, possible new applications, and necessity of modification. Develop, coordinate, and monitor all aspects of production, including selection of manufacturing methods, fabrication, and operation of product designs. Specify system components or direct modification of products to ensure conformance with engineering design and performance specifications.

Education/Training Required: Bachelor's degree. **Education and Training Program:** Mechanical Engineering. **Knowledge/Courses:** Design; Engineering and Technology; Physics; Mechanical Devices; Production and Processing; Mathematics.

Personality Type: Investigative-Realistic-Conventional. **Career Cluster:** 15 Science, Technology, Engineering, and Mathematics. **Career Pathway:** 15.1 Engineering and

Technology. **Other Jobs in This Pathway:** Architectural and Engineering Managers; Automotive Engineers; Biochemical Engineers; Biofuels/Biodiesel Technology and Product Development Managers; Civil Engineers; Cost Estimators; Education, Training, and Library Workers, All Other; Electrical Engineers; Electronics Engineers, Except Computer; Energy Engineers; Engineers, All Other; Fuel Cell Engineers; Human Factors Engineers and Ergonomists; Industrial Engineers; Manufacturing Engineers; Mechatronics Engineers; Microsystems Engineers; Nanosystems Engineers; Photonics Engineers; Radio Frequency Identification Device Specialists; Robotics Engineers; Solar Energy Systems Engineers; Transportation Engineers; Validation Engineers; Wind Energy Engineers; others.

Job Specialization: Automotive Engineers

Develop new or improved designs for vehicle structural members, engines, transmissions, and other vehicle systems using computer-assisted design technology. Direct building, modification, and testing of vehicle and components. Read current literature, attend meetings or conferences, and talk with colleagues to stay abreast of new technology and competitive products. Establish production or quality control standards. Prepare and present technical or project status reports. Develop or implement operating methods and procedures. Write, review, or maintain engineering documentation. Conduct research studies to develop new concepts in automotive engineering. Coordinate production activities with other functional units such as procurement, maintenance, and quality control. Provide technical direction to other engineers or engineering support personnel. Perform failure, variation, or root cause analyses. Develop or integrate control feature requirements. Develop engineering specifications and cost estimates for automotive design concepts. Develop calibration methodologies, test methodologies, or tools. Conduct automotive design reviews. Calibrate vehicle systems, including control algorithms and other software systems. Build models for algorithm and control feature verification testing. Alter or modify designs to obtain specified functional and operational performance. Design or analyze automobile systems in areas such as aerodynamics, alternate fuels, ergonomics, hybrid power, brakes, transmissions, steering, calibration, safety, and diagnostics. Conduct or direct system-level automotive testing.

Education/Training Required: Bachelor's degree. **Education and Training Program:** Mechanical Engineering. **Knowledge/Courses:** No data available.

Personality Type: No data available. **Career Cluster:** 15 Science, Technology, Engineering, and Mathematics. **Career Pathway:** 15.1 Engineering and Technology. **Other Jobs in This Pathway:** Architectural and Engineering Managers; Biochemical Engineers; Biofuels/Biodiesel Technology and Product Development Managers; Civil Engineers; Cost Estimators; Education, Training, and Library Workers, All Other; Electrical Engineers; Electronics Engineers, Except Computer; Energy Engineers; Engineers, All Other; Fuel Cell Engineers; Human Factors Engineers and Ergonomists; Industrial Engineers; Manufacturing Engineers; Mechanical Engineers; Mechatronics Engineers; Microsystems Engineers; Nanosystems Engineers; Photonics Engineers; Radio Frequency Identification Device Specialists; Robotics Engineers; Solar Energy Systems

Engineers; Transportation Engineers; Validation Engineers; Wind Energy Engineers; others.

Job Specialization: Fuel Cell Engineers

Design, evaluate, modify, and construct fuel cell components and systems for transportation, stationary, or portable applications. Write technical reports or proposals related to engineering projects. Read current literature, attend meetings or conferences, and talk with colleagues to stay abreast of new technology and competitive products. Prepare test stations, instrumentation, or data acquisition systems for use in specific tests. Plan or implement cost reduction or product improvement projects in collaboration with other engineers, suppliers, support personnel, or customers. Coordinate engineering or test schedules with departments outside engineering, such as manufacturing. Validate design of fuel cells, fuel cell components, or fuel cell systems. Authorize the release of parts or subsystems for production. Simulate or model fuel cell, motor, or other system information using simulation software programs. Recommend or implement changes to fuel cell system design. Provide technical consultation or direction related to the development or production of fuel cell systems. Plan or conduct experiments to validate new materials, optimize startup protocols, reduce conditioning time, or examine contaminant tolerance. Manage hybrid system architecture, including sizing of components such as fuel cells, energy storage units, and electric drives, for fuel cell battery hybrids. Integrate electric drive subsystems with other vehicle systems to optimize performance or mitigate faults. Identify and define the vehicle and system integration challenges for fuel cell vehicles.

Education/Training Required: Bachelor's degree. **Education and Training Program:** Mechanical Engineering. **Knowledge/Courses:** No data available.

Personality Type: No data available. **Career Cluster:** 15 Science, Technology, Engineering, and Mathematics. **Career Pathway:** 15.1 Engineering and Technology. **Other Jobs in This Pathway:** Architectural and Engineering Managers; Automotive Engineers; Biochemical Engineers; Biofuels/ Biodiesel Technology and Product Development Managers; Civil Engineers; Cost Estimators; Education, Training, and Library Workers, All Other; Electrical Engineers; Electronics Engineers, Except Computer; Energy Engineers; Engineers, All Other; Human Factors Engineers and Ergonomists; Industrial Engineers; Manufacturing Engineers; Mechanical Engineers; Mechatronics Engineers; Microsystems Engineers; Nanosystems Engineers; Photonics Engineers; Radio Frequency Identification Device Specialists; Robotics Engineers; Solar Energy Systems Engineers; Transportation Engineers; Validation Engineers; Wind Energy Engineers; others.

Medical and Clinical Laboratory Technicians

❀ Annual Earnings: $36,280

❀ Earnings Growth Potential: Low (33.3%)

❀ Growth: 16.1%

❀ Annual Job Openings: 5,460

❀ Self-Employed: 0.2%

Skills—Most Important: Science Skills; Equipment Use/Maintenance Skills.

Perform routine medical laboratory tests for the diagnosis, treatment, and prevention of disease. May work under the supervision of a medical technologist. Conduct chemical analyses of body fluids, such as blood and urine, using microscope or automatic analyzer to detect abnormalities or diseases and enter findings into computer. Conduct blood tests for transfusion purposes and perform blood counts. Examine cells stained with dye to locate abnormalities. Set up, maintain, calibrate, clean, and test sterility of medical laboratory equipment. Analyze the results of tests and experiments to ensure conformity to specifications using special mechanical and electrical devices. Analyze and record test data to issue reports that use charts, graphs, and narratives. Consult with a pathologist to determine a final diagnosis when abnormal cells are found. Prepare standard volumetric solutions and reagents to be combined with samples following standardized formulas or experimental procedures. Inoculate fertilized eggs, broths, or other bacteriological media with organisms. Collect blood or tissue samples from patients, observing principles of asepsis to obtain blood sample. Obtain specimens and cultivate, isolate, and identify microorganisms for analysis. Cut, stain, and mount tissue samples for examination by pathologists. Perform medical research to further control and cure disease. Test raw materials, processes, and finished products to determine quality and quantity of materials or characteristics of a substance. Supervise and instruct other technicians and laboratory assistants.

Education/Training Required: Associate degree. **Education and Training Programs:** Blood Bank Technology Specialist Training; Clinical/Medical Laboratory Assistant Training; Clinical/Medical Laboratory Technician; Hematology Technology/Technician;

Histologic Technician Training. **Knowledge/ Courses:** Chemistry; Medicine and Dentistry; Biology; Mechanical Devices; Computers and Electronics; Production and Processing.

Personality Type: Realistic-Investigative-Conventional. **Career Cluster:** 08 Health Science. **Career Pathways:** 08.1 Therapeutic Services; 08.2 Diagnostics Services. **Other Jobs in These Pathways:** Clinical Psychologists; Counseling Psychologists; Cytogenetic Technologists; Cytotechnologists; Dental Assistants; Dental Hygienists; Dentists, General; Emergency Medical Technicians and Paramedics; Endoscopy Technicians; Healthcare Support Workers, All Other; Histotechnologists and Histologic Technicians; Home Health Aides; Licensed Practical and Licensed Vocational Nurses; Massage Therapists; Medical and Clinical Laboratory Technologists; Medical and Health Services Managers; Medical Assistants; Medical Secretaries; Pharmacists; Pharmacy Technicians; Radiologic Technologists; School Psychologists; Social and Human Service Assistants; Speech-Language Pathologists; Speech-Language Pathology Assistants; others.

Medical and Clinical Laboratory Technologists

* Annual Earnings: $56,130
* Earnings Growth Potential: Low (30.9%)
* Growth: 11.9%
* Annual Job Openings: 5,330
* Self-Employed: 0.2%

Skills—Most Important: Science Skills; Mathematics Skills; Equipment Use/ Maintenance Skills. **Other High-Level Skills:**

Communication Skills; Thought-Processing Skills; Management Skills; Social Skills.

Perform complex medical laboratory tests for diagnosis, treatment, and prevention of disease. May train or supervise staff. Analyze laboratory findings to check the accuracy of the results. Conduct chemical analysis of body fluids, including blood, urine, and spinal fluid, to determine presence of normal and abnormal components. Operate, calibrate, and maintain equipment used in quantitative and qualitative analysis, such as spectrophotometers, calorimeters, flame photometers, and computer-controlled analyzers. Enter data from analysis of medical tests and clinical results into computer for storage. Analyze samples of biological material for chemical content or reaction. Establish and monitor programs to ensure the accuracy of laboratory results. Set up, clean, and maintain laboratory equipment. Provide technical information about test results to physicians, family members, and researchers. Supervise, train, and direct lab assistants, medical and clinical laboratory technicians and technologists, and other medical laboratory workers engaged in laboratory testing. Develop, standardize, evaluate, and modify procedures, techniques, and tests used in the analysis of specimens and in medical laboratory experiments. Cultivate, isolate, and assist in identifying microbial organisms and perform various tests on these microorganisms. Study blood samples to determine the number of cells and their morphology as well as the blood group, type, and compatibility for transfusion purposes.

Education/Training Required: Bachelor's degree. **Education and Training Programs:** Clinical Laboratory Science/Medical Technology/Technologist; Clinical/Medical Laboratory Science and Allied Professions,

Other; Cytogenetics/Genetics/Clinical Genetics Technology/Technologist; Cytotechnology/Cytotechnologist; Histologic Technology/Histotechnologist; Renal/Dialysis Technologist/Technician. **Knowledge/Courses:** Biology; Chemistry; Medicine and Dentistry; Mechanical Devices; Clerical Practices; Mathematics.

Personality Type: Investigative-Realistic-Conventional. **Career Cluster:** 08 Health Science. **Career Pathway:** 08.2 Diagnostics Services. **Other Jobs in This Pathway:** Ambulance Drivers and Attendants, Except Emergency Medical Technicians; Anesthesiologist Assistants; Cardiovascular Technologists and Technicians; Cytogenetic Technologists; Cytotechnologists; Diagnostic Medical Sonographers; Emergency Medical Technicians and Paramedics; Endoscopy Technicians; Health Diagnosing and Treating Practitioners, All Other; Health Technologists and Technicians, All Other; Healthcare Practitioners and Technical Workers, All Other; Histotechnologists and Histologic Technicians; Medical and Clinical Laboratory Technicians; Medical and Health Services Managers; Medical Assistants; Medical Equipment Preparers; Neurodiagnostic Technologists; Nuclear Medicine Technologists; Ophthalmic Laboratory Technicians; Physical Scientists, All Other; Physician Assistants; Radiologic Technicians; Radiologic Technologists; Surgical Technologists; Veterinary Assistants and Laboratory Animal Caretakers; others.

Job Specialization: Cytogenetic Technologists

Analyze chromosomes found in biological specimens such as amniotic fluids, bone marrow, and blood to aid in the study, diagnosis, or treatment of genetic diseases.

Develop and implement training programs for trainees, medical students, resident physicians, or post-doctoral fellows. Stain slides to make chromosomes visible for microscopy. Summarize test results and report to appropriate authorities. Select or prepare specimens and media for cell cultures using aseptic techniques, knowledge of medium components, or cell nutritional requirements. Select banding methods to permit identification of chromosome pairs. Identify appropriate methods of specimen collection, preservation, or transport. Prepare slides of cell cultures following standard procedures. Select appropriate methods of preparation and storage of media to maintain potential of hydrogen, sterility, or ability to support growth. Harvest cell cultures using substances such as mitotic arrestants, cell-releasing agents, and cell fixatives. Create chromosome images using computer imaging systems. Determine optimal time sequences and methods for manual or robotic cell harvests.

Education/Training Required: Bachelor's degree. **Education and Training Programs:** Clinical Laboratory Science/Medical Technology/Technologist; Cytogenetics/Genetics/Clinical Genetics Technology/Technologist. **Knowledge/Courses:** Biology; Chemistry; Medicine and Dentistry; Education and Training.

Personality Type: Investigative-Realistic-Conventional. **Career Cluster:** 08 Health Science. **Career Pathway:** 08.2 Diagnostics Services. **Other Jobs in This Pathway:** Ambulance Drivers and Attendants, Except Emergency Medical Technicians; Anesthesiologist Assistants; Cardiovascular Technologists and Technicians; Cytotechnologists; Diagnostic Medical Sonographers; Emergency Medical Technicians and Paramedics; Endoscopy

Technicians; Health Diagnosing and Treating Practitioners, All Other; Health Technologists and Technicians, All Other; Healthcare Practitioners and Technical Workers, All Other; Histotechnologists and Histologic Technicians; Medical and Clinical Laboratory Technicians; Medical and Clinical Laboratory Technologists; Medical and Health Services Managers; Medical Assistants; Medical Equipment Preparers; Neurodiagnostic Technologists; Nuclear Medicine Technologists; Ophthalmic Laboratory Technicians; Physical Scientists, All Other; Physician Assistants; Radiologic Technicians; Radiologic Technologists; Surgical Technologists; Veterinary Assistants and Laboratory Animal Caretakers; others.

Job Specialization: Cytotechnologists

Stain, mount, and study cells to detect evidence of cancer, hormonal abnormalities, and other pathological conditions following established standards and practices. Examine cell samples to detect abnormalities in the color, shape, or size of cellular components and patterns. Examine specimens using microscopes to evaluate specimen quality. Prepare and analyze samples, such as Papanicolaou smear body fluids and fine needle aspirations to detect abnormal conditions. Provide patient clinical data or microscopic findings to assist pathologists in the preparation of pathology reports. Assist pathologists or other physicians to collect cell samples such as by fine needle aspiration biopsies. Document specimens by verifying patients' and specimens' information. Maintain effective laboratory operations by adhering to standards of specimen collection, preparation, or laboratory safety. Submit slides with abnormal cell structures to pathologists for further examination. Adjust, maintain, or repair laboratory equipment such as microscopes. Assign

tasks or coordinate task assignments to ensure adequate performance of laboratory activities.

Education/Training Required: Bachelor's degree. **Education and Training Programs:** Clinical Laboratory Science/Medical Technology/Technologist; Cytotechnology/Cytotechnologist. **Knowledge/Courses:** Biology; Medicine and Dentistry; Chemistry; Clerical.

Personality Type: Investigative-Realistic. **Career Cluster:** 08 Health Science. **Career Pathway:** 08.2 Diagnostics Services. **Other Jobs in This Pathway:** Ambulance Drivers and Attendants, Except Emergency Medical Technicians; Anesthesiologist Assistants; Cardiovascular Technologists and Technicians; Cytogenetic Technologists; Diagnostic Medical Sonographers; Emergency Medical Technicians and Paramedics; Endoscopy Technicians; Health Diagnosing and Treating Practitioners, All Other; Health Technologists and Technicians, All Other; Healthcare Practitioners and Technical Workers, All Other; Histotechnologists and Histologic Technicians; Medical and Clinical Laboratory Technicians; Medical and Clinical Laboratory Technologists; Medical and Health Services Managers; Medical Assistants; Medical Equipment Preparers; Neurodiagnostic Technologists; Nuclear Medicine Technologists; Ophthalmic Laboratory Technicians; Physical Scientists, All Other; Physician Assistants; Radiologic Technicians; Radiologic Technologists; Surgical Technologists; Veterinary Assistants and Laboratory Animal Caretakers; others.

Job Specialization: Histotechnologists and Histologic Technicians

Prepare histologic slides from tissue sections for microscopic examination and diagnosis

M

by pathologists. May assist in research studies. Cut sections of body tissues for microscopic examination using microtomes. Embed tissue specimens into paraffin wax blocks or infiltrate tissue specimens with wax. Freeze tissue specimens. Mount tissue specimens on glass slides. Stain tissue specimens with dyes or other chemicals to make cell details visible under microscopes. Examine slides under microscopes to ensure tissue preparation meets laboratory requirements. Identify tissue structures or cell components to be used in the diagnosis, prevention, or treatment of diseases. Operate computerized laboratory equipment to dehydrate, decalcify, or microincinerate tissue samples. Perform procedures associated with histochemistry to prepare specimens for immunofluorescence or microscopy. Maintain laboratory equipment such as microscopes, mass spectrometers, microtomes, immunostainers, tissue processors, embedding centers, and water baths. Prepare or use prepared tissue specimens for teaching, research, or diagnostic purposes.

Education/Training Required: Associate degree. **Education and Training Programs:** Clinical Laboratory Science/Medical Technology/Technologist; Clinical/Medical Laboratory Science and Allied Professions, Other; Cytogenetics/Genetics/Clinical Genetics Technology/Technologist; Cytotechnology/ Cytotechnologist; Histologic Technology/ Histotechnologist; Renal/Dialysis Technologist/ Technician. **Knowledge/Courses:** Biology; Chemistry; Medicine and Dentistry; Production and Processing; Mechanical Devices; Education and Training.

Personality Type: Realistic-Investigative-Conventional. **Career Cluster:** 08 Health Science. **Career Pathway:** 08.2 Diagnostics Services. **Other Jobs in This Pathway:**

Ambulance Drivers and Attendants, Except Emergency Medical Technicians; Anesthesiologist Assistants; Cardiovascular Technologists and Technicians; Cytogenetic Technologists; Cytotechnologists; Diagnostic Medical Sonographers; Emergency Medical Technicians and Paramedics; Endoscopy Technicians; Health Diagnosing and Treating Practitioners, All Other; Health Technologists and Technicians, All Other; Healthcare Practitioners and Technical Workers, All Other; Medical and Clinical Laboratory Technicians; Medical and Clinical Laboratory Technologists; Medical and Health Services Managers; Medical Assistants; Medical Equipment Preparers; Neurodiagnostic Technologists; Nuclear Medicine Technologists; Ophthalmic Laboratory Technicians; Physical Scientists, All Other; Physician Assistants; Radiologic Technicians; Radiologic Technologists; Surgical Technologists; Veterinary Assistants and Laboratory Animal Caretakers; others.

Medical and Health Services Managers

* Annual Earnings: $84,270
* Earnings Growth Potential: Medium (39.1%)
* Growth: 16.0%
* Annual Job Openings: 9,940
* Self-Employed: 6.0%

Skills—Most Important: Science Skills; Management Skills; Thought-Processing Skills. **Other High-Level Skills:** Social Skills; Communication Skills; Mathematics Skills.

Plan, direct, or coordinate medicine and health services in hospitals, clinics, managed care organizations, public health agencies, or

similar organizations. Direct, supervise, and evaluate work activities of medical, nursing, technical, clerical, service, maintenance, and other personnel. Establish objectives and evaluative or operational criteria for units they manage. Direct or conduct recruitment, hiring, and training of personnel. Develop and maintain computerized record management systems to store and process data such as personnel activities and information and to produce reports. Develop and implement organizational policies and procedures for the facility or medical unit. Conduct and administer fiscal operations, including accounting, planning budgets, authorizing expenditures, establishing rates for services, and coordinating financial reporting. Establish work schedules and assignments for staff according to workload, space, and equipment availability. Maintain communication between governing boards, medical staff, and department heads by attending board meetings and coordinating interdepartmental functioning.

Education/Training Required: Work experience plus degree. **Education and Training Programs:** Community Health and Preventive Medicine; Health and Medical Administrative Services, Other; Health Information/Medical Records Administration/ Administrator; Health Services Administration; Health Unit Manager/Ward Supervisor Training; Health/Health Care Administration/ Management; Hospital and Health Care Facilities Administration/Management; Public Health, General. **Knowledge/Courses:** Economics and Accounting; Personnel and Human Resources; Administration and Management; Sales and Marketing; Medicine and Dentistry; Law and Government.

Personality Type: Enterprising-Conventional-Social. **Career Cluster:** 08 Health Science. **Career Pathways:** 08.1 Therapeutic Services; 08.2 Diagnostics Services; 08.3 Health Informatics. **Other Jobs in These Pathways:** Cytogenetic Technologists; Cytotechnologists; Dental Assistants; Dental Hygienists; Emergency Medical Technicians and Paramedics; Endoscopy Technicians; Engineers, All Other; Executive Secretaries and Executive Administrative Assistants; First-Line Supervisors of Office and Administrative Support Workers; Healthcare Support Workers, All Other; Histotechnologists and Histologic Technicians; Home Health Aides; Licensed Practical and Licensed Vocational Nurses; Medical and Clinical Laboratory Technologists; Medical Assistants; Medical Records and Health Information Technicians; Medical Secretaries; Pharmacists; Pharmacy Technicians; Physical Therapists; Public Relations Specialists; Radiologic Technologists; Receptionists and Information Clerks; Social and Human Service Assistants; Speech-Language Pathology Assistants; others.

Medical Assistants

- ❋ Annual Earnings: $28,860
- ❋ Earnings Growth Potential: Low (27.9%)
- ❋ Growth: 33.9%
- ❋ Annual Job Openings: 21,780
- ❋ Self-Employed: 0.0%

Skills—Most Important: Science Skills; Social Skills; Communication Skills. **Other High-Level Skills:** Thought-Processing Skills; Equipment Use/Maintenance Skills.

Perform administrative and certain clinical duties under the direction of physicians.

Administrative duties may include scheduling appointments, maintaining medical records, billing, and coding for insurance purposes. Clinical duties may include taking and recording vital signs and medical histories, preparing patients for examination, drawing blood, and administering medications as directed by physician. Interview patients to obtain medical information and measure their vital signs, weight, and height. Show patients to examination rooms and prepare them for the physician. Record patients' medical history, vital statistics, and information such as test results in medical records. Prepare and administer medications as directed by a physician. Collect blood, tissue, or other laboratory specimens; log the specimens; and prepare them for testing. Explain treatment procedures, medications, diets, and physicians' instructions to patients. Help physicians examine and treat patients, handing them instruments and materials or performing such tasks as giving injections or removing sutures. Authorize drug refills and provide prescription information to pharmacies. Prepare treatment rooms for patient examinations, keeping the rooms neat and clean. Clean and sterilize instruments and dispose of contaminated supplies. Schedule appointments for patients. Change dressings on wounds. Greet and log in patients arriving at office or clinic. Contact medical facilities or departments to schedule patients for tests or admission. Perform general office duties such as answering telephones, taking dictation, or completing insurance forms. Inventory and order medical, lab, or office supplies and equipment. Perform routine laboratory tests and sample analyses. Set up medical laboratory equipment.

Education/Training Required: Moderate-term on-the-job training. **Education and Training Programs:** Allied Health and Medical Assisting Services, Other; Anesthesiologist Assistant Training; Chiropractic Assistant/Technician Training; Medical Administrative/Executive Assistant and Medical Secretary Training; Medical Insurance Coding Specialist/Coder Training; Medical Office Assistant/Specialist Training; Medical Office Management/Administration; Medical Reception/Receptionist; Medical/Clinical Assistant Training; Ophthalmic Technician/Technologist Training; Optometric Technician/Assistant Training; Orthoptics/Orthoptist. **Knowledge/Courses:** Medicine and Dentistry; Clerical Practices; Psychology; Therapy and Counseling; Customer and Personal Service; Public Safety and Security.

Personality Type: Social-Conventional-Realistic. **Career Cluster:** 08 Health Science. **Career Pathways:** 08.2 Diagnostics Services; 08.3 Health Informatics. **Other Jobs in These Pathways:** Clinical Psychologists; Cytogenetic Technologists; Cytotechnologists; Editors; Emergency Medical Technicians and Paramedics; Endoscopy Technicians; Engineers, All Other; Executive Secretaries and Executive Administrative Assistants; First-Line Supervisors of Office and Administrative Support Workers; Health Technologists and Technicians, All Other; Histotechnologists and Histologic Technicians; Medical and Clinical Laboratory Technicians; Medical and Clinical Laboratory Technologists; Medical and Health Services Managers; Medical Records and Health Information Technicians; Medical Secretaries; Medical Transcriptionists; Mental Health Counselors; Physical Therapists; Public Relations Specialists; Radiologic Technologists; Receptionists and Information Clerks; Rehabilitation Counselors; Substance Abuse and Behavioral Disorder Counselors; Surgical Technologists; others.

Medical Equipment Preparers

❋ Annual Earnings: $29,490

❋ Earnings Growth Potential: Low (30.6%)

❋ Growth: 12.8%

❋ Annual Job Openings: 1,120

❋ Self-Employed: 3.0%

Skills—Most Important: Installation Skills; Equipment Use/Maintenance Skills.

Prepare, sterilize, install, or clean laboratory or health-care equipment. May perform routine laboratory tasks and operate or inspect equipment. Organize and assemble routine and specialty surgical instrument trays and other sterilized supplies, filling special requests as needed. Clean instruments to prepare them for sterilization. Operate and maintain steam autoclaves, keeping records of loads completed, items in loads, and maintenance procedures performed. Record sterilizer test results. Start equipment and observe gauges and equipment operation to detect malfunctions and to ensure equipment is operating to standards. Examine equipment to detect leaks, worn or loose parts, or other indications of disrepair. Report defective equipment to appropriate supervisors or staff. Check sterile supplies to ensure that they are not outdated. Attend hospital in-service programs. Purge wastes from equipment by connecting equipment to water sources and flushing water through systems. Stock crash carts or other medical supplies.

Education/Training Required: Short-term on-the-job training. **Education and Training Programs:** Allied Health and Medical Assisting Services, Other; Medical/Clinical Assistant Training. **Knowledge/Courses:** Production and Processing; Chemistry; Customer and Personal Service; Biology; Medicine and Dentistry; Public Safety and Security.

Personality Type: Realistic-Conventional-Investigative. **Career Cluster:** 08 Health Science. **Career Pathways:** 08.1 Therapeutic Services; 08.2 Diagnostics Services. **Other Jobs in These Pathways:** Clinical Psychologists; Counseling Psychologists; Cytogenetic Technologists; Cytotechnologists; Dental Assistants; Dental Hygienists; Dentists, General; Emergency Medical Technicians and Paramedics; Endoscopy Technicians; Healthcare Support Workers, All Other; Histotechnologists and Histologic Technicians; Home Health Aides; Licensed Practical and Licensed Vocational Nurses; Massage Therapists; Medical and Clinical Laboratory Technicians; Medical and Clinical Laboratory Technologists; Medical and Health Services Managers; Medical Assistants; Medical Secretaries; Pharmacists; Pharmacy Technicians; Radiologic Technologists; School Psychologists; Social and Human Service Assistants; Speech-Language Pathology Assistants; others.

Medical Equipment Repairers

❋ Annual Earnings: $44,490

❋ Earnings Growth Potential: High (41.5%)

❋ Growth: 27.2%

❋ Annual Job Openings: 2,320

❋ Self-Employed: 16.4%

Skills—Most Important: Equipment Use/ Maintenance Skills; Mathematics Skills; Science Skills. **Other High-Level Skills:** Management Skills; Thought-Processing Skills; Social Skills; Communication Skills.

Test, adjust, or repair biomedical or electromedical equipment. Test and calibrate components and equipment following manufacturers' manuals and troubleshooting techniques using hand tools, power tools and measuring devices. Keep records of maintenance, repair, and required updates of equipment. Inspect and test malfunctioning medical and related equipment following manufacturers' specifications using test and analysis instruments. Disassemble malfunctioning equipment and remove, repair, and replace defective parts such as motors, clutches, or transformers. Perform preventive maintenance or service such as cleaning, lubricating, and adjusting equipment. Test, evaluate, and classify excess or in-use medical equipment and determine serviceability, condition, and disposition in accordance with regulations. Examine medical equipment and facility's structural environment and check for proper use of equipment to protect patients and staff from electrical or mechanical hazards and to ensure compliance with safety regulations. Study technical manuals and attend training sessions provided by equipment manufacturers to maintain current knowledge. Solder loose connections. Explain and demonstrate correct operation and preventive maintenance of medical equipment to personnel. Evaluate technical specifications to identify equipment and systems best suited for intended use and possible purchase based on specifications, user needs, and technical requirements.

Education/Training Required: Associate degree. **Education and Training Program:** Biomedical Technology/Technician. **Knowledge/Courses:** Mechanical Devices; Engineering and Technology; Physics; Telecommunications; Computers and Electronics; Chemistry.

Personality Type: Realistic-Investigative-Conventional. **Career Cluster:** 13

Manufacturing. **Career Pathway:** 13.3 Maintenance, Installation, and Repair. **Other Jobs in This Pathway:** Aircraft Mechanics and Service Technicians; Automotive Specialty Technicians; Biological Technicians; Civil Engineering Technicians; Computer, Automated Teller, and Office Machine Repairers; Electrical and Electronic Equipment Assemblers; Electrical and Electronics Repairers, Commercial and Industrial Equipment; Electrical Engineering Technicians; Electrical Engineering Technologists; Electromechanical Engineering Technologists; Electronics Engineering Technicians; Electronics Engineering Technologists; Engineering Technicians, Except Drafters, All Other; Fuel Cell Technicians; Helpers—Installation, Maintenance, and Repair Workers; Industrial Engineering Technologists; Industrial Machinery Mechanics; Installation, Maintenance, and Repair Workers, All Other; Manufacturing Engineering Technologists; Manufacturing Production Technicians; Mapping Technicians; Mechanical Engineering Technologists; Mobile Heavy Equipment Mechanics, Except Engines; Telecommunications Line Installers and Repairers; Tire Repairers and Changers; others.

Medical Scientists, Except Epidemiologists

- Annual Earnings: $76,700
- Earnings Growth Potential: High (45.8%)
- Growth: 40.4%
- Annual Job Openings: 6,620
- Self-Employed: 2.5%

Skills—Most Important: Science Skills; Mathematics Skills; Thought-Processing Skills.

Other High-Level Skills: Communication Skills; Social Skills; Management Skills; Equipment Use/Maintenance Skills.

Conduct research dealing with the understanding of human diseases and the improvement of human health. Engage in clinical investigation or other research, production, technical writing, or related activities. Conduct research to develop methodologies, instrumentation, and procedures for medical application, analyzing data and presenting findings. Plan and direct studies to investigate human or animal disease, preventive methods, and treatments for disease. Follow strict safety procedures when handling toxic materials to avoid contamination. Evaluate effects of drugs, gases, pesticides, parasites, and microorganisms at various levels. Teach principles of medicine and medical and laboratory procedures to physicians, residents, students, and technicians. Prepare and analyze organ, tissue, and cell samples to identify toxicity, bacteria, or microorganisms or to study cell structure. Standardize drug dosages, methods of immunization, and procedures for manufacture of drugs and medicinal compounds. Investigate cause, progress, life cycle, or mode of transmission of diseases or parasites. Confer with health department, industry personnel, physicians, and others to develop health safety standards and public health improvement programs. Study animal and human health and physiological processes. Consult with and advise physicians, educators, researchers, and others on medical applications of physics, biology, and chemistry. Use equipment such as atomic absorption spectrometers, electron microscopes, flow cytometers, and chromatography systems.

Education/Training Required: Doctoral degree. **Education and Training Programs:**

Anatomy; Biochemistry; Biomedical Sciences, General; Biophysics; Biostatistics; Cardiovascular Science; Cell Physiology; Cell/Cellular Biology and Histology; Endocrinology; Environmental Toxicology; Epidemiology; Exercise Physiology; Human/Medical Genetics; Immunology; Medical Microbiology and Bacteriology; Medical Science; Molecular Biology; Molecular Pharmacology; Molecular Physiology; Molecular Toxicology; Neuropharmacology; Oncology and Cancer Biology; Pathology/Experimental Pathology; Pharmacology; Pharmacology and Toxicology; Pharmacology and Toxicology, Other; Physiology, General; Physiology, Pathology, and Related Sciences, Other; Reproductive Biology; Toxicology; Vision Science/Physiological Optics. **Knowledge/Courses:** Biology; Medicine and Dentistry; Chemistry; Communications and Media; Personnel and Human Resources; Mathematics.

Personality Type: Investigative-Realistic-Artistic. **Career Clusters:** 08 Health Science; 15 Science, Technology, Engineering, and Mathematics. **Career Pathways:** 08.1 Therapeutic Services; 15.2 Science and Mathematics. **Other Jobs in These Pathways:** Architectural and Engineering Managers; Biofuels/Biodiesel Technology and Product Development Managers; Clinical Psychologists; Community and Social Service Specialists, All Other; Counseling Psychologists; Dental Assistants; Dental Hygienists; Dentists, General; Education, Training, and Library Workers, All Other; Healthcare Support Workers, All Other; Home Health Aides; Licensed Practical and Licensed Vocational Nurses; Low Vision Therapists, Orientation and Mobility Specialists, and Vision Rehabilitation Therapists; Massage Therapists; Medical and Clinical Laboratory Technicians; Medical and Health Services

Managers; Medical Secretaries; Occupational Therapists; Pharmacists; Pharmacy Technicians; Radiologic Technologists; School Psychologists; Social and Human Service Assistants; Speech-Language Pathologists; Speech-Language Pathology Assistants; others.

Medical Secretaries

* Annual Earnings: $30,530
* Earnings Growth Potential: Low (30.5%)
* Growth: 26.6%
* Annual Job Openings: 18,900
* Self-Employed: 1.4%

Skills—Most Important: Communication Skills; Social Skills.

Perform secretarial duties using specific knowledge of medical terminology and hospital, clinical, or laboratory procedures. Schedule and confirm patient diagnostic appointments, surgeries, and medical consultations. Compile and record medical charts, reports, and correspondence. Answer telephones and direct calls. Receive and route messages and documents such as laboratory results to appropriate staff. Greet visitors, ascertain purpose of visit, and direct them to appropriate staff. Interview patients to complete documents, case histories, and forms such as intake and insurance forms. Maintain medical records, technical library, and correspondence files. Operate office equipment such as voicemail and use word processing, spreadsheet, and other software applications to prepare reports, invoices, financial statements, letters, case histories, and medical records. Transmit correspondence and medical records by mail, e-mail, or fax. Perform various clerical and administrative functions, such as ordering and maintaining an inventory of supplies. Arrange hospital admissions for patients. Transcribe recorded messages and practitioners' diagnoses and recommendations into patients' medical records. Perform bookkeeping duties, such as doing credits and collections, preparing and sending financial statements and bills, and keeping financial records. Complete insurance and other claim forms.

Education/Training Required: Moderate-term on-the-job training. **Education and Training Programs:** Medical Administrative/Executive Assistant and Medical Secretary Training; Medical Insurance Specialist/Medical Biller Training; Medical Office Assistant/Specialist Training. **Knowledge/Courses:** Clerical Practices; Medicine and Dentistry; Customer and Personal Service; Computers and Electronics; Economics and Accounting.

Personality Type: Conventional-Social. **Career Cluster:** 08 Health Science. **Career Pathways:** 08.3 Health Informatics; 08.1 Therapeutic Services. **Other Jobs in These Pathways:** Clinical Psychologists; Counseling Psychologists; Dental Assistants; Dental Hygienists; Editors; Engineers, All Other; Executive Secretaries and Executive Administrative Assistants; First-Line Supervisors of Office and Administrative Support Workers; Healthcare Support Workers, All Other; Home Health Aides; Licensed Practical and Licensed Vocational Nurses; Medical and Clinical Laboratory Technicians; Medical and Health Services Managers; Medical Assistants; Medical Records and Health Information Technicians; Pharmacists; Pharmacy Technicians; Physical Therapists; Public Relations Specialists; Rehabilitation Counselors; Radiologic Technologists; Receptionists and Information Clerks; Rehabilitation Counselors;

School Psychologists; Social and Human Service Assistants; Speech-Language Pathology Assistants; others.

Middle School Teachers, Except Special and Career/Technical Education

* Annual Earnings: $51,960
* Earnings Growth Potential: Low (32.7%)
* Growth: 15.3%
* Annual Job Openings: 25,110
* Self-Employed: 0.0%

Skills—Most Important: Social Skills; Communication Skills; Thought-Processing Skills. **Other High-Level Skills:** Mathematics Skills; Management Skills.

Teach students in public or private schools in one or more subjects at the middle, intermediate, or junior high level, which falls between elementary and senior high school as defined by applicable state laws and regulations. Establish and enforce rules for behavior and procedures for maintaining order among students. Adapt teaching methods and instructional materials to meet students' varying needs and interests. Instruct through lectures, discussions, and demonstrations in one or more subjects, such as English, mathematics, or social studies. Prepare, administer, and grade tests and assignments to evaluate students' progress. Establish clear objectives for all lessons, units, and projects and communicate these objectives to students. Plan and conduct activities for a balanced program of instruction, demonstration, and work time that provides students with opportunities to observe, question, and investigate. Maintain accurate, complete, and correct student records as required by laws, district policies, and administrative regulations. Observe and evaluate students' performance, behavior, social development, and physical health. Prepare materials and classrooms for class activities.

Education/Training Required: Bachelor's degree. **Education and Training Programs:** Art Teacher Education; Computer Teacher Education; English/Language Arts Teacher Education; Family and Consumer Sciences/Home Economics Teacher Education; Foreign Language Teacher Education; Health Occupations Teacher Education; Health Teacher Education; History Teacher Education; Junior High/Intermediate/Middle School Education and Teaching; Mathematics Teacher Education; Music Teacher Education; Physical Education Teaching and Coaching; Reading Teacher Education; Science Teacher Education/General Science Teacher Education; Social Science Teacher Education; Social Studies Teacher Education; Teacher Education and Professional Development, Specific Subject Areas, Other; Technology Teacher Education/Industrial Arts Teacher Education. **Knowledge/Courses:** History and Archeology; Education and Training; Sociology and Anthropology; Fine Arts; Philosophy and Theology; English Language.

Personality Type: Social-Artistic. **Career Cluster:** 05 Education and Training. **Career Pathway:** 05.3 Teaching/Training. **Other Jobs in This Pathway:** Adult Basic and Secondary Education and Literacy Teachers and Instructors; Athletes and Sports Competitors; Audio-Visual and Multimedia Collections Specialists; Career/Technical Education Teachers, Middle School; Career/Technical Education Teachers, Secondary School; Chemists; Coaches and Scouts;

Dietitians and Nutritionists; Elementary School Teachers, Except Special Education; Fitness Trainers and Aerobics Instructors; Historians; Instructional Coordinators; Instructional Designers and Technologists; Interpreters and Translators; Kindergarten Teachers, Except Special Education; Librarians; Physicists; Preschool Teachers, Except Special Education; Recreation Workers; Secondary School Teachers, Except Special and Career/Technical Education; Self-Enrichment Education Teachers; Teacher Assistants; Teachers and Instructors, All Other; Tutors.

Millwrights

- ❋ Annual Earnings: $48,360
- ❋ Earnings Growth Potential: Low (35.7%)
- ❋ Growth: 1.4%
- ❋ Annual Job Openings: 980
- ❋ Self-Employed: 0.0%

Skills—Most Important: Installation Skills; Equipment Use/Maintenance Skills; Mathematics Skills. **Other High-Level Skills:** Social Skills; Management Skills; Thought-Processing Skills.

Install, dismantle, or move machinery and heavy equipment according to layout plans, blueprints, or other drawings. Replace defective parts of machine or adjust clearances and alignment of moving parts. Align machines and equipment using hoists, jacks, hand tools, squares, rules, micrometers, and plumb bobs. Connect power unit to machines or steam piping to equipment and test unit to evaluate its mechanical operation. Assemble and install equipment using hand tools and power tools. Position steel beams to support bedplates of

machines and equipment using blueprints and schematic drawings to determine work procedures. Signal crane operator to lower basic assembly units to bedplate and align unit to centerline. Insert shims, adjust tension on nuts and bolts, or position parts using hand tools and measuring instruments to set specified clearances between moving and stationary parts. Move machinery and equipment using hoists, dollies, rollers, and trucks. Attach moving parts and subassemblies to basic assembly unit using hand tools and power tools.

Education/Training Required: Long-term on-the-job training. **Education and Training Programs:** Heavy/Industrial Equipment Maintenance Technologies, Other; Industrial Mechanics and Maintenance Technology. **Knowledge/Courses:** Mechanical Devices; Building and Construction; Physics; Design; Engineering and Technology; Mathematics.

Personality Type: Realistic-Conventional-Investigative. **Career Cluster:** 13 Manufacturing. **Career Pathway:** 13.3 Maintenance, Installation, and Repair. **Other Jobs in This Pathway:** Aircraft Mechanics and Service Technicians; Automotive Specialty Technicians; Biological Technicians; Civil Engineering Technicians; Computer, Automated Teller, and Office Machine Repairers; Electrical and Electronic Equipment Assemblers; Electrical and Electronics Repairers, Commercial and Industrial Equipment; Electrical Engineering Technicians; Electrical Engineering Technologists; Electromechanical Engineering Technologists; Electronics Engineering Technicians; Electronics Engineering Technologists; Engineering Technicians, Except Drafters, All Other; Fuel Cell Technicians; Helpers—Installation, Maintenance, and Repair Workers; Industrial Engineering

Technologists; Industrial Machinery Mechanics; Installation, Maintenance, and Repair Workers, All Other; Manufacturing Engineering Technologists; Manufacturing Production Technicians; Mapping Technicians; Mechanical Engineering Technologists; Mobile Heavy Equipment Mechanics, Except Engines; Telecommunications Line Installers and Repairers; Tire Repairers and Changers; others.

Mining and Geological Engineers, Including Mining Safety Engineers

* Annual Earnings: $82,870
* Earnings Growth Potential: Medium (40.9%)
* Growth: 15.2%
* Annual Job Openings: 260
* Self-Employed: 0.0%

Skills—Most Important: Science Skills; Technology/Programming Skills; Mathematics Skills. **Other High-Level Skills:** Management Skills; Thought-Processing Skills; Communication Skills; Social Skills; Equipment Use/Maintenance Skills.

Determine the location and plan the extraction of coal, metallic ores, nonmetallic minerals, and building materials such as stone and gravel. Work involves conducting preliminary surveys of deposits or undeveloped mines and planning their development; examining deposits or mines to determine whether they can be worked at a profit; making geological and topographical surveys; evolving methods of mining best suited to character, type, and size of deposits; and supervising mining operations. Inspect mining areas for unsafe structures, equipment, and working conditions. Select locations and

plan underground or surface mining operations, specifying processes, labor usage, and equipment that will result in safe, economical, and environmentally sound extraction of minerals and ores. Examine maps, deposits, drilling locations, or mines to determine the location, size, accessibility, contents, value, and potential profitability of mineral, oil, and gas deposits. Prepare schedules, reports, and estimates of the costs involved in developing and operating mines. Monitor mine production rates to assess operational effectiveness. Design, implement, and monitor the development of mines, facilities, systems, or equipment. Select or develop mineral location, extraction, and production methods based on factors such as safety, cost, and deposit characteristics. Prepare technical reports for use by mining, engineering, and management personnel.

Education/Training Required: Bachelor's degree. **Education and Training Program:** Mining and Mineral Engineering. **Knowledge/Courses:** Engineering and Technology; Design; Physics; Geography; Building and Construction; Chemistry.

Personality Type: Investigative-Realistic-Enterprising. **Career Cluster:** 15 Science, Technology, Engineering, and Mathematics. **Career Pathway:** 15.1 Engineering and Technology. **Other Jobs in This Pathway:** Architectural and Engineering Managers; Automotive Engineers; Biochemical Engineers; Biofuels/Biodiesel Technology and Product Development Managers; Civil Engineers; Cost Estimators; Electrical Engineers; Electronics Engineers, Except Computer; Energy Engineers; Engineers, All Other; Fuel Cell Engineers; Human Factors Engineers and Ergonomists; Industrial Engineers; Manufacturing Engineers; Mechanical Engineers; Mechatronics Engineers;

Microsystems Engineers; Nanosystems Engineers; Photonics Engineers; Radio Frequency Identification Device Specialists; Robotics Engineers; Solar Energy Systems Engineers; Transportation Engineers; Validation Engineers; Wind Energy Engineers; others.

Mobile Heavy Equipment Mechanics, Except Engines

❋ Annual Earnings: $44,830

❋ Earnings Growth Potential: Low (33.7%)

❋ Growth: 8.7%

❋ Annual Job Openings: 3,770

❋ Self-Employed: 5.8%

Skills—Most Important: Equipment Use/Maintenance Skills; Installation Skills; Management Skills. **Other High-Level Skills:** Thought-Processing Skills; Social Skills.

Diagnose, adjust, repair, or overhaul mobile mechanical, hydraulic, and pneumatic equipment, such as cranes, bulldozers, graders, and conveyors, used in construction, logging, and surface mining. Repair and replace damaged or worn parts. Dismantle and reassemble heavy equipment using hoists and hand tools. Operate and inspect machines or heavy equipment to diagnose defects. Test mechanical products and equipment after repair or assembly to ensure proper performance and compliance with manufacturers' specifications. Clean, lubricate, and perform other routine maintenance work on equipment and vehicles. Read and understand operating manuals, blueprints, and technical drawings. Overhaul and test machines or equipment to ensure operating efficiency. Fit bearings to adjust, repair, or overhaul mobile mechanical, hydraulic, and pneumatic equipment. Diagnose faults or malfunctions to determine required repairs using engine diagnostic equipment such as computerized test equipment and calibration devices. Examine parts for damage or excessive wear using micrometers and gauges. Repair, rewire, and troubleshoot electrical systems. Schedule maintenance for industrial machines and equipment and keep equipment service records. Research, order, and maintain parts inventory for services and repairs. Adjust, maintain, and repair or replace subassemblies, such as transmissions and crawler heads, using hand tools, jacks, and cranes. Clean parts by spraying them with grease solvent or immersing them in tanks of solvent. Weld or solder broken parts and structural members using electric or gas welders and soldering tools.

Education/Training Required: Long-term on-the-job training. **Education and Training Programs:** Agricultural Mechanics and Equipment/Machine Technology; Heavy Equipment Maintenance Technology/Technician . **Knowledge/Courses:** Mechanical Devices; Physics; Building and Construction; Engineering and Technology; Design; Transportation.

Personality Type: Realistic-Conventional. **Career Clusters:** 01 Agriculture, Food, and Natural Resources; 13 Manufacturing. **Career Pathways:** 01.4 Power Structure and Technical Systems; 13.3 Maintenance, Installation, and Repair. **Other Jobs in These Pathways:** Aircraft Mechanics and Service Technicians; Automotive Specialty Technicians; Biological Technicians; Civil Engineering Technicians; Computer, Automated Teller, and Office Machine Repairers; Electrical and Electronic Equipment Assemblers; Electrical and Electronics Repairers, Commercial and

Industrial Equipment; Electrical Engineering Technicians; Electrical Engineering Technologists; Electromechanical Engineering Technologists; Electronics Engineering Technicians; Electronics Engineering Technologists; Engineering Technicians, Except Drafters, All Other; Fuel Cell Technicians; Helpers—Installation, Maintenance, and Repair Workers; Industrial Engineering Technologists; Industrial Machinery Mechanics; Installation, Maintenance, and Repair Workers, All Other; Manufacturing Engineering Technologists; Manufacturing Production Technicians; Mapping Technicians; Mechanical Engineering Technologists; Nanotechnology Engineering Technicians; Telecommunications Line Installers and Repairers; Tire Repairers and Changers; others.

Natural Sciences Managers

- ❋ Annual Earnings: $116,020
- ❋ Earnings Growth Potential: High (42.0%)
- ❋ Growth: 15.5%
- ❋ Annual Job Openings: 2,010
- ❋ Self-Employed: 0.0%

Skills—Most Important: Science Skills; Management Skills; Mathematics Skills. **Other High-Level Skills:** Communication Skills; Thought-Processing Skills; Social Skills; Technology/Programming Skills.

Plan, direct, or coordinate activities, including research and development, in such fields as life sciences, physical sciences, mathematics, and statistics. Confer with scientists, engineers, regulators, and others to plan and review projects and to provide technical assistance. Develop client relationships and communicate with clients to explain proposals, present research findings, establish specifications, or discuss project status. Plan and direct research, development, and production activities. Prepare project proposals. Design and coordinate successive phases of problem analysis, solution proposals, and testing. Review project activities and prepare and review research, testing, and operational reports. Hire, supervise, and evaluate engineers, technicians, researchers, and other staff. Determine scientific and technical goals within broad outlines provided by top management and make detailed plans to accomplish these goals. Develop and implement policies, standards, and procedures for the architectural, scientific, and technical work performed to ensure regulatory compliance and operations enhancement. Develop innovative technology and train staff for its implementation. Provide for stewardship of plant and animal resources and habitats, studying land use, monitoring animal populations, or providing shelter, resources, and medical treatment for animals. Recruit personnel and oversee the development and maintenance of staff competence. Advise and assist in obtaining patents or meeting other legal requirements.

Education/Training Required: Work experience plus degree. **Education and Training Programs:** Acoustics; Analytical Chemistry; Anatomy; Animal Genetics; Animal Physiology; Astronomy; Astrophysics; Atmospheric Chemistry and Climatology; Atmospheric Physics and Dynamics; Atmospheric Sciences and Meteorology, General; Atomic Physics; Biochemistry; Biological and Physical Sciences; Biology, General; Biometry; Biophysics; Biopsychology; Biostatistics; Biotechnology; Botany; Cell Biology and Histology; Chemistry, General; Ecology; Elementary Particle Physics; Entomology;

Evolutionary Biology; Geochemistry; Geochemistry and Petrology; Geology/Earth Science, General; Geophysics and Seismology; Hydrology and Water Resources Science; Inorganic Chemistry; Marine Biology and Biological Oceanography; Meteorology; Microbiology, General; Molecular Biology; Natural Sciences; Nuclear Physics; Nutrition Sciences; Oceanography, Chemical and Physical; Optics; Organic Chemistry; Paleontology; Parasitology; Pathology; Pharmacology; Physical Chemistry; Physical Sciences; Physics, General; Planetary Astronomy and Science; Plant Genetics; Plant Pathology; Plant Physiology; Plasma and High-Temperature Physics; Polymer Chemistry; Radiation Biology; Science, Technology, and Society; Theoretical and Mathematical Physics; Toxicology; Virology; Zoology; others. **Knowledge/Courses:** Biology; Chemistry; Engineering and Technology; Law and Government; Administration and Management; Physics.

Personality Type: Enterprising-Investigative. **Career Clusters:** 04 Business, Management, and Administration; 15 Science, Technology, Engineering, and Mathematics. **Career Pathways:** 15.2 Science and Mathematics; 04.2 Business, Financial Management, and Accounting; 04.4 Business Analysis. **Other Jobs in These Pathways:** Accountants; Architectural and Engineering Managers; Auditors; Billing and Posting Clerks; Billing, Cost, and Rate Clerks; Biofuels/Biodiesel Technology and Product Development Managers; Bookkeeping, Accounting, and Auditing Clerks; Brownfield Redevelopment Specialists and Site Managers; Community and Social Service Specialists, All Other; Compliance Managers; Computer and Information Systems Managers; Education, Training, and Library Workers, All Other; Financial Analysts; Financial Managers, Branch

or Department; Investment Fund Managers; Loss Prevention Managers; Managers, All Other; Payroll and Timekeeping Clerks; Regulatory Affairs Managers; Security Managers; Statement Clerks; Supply Chain Managers; Treasurers and Controllers; Wind Energy Operations Managers; Wind Energy Project Managers; others.

Job Specialization: Clinical Research Coordinators

Plan, direct, or coordinate clinical research projects. Direct the activities of workers engaged in clinical research projects to ensure compliance with protocols and overall clinical objectives. May evaluate and analyze clinical data. Review scientific literature, participate in continuing education activities, or attend conferences and seminars to maintain current knowledge of clinical studies affairs and issues. Prepare for or participate in quality assurance audits conducted by study sponsors, federal agencies, or specially designated review groups. Participate in preparation and management of research budgets and monetary disbursements. Confer with health-care professionals to determine the best recruitment practices for studies. Track enrollment status of subjects and document dropout information such as dropout causes and subject contact efforts. Review proposed study protocols to evaluate factors such as sample collection processes, data management plans, and potential subject risks. Record adverse event and side effect data and confer with investigators on the reporting of events to oversight agencies. Prepare study-related documentation such as protocol worksheets, procedural manuals, adverse event reports, institutional review board documents, and progress reports. Participate in the development of study protocols including guidelines for administration or data collection procedures. Oversee subject enrollment to ensure that informed consent is properly obtained and documented. Order drugs or devices necessary for study completion. Instruct research staff in scientific and procedural aspects of studies including standards of care, informed consent procedures, or documentation procedures.

Education/Training Required: Work experience in a related occupation. **Education and Training Programs:** Biometry/Biometrics; Biostatistics; Biotechnology; Cell/Cellular Biology and Anatomical Sciences, Other; Immunology; Medical Microbiology and Bacteriology; Microbiology, General; Nutrition Sciences; Parasitology; Pathology/Experimental Pathology; Pharmacology; Statistics, General; Toxicology; Virology. **Knowledge/Courses:** Medicine and Dentistry; Biology; Administration and Management; Clerical Practices; English Language; Law and Government.

Personality Type: Enterprising-Investigative-Conventional. **Career Cluster:** 15 Science, Technology, Engineering, and Mathematics. **Career Pathway:** 15.2 Science and Mathematics. **Other Jobs in This Pathway:** Architectural and Engineering Managers; Biochemists and Biophysicists; Biofuels/Biodiesel Technology and Product Development Managers; Bioinformatics Scientists; Biological Scientists, All Other; Biologists; Biostatisticians; Chemists; Clinical Data Managers; Community and Social Service Specialists, All Other; Dietitians and Nutritionists; Education, Training, and Library Workers, All Other; Geneticists; Geoscientists, Except Hydrologists and Geographers; Medical Scientists, Except Epidemiologists; Molecular and Cellular Biologists; Natural Sciences Managers; Operations Research Analysts; Physical Scientists, All Other; Social Scientists and Related Workers, All Other; Statisticians; Survey Researchers; Transportation Planners; Water Resource Specialists; Zoologists and Wildlife Biologists; others.

Job Specialization: Water Resource Specialists

Design or implement programs and strategies related to water resource issues, such as supply, quality, and regulatory compliance issues. Supervise teams of workers who capture water from wells and rivers. Review or evaluate designs for water detention facilities, storm drains, flood control facilities, or other hydraulic structures. Negotiate for water rights with communities or water facilities to meet water supply demands. Perform hydrologic, hydraulic, or water quality modeling. Compile water resource data, using geographic information systems or global position systems software. Compile and maintain documentation on the health of a body of water. Write proposals, project reports, informational brochures, or other documents on wastewater purification, water supply and demand, or other water resource subjects. Recommend new or revised policies, procedures, or regulations to support water resource or conservation goals. Provide technical expertise to assist communities in the development or implementation of storm water monitoring or other water programs. Present water resource proposals to government, public interest groups, or community groups. Identify methods for distributing purified wastewater into rivers, streams, or oceans. Monitor water use, demand, or quality in a geographic area. Identify and characterize specific causes or sources of water pollution. Develop plans to protect watershed health or rehabilitate watersheds. Develop or implement standardized water monitoring and assessment methods.

Education/Training Required: Work experience plus degree. **Education and Training Programs:** Geochemistry; Geological and Earth Sciences/Geosciences, Other; Geology/Earth Science, General; Hydrology and Water Resources Science; Oceanography, Chemical and Physical. **Knowledge/Courses:** No data available.

Personality Type: No data available. **Career Cluster:** 15 Science, Technology, Engineering, and Mathematics. **Career Pathway:** 15.2 Science and Mathematics. **Other Jobs in This Pathway:** Architectural and Engineering Managers; Biochemists and Biophysicists; Biofuels/Biodiesel Technology and Product Development Managers; Bioinformatics Scientists; Biological Scientists, All Other; Biologists; Biostatisticians; Chemists; Clinical Data Managers; Clinical Research Coordinators; Community and Social Service Specialists, All Other; Dietitians and Nutritionists; Education, Training, and Library Workers, All Other; Geneticists; Geoscientists, Except Hydrologists and Geographers; Medical Scientists, Except Epidemiologists; Molecular and Cellular Biologists; Natural Sciences Managers; Operations Research Analysts; Physical Scientists, All Other; Social Scientists and Related Workers, All Other; Statisticians; Survey Researchers; Transportation Planners; Zoologists and Wildlife Biologists; others.

Network and Computer Systems Administrators

* Annual Earnings: $69,160
* Earnings Growth Potential: Medium (38.7%)
* Growth: 23.2%
* Annual Job Openings: 13,550
* Self-Employed: 0.8%

Skills—Most Important: Technology/Programming Skills; Equipment Use/Maintenance Skills; Installation Skills. **Other High-Level Skills:** Thought-Processing Skills; Mathematics Skills; Management Skills; Communication Skills; Social Skills.

Install, configure, and support organizations' local area networks, wide area networks, and Internet systems or segments of network systems. Maintain network hardware and software. Monitor networks to ensure network availability to all system users and perform necessary maintenance to support network availability. May supervise other network support and client server specialists and plan, coordinate, and implement network security measures. Perform data backups and disaster recovery operations. Maintain and administer computer networks and related computing environments including computer hardware, systems software, applications software, and all configurations. Plan, coordinate, and implement network security measures to protect data, software, and hardware. Operate master consoles to monitor the performance of computer systems and networks and to coordinate computer network access and use. Perform routine network startup and shutdown procedures, and maintain control records. Design, configure, and test computer hardware, networking software, and operating system software. Recommend changes to improve systems and network configurations and determine hardware or software requirements related to such changes. Confer with network users about how to solve existing system problems. Monitor network performance to determine whether adjustments need to be made and to determine where changes will need to be made in the future. Train people in computer system use. Load computer tapes and disks and install software and printer paper or forms. Gather data pertaining to customer needs and use the information to identify, predict, interpret, and evaluate system and network requirements. Analyze equipment performance records to determine the need for repair or replacement. Maintain logs related to network functions as well as maintenance and repair records. Maintain an inventory of parts for emergency repairs.

Education/Training Required: Bachelor's degree. **Education and Training Programs:** Network and System Administration/Administrator; System, Networking, and LAN/WAN Management/Manager. **Knowledge/Courses:** Telecommunications; Computers and Electronics; Clerical Practices; Administration and Management; Engineering and Technology.

Personality Type: Investigative-Realistic-Conventional. **Career Cluster:** 11 Information Technology. **Career Pathways:** 11.4 Programming and Software Development; 11.2 Information Support Services; 11.1 Network Systems. **Other Jobs in These Pathways:** Architectural and Engineering Managers; Bioinformatics Scientists; Computer and Information Systems Managers; Computer Hardware Engineers; Computer Numerically Controlled Machine Tool Programmers, Metal and Plastic; Computer Operators; Graphic Designers; Multimedia Artists and Animators;

Remote Sensing Scientists and Technologists; Remote Sensing Technicians.

Occupational Therapists

* Annual Earnings: $72,320
* Earnings Growth Potential: Low (32.4%)
* Growth: 25.6%
* Annual Job Openings: 4,580
* Self-Employed: 7.0%

Skills—Most Important: Science Skills; Communication Skills; Social Skills. **Other High-Level Skills:** Thought-Processing Skills; Management Skills; Equipment Use/Maintenance Skills.

Assess, plan, organize, and participate in rehabilitative programs that help restore vocational, homemaking, and daily living skills as well as general independence to disabled persons. Evaluate patients' progress and prepare reports that detail progress. Test and evaluate patients' physical and mental abilities and analyze medical data to determine realistic rehabilitation goals for patients. Select activities that will help individuals learn work and life-management skills within limits of their mental and physical capabilities. Plan, organize, and conduct occupational therapy programs in hospital, institutional, or community settings to help rehabilitate those impaired because of illness, injury, or psychological or developmental problems. Recommend changes in patients' work or living environments consistent with their needs and capabilities. Consult with rehabilitation team to select activity programs and coordinate occupational therapy with other therapeutic activities. Help clients improve decision making, abstract reasoning, memory, sequencing, coordination and perceptual skills using computer programs. Develop and participate in health promotion programs, group activities, or discussions to promote client health, facilitate social adjustment, alleviate stress, and prevent physical or mental disability. Provide training and supervision in therapy techniques and objectives for students and nurses and other medical staff. Design and create or requisition special supplies and equipment, such as splints, braces, and computer-aided adaptive equipment.

Education/Training Required: Master's degree. **Education and Training Program:** Occupational Therapy/Therapist. **Knowledge/ Courses:** Therapy and Counseling; Psychology; Sociology and Anthropology; Medicine and Dentistry; Biology; Philosophy and Theology.

Personality Type: Social-Investigative. **Career Cluster:** 08 Health Science. **Career Pathway:** 08.1 Therapeutic Services. **Other Jobs in This Pathway:** Clinical Psychologists; Community and Social Service Specialists, All Other; Counseling Psychologists; Dental Assistants; Dental Hygienists; Dentists, General; Health Technologists and Technicians, All Other; Healthcare Support Workers, All Other; Home Health Aides; Licensed Practical and Licensed Vocational Nurses; Low Vision Therapists, Orientation and Mobility Specialists, and Vision Rehabilitation Therapists; Massage Therapists; Medical and Clinical Laboratory Technicians; Medical and Health Services Managers; Medical Scientists, Except Epidemiologists; Medical Secretaries; Ophthalmic Medical Technologists; Pharmacists; Pharmacy Technicians; Radiologic Technologists; School Psychologists; Social and Human Service Assistants; Speech-Language Pathologists; Speech-Language Pathology Assistants; Substance Abuse and Behavioral Disorder Counselors; others.

Job Specialization: Low Vision Therapists, Orientation and Mobility Specialists, and Vision Rehabilitation Therapists

Provide therapy to patients with visual impairments to improve their functioning in daily life activities. May train patients in activities such as computer use, communication skills, or home-management skills. Teach cane skills including cane use with a guide, diagonal techniques, and two-point touches. Refer clients to services, such as eye care, health care, rehabilitation, and counseling, to enhance visual and life functioning or when condition exceeds scope of practice. Provide consultation, support, or education to groups such as parents and teachers. Participate in professional development activities such as reading literature, continuing education, attending conferences, and collaborating with colleagues. Obtain, distribute, or maintain low vision devices. Design instructional programs to improve communication using devices such as slates and styluses, braillers, keyboards, adaptive handwriting devices, talking book machines, digital books, and optical character readers. Collaborate with specialists, such as rehabilitation counselors, speech pathologists, and occupational therapists, to provide client solutions.

Education/Training Required: Master's degree. **Education and Training Program:** Occupational Therapy/Therapist. **Knowledge/ Courses:** Therapy and Counseling; Psychology; Sociology and Anthropology; Education and Training; Transportation; Medicine and Dentistry.

Personality Type: Social-Investigative-Realistic. **Career Cluster:** 08 Health Science. **Career Pathway:** 08.1 Therapeutic Services. **Other Jobs in This Pathway:** Clinical Psychologists;

Community and Social Service Specialists, All Other; Counseling Psychologists; Dental Assistants; Dental Hygienists; Dentists, General; Health Technologists and Technicians, All Other; Healthcare Support Workers, All Other; Home Health Aides; Licensed Practical and Licensed Vocational Nurses; Massage Therapists; Medical and Clinical Laboratory Technicians; Medical and Health Services Managers; Medical Scientists, Except Epidemiologists; Medical Secretaries; Occupational Therapists; Ophthalmic Medical Technologists; Pharmacists; Pharmacy Technicians; Radiologic Technologists; School Psychologists; Social and Human Service Assistants; Speech-Language Pathologists; Speech-Language Pathology Assistants; Substance Abuse and Behavioral Disorder Counselors; others.

Operating Engineers and Other Construction Equipment Operators

- Annual Earnings: $40,400
- Earnings Growth Potential: Low (34.5%)
- Growth: 12.0%
- Annual Job Openings: 11,820
- Self-Employed: 3.4%

Skills—Most Important: Equipment Use/ Maintenance Skills.

Operate one or several types of power construction equipment, such as motor graders, bulldozers, scrapers, compressors, pumps, derricks, shovels, tractors, or front-end loaders, to excavate, move, and grade earth; erect structures; or pour concrete or other hard-surface pavement. May repair and maintain equipment. Learn and follow safety regulations. Take actions to avoid potential hazards and obstructions such as utility lines, other equipment, other workers, and falling objects. Adjust handwheels and depress pedals to control attachments such as blades, buckets, scrapers, and swing booms. Start engines; move throttles, switches, and levers; and depress pedals to operate machines such as bulldozers, trench excavators, road graders, and backhoes. Locate underground services, such as pipes and wires, prior to beginning work. Monitor operations to ensure that health and safety standards are met. Align machines, cutterheads, or depth gauge makers with reference stakes and guidelines or ground. Position equipment following hand signals of other workers. Load and move dirt, rocks, equipment, and materials using trucks, crawler tractors, power cranes, shovels, graders, and related equipment. Drive and maneuver equipment equipped with blades in successive passes over working areas to remove topsoil, vegetation, and rocks and to distribute and level earth or terrain. Coordinate machine actions with other activities, positioning or moving loads in response to hand or audio signals from crew members. Repair and maintain equipment, making emergency adjustments or assisting with major repairs. Operate tractors and bulldozers to perform such tasks as clearing land, mixing sludge, trimming backfills, and building roadways and parking lots.

Education/Training Required: Moderate-term on-the-job training. **Education and Training Programs:** Construction/Heavy Equipment/ Earthmoving Equipment Operation; Mobile Crane Operation/Operator. **Knowledge/ Courses:** Building and Construction; Mechanical Devices; Engineering and Technology; Design; Production and Processing; Public Safety and Security.

Personality Type: Realistic-Conventional-Investigative. **Career Clusters:** 02 Architecture and Construction; 16 Transportation, Distribution, and Logistics. **Career Pathways:** 16.1 Transportation Operations; 02.2 Construction. **Other Jobs in These Pathways:** Automotive Master Mechanics; Bus Drivers, School or Special Client; Bus Drivers, Transit and Intercity; Cement Masons and Concrete Finishers; Construction Carpenters; Construction Laborers; Construction Managers; Cost Estimators; Drywall and Ceiling Tile Installers; Electricians; First-Line Supervisors of Construction Trades and Extraction Workers; First-Line Supervisors of Helpers, Laborers, and Material Movers, Hand; First-Line Supervisors of Transportation and Material-Moving Machine and Vehicle Operators; Heating and Air Conditioning Mechanics and Installers; Heavy and Tractor-Trailer Truck Drivers; Laborers and Freight, Stock, and Material Movers, Hand; Light Truck or Delivery Services Drivers; Painters, Construction and Maintenance; Pipe Fitters and Steamfitters; Plumbers; Refrigeration Mechanics and Installers; Roofers; Rough Carpenters; Solar Energy Installation Managers; Taxi Drivers and Chauffeurs; others.

Operations Research Analysts

- ❋ Annual Earnings: $70,960
- ❋ Earnings Growth Potential: High (43.7%)
- ❋ Growth: 22.0%
- ❋ Annual Job Openings: 3,220
- ❋ Self-Employed: 0.2%

Skills—Most Important: Mathematics Skills; Science Skills; Thought-Processing Skills. **Other High-Level Skills:** Technology/Programming Skills; Communication Skills; Management Skills; Social Skills.

Formulate and apply mathematical modeling and other optimizing methods using a computer to develop and interpret information that assists management with decision making, policy formulation, or other managerial functions. May develop related software, service, or products. Frequently concentrates on collecting and analyzing data and developing decision support software. May develop and supply optimal time, cost, or logistics networks for program evaluation, review, or implementation. Formulate mathematical or simulation models of problems, relating constants and variables, restrictions, alternatives, conflicting objectives, and their numerical parameters. Perform validation and testing of models to ensure adequacy and reformulate models as necessary. Collaborate with senior managers and decision makers to identify and solve problems and to clarify management objectives. Define data requirements and gather and validate information, applying judgment and statistical tests. Study and analyze information about alternative courses of action to determine which plan will offer the best outcomes. Prepare management reports defining and evaluating problems and recommending solutions. Break systems into their component parts, assign numerical values to each component, and examine the mathematical relationships between them. Specify manipulative or computational methods to be applied to models. Observe the current system in operation and gather and analyze information about the parts of component problems. Design, conduct, and evaluate experimental operational models in cases where models cannot be developed from existing data. Develop and apply time and cost networks to plan, control, and review large projects. Develop business methods and procedures, including accounting systems, file systems, office systems, logistics systems, and production schedules.

Education/Training Required: Master's degree. **Education and Training Programs:** Management Science; Management Sciences and Quantitative Methods, Other; Operations Research. **Knowledge/Courses:** Mathematics; Computers and Electronics; Engineering and Technology; Production and Processing; Economics and Accounting; Transportation.

Personality Type: Investigative-Conventional-Enterprising. **Career Clusters:** 04 Business, Management, and Administration; 15 Science, Technology, Engineering, and Mathematics. **Career Pathways:** 04.1 Management; 04.4 Business Analysis; 15.2 Science and Mathematics. **Other Jobs in These Pathways:** Brownfield Redevelopment Specialists and Site Managers; Business Continuity Planners; Business Operations Specialists, All Other; Chief Executives; Chief Sustainability Officers; Compliance Managers; Computer and Information Systems Managers; Construction Managers; Customs Brokers; Energy Auditors; First-Line Supervisors of Office and Administrative Support Workers; General and Operations Managers; Investment Fund Managers; Loss Prevention Managers; Management Analysts; Managers, All Other; Public Relations Specialists; Regulatory Affairs Managers; Sales Managers; Security Management Specialists; Security Managers; Supply Chain Managers; Sustainability Specialists; Wind Energy Operations Managers; Wind Energy Project Managers; others.

Optometrists

- ❋ Annual Earnings: $94,990
- ❋ Earnings Growth Potential: High (47.8%)
- ❋ Growth: 24.4%
- ❋ Annual Job Openings: 2,010
- ❋ Self-Employed: 24.6%

Skills—Most Important: Science Skills; Mathematics Skills; Thought-Processing Skills. **Other High-Level Skills:** Communication Skills; Social Skills; Equipment Use/Maintenance Skills; Management Skills.

Diagnose, manage, and treat conditions and diseases of the human eye and visual system. Examine eyes and visual systems, diagnose problems or impairments, prescribe corrective lenses, and provide treatment. May prescribe therapeutic drugs to treat eye conditions. Examine eyes, using observation, instruments, and pharmaceutical agents, to determine visual acuity and perception, focus, and coordination and to diagnose diseases and other abnormalities such as glaucoma or color blindness. Analyze test results and develop a treatment plan. Prescribe, supply, fit, and adjust eyeglasses, contact lenses, and other vision aids. Prescribe medications to treat eye diseases if state laws permit. Educate and counsel patients on contact lens care, visual hygiene, lighting arrangements, and safety factors. Consult with and refer patients to ophthalmologist or other health-care practitioner if additional medical treatment is necessary. Remove foreign bodies from the eye. Provide patients undergoing eye surgeries, such as cataract and laser vision correction, with pre- and post-operative care. Prescribe therapeutic procedures to correct or conserve vision. Provide vision therapy and low vision rehabilitation.

Education/Training Required: First professional degree. **Education and Training Program:** Optometry (OD). **Knowledge/ Courses:** Medicine and Dentistry; Biology; Therapy and Counseling; Physics; Sales and Marketing; Economics and Accounting.

Personality Type: Investigative-Social-Realistic. **Career Cluster:** 08 Health Science. **Career Pathway:** 08.1 Therapeutic Services. **Other Jobs in This Pathway:** Clinical Psychologists; Community and Social Service Specialists, All Other; Counseling Psychologists; Dental Assistants; Dental Hygienists; Dentists, General; Health Technologists and Technicians, All Other; Healthcare Support Workers, All Other; Home Health Aides; Licensed Practical and Licensed Vocational Nurses; Low Vision Therapists, Orientation and Mobility Specialists, and Vision Rehabilitation Therapists; Massage Therapists; Medical and Clinical Laboratory Technicians; Medical and Health Services Managers; Medical Scientists, Except Epidemiologists; Medical Secretaries; Occupational Therapists; Pharmacists; Pharmacy Technicians; Radiologic Technologists; School Psychologists; Social and Human Service Assistants; Speech-Language Pathologists; Speech-Language Pathology Assistants; Substance Abuse and Behavioral Disorder Counselors; others.

Orthodontists

- Annual Earnings: 166,400+
- Earnings Growth Potential: Cannot be calculated
- Growth: 19.7%
- Annual Job Openings: 360
- Self-Employed: 28.1%

Skills—Most Important: Science Skills; Communication Skills; Thought-Processing Skills. **Other High-Level Skills:** Social Skills; Management Skills; Equipment Use/ Maintenance Skills.

Examine, diagnose, and treat dental malocclusions and oral cavity anomalies. Design and fabricate appliances to realign teeth and jaws to produce and maintain normal function and to improve appearance. Fit dental appliances in patients' mouths to alter the position and relationship of teeth and jaws and to realign teeth. Study diagnostic records such as medical/dental histories, plaster models of the teeth, photos of a patient's face and teeth, and X-rays to develop patient treatment plans. Diagnose teeth and jaw or other dental-facial abnormalities. Prepare diagnostic and treatment records. Examine patients to assess abnormalities of jaw development, tooth position, and other dental-facial structures. Adjust dental appliances periodically to produce and maintain normal function. Provide patients with proposed treatment plans and cost estimates. Instruct dental officers and technical assistants in orthodontic procedures and techniques. Coordinate orthodontic services with other dental and medical services. Design and fabricate appliances, such as space maintainers, retainers, and labial and lingual arch wires.

Education/Training Required: First professional degree. **Education and Training Programs:** Orthodontics Specialty; Orthodontics/Orthodontology. **Knowledge/Courses:** Medicine and Dentistry; Biology; Sales and Marketing; Economics and Accounting; Personnel and Human Resources; Customer and Personal Service.

Personality Type: Investigative-Realistic-Social. **Career Cluster:** 08 Health Science. **Career Pathway:** 08.1 Therapeutic Services. **Other Jobs in This Pathway:** Clinical Psychologists; Counseling Psychologists; Dental Assistants; Dental Hygienists; Dentists, All Other Specialists; Dentists, General; Home Health Aides; Licensed Practical and Licensed Vocational Nurses; Low Vision Therapists, Orientation and Mobility Specialists, and Vision Rehabilitation Therapists; Massage Therapists; Medical and Clinical Laboratory Technicians; Medical and Health Services Managers; Medical Scientists, Except Epidemiologists; Medical Secretaries; Occupational Therapists; Orthodontists; Pharmacists; Pharmacy Technicians; Prosthodontists; Radiologic Technologists; School Psychologists; Social and Human Service Assistants; Speech-Language Pathologists; Speech-Language Pathology Assistants; Substance Abuse and Behavioral Disorder Counselors; others.

Paralegals and Legal Assistants

❋ Annual Earnings: $46,680

❋ Earnings Growth Potential: Medium (36.9%)

❋ Growth: 28.1%

❋ Annual Job Openings: 10,400

❋ Self-Employed: 3.2%

Skills—Most Important: Communication Skills.

Assist lawyers by researching legal precedent, investigating facts, or preparing legal documents. Conduct research to support a legal proceeding, to formulate a defense, or to initiate legal action. Prepare affidavits or other documents, such as legal correspondence, and organize and maintain documents in paper or electronic filing system. Prepare for trial by performing tasks such as organizing exhibits. Prepare legal documents, including briefs, pleadings, appeals, wills, contracts, and real estate closing statements. Meet with clients and other professionals to discuss details of case. File pleadings with court clerk. Gather and analyze research data, such as statutes; decisions; and legal articles, codes, and documents. Call on witnesses to testify at hearings. Investigate facts and law of cases and search pertinent sources, such as public records, to determine causes of action and to prepare cases. Direct and coordinate law office activity, including delivery of subpoenas. Appraise and inventory real and personal property for estate planning.

Education/Training Required: Associate degree. **Education and Training Program:** Legal Assistant/Paralegal Training. **Knowledge/Courses:** Clerical Practices; Law and Government; English Language; Computers and Electronics; Communications and Media.

Personality Type: Conventional-Investigative-Enterprising. **Career Cluster:** 12 Law, Public Safety, Corrections, and Security. **Career Pathway:** 12.5 Legal Services. **Other Jobs in This Pathway:** Administrative Law Judges, Adjudicators, and Hearing Officers; Arbitrators, Mediators, and Conciliators; Court Reporters; Farm and Home Management Advisors; Judges, Magistrate Judges, and Magistrates; Lawyers; Legal Secretaries; Legal Support Workers, All Other; Title Examiners, Abstractors, and Searchers.

Personal Financial Advisors

* Annual Earnings: $64,750
* Earnings Growth Potential: High (49.6%)
* Growth: 30.1%
* Annual Job Openings: 8,530
* Self-Employed: 29.3%

Skills—Most Important: Mathematics Skills; Communication Skills; Thought-Processing Skills. **Other High-Level Skills:** Social Skills; Management Skills.

Advise clients on financial plans using knowledge of tax and investment strategies, securities, insurance, pension plans, and real estate. Duties include assessing clients' assets, liabilities, cash flows, insurance coverages, tax statuses, and financial objectives to establish investment strategies. Prepare and interpret for clients information such as investment performance reports, financial document summaries, and income projections. Recommend strategies clients can use to achieve their financial goals and objectives, including specific recommendations in such areas as cash management, insurance coverage, and investment planning. Build and maintain client bases, keeping client plans up-to-date and recruiting new clients on an ongoing basis. Devise debt liquidation plans that include payoff priorities and timelines. Implement financial planning recommendations or refer clients to someone who can assist them with plan implementation. Interview clients to determine their current income, expenses, insurance coverage, tax status, financial objectives, risk tolerance, and other information needed to develop a financial plan. Monitor financial market trends to ensure that plans are effective and to identify necessary updates. Explain and document for clients the types of services that are to be provided and the responsibilities to be taken by the personal financial advisor. Explain to individuals and groups the details of financial assistance available to college and university students, such as loans, grants, and scholarships. Guide clients in gathering information such as bank account records, income tax returns, life and disability insurance records, pension plan information, and wills.

Education/Training Required: Bachelor's degree. **Education and Training Programs:** Finance, General; Financial Planning and Services. **Knowledge/Courses:** Economics and Accounting; Sales and Marketing; Law and Government; Customer and Personal Service; Mathematics; Computers and Electronics.

Personality Type: Enterprising-Conventional-Social. **Career Cluster:** 06 Finance. **Career Pathway:** 06.1 Financial and Investment Planning. **Other Jobs in This Pathway:** Budget Analysts; Credit Analysts; Financial Analysts; Financial Managers, Branch or Department; Financial Quantitative Analysts; Financial Specialists, All Other; Fraud Examiners, Investigators and Analysts; Investment Underwriters; Loan Counselors;

Risk Management Specialists; Sales Agents, Financial Services; Sales Agents, Securities and Commodities; Securities and Commodities Traders; Securities, Commodities, and Financial Services Sales Agents; Treasurers and Controllers.

Petroleum Engineers

- ❋ Annual Earnings: $114,080
- ❋ Earnings Growth Potential: High (44.4%)
- ❋ Growth: 18.4%
- ❋ Annual Job Openings: 860
- ❋ Self-Employed: 0.4%

Skills—Most Important: Science Skills; Mathematics Skills; Management Skills. **Other High-Level Skills:** Thought-Processing Skills; Communication Skills; Technology/ Programming Skills; Social Skills; Equipment Use/Maintenance Skills.

Devise methods to improve oil and gas well production and determine the need for new or modified tool designs. Oversee drilling and offer technical advice to achieve economical and satisfactory progress. Assess costs and estimate the production capabilities and economic value of oil and gas wells to evaluate the economic viability of potential drilling sites. Monitor production rates and plan rework processes to improve production. Analyze data to recommend placement of wells and supplementary processes to enhance production. Specify and supervise well modification and stimulation programs to maximize oil and gas recovery. Direct and monitor the completion and evaluation of wells, well testing, or well surveys. Assist engineering and other personnel to solve operating problems.

Develop plans for oil and gas field drilling and for product recovery and treatment. Maintain records of drilling and production operations. Confer with scientific, engineering, and technical personnel to resolve design, research, and testing problems. Write technical reports for engineering and management personnel. Evaluate findings to develop, design, or test equipment or processes.

Education/Training Required: Bachelor's degree. **Education and Training Program:** Petroleum Engineering. **Knowledge/Courses:** Engineering and Technology; Physics; Geography; Chemistry; Economics and Accounting; Design.

Personality Type: Investigative-Realistic-Conventional. **Career Cluster:** 15 Science, Technology, Engineering, and Mathematics. **Career Pathway:** 15.1 Engineering and Technology. **Other Jobs in This Pathway:** Architectural and Engineering Managers; Automotive Engineers; Biochemical Engineers; Biofuels/Biodiesel Technology and Product Development Managers; Civil Engineers; Cost Estimators; Electrical Engineers; Electronics Engineers, Except Computer; Energy Engineers; Engineers, All Other; Fuel Cell Engineers; Human Factors Engineers and Ergonomists; Industrial Engineers; Manufacturing Engineers; Mechanical Engineers; Mechatronics Engineers; Microsystems Engineers; Nanosystems Engineers; Photonics Engineers; Radio Frequency Identification Device Specialists; Robotics Engineers; Solar Energy Systems Engineers; Transportation Engineers; Validation Engineers; Wind Energy Engineers; others.

Pharmacists

- ❋ Annual Earnings: $111,570
- ❋ Earnings Growth Potential: Low (26.4%)
- ❋ Growth: 17.0%
- ❋ Annual Job Openings: 10,580
- ❋ Self-Employed: 0.6%

Skills—Most Important: Science Skills; Communication Skills; Management Skills. **Other High-Level Skills:** Social Skills; Mathematics Skills; Thought-Processing Skills.

Compound and dispense medications following prescriptions issued by physicians, dentists, or other authorized medical practitioners. Review prescriptions to assure accuracy, to ascertain the needed ingredients, and to evaluate their suitability. Provide information and advice on drug interactions, side effects, dosage, and storage. Assess the identity, strength, and purity of medications. Maintain records, such as pharmacy files, patient profiles, charge system files, inventories, control records for radioactive nuclei, and registries of poisons, narcotics, and controlled drugs. Compound and dispense medications as prescribed by calculating, weighing, measuring, and mixing ingredients or oversee these activities. Plan, implement, and maintain procedures for mixing, packaging, and labeling pharmaceuticals according to policy and legal requirements to ensure quality, security, and proper disposal. Teach pharmacy students serving as interns in preparation for their graduation or licensure. Advise customers on the selection of medication brands, medical equipment, and health-care supplies. Provide specialized services to help patients manage conditions such as diabetes, asthma, smoking cessation, or high blood pressure. Collaborate with other health-care professionals to plan, monitor, review, and evaluate the quality and effectiveness of drugs and drug regimens, providing advice on drug applications and characteristics. Analyze prescribing trends to monitor patient compliance and to prevent excessive usage or harmful interactions.

Education/Training Required: First professional degree. **Education and Training Programs:** Clinical, Hospital, and Managed Care Pharmacy (MS, PhD); Industrial and Physical Pharmacy and Cosmetic Sciences (MS, PhD); Medicinal and Pharmaceutical Chemistry (MS, PhD); Natural Products Chemistry and Pharmacognosy (MS, PhD); Pharmaceutics and Drug Design (MS, PhD); Pharmacoeconomics/Pharmaceutical Economics (MS, PhD); Pharmacy (PharmD [USA], PharmD or BS/BPharm [Canada]); Pharmacy Administration and Pharmacy Policy and Regulatory Affairs (MS, PhD); Pharmacy, Pharmaceutical Sciences, and Administration, Other. **Knowledge/Courses:** Biology; Medicine and Dentistry; Chemistry; Therapy and Counseling; Psychology; Clerical.

Personality Type: Investigative-Conventional-Social. **Career Cluster:** 08 Health Science. **Career Pathways:** 08.1 Therapeutic Services; 08.5 Biotechnology Research and Development. **Other Jobs in These Pathways:** Clinical Psychologists; Community and Social Service Specialists, All Other; Counseling Psychologists; Dental Assistants; Dental Hygienists; Dentists, General; Health Technologists and Technicians, All Other; Healthcare Support Workers, All Other; Home Health Aides; Licensed Practical and Licensed Vocational Nurses; Low Vision Therapists, Orientation and Mobility Specialists, and Vision Rehabilitation

Therapists; Massage Therapists; Medical and Clinical Laboratory Technicians; Medical and Health Services Managers; Medical Scientists, Except Epidemiologists; Medical Secretaries; Occupational Therapists; Ophthalmic Medical Technologists; Pharmacy Technicians; Radiologic Technologists; School Psychologists; Social and Human Service Assistants; Speech-Language Pathologists; Speech-Language Pathology Assistants; Substance Abuse and Behavioral Disorder Counselors; others.

Pharmacy Technicians

* Annual Earnings: $28,400
* Earnings Growth Potential: Low (30.1%)
* Growth: 30.6%
* Annual Job Openings: 18,200
* Self-Employed: 0.2%

Skills—Most Important: Mathematics Skills; Social Skills; Communication Skills.

Prepare medications under the direction of a pharmacist. May measure, mix, count out, label, and record amounts and dosages of medications. Receive written prescription or refill requests and verify that information is complete and accurate. Establish and maintain patient profiles, including lists of medications taken by patients. Maintain proper storage and security conditions for drugs. Prepack bulk medicines, fill bottles with prescribed medications, and type and affix labels. Answer telephones, responding to questions or requests. Mix pharmaceutical preparations according to written prescriptions. Clean and help maintain equipment and work areas and sterilize glassware according to prescribed methods. Price and file prescriptions that have been filled. Receive and store incoming supplies, verify quantities against invoices, check for outdated medications in current inventory, and inform supervisors of stock needs and shortages. Assist customers by answering simple questions, locating items, or referring them to the pharmacist for medication information. Order, label, and count stock of medications, chemicals, and supplies and enter inventory data into computer. Operate cash registers to accept payment from customers. Transfer medication from vials to the appropriate number of sterile, disposable syringes using aseptic techniques. Supply and monitor robotic machines that dispense medicine into containers and label the containers. Prepare and process medical insurance claim forms and records. Deliver medications and pharmaceutical supplies to patients, nursing stations, or surgery.

Education/Training Required: Moderate-term on-the-job training. **Education and Training Program:** Pharmacy Technician/Assistant Training. **Knowledge/Courses:** Medicine and Dentistry; Clerical Practices; Computers and Electronics; Customer and Personal Service; Chemistry; Mathematics.

Personality Type: Conventional-Realistic. **Career Cluster:** 08 Health Science. **Career Pathway:** 08.1 Therapeutic Services. **Other Jobs in This Pathway:** Clinical Psychologists; Community and Social Service Specialists, All Other; Counseling Psychologists; Dental Assistants; Dental Hygienists; Dentists, General; Health Technologists and Technicians, All Other; Healthcare Support Workers, All Other; Home Health Aides; Licensed Practical and Licensed Vocational Nurses; Low Vision Therapists, Orientation and Mobility Specialists, and Vision Rehabilitation Therapists; Massage Therapists; Medical and

Clinical Laboratory Technicians; Medical and Health Services Managers; Medical Scientists, Except Epidemiologists; Medical Secretaries; Occupational Therapists; Ophthalmic Medical Technologists; Pharmacists; Radiologic Technologists; School Psychologists; Social and Human Service Assistants; Speech-Language Pathologists; Speech-Language Pathology Assistants; Substance Abuse and Behavioral Disorder Counselors; others.

Physical Therapist Assistants

❋ Annual Earnings: $49,690

❋ Earnings Growth Potential: Medium (37.5%)

❋ Growth: 33.3%

❋ Annual Job Openings: 3,050

❋ Self-Employed: 1.3%

Skills—Most Important: Science Skills; Social Skills; Communication Skills. **Other High-Level Skills:** Thought-Processing Skills; Equipment Use/Maintenance Skills.

Assist physical therapists in providing physical therapy treatments and procedures. May, in accordance with state laws, assist in the development of treatment plans, carry out routine functions, document the progress of treatment, and modify specific treatments in accordance with patient status and within the scope of treatment plans established by physical therapists. Generally requires formal training. Instruct, motivate, safeguard, and assist patients as they practice exercises and functional activities. Confer with physical therapy staff or others to discuss and evaluate patient information for planning, modifying, and coordinating treatment. Administer active and passive manual therapeutic exercises, therapeutic massage, and heat, light, sound, water, and electrical modality treatments, such as ultrasound. Observe patients during treatments to compile and evaluate data on patients' responses and progress and report to physical therapist. Measure patients' range-of-joint motion, body parts, and vital signs to determine effects of treatments or for patient evaluations. Secure patients into or onto therapy equipment. Fit patients for orthopedic braces, prostheses, and supportive devices, such as crutches. Train patients in the use of orthopedic braces, prostheses, or supportive devices. Transport patients to and from treatment areas, lifting and transferring them according to positioning requirements. Monitor operation of equipment and record use of equipment and administration of treatment. Clean work area and check and store equipment after treatment. Assist patients to dress, undress, or put on and remove supportive devices, such as braces, splints, and slings. Administer traction to relieve neck and back pain using intermittent and static traction equipment.

Education/Training Required: Associate degree. **Education and Training Program:** Physical Therapy Technician/Assistant Training. **Knowledge/Courses:** Therapy and Counseling; Medicine and Dentistry; Psychology; Biology; Customer and Personal Service; Education and Training.

Personality Type: Social-Realistic-Investigative. **Career Cluster:** 08 Health Science. **Career Pathway:** 08.1 Therapeutic Services. **Other Jobs in This Pathway:** Clinical Psychologists; Community and Social Service Specialists, All Other; Counseling Psychologists; Dental Assistants; Dental Hygienists; Dentists, General; Health Technologists and Technicians, All Other; Healthcare Support Workers, All

Other; Home Health Aides; Licensed Practical and Licensed Vocational Nurses; Low Vision Therapists, Orientation and Mobility Specialists, and Vision Rehabilitation Therapists; Massage Therapists; Medical and Clinical Laboratory Technicians; Medical and Health Services Managers; Medical Scientists, Except Epidemiologists; Medical Secretaries; Occupational Therapists; Pharmacists; Pharmacy Technicians; Radiologic Technologists; School Psychologists; Social and Human Service Assistants; Speech-Language Pathologists; Speech-Language Pathology Assistants; Substance Abuse and Behavioral Disorder Counselors; others.

Physical Therapists

- ❋ Annual Earnings: $76,310
- ❋ Earnings Growth Potential: Low (29.7%)
- ❋ Growth: 30.3%
- ❋ Annual Job Openings: 7,860
- ❋ Self-Employed: 8.0%

Skills—Most Important: Science Skills; Social Skills; Communication Skills. **Other High-Level Skills:** Thought-Processing Skills; Management Skills; Equipment Use/Maintenance Skills.

Assess, plan, organize, and participate in rehabilitative programs that improve mobility, relieve pain, increase strength, and decrease or prevent deformity of patients suffering from disease or injury. Plan, prepare, and carry out individually designed programs of physical treatment to maintain, improve, or restore physical functioning, alleviate pain, and prevent physical dysfunction in patients. Perform and document an initial exam, evaluating data to identify problems and determine a diagnosis prior to intervention. Evaluate effects of treatment at various stages and adjust treatments to achieve maximum benefit. Administer manual exercises, massage, or traction to help relieve pain, increase patient strength, or decrease or prevent deformity or crippling. Instruct patient and family in treatment procedures to be continued at home. Confer with the patient, medical practitioners, and others to plan, implement, and assess the intervention program. Review physician's referral and patient's medical records to help determine diagnosis and physical therapy treatment. Obtain patients' informed consent to proposed interventions. Record prognosis, treatment, response, and progress in patient's chart or enter information into computer. Discharge patient from physical therapy when goals or projected outcomes have been attained and provide for appropriate follow-up care or referrals. Test and measure patient's strength, motor development and function, sensory perception, functional capacity, and respiratory and circulatory efficiency and record data. Identify and document goals, anticipated progress, and plans for reevaluation.

Education/Training Required: Master's degree. **Education and Training Programs:** Kinesiotherapy/Kinesiotherapist; Physical Therapy/Therapist. **Knowledge/Courses:** Therapy and Counseling; Medicine and Dentistry; Psychology; Education and Training; Biology; Customer and Personal Service.

Personality Type: Social-Investigative-Realistic. **Career Cluster:** 08 Health Science. **Career Pathway:** 08.3 Health Informatics. **Other Jobs in This Pathway:** Clinical Psychologists; Dental Laboratory Technicians; Editors; Engineers, All Other; Executive Secretaries and Executive Administrative Assistants; Fine Artists, Including Painters, Sculptors, and Illustrators; First-Line Supervisors of Office and Administrative Support Workers; Health Educators; Medical and Health Services Managers; Medical Appliance Technicians; Medical Assistants; Medical Records and Health Information Technicians; Medical Secretaries; Medical Transcriptionists; Mental Health Counselors; Occupational Health and Safety Specialists; Occupational Health and Safety Technicians; Psychiatric Aides; Psychiatric Technicians; Public Relations Specialists; Receptionists and Information Clerks; Recreational Therapists; Rehabilitation Counselors; Substance Abuse and Behavioral Disorder Counselors; Therapists, All Other; others.

Physician Assistants

❋ Annual Earnings: $86,410

❋ Earnings Growth Potential: Low (33.5%)

❋ Growth: 39.0%

❋ Annual Job Openings: 4,280

❋ Self-Employed: 1.4%

Skills—Most Important: Science Skills; Social Skills; Communication Skills. **Other High-Level Skills:** Thought-Processing Skills; Mathematics Skills; Management Skills.

Under the supervision of physicians, provide health-care services typically performed by a physician. Conduct complete physicals, provide treatment, and counsel patients. May in some cases prescribe medication. Must graduate from an accredited educational program for physician assistants. Examine patients to obtain information about their physical condition. Make tentative diagnoses and decisions about management and treatment of patients. Interpret diagnostic test results for deviations from normal. Obtain, compile, and record patient medical data, including health history, progress notes, and results of physical examination. Administer or order diagnostic tests, such as X-ray, electrocardiogram, and laboratory tests. Prescribe therapy or medication with physician approval. Perform therapeutic procedures, such as injections, immunizations, suturing and wound care, and infection management. Instruct and counsel patients about prescribed therapeutic regimens, normal growth and development, family planning, emotional problems of daily living, and health maintenance. Provide physicians with assistance during surgery or complicated medical procedures. Supervise and coordinate activities of technicians and technical assistants. Visit and observe patients on hospital rounds or house calls, updating charts, ordering therapy, and reporting back to physician. Order medical and laboratory supplies and equipment.

Education/Training Required: Master's degree. **Education and Training Program:** Physician Assistant Training. **Knowledge/Courses:** Medicine and Dentistry; Biology; Therapy and Counseling; Psychology; Chemistry; Sociology and Anthropology.

Personality Type: Social-Investigative-Realistic. **Career Cluster:** 08 Health Science. **Career Pathway:** 08.2 Diagnostics Services. **Other Jobs in This Pathway:** Ambulance Drivers and Attendants, Except Emergency Medical Technicians; Anesthesiologist Assistants; Cardiovascular Technologists and Technicians; Cytogenetic Technologists; Cytotechnologists; Diagnostic Medical Sonographers; Emergency Medical Technicians and Paramedics;

P

Endoscopy Technicians; Health Diagnosing and Treating Practitioners, All Other; Health Technologists and Technicians, All Other; Healthcare Practitioners and Technical Workers, All Other; Histotechnologists and Histologic Technicians; Medical and Clinical Laboratory Technicians; Medical and Clinical Laboratory Technologists; Medical and Health Services Managers; Medical Assistants; Medical Equipment Preparers; Neurodiagnostic Technologists; Nuclear Medicine Technologists; Ophthalmic Laboratory Technicians; Physical Scientists, All Other; Radiologic Technicians; Radiologic Technologists; Surgical Technologists; Veterinary Assistants and Laboratory Animal Caretakers; others.

Job Specialization: Anesthesiologist Assistants

Assist anesthesiologists in the administration of anesthesia for surgical and non-surgical procedures. Monitor patient status and provide patient care during surgical treatment. Verify availability of operating room supplies, medications, and gases. Provide clinical instruction, supervision, or training to staff in areas such as anesthesia practices. Collect samples or specimens for diagnostic testing. Participate in seminars, workshops, or other professional activities to keep abreast of developments in anesthesiology. Collect and document patients' pre-anesthetic health histories. Provide airway management interventions including tracheal intubation, fiber optics, or ventilary support. Respond to emergency situations by providing cardiopulmonary resuscitation, basic cardiac life support, advanced cardiac life support, or pediatric advanced life support. Monitor and document patients' progress during post-anesthesia period. Pretest and calibrate

anesthesia delivery systems and monitors. Assist anesthesiologists in monitoring electrocardiogram, direct arterial pressure, central venous pressure, arterial blood gas, hematocrit, or routine measurement of temperature, respiration, blood pressure, and heart rate. Assist in the provision of advanced life support techniques including procedures high-frequency ventilation or intra-arterial cardiovascular assistance devices. Assist anesthesiologists in performing anesthetic procedures such as epidural and spinal injections.

Education/Training Required: Master's degree. **Education and Training Program:** Physician Assistant Training. **Knowledge/Courses:** No data available.

Personality Type: Realistic-Social-Investigative. **Career Cluster:** 08 Health Science. **Career Pathway:** 08.2 Diagnostics Services. **Other Jobs in This Pathway:** Ambulance Drivers and Attendants, Except Emergency Medical Technicians; Cardiovascular Technologists and Technicians; Cytogenetic Technologists; Cytotechnologists; Diagnostic Medical Sonographers; Emergency Medical Technicians and Paramedics; Endoscopy Technicians; Health Diagnosing and Treating Practitioners, All Other; Health Technologists and Technicians, All Other; Healthcare Practitioners and Technical Workers, All Other; Histotechnologists and Histologic Technicians; Medical and Clinical Laboratory Technicians; Medical and Clinical Laboratory Technologists; Medical and Health Services Managers; Medical Assistants; Medical Equipment Preparers; Neurodiagnostic Technologists; Nuclear Medicine Technologists; Ophthalmic Laboratory Technicians; Physical Scientists, All Other; Physician Assistants; Radiologic

Technicians; Radiologic Technologists; Surgical Technologists; Veterinary Assistants and Laboratory Animal Caretakers; others.

Physicists

* Annual Earnings: $106,370
* Earnings Growth Potential: High (44.7%)
* Growth: 15.9%
* Annual Job Openings: 690
* Self-Employed: 0.0%

Skills—Most Important: Science Skills; Mathematics Skills; Technology/ Programming Skills. **Other High-Level Skills:** Communication Skills; Thought-Processing Skills; Social Skills; Management Skills; Equipment Use/Maintenance Skills.

Conduct research into phases of physical phenomena, develop theories and laws on basis of observation and experiments, and devise methods to apply laws and theories to industry and other fields. Perform complex calculations as part of the analysis and evaluation of data using computers. Describe and express observations and conclusions in mathematical terms. Analyze data from research to detect and measure physical phenomena. Report experimental results by writing papers for scientific journals or by presenting information at scientific conferences. Design computer simulations to model physical data so that it can be better understood. Collaborate with other scientists in the design, development, and testing of experimental, industrial, or medical equipment, instrumentation, and procedures. Direct testing and monitoring of contamination of radioactive equipment and recording of personnel and plant area radiation exposure data. Observe the structure and properties of matter and the transformation and propagation of energy using equipment such as masers, lasers, and telescopes to explore and identify the basic principles governing these phenomena. Develop theories and laws on the basis of observation and experiments and apply these theories and laws to problems in areas such as nuclear energy, optics, and aerospace technology. Teach physics to students. Develop manufacturing, assembly, and fabrication processes of lasers, masers, infrared, and other light-emitting and light-sensitive devices.

Education/Training Required: Doctoral degree. **Education and Training Programs:** Acoustics; Astrophysics; Atomic/Molecular Physics; Condensed Matter and Materials Physics; Elementary Particle Physics; Health/ Medical Physics; Nuclear Physics; Optics/ Optical Sciences; Physics, General; Physics, Other; Plasma and High-Temperature Physics; Theoretical and Mathematical Physics. **Knowledge/Courses:** Physics; Mathematics; Engineering and Technology; Computers and Electronics; English Language; Telecommunications.

Personality Type: Investigative-Realistic. **Career Clusters:** 05 Education and Training; 15 Science, Technology, Engineering, and Mathematics. **Career Pathways:** 15.2 Science and Mathematics; 05.3 Teaching/Training. **Other Jobs in These Pathways:** Adult Basic and Secondary Education and Literacy Teachers and Instructors; Architectural and Engineering Managers; Biofuels/Biodiesel Technology and Product Development Managers; Biologists; Career/Technical Education Teachers, Secondary School; Chemists; Coaches and Scouts; Community and Social Service Specialists, All Other; Education, Training, and Library Workers, All Other; Elementary School Teachers, Except Special Education; Fitness Trainers and Aerobics Instructors; Instructional Coordinators; Instructional Designers and Technologists; Kindergarten Teachers, Except Special Education; Librarians; Medical Scientists, Except Epidemiologists; Middle School Teachers, Except Special and Career/Technical Education; Operations Research Analysts; Preschool Teachers, Except Special Education; Recreation Workers; Secondary School Teachers, Except Special and Career/Technical Education; Self-Enrichment Education Teachers; Teacher Assistants; Teachers and Instructors, All Other; Tutors; others.

Plumbers, Pipefitters, and Steamfitters

- ❋ Annual Earnings: $46,660
- ❋ Earnings Growth Potential: Medium (40.9%)
- ❋ Growth: 15.3%
- ❋ Annual Job Openings: 17,550
- ❋ Self-Employed: 12.3%

Skills—Most Important: Equipment Use/Maintenance Skills; Installation Skills; Mathematics Skills. **Other High-Level Skills:** Thought-Processing Skills; Management Skills; Social Skills.

Job Specialization: Pipe Fitters and Steamfitters

Lay out, assemble, install, and maintain pipe systems, pipe supports, and related hydraulic and pneumatic equipment for steam, hot water, heating, cooling, lubricating, sprinkling, and industrial production and processing systems. Cut, thread, and hammer pipe to specifications using tools such as saws, cutting torches, and pipe threaders and benders. Assemble and secure pipes, tubes, fittings, and related equipment according to specifications by welding, brazing, cementing, soldering, and threading joints. Attach pipes to walls, structures, and fixtures, such as radiators or tanks, using brackets, clamps, tools, or welding equipment. Inspect, examine, and test installed systems and pipe lines using pressure gauge, hydrostatic testing, observation, or other methods. Measure and mark pipes for cutting and threading. Lay out full-scale drawings of pipe systems, supports, and related equipment following blueprints. Plan pipe system layout, installation, or repair according to specifications. Select pipe sizes and types and related materials, such as supports, hangers, and hydraulic cylinders according to specifications.

Education/Training Required: Long-term on-the-job training. **Education and Training Programs:** Pipefitting/Pipefitter and Sprinkler Fitter; Plumbing and Related Water Supply Services, Other; Plumbing Technology/Plumber. **Knowledge/Courses:** Building and Construction; Mechanical Devices; Physics; Design; Engineering and Technology; Chemistry.

Personality Type: Realistic-Conventional. **Career Cluster:** 02 Architecture and Construction. **Career Pathway:** 02.2 Construction. **Other Jobs in This Pathway:** Brickmasons and Blockmasons; Cement Masons and Concrete Finishers; Construction and Building Inspectors; Construction Carpenters; Construction Laborers; Construction Managers; Cost Estimators; Drywall and Ceiling Tile Installers; Electrical Power-Line Installers and Repairers; Electricians; Engineering Technicians,

Except Drafters, All Other; Excavating and Loading Machine and Dragline Operators; First-Line Supervisors of Construction Trades and Extraction Workers; Heating and Air Conditioning Mechanics and Installers; Helpers—Carpenters; Helpers—Electricians; Helpers—Pipelayers, Plumbers, Pipefitters, and Steamfitters; Highway Maintenance Workers; Operating Engineers and Other Construction Equipment Operators; Painters, Construction and Maintenance; Plumbers; Refrigeration Mechanics and Installers; Roofers; Rough Carpenters; Solar Energy Installation Managers; others.

Job Specialization: Plumbers

Assemble, install, and repair pipes, fittings, and fixtures of heating, water, and drainage systems according to specifications and plumbing codes. Assemble pipe sections, tubing, and fittings using couplings; clamps; screws; bolts; cement; plastic solvent; caulking; or soldering, brazing, and welding equipment. Fill pipes or plumbing fixtures with water or air and observe pressure gauges to detect and locate leaks. Review blueprints and building codes and specifications to determine work details and procedures. Prepare written work cost estimates and negotiate contracts. Study building plans and inspect structures to assess material and equipment needs, to establish the sequence of pipe installations, and to plan installation around obstructions such as electrical wiring. Keep records of assignments and produce detailed work reports. Perform complex calculations and planning for special or very large jobs. Locate and mark the position of pipe installations, connections, passage holes, and fixtures in structures using measuring instruments such as rulers and levels. Measure, cut, thread, and bend pipe to required angle

using hand and power tools or machines such as pipe cutters, pipe-threading machines, and pipe-bending machines. Install pipe assemblies, fittings, valves, appliances such as dishwashers and water heaters and fixtures such as sinks and toilets using hand and power tools. Cut openings in structures to accommodate pipes and pipe fittings using hand and power tools. Hang steel supports from ceiling joists to hold pipes in place.

Education/Training Required: Long-term on-the-job training. **Education and Training Programs:** Pipefitting/Pipefitter and Sprinkler Fitter; Plumbing and Related Water Supply Services, Other; Plumbing Technology/Plumber. **Knowledge/Courses:** Building and Construction; Mechanical Devices; Physics; Design; Engineering and Technology; Customer and Personal Service.

Personality Type: Realistic-Conventional-Investigative. **Career Cluster:** 02 Architecture and Construction. **Career Pathway:** 02.2 Construction. **Other Jobs in This Pathway:** Brickmasons and Blockmasons; Cement Masons and Concrete Finishers; Construction and Building Inspectors; Construction Carpenters; Construction Laborers; Construction Managers; Cost Estimators; Drywall and Ceiling Tile Installers; Electrical Power-Line Installers and Repairers; Electricians; Engineering Technicians, Except Drafters, All Other; Excavating and Loading Machine and Dragline Operators; First-Line Supervisors of Construction Trades and Extraction Workers; Heating and Air Conditioning Mechanics and Installers; Helpers—Carpenters; Helpers—Electricians; Helpers—Pipelayers, Plumbers, Pipefitters, and Steamfitters; Highway Maintenance Workers; Operating Engineers and Other Construction Equipment Operators; Painters, Construction and Maintenance; Pipe Fitters and Steamfitters; Refrigeration Mechanics and Installers; Roofers; Rough Carpenters; Solar Energy Installation Managers; others.

Police and Sheriff's Patrol Officers

❋ Annual Earnings: $53,540

❋ Earnings Growth Potential: Medium (40.8%)

❋ Growth: 8.7%

❋ Annual Job Openings: 22,790

❋ Self-Employed: 0.0%

Skills—Most Important: Social Skills; Communication Skills; Thought-Processing Skills. **Other High-Level Skills:** Management Skills; Equipment Use/Maintenance Skills.

Job Specialization: Police Patrol Officers

Patrol assigned areas to enforce laws and ordinances, regulate traffic, control crowds, prevent crime, and arrest violators. Provide for public safety by maintaining order, responding to emergencies, protecting people and property, enforcing motor vehicle and criminal laws, and promoting good community relations. Identify, pursue, and arrest suspects and perpetrators of criminal acts. Record facts to prepare reports that document incidents and activities. Review facts of incidents to determine if criminal act or statute violations were involved. Render aid to accident victims and other persons requiring first aid for physical injuries. Testify in court to present evidence or act as witness in traffic and criminal cases. Evaluate complaint and emergency-request information to determine response requirements. Patrol specific area

on foot, horseback, or motorized conveyance, responding promptly to calls for assistance. Monitor, note, report, and investigate suspicious persons and situations, safety hazards, and unusual or illegal activity in patrol area. Investigate traffic accidents and other accidents to determine causes and to determine if a crime has been committed. Photograph or draw diagrams of crime or accident scenes and interview principals and eyewitnesses. Monitor traffic to ensure motorists observe traffic regulations and exhibit safe driving procedures. Relay complaint and emergency-request information to appropriate agency dispatchers. Issue citations or warnings to violators of motor vehicle ordinances. Direct traffic flow and reroute traffic in emergencies.

Education/Training Required: Long-term on-the-job training. **Education and Training Programs:** Criminal Justice/Police Science; Criminalistics and Criminal Science. **Knowledge/Courses:** Psychology; Public Safety and Security; Law and Government; Customer and Personal Service; Therapy and Counseling; Sociology and Anthropology.

Personality Type: Realistic-Enterprising-Conventional. **Career Cluster:** 12 Law, Public Safety, Corrections, and Security. **Career Pathway:** 12.4 Law Enforcement Services. **Other Jobs in This Pathway:** Bailiffs; Correctional Officers and Jailers; Criminal Investigators and Special Agents; First-Line Supervisors of Police and Detectives; Forensic Science Technicians; Immigration and Customs Inspectors; Intelligence Analysts; Police Detectives; Police Identification and Records Officers; Remote Sensing Scientists and Technologists; Sheriffs and Deputy Sheriffs.

Job Specialization: Sheriffs and Deputy Sheriffs

Enforce law and order in rural or unincorporated districts or serve legal processes of courts. May patrol courthouse, guard court or grand jury, or escort defendants. Drive vehicles or patrol specific areas to detect law violators, issue citations, and make arrests. Investigate illegal or suspicious activities. Verify that the proper legal charges have been made against law offenders. Execute arrest warrants, locating and taking persons into custody. Record daily activities and submit logs and other related reports and paperwork to appropriate authorities. Patrol and guard courthouses, grand jury rooms, or assigned areas to provide security, enforce laws, maintain order, and arrest violators. Notify patrol units to take violators into custody or to provide needed assistance or medical aid. Place people in protective custody. Take control of accident scenes to maintain traffic flow, to assist accident victims, and to investigate causes. Serve statements of claims, subpoenas, summonses, orders to pay alimony, and other court orders. Question individuals entering secured areas to determine their business, directing and rerouting individuals as necessary. Transport or escort prisoners and defendants en route to courtrooms, prisons or jails, attorneys' offices, or medical facilities. Locate and confiscate real or personal property as directed by court order. Manage jail operations and tend to jail inmates.

Education/Training Required: Long-term on-the-job training. **Education and Training Programs:** Criminal Justice/Police Science; Criminalistics and Criminal Science. **Knowledge/Courses:** Public Safety and Security; Law and Government; Telecommunications; Psychology; Therapy and Counseling; Philosophy and Theology.

Personality Type: Enterprising-Realistic-Social. **Career Cluster:** 12 Law, Public Safety, Corrections, and Security. **Career Pathways:** 12.4 Law Enforcement Services; 12.3 Security and Protective Services. **Other Jobs in These Pathways:** Animal Control Workers; Bailiffs; Correctional Officers and Jailers; Criminal Investigators and Special Agents; Crossing Guards; First-Line Supervisors of Police and Detectives; First-Line Supervisors of Protective Service Workers, All Other; Forensic Science Technicians; Forest Firefighters; Gaming Surveillance Officers and Gaming Investigators; Immigration and Customs Inspectors; Intelligence Analysts; Lifeguards, Ski Patrol, and Other Recreational Protective Service Workers; Parking Enforcement Workers; Police Detectives; Police Identification and Records Officers; Police Patrol Officers; Police, Fire, and Ambulance Dispatchers; Private Detectives and Investigators; Remote Sensing Scientists and Technologists; Retail Loss Prevention Specialists; Security Guards; Transit and Railroad Police.

Political Scientists

* Annual Earnings: $107,420
* Earnings Growth Potential: Very high (54.6%)
* Growth: 19.4%
* Annual Job Openings: 280
* Self-Employed: 1.4%

Skills—Most Important: Science Skills; Communication Skills; Thought-Processing Skills. **Other High-Level Skills:** Mathematics Skills; Social Skills; Management Skills.

Study the origin, development, and operation of political systems. Research a wide range of

subjects, such as relations between the United States and foreign countries, the beliefs and institutions of foreign nations, or the politics of small towns or a major metropolis. May study topics such as public opinion, political decision making, and ideology. May analyze the structure and operation of governments as well as various political entities. May conduct public opinion surveys, analyze election results, or analyze public documents. Teach political science. Disseminate research results through academic publications, written reports, or public presentations. Identify issues for research and analysis. Develop and test theories using information from interviews, newspapers, periodicals, case law, historical papers, polls, and/or statistical sources. Maintain current knowledge of government policy decisions. Collect, analyze, and interpret data such as election results and public opinion surveys; report on findings, recommendations, and conclusions. Interpret and analyze policies, public issues, legislation, and/or the operations of governments, businesses, and organizations. Evaluate programs and policies and make related recommendations to institutions and organizations. Write drafts of legislative proposals and prepare speeches, correspondence, and policy papers for government use. Forecast political, economic, and social trends. Consult with and advise government officials, civic bodies, research agencies, the media, political parties, and others concerned with political issues. Provide media commentary and/or criticism on public policy and political issues and events.

Education/Training Required: Master's degree. **Education and Training Programs:** American Government and Politics (United States); Canadian Government and Politics; International Relations and Affairs;

International/Global Studies; Political Science and Government, General; Political Science and Government, Other. **Knowledge/Courses:** History and Archeology; Law and Government; Philosophy and Theology; Sociology and Anthropology; Foreign Language; Geography.

Personality Type: Investigative-Artistic-Social. **Career Clusters:** 07 Government and Public Administration; 15 Science, Technology, Engineering, and Mathematics. **Career Pathways:** 15.2 Science and Mathematics; 07.1 Governance. **Other Jobs in These Pathways:** Administrative Services Managers; Architectural and Engineering Managers; Biofuels/Biodiesel Technology and Product Development Managers; Biologists; Chemists; Chief Executives; Chief Sustainability Officers; Clinical Research Coordinators; Community and Social Service Specialists, All Other; Compliance Managers; Dietitians and Nutritionists; Education, Training, and Library Workers, All Other; General and Operations Managers; Legislators; Managers, All Other; Mapping Technicians; Medical Scientists, Except Epidemiologists; Natural Sciences Managers; Operations Research Analysts; Regulatory Affairs Managers; Reporters and Correspondents; Social and Community Service Managers; Storage and Distribution Managers; Surveying Technicians; Transportation Managers; others.

Preschool Teachers, Except Special Education

- ❈ Annual Earnings: $25,700
- ❈ Earnings Growth Potential: Low (33.1%)
- ❈ Growth: 19.0%
- ❈ Annual Job Openings: 17,830
- ❈ Self-Employed: 1.4%

Skills—Most Important: Social Skills; Thought-Processing Skills; Management Skills.

Instruct children (normally up to 5 years of age) in activities designed to promote social, physical, and intellectual growth needed for primary school in preschool, day-care center, or other child development facility. May be required to hold state certification. Provide a variety of materials and resources for children to explore, manipulate, and use, both in learning activities and in imaginative play. Attend to children's basic needs by feeding them, dressing them, and changing their diapers. Teach basic skills such as color, shape, number and letter recognition, personal hygiene, and social skills. Establish and enforce rules for behavior and procedures for maintaining order. Read books to entire classes or to small groups. Organize and lead activities designed to promote physical, mental, and social development, such as games, arts and crafts, music, storytelling, and field trips. Observe and evaluate children's performance, behavior, social development, and physical health. Identify children showing signs of emotional, developmental, or health-related problems and discuss them with supervisors, parents or guardians, and child development specialists.

Education/Training Required: Postsecondary vocational training. **Education and Training Programs:** Child Care and Support Services Management; Early Childhood Education and Teaching. **Knowledge/Courses:** Philosophy and Theology; Therapy and Counseling; Sociology and Anthropology; Geography; Customer and Personal Service; Psychology.

Personality Type: Social-Artistic. **Career Clusters:** 05 Education and Training; 10 Human Services. **Career Pathways:** 05.3 Teaching/Training; 10.1 Early Childhood Development and Services. **Other Jobs in These Pathways:** Adult Basic and Secondary Education and Literacy Teachers and Instructors; Athletes and Sports Competitors; Audio-Visual and Multimedia Collections Specialists; Career/Technical Education Teachers, Middle School; Career/Technical Education Teachers, Secondary School; Chemists; Coaches and Scouts; Dietitians and Nutritionists; Elementary School Teachers, Except Special Education; Farm and Home Management Advisors; Fitness Trainers and Aerobics Instructors; Historians; Instructional Coordinators; Instructional Designers and Technologists; Interpreters and Translators; Kindergarten Teachers, Except Special Education; Librarians; Middle School Teachers, Except Special and Career/Technical Education; Physicists; Recreation Workers; Secondary School Teachers, Except Special and Career/Technical Education; Self-Enrichment Education Teachers; Teacher Assistants; Teachers and Instructors, All Other; Tutors.

P

Probation Officers and Correctional Treatment Specialists

* Annual Earnings: $47,200
* Earnings Growth Potential: Low (34.5%)
* Growth: 19.3%
* Annual Job Openings: 4,180
* Self-Employed: 0.3%

Skills—Most Important: Social Skills; Communication Skills; Thought-Processing Skills.

Provide social services to assist in rehabilitation of law offenders in custody or on probation or parole. Make recommendations for actions involving formulation of rehabilitation plan and treatment of offender, including conditional release and education and employment stipulations. Prepare and maintain case folder for each assigned inmate or offender. Write reports describing offenders' progress. Inform offenders or inmates of requirements of conditional release, such as office visits, restitution payments, or educational and employment stipulations. Discuss with offenders how such issues as drug and alcohol abuse and anger management problems might have played roles in their criminal behavior. Gather information about offenders' backgrounds by talking to offenders, their families and friends, and other people who have relevant information. Develop rehabilitation programs for assigned offenders or inmates, establishing rules of conduct, goals, and objectives. Develop liaisons and networks with other parole officers, community agencies, correctional institutions, psychiatric facilities, and after-care agencies to

plan for helping offenders with life adjustments. Arrange for medical, mental health, or substance abuse treatment services according to individual needs or court orders. Assist offenders or inmates detainers, sentences in other jurisdictions, writs, and applications for social assistance. Arrange for postrelease services, such as employment, housing, counseling, education, and social activities. Recommend remedial action or initiate court action in response to noncompliance with terms of probation or parole.

Education/Training Required: Bachelor's degree. **Education and Training Program:** Social Work. **Knowledge/Courses:** Therapy and Counseling; Sociology and Anthropology; Psychology; Law and Government; Public Safety and Security; Philosophy and Theology.

Personality Type: Social-Enterprising-Conventional. **Career Cluster:** 10 Human Services. **Career Pathway:** 10.3 Family and Community Services. **Other Jobs in This Pathway:** Chief Executives; Child, Family, and School Social Workers; Childcare Workers; City and Regional Planning Aides; Counselors, All Other; Eligibility Interviewers, Government Programs; Farm and Home Management Advisors; Legislators; Managers, All Other; Marriage and Family Therapists; Nannies; Personal Care Aides; Protective Service Workers, All Other; Social and Community Service Managers; Social Science Research Assistants; Social Scientists and Related Workers, All Other; Social Workers, All Other; Sociologists; Supply Chain Managers.

Producers and Directors

* Annual Earnings: $68,440
* Earnings Growth Potential: Very high (53.0%)
* Growth: 9.8%
* Annual Job Openings: 4,040
* Self-Employed: 20.1%

Skills—Most Important: Because this occupation is highly diverse, separate lists of skills are provided for each job specialization.

Job Specialization: Directors— Stage, Motion Pictures, Television, and Radio

Interpret script, conduct rehearsals, and direct activities of cast and technical crew for stage, motion pictures, television, or radio programs. Direct live broadcasts, films, and recordings or nonbroadcast programming for public entertainment or education. Supervise and coordinate the work of camera, lighting, design, and sound crew members. Confer with technical directors, managers, crew members, and writers to discuss details of production, such as photography, script, music, sets, and costumes. Plan details such as framing, composition, camera movement, sound, and actor movement for each shot or scene. Establish pace of programs and sequences of scenes according to time requirements and cast and set accessibility. Identify and approve equipment and elements required for productions, such as scenery, lights, props, costumes, choreography, and music. Select plays or scripts for production and determine how material should be interpreted and performed. Compile cue words and phrases. Cue announcers, cast members, and technicians during performances.

Skills—Most Important: Social Skills; Communication Skills; Management Skills. **Other High-Level Skills:** Thought-Processing Skills.

Education/Training Required: Work experience plus degree. **Education and Training Programs:** Cinematography and Film/Video Production; Directing and Theatrical Production; Drama and Dramatics/Theatre Arts, General; Dramatic/ Theatre Arts and Stagecraft, Other; Film/Cinema/ Video Studies; Radio and Television. **Knowledge/ Courses:** Communications and Media; Fine Arts; Telecommunications; Production and Processing; Computers and Electronics; Engineering and Technology.

Personality Type: Enterprising-Artistic. **Career Cluster:** 03 Arts, Audio/Video Technology, and Communications. **Career Pathways:** 03.5 Journalism and Broadcasting; 03.4 Performing Arts. **Other Jobs in These Pathways:** Actors; Artists and Related Workers, All Other; Audio and Video Equipment Technicians; Broadcast Technicians; Camera Operators, Television, Video, and Motion Picture; Copy Writers; Editors; Entertainers and Performers, Sports and Related Workers, All Other; Film and Video Editors; Managers, All Other; Media and Communication Workers, All Other; Music Composers and Arrangers; Music Directors; Musicians, Instrumental; Photographers; Poets, Lyricists and Creative Writers; Producers; Program Directors; Public Relations Specialists; Radio and Television Announcers; Reporters and Correspondents; Singers; Talent Directors; Technical Directors/ Managers; Technical Writers; others.

Job Specialization: Producers

Plan and coordinate various aspects of radio, television, stage, or motion picture production, such as selecting script;

coordinating writing, directing, and editing; and arranging financing. Coordinate the activities of writers, directors, managers, and other personnel throughout the production process. Monitor postproduction processes to ensure accurate completion of details. Conduct meetings with staff to discuss production progress and to ensure production objectives are attained. Resolve personnel problems that arise during the production process by acting as liaisons between dissenting parties. Review film, recordings, or rehearsals to ensure conformance to production and broadcast standards. Perform administrative duties, such as preparing operational reports, distributing rehearsal call sheets and script copies, and arranging for rehearsal quarters. Write and edit news stories from information collected by reporters and other sources. Research production topics using the Internet, video archives, and other sources. Perform management activities such as budgeting, scheduling, planning, and marketing. Determine production size, content, and budget, establishing details such as production schedules and management policies. Compose and edit scripts or provide screenwriters with story outlines from which scripts can be written. Produce shows for special occasions, such as holidays or testimonials. Write and submit proposals to bid on contracts for projects. Hire directors, principal cast members, and key production staff members. Arrange financing for productions. Select plays, scripts, books, or ideas to be produced.

Skills—Most Important: Management Skills; Social Skills; Communication Skills. **Other High-Level Skills:** Thought-Processing Skills; Mathematics Skills.

Education/Training Required: Work experience plus degree. **Education and Training Programs:** Cinematography and Film/Video Production; Directing and Theatrical Production; Drama and Dramatics/Theatre Arts, General; Dramatic/Theatre Arts and Stagecraft, Other; Film/Cinema/Video Studies; Radio and Television. **Knowledge/Courses:** Communications and Media; Fine Arts; Philosophy and Theology; Sociology and Anthropology; History and Archeology; Geography.

Personality Type: Enterprising-Artistic. **Career Cluster:** 03 Arts, Audio/Video Technology, and Communications. **Career Pathways:** 03.4 Performing Arts; 03.5 Journalism and Broadcasting. **Other Jobs in These Pathways:** Actors; Artists and Related Workers, All Other; Audio and Video Equipment Technicians; Broadcast Technicians; Camera Operators, Television, Video, and Motion Picture; Copy Writers; Directors—Stage, Motion Pictures, Television, and Radio; Editors; Entertainers and Performers, Sports and Related Workers, All Other; Film and Video Editors; Managers, All Other; Media and Communication Workers, All Other; Music Composers and Arrangers; Music Directors; Musicians, Instrumental; Photographers; Poets, Lyricists and Creative Writers; Program Directors; Public Relations Specialists; Radio and Television Announcers; Reporters and Correspondents; Singers; Talent Directors; Technical Directors/Managers; Technical Writers; others.

Job Specialization: Program Directors

Direct and coordinate activities of personnel engaged in preparation of radio or television station program schedules and programs such as sports or news. Plan and schedule programming and event coverage based on broadcast length, time availability, and other factors such as community needs, ratings data, and viewer demographics. Monitor and review programming to ensure that schedules are met, guidelines are adhered to, and performances are of adequate quality. Direct and coordinate activities of personnel engaged in broadcast news, sports, or programming. Check completed program logs for accuracy and conformance with FCC rules and regulations and resolve program log inaccuracies. Establish work schedules and assign work to staff members. Coordinate activities between departments, such as news and programming. Perform personnel duties such as hiring staff and evaluating work performance. Evaluate new and existing programming for suitability and to assess the need for changes using information such as audience surveys and feedback. Develop budgets for programming and broadcasting activities and monitor expenditures to ensure that they remain within budget. Confer with directors and production staff to discuss issues such as production and casting problems, budgets, policies, and news coverage. Select, acquire, and maintain programs, music, films, and other needed materials and obtain legal clearances for their use. Monitor network transmissions for advisories concerning daily program schedules, program content, special feeds, and/or program changes.

Skills—Most Important: Management Skills; Thought-Processing Skills; Social Skills. **Other High-Level Skills:** Communication Skills.

Education/Training Required: Work experience plus degree. **Education and Training Programs:** Cinematography and Film/Video Production; Directing and Theatrical Production; Drama and Dramatics/Theatre Arts, General; Dramatic/Theatre Arts and Stagecraft, Other; Film/Cinema/Video Studies; Radio and Television. **Knowledge/Courses:**

Telecommunications; Communications and Media; Clerical Practices; Computers and Electronics; Personnel and Human Resources; Engineering and Technology.

Personality Type: Enterprising-Conventional-Artistic. **Career Cluster:** 03 Arts, Audio/Video Technology, and Communications. **Career Pathways:** 03.4 Performing Arts; 03.5 Journalism and Broadcasting. **Other Jobs in These Pathways:** Actors; Artists and Related Workers, All Other; Audio and Video Equipment Technicians; Broadcast Technicians; Camera Operators, Television, Video, and Motion Picture; Copy Writers; Directors—Stage, Motion Pictures, Television, and Radio; Editors; Entertainers and Performers, Sports and Related Workers, All Other; Film and Video Editors; Managers, All Other; Media and Communication Workers, All Other; Music Composers and Arrangers; Music Directors; Musicians, Instrumental; Photographers; Poets, Lyricists and Creative Writers; Producers; Public Relations Specialists; Radio and Television Announcers; Reporters and Correspondents; Singers; Talent Directors; Technical Directors/Managers; Technical Writers; others.

Job Specialization: Talent Directors

Audition and interview performers to select most appropriate talent for parts in stage, television, radio, or motion picture productions. Review performer information such as photos, resumes, voice tapes, videos, and union membership to decide whom to audition for parts. Read scripts and confer with producers to determine the types and numbers of performers required for a production. Select performers for roles or submit lists of suitable performers to producers or directors for final selection. Audition and interview performers to match their attributes to specific roles or to increase the pool of acting talent. Maintain talent files that include information such as performers' specialties, past performances, and availability. Prepare actors for auditions by providing scripts and information about roles and casting requirements. Serve as liaisons between directors, actors, and agents. Attend or view productions to maintain knowledge of available actors. Negotiate contract agreements with performers, with agents, or between performers and agents or production companies. Contact agents and actors to provide notification of audition and performance opportunities and to set up audition times. Hire and supervise workers who help locate people with specified attributes and talents. Arrange for and/or design screen tests or auditions for prospective performers. Locate performers or extras for crowd and background scenes and stand-ins or photo doubles for actors by direct contact or through agents.

Skills—Most Important: Social Skills; Communication Skills; Management Skills. **Other High-Level Skills:** Thought-Processing Skills.

Education/Training Required: Long-term on-the-job training. **Education and Training Programs:** Cinematography and Film/Video Production; Directing and Theatrical Production; Drama and Dramatics/Theatre Arts, General; Dramatic/Theatre Arts and Stagecraft, Other; Film/Cinema/Video Studies; Radio and Television. **Knowledge/Courses:** Fine Arts; Communications and Media; Clerical Practices; Sales and Marketing; Computers and Electronics; Telecommunications.

Personality Type: Enterprising-Artistic. **Career Cluster:** 03 Arts, Audio/Video Technology, and Communications. **Career Pathways:**

03.4 Performing Arts; 03.5 Journalism and Broadcasting. **Other Jobs in These Pathways:** Actors; Artists and Related Workers, All Other; Audio and Video Equipment Technicians; Broadcast Technicians; Camera Operators, Television, Video, and Motion Picture; Copy Writers; Directors—Stage, Motion Pictures, Television, and Radio; Editors; Entertainers and Performers, Sports and Related Workers, All Other; Film and Video Editors; Managers, All Other; Media and Communication Workers, All Other; Music Composers and Arrangers; Music Directors; Musicians, Instrumental; Photographers; Poets, Lyricists and Creative Writers; Producers; Program Directors; Public Relations Specialists; Radio and Television Announcers; Reporters and Correspondents; Singers; Technical Directors/Managers; Technical Writers; others.

Job Specialization: Technical Directors/Managers

Coordinate activities of technical departments, such as taping, editing, engineering, and maintenance to produce radio or television programs. Test equipment to ensure proper operation. Monitor broadcasts to ensure that programs conform to station or network policies and regulations. Observe pictures through monitors and direct camera and video staff on shading and composition. Act as liaisons between engineering and production departments. Supervise and assign duties to workers engaged in technical control and production of radio and television programs. Schedule use of studio and editing facilities for producers and engineering and maintenance staff. Confer with operations directors to formulate and maintain fair and attainable technical policies for programs. Train workers in use of equipment such as switchers, cameras, monitors, microphones, and lights. Discuss filter options, lens choices, and the visual effects of objects being filmed with photography directors and video operators.

Skills—Most Important: Management Skills; Social Skills; Thought-Processing Skills. **Other High-Level Skills:** Communication Skills; Equipment Use/Maintenance Skills.

Education/Training Required: Long-term on-the-job training. **Education and Training Programs:** Cinematography and Film/Video Production; Directing and Theatrical Production; Drama and Dramatics/Theatre Arts, General; Dramatic/Theatre Arts and Stagecraft, Other; Film/Cinema/Video Studies; Radio and Television. **Knowledge/Courses:** Communications and Media; Telecommunications; Fine Arts; Engineering and Technology; Production and Processing; Computers and Electronics.

Personality Type: Enterprising-Realistic-Conventional. **Career Cluster:** 03 Arts, Audio/Video Technology, and Communications. **Career Pathways:** 03.1 Audio and Video Technology and Film; 03.4 Performing Arts; 03.5 Journalism and Broadcasting. **Other Jobs in These Pathways:** Actors; Audio and Video Equipment Technicians; Broadcast Technicians; Commercial and Industrial Designers; Copy Writers; Directors—Stage, Motion Pictures, Television, and Radio; Editors; Entertainers and Performers, Sports and Related Workers, All Other; Graphic Designers; Managers, All Other; Media and Communication Workers, All Other; Multimedia Artists and Animators; Music Composers and Arrangers; Music Directors; Musicians, Instrumental; Photographers; Poets, Lyricists and Creative Writers; Producers; Program Directors; Public Relations Specialists; Radio and Television Announcers; Reporters and Correspondents; Singers; Talent Directors; Technical Writers; others.

Prosthodontists

- ❋ Annual Earnings: $118,400
- ❋ Earnings Growth Potential: Very high (65.1%)
- ❋ Growth: 26.4%
- ❋ Annual Job Openings: 30
- ❋ Self-Employed: 27.9%

Skills—Most Important: Science Skills; Social Skills; Thought-Processing Skills. **Other High-Level Skills:** Management Skills; Communication Skills.

Construct oral prostheses to replace missing teeth and other oral structures to correct natural and acquired deformation of mouth and jaws; to restore and maintain oral function, such as chewing and speaking; and to improve appearance. Replace missing teeth and associated oral structures with permanent fixtures, such as crowns and bridges, or removable fixtures, such as dentures. Fit prostheses to patients, making necessary adjustments and modifications. Design and fabricate dental prostheses or supervise dental technicians and laboratory bench workers who construct the devices. Measure and take impressions of patients' jaws and teeth to determine the shape and size of dental prostheses using face bows, dental articulators, recording devices, and other materials. Collaborate with general dentists, specialists, and other health professionals to develop solutions to dental and oral health concerns. Repair, reline, and/or rebase dentures. Restore function and aesthetics to traumatic injury victims or to individuals with diseases or birth defects. Use bonding technology on the surface of the teeth to change tooth shape or to close gaps. Treat facial pain and jaw joint problems. Place veneers on teeth to conceal defects. Bleach discolored teeth.

Education/Training Required: First professional degree. **Education and Training Programs:** Prosthodontics Specialty; Prosthodontics/Prosthodontology (Cert., MS, PhD). **Knowledge/Courses:** Medicine and Dentistry; Biology; Chemistry; Psychology; Engineering and Technology; Sales and Marketing.

Personality Type: Investigative-Realistic. **Career Cluster:** 08 Health Science. **Career Pathway:** 08.1 Therapeutic Services. **Other Jobs in This Pathway:** Clinical Psychologists; Counseling Psychologists; Dental Assistants; Dental Hygienists; Dentists, All Other Specialists; Dentists, General; Home Health Aides; Licensed Practical and Licensed Vocational Nurses; Low Vision Therapists, Orientation and Mobility Specialists, and Vision Rehabilitation Therapists; Massage Therapists; Medical and Clinical Laboratory Technicians; Medical and Health Services Managers; Medical Scientists, Except Epidemiologists; Medical Secretaries; Occupational Therapists; Pharmacists; Oral and Maxillofacial Surgeons; Orthodontists; Pharmacy Technicians; Radiologic Technologists; School Psychologists; Social and Human Service Assistants; Speech-Language Pathologists; Speech-Language Pathology Assistants; Substance Abuse and Behavioral Disorder Counselors; others.

Public Relations and Fundraising Managers

- ❋ Annual Earnings: $91,810
- ❋ Earnings Growth Potential: High (45.8%)
- ❋ Growth: 12.9%
- ❋ Annual Job Openings: 2,060
- ❋ Self-Employed: 0.0%

Skills—Most Important: Management Skills; Social Skills; Communication Skills. **Other High-Level Skills:** Thought-Processing Skills; Mathematics Skills.

Plan and direct public relations programs designed to create and maintain a favorable public image for employer or client or, if engaged in fundraising, plan and direct activities to solicit and maintain funds for special projects and nonprofit organizations. Establish and maintain effective working relationships with clients, government officials, and media representatives and use these relationships to develop new business opportunities. Write interesting and effective press releases, prepare information for media kits, and develop and maintain company Internet or intranet Web pages. Identify main client groups and audiences, determine the best way to communicate publicity information to them, and develop and implement a communication plan. Assign, supervise, and review the activities of public relations staff. Develop and maintain the company's corporate image and identity, which includes the use of logos and signage. Respond to requests for information about employers' activities or status. Direct activities of external agencies, establishments, and departments that develop and implement communication strategies and information programs. Manage communications budgets.

Education/Training Required: Work experience plus degree. **Education and Training Program:** Public Relations/Image Management. **Knowledge/Courses:** Sales and Marketing; Communications and Media; Customer and Personal Service; Personnel and Human Resources; English Language; Administration and Management.

Personality Type: Enterprising-Artistic. **Career Cluster:** 04 Business, Management, and Administration. **Career Pathway:** 04.1 Management. **Other Jobs in This Pathway:** Brownfield Redevelopment Specialists and Site Managers; Business Continuity Planners; Business Operations Specialists, All Other; Chief Executives; Chief Sustainability Officers; Compliance Managers; Computer and Information Systems Managers; Construction Managers; Customs Brokers; Energy Auditors; First-Line Supervisors of Office and Administrative Support Workers; General and Operations Managers; Investment Fund Managers; Loss Prevention Managers; Management Analysts; Managers, All Other; Public Relations Specialists; Regulatory Affairs Managers; Sales Managers; Security Management Specialists; Security Managers; Supply Chain Managers; Sustainability Specialists; Wind Energy Operations Managers; Wind Energy Project Managers; others.

Public Relations Specialists

* Annual Earnings: $52,090
* Earnings Growth Potential: High (41.3%)
* Growth: 24.0%
* Annual Job Openings: 13,130
* Self-Employed: 4.5%

Skills—Most Important: Social Skills; Communication Skills; Thought-Processing Skills. **Other High-Level Skills:** Management Skills.

Engage in promoting or creating goodwill for individuals, groups, or organizations by writing or selecting favorable publicity material and releasing it through various communications media. May prepare and arrange displays and make speeches. Respond to requests for information from the media or designate another appropriate spokesperson or information source. Study the objectives, promotional policies, and needs of organizations to develop public relations strategies that will influence public opinion or promote ideas, products, and services. Plan and direct development and communication of informational programs to maintain favorable public and stockholder perceptions of an organization's accomplishments and agenda. Establish and maintain cooperative relationships with representatives of community, consumer, employee, and public interest groups. Prepare or edit organizational publications for internal and external audiences, including employee newsletters and stockholders' reports. Coach client representatives in effective communication with the public and with employees. Confer with production and support personnel to produce or coordinate production of advertisements and promotions.

Education/Training Required: Bachelor's degree. **Education and Training Programs:** Family and Consumer Sciences/Human Sciences Communication; Health Communication; Political Communication; Public Relations/Image Management; Speech Communication and Rhetoric. **Knowledge/Courses:** Communications and Media; Sales and Marketing; English Language; Geography; Computers and Electronics; Customer and Personal Service.

Personality Type: Enterprising-Artistic-Social. **Career Clusters:** 03 Arts, Audio/Video Technology, and Communications; 04 Business, Management, and Administration; 08 Health Science; 10 Human Services. **Career Pathways:** 03.5 Journalism and Broadcasting; 04.1 Management; 10.5 Consumer Services Career; 08.3 Health Informatics. **Other Jobs in These Pathways:** Brownfield Redevelopment Specialists and Site Managers; Business Continuity Planners; Business Operations Specialists, All Other; Compliance Managers; Construction Managers; Customs Brokers; Energy Auditors; Executive Secretaries and Executive Administrative Assistants; First-Line Supervisors of Office and Administrative Support Workers; First-Line Supervisors of Retail Sales Workers; General and Operations Managers; Investment Fund Managers; Loss Prevention Managers; Management Analysts; Managers, All Other; Medical Assistants; Medical Secretaries; Receptionists and Information Clerks; Regulatory Affairs Managers; Security Management Specialists; Security Managers; Supply Chain Managers; Sustainability Specialists; Wind Energy Operations Managers; Wind Energy Project Managers; others.

Purchasing Agents, Except Wholesale, Retail, and Farm Products

* Annual Earnings: $56,580
* Earnings Growth Potential: Medium (38.0%)
* Growth: 13.9%
* Annual Job Openings: 11,860
* Self-Employed: 1.4%

Skills—Most Important: Management Skills; Thought-Processing Skills; Mathematics Skills. **Other High-Level Skills:** Communication Skills; Social Skills.

Purchase machinery, equipment, tools, parts, supplies, or services necessary for the operation of an establishment. Purchase raw or semi-finished materials for manufacturing. Purchase the highest quality merchandise at the lowest possible price and in correct amounts. Prepare purchase orders, solicit bid proposals, and review requisitions for goods and services. Research and evaluate suppliers based on price, quality, selection, service, support, availability, reliability, production and distribution capabilities, and the supplier's reputation and history. Analyze price proposals, financial reports, and other data and information to determine reasonable prices. Monitor and follow applicable laws and regulations. Negotiate, renegotiate, and administer contracts with suppliers, vendors, and other representatives. Monitor shipments to ensure that goods come in on time and resolve problems related to undelivered goods. Confer with staff, users, and vendors to discuss defective or unacceptable goods or services and determine corrective action. Evaluate and monitor contract performance to ensure compliance with contractual obligations and to determine need for changes. Maintain and review computerized or manual records of items purchased, costs, deliveries, product performance, and inventories. Review catalogs, industry periodicals, directories, trade journals, and Internet sites and consult with other department personnel to locate necessary goods and services. Study sales records and inventory levels of stock to develop strategic purchasing programs that facilitate employee access to supplies.

Education/Training Required: Long-term on-the-job training. **Education and Training Programs:** Insurance; Merchandising and Buying Operations; Sales, Distribution, and Marketing Operations, General. **Knowledge/Courses:** Economics and Accounting; Transportation; Law and Government; Production and Processing; Clerical Practices; Administration and Management.

Personality Type: Conventional-Enterprising. **Career Cluster:** 14 Marketing, Sales, and Service. **Career Pathway:** 14.3 Buying and Merchandising. **Other Jobs in This Pathway:** Retail Salespersons; Sales Representatives, Wholesale and Manufacturing, Except Technical and Scientific Products; Telemarketers; Wholesale and Retail Buyers, Except Farm Products.

Radiation Therapists

* Annual Earnings: $74,980
* Earnings Growth Potential: Low (32.0%)
* Growth: 27.1%
* Annual Job Openings: 690
* Self-Employed: 0.0%

Skills—Most Important: Science Skills; Equipment Use/Maintenance Skills; Mathematics Skills. **Other High-Level Skills:** Social Skills; Thought-Processing Skills; Communication Skills; Management Skills.

Provide radiation therapy to patients as prescribed by radiologists according to established practices and standards. Duties may include reviewing prescriptions and diagnoses; acting as liaisons with physicians and supportive care personnel; preparing equipment such as immobilization, treatment, and protection devices; and maintaining records, reports, and files. May assist in dosimetry procedures and tumor localization. Administer prescribed doses of radiation to specific body parts using radiation therapy equipment according to established practices and standards. Position patients for treatment with accuracy according to prescription. Enter data into computer and set controls to operate and adjust equipment and regulate dosage. Follow principles of radiation protection for patient, self, and others. Maintain records, reports, and files, including such information as radiation dosages, equipment settings, and patients' reactions. Review prescription, diagnosis, patient chart, and identification. Conduct most treatment sessions independently in accordance with the long-term treatment plan and under the general direction of the patient's physician. Check radiation therapy equipment to ensure proper operation. Observe and reassure patients during treatment and report unusual reactions to physician or turn equipment off if unexpected adverse reactions occur. Check for side effects such as skin irritation, nausea, and hair loss to assess patients' reaction to treatment. Educate, prepare, and reassure patients and their families by answering questions, providing physical assistance, and reinforcing physicians' advice on treatment reactions and post-treatment care. Calculate treatment dosages delivered during each session.

R

Prepare and construct equipment, such as immobilization, treatment, and protection devices. Photograph treated area of patient and process film.

Education/Training Required: Associate degree. **Education and Training Program:** Medical Radiologic Technology/Science—Radiation Therapist. **Knowledge/Courses:** Medicine and Dentistry; Biology; Physics; Psychology; Philosophy and Theology; Therapy and Counseling.

Personality Type: Social-Realistic-Conventional. **Career Cluster:** 08 Health Science. **Career Pathway:** 08.2 Diagnostics Services. **Other Jobs in This Pathway:** Ambulance Drivers and Attendants, Except Emergency Medical Technicians; Anesthesiologist Assistants; Cardiovascular Technologists and Technicians; Cytogenetic Technologists; Cytotechnologists; Diagnostic Medical Sonographers; Emergency Medical Technicians and Paramedics; Endoscopy Technicians; Health Diagnosing and Treating Practitioners, All Other; Health Technologists and Technicians, All Other; Healthcare Practitioners and Technical Workers, All Other; Histotechnologists and Histologic Technicians; Medical and Clinical Laboratory Technicians; Medical and Clinical Laboratory Technologists; Medical and Health Services Managers; Medical Assistants; Medical Equipment Preparers; Neurodiagnostic Technologists; Ophthalmic Laboratory Technicians; Physical Scientists, All Other; Physician Assistants; Radiologic Technicians; Radiologic Technologists; Surgical Technologists; Veterinary Assistants and Laboratory Animal Caretakers; others.

Radiologic Technologists

❋ Annual Earnings: $54,340

❋ Earnings Growth Potential: Low (32.8%)

❋ Growth: 17.2%

❋ Annual Job Openings: 6,800

❋ Self-Employed: 0.8%

Skills—Most Important: Science Skills; Social Skills; Equipment Use/Maintenance Skills. **Other High-Level Skills:** Mathematics Skills; Thought-Processing Skills.

Take X-rays and CAT scans or administer nonradioactive materials into patient's bloodstream for diagnostic purposes. Includes technologists who specialize in other modalities, such as computed tomography and magnetic resonance. Includes workers whose primary duties are to demonstrate portions of the human body on X-ray film or fluoroscopic screen. Review and evaluate developed X-rays, videotape, or computer-generated information to determine if images are satisfactory for diagnostic purposes. Use radiation safety measures and protection devices to comply with government regulations and to ensure safety of patients and staff. Explain procedures and observe patients to ensure safety and comfort during scan. Operate or oversee operation of radiologic and magnetic imaging equipment to produce images of the body for diagnostic purposes. Position and immobilize patient on examining table. Position imaging equipment and adjust controls to set exposure time and distance according to specification of examination. Key commands and data into computer to document and specify scan sequences, adjust transmitters and receivers, or photograph certain images. Monitor video display of area being scanned and adjust density or contrast to improve picture quality. Monitor patients' conditions and reactions, reporting abnormal signs to physician. Set up examination rooms, ensuring that necessary equipment is ready. Prepare and administer oral or injected contrast media to patients. Take thorough and accurate patient medical histories. Remove and process film. Record, process, and maintain patient data and treatment records and prepare reports. Coordinate work with clerical personnel or other technologists. Demonstrate new equipment, procedures, and techniques to staff.

Education/Training Required: Associate degree. **Education and Training Programs:** Allied Health Diagnostic, Intervention, and Treatment Professions, Other; Medical Radiologic Technology/Science—Radiation Therapist; Radiologic Technology/Science—Radiographer. **Knowledge/Courses:** Medicine and Dentistry; Physics; Customer and Personal Service; Biology; Psychology; Chemistry.

Personality Type: Realistic-Social. **Career Cluster:** 08 Health Science. **Career Pathways:** 08.2 Diagnostics Services; 08.1 Therapeutic Services. **Other Jobs in These Pathways:** Clinical Psychologists; Counseling Psychologists; Cytogenetic Technologists; Cytotechnologists; Dental Assistants; Dental Hygienists; Dentists, General; Emergency Medical Technicians and Paramedics; Endoscopy Technicians; Healthcare Support Workers, All Other; Histotechnologists and Histologic Technicians; Home Health Aides; Licensed Practical and Licensed Vocational Nurses; Massage Therapists; Medical and Clinical Laboratory Technicians; Medical and Clinical Laboratory Technologists; Medical and Health Services Managers; Medical Assistants; Medical Secretaries; Pharmacists; Pharmacy Technicians; School Psychologists; Social and Human Service Assistants; Speech-Language Pathologists; Speech-Language Pathology Assistants; others.

Rail Car Repairers

* Annual Earnings: $47,410
* Earnings Growth Potential: Medium (40.1%)
* Growth: 6.5%
* Annual Job Openings: 590
* Self-Employed: 5.6%

Skills—Most Important: Installation Skills; Equipment Use/Maintenance Skills.

Diagnose, adjust, repair, or overhaul railroad rolling stock, mine cars, or mass-transit rail cars. Repair or replace defective or worn parts such as bearings, pistons, and gears using hand tools, torque wrenches, power tools, and welding equipment. Test units for operability before and after repairs. Record conditions of cars and repair and maintenance work performed or to be performed. Remove locomotives, car mechanical units, or other components using pneumatic hoists and jacks, pinch bars, hand tools, and cutting torches. Inspect components such as bearings, seals, gaskets, wheels, and coupler assemblies to determine if repairs are needed. Inspect the interior and exterior of rail cars to identify defects and to determine the extent of wear and damage. Adjust repaired or replaced units to ensure proper operation. Perform scheduled maintenance and clean units and components. Repair, fabricate, and install steel or wood fittings using blueprints, shop sketches, and instruction manuals. Repair and maintain electrical and electronic controls for propulsion and braking systems. Disassemble units such as water pumps, control valves, and compressors so that repairs can be made. Measure diameters of axle wheel seats, using micrometers, and mark dimensions on axles so that wheels can be bored to specified dimensions. Align car sides for installation of car ends and crossties using width gauges, turnbuckles, and wrenches. Replace defective wiring and insulation and tighten electrical connections.

Education/Training Required: Long-term on-the-job training. **Education and Training Program:** Heavy Equipment Maintenance Technology/Technician. **Knowledge/Courses:** Mechanical Devices; Public Safety and Security; Production and Processing.

Personality Type: Realistic-Conventional-Investigative. **Career Cluster:** 13 Manufacturing. **Career Pathway:** 13.3 Maintenance, Installation, and Repair. **Other Jobs in This Pathway:** Aircraft Mechanics and Service Technicians; Automotive Specialty Technicians; Biological Technicians; Civil Engineering Technicians; Computer, Automated Teller, and Office Machine Repairers; Electrical and Electronic Equipment Assemblers; Electrical and Electronics Repairers, Commercial and Industrial Equipment; Electrical Engineering Technicians; Electrical Engineering Technologists; Electromechanical Engineering Technologists; Electronics Engineering Technicians; Electronics Engineering Technologists; Engineering Technicians, Except Drafters, All Other; Fuel Cell Technicians; Helpers—Installation, Maintenance, and Repair Workers; Industrial Engineering Technologists; Industrial Machinery Mechanics; Installation, Maintenance, and Repair Workers, All Other; Manufacturing Engineering Technologists; Manufacturing Production Technicians; Mapping Technicians; Mechanical Engineering Technologists; Mobile Heavy Equipment Mechanics, Except Engines; Telecommunications Line Installers and Repairers; Tire Repairers and Changers; others.

Real Estate Sales Agents

- ❋ Annual Earnings: $40,030
- ❋ Earnings Growth Potential: High (48.9%)
- ❋ Growth: 16.2%
- ❋ Annual Job Openings: 12,830
- ❋ Self-Employed: 58.3%

Skills—Most Important: Social Skills; Mathematics Skills; Communication Skills. **Other High-Level Skills:** Thought-Processing Skills.

Rent, buy, or sell property for clients. Perform duties such as studying property listings, interviewing prospective clients, accompanying clients to property site, discussing conditions of sale, and drawing up real estate contracts. Includes agents who represent buyer. Present purchase offers to sellers for consideration. Act as an intermediary in negotiations between buyers and sellers, generally representing one or the other. Compare a property with similar properties that have recently sold to determine its competitive market price. Advise clients on market conditions, prices, mortgages, legal requirements, and related matters. Promote sales of properties through advertisements, open houses, and participation in multiple listing services. Accompany buyers during visits to and inspections of property, advising them on the suitability and value of the homes they are visiting. Confer with escrow companies, lenders, home inspectors, and pest control operators to ensure that terms and conditions of purchase agreements are met before closing dates. Prepare documents such as representation contracts, purchase agreements, closing statements, deeds, and leases. Interview clients to determine what kinds of properties they are seeking. Coordinate property closings, overseeing signing of documents and disbursement of funds. Generate lists of properties that are compatible with buyers' needs and financial resources. Contact property owners and advertise services to solicit property sales listings. Arrange for title searches to determine whether clients have clear property titles. Display commercial, industrial, agricultural, and residential properties to clients and explain their features.

Education/Training Required: Postsecondary vocational training. **Education and Training Program:** Real Estate. **Knowledge/Courses:** Sales and Marketing; Customer and Personal Service; Law and Government; Building and Construction; Economics and Accounting; Computers and Electronics.

Personality Type: Enterprising-Conventional. **Career Cluster:** 14 Marketing, Sales, and Service. **Career Pathway:** 14.2 Professional Sales and Marketing. **Other Jobs in This Pathway:** Cashiers; Counter and Rental Clerks; Door-To-Door Sales Workers, News and Street Vendors, and Related Workers; Driver/Sales Workers; Energy Brokers; First-Line Supervisors of Non-Retail Sales Workers; First-Line Supervisors of Retail Sales Workers; Hotel, Motel, and Resort Desk Clerks; Marketing Managers; Marking Clerks; Online Merchants; Order Fillers, Wholesale and Retail Sales; Parts Salespersons; Property, Real Estate, and Community Association Managers; Reservation and Transportation Ticket Agents and Travel Clerks; Retail Salespersons; Sales and Related Workers, All Other; Sales Representatives, Services, All Other; Sales Representatives, Wholesale and

Manufacturing, Except Technical and Scientific Products; Sales Representatives, Wholesale and Manufacturing, Technical and Scientific Products; Solar Sales Representatives and Assessors; Stock Clerks—Stockroom, Warehouse, or Storage Yard; Stock Clerks, Sales Floor; Telemarketers; Wholesale and Retail Buyers, Except Farm Products; others.

Refuse and Recyclable Material Collectors

* Annual Earnings: $32,640
* Earnings Growth Potential: High (42.6%)
* Growth: 18.6%
* Annual Job Openings: 7,110
* Self-Employed: 11.8%

Skills—Most Important: Equipment Use/Maintenance Skills.

Collect and dump refuse or recyclable materials from containers into truck. May drive truck. Inspect trucks prior to beginning routes to ensure safe operating condition. Refuel trucks and add other fluids, such as oil. Drive to disposal sites to empty trucks that have been filled. Fill out reports for defective equipment. Drive trucks along established routes through residential streets and alleys or through business and industrial areas. Operate equipment that compresses the collected refuse. Operate automated or semi-automated hoisting devices that raise refuse bins and dump contents into openings in truck bodies. Dismount garbage trucks to collect garbage and remount trucks to ride to the next collection point. Communicate with dispatchers on delays, unsafe sites, accidents, equipment breakdowns, and other maintenance problems. Keep informed of road

R

and weather conditions to determine how routes will be affected. Tag garbage or recycling containers to inform customers of problems such as excess garbage or inclusion of items that are not permitted. Clean trucks and compactor bodies after routes have been completed. Sort items set out for recycling and throw materials into designated truck compartments. Organize schedules for refuse collection. Provide quotes for refuse collection contracts.

Education/Training Required: Short-term on-the-job training. **Education and Training Programs:** No related CIP programs; this job is learned through informal short-term on-the-job training. **Knowledge/Courses:** Transportation; Customer and Personal Service.

Personality Type: Realistic-Conventional. **Career Cluster:** 01 Agriculture, Food, and Natural Resources. **Career Pathway:** 01.5 Natural Resources Systems. **Other Jobs in This Pathway:** Climate Change Analysts; Conveyor Operators and Tenders; Derrick Operators, Oil and Gas; Engineering Technicians, Except Drafters, All Other; Environmental Economists; Environmental Restoration Planners; Environmental Science and Protection Technicians, Including Health; Environmental Scientists and Specialists, Including Health; Fishers and Related Fishing Workers; Forest and Conservation Technicians; Geological Sample Test Technicians; Geophysical Data Technicians; Helpers—Extraction Workers; Industrial Ecologists; Industrial Truck and Tractor Operators; Logging Equipment Operators; Mechanical Engineering Technicians; Park Naturalists; Range Managers; Recreation Workers; Rotary Drill Operators, Oil and Gas; Service Unit Operators, Oil, Gas, and Mining; Soil and Water Conservationists; Wellhead Pumpers; Zoologists and Wildlife Biologists; others.

Registered Nurses

- ❋ Annual Earnings: $64,690
- ❋ Earnings Growth Potential: Low (31.7%)
- ❋ Growth: 22.2%
- ❋ Annual Job Openings: 103,900
- ❋ Self-Employed: 0.6%

Skills—Most Important: Science Skills; Social Skills; Thought-Processing Skills. **Other High-Level Skills:** Communication Skills; Mathematics Skills; Management Skills; Equipment Use/Maintenance Skills.

Assess patient health problems and needs, develop and implement nursing care plans, and maintain medical records. Administer nursing care to ill, injured, convalescent, or disabled patients. May advise patients on health maintenance and disease prevention or provide case management. Licensing or registration required. Includes advance practice nurses such as nurse practitioners, clinical nurse specialists, certified nurse midwives, and certified registered nurse anesthetists. Advanced practice nursing is practiced by RNs who have specialized formal, post-basic education and who function in highly autonomous and specialized roles. Maintain accurate, detailed reports and records. Monitor, record, and report symptoms and changes in patients' conditions. Record patients' medical information and vital signs. Modify patient treatment plans as indicated by patients' responses and conditions. Consult and coordinate with health-care team members to assess, plan, implement, and evaluate patient care plans. Order, interpret, and evaluate diagnostic tests to identify and assess patients' conditions. Monitor all aspects of patient care, including diet and physical activity. Direct and supervise less-skilled nursing or health-care personnel or supervise a particular unit. Prepare patients for and assist with examinations and treatments. Observe nurses and visit patients to ensure proper nursing care. Assess the needs of individuals, families, or communities, including assessment of individuals' home or work environments to identify potential health or safety problems. Instruct individuals, families, and other groups on topics such as health education, disease prevention, and childbirth and develop health improvement programs. Prepare rooms, sterile instruments, equipment, and supplies and ensure that stock of supplies is maintained. Inform physician of patients' conditions during anesthesia. Administer local, inhalation, intravenous, and other anesthetics. Provide health care, first aid, immunizations, and assistance in convalescence and rehabilitation in locations such as schools, hospitals, and industry.

Education/Training Required: Associate degree. **Education and Training Programs:** Adult Health Nurse/Nursing; Clinical Nurse Specialist Training; Critical Care Nursing; Family Practice Nurse/Nursing; Maternal/Child Health and Neonatal Nurse/Nursing; Nurse Anesthetist Training; Nurse Midwife/Nursing Midwifery; Nursing Science; Occupational and Environmental Health Nursing; Pediatric Nurse/Nursing; Perioperative/Operating Room and Surgical Nurse/Nursing; Psychiatric/Mental Health Nurse/Nursing; Public Health/Community Nurse/Nursing; Registered Nursing/Registered Nurse Training. **Knowledge/Courses:** Psychology; Medicine and Dentistry; Therapy and Counseling; Biology; Philosophy and Theology; Sociology and Anthropology.

Personality Type: Social-Investigative-Conventional. **Career Cluster:** 08 Health Science. **Career Pathway:** 08.1 Therapeutic Services. **Other Jobs in This Pathway:** Clinical Psychologists; Community and Social Service Specialists, All Other; Counseling Psychologists; Dental Assistants; Dental Hygienists; Dentists, General; Health Technologists and Technicians, All Other; Healthcare Support Workers, All Other; Home Health Aides; Licensed Practical and Licensed Vocational Nurses; Low Vision Therapists, Orientation and Mobility Specialists, and Vision Rehabilitation Therapists; Massage Therapists; Medical and Clinical Laboratory Technicians; Medical and Health Services Managers; Medical Scientists, Except Epidemiologists; Medical Secretaries; Occupational Therapists; Pharmacists; Pharmacy Technicians; Radiologic Technologists; School Psychologists; Social and Human Service Assistants; Speech-Language Pathologists; Speech-Language Pathology Assistants; Substance Abuse and Behavioral Disorder Counselors; others.

Job Specialization: Acute Care Nurses

Provide advanced nursing care for patients with acute conditions such as heart attacks, respiratory distress syndrome, or shock. May care for pre- and post-operative patients or perform advanced, invasive diagnostic or therapeutic procedures. Analyze the indications, contraindications, risk complications, and cost-benefit tradeoffs of therapeutic interventions. Diagnose acute or chronic conditions that could result in rapid physiological deterioration or life-threatening instability. Distinguish between normal and abnormal developmental and age-related physiological and behavioral changes in

R

acute, critical, and chronic illness. Manage patients' pain relief and sedation by providing pharmacologic and non-pharmacologic interventions, monitoring patients' responses, and changing care plans accordingly. Interpret information obtained from electrocardiograms or radiographs. Perform emergency medical procedures, such as basic cardiac life support, advanced cardiac life support, and other condition-stabilizing interventions. Assess urgent and emergent health conditions using both physiologically and technologically derived data. Adjust settings on patients' assistive devices such as temporary pacemakers. Assess the impact of illnesses or injuries on patients' health, function, growth, development, nutrition, sleep, rest, quality of life, or family, social, and educational relationships. Collaborate with members of multidisciplinary health-care teams to plan, manage, or assess patient treatments. Discuss illnesses and treatments with patients and family members.

Education/Training Required: Associate degree. **Education and Training Program:** Critical Care Nursing. **Knowledge/Courses:** Therapy and Counseling; Medicine and Dentistry; Psychology; Biology; Sociology and Anthropology; Philosophy and Theology.

Personality Type: Social-Investigative-Realistic. **Career Cluster:** 08 Health Science. **Career Pathway:** 08.1 Therapeutic Services. **Other Jobs in This Pathway:** Clinical Psychologists; Community and Social Service Specialists, All Other; Counseling Psychologists; Dental Assistants; Dental Hygienists; Dentists, General; Health Technologists and Technicians, All Other; Healthcare Support Workers, All Other; Home Health Aides; Licensed Practical and Licensed Vocational Nurses; Low Vision Therapists, Orientation and Mobility Specialists, and Vision Rehabilitation Therapists; Massage Therapists; Medical and Clinical Laboratory Technicians; Medical and Health Services Managers; Medical Scientists, Except Epidemiologists; Medical Secretaries; Occupational Therapists; Pharmacists; Pharmacy Technicians; Radiologic Technologists; School Psychologists; Social and Human Service Assistants; Speech-Language Pathologists; Speech-Language Pathology Assistants; Substance Abuse and Behavioral Disorder Counselors; others.

Job Specialization: Advanced Practice Psychiatric Nurses

Provide advanced nursing care for patients with psychiatric disorders. May provide psychotherapy under the direction of a psychiatrist. Teach classes in mental health topics such as stress reduction. Participate in activities aimed at professional growth and development including conferences or continuing education activities. Direct or provide home health services. Monitor the use and status of medical and pharmaceutical supplies. Develop practice protocols for mental health problems based on review and evaluation of published research. Develop, implement, or evaluate programs such as outreach activities, community mental health programs, and crisis situation response activities. Treat patients for routine physical health problems. Write prescriptions for psychotropic medications as allowed by state regulations and collaborative practice agreements. Refer patients requiring more specialized or complex treatment to psychiatrists, primary care physicians, or other medical specialists. Provide routine physical health screenings to detect or monitor problems such as heart disease and diabetes. Participate in treatment team conferences on diagnosis or treatment of difficult cases. Interpret diagnostic or laboratory tests such as electrocardiograms and renal-functioning tests. Evaluate patients' behavior to formulate diagnoses or assess treatments. Develop and implement treatment plans. Monitor patients' medication usage and results. Educate patients and family members about mental health and medical conditions, preventive health measures, medications, or treatment plans.

Education/Training Required: Master's degree. **Education and Training Program:** Psychiatric/ Mental Health Nurse Training/Nursing. **Knowledge/Courses:** Therapy and Counseling; Psychology; Medicine and Dentistry; Sociology and Anthropology; Philosophy and Theology; Biology.

Personality Type: Social-Investigative. **Career Cluster:** 08 Health Science. **Career Pathway:** 08.1 Therapeutic Services. **Other Jobs in This Pathway:** Clinical Psychologists; Community and Social Service Specialists, All Other; Counseling Psychologists; Dental Assistants; Dental Hygienists; Dentists, General; Health Technologists and Technicians, All Other; Healthcare Support Workers, All Other; Home Health Aides; Licensed Practical and Licensed Vocational Nurses; Low Vision Therapists, Orientation and Mobility Specialists, and Vision Rehabilitation Therapists; Massage Therapists; Medical and Clinical Laboratory Technicians; Medical and Health Services Managers; Medical Scientists, Except Epidemiologists; Medical Secretaries; Occupational Therapists; Pharmacists; Pharmacy Technicians; Radiologic Technologists; School Psychologists; Social and Human Service Assistants; Speech-Language Pathologists; Speech-Language Pathology Assistants; Substance Abuse and Behavioral Disorder Counselors; others.

Job Specialization: Clinical Nurse Specialists

Plan, direct, or coordinate daily patient care activities in a clinical practice. Ensure adherence to established clinical policies, protocols, regulations, and standards. Coordinate or conduct educational programs or in-service training sessions on topics such as clinical procedures. Observe, interview, and assess patients to identify care needs. Evaluate the quality and effectiveness of nursing practice or organizational systems. Provide direct care by performing comprehensive health assessments, developing differential diagnoses, conducting specialized tests, or prescribing medications or treatments. Provide specialized direct and indirect care to inpatients and outpatients in a designated specialty such as obstetrics, neurology, oncology, or neonatal care. Maintain departmental policies, procedures, objectives, or infection-control standards. Collaborate with other health-care professionals and service providers to ensure optimal patient care. Develop nursing service philosophies, goals, policies, priorities, or procedures. Develop, implement, or evaluate standards of nursing practice in specialty area such as pediatrics, acute care, and geriatrics. Develop or assist others in development of care and treatment plans. Make clinical recommendations to physicians, other health-care providers, insurance companies, patients, or health-care organizations. Plan, evaluate, or modify treatment programs based on information gathered by observing and interviewing patients or by analyzing patient records. Present clients with information required to make informed health-care and treatment decisions.

Education/Training Required: Master's degree. **Education and Training Program:** Clinical Nurse Specialist Training. **Knowledge/Courses:** Medicine and Dentistry; Biology; Therapy and Counseling; Psychology; Sociology and Anthropology; Philosophy and Theology.

Personality Type: Enterprising-Social-Conventional. **Career Cluster:** 08 Health Science. **Career Pathways:** 08.3 Health Informatics; 08.1 Therapeutic Services. **Other Jobs in These Pathways:** Clinical Psychologists; Counseling Psychologists; Dental Assistants; Dental Hygienists; Editors; Engineers, All Other; Executive Secretaries and Executive Administrative Assistants; First-Line Supervisors of Office and Administrative Support Workers; Healthcare Support Workers, All Other; Home Health Aides; Licensed Practical and Licensed Vocational Nurses; Medical and Clinical Laboratory Technicians; Medical and Health Services Managers; Medical Assistants; Medical Records and Health Information Technicians; Medical Secretaries; Pharmacists; Pharmacy Technicians; Physical Therapists; Public Relations Specialists; Radiologic Technologists; Receptionists and Information Clerks; School Psychologists; Social and Human Service Assistants; Speech-Language Pathology Assistants; others.

Job Specialization: Critical Care Nurses

Provide advanced nursing care for patients in critical or coronary care units. Identify patients' age-specific needs and alter care plans as necessary to meet those needs. Provide post-mortem care. Evaluate patients' vital signs and laboratory data to determine emergency intervention needs. Perform approved therapeutic or diagnostic procedures based on patients' clinical status. Administer blood and blood products, monitoring patients for signs and symptoms related to transfusion reactions. Administer medications intravenously, by injection, orally, through gastric tubes, or by other methods. Advocate for patients' and families' needs or provide emotional support for patients and their families. Set up and monitor medical equipment and devices such as cardiac monitors, mechanical ventilators and alarms, oxygen delivery devices, transducers, and pressure lines. Monitor patients' fluid intake and output to detect emerging problems such as fluid and electrolyte imbalances. Monitor patients for changes in status and indications of conditions such as sepsis or shock and institute appropriate interventions. Assess patients' pain levels and sedation requirements. Assess patients' psychosocial status and needs including areas such as sleep patterns, anxiety, grief, anger, and support systems. Collaborate with other health-care professionals to develop and revise treatment plans based on identified needs and assessment data. Collect specimens for laboratory tests. Compile and analyze data obtained from monitoring or diagnostic tests.

Education/Training Required: Associate degree. **Education and Training Program:** Critical Care Nursing. **Knowledge/Courses:** Medicine and Dentistry; Biology; Psychology; Therapy and Counseling; Sociology and Anthropology; Philosophy and Theology.

Personality Type: Social-Investigative-Realistic. **Career Cluster:** 08 Health Science. **Career Pathway:** 08.1 Therapeutic Services. **Other Jobs in This Pathway:** Clinical Psychologists; Community and Social Service Specialists, All Other; Counseling Psychologists; Dental Assistants; Dental Hygienists; Dentists, General; Health Technologists and Technicians, All Other; Healthcare Support Workers, All Other; Home Health Aides; Licensed Practical and Licensed Vocational Nurses; Low Vision Therapists, Orientation and

Mobility Specialists, and Vision Rehabilitation Therapists; Massage Therapists; Medical and Clinical Laboratory Technicians; Medical and Health Services Managers; Medical Scientists, Except Epidemiologists; Medical Secretaries; Occupational Therapists; Pharmacists; Pharmacy Technicians; Radiologic Technologists; School Psychologists; Social and Human Service Assistants; Speech-Language Pathologists; Speech-Language Pathology Assistants; Substance Abuse and Behavioral Disorder Counselors; others.

Respiratory Therapists

* Annual Earnings: $54,280
* Earnings Growth Potential: Low (26.3%)
* Growth: 20.9%
* Annual Job Openings: 4,140
* Self-Employed: 0.0%

Skills—Most Important: Science Skills; Equipment Use/Maintenance Skills; Social Skills. **Other High-Level Skills:** Communication Skills; Thought-Processing Skills; Mathematics Skills; Management Skills.

Assess, treat, and care for patients with breathing disorders. Assume primary responsibility for all respiratory care modalities, including the supervision of respiratory therapy technicians. Initiate and conduct therapeutic procedures; maintain patient records; and select, assemble, check, and operate equipment. Provide emergency care, including artificial respiration, external cardiac massage and assistance with cardiopulmonary resuscitation. Monitor patient's physiological responses to therapy, such as vital signs, arterial blood gases, and blood chemistry changes and consult with physician if adverse reactions occur. Read prescription, measure arterial blood gases, and review patient information to assess patient condition. Set up and operate devices such as mechanical ventilators, therapeutic gas administration apparatus, environmental control systems, and aerosol generators following specified parameters of treatment. Enforce safety rules and ensure careful adherence to physicians' orders. Explain treatment procedures to patients to gain cooperation and allay fears. Maintain charts that contain patients' pertinent identification and therapy information. Relay blood analysis results to a physician. Work as part of a team of physicians, nurses, and other health-care professionals to manage patient care by assisting with medical procedures and related duties. Inspect, clean, test, and maintain respiratory therapy equipment to ensure equipment is functioning safely and efficiently, ordering repairs when necessary. Make emergency visits to resolve equipment problems. Educate patients and their families about their conditions and teach appropriate disease management techniques, such as breathing exercises and the use of medications and respiratory equipment.

Education/Training Required: Associate degree. **Education and Training Program:** Respiratory Care Therapy/Therapist. **Knowledge/Courses:** Medicine and Dentistry; Biology; Customer and Personal Service; Therapy and Counseling; Psychology; Chemistry.

Personality Type: Social-Investigative-Realistic. **Career Cluster:** 08 Health Science. **Career Pathway:** 08.1 Therapeutic Services. **Other Jobs in This Pathway:** Clinical Psychologists; Community and Social Service Specialists, All Other; Counseling Psychologists; Dental

R

Assistants; Dental Hygienists; Dentists, General; Health Technologists and Technicians, All Other; Healthcare Support Workers, All Other; Home Health Aides; Licensed Practical and Licensed Vocational Nurses; Low Vision Therapists, Orientation and Mobility Specialists, and Vision Rehabilitation Therapists; Massage Therapists; Medical and Clinical Laboratory Technicians; Medical and Health Services Managers; Medical Scientists, Except Epidemiologists; Medical Secretaries; Occupational Therapists; Pharmacists; Pharmacy Technicians; Radiologic Technologists; School Psychologists; Social and Human Service Assistants; Speech-Language Pathologists; Speech-Language Pathology Assistants; Substance Abuse and Behavioral Disorder Counselors; others.

Sales Engineers

* Annual Earnings: $87,390
* Earnings Growth Potential: Medium (40.6%)
* Growth: 8.8%
* Annual Job Openings: 3,500
* Self-Employed: 0.0%

Skills—Most Important: Social Skills; Mathematics Skills; Technology/Programming Skills. **Other High-Level Skills:** Thought-Processing Skills; Communication Skills; Management Skills; Equipment Use/Maintenance Skills.

Sell business goods or services, the selling of which requires a technical background equivalent to a baccalaureate degree in engineering. Plan and modify product configurations to meet customer needs. Collaborate with sales teams to understand customer requirements, to promote the sale of company products, and to provide sales support.

Confer with customers and engineers to assess equipment needs and to determine system requirements. Secure and renew orders and arrange delivery. Develop, present, or respond to proposals for specific customer requirements, including request for proposal responses and industry-specific solutions. Sell products requiring extensive technical expertise and support for installation and use, such as material handling equipment, numerical-control machinery, and computer systems. Diagnose problems with installed equipment. Recommend improved materials or machinery to customers, documenting how such changes will lower costs or increase production. Prepare and deliver technical presentations that explain products or services to customers and prospective customers. Provide technical and nontechnical support and services to clients or other staff members on the use, operation, and maintenance of equipment. Research and identify potential customers for products or services. Visit prospective buyers at commercial, industrial, or other establishments to show samples or catalogs and to inform them about product pricing, availability, and advantages. Create sales or service contracts for products or services. Arrange for demonstrations or trial installations of equipment.

Education/Training Required: Bachelor's degree. **Education and Training Program:** Selling Skills and Sales Operations. **Knowledge/Courses:** Sales and Marketing; Engineering and Technology; Design; Physics; Computers and Electronics; Customer and Personal Service.

Personality Type: Enterprising-Realistic-Investigative. **Career Cluster:** 14 Marketing, Sales, and Service. **Career Pathway:** 14.2 Professional Sales and Marketing. **Other Jobs in This Pathway:** Cashiers; Counter and Rental Clerks; Door-To-Door Sales Workers, News and Street Vendors, and Related Workers; Driver/Sales

Workers; Energy Brokers; First-Line Supervisors of Non-Retail Sales Workers; First-Line Supervisors of Retail Sales Workers; Hotel, Motel, and Resort Desk Clerks; Marketing Managers; Marking Clerks; Online Merchants; Order Fillers, Wholesale and Retail Sales; Parts Salespersons; Property, Real Estate, and Community Association Managers; Real Estate Sales Agents; Reservation and Transportation Ticket Agents and Travel Clerks; Retail Salespersons; Sales and Related Workers, All Other; Sales Representatives, Services, All Other; Sales Representatives, Wholesale and Manufacturing, Except Technical and Scientific Products; Sales Representatives, Wholesale and Manufacturing, Technical and Scientific Products; Solar Sales Representatives and Assessors; Stock Clerks—Stockroom, Warehouse, or Storage Yard; Stock Clerks, Sales Floor; Telemarketers; others.

Sales Managers

❋ Annual Earnings: $98,530

❋ Earnings Growth Potential: High (49.3%)

❋ Growth: 14.9%

❋ Annual Job Openings: 12,660

❋ Self-Employed: 4.2%

Skills—Most Important: Management Skills; Social Skills; Thought-Processing Skills. **Other High-Level Skills:** Mathematics Skills; Communication Skills.

Direct the actual distribution or movement of products or services to customers. Coordinate sales distribution by establishing sales territories, quotas, and goals and establish training programs for sales representatives. Analyze sales statistics gathered by staff to determine sales potential and inventory requirements and monitor customer preferences. Resolve customer complaints on sales and service. Monitor customer preferences to determine focus of sales efforts. Direct and coordinate activities involving sales of manufactured products, services, commodities, real estate, or other subjects of sale. Determine price schedules and discount rates. Review operational records and reports to project sales and determine profitability. Direct, coordinate, and review activities in sales and service accounting and recordkeeping and in receiving and shipping operations. Confer or consult with department heads to plan advertising services and to secure information on equipment and customer specifications. Advise dealers and distributors on policies and operating procedures to ensure functional effectiveness of business. Prepare budgets and approve budget expenditures. Represent company at trade association meetings to promote products.

Education/Training Required: Work experience plus degree. **Education and Training Programs:** Business Administration and Management, General; Business/Commerce, General; Consumer Merchandising/Retailing Management; Marketing, Other; Marketing/Marketing Management, General. **Knowledge/Courses:** Sales and Marketing; Personnel and Human Resources; Economics and Accounting; Administration and Management; Customer and Personal Service; Psychology.

Personality Type: Enterprising-Conventional. **Career Clusters:** 04 Business, Management, and Administration; 10 Human Services; 14 Marketing, Sales, and Service. **Career Pathways:** 14.1 Management and Entrepreneurship; 10.5 Consumer Services Career; 14.4 Marketing Communications and Promotion; 04.1

Management. **Other Jobs in These Pathways:** Brownfield Redevelopment Specialists and Site Managers; Business Continuity Planners; Business Operations Specialists, All Other; Chief Executives; Chief Sustainability Officers; Compliance Managers; Computer and Information Systems Managers; Construction Managers; Customs Brokers; Energy Auditors; First-Line Supervisors of Office and Administrative Support Workers; First-Line Supervisors of Retail Sales Workers; General and Operations Managers; Investment Fund Managers; Loss Prevention Managers; Management Analysts; Managers, All Other; Public Relations Specialists; Regulatory Affairs Managers; Security Management Specialists; Security Managers; Supply Chain Managers; Sustainability Specialists; Wind Energy Operations Managers; Wind Energy Project Managers; others.

Sales Representatives, Wholesale and Manufacturing, Technical and Scientific Products

* Annual Earnings: $73,710
* Earnings Growth Potential: High (50.2%)
* Growth: 9.7%
* Annual Job Openings: 14,230
* Self-Employed: 3.6%

Skills—Most Important: Social Skills; Communication Skills; Management Skills. **Other High-Level Skills:** Mathematics Skills; Thought-Processing Skills.

Sell goods for wholesalers or manufacturers where technical or scientific knowledge is required in such areas as biology, engineering, chemistry, and electronics that is normally obtained from at least two years of postsecondary education. Contact new and existing customers to discuss their needs and to explain how these needs could be met by specific products and services. Answer customers' questions about products, prices, availability, product uses, and credit terms. Quote prices, credit terms, and other bid specifications. Emphasize product features based on analyses of customers' needs and on technical knowledge of product capabilities and limitations. Negotiate prices and terms of sales and service agreements. Maintain customer records. Identify prospective customers by using business directories, following leads from existing clients, participating in organizations and clubs, and attending trade shows and conferences. Prepare sales contracts for orders and submit orders for processing. Select the correct products or assist customers in making product selections, based on customers' needs, product specifications, and applicable regulations.

Education/Training Required: Work experience in a related occupation. **Education and Training Programs:** Business, Management, Marketing, and Related Support Services, Other; Selling Skills and Sales Operations. **Knowledge/Courses:** Sales and Marketing; Customer and Personal Service; Production and Processing; Administration and Management; Transportation; Computers and Electronics.

Personality Type: Enterprising-Conventional. **Career Cluster:** 14 Marketing, Sales, and Service. **Career Pathway:** 14.2 Professional Sales and Marketing. **Other Jobs in This Pathway:** Cashiers; Counter and Rental Clerks; Door-To-Door Sales Workers, News and Street Vendors, and Related Workers; Driver/ Sales Workers; Energy Brokers; First-Line

Supervisors of Non-Retail Sales Workers; First-Line Supervisors of Retail Sales Workers; Hotel, Motel, and Resort Desk Clerks; Marketing Managers; Marking Clerks; Online Merchants; Order Fillers, Wholesale and Retail Sales; Parts Salespersons; Property, Real Estate, and Community Association Managers; Real Estate Sales Agents; Reservation and Transportation Ticket Agents and Travel Clerks; Retail Salespersons; Sales and Related Workers, All Other; Sales Representatives, Services, All Other; Sales Representatives, Wholesale and Manufacturing, Except Technical and Scientific Products; Solar Sales Representatives and Assessors; Stock Clerks—Stockroom, Warehouse, or Storage Yard; Stock Clerks, Sales Floor; Telemarketers; Wholesale and Retail Buyers, Except Farm Products; others.

Job Specialization: Solar Sales Representatives and Assessors

Contact new or existing customers to determine their solar equipment needs, suggest systems or equipment, or estimate costs. Generate solar energy customer leads to develop new accounts. Prepare proposals, quotes, contracts, or presentations for potential solar customers. Select solar energy products, systems, or services for customers based on electrical energy requirements, site conditions, price, or other factors. Assess sites to determine suitability for solar equipment using tape measures, compasses, and computer software. Calculate potential solar resources or solar array production for a particular site considering issues such as climate, shading, and roof orientation. Create customized energy-management packages to satisfy customer needs. Develop marketing or strategic plans for sales territories. Gather information from prospective customers to identify their solar

energy needs. Prepare or review detailed design drawings, specifications, or lists related to solar installations. Provide customers with information such as quotes, orders, sales, shipping, warranties, credit, funding options, incentives, or tax rebates. Provide technical information about solar power, solar systems, equipment, and services to potential customers or dealers. Take quote requests or orders from dealers or customers. Demonstrate use of solar and related equipment to customers or dealers.

Education/Training Required: Work experience in a related occupation. **Education and Training Programs:** Business, Management, Marketing, and Related Support Services, Other; Selling Skills and Sales Operations. **Knowledge/Courses:** No data available.

Personality Type: No data available. **Career Cluster:** 14 Marketing, Sales, and Service. **Career Pathway:** 14.2 Professional Sales and Marketing. **Other Jobs in This Pathway:** Cashiers; Counter and Rental Clerks; Door-To-Door Sales Workers, News and Street Vendors, and Related Workers; Driver/Sales Workers; Energy Brokers; First-Line Supervisors of Non-Retail Sales Workers; First-Line Supervisors of Retail Sales Workers; Hotel, Motel, and Resort Desk Clerks; Marketing Managers; Marking Clerks; Online Merchants; Order Fillers, Wholesale and Retail Sales; Parts Salespersons; Property, Real Estate, and Community Association Managers; Real Estate Sales Agents; Reservation and Transportation Ticket Agents and Travel Clerks; Retail Salespersons; Sales and Related Workers, All Other; Sales Representatives, Services, All Other; Sales Representatives, Wholesale and Manufacturing, Except Technical and Scientific Products; Sales Representatives, Wholesale and Manufacturing,

Technical and Scientific Products; Stock Clerks—Stockroom, Warehouse, or Storage Yard; Stock Clerks, Sales Floor; Telemarketers; Wholesale and Retail Buyers, Except Farm Products; others.

Secondary School Teachers, Except Special and Career/Technical Education

* Annual Earnings: $53,230
* Earnings Growth Potential: Low (34.2%)
* Growth: 8.9%
* Annual Job Openings: 41,240
* Self-Employed: 0.0%

Skills—Most Important: Social Skills; Communication Skills; Thought-Processing Skills. **Other High-Level Skills:** Mathematics Skills; Management Skills.

Instruct students in secondary public or private schools in one or more subjects at the secondary level, such as English, mathematics, or social studies. May be designated according to subject matter specialty, such English teachers. Establish and enforce rules for behavior and procedures for maintaining order among students. Instruct through lectures, discussions, and demonstrations in one or more subjects, such as English, mathematics, or social studies. Establish clear objectives for all lessons, units, and projects and communicate those objectives to students. Prepare, administer, and grade tests and assignments to evaluate students' progress. Prepare materials and classrooms for class activities. Adapt teaching methods and instructional materials to meet students' varying needs and interests. Maintain accurate and complete student records as required by laws, district policies, and administrative regulations. Assign and grade classwork and homework. Observe and evaluate students' performance, behavior, social development, and physical health. Enforce all administration policies and rules governing students.

Education/Training Required: Bachelor's degree. **Education and Training Programs:** Agricultural Teacher Education; Art Teacher Education; Biology Teacher Education; Business Teacher Education; Chemistry Teacher Education; Computer Teacher Education; Drama and Dance Teacher Education; Driver and Safety Teacher Education; English/Language Arts Teacher Education; Family and Consumer Sciences/Home Economics Teacher Education; Foreign Language Teacher Education; French Language Teacher Education; Geography Teacher Education; German Language Teacher Education; Health Occupations Teacher Education; Health Teacher Education; History Teacher Education; Junior High/Intermediate/Middle School Education and Teaching; Latin Teacher Education; Mathematics Teacher Education; Music Teacher Education; Physical Education Teaching and Coaching; Physics Teacher Education; Reading Teacher Education; Sales and Marketing Operations/Marketing and Distribution Teacher Education; Science Teacher Education; Secondary Education and Teaching; Social Science Teacher Education; Social Studies Teacher Education; Spanish Language Teacher Education; Speech Teacher Education; Teacher Education, Multiple Levels; Technology Teacher Education/Industrial Arts Teacher Education; others. **Knowledge/Courses:** History and Archeology; Philosophy and Theology; Sociology and Anthropology; Fine Arts; Education and Training; Therapy and Counseling.

Personality Type: Social-Artistic-Enterprising.
Career Cluster: 05 Education and Training.
Career Pathway: 05.3 Teaching/Training.
Other Jobs in This Pathway: Adult Basic and Secondary Education and Literacy Teachers and Instructors; Athletes and Sports Competitors; Audio-Visual and Multimedia Collections Specialists; Career/Technical Education Teachers, Middle School; Career/Technical Education Teachers, Secondary School; Chemists; Coaches and Scouts; Dietitians and Nutritionists; Elementary School Teachers, Except Special Education; Fitness Trainers and Aerobics Instructors; Historians; Instructional Coordinators; Instructional Designers and Technologists; Interpreters and Translators; Kindergarten Teachers, Except Special Education; Librarians; Middle School Teachers, Except Special and Career/Technical Education; Physicists; Preschool Teachers, Except Special Education; Recreation Workers; Self-Enrichment Education Teachers; Teacher Assistants; Teachers and Instructors, All Other; Tutors.

Securities, Commodities, and Financial Services Sales Agents

* Annual Earnings: $70,190

* Earnings Growth Potential: Very high (55.4%)

* Growth: 9.3%

* Annual Job Openings: 12,680

* Self-Employed: 15.4%

Skills—Most Important: Mathematics Skills; Communication Skills; Social Skills. **Other High-Level Skills:** Thought-Processing Skills; Management Skills.

Job Specialization: Sales Agents, Financial Services

Sell financial services such as loan, tax, and securities counseling to customers of financial institutions and business establishments. Determine customers' financial services needs and prepare proposals to sell services that address these needs. Contact prospective customers to present information and explain services. Sell services and equipment, such as trusts, investments, and check-processing services. Prepare forms or agreements to complete sales. Develop prospects from current commercial customers, referral leads, and sales and trade meetings. Review business trends to advise customers on expected fluctuations. Make presentations on financial services to groups to attract new clients. Evaluate costs and revenue from agreements to determine continued profitability.

Education/Training Required: Bachelor's degree. **Education and Training Programs:** Business and Personal/Financial Services Marketing Operations; Financial Planning and Services; Investments and Securities. **Knowledge/Courses:** Sales and Marketing; Economics and Accounting; Customer and Personal Service; Law and Government; Mathematics; Personnel and Human Resources.

Personality Type: Enterprising-Conventional.
Career Cluster: 06 Finance. **Career Pathway:** 06.1 Financial and Investment Planning. **Other Jobs in This Pathway:** Budget Analysts; Credit Analysts; Financial Analysts; Financial Managers, Branch or Department; Financial Quantitative Analysts; Financial Specialists, All Other; Fraud Examiners, Investigators and Analysts; Investment Underwriters; Loan Counselors; Personal Financial Advisors; Risk Management Specialists; Sales Agents, Securities

and Commodities; Securities and Commodities Traders; Securities, Commodities, and Financial Services Sales Agents; Treasurers and Controllers.

Job Specialization: Sales Agents, Securities and Commodities

Buy and sell securities in investment and trading firms and develop and implement financial plans for individuals, businesses, and organizations. Complete sales order tickets and submit for processing of client-requested transactions. Record transactions accurately and keep clients informed about transactions. Interview clients to determine clients' assets, liabilities, cash flow, insurance coverage, tax status, and financial objectives. Develop financial plans based on analysis of clients' financial status and discuss financial options with clients. Review all securities transactions to ensure accuracy of information and that trades conform to regulations of governing agencies. Offer advice on the purchase or sale of particular securities. Relay buy or sell orders to securities exchanges or to firm trading departments. Identify potential clients using advertising campaigns, mailing lists, and personal contacts. Review financial periodicals, stock and bond reports, business publications, and other material to identify potential investments for clients and to keep abreast of trends affecting market conditions. Contact prospective customers to determine customer needs, present information, and explain available services. Prepare documents needed to implement plans selected by clients. Analyze market conditions to determine optimum times to execute securities transactions. Explain stock market terms and trading practices to clients. Inform and advise concerned parties on fluctuations and securities transactions affecting plans or accounts. Calculate costs for billings and commissions.

Education/Training Required: Bachelor's degree. **Education and Training Programs:** Business and Personal/Financial Services Marketing Operations; Financial Planning and Services; Investments and Securities. **Knowledge/Courses:** Economics and Accounting; Customer and Personal Service; Sales and Marketing; Clerical Practices; Law and Government; Mathematics.

Personality Type: Enterprising-Conventional. **Career Cluster:** 06 Finance. **Career Pathway:** 06.1 Financial and Investment Planning. **Other Jobs in This Pathway:** Budget Analysts; Credit Analysts; Financial Analysts; Financial Managers, Branch or Department; Financial Quantitative Analysts; Financial Specialists, All Other; Fraud Examiners, Investigators and Analysts; Investment Underwriters; Loan Counselors; Personal Financial Advisors; Risk Management Specialists; Sales Agents, Financial Services; Securities and Commodities Traders; Securities, Commodities, and Financial Services Sales Agents; Treasurers and Controllers.

Job Specialization: Securities and Commodities Traders

Buy and sell securities and commodities to transfer debt, capital, or risk. Establish and negotiate unit prices and terms of sale. Agree on buying or selling prices at optimal levels for clients. Buy or sell stocks, bonds, commodity futures, foreign currencies, or other securities at stock exchanges on behalf of investment dealers. Make bids and offers to buy or sell securities. Analyze target companies and investment opportunities to inform investment decisions. Develop and maintain supplier and customer relationships. Devise trading, option, and hedge strategies. Identify opportunities and develop channels for purchase or sale of securities or commodities. Inform other traders, managers, or customers of market conditions, including volume, price, competition, and dynamics. Monitor markets and positions. Process paperwork for special orders, including margin and option purchases. Receive sales order tickets and inspect forms to determine accuracy of information. Report all positions or trading results. Review securities transactions to ensure conformance to regulations.

Education/Training Required: Bachelor's degree. **Education and Training Programs:** Business and Personal/Financial Services Marketing Operations; Financial Planning and Services; Investments and Securities. **Knowledge/Courses:** No data available.

Personality Type: Enterprising-Conventional. **Career Cluster:** 06 Finance. **Career Pathway:** 06.1 Financial and Investment Planning. **Other Jobs in This Pathway:** Budget Analysts; Credit Analysts; Financial Analysts; Financial Managers, Branch or Department; Financial Quantitative Analysts; Financial Specialists, All Other; Fraud Examiners, Investigators and Analysts; Investment Underwriters; Loan Counselors; Personal Financial Advisors; Risk Management Specialists; Sales Agents, Financial Services; Sales Agents, Securities and Commodities; Securities, Commodities, and Financial Services Sales Agents; Treasurers and Controllers.

Security and Fire Alarm Systems Installers

- ✸ Annual Earnings: $38,500
- ✸ Earnings Growth Potential: Low (35.4%)
- ✸ Growth: 24.8%
- ✸ Annual Job Openings: 2,780
- ✸ Self-Employed: 6.3%

Skills—Most Important: Installation Skills; Equipment Use/Maintenance Skills; Social Skills.

Install, program, maintain, and repair security and fire alarm wiring and equipment. Ensure that work is in accordance with relevant codes. Examine systems to locate problems such as loose connections or broken insulation. Test backup batteries, keypad programming, sirens, and all security features to ensure proper functioning and to diagnose malfunctions. Mount and fasten control panels, door and window contacts, sensors, and video cameras and attach electrical and telephone wiring to connect components. Install, maintain, or repair security systems, alarm devices, and related equipment following blueprints of electrical layouts and building plans. Feed cables through access holes, roof spaces, and cavity walls to reach fixture outlets. Then position and terminate cables, wires, and strapping. Inspect installation sites and study work orders, building plans, and installation manuals to determine materials requirements and installation procedures. Adjust sensitivity of units based on room structures and manufacturers' recommendations using programming keypads. Test and repair circuits and sensors, following wiring and system specifications. Drill holes for wiring in wall studs, joists, ceilings, and floors.

Demonstrate systems for customers and explain details such as the causes and consequences of false alarms. Consult with clients to assess risks and to determine security requirements. Keep informed of new products and developments. Mount raceways and conduits and fasten wires to wood framing using staplers. Prepare documents such as invoices and warranties.

Education/Training Required: Postsecondary vocational training. **Education and Training Programs:** Electrician; Security System Installation, Repair, and Inspection Technology/Technician. **Knowledge/Courses:** Telecommunications; Building and Construction; Mechanical Devices; Computers and Electronics; Public Safety and Security; Design.

Personality Type: Realistic-Conventional. **Career Cluster:** 02 Architecture and Construction. **Career Pathways:** 02.3 Maintenance/Operations; 02.2 Construction. **Other Jobs in These Pathways:** Brickmasons and Blockmasons; Cement Masons and Concrete Finishers; Construction and Building Inspectors; Construction Carpenters; Construction Laborers; Construction Managers; Cost Estimators; Drywall and Ceiling Tile Installers; Electrical Power-Line Installers and Repairers; Electricians; Engineering Technicians, Except Drafters, All Other; First-Line Supervisors of Construction Trades and Extraction Workers; Heating and Air Conditioning Mechanics and Installers; Helpers—Carpenters; Helpers—Electricians; Helpers—Pipelayers, Plumbers, Pipefitters, and Steamfitters; Highway Maintenance Workers; Operating Engineers and Other Construction Equipment Operators; Painters, Construction and Maintenance; Pipe Fitters and Steamfitters; Plumbers; Refrigeration Mechanics and Installers; Roofers; Rough Carpenters; Solar Energy Installation Managers; others.

Self-Enrichment Education Teachers

- ✳ Annual Earnings: $36,340
- ✳ Earnings Growth Potential: High (48.3%)
- ✳ Growth: 32.0%
- ✳ Annual Job Openings: 12,030
- ✳ Self-Employed: 17.3%

Skills—Most Important: Thought-Processing Skills; Communication Skills; Social Skills.

Teach or instruct courses other than those that normally lead to an occupational objective or degree. Courses may include self-improvement, nonvocational, and nonacademic subjects. Teaching may or may not take place in a traditional educational institution. Adapt teaching methods and instructional materials to meet students' varying needs and interests. Conduct classes, workshops, and demonstrations and provide individual instruction to teach topics and skills such as cooking, dancing, writing, physical fitness, photography, personal finance, and flying. Monitor students' performance to make suggestions for improvement and to ensure that they satisfy course standards, training requirements, and objectives. Observe students to determine qualifications, limitations, abilities, interests, and other individual characteristics. Instruct students individually and in groups using various teaching methods such as lectures, discussions, and demonstrations. Establish clear objectives for all lessons, units, and projects and communicate those objectives to students. Prepare students for further development by encouraging them to explore learning opportunities and to persevere with challenging tasks. Prepare materials and classrooms for class activities. Enforce policies and rules governing students. Plan and conduct activities for a balanced program of instruction, demonstration, and work time that provides students with opportunities to observe, question, and investigate. Prepare instructional program objectives, outlines, and lesson plans.

Education/Training Required: Work experience in a related occupation. **Education and Training Program:** Adult and Continuing Education and Teaching. **Knowledge/ Courses:** Education and Training; Fine Arts; Communications and Media; Customer and Personal Service; Sales and Marketing; English Language.

Personality Type: Social-Artistic-Enterprising. **Career Cluster:** 05 Education and Training. **Career Pathway:** 05.3 Teaching/Training. **Other Jobs in This Pathway:** Adult Basic and Secondary Education and Literacy Teachers and Instructors; Athletes and Sports Competitors; Audio-Visual and Multimedia Collections Specialists; Career/Technical Education Teachers, Middle School; Career/ Technical Education Teachers, Secondary School; Chemists; Coaches and Scouts; Dietitians and Nutritionists; Elementary School Teachers, Except Special Education; Fitness Trainers and Aerobics Instructors; Historians; Instructional Coordinators; Instructional Designers and Technologists; Interpreters and Translators; Kindergarten Teachers, Except Special Education; Librarians; Middle School Teachers, Except Special and Career/Technical Education; Physicists; Preschool Teachers, Except Special Education; Recreation Workers; Secondary School Teachers, Except Special and Career/Technical Education; Teacher Assistants; Teachers and Instructors, All Other; Tutors.

Ship Engineers

- ✳ Annual Earnings: $65,880
- ✳ Earnings Growth Potential: High (42.1%)
- ✳ Growth: 18.6%
- ✳ Annual Job Openings: 700
- ✳ Self-Employed: 0.0%

Skills—Most Important: Equipment Use/ Maintenance Skills; Science Skills; Management Skills. **Other High-Level Skills:** Thought-Processing Skills.

Supervise and coordinate activities of crew engaged in operating and maintaining engines; boilers; deck machinery; and electrical, sanitary, and refrigeration equipment aboard ship. Record orders for changes in ship speed and direction and note gauge readings and test data, such as revolutions per minute and voltage output, in engineering logs and bellbooks. Install engine controls, propeller shafts, and propellers. Perform and participate in emergency drills. Fabricate engine replacement parts such as valves, stay rods, and bolts using metalworking machinery. Operate and maintain off-loading liquid pumps and valves. Maintain and repair engines, electric motors, pumps, winches, and other mechanical and electrical equipment or assist other crew members with maintenance and repair duties. Maintain electrical power, heating, ventilation, refrigeration, water, and sewerage systems. Monitor and test operations of engines and other equipment so that malfunctions and their causes can be identified. Monitor engine, machinery, and equipment indicators when vessels are underway and report abnormalities to appropriate shipboard staff. Start engines to propel ships and regulate engines and power transmissions to control speeds of ships according to directions from captains or bridge computers. Order and receive engine room's stores such as oil and spare parts; maintain inventories and record usage of supplies. Act as a liaison between a ship's captain and shore personnel to ensure that schedules and budgets are maintained and that the ship is operated safely and efficiently. Clean engine parts and keep engine rooms clean.

Education/Training Required: Work experience in a related occupation. **Education and Training Program:** Marine Maintenance/Fitter and Ship Repair Technology/Technician. **Knowledge/Courses:** Mechanical Devices; Building and Construction; Engineering and Technology; Transportation; Chemistry; Public Safety and Security.

Personality Type: Realistic-Conventional-Enterprising. **Career Cluster:** 16 Transportation, Distribution, and Logistics. **Career Pathway:** 16.1 Transportation Operations. **Other Jobs in This Pathway:** Airline Pilots, Copilots, and Flight Engineers; Automotive and Watercraft Service Attendants; Automotive Master Mechanics; Bus Drivers, School or Special Client; Bus Drivers, Transit and Intercity; Commercial Pilots; Crane and Tower Operators; First-Line Supervisors of Helpers, Laborers, and Material Movers, Hand; First-Line Supervisors of Transportation and Material-Moving Machine and Vehicle Operators; Freight and Cargo Inspectors; Heavy and Tractor-Trailer Truck Drivers; Laborers and Freight, Stock, and Material Movers, Hand; Light Truck or Delivery Services Drivers; Mates—Ship, Boat, and Barge; Motor Vehicle Operators, All Other; Operating Engineers and Other Construction Equipment Operators; Parking Lot Attendants; Pilots, Ship; Railroad Conductors and Yardmasters; Sailors

and Marine Oilers; Ship and Boat Captains; Storage and Distribution Managers; Taxi Drivers and Chauffeurs; Transportation Managers; Transportation Workers, All Other; others.

Social and Community Service Managers

⚜ Annual Earnings: $57,950
⚜ Earnings Growth Potential: Medium (40.8%)
⚜ Growth: 13.8%
⚜ Annual Job Openings: 4,820
⚜ Self-Employed: 3.1%

Skills—Most Important: Management Skills; Science Skills; Social Skills. **Other High-Level Skills:** Thought-Processing Skills; Mathematics Skills; Communication Skills.

Plan, organize, or coordinate the activities of a social service program or community outreach organization. Oversee the program or organization's budget and policies on participant involvement, program requirements, and benefits. Work may involve directing social workers, counselors, or probation officers. Evaluate the work of staff and volunteers to ensure that programs are of appropriate quality and that resources are used effectively. Provide direct service and support to individuals or clients, such as handling a referral for child advocacy issues, conducting a needs evaluation, or resolving complaints. Recruit, interview, and hire or sign up volunteers and staff. Establish and maintain relationships with other agencies and organizations in the community to meet community needs and to ensure that services are not duplicated. Establish and oversee administrative procedures to meet objectives set by boards of directors or senior management. Direct activities of professional and technical staff members and volunteers. Plan and administer budgets for programs, equipment, and support services. Participate in the determination of organizational policies on such issues as participant eligibility, program requirements, and program benefits.

Education/Training Required: Bachelor's degree. **Education and Training Programs:** Business Administration and Management, General; Business, Management, Marketing, and Related Support Services, Other; Business/Commerce, General; Community Organization and Advocacy; Entrepreneurship/Entrepreneurial Studies; Human Services, General; Non-Profit/Public/Organizational Management; Public Administration. **Knowledge/Courses:** Therapy and Counseling; Psychology; Sociology and Anthropology; Philosophy and Theology; Personnel and Human Resources; Customer and Personal Service.

Personality Type: Enterprising-Social. **Career Clusters:** 04 Business, Management, and Administration; 07 Government and Public Administration; 10 Human Services. **Career Pathways:** 04.1 Management; 07.1 Governance; 10.3 Family and Community Services; 07.7 Public Management and Administration. **Other Jobs in These Pathways:** Brownfield Redevelopment Specialists and Site Managers; Business Continuity Planners; Business Operations Specialists, All Other; Chief Executives; Chief Sustainability Officers; Childcare Workers; Compliance Managers; Construction Managers; Customs Brokers; Energy Auditors; First-Line Supervisors of Office and Administrative Support Workers; General and Operations Managers; Investment Fund Managers; Loss Prevention Managers; Management Analysts; Managers, All Other;

Nannies; Personal Care Aides; Regulatory Affairs Managers; Security Management Specialists; Security Managers; Supply Chain Managers; Sustainability Specialists; Wind Energy Operations Managers; Wind Energy Project Managers; others.

Social Science Research Assistants

- ❋ Annual Earnings: $37,230
- ❋ Earnings Growth Potential: High (42.6%)
- ❋ Growth: 17.8%
- ❋ Annual Job Openings: 1,270
- ❋ Self-Employed: 1.5%

Skills—Most Important: Science Skills; Mathematics Skills; Technology/Programming Skills. **Other High-Level Skills:** Communication Skills; Thought-Processing Skills; Social Skills; Management Skills.

Assist social scientists in laboratory, survey, and other social research. May perform publication activities, laboratory analysis, quality control, or data management. Normally these individuals work under the direct supervision of social scientists and assist in those activities that are more routine. Code data in preparation for computer entry. Provide assistance in the design of survey instruments such as questionnaires. Prepare, manipulate, and manage extensive databases. Prepare tables, graphs, fact sheets, and written reports summarizing research results. Obtain informed consent of research subjects and/or their guardians. Edit and submit protocols and other required research documentation. Screen potential subjects to determine their suitability as study participants. Conduct Internet-based and library research. Supervise the work of survey interviewers. Perform descriptive and multivariate statistical analyses of data. Recruit and schedule research participants. Develop and implement research quality control procedures. Track research participants and perform necessary follow-up tasks. Verify the accuracy and validity of data entered in databases; correct errors. Track laboratory supplies and expenses such as participant reimbursement. Provide assistance with the preparation of project-related reports, manuscripts, and presentations. Present research findings to groups of people. Perform needs assessments and/or consult with clients to determine the research and information required. Allocate and manage laboratory space and resources.

Education/Training Required: Associate degree. **Education and Training Program:** Social Sciences, General. **Knowledge/Courses:** Psychology; Sociology and Anthropology; Clerical Practices; Computers and Electronics; English Language; Communications and Media.

Personality Type: Conventional-Investigative. **Career Cluster:** 10 Human Services. **Career Pathway:** 10.3 Family and Community Services. **Other Jobs in This Pathway:** Chief Executives; Child, Family, and School Social Workers; Childcare Workers; City and Regional Planning Aides; Counselors, All Other; Eligibility Interviewers, Government Programs; Farm and Home Management Advisors; Legislators; Managers, All Other; Marriage and Family Therapists; Nannies; Personal Care Aides; Probation Officers and Correctional Treatment Specialists; Protective Service Workers, All Other; Social and Community Service Managers; Social Scientists and Related Workers, All Other; Social Workers, All Other; Sociologists; Supply Chain Managers.

Job Specialization: City and Regional Planning Aides

Compile data from various sources, such as maps, reports, and field and file investigations, for use by city planner in making planning studies. Prepare, maintain, and update files and records, including land use data and statistics. Respond to public inquiries and complaints. Research, compile, analyze, and organize information from maps, reports, investigations, and books for use in reports and special projects. Prepare, develop, and maintain maps and databases. Serve as liaison between planning department and other departments and agencies. Prepare reports using statistics, charts, and graphs to illustrate planning studies in areas such as population, land use, or zoning. Participate in and support team planning efforts. Provide and process zoning and project permits and applications. Perform clerical duties such as composing, typing, and proofreading documents; scheduling appointments and meetings; handling mail; and posting public notices. Conduct interviews, surveys, and site inspections on factors that affect land usage, such as zoning, traffic flow, and housing. Perform code enforcement tasks. Inspect sites and review plans for minor development permit applications.

Education/Training Required: Associate degree. **Education and Training Program:** Social Sciences, General. **Knowledge/ Courses:** Geography; History and Archeology; Design; Law and Government; Building and Construction; Sociology and Anthropology.

Personality Type: Conventional-Realistic. **Career Cluster:** 10 Human Services. **Career Pathway:** 10.3 Family and Community Services. **Other Jobs in This Pathway:** Chief Executives; Child, Family, and School Social Workers;

Childcare Workers; Counselors, All Other; Eligibility Interviewers, Government Programs; Farm and Home Management Advisors; Legislators; Managers, All Other; Marriage and Family Therapists; Nannies; Personal Care Aides; Probation Officers and Correctional Treatment Specialists; Protective Service Workers, All Other; Social and Community Service Managers; Social Science Research Assistants; Social Scientists and Related Workers, All Other; Social Workers, All Other; Sociologists; Supply Chain Managers.

Social Scientists and Related Workers, All Other

* Annual Earnings: $74,620
* Earnings Growth Potential: High (41.8%)
* Growth: 22.5%
* Annual Job Openings: 2,380
* Self-Employed: 1.5%

Skills—Most Important: Mathematics Skills; Management Skills; Thought-Processing Skills. **Other High-Level Skills:** Communication Skills; Social Skills; Science Skills.

This occupation includes all social scientists and related workers not listed separately. Because this is a highly diverse occupation, no data is available for some information topics.

Education/Training Required: Master's degree. **Education and Training Program:** Social Sciences, Other. **Career Clusters:** 10 Human Services; 15 Science, Technology, Engineering, and Mathematics. **Career Pathways:** 15.2 Science and Mathematics; 10.3 Family and Community Services. **Other Jobs in These Pathways:** Anthropologists; Archeologists;

Architectural and Engineering Managers; Archivists; Astronomers; Atmospheric and Space Scientists; Biochemists and Biophysicists; Biofuels/Biodiesel Technology and Product Development Managers; Bioinformatics Scientists; Biological Scientists, All Other; Biologists; Biostatisticians; Cartographers and Photogrammetrists; Chemists; Chief Executives; Child, Family, and School Social Workers; Childcare Workers; City and Regional Planning Aides; Clinical Data Managers; Clinical Research Coordinators; Community and Social Service Specialists, All Other; Counselors, All Other; Curators; Dietitians and Nutritionists; Economists; Education, Training, and Library Workers, All Other; Eligibility Interviewers, Government Programs; Environmental Economists; Epidemiologists; others.

Job Specialization: Transportation Planners

Prepare studies for proposed transportation projects. Gather, compile, and analyze data. Study the use and operation of transportation systems. Develop transportation models or simulations. Prepare or review engineering studies or specifications. Represent jurisdictions in the legislative or administrative approval of land development projects. Prepare necessary documents to obtain project approvals or permits. Direct urban traffic counting programs. Develop or test new methods or models of transportation analysis. Analyze transportation-related consequences of federal and state legislative proposals. Analyze information from traffic counting programs. Review development plans for transportation system effects, infrastructure requirements, or compliance with applicable transportation regulations. Prepare reports or recommendations on transportation planning. Produce environmental documents, such as environmental assessments or environmental impact statements. Participate in public meetings or hearings to explain planning proposals, to gather feedback from those affected by projects, or to achieve consensus on project designs. Document and evaluate transportation project needs and costs. Develop design ideas for new or improved transport infrastructure, such as junction improvements, pedestrian projects, bus facilities, and car parking areas. Develop computer models to address transportation planning issues. Design transportation surveys to identify areas of public concern. Analyze and interpret data from traffic-modeling software, geographic information systems, or associated databases.

Education/Training Required: Master's degree. **Education and Training Program:** City/Urban, Community, and Regional Planning. **Knowledge/Courses:** Geography; Transportation; Law and Government; Design; History and Archeology; Sociology and Anthropology.

Personality Type: Investigative-Conventional-Realistic. **Career Cluster:** 15 Science, Technology, Engineering, and Mathematics. **Career Pathway:** 15.2 Science and Mathematics. **Other Jobs in This Pathway:** Architectural and Engineering Managers; Biochemists and Biophysicists; Biofuels/Biodiesel Technology and Product Development Managers; Bioinformatics Scientists; Biological Scientists, All Other; Biologists; Biostatisticians; Chemists; Clinical Data Managers; Clinical Research Coordinators; Community and Social Service Specialists, All Other; Dietitians and Nutritionists; Education, Training, and Library Workers, All Other; Geneticists; Geoscientists, Except Hydrologists and Geographers; Medical Scientists, Except Epidemiologists; Molecular and Cellular Biologists; Natural Sciences

Managers; Operations Research Analysts; Physical Scientists, All Other; Social Scientists and Related Workers, All Other; Statisticians; Survey Researchers; Water Resource Specialists; Zoologists and Wildlife Biologists; others.

Software Developers, Applications

- ❋ Annual Earnings: $87,790
- ❋ Earnings Growth Potential: Medium (38.1%)
- ❋ Growth: 34.0%
- ❋ Annual Job Openings: 21,840
- ❋ Self-Employed: 2.7%

Skills—Most Important: Technology/Programming Skills; Mathematics Skills; Science Skills. **Other High-Level Skills:** Thought-Processing Skills; Equipment Use/Maintenance Skills; Communication Skills; Social Skills; Management Skills.

Develop, create, and modify general computer applications software or specialized utility programs. Analyze user needs and develop software solutions. Design software or customize software for client use with the aim of optimizing operational efficiency. May analyze and design databases within an application area, working individually or coordinating database development as part of a team. Confer with systems analysts, engineers, programmers, and others to design system and to obtain information on project limitations and capabilities, performance requirements, and interfaces. Modify existing software to correct errors, allow it to adapt to new hardware, or to improve its performance. Analyze user needs and software requirements to determine feasibility of design within time and cost constraints. Consult with customers about software system design and maintenance. Coordinate software system installation and monitor equipment functioning to ensure specifications are met. Design, develop, and modify software systems using scientific analysis and mathematical models to predict and measure outcome and consequences of design. Develop and direct software system testing and validation procedures, programming, and documentation. Analyze information to determine, recommend, and plan computer specifications and layouts and peripheral equipment modifications. Supervise the work of programmers, technologists, and technicians and other engineering and scientific personnel. Obtain and evaluate information on factors such as reporting formats required, costs, and security needs to determine hardware configuration. Determine system performance standards. Train users to use new or modified equipment. Store, retrieve, and manipulate data for analysis of system capabilities and requirements. Specify power supply requirements and configuration.

Education/Training Required: Bachelor's degree. **Education and Training Programs:** Computer Graphics; Computer Science; Computer Software and Media Applications, Other; Data Modeling/Warehousing and Database Administration; Modeling, Virtual Environments and Simulation; Web Page, Digital/Multimedia, and Information Resources Design. **Knowledge/Courses:** Computers and Electronics; Mathematics; Engineering and Technology; Design; English Language.

Personality Type: Investigative-Realistic-Conventional. **Career Cluster:** 11 Information Technology. **Career Pathways:** 11.4 Programming and Software Development; 13.3 Maintenance, Installation, and Repair; 11.3

Interactive Media; 11.2 Information Support Services; 11.1 Network Systems; 08.3 Health Informatics; 15.2 Science and Mathematics. **Other Jobs in These Pathways:** Architectural and Engineering Managers; Automotive Specialty Technicians; Biofuels/Biodiesel Technology and Product Development Managers; Clinical Psychologists; Computer and Information Systems Managers; Computer, Automated Teller, and Office Machine Repairers; Electrical and Electronic Equipment Assemblers; Electrical Engineering Technicians; Electronics Engineering Technicians; Engineers, All Other; Executive Secretaries and Executive Administrative Assistants; First-Line Supervisors of Office and Administrative Support Workers; Graphic Designers; Helpers—Installation, Maintenance, and Repair Workers; Industrial Machinery Mechanics; Installation, Maintenance, and Repair Workers, All Other; Medical and Health Services Managers; Medical Assistants; Medical Records and Health Information Technicians; Medical Secretaries; Mobile Heavy Equipment Mechanics, Except Engines; Physical Therapists; Public Relations Specialists; Receptionists and Information Clerks; Telecommunications Line Installers and Repairers; others.

Software Developers, Systems Software

❋ Annual Earnings: $94,180

❋ Earnings Growth Potential: Low (35.2%)

❋ Growth: 30.4%

❋ Annual Job Openings: 15,340

❋ Self-Employed: 2.7%

Skills—Most Important: Technology/Programming Skills; Science Skills;

Mathematics Skills. **Other High-Level Skills:** Thought-Processing Skills; Communication Skills; Social Skills; Management Skills; Equipment Use/Maintenance Skills.

Research, design, develop, and test operating systems—develop software, compilers, and network distribution software for medical, industrial, military, communications, aerospace, business, scientific, and general computing applications. Set operational specifications and formulate and analyze software requirements. Apply principles and techniques of computer science, engineering, and mathematical analysis. Modify existing software to correct errors, to adapt it to new hardware, or to upgrade interfaces and improve performance. Design and develop software systems using scientific analysis and mathematical models to predict and measure outcome and consequences of design. Consult with engineering staff to evaluate interface between hardware and software, develop specifications and performance requirements, and resolve customer problems. Analyze information to determine, recommend, and plan installation of a new system or modification of an existing system. Develop and direct software system testing and validation procedures. Direct software programming and development of documentation. Consult with customers or other departments on project status, proposals, and technical issues such as software system design and maintenance. Advise customer about or perform maintenance of software system. Coordinate installation of software system. Monitor functioning of equipment to ensure system operates in conformance with specifications. Store, retrieve, and manipulate data for analysis of system capabilities and requirements. Confer with data processing and project managers to obtain information on

limitations and capabilities for data processing projects. Prepare reports and correspondence on project specifications, activities, and status. Evaluate factors such as reporting formats required, cost constraints, and need for security restrictions to determine hardware configuration.

Education/Training Required: Bachelor's degree. **Education and Training Programs:** Computer Graphics; Computer Science; Computer Software and Media Applications, Other; Data Modeling/Warehousing and Database Administration; Modeling, Virtual Environments and Simulation; Web Page, Digital/Multimedia, and Information Resources Design. **Knowledge/Courses:** Computers and Electronics; Engineering and Technology; Design; Telecommunications; Mathematics; Communications and Media.

Personality Type: Investigative-Conventional-Realistic. **Career Cluster:** 11 Information Technology. **Career Pathways:** 11.2 Information Support Services; 11.3 Interactive Media; 11.1 Network Systems; 11.4 Programming and Software Development. **Other Jobs in These Pathways:** Architectural and Engineering Managers; Bioinformatics Scientists; Computer and Information Systems Managers; Computer Hardware Engineers; Computer Numerically Controlled Machine Tool Programmers, Metal and Plastic; Computer Operators; Graphic Designers; Multimedia Artists and Animators; Remote Sensing Scientists and Technologists; Remote Sensing Technicians.

Special Education Teachers, Middle School

* Annual Earnings: $53,440
* Earnings Growth Potential: Low (32.0%)
* Growth: 18.1%
* Annual Job Openings: 4,410
* Self-Employed: 0.2%

Skills—Most Important: Social Skills; Thought-Processing Skills; Communication Skills. **Other High-Level Skills:** Management Skills.

Teach middle school subjects to educationally and physically handicapped students. Includes teachers who specialize and work with audibly and visually handicapped students and those who teach basic academic and life processes skills to the mentally impaired. Establish and enforce rules for behavior and policies and procedures to maintain order among students. Maintain accurate and complete student records and prepare reports on children and activities as required by laws, district policies, and administrative regulations. Prepare materials and classrooms for class activities. Confer with parents, administrators, testing specialists, social workers, and professionals to develop individual educational plans designed to promote students' educational, physical, and social development. Develop and implement strategies to meet the needs of students with a variety of handicapping conditions. Teach socially acceptable behavior, employing techniques such as behavior modification and positive reinforcement. Modify the general education curriculum for special-needs students based on a variety of instructional techniques and instructional technology. Employ special educational strategies and techniques during instruction to improve the development of sensory- and perceptual-motor skills, language, cognition, and memory. Confer with parents or guardians, other teachers, counselors, and administrators to resolve students' behavioral and academic problems. Instruct through lectures, discussions, and demonstrations in one or more subjects, such as English, mathematics, or social studies.

Education/Training Required: Bachelor's degree. **Education and Training Program:** Education/Teaching of Individuals in Junior High/Middle School Special Education Programs. **Knowledge/Courses:** Therapy and Counseling; History and Archeology; Psychology; Education and Training; Geography; Philosophy and Theology.

Personality Type: Social-Artistic. **Career Cluster:** 05 Education and Training. **Career Pathway:** 05.3 Teaching/Training. **Other Jobs in This Pathway:** Adult Basic and Secondary Education and Literacy Teachers and Instructors; Athletes and Sports Competitors; Audio-Visual and Multimedia Collections Specialists; Career/Technical Education Teachers, Middle School; Career/Technical Education Teachers, Secondary School; Chemists; Coaches and Scouts; Dietitians and Nutritionists; Elementary School Teachers, Except Special Education; Fitness Trainers and Aerobics Instructors; Historians; Instructional Coordinators; Instructional Designers and Technologists; Interpreters and Translators; Kindergarten Teachers, Except Special Education; Librarians; Middle School Teachers, Except Special and Career/Technical Education; Physicists; Preschool Teachers, Except Special Education; Recreation Workers; Secondary School Teachers, Except Special and

Career/Technical Education; Self-Enrichment Education Teachers; Teacher Assistants; Teachers and Instructors, All Other; Tutors.

Special Education Teachers, Secondary School

- ❋ Annual Earnings: $54,810
- ❋ Earnings Growth Potential: Low (33.2%)
- ❋ Growth: 13.3%
- ❋ Annual Job Openings: 5,750
- ❋ Self-Employed: 0.2%

Skills—Most Important: Social Skills; Thought-Processing Skills; Communication Skills. **Other High-Level Skills:** Mathematics Skills.

Teach secondary school subjects to educationally and physically handicapped students. Includes teachers who specialize and work with audibly and visually handicapped students and those who teach basic academic and life processes skills to the mentally impaired. Maintain accurate and complete student records and prepare reports on children and activities as required by laws, district policies, and administrative regulations. Teach socially acceptable behavior, employing techniques such as behavior modification and positive reinforcement. Prepare materials and classrooms for class activities. Establish and enforce rules for behavior and policies and procedures to maintain order among students. Confer with parents, administrators, testing specialists, social workers, and professionals to develop individual educational plans designed to promote students' educational, physical, and social development. Instruct through lectures, discussions, and demonstrations in one or more

subjects, such as English, mathematics, or social studies. Employ special educational strategies and techniques during instruction to improve the development of sensory- and perceptual-motor skills, language, cognition, and memory.

Education/Training Required: Bachelor's degree. **Education and Training Program:** Education/Teaching of Individuals in Secondary Special Education Programs. **Knowledge/Courses:** Therapy and Counseling; History and Archeology; Psychology; Geography; Philosophy and Theology; Sociology and Anthropology.

Personality Type: Social-Investigative. **Career Cluster:** 05 Education and Training. **Career Pathway:** 05.3 Teaching/Training. **Other Jobs in This Pathway:** Adult Basic and Secondary Education and Literacy Teachers and Instructors; Athletes and Sports Competitors; Audio-Visual and Multimedia Collections Specialists; Career/Technical Education Teachers, Middle School; Career/Technical Education Teachers, Secondary School; Chemists; Coaches and Scouts; Dietitians and Nutritionists; Elementary School Teachers, Except Special Education; Fitness Trainers and Aerobics Instructors; Historians; Instructional Coordinators; Instructional Designers and Technologists; Interpreters and Translators; Kindergarten Teachers, Except Special Education; Librarians; Middle School Teachers, Except Special and Career/Technical Education; Physicists; Preschool Teachers, Except Special Education; Recreation Workers; Secondary School Teachers, Except Special and Career/Technical Education; Self-Enrichment Education Teachers; Teacher Assistants; Teachers and Instructors, All Other; Tutors.

Speech-Language Pathologists

❋ Annual Earnings: $66,920

❋ Earnings Growth Potential: Low (35.8%)

❋ Growth: 18.5%

❋ Annual Job Openings: 4,380

❋ Self-Employed: 9.0%

Skills—Most Important: Science Skills; Communication Skills; Thought-Processing Skills. **Other High-Level Skills:** Social Skills; Mathematics Skills; Management Skills; Equipment Use/Maintenance Skills.

Assess and treat persons with speech, language, voice, and fluency disorders. May select alternative communication systems and teach their use. May perform research related to speech and language problems. Monitor patients' progress and adjust treatments accordingly. Evaluate hearing or speech and language test results, barium swallow results, and medical or background information to diagnose and plan treatment for speech, language, fluency, voice, and swallowing disorders. Administer hearing or speech and language evaluations, tests, or examinations to patients to collect information on type and degree of impairments using written and oral tests and special instruments. Write reports and maintain proper documentation of information, such as client Medicaid and billing records and caseload activities, including the initial evaluation, treatment, progress, and discharge of clients. Develop and implement treatment plans for problems such as stuttering, delayed language, swallowing disorders, and inappropriate pitch or harsh voice problems based on own assessments and recommendations of physicians, psychologists, or social workers. Develop individual or group activities and programs in schools to deal with behavior, speech, language, or swallowing problems. Participate in and write reports for meetings on patients' progress, such as individualized educational planning meetings, in-service meetings, or intervention assistance team meetings. Complete administrative responsibilities, such as coordinating paperwork, scheduling case management activities, or writing lesson plans.

Education/Training Required: Master's degree. **Education and Training Programs:** Audiology/Audiologist and Speech-Language Pathology/Pathologist; Communication Disorders Sciences and Services, Other; Communication Disorders, General; Communication Sciences and Disorders, General; Speech-Language Pathology/Pathologist. **Knowledge/Courses:** Therapy and Counseling; English Language; Psychology; Sociology and Anthropology; Education and Training; Medicine and Dentistry.

Personality Type: Social-Investigative-Artistic. **Career Cluster:** 08 Health Science. **Career Pathway:** 08.1 Therapeutic Services. **Other Jobs in This Pathway:** Clinical Psychologists; Community and Social Service Specialists, All Other; Counseling Psychologists; Dental Assistants; Dental Hygienists; Dentists, General; Health Technologists and Technicians, All Other; Healthcare Support Workers, All Other; Home Health Aides; Licensed Practical and Licensed Vocational Nurses; Low Vision Therapists, Orientation and Mobility Specialists, and Vision Rehabilitation Therapists; Massage Therapists; Medical and Clinical Laboratory Technicians; Medical and Health Services Managers; Medical Scientists, Except Epidemiologists; Medical Secretaries; Occupational Therapists; Ophthalmic Medical

Technologists; Pharmacists; Pharmacy Technicians; Radiologic Technologists; School Psychologists; Social and Human Service Assistants; Speech-Language Pathology Assistants; Substance Abuse and Behavioral Disorder Counselors; others.

Statisticians

❋ Annual Earnings: $72,830

❋ Earnings Growth Potential: High (46.3%)

❋ Growth: 13.1%

❋ Annual Job Openings: 960

❋ Self-Employed: 2.8%

Skills—Most Important: Mathematics Skills; Science Skills; Technology/Programming Skills. **Other High-Level Skills:** Thought-Processing Skills; Communication Skills; Management Skills; Social Skills.

Engage in the development of mathematical theory or apply statistical theory and methods to collect, organize, interpret, and summarize numerical data to provide usable information. May specialize in fields such as biostatistics, agricultural statistics, business statistics, economic statistics, or other fields. Report results of statistical analyses, including information in the form of graphs, charts, and tables. Process large amounts of data for statistical modeling and graphic analysis. Identify relationships and trends in data as well as factors that could affect the results of research. Analyze and interpret statistical data to identify significant differences in relationships among sources of information. Prepare data for processing by organizing information, checking for any inaccuracies, and adjusting and weighting the raw data. Evaluate the statistical methods and procedures used to obtain data to ensure validity, applicability, efficiency, and accuracy. Evaluate sources of information to determine any limitations in reliability or usability. Plan data collection methods for specific projects and determine the types and sizes of sample groups to be used. Design research projects that apply valid scientific techniques and utilize information obtained from baselines or historical data to structure uncompromised and efficient analyses. Develop an understanding of fields to which statistical methods are to be applied to determine whether methods and results are appropriate. Supervise and provide instructions for workers collecting and tabulating data. Apply sampling techniques or utilize complete enumeration bases to determine and define groups to be surveyed.

Education/Training Required: Master's degree. **Education and Training Programs:** Applied Mathematics, General; Biostatistics; Business Statistics; Mathematical Statistics and Probability; Mathematics, General; Statistics, General; Statistics, Other. **Knowledge/Courses:** Mathematics; Computers and Electronics; English Language; Law and Government; Education and Training.

Personality Type: Conventional-Investigative. **Career Clusters:** 04 Business, Management, and Administration; 15 Science, Technology, Engineering, and Mathematics. **Career Pathways:** 15.2 Science and Mathematics; 04.2 Business Financial Management and Accounting. **Other Jobs in These Pathways:** Accountants; Architectural and Engineering Managers; Auditors; Billing and Posting Clerks; Billing, Cost, and Rate Clerks; Biofuels/Biodiesel Technology and Product Development Managers; Bookkeeping, Accounting, and Auditing Clerks; Brownfield Redevelopment

Specialists and Site Managers; Community and Social Service Specialists, All Other; Compliance Managers; Education, Training, and Library Workers, All Other; Financial Analysts; Financial Managers, Branch or Department; Investment Fund Managers; Loss Prevention Managers; Managers, All Other; Medical Scientists, Except Epidemiologists; Payroll and Timekeeping Clerks; Regulatory Affairs Managers; Security Managers; Statement Clerks; Supply Chain Managers; Treasurers and Controllers; Wind Energy Operations Managers; Wind Energy Project Managers; others.

Job Specialization: Biostatisticians

Develop and apply biostatistical theory and methods to the study of life sciences. Write research proposals or grant applications for submission to external bodies. Teach graduate or continuing education courses or seminars in biostatistics. Read current literature, attend meetings or conferences, and talk with colleagues to keep abreast of methodological or conceptual developments in fields such as biostatistics, pharmacology, life sciences, and social sciences. Prepare statistical data for inclusion in reports to data-monitoring committees, federal regulatory agencies, managers, or clients. Prepare articles for publication or presentation at professional conferences. Calculate sample size requirements for clinical studies. Determine project plans, timelines, or technical objectives for statistical aspects of biological research studies. Assign work to biostatistical assistants or programmers. Write program code to analyze data using statistical analysis software.

Education/Training Required: Master's degree. **Education and Training Programs:** Applied Mathematics, General; Biostatistics; Business Statistics; Mathematical Statistics and Probability; Mathematics, General; Statistics, General; Statistics, Other. **Knowledge/ Courses:** Mathematics; Biology; Computers and Electronics; Medicine and Dentistry; English Language; Education and Training.

Personality Type: Investigative-Conventional. **Career Cluster:** 15 Science, Technology, Engineering, and Mathematics. **Career Pathway:** 15.2 Science and Mathematics. **Other Jobs in This Pathway:** Architectural and Engineering Managers; Biochemists and Biophysicists; Biofuels/Biodiesel Technology and Product Development Managers; Bioinformatics Scientists; Biological Scientists, All Other; Biologists; Chemists; Clinical Data Managers; Clinical Research Coordinators; Community and Social Service Specialists, All Other; Dietitians and Nutritionists; Education, Training, and Library Workers, All Other; Geneticists; Geoscientists, Except Hydrologists and Geographers; Medical Scientists, Except Epidemiologists; Molecular and Cellular Biologists; Natural Sciences Managers; Operations Research Analysts; Physical Scientists, All Other; Social Scientists and Related Workers, All Other; Statisticians; Survey Researchers; Transportation Planners; Water Resource Specialists; Zoologists and Wildlife Biologists; others.

Job Specialization: Clinical Data Managers

Apply knowledge of health care and database management to analyze clinical data and to identify and report trends. Provide support and information to functional areas such as marketing, clinical monitoring, and medical affairs. Evaluate processes and technologies and suggest revisions to increase productivity and efficiency. Develop technical specifications for data management programming and communicate needs to information technology staff. Contribute to the compilation, organization, and production of protocols, clinical study reports, regulatory submissions, or other controlled documentation. Write work instruction manuals, data capture guidelines, or standard operating procedures. Track the flow of work forms including in-house data flow or electronic forms transfer. Train staff on technical procedures or software program usage. Supervise the work of data management project staff. Prepare data analysis listings and activity, performance, or progress reports. Perform quality control audits to ensure accuracy, completeness, or proper usage of clinical systems and data.

Education/Training Required: Bachelor's degree. **Education and Training Programs:** Applied Mathematics, General; Biostatistics; Business Statistics; Mathematical Statistics and Probability; Mathematics, General; Statistics, General; Statistics, Other. **Knowledge/Courses:** Medicine and Dentistry; Biology; Clerical Practices; Administration and Management; Computers and Electronics.

Personality Type: Conventional-Investigative. **Career Cluster:** 15 Science, Technology, Engineering, and Mathematics. **Career Pathway:** 15.2 Science and Mathematics. **Other Jobs in This Pathway:** Architectural and Engineering Managers; Biochemists and Biophysicists; Biofuels/Biodiesel Technology and Product Development Managers; Bioinformatics Scientists; Biological Scientists, All Other; Biologists; Biostatisticians; Chemists; Clinical Research Coordinators; Community and Social Service Specialists, All Other; Dietitians and Nutritionists; Education, Training, and Library Workers, All Other; Geneticists; Geoscientists, Except Hydrologists and Geographers; Medical Scientists, Except Epidemiologists; Molecular and Cellular Biologists; Natural Sciences Managers; Operations Research Analysts; Physical Scientists, All Other; Social Scientists and Related Workers, All Other; Statisticians; Survey Researchers; Transportation Planners; Water Resource Specialists; Zoologists and Wildlife Biologists; others.

Supervisors of Construction and Extraction Workers

* Annual Earnings: $58,680
* Earnings Growth Potential: Medium (38.3%)
* Growth: 15.4%
* Annual Job Openings: 24,220
* Self-Employed: 19.0%

Skills—Most Important: Equipment Use/Maintenance Skills; Management Skills; Social Skills. **Other High-Level Skills:** Thought-Processing Skills; Mathematics Skills; Communication Skills.

Directly supervise and coordinate activities of construction or extraction workers. Examine and inspect work progress, equipment, and construction sites to verify safety and to ensure that specifications are met. Read specifications such as blueprints to determine construction requirements and to plan procedures. Estimate material and worker requirements to complete jobs. Supervise, coordinate, and schedule the activities of construction or extractive workers. Confer with managerial and technical personnel, other departments, and contractors to resolve problems and to coordinate activities. Order or requisition materials and supplies. Locate, measure, and mark site locations and placement of structures and equipment using measuring and marking equipment. Record information such as personnel, production, and operational data on specified forms and reports. Assign work to employees based on material and worker requirements of specific jobs. Provide assistance to workers engaged in construction or extraction activities using hand tools and equipment. Train workers in construction methods, operation of equipment, safety procedures, and company policies. Analyze worker and production problems and recommend solutions, such as improving production methods or implementing motivational plans. Arrange for repairs of equipment and machinery. Suggest or initiate personnel actions such as promotions, transfers, and hires.

Education/Training Required: Work experience in a related occupation. **Education and Training Programs:** Blasting/Blaster; Building/Construction Finishing, Management, and Inspection, Other; Building/Construction Site Management/Manager; Building/Home/Construction Inspection/Inspector; Building/Property Maintenance; Carpentry/Carpenter; Concrete Finishing/Concrete Finisher; Construction Trades, Other; Drywall Installation/Drywaller; Electrical and Power Transmission Installation/Installer, General; Electrical and Power Transmission Installers, Other; Electrician; Glazier Training; Lineworker; Masonry/Mason Training; Painting/Painter and Wall Coverer Training; Plumbing Technology/Plumber; Roofer Training; Well Drilling/Driller. **Knowledge/Courses:** Building and Construction; Mechanical Devices; Design; Engineering and Technology; Production and Processing; Public Safety and Security.

Personality Type: Enterprising-Realistic-Conventional. **Career Cluster:** 02 Architecture and Construction. **Career Pathway:** 02.2

Construction. **Other Jobs in This Pathway:** Brickmasons and Blockmasons; Cement Masons and Concrete Finishers; Construction and Building Inspectors; Construction Carpenters; Construction Laborers; Construction Managers; Cost Estimators; Drywall and Ceiling Tile Installers; Electrical Power-Line Installers and Repairers; Electricians; Engineering Technicians, Except Drafters, All Other; Excavating and Loading Machine and Dragline Operators; Heating and Air Conditioning Mechanics and Installers; Helpers—Carpenters; Helpers—Electricians; Helpers—Pipelayers, Plumbers, Pipefitters, and Steamfitters; Highway Maintenance Workers; Operating Engineers and Other Construction Equipment Operators; Painters, Construction and Maintenance; Pipe Fitters and Steamfitters; Plumbers; Refrigeration Mechanics and Installers; Roofers; Rough Carpenters; Solar Energy Installation Managers; others.

Job Specialization: Solar Energy Installation Managers

Direct work crews installing residential or commercial solar photovoltaic or thermal systems. Plan and coordinate installations of photovoltaic solar and solar thermal systems to ensure conformance to codes. Supervise solar installers, technicians, and subcontractors for solar installation projects to ensure compliance with safety standards. Assess potential solar installation sites to determine feasibility and design requirements. Assess system performance or functionality at the system, subsystem, and component levels. Coordinate or schedule building inspections for solar installation projects. Monitor work of contractors and subcontractors to ensure projects conform to plans, specifications, schedules, or budgets. Perform start-up of systems for testing or customer implementation. Provide technical assistance to installers, technicians, or other solar professionals in areas such as solar electric systems, solar thermal systems, electrical systems, and mechanical systems. Visit customer sites to determine solar system needs, requirements, or specifications. Develop and maintain system architecture, including all piping, instrumentation, or process flow diagrams. Estimate materials, equipment, and personnel needed for residential or commercial solar installation projects. Evaluate subcontractors or subcontractor bids for quality, cost, and reliability. Identify means to reduce costs, minimize risks, or increase efficiency of solar installation projects. Prepare solar installation project proposals, quotes, budgets, or schedules.

Education/Training Required: Work experience in a related occupation. **Education and Training Programs:** Blasting/Blaster; Building/Construction Finishing, Management, and Inspection, Other; Building/Construction Site Management/Manager; Building/Home/Construction Inspection/Inspector; Building/Property Maintenance; Carpentry/Carpenter; Concrete Finishing/Concrete Finisher; Construction Trades, Other; Drywall Installation/Drywaller; Electrical and Power Transmission Installation/Installer, General; Electrical and Power Transmission Installers, Other; Electrician; Glazier Training; Lineworker; Masonry/Mason Training; Painting/Painter and Wall Coverer Training; Plumbing Technology/Plumber; Roofer Training; Well Drilling/Driller. **Knowledge/Courses:** No data available.

Personality Type: No data available. **Career Cluster:** 02 Architecture and Construction. **Career Pathway:** 02.2 Construction. **Other Jobs in This Pathway:** Brickmasons and Blockmasons; Cement Masons and Concrete Finishers; Construction and Building Inspectors; Construction Carpenters; Construction Laborers; Construction Managers; Cost Estimators; Drywall and Ceiling Tile Installers; Electrical Power-Line Installers and Repairers; Electricians; Engineering Technicians, Except Drafters, All Other; Excavating and Loading Machine and Dragline Operators; First-Line Supervisors of Construction Trades and Extraction Workers; Heating and Air Conditioning Mechanics and Installers; Helpers—Carpenters; Helpers—Electricians; Helpers—Pipelayers, Plumbers, Pipefitters, and Steamfitters; Highway Maintenance Workers; Operating Engineers and Other Construction Equipment Operators; Painters, Construction and Maintenance; Pipe Fitters and Steamfitters; Plumbers; Refrigeration Mechanics and Installers; Roofers; Rough Carpenters; others.

Surgical Technologists

- Annual Earnings: $39,920
- Earnings Growth Potential: Low (29.6%)
- Growth: 25.3%
- Annual Job Openings: 4,630
- Self-Employed: 0.2%

Skills—Most Important: Equipment Use/Maintenance Skills; Management Skills; Social Skills. **Other High-Level Skills:** Mathematics Skills; Communication Skills; Thought-Processing Skills.

Assist in operations under the supervision of surgeons, registered nurses, or other surgical personnel. May help set up operating rooms; prepare and transport patients for surgery; adjust lights and equipment; pass instruments

and other supplies to surgeons and surgeons'
assistants; hold retractors; cut sutures; and
help count sponges, needles, supplies, and
instruments. Scrub arms and hands and assist
the surgical team to scrub and put on gloves,
masks, and surgical clothing. Position patients
on the operating table and cover them with
sterile surgical drapes to prevent exposure.
Provide technical assistance to surgeons, surgical
nurses, and anesthesiologists. Wash and sterilize
equipment using germicides and sterilizers.
Prepare, care for, and dispose of tissue specimens
taken for laboratory analysis. Clean and restock
the operating room, placing equipment and
supplies and arranging instruments according
to instruction. Prepare dressings or bandages
and apply or assist with their application
following surgery. Operate, assemble, adjust, or
monitor sterilizers, lights, suction machines, and
diagnostic equipment to ensure proper operation.
Monitor and continually assess operating room
conditions, including patient and surgical team
needs. Observe patients' vital signs to assess
physical condition. Maintain supply of fluids,
such as plasma, saline, blood, and glucose, for
use during operations. Maintain files and records
of surgical procedures.

Education/Training Required: Postsecondary
vocational training. **Education and Training
Programs:** Pathology/Pathologist Assistant
Training; Surgical Technology/Technologist.
Knowledge/Courses: Medicine and Dentistry;
Biology; Psychology; Chemistry; Therapy and
Counseling; Customer and Personal Service.

Personality Type: Realistic-Social-
Conventional. **Career Cluster:** 08 Health
Science. **Career Pathway:** 08.2 Diagnostics
Services. **Other Jobs in This Pathway:**
Ambulance Drivers and Attendants,
Except Emergency Medical Technicians;

Anesthesiologist Assistants; Cardiovascular
Technologists and Technicians; Cytogenetic
Technologists; Cytotechnologists; Diagnostic
Medical Sonographers; Emergency Medical
Technicians and Paramedics; Endoscopy
Technicians; Health Diagnosing and Treating
Practitioners, All Other; Health Technologists
and Technicians, All Other; Healthcare
Practitioners and Technical Workers, All Other;
Histotechnologists and Histologic Technicians;
Medical and Clinical Laboratory Technicians;
Medical and Clinical Laboratory Technologists;
Medical and Health Services Managers;
Medical Assistants; Medical Equipment
Preparers; Neurodiagnostic Technologists;
Nuclear Medicine Technologists; Ophthalmic
Laboratory Technicians; Physical Scientists,
All Other; Physician Assistants; Radiologic
Technicians; Radiologic Technologists;
Veterinary Assistants and Laboratory Animal
Caretakers; others.

Survey Researchers

* Annual Earnings: $36,050
* Earnings Growth Potential: High (48.2%)
* Growth: 30.3%
* Annual Job Openings: 1,340
* Self-Employed: 6.7%

Skills—Most Important: Mathematics Skills;
Science Skills; Technology/Programming Skills.
Other High-Level Skills: Communication
Skills; Thought-Processing Skills; Social Skills;
Management Skills.

**Design or conduct surveys. May supervise
interviewers who conduct the survey in
person or over the telephone. May present
survey results to client.** Prepare and present

summaries and analyses of survey data, including tables, graphs, and fact sheets that describe survey techniques and results. Consult with clients to identify survey needs and specific requirements, such as special samples. Analyze data from surveys, old records, or case studies using statistical software. Review, classify, and record survey data in preparation for computer analysis. Conduct research to gather information about survey topics. Conduct surveys and collect data, using methods such as interviews, questionnaires, focus groups, market analysis surveys, public opinion polls, literature reviews, and file reviews. Collaborate with other researchers in the planning, implementation, and evaluation of surveys. Direct and review the work of staff members, including survey support staff and interviewers who gather survey data. Monitor and evaluate survey progress and performance using sample disposition reports and response rate calculations. Produce documentation of the questionnaire development process, data collection methods, sampling designs, and decisions related to sample statistical weighting. Determine and specify details of survey projects, including sources of information, procedures to be used, and the design of survey instruments and materials. Support, plan, and coordinate operations for single or multiple surveys. Direct updates and changes in survey implementation and methods. Hire and train recruiters and data collectors.

Education/Training Required: Bachelor's degree. **Education and Training Programs:** Applied Economics; Business/Managerial Economics; Economics, General; Marketing Research. **Knowledge/Courses:** Sociology and Anthropology; Sales and Marketing; Personnel and Human Resources; Mathematics; Administration and Management; English Language.

Personality Type: Investigative-Conventional-Enterprising. **Career Clusters:** 04 Business, Management, and Administration; 14 Marketing, Sales, and Service; 15 Science, Technology, Engineering, and Mathematics. **Career Pathways:** 15.2 Science and Mathematics; 04.1 Management; 14.5 Marketing Information Management and Research. **Other Jobs in These Pathways:** Brownfield Redevelopment Specialists and Site Managers; Business Continuity Planners; Business Operations Specialists, All Other; Chief Executives; Chief Sustainability Officers; Compliance Managers; Computer and Information Systems Managers; Construction Managers; Customs Brokers; Energy Auditors; First-Line Supervisors of Office and Administrative Support Workers; First-Line Supervisors of Retail Sales Workers; General and Operations Managers; Investment Fund Managers; Loss Prevention Managers; Management Analysts; Managers, All Other; Regulatory Affairs Managers; Sales Managers; Security Management Specialists; Security Managers; Supply Chain Managers; Sustainability Specialists; Wind Energy Operations Managers; Wind Energy Project Managers; others.

Surveying and Mapping Technicians

* Annual Earnings: $37,900
* Earnings Growth Potential: Medium (38.1%)
* Growth: 20.4%
* Annual Job Openings: 2,940
* Self-Employed: 5.6%

Skills—Most Important: Mathematics Skills; Technology/Programming Skills; Equipment

Use/Maintenance Skills. **Other High-Level Skills:** Management Skills; Thought-Processing Skills; Communication Skills; Social Skills.

Job Specialization: Mapping Technicians

Calculate mapmaking information from field notes and draw and verify accuracy of topographical maps. Check all layers of maps to ensure accuracy, identifying and marking errors and making corrections. Determine scales, line sizes, and colors to be used for hard copies of computerized maps using plotters. Monitor mapping work and the updating of maps to ensure accuracy, the inclusion of new and/or changed information, and compliance with rules and regulations. Identify and compile database information to create maps in response to requests. Produce and update overlay maps to show information boundaries, water locations, and topographic features on various base maps and at different scales. Trace contours and topographic details to generate maps that denote specific land and property locations and geographic attributes. Lay out and match aerial photographs in sequences in which they were taken and identify areas missing from photographs. Compare topographical features and contour lines with images from aerial photographs, old maps, and other reference materials to verify the accuracy of their identification. Compute and measure scaled distances between reference points to establish relative positions of adjoining prints and enable the creation of photographic mosaics. Research resources such as survey maps and legal descriptions to verify property lines and to obtain information needed for mapping.

Education/Training Required: Moderate-term on-the-job training. **Education and Training**

Programs: Geographic Information Science and Cartography; Surveying Technology/Surveying. **Knowledge/Courses:** Geography; Design; Computers and Electronics; Engineering and Technology; Mathematics; Clerical.

Personality Type: Conventional-Realistic. **Career Clusters:** 07 Government and Public Administration; 13 Manufacturing. **Career Pathways:** 07.1 Governance; 13.3 Maintenance, Installation, and Repair. **Other Jobs in These Pathways:** Administrative Services Managers; Aircraft Mechanics and Service Technicians; Automotive Specialty Technicians; Biological Technicians; Chief Executives; Chief Sustainability Officers; Civil Engineering Technicians; Compliance Managers; Computer, Automated Teller, and Office Machine Repairers; Electrical and Electronic Equipment Assemblers; Electrical and Electronics Repairers, Commercial and Industrial Equipment; Electrical Engineering Technicians; Electronics Engineering Technicians; General and Operations Managers; Helpers—Installation, Maintenance, and Repair Workers; Industrial Machinery Mechanics; Installation, Maintenance, and Repair Workers, All Other; Managers, All Other; Mobile Heavy Equipment Mechanics, Except Engines; Regulatory Affairs Managers; Social and Community Service Managers; Storage and Distribution Managers; Telecommunications Line Installers and Repairers; Tire Repairers and Changers; Transportation Managers; others.

Job Specialization: Surveying Technicians

Adjust and operate surveying instruments such as theodolite and electronic distance-measuring equipment and compile notes, make sketches, and enter data into computers.

Compile information necessary to stake projects for construction using engineering plans. Run rods for benches and cross-section elevations. Position and hold the vertical rods, or targets, that theodolite operators use for sighting to measure angles, distances, and elevations. Record survey measurements and descriptive data using notes, drawings, sketches, and inked tracings. Perform calculations to determine earth curvature corrections, atmospheric impacts on measurements, traverse closures and adjustments, azimuths, level runs, and placement of markers. Conduct surveys to ascertain the locations of natural features and man-made structures on the Earth's surface, underground, and underwater using electronic distance-measuring equipment and other surveying instruments. Search for section corners, property irons, and survey points. Operate and manage land-information computer systems, performing tasks such as storing data, making inquiries, and producing plots and reports. Direct and supervise work of subordinate members of surveying parties. Set out and recover stakes, marks, and other monumentation. Lay out grids and determine horizontal and vertical controls. Compare survey computations with applicable standards to determine adequacy of data. Collect information needed to carry out new surveys using source maps, previous survey data, photographs, and computer records.

Education/Training Required: Moderate-term on-the-job training. **Education and Training Programs:** Geographic Information Science and Cartography; Surveying Technology/Surveying. **Knowledge/Courses:** Geography; Design; Building and Construction; Mathematics; Law and Government; Engineering and Technology.

Personality Type: Realistic-Conventional. **Career Clusters:** 02 Architecture and Construction; 07 Government and Public Administration. **Career Pathways:** 02.1 Design/Pre-Construction; 07.1 Governance. **Other Jobs in These Pathways:** Administrative Services Managers; Architects, Except Landscape and Naval; Architectural and Engineering Managers; Architectural Drafters; Chief Executives; Chief Sustainability Officers; Civil Drafters; Civil Engineering Technicians; Compliance Managers; Electrical Drafters; Electronic Drafters; Engineering Technicians, Except Drafters, All Other; Engineers, All Other; General and Operations Managers; Geodetic Surveyors; Interior Designers; Legislators; Managers, All Other; Mapping Technicians; Mechanical Drafters; Regulatory Affairs Managers; Reporters and Correspondents; Social and Community Service Managers; Storage and Distribution Managers; Transportation Managers; others.

Technical Writers

* Annual Earnings: $63,280
* Earnings Growth Potential: High (41.3%)
* Growth: 18.2%
* Annual Job Openings: 1,680
* Self-Employed: 2.0%

Skills—Most Important: Communication Skills; Thought-Processing Skills.

Write technical materials, such as equipment manuals, appendices, or operating and maintenance instructions. May assist in layout work. Organize material and complete writing assignment according to set standards on order, clarity, conciseness, style, and terminology. Maintain records and files of work and revisions.

Edit, standardize, or make changes to material prepared by other writers or establishment personnel. Confer with customer representatives, vendors, plant executives, or publisher to establish technical specifications and to determine subject material to be developed for publication. Review published materials and recommend revisions or changes in scope, format, content, and methods of reproduction and binding. Select photographs, drawings, sketches, diagrams, and charts to illustrate material. Study drawings, specifications, mockups, and product samples to integrate and delineate technology, operating procedure, and production sequence and detail. Interview production and engineering personnel and read journals and other material to become familiar with product technologies and production methods. Observe production, developmental, and experimental activities to determine operating procedure and detail. Arrange for typing, duplication, and distribution of material. Assist in laying out material for publication. Analyze developments in specific field to determine need for revisions in previously published materials and development of new material. Review manufacturers' and trade catalogs, drawings, and other data relative to operation, maintenance, and service of equipment.

Education/Training Required: Bachelor's degree. **Education and Training Programs:** Business/Corporate Communications; Speech Communication and Rhetoric. **Knowledge/ Courses:** Communications and Media; Clerical Practices; English Language; Computers and Electronics; Education and Training; Engineering and Technology.

Personality Type: Artistic-Investigative-Conventional. **Career Clusters:** 03 Arts, Audio/ Video Technology, and Communications; 04 Business, Management, and Administration.

Career Pathways: 03.5 Journalism and Broadcasting; 04.5 Marketing. **Other Jobs in These Pathways:** Advertising Sales Agents; Audio and Video Equipment Technicians; Broadcast News Analysts; Broadcast Technicians; Camera Operators, Television, Video, and Motion Picture; Copy Writers; Directors—Stage, Motion Pictures, Television, and Radio; Editors; Film and Video Editors; Media and Communication Workers, All Other; Photographers; Producers; Program Directors; Public Address System and Other Announcers; Public Relations Specialists; Radio and Television Announcers; Reporters and Correspondents; Sound Engineering Technicians; Talent Directors; Technical Directors/Managers.

Telecommunications Equipment Installers and Repairers, Except Line Installers

- ❈ Annual Earnings: $54,710
- ❈ Earnings Growth Potential: High (43.0%)
- ❈ Growth: –0.2%
- ❈ Annual Job Openings: 3,560
- ❈ Self-Employed: 4.0%

Skills—Most Important: Installation Skills; Equipment Use/Maintenance Skills; Technology/ Programming Skills. **Other High-Level Skills:** Thought-Processing Skills; Social Skills.

Set up, rearrange, or remove switching and dialing equipment used in central offices. Service or repair telephones and other communication equipment on customers' properties. May install equipment in new locations or install wiring and telephone jacks in buildings under construction. Note differences in wire and cable colors so that work can be performed correctly. Test circuits and components of malfunctioning telecommunications equipment to isolate sources of malfunctions using test meters, circuit diagrams, polarity probes, and other hand tools. Test repaired, newly installed, or updated equipment to ensure that it functions properly and conforms to specifications using test equipment and observation. Drive crew trucks to and from work areas. Inspect equipment on a regular basis to ensure proper functioning. Repair or replace faulty equipment such as defective and damaged telephones, wires, switching system components, and associated equipment. Remove and remake connections to change circuit layouts, following work orders or diagrams. Demonstrate equipment to customers and explain how it is to be used and respond to inquiries or complaints. Analyze test readings, computer printouts, and trouble reports to determine equipment repair needs and required repair methods. Adjust or modify equipment to enhance equipment performance or to respond to customer requests. Request support from technical service centers when on-site procedures fail to solve installation or maintenance problems. Remove loose wires and other debris after work is completed. Communicate with bases, using telephones or two-way radios to receive instructions or technical advice or to report equipment status.

Education/Training Required: Postsecondary vocational training. **Education and Training Program:** Communications Systems Installation and Repair Technology. **Knowledge/Courses:** Telecommunications; Mechanical Devices; Computers and Electronics; Engineering and Technology; Design; Public Safety and Security.

Personality Type: Realistic-Investigative-Conventional. **Career Cluster:** 03 Arts, Audio/Video Technology, and Communications.

Career Pathway: 03.6 Telecommunications. **Other Jobs in This Pathway:** Broadcast Technicians; Communications Equipment Operators, All Other; Electronic Home Entertainment Equipment Installers and Repairers; Film and Video Editors; Media and Communication Workers, All Other; Radio Mechanics; Radio Operators; Radio, Cellular, and Tower Equipment Installers and Repairers; Sound Engineering Technicians.

Training and Development Specialists

- Annual Earnings: $54,160
- Earnings Growth Potential: High (42.6%)
- Growth: 23.3%
- Annual Job Openings: 10,710
- Self-Employed: 1.6%

Skills—Most Important: Science Skills; Thought-Processing Skills; Social Skills. **Other High-Level Skills:** Communication Skills; Management Skills.

Conduct training and development programs for employees. Keep up with developments in area of expertise by reading current journals, books, and magazine articles. Present information using a variety of instructional techniques and formats such as role playing, simulations, team exercises, group discussions, videos, and lectures. Schedule classes based on availability of classrooms, equipment, and instructors. Organize and develop or obtain training procedure manuals and guides and course materials such as handouts and visual materials. Offer specific training programs to help workers maintain or improve job skills. Monitor, evaluate, and record training activities and program effectiveness.

Attend meetings and seminars to obtain information for use in training programs or to inform management of training program status. Coordinate recruitment and placement of training program participants. Evaluate training materials prepared by instructors, such as outlines, text, and handouts. Develop alternative training methods if expected improvements are not seen. Assess training needs through surveys, interviews with employees, focus groups, or consultation with managers, instructors, or customer representatives. Screen, hire, and assign workers to positions based on qualifications. Select and assign instructors to conduct training.

Education/Training Required: Work experience plus degree. **Education and Training Program:** Human Resources Development. **Knowledge/Courses:** Education and Training; Sociology and Anthropology; Sales and Marketing; Clerical Practices; Personnel and Human Resources; Psychology.

Personality Type: Social-Artistic-Conventional. **Career Clusters:** 04 Business, Management, and Administration; 05 Education and Training. **Career Pathway:** 04.3 Human Resources. **Other Jobs in This Pathway:** Human Resources Specialists.

Transportation Inspectors

- ❋ Annual Earnings: $57,640
- ❋ Earnings Growth Potential: High (46.3%)
- ❋ Growth: 18.4%
- ❋ Annual Job Openings: 1,130
- ❋ Self-Employed: 4.2%

Skills—Most Important: Science Skills; Equipment Use/Maintenance Skills; Thought-Processing Skills. **Other High-Level**

Skills: Management Skills; Social Skills; Communication Skills.

Job Specialization: Aviation Inspectors

Inspect aircraft, maintenance procedures, air navigational aids, air traffic controls, and communications equipment to ensure conformance with federal safety regulations. Inspect work of aircraft mechanics performing maintenance, modification, or repair and overhaul of aircraft and aircraft mechanical systems to ensure adherence to standards and procedures. Start aircraft and observe gauges, meters, and other instruments to detect evidence of malfunctions. Examine aircraft access plates and doors for security. Examine landing gear, tires, and exteriors of fuselage, wings, and engines for evidence of damage or corrosion and to determine whether repairs are needed. Prepare and maintain detailed repair, inspection, investigation, and certification records and reports. Inspect new, repaired, or modified aircraft to identify damage or defects and to assess airworthiness and conformance to standards using checklists, hand tools, and test instruments. Examine maintenance records and flight logs to determine if service and maintenance checks and overhauls were performed at prescribed intervals. Recommend replacement, repair, or modification of aircraft equipment. Recommend changes in rules, policies, standards, and regulations based on knowledge of operating conditions, aircraft improvements, and other factors. Issue pilot's licenses to individuals meeting standards. Investigate air accidents and complaints to determine causes. Observe flight activities of pilots to assess flying skills and to ensure conformance to flight and safety regulations.

Education/Training Required: Work experience in a related occupation. **Education and Training Program:** Aircraft Powerplant Technology/Technician. **Knowledge/Courses:** Mechanical Devices; Physics; Transportation; Chemistry; Design; Law and Government.

Personality Type: Realistic-Conventional-Investigative. **Career Cluster:** 16 Transportation, Distribution, and Logistics. **Career Pathways:** 16.1 Transportation Operations; 16.5 Transportation Systems/Infrastructure Planning, Management, and Regulation. **Other Jobs in These Pathways:** Airline Pilots, Copilots, and Flight Engineers; Automotive and Watercraft Service Attendants; Automotive Master Mechanics; Bus Drivers, School or Special Client; Bus Drivers, Transit and Intercity; Commercial Pilots; Crane and Tower Operators; First-Line Supervisors of Helpers, Laborers, and Material Movers, Hand; First-Line Supervisors of Transportation and Material-Moving Machine and Vehicle Operators; Freight and Cargo Inspectors; Heavy and Tractor-Trailer Truck Drivers; Laborers and Freight, Stock, and Material Movers, Hand; Light Truck or Delivery Services Drivers; Mates—Ship, Boat, and Barge; Motor Vehicle Operators, All Other; Operating Engineers and Other Construction Equipment Operators; Parking Lot Attendants; Pilots, Ship; Railroad Conductors and Yardmasters; Sailors and Marine Oilers; Ship and Boat Captains; Storage and Distribution Managers; Taxi Drivers and Chauffeurs; Transportation Managers; Transportation Workers, All Other; others.

Job Specialization: Freight and Cargo Inspectors

Inspect the handling, storage, and stowing of freight and cargoes. Check temperatures and humidities of shipping and storage areas to ensure that they are at appropriate levels to protect cargo. Advise crews in techniques of stowing dangerous and heavy cargo. Calculate gross and net tonnage, hold capacities, volumes of stored fuel and water, cargo weights, and ship stability factors using mathematical formulas. Record details about freight conditions, handling of freight, and problems encountered. Recommend remedial procedures to correct violations found during inspections. Prepare and submit reports after completion of freight shipments. Post warning signs on vehicles containing explosives or flammable or radioactive materials. Observe loading of freight to ensure that crews comply with procedures. Notify workers of any special treatment required for shipments. Issue certificates of compliance for vessels without violations. Inspect shipments to ensure that freight is securely braced and blocked. Inspect loaded cargo, cargo lashed to decks or in storage facilities, and cargo-handling devices to determine compliance with health and safety regulations and need for maintenance. Direct crews to reload freight or to insert additional bracing or packing as necessary. Determine types of licenses and safety equipment required and compute applicable fees such as tolls and wharfage fees. Determine cargo transportation capabilities by reading documents that set forth cargo loading and securing procedures, capacities, and stability factors.

Education/Training Required: Work experience in a related occupation. **Education and Training Programs:** No related CIP programs; this job is learned through work experience in a related occupation. **Knowledge/ Courses:** Transportation; Engineering and Technology; Public Safety and Security; Physics; Geography; Mechanical.

Personality Type: Realistic-Conventional. **Career Cluster:** 16 Transportation, Distribution, and Logistics. **Career Pathways:** 16.5 Transportation Systems/Infrastructure Planning, Management, and Regulation; 16.1 Transportation Operations. **Other Jobs in These Pathways:** Airline Pilots, Copilots, and Flight Engineers; Automotive and Watercraft Service Attendants; Automotive Master Mechanics; Bus Drivers, School or Special Client; Bus Drivers, Transit and Intercity; Commercial Pilots; Crane and Tower Operators; First-Line Supervisors of Helpers, Laborers, and Material Movers, Hand; First-Line Supervisors of Transportation and Material-Moving Machine and Vehicle Operators; Heavy and Tractor-Trailer Truck Drivers; Laborers and Freight, Stock, and Material Movers, Hand; Light Truck or Delivery Services Drivers; Mates—Ship, Boat, and Barge; Motor Vehicle Operators, All Other; Operating Engineers and Other Construction Equipment Operators; Parking Lot Attendants; Pilots, Ship; Railroad Conductors and Yardmasters; Sailors and Marine Oilers; Ship and Boat Captains; Storage and Distribution Managers; Taxi Drivers and Chauffeurs; Transportation Inspectors; Transportation Managers; Transportation Workers, All Other; others.

Job Specialization: Transportation Vehicle, Equipment, and Systems Inspectors, Except Aviation

Inspect and monitor transportation equipment, vehicles, or systems to ensure compliance with regulations and safety standards. Conduct vehicle or transportation equipment tests using diagnostic equipment. Investigate and make recommendations on carrier requests for waiver of federal standards. Prepare reports on investigations or inspections and actions taken. Issue notices and recommend corrective actions when infractions or problems are found. Investigate incidents or violations, such as delays, accidents, and equipment failures. Investigate complaints on safety violations. Inspect repairs to transportation vehicles and equipment to ensure that repair work was performed properly. Examine transportation vehicles, equipment, or systems to detect damage, wear, or malfunction. Inspect vehicles and other equipment for evidence of abuse, damage, or mechanical malfunction. Examine carrier operating rules, employee qualification guidelines, and carrier training and testing programs for compliance with regulations or safety standards. Inspect vehicles or equipment to ensure compliance with rules, standards, or regulations.

Education/Training Required: Work experience in a related occupation. **Education and Training Programs:** No related CIP programs; this job is learned through work experience in a related occupation. **Knowledge/ Courses:** Mechanical Devices; Transportation; Public Safety and Security; Engineering and Technology; Administration and Management; Physics.

Personality Type: Realistic-Conventional-Investigative. **Career Cluster:** 16 Transportation, Distribution, and Logistics. **Career Pathways:** 16.1 Transportation Operations; 16.5 Transportation Systems/ Infrastructure Planning, Management, and Regulation. **Other Jobs in These Pathways:** Airline Pilots, Copilots, and Flight Engineers; Automotive and Watercraft Service Attendants; Automotive Master Mechanics; Bus Drivers, School or Special Client; Bus Drivers, Transit and Intercity; Commercial Pilots; Crane and Tower Operators; First-Line Supervisors of Helpers, Laborers, and Material Movers, Hand; First-Line Supervisors of Transportation and Material-Moving Machine and Vehicle Operators; Freight and Cargo Inspectors; Heavy and Tractor-Trailer Truck Drivers; Laborers and Freight, Stock, and Material Movers, Hand; Light Truck or Delivery Services Drivers; Mates—Ship, Boat, and Barge; Motor Vehicle Operators, All Other; Operating Engineers and Other Construction Equipment Operators; Parking Lot Attendants; Pilots, Ship; Railroad Conductors and Yardmasters; Sailors and Marine Oilers; Ship and Boat Captains; Storage and Distribution Managers; Taxi Drivers and Chauffeurs; Transportation Managers; Transportation Workers, All Other; others.

Veterinarians

- ✽ Annual Earnings: $82,040
- ✽ Earnings Growth Potential: Medium (39.2%)
- ✽ Growth: 32.9%
- ✽ Annual Job Openings: 3,020
- ✽ Self-Employed: 6.9%

Skills—Most Important: Science Skills; Communication Skills; Thought-Processing Skills. **Other High-Level Skills:** Social Skills; Management Skills; Mathematics Skills; Equipment Use/Maintenance Skills.

Diagnose and treat diseases and dysfunctions of animals. May engage in a particular function, such as research and development, consultation, administration, technical writing, sale or production of commercial products, or rendering of technical services to commercial firms or other organizations. Includes veterinarians who inspect livestock.

Treat sick or injured animals by prescribing medication, setting bones, dressing wounds, or performing surgery. Examine animals to detect and determine the nature of diseases or injuries. Provide care to a wide range of animals or specialize in a particular species, such as horses or exotic birds. Inoculate animals against diseases such as rabies and distemper. Advise animal owners on sanitary measures, feeding, general care, medical conditions, and treatment options. Operate diagnostic equipment such as radiographic and ultrasound equipment and interpret the resulting images. Educate the public about diseases that can be spread from animals to humans. Collect body tissue, feces, blood, urine, or other body fluids for examination and analysis. Attend lectures, conferences, and continuing education courses. Euthanize animals. Train and supervise workers who handle and care for animals. Conduct postmortem studies and analyses to determine the causes of animals' deaths. Specialize in a particular type of treatment such as dentistry, pathology, nutrition, surgery, microbiology, or internal medicine. Direct the overall operations of animal hospitals, clinics, or mobile services to farms. Drive mobile clinic vans to farms so that health problems can be treated or prevented.

Education/Training Required: First professional degree. **Education and Training Programs:** Comparative and Laboratory Animal Medicine; Laboratory Animal Medicine; Large Animal/Food Animal and Equine Surgery and Medicine; Small/Companion Animal Surgery and Medicine; Theriogenology; Veterinary Anatomy; Veterinary Anesthesiology; Veterinary Dentistry; Veterinary Dermatology; Veterinary Emergency and Critical Care Medicine; Veterinary Infectious Diseases; Veterinary Internal Medicine; Veterinary Medicine; Veterinary Microbiology; Veterinary

Microbiology and Immunobiology; Veterinary Nutrition; Veterinary Ophthalmology; Veterinary Pathology; Veterinary Pathology and Pathobiology; Veterinary Physiology; Veterinary Practice; Veterinary Preventive Medicine; Veterinary Preventive Medicine Epidemiology and Public Health; Veterinary Radiology; Veterinary Sciences/Veterinary Clinical Sciences, General; Veterinary Surgery; Veterinary Toxicology; Veterinary Toxicology and Pharmacology; Zoological Medicine; others. **Knowledge/Courses:** Medicine and Dentistry; Biology; Chemistry; Therapy and Counseling; Sales and Marketing; Personnel and Human Resources.

Personality Type: Investigative-Realistic. **Career Clusters:** 01 Agriculture, Food, and Natural Resources; 08 Health Science. **Career Pathways:** 08.1 Therapeutic Services; 01.3 Animal Systems. **Other Jobs in These Pathways:** Biologists; Clinical Psychologists; Community and Social Service Specialists, All Other; Counseling Psychologists; Dental Assistants; Dental Hygienists; Dentists, General; Healthcare Support Workers, All Other; Home Health Aides; Licensed Practical and Licensed Vocational Nurses; Low Vision Therapists, Orientation and Mobility Specialists, and Vision Rehabilitation Therapists; Massage Therapists; Medical and Clinical Laboratory Technicians; Medical and Health Services Managers; Medical Scientists, Except Epidemiologists; Medical Secretaries; Nonfarm Animal Caretakers; Occupational Therapists; Pharmacists; Pharmacy Technicians; Radiologic Technologists; School Psychologists; Social and Human Service Assistants; Speech-Language Pathologists; Speech-Language Pathology Assistants; others.

Water and Wastewater Treatment Plant and System Operators

- ❋ Annual Earnings: $40,770
- ❋ Earnings Growth Potential: Medium (39.0%)
- ❋ Growth: 19.8%
- ❋ Annual Job Openings: 4,690
- ❋ Self-Employed: 0.0%

Skills—Most Important: Equipment Use/Maintenance Skills; Mathematics Skills; Thought-Processing Skills.

Operate or control an entire process or system of machines, often through the use of control boards, to transfer or treat water or liquid waste. Add chemicals such as ammonia, chlorine, or lime to disinfect and deodorize water and other liquids. Inspect equipment or monitor operating conditions, meters, and gauges to determine load requirements and detect malfunctions. Collect and test water and sewage samples using test equipment and color analysis standards. Record operational data, personnel attendance, or meter and gauge readings on specified forms. Operate and adjust controls on equipment to purify and clarify water, process or dispose of sewage, and generate power. Maintain, repair, and lubricate equipment using hand tools and power tools. Clean and maintain tanks, filter beds, and other work areas using hand tools and power tools.

Education/Training Required: Long-term on-the-job training. **Education and Training Program:** Water Quality and Wastewater Treatment Management and Recycling Technology/Technician. **Knowledge/Courses:** Physics; Building and Construction; Mechanical Devices; Biology; Chemistry; Engineering and Technology.

W

Personality Type: Realistic-Conventional. **Career Cluster:** 01 Agriculture, Food, and Natural Resources. **Career Pathway:** 01.6 Environmental Service Systems. **Other Jobs in This Pathway:** Environmental Engineering Technicians; Hazardous Materials Removal Workers; Occupational Health and Safety Specialists.

Writers and Authors

* Annual Earnings: $55,420
* Earnings Growth Potential: High (48.4%)
* Growth: 14.8%
* Annual Job Openings: 5,420
* Self-Employed: 69.4%

Skills—Most Important: Communication Skills; Social Skills; Thought-Processing Skills. **Other High-Level Skills:** Management Skills.

Job Specialization: Copy Writers

Write advertising copy for use by publication or broadcast media to promote sale of goods and services. Write to customers in their terms and on their level so that the advertiser's sales message is more readily received. Discuss the product, advertising themes and methods, and any changes that should be made in advertising copy with the client. Write advertising copy for use by publication, broadcast, or Internet media to promote the sale of goods and services. Present drafts and ideas to clients. Vary language and tone of messages based on product and medium. Consult with sales, media, and marketing representatives to obtain information on product or service and discuss style and length of advertising copy. Edit or rewrite existing copy as necessary and submit copy for

approval by supervisor. Develop advertising campaigns for a wide range of clients, working with an advertising agency's creative director and art director to determine the best way to present advertising information.

Education/Training Required: Bachelor's degree. **Education and Training Programs:** Broadcast Journalism; Business/Corporate Communications; Communication, Journalism, and Related Programs, Other; Family and Consumer Sciences/Human Sciences Communication; Journalism; Mass Communication/Media Studies; Playwriting and Screenwriting; Speech Communication and Rhetoric. **Knowledge/Courses:** Sales and Marketing; Communications and Media; English Language; Clerical Practices; Computers and Electronics; Administration and Management.

Personality Type: Enterprising-Artistic. **Career Cluster:** 03 Arts, Audio/Video Technology, and Communications. **Career Pathway:** 03.5 Journalism and Broadcasting. **Other Jobs in This Pathway:** Audio and Video Equipment Technicians; Broadcast News Analysts; Broadcast Technicians; Camera Operators, Television, Video, and Motion Picture; Directors—Stage, Motion Pictures, Television, and Radio; Editors; Film and Video Editors; Media and Communication Workers, All Other; Photographers; Producers; Program Directors; Public Address System and Other Announcers; Public Relations Specialists; Radio and Television Announcers; Reporters and Correspondents; Sound Engineering Technicians; Talent Directors; Technical Directors/Managers; Technical Writers.

Job Specialization: Poets, Lyricists, and Creative Writers

Create original written works, such as scripts, essays, prose, poetry, or song lyrics, for publication or performance. Revise written material to meet personal standards and to satisfy needs of clients, publishers, directors, or producers. Choose subject matter and suitable form to express personal feelings and experiences or ideas or to narrate stories or events. Plan project arrangements or outlines and organize material accordingly. Prepare works in appropriate format for publication and send them to publishers or producers. Follow procedures to get copyrights for completed work. Write fiction or nonfiction prose such as short stories, novels, biographies, articles, descriptive or critical analyses, and essays. Develop factors such as themes, plots, characterizations, psychological analyses, historical environments, action, and dialogue to create material. Confer with clients, editors, publishers, or producers to discuss changes or revisions to written material. Conduct research to obtain factual information and authentic detail using sources such as newspaper accounts, diaries, and interviews. Write narrative, dramatic, lyric, or other types of poetry for publication. Attend book launches and publicity events or conduct public readings. Write words to fit musical compositions, including lyrics for operas, musical plays, and choral works. Adapt text to accommodate musical requirements of composers and singers. Teach writing classes. Write humorous material for publication or for performances such as comedy routines, gags, and comedy shows.

Education/Training Required: Bachelor's degree. **Education and Training Programs:** Broadcast Journalism; Business/Corporate Communications; Communication, Journalism, and Related Programs, Other; Family and Consumer Sciences/Human Sciences Communication; Journalism; Mass Communication/Media Studies; Playwriting and Screenwriting; Speech Communication and Rhetoric. **Knowledge/Courses:** Fine Arts; Communications and Media; Philosophy and Theology; Sociology and Anthropology; Sales and Marketing; History and Archeology.

Personality Type: Artistic-Investigative. **Career Cluster:** 03 Arts, Audio/Video Technology, and Communications. **Career Pathway:** 03.4 Performing Arts. **Other Jobs in This Pathway:** Actors; Artists and Related Workers, All Other; Choreographers; Craft Artists; Dancers; Designers, All Other; Directors—Stage, Motion Pictures, Television, and Radio; Entertainers and Performers, Sports and Related Workers, All Other; Managers, All Other; Music Composers and Arrangers; Music Directors; Musicians, Instrumental; Producers; Program Directors; Set and Exhibit Designers; Singers; Talent Directors; Technical Directors/Managers.

W

Index

M

N